D0996956

Adolescence

Adolescence
Development During a Global Era

EDITED BY

Dena Phillips Swanson, Malik Chaka Edwards and

Margaret Beale Spencer

AMSTERDAM • BOSTON • HEIDELBERG • LONDON
NEW YORK • OXFORD • PARIS • SAN DIEGO
SAN FRANCISCO • SINGAPORE • SYDNEY • TOKYO
Academic Press is an imprint of Elsevier

Academic Press is an imprint of Elsevier
30 Corporate Drive, Suite 400, Burlington, MA 01803, USA
525 B Street, Suite 1900, San Diego, California 92101-4495, USA
84 Theobald's Road, London WC1X 8RR, UK

Notices
Knowledge and best practice in this field are constantly changing. As new research and experience broaden our
understanding, changes in research methods, professional practices, or medical treatment may become
necessary.

Practitioners and researchers must always rely on their own experience and knowledge in evaluating and
using any information, methods, compounds, or experiments described herein. In using such information or
methods they should be mindful of their own safety and the safety of others, including parties for whom they
have a professional responsibility.

To the fullest extent of the law, neither the Publisher nor the authors, contributors, or editors, assume any
liability for any injury and/or damage to persons or property as a matter of products liability, negligence or
otherwise, or from any use or operation of any methods, products, instructions, or ideas contained in the
material herein.

Library of Congress Cataloging-in-Publication Data
Application Submitted

British Library Cataloguing-in-Publication Data
A catalogue record for this book is available from the British Library.

ISBN: 978-0-12-374424-1

For information on all Academic Press publications
visit our Web site at www.elsevierdirect.com

Printed in the United States of America
10   11   12   13   14   9   8   7   6   5   4   3   2   1

Contents

UNIT 4 STRUCTURING AND FACILITATING SUPPORTIVE SYSTEMS

Contributors

Lynn Bridgers
St. Norbert College, De Pere, Wisconsin, USA

Casey Erin Clardy
Fuller Theological Seminary, School of Psychology, Pasadena, California 91101, USA

Donna DeGennaro
UMass Boston, Boston, Massachusetts 02125-3393, USA

Lisa Bouillion Diaz
University of Illinois at Urbana-Champaign, Champaign, Illinois 61820, USA

Tiffany Dovydaitis
Center for Health Equity Research, The University of Pennsylvania School of Nursing, Philadelphia, Pennsylvania 19104-4217, USA

Davido Dupree
University of Pennsylvania, Philadelphia, Pennsylvania 19104-3325, USA

Malik Chaka Edwards
Charlotte School of Law, Charlotte, North Carolina 28208, USA

Tyhesha Goss Elmore
University of Pennsylvania, Philadelphia, Pennsylvania 19104, USA

Edward M. Epstein
University of Pennsylvania, Philadelphia, Pennsylvania 19104, USA

Marybeth Gasman
Graduate School of Education, University of Pennsylvania, Philadelphia, Pennsylvania 19104, USA

Camara Jules P. Harrell
Department of Psychology, Howard University, Washington, District of Colombia 20059, USA

Cherise A. Harris
Department of Sociology, Connecticut College, Connecticut 06320, USA

Cleopatra Y. Jacobs Johnson
University of Pennsylvania, Philadelphia, Pennsylvania 19104, USA

Grace Kao
Department of Sociology, University of Pennsylvania, Philadelphia, Pennsylvania 19104-6299, USA

Tina J. Kauh
Public/Private Ventures, Philadelphia, Pennsylvania 19103, USA

Pamela Ebstyne King
Fuller Theological Seminary, School of Psychology, Pasadena, California 91101, USA

Michele Muñoz-Miller
University of Pennsylvania, Philadelphia, Pennsylvania 19104, USA

Enrique Neblett
Department of Psychology, The University of North Carolina, Chapel Hill, North Carolina 27599, USA

Norman A. Newberg
Graduate School of Education, University of Pennsylvania, Philadelphia, Pennsylvania 19104, USA

Ikechukwu Onyewuenyi
Department of Psychology, The University of Pittsburgh, Pittsburgh, Pennsylvania 15260, USA

Erin L. Pickreign
Mt. Hope Family Center, University of Rochester, Rochester, New York 14608, USA

Jenel Sánchez Ramos
Fuller Theological Seminary, School of Psychology, Pasadena, California 91101, USA

Kerry Ann Rockquemore
Department of African American Studies, University of Illinois, Chicago, Illinois 60607, USA

Monica L. Rodriguez
Department of Psychology, University at Albany, State University of New York, Albany, New York 12222, USA

Mary Lou de Leon Siantz
Diversity and Cultural Affairs, The University of Pennsylvania School of Nursing, Philadelphia, Pennsylvania 19104-4217, USA

John Snarey
Center for Research in Faith & Moral Development, Emory University, Atlanta, Georgia 30322, USA

Margaret Beale Spencer
Department of Comparative Human Development, and Committee on Education, University of Chicago, Illinois 60637, USA

Tirzah R. Spencer
University of North Carolina, Chapel Hill, North Carolina 27599, USA

Dena Phillips Swanson
Warner School of Education and Human Development, University of Rochester, Rochester, New York 14627, USA

Ronald D. Taylor
Department of Psychology, Temple University, Philadelphia, Pennsylvania 19122-6085, USA

Carol Cuthbertson Thompson
Rowan University, Glassboro, New Jersey 08028, USA

Sheree L. Toth
Mt. Hope Family Center, University of Rochester, Rochester, New York 14608, USA

Kristin Turney
School of Public Health, University of Michigan, Ann Arbor, Michigan 48109-2029, USA

Nicole J. Walden
University at Albany, State University of New York, Albany, New York 12222, USA

Preface

Contemporary social policies in the United States have shaped perceptions of and opportunities for youth since child labor laws, compulsory education, and juvenile justice were initiated immediately preceding the twentieth century. These policies separated adolescence from adulthood. They also ushered in an era of age-differentiated expectations and an increasingly longer transition into adulthood. By the twenty-first century, these expectations were widely accepted as part of adolescents' normal development as well as representing sources of youths' unique challenges. The decades between the twentieth and twenty-first century saw an evolution from agricultural to industrial to technological industries, shaped the work force youth were being prepared to enter, and conceptually, created a moratorium for needed youthful role exploration. Opportunities afforded in support of role exploration include youths' decision-making practice options albeit, and most importantly, without the punitive affective consequences frequently linked with adulthood status. Concurrently, challenges and shifts occurred in the social consciousness of the country that continued to shape opportunities accessible to youth in preparation for their future adult roles in a rapidly changing society. These are most noted in policies on school desegregation, immigration laws, the "war on poverty," and an emerging focus on the needs of urban communities. Other policies reflecting social perceptions of adolescence include shifts in the legal drinking age and debates over the age to prosecute a minor as an adult. These societal struggles in some ways acknowledge a recognized need to reevaluate and support youth experiences. Youth-focused policies along with the processes designed to implement them and enhance developmental gains, however, have consistently been differentially applied based upon youths' group membership and status in society. This has greatly contributed to variability in developmental processes, experiences actually had in diverse social contexts, and patterns of outcomes achieved.

Accordingly, variations in experiences may be due to the social status ascribed to particular social markers (e.g., gender) or some combination (e.g., highly privileged Caucasian youth [albeit frequently unacknowledged]; negatively stereotyped African American youth; and model minority stereotyped Asian American youth). Unavoidably, "status" is linked with human development processes and thus encompasses the role and implications of biological, cognitive, and socioemotional transitions. While understanding that these processes are relevant for all youth, their impact may be distinctive based upon a youth's group status in society (e.g., their valued or devalued position and its intergenerational stability over time); status influences the nature of experiences as individuals interact with the multiple levels of their social and physical environment. Thus, as a function of group status perceptions and experiences of youth and their families, irrespective of normative needs and developmental tasks, the consequent privileges or extra risks experienced require consideration. That is, thoughtfully planned initiatives require a consideration of the physical and sociopolitical contexts salient for diverse youth given their unavoidably integrated biological, socioemotional, and cognitive domains of development.

Substantively, this conceptual framing of adolescence, given our expectations for youths' uniform and successful completion of developmental tasks, affords specific benefits. It allows us to see the world through their eyes. The conceptual orientation allows us to recognize *and* account for youths' simultaneous domains of development, which impact their ways of viewing the world and forming responses to life's everyday demands as developmental tasks (see Havighurst, 1953): stated bluntly, perception matters. Accordingly, how individuals see the world, make meaning of their observations, respond to normal expectations for competence and efficacy, considered together have life course implications. The particular perspective taken (or conceptual framing embraced) is critical and applicable whether contemplating research questions, discerning relevant constructs for measuring process or outcome variables, designing trainings for teachers and service providers, deliberating philanthropic or federal funding initiatives, or thinking through valid and authentic evaluations regarding their efficacy for all. In other words, irrespective of the specific focus (e.g., research questions, research methodologies, training character, or funding decisions), *how one thinks about and makes meaning of a phenomenon, task, or issue matters.*

Thus, a primary goal of this book is to provide a strong basis for understanding developmental processes and human vulnerability variability. *Human vulnerability is a life course characteristic and refers to the dilemma of having both risk factors (i.e., the constant confrontation of challenges) to contend with as well as the availability of protective factors (i.e., the latter function as sources support)* (see Anthony, 1974; Spencer, 2008). This volume's focus is primarily on the character of vulnerability, its particular manifestation during adolescence, and its sociopolitical ramifications for diverse youths' everyday twenty-first century experiences. Our general emphasis is on *diverse youth. We refer both to identifiable "minority youth" of color (e.g., Latino and African American) as well as Caucasian youth and some ethnicities of Asian Americans (e.g., Taiwanese, Chinese, Japanese) who are able to claim an underacknowledged protective factor status of White privilege or "model minority" positive stereotype.*

THE VOLUME'S DESIGN

As an edited compilation, this volume attempts to integrate the noted adolescent realities including their normative and nonnormative aspects. Most important, we explore the impact of contemporary issues, including frequently "underaddressed normative challenges." At the same time, we give attention to the "more stable" and frequently intergenerationally transmitted and socially constructed realities, including uneven resource distribution and stable support-*inaccessibility outcomes*, as well as significant and frequently unacknowledged privilege (e.g., see Luthar & Lattendresse, 2002). It is our view that incorporating and addressing youths' broadly diverse sociopolitical realities are needed for understanding their responses to them. Thus, we view it as a critical stance to incorporate and address the sociopolitical and pyschohistorical factors, especially within the United States, that impact the context in which adolescent development occurs. In particular, there has been little focus on the salience of issues such as immigration, technological shifts, and other sources of group variation and experiences such as the role of faith and spirituality (see Bridgers & Snarey; King et al., this volume). Although inconsistently acknowledged, as noted, all impact the climate and opportunities available to developing adolescents (see Spencer et al., 2006). Accordingly, with that said, the volume attempts to address some of these issues as a conceptual strategy. A goal is to understand how *sociological and political factors, as contextual forces, interact with and influence psychological experiences and pyschohistorical processes as experienced by young people engaged in confronting normal human development tasks.* We have, for example, a generation developing in a "technology-infused world" where in- and out-of-school time is "increasingly mediated by new communication technologies" (see Diaz et al., this volume). Emerging research explores the impact this will have in exacerbating social inequities or supporting developmental processes (see Dupree, this volume).

Our foundational perspective concerning the importance and unavoidability of human vulnerability (i.e., the normative presence of both risks and protective factors) represents the ordering of the volume's content. The text's topical content and its thematic ordering by unit category addresses *Normative Development* (Unit 1), *Contextual Processes* (Unit 2), *Developmental Challenges* (Unit 3), and *Supportive Systems* (Unit 4). As conceptualized, the working assumption concerning human vulnerability (i.e., all humans possess varying levels of both risks and protective factors) defines the volume's organization. It represents a particular theoretical orientation, conceptual grounding, cultural-contextual commitment, and a multidisciplinary approach. The framing perspective emphasizes the foundational role of human perceptions and meaning-making processes which occurs across the life course as human development unfolds within unavoidable individual-context interactions (see Bronfenbrenner 1989; Spencer, 2008; Spencer et al., 2006).

REFERENCES

Anthony, E. J. (1974). Introduction: The syndrome of the psychologically vulnerable child. In E. J. Anthony & C. Koupernik (Eds.), *The child in his family: Children at psychiatric risk* (pp. 103–148). New York: Wiley Publishers.

Bronfenbrenner, U. (1989). Ecological systems theory. In R. Vasta (Ed.), *Annals of child development* (pp. 187–248). Greenwich, CT: JAI.

Havighurst, R. J. (1953). *Human development and education.* New York: McKay.

Luthar, S. S., & Lattendresse, S. J. (2002). Adolescent risk: The cost of affluence. *New Directions for Youth Development, 95,* 101–121.

Spencer, M. B. (2008). Phenomenology and ecological systems theory: Development of diverse groups. In W. Damon & R. Lerner (Eds.), *Child and adolescent development: An advanced course* (chap. 19, pp. 696–735). New York: Wiley Publishers.

Spencer, M. B., Harpalani, V., Cassidy, E., Jacobs, C., Donde, S., Goss, T., et al. (2006). Understanding vulnerability and resilience from a normative development perspective: Implications for racially and ethnically diverse youth. In D. Cicchetti & E. Cohen (Eds.), *Handbook of developmental psychopathology* (Vol. 1, pp. 627–672). Hoboken, NJ: Wiley Publishers.

Foreword

Much of what is written about adolescent development takes the perspective of a single discipline: anthropology, biology, psychology, or sociology. A major strength of this book is its interdisciplinary approach. The editors and contributors integrate the research and theory from multiple disciplines and perspectives into their comprehensive treatment of adolescent development. Their approach to "normative development" emphasizes contextual factors, developmental challenges, and supportive systems that impact adolescent development. In their usage, normative does not mean typical or average; it means that normal human development occurs within specific biological and social contexts. The outcomes may differ considerably depending upon the demands of the varying biosocial environments.

In an earlier book, Spencer, Brookins, and Allen (1985) focused on African American children and youth. In my Foreword to *Beginnings*, I wrote "black child development is viewed from the perspective of the social ecology of black life experiences" (p. xii). This was a welcome change from the normative stance of most previous research. The authors were "saying that each group must be understood from the context of its historical experiences and current circumstances. The influences of race, ethnicity, and class on socialization patterns and family styles must be viewed from a variety of perspectives, free of the implicit ethnocentrism that idealizes the middle-class Anglo-European life style" (p. xv). The editors and contributors to *Adolescence: Development in a Global Era* embrace this inclusive approach by focusing on a culturally broad spectrum of youth (majority and minority youth in context). While acknowledging that cognitive, biological, affective, and psychological developmental processes are relevant for all youth, it is important to these authors that readers understand that adolescent development is strongly impacted by a youth's position in society.

Youth in the twenty-first century face new challenges as well as those traditionally associated with adolescence. In addition to learning to be independent and productive individuals within a specific social context or community, youth today are being asked to prepare themselves for a technologically sophisticated global society that is not limited by national or international boundaries. Access to communication devices that make it as easy to communicate with someone in Hong Kong as in the next room raises questions about parental control and the impact of international political and social processes on the developmental transitions of twenty-first century youth.

Recent social and political developments within the United States also pose challenges for today's youth. What does it mean to come of age during an economic depression? Are the experiences of the "Great Depression" of the 1930s relevant to understanding the impact of the current economic meltdown on adolescent development in contemporary America? How does the election of an African American, Barack Obama, as President of the United

States affect the sociohistorical perceptions of youths of all racial/ethnic/class backgrounds? Has progress in race relations broadened the aspirations of African American and Latino/a adolescents? Have perceptions of "glass ceilings" for women and minorities changed as opportunities have expanded? I agree with the editors of *Adolescence: Development in a Global Era* that it is important to address the sociopolitical and psychohistorical factors within the United States that impact the context in which development occurs.

The chapters in this book provide comprehensive and insightful syntheses of research on biological processes, cognitive processes, psychosocial processes, and historical processes. Unit 1 focuses on developmental transitions and introduces the foundation for the conceptual themes addressed in the volume. In Chapter 2, literature from epidemiology, biology, and developmental psychology is presented. Among the models and studies examined, Krieger's (2001) ecosocial model is especially helpful in framing the bidirectional approach to discussing how psychosocial factors influence biological outcomes and biological processes influence psychosocial outcomes. Chapter 3, "Cognitive Processes," addresses links between technological innovations (especially in communications) and cognitive developmental processes. PVEST (Phenomenological Variation of Ecological Systems Theory) is used as a foundation for exploring a socially conscious and culturally relevant theory of cognitive development during this period of rapid globalization. The focus of Chapter 4 is on psychosocial processes associated with normative development and cultural influences on these processes from early to late adolescence. Emphasis is placed on the transition through adolescence involving shifts in expected behaviors, changes in social networks, and defining one's identity.

Unit 2, "Contexts of Development: Socialization Processes," includes chapters on historical perspectives, leisure and technological influences, educating adolescents, foundations of faith, multicultural perspectives of self and racial identity, immigration and well-being, socializing relationships, and adolescent health in the African American community. Issues of faith and immigration are welcome additions to the study of adolescent development. These chapters provide a broad perspective on social and historical factors that affect identity development and sense of self among diverse adolescents.

Unit 3, "Confronting Normative Challenges: Risk, Resilience, Privilege, and Coping," includes chapters on civic and family support responsibilities, social context and adolescent school engagement, and religious and spiritual development in diverse adolescents. These chapters explore civic engagement, school engagement, and emerging conceptual differences between spiritual and religious development. Special attention is given to the role of culture and ethnicity, in addition to other sociopolitical and contemporary influences.

Unit 4, "Structuring and Facilitating Supportive Systems," includes chapters on the treatment of adolescent psychopathology, juvenile justice, and youth-focused prevention programming. The focus of this unit is translating research results into strategies for practice and social policies. One wonders if politicians and other policy makers had access to appropriate research results they would see the fallacies in No Child Left Behind or Zero Tolerance policies.

In spite of the fact that many changes in social patterns have occurred since the *Brown* decision of 1954 and the Civil Rights legislation of the 1960s, some of the same issues faced by diverse youths in the middle of the twentieth century still pose obstacles to adolescent development early in the twenty-first century. Among these issues are widespread income inequality; inequality in access to high-quality health care; inequality in exposure to environmental hazards; segregated housing patterns associated with concentrated poverty; inequality in access to high-quality education; large gaps in educational achievement and attainment; the overrepresentation of youths of color in special education; the overrepresentation of youths of color in the juvenile and criminal justice systems; and the continuing presence of racial, ethnic, gender, and social class discrimination in American social institutions. Can we identify and implement strategic programs that enable adolescents across all spectrums of the social structure to develop to their full potential? That is the challenge posed by the research presented in this book.

Some of the topics explored in this book have been the focus of previous scholars: Urie Bronfenbrenner (ecology), Glenn Elder (life span development), E. Franklin Frazier (the black family), Allison Davis (child-rearing practices, ability testing), Robert Havighurst (adolescent development), and Kenneth and Mamie Clark (racial self-image). The research in this book, while acknowledging previous scholars, demonstrates how much the field has developed during the last 60 years. The integration of brain research and other recent biological and ecological research with anthropological, sociological, and psychological research into a multidisciplinary body of work that brings together in one volume the latest scientific knowledge on adolescent development is an important contribution to research and practice. This book should be widely read by students, researchers, and practitioners who are interested in improving our understanding of adolescent development.

Edgar G. Epps

Marshall Field IV Professor of Urban Education Emeritus, The University of Chicago, and
Professor, Department of Educational Policy and Community Studies, The University of
Wisconsin-Milwaukee
August 31, 2009

REFERENCES

Krieger, N. (2001). Theories for social epidemiology in the 21st century: An ecosocial perspective. *International Journal of Epidemiology, 30*, 668–677.

Spencer, M. B., Brookins, G. K., & Allen, W. R. (1985). *Beginnings: The social and affective development of Black children.* Hillsdale, NJ: Lawrence Erlbaum.

Chapter 1

Sociopolitical contexts of development

Margaret Beale Spencer
University of Chicago, Chicago, Illinois, USA

Dena Phillips Swanson
University of Rochester, Rochester, New York, USA

Malik Chaka Edwards
Charlotte Law School, Charlotte, North Carolina, USA

Excluding the first 2 years of life, there are few periods of the life course more eventful, labile, and responsive to context features than adolescence. The rapid and pronounced shifts in cognitive, physical, and socio-emotional growth and development are associated with significant biological matura-tion. These sources of change, as well as youths' navigation across and involvement in diverse settings, matter profoundly. Physical examples of con-texts include neighborhoods, work apprenticeship sites, organizational local-ities (e.g., 4-H, Scouting), and activity settings (e.g., skate board spaces, swimming pools, basketball courts, service learning settings, bowling alleys, Police Athletic League [PAL] locales, car repair hangouts). Also salient within the optional contexts and sites are the adults who are responsible for monitoring and maintaining the diverse settings that include teaching, admin-istrative, and support staff members (i.e., those who might not necessarily be perceived by youth as socially and emotionally important and support-providing individuals). Also important as context features, although infre-quently thought about as salient in youths' navigated space, are the attitudes, training pedagogy, philosophical stances, stereotypes, and belief systems of the adult police and public transportation officers, service provider security persons, and others responsible for modeling and maintaining order as well as providing safety and security in public spaces. The fact that many adults (e.g., police officers) comprising adolescent contextual experiences are paid through tax dollars, *politically positions* them. In addition, their direct and relational interaction with adolescents *socially positions* them. The role of

Adolescence: Development During a Global Era

public transportation security persons, along with municipal police officers, remains especially significant through the adult years. Their salience is particularly obvious given the nation's burgeoning incarceration rate, which continues to be one of the highest in the world.

The previously described role (i.e., public safety personnel) represents a publicly paid, local representative and salient model of a community's legal system that is sworn to serve and protect public spaces. These spaces are frequently "criss-crossed" by youth who are generally without direct adult supervision. Thus, as representatives of public policy, officers of the law and adult models are present within, between, and across youths' navigated spaces. The quality of encounters (i.e., both perceived and experienced) has salience for and *contributes to youths' sociopolitical beliefs* and *behavioral orientations.* To illustrate, a significant number of males, in particular (expressed with varying levels of intensity), have a propensity to expect respect from others and cope by resorting to hypermasculine response styles in response to colloquially and variously expressed peer pressure to "man up" when disrespected (see Spencer, 1999, 2005; Spencer, Fegley, Harpalani, & Seaton, 2004; Swanson, Cunningham, & Spencer, 2005). Together the multiple sources of influence play significant and unavoidable roles in the progressive complexity associated with youth development during adolescence.

1.1. GENERAL INTRODUCTION AND OVERVIEW: HUMAN DEVELOPMENT ACROSS CONTEXT-SHARING DIVERSE GROUPS

In acknowledging the complexities of human development from a life span perspective, Baltes (1987) describes three primary influences which, along with biological and environmental determinants, take collective responsibility for explaining how individuals develop over time. The three sources of sway and significance include history-graded, age-graded, and nonnormative influences.

History-graded influences are associated with historical time and define the biocultural context of development. A cogent and contemporary example of history-graded influences reflecting sociopolitical forces on adolescent development has been immigration law changes. In fact, both American immigration law changes and the magnitude of technology innovations have expanded the contexts of development. Age-graded (i.e., normative) influences continue to be important and represent factors strongly associated with chronological age. That is, they afford a level of predictability in terms of their onset, direction, and duration (e.g., youths' apprenticeship needs and opportunities, which prepare them for adult work; critical role experimentation options [albeit without long-term consequences] as well as the exploration of career and work roles). Nonnormative influences are characterized as events, patterns, and sequences that are not applicable to most individuals or associated with a dimension of developmental time (i.e., immigration experiences, the experiences of American youth living through "9/11" and residing in the northeastern region of the United States, significant illness associated with the recent flu epidemic), whether ontogenetic or historical. These influences, in essence, do not follow a common and predictable course across development. The following sections provide a more detailed discussion of these influences as linked to adolescent development.

1.1.1. **History-graded influences**

History-graded influences are impacted by ideological, demographic, and other social context variables. This was evidenced by the *1965 Immigration Act*, which eliminated country-specific immigration quotas and ushered in an era of increased immigration to the United States. This resulted in clear demographic shifts, with the largest number of immigrants since the Act's passage not coming from Europe, but from Africa, Asia, the Caribbean and Latin America; in fact, for the latter group of nations noted, the changes include the largest number of immigrants coming from Mexico followed by East and Southeast Asia (Camarota, 2007).

This shift in demography resulted in a shift in American mythology. The American "melting pot" myth has been deconstructed for better describing what it means to be a nation of immigrants. As a nation, having clarity about the meaning of this status has significance, not just for White privilege, but for the larger "Black-White" relational paradigm as well. Blacks are no longer the largest minority, and by 2042 Whites will no longer be the majority (Bernstein & Edwards, 2008). What are the results of such a shift? Does the conception of Asians as model minorities give them "honorary whiteness?" If so, which Asians get this privilege? Blackness also needs to be unpacked, as evidenced by contemporary questions of whether U.S. President Obama's Kenyan father and Kansas-born White mother make him Black even if he is "African American."

As noted in Jacobs et al. (Chapter 10), one in five children in the United States is an immigrant or the child of immigrant parents. As a result, immigration accounts for practically all of the increase in public school enrollment over the past two decades (Camarota, 2007). While one would logically expect increases in bilingual education and greater diversity in employment, this is not always the case. California is the most diverse state in the country but passed Proposition 227 in 1998, which required that "all children in California public schools shall be taught English, and be placed in English language classrooms. The proposition requires that children who are English learners shall be educated through sheltered English immersion opportunities during a temporary transition period, which will normally not exceed one year" (see California Secretary of State, 1998). A similar law was passed in Arizona in 2000, and similar ballot initiatives are being organized around the country.

It is counterintuitive that we are witnessing the development of language immersion programs in magnet schools to attract privileged parents into low-income schools. As a result of the noted strategy, bilingualism has become privileged in ways that do not acknowledge its protective factors or communal meaning. Perhaps its embracement construes its perception and function as yet another protective factor.

Impact of expanded media and technology influences on adolescents. Frand (2000) reports that "most students entering college today are younger than the microcomputer, are more comfortable working on a keyboard than writing in a spiral notebook, and happier reading from a computer screen than from paper in hand. For them, constant connectivity—being in touch with friends and family at any time and from any place—is of utmost importance" (p. 15). As reported by Howe and Strauss (2000), youth born in or following 1982 are seen as virtually matchless in their uniqueness and, in fact, are described as totally unlike previous generations and are often referred to as *Millennials*. The term *Millennials* was adopted as a strategy to capture and understand the first postcomputer generation. They are the first native speakers of technology, and their foundation is digital versus analog. Many researchers are attempting to understand the implications of this "information age mindset" (Frand, 2000, p. 16). Millennials' core personality traits have been identified as confident, conventional, sheltered, team-oriented, achieving, and pressured (Cooney, 2007-2008, p. 506). They are "ambitious, demanding, and they question everything" but authority (Cooney).

For educational purposes, it may be critical to recognize that they are students who have an exploratory style of learning which causes them not only to retain information better but to use it in creative and innovative ways (Cooney, 2007-2008). Because Millennials developed using interactive technology such as the Internet, they are less likely to use instructions as a guide and, alternatively, make use of trial-and-error techniques until successful. According to Cooney, "they are oriented to inductive reasoning, formulating hypotheses and figuring out rules; they crave interactivity and may need to be encouraged to stop experiencing and spend time reflecting" (p. 506). This knowledge sets a psychohistorical moment, although it is still important to unpack the broad developmental implications.

1.1.2. **Age-graded influences**

The concept of normative development implies commonalities across processes and experiences shared by individuals within a given age range. Age-graded (i.e., normative) influences subsequently assume predictability in their onset, direction, and duration across groups. These are strongly tied to social expectations regarding timing of developmental expectations. School transitions are age-graded experiences associated with socially defined expectations but that also influence subsequent experiences. Accordingly, some school districts have implemented "social promotions" to minimize the deleterious social effects of academically retained students being "off-time" and in classes with socially or physically less developed students. For American youth, obtaining a license to drive is a developmental marker and provides an illustration of age-graded influences affected by context features.

As a traditional marker of impending adult status, obtaining a driver's license communicates different meanings to varying members of diverse ethnic groups. To illustrate, for Caucasian youth, more generally, or for some economically privileged teens, obtaining a driver's license may have meaning as an important "adult transitioning marker." In contrast, as a historical and traditional "pending adulthood transition marker," it may represent an "angst-generating developmental transition." More specifically, given the dissimilar sociopolitical realities for Black or Hispanic adolescent males (i.e., independent of wealth status), the different inferred perceptions, anxieties, and experiences of parents and other socializing adults are authentic. Their social awareness communicates, on the one hand, a heightened sense of vulnerability for some in contrast to beliefs about anticipated and expanding autonomy for others. Thus, a traditional adolescent marker heralding an impending transition to adulthood status may be enjoyed as "celebratory" for some (e.g., Caucasian, Asian youth) and a source of angst for others (e.g., being picked up by police due to underacknowledged racial profiling). Thus, for particular parents and youth, political and social realities reinforce unavoidable inferences concerning daily rituals and social realities for their youth as each young person navigates social space. This simple fact has huge parental socialization consequences (e.g., see Hughes et al., 2006) and political implications as youths' maturational processes make their capacity for inference making concerning inequities unavoidable.

1.1.3. **Nonnormative influences**

Undoubtedly, youths' experiences in different contexts, given each setting's varying character, are quite foundational to the outcomes and processes of human development. Male youth of color, for example, may use a bravado (i.e., hypermasculinity) orientation as a coping strategy in preparation for expected disrespect or harassment (Spencer, 1999; Stevenson, 2003). Normal maturation and associated inference making in the physical, socio-emotional, and cognitive domains contribute to the nature of individual context interactions and are especially evident during adolescence. What makes them particularly significant is that many social exchanges and events occur when youth are either alone or with peer group members. That is, progressively fewer exchanges occur while under the direct supervision of parents; thus, parental monitoring means something very different during adolescence (see Spencer, Dupree, Swanson, & Cunningham, 1996). Importantly, other socializing adults become equally or more salient. The nature of the interactions and youths' psychological preparation for them (i.e., the nature of cultural socialization, including spirituality and faith group experiences; perceptions of parental monitoring [see Spencer, Dupree, et al., 1996]) have important implications for positive youth development (see Blum, 2003; Damon, 2004; Lerner, Theokas, & Bobek, 2005) and resiliency (i.e., obtaining good outcomes in the face of normative and nonnormative challenges; see Spencer, 2006, 2008a). Accordingly, the character of outcomes produced has consequences for successful adulthood transitions.

While navigating across diverse settings, and given the several sources of rapid growth and maturation, youths' *perceptions of their contexts and interactions within them have implications for how they make sense of their lives*. The "making sense" process plays a role in decisions about how to address the important normative tasks associated with the adolescent period (Havighurst, 1953). The satisfactory completion of development-stage-specific expectations is critical given normative anticipation of youths' physical and psychological well-being as each pursues effectance motivation (see White, 1959, 1960). The latter source of unavoidable psychological drive is consistent with their pursuit of successful competence formation processes (see White). Of course, youths' membership in diverse groups (e.g., variable as a function of ethnicity, gender, immigration status, race, level of privilege, and combinations of same) further complicates the process. Experiences resulting from group membership, which are not consistent with "age-graded" expectations, contribute to nonnormative influences (e.g., language brokering among youth of immigrant parents, exposure to community violence, managing a chronic illness).

As suggested, group membership may be associated with an individual's gender, ethnicity, immigration status, skin color, conspicuous privilege, neighborhood location, faith group, or some combination of these.

Particularly in peer groups, youths' attendant experiences within groups and between them can be contributed to by multiple factors. For example, the variations may be due to similarities and differences evident either between groups (e.g., groups' differential treatment) or from within (e.g., as a function of perceived physical attractiveness, pubertal timing, gender). Each is important as members exchange feedback, infer assumptions about the self, and navigate through diverse contexts. Youths' awareness of others and inferences made about them (i.e., both collectively and individually) are unavoidable. Undoubtedly, and independently of whether formally acknowledged as a social concern, a signal political aspect of group membership is the unique experiences had by individual members as a function of the group's perceived status.

The situation is construed as "political" because differences in perceptions of status are *informal demarcations*. The clarification is critical given the frequently referred to and copious *formally held democratic beliefs* concerning equal treatment and equal access for all citizens. Further, because the differences in experiences are generally under- or unacknowledged by most, youths' preparations to make sense of and to cope with "differences felt or inferred" are critical. The unavoidable awareness of social disparities, experienced by youths themselves, potentially increase the level of normative risks generally confronted as a consequence. They are important and have implications for youths' subsequent meaning making, problem solving, and the character of their coping efforts, including their emergent sense of self. The knowledge and insights about the multiple identifications provide clarity about an emergent as well as stable achieved identity.

A signal political aspect of the many social groupings has to do with youths' awareness of lived versus reported or acknowledged disparities. It is important to understand youths' level of consciousness of stated laws and rights taught in high-school civics classes versus their *daily experiences of the law and its consistency of application* (see Spencer, 2008b). That is, although generally unacknowledged, as noted, significant differences remain in how laws and policies are practiced, modeled, and explained in everyday exchanges as their intended and unintended impact may contribute to hostile environments (Chestang, 1972). That is, for the United States of America, the nation's history is based upon the democratic belief and "social ideal" concerning equality of opportunity and equity regarding access. The latter issue, in particular, gained social and political significance following the Civil Rights Era. However, too frequently, adolescents and their families may, in fact, perceive and experience unequal treatment. Groups may have less access to resources and opportunities actually needed for maximizing generally valued—and assumed to be normative—outcomes for all citizens (i.e., consistent achievement along with successful and healthy life-course development). The unacknowledged dilemma of unequal access is a political reality which, we believe, is of special salience during adolescence given youths' capacity for more abstract reasoning, sense of fairness, and the fact that their development requires more frequent independent navigation of social spaces and broadly diverse physical places.

Thus, foundational and ongoing supports afforded youth by families and communities, as well as assistance promised by education (i.e., achievement pursuits), social services, philanthropic, and public health service systems, to name but a few, *matter deeply*. Each represents critical options for youths' successful transition into and through adulthood. Equally important, youths' early and prior experiences are significant. Specifically, youths' personal history of multilevel influences encountered during the infancy, early, and middle childhood periods become internalized and are *manifested as a particular quality of adolescent human vulnerability* (i.e., the unavoidable presence of both risk factor burden as well as protective factor presence) (see Anthony, 1974; Baltes, 1987; Spencer, Harpalani, Cassidy, Jacobs, et al., 2006).

1.2. INTRODUCTION TO THE CONCEPTUAL ORIENTATION

By adolescence, youths' ego and intellectual functioning are integrated with the net consequences of unique supports and cumulative challenges addressed given their developmental tasks from earlier periods of development (i.e., during infancy, toddlerhood, preschool, and middle childhood). Outcomes from the several sets of normative developmental challenges confronted are internalized; in general and too frequently, they become unavoidably integrated and adopted ... also classically described by James as habit (see James, 1902). Thus, the character and specifics of the net vulnerability associated with prior periods of development then represent the current stage's degree of risk (e.g., inadequate learning of literacy skills; beliefs concerning "earned or deserved conspicuous privilege") and character of protective factors present (e.g., emerging sense of purpose, spirituality, confidence, and positive identifications).

Given its frequent stereotypic presentation in the media, adolescent vulnerability is evident and manifest both psychosocially (e.g., a hypermasculine or bravado response style as an aspect of male youths' ongoing identity process), as well as behaviorally (e.g., bravado or stylistically aggressive). In fact, frequently viewed as an expressive and evident "style," adolescent identity expression is often viewed with trepidation and foreboding by parents, teachers, and most socializing adults! That said, and as suggested by the foundational perspective guiding our understanding of contemporary adolescence, we assert that *all humans are vulnerable* (possess both risk and protective factors) and take on particular behavioral styles in response to normative and nonnormative challenges. Of course, the redundant use of a particular reactive style suggests a psychosocial internalization of the coping behavior, which ultimately becomes expressed as an identity. It is critical to keep in mind that its manifestation varies both as a behavior and psychological reaction given one's success in coping with unavoidable human vulnerability (i.e., especially given age-graded developmental tasks) (see Havighurst, 1953). In fact, it may be that the behavioral expressions of vulnerability during adolescence, as responded to by parents and socializing adults, is unparalleled in significance except, perhaps, for parental reactions to young children's period of "the terrible twos!"

Our point is that the manifestations of vulnerability (i.e., its behavioral character, stylistic manifestation or "framing") generate various, and frequently derisive, reactions for diverse groups of youth. However, even when youthful coping behaviors "look the same" (e.g., the quality and theme of youthful music and its often loud volume!), too frequently, their inferred intent or character is interpreted based on the peer group demographics (see Tinsley, Wilson, & Spencer, in press) and everyday social experiences of diverse youth. For example, the social relational efforts of groups of minority youth often place them in jeopardy. When socially organized in the neighborhood as a peer group, the effort may not be viewed as a group of bored adolescents entertaining each other and themselves but, alternatively and too frequently, these youth may instead be saddled with interpretations of ill intentions. This is less likely to be the case for perceptions about groups of Caucasian or privileged young people living in suburban or gated communities. As suggested, the former group of adolescents, especially youth of color and males, may be regarded by patrolling police as frightening and threatening Black or Hispanic *men* (see Lee, Spencer, & Harpalani, 2003; Spencer, 2001a, 2001b; Swanson, Cunningham, & Spencer, 2003). This is in contrast to perceptions of youth as bored "growing boys"...*just being boys* (!). In the latter instance, what might be, in fact, high-risk behavior is viewed as youths' innocent experimentation with roles in preparation for adulthood transitions—a normal and necessary part of the identity formation process. In fact—in most cases and at best—such young people are asked to "move along." Alternatively, other groups found in the same situation (i.e., socializing with friends and viewed as loiterers) may receive clear threats in addition to the admonition to "move along," including, too often, implicit or explicit threats of incarceration.

As one of multiple stereotyping problems and sources of significant risk, the dilemma of "adultifying" particular young people and "imputing negative intent" continues to be a theme generally not addressed in developmental science. It is no minor omission, since the problem, as a virtually normative theme, has important implications for youths' growth, development, and youth policy. That is, as a sociopolitical theme and source of context variability, the formal stance of a democratic system is that everyone is treated equally and fairly. Too frequently, the added risk engendered by the imposition of, for example, "a Black tax" (i.e., the added costs of social functioning for Black people or people of color, more generally) is neither accounted for in research designs nor acknowledged.

Thus, inequity is generally not recognized, nor it is included in the constructs researched or analyzed when exploring between-group differences obtained from research programs when outcomes expected are the same (e.g., academic achievement, employment, incarceration statistics, physical health [obesity status, hypertension], status outcomes). We suggest salient consequences for the unacknowledged problem of "a Black tax" for some and its absence for others.

As a cyclical dilemma, then, the chronic invisibility of additional sources of youth risk status often associated with social status (e.g., greater risks encountered or fewer protective factors accessible) has implications for the character and importance of parental socialization (see Hughes et al., 2006). That is, an aspect of effective parenting for some includes preparing offspring for differential treatment, including appropriate responses when navigating diverse social settings in *American towns and cities*. The consequent and minimally understood anger and frustration felt by many youth has been addressed by some social scientists (e.g., see Stevenson, 2003), although the dilemma remains generally ignored. On the other hand, the privileging beliefs internalized by other youth have been recently addressed by Luthar and colleagues, as well as McIntosh (e.g., Luthar & Latendresse, 2002; McIntosh, 1989). In fact, and most importantly in both cases, youths' responsive strategies for coping with situations of significant risk or implicit beliefs of power and "earned privileges" (i.e., unacknowledged beliefs concerning expected supports) become stable. Representing one extreme, they are internalized as critical elements of the identity formation process and may communicate varying gradations of internalized privileging beliefs.

At another extreme, youths' context-associated experiences of heightened risk may promote *severe sensitivity and hypervigilance* around issues of respect which, unavoidably and recursively, also contribute to what happens in schools or with socializing adults more generally (i.e., reactive coping, which is frequently misinterpreted as indifference, disinterest, or dangerous behavior). Examples would be police harassment on public transportation and in neighborhoods or public schools' failure to provide the level of academic support needed and expected. In fact, the lack of school support has been hypothesized as emanating from teachers' own fears or feelings of inadequacy to teach in contemporary urban centers (e.g., see Hafiz, 2010). Thus teachers' own unacknowledged professional and personal support needs may inadvertently contribute to interpersonally negative settings as experienced by students (e.g., see Dell'Angelo, 2009). Unfortunately, such situations merely heighten youths' level of vulnerability (i.e., more risks experienced and even fewer supports proffered (see Spencer, 1999, 2008b; Swanson et al., 2003) As viewed classically by James (1902) more than a century ago, humans' redundant use of productive and unproductive strategies become habit. That is, they become part of more general psychosocial processes and, very importantly, demonstrate stability and stridency over time as one's identity. The observation is also consistent with Eriksonian notions suggesting that adolescents would rather sustain a negative identity (i.e., as viewed by others) versus tolerate the insecurity of lacking an achieved identity (see Erikson, 1964). Thus the net impact on, or degree of, vulnerability may change. There may be an increasingly high level of risk attained by youth without a concomitant change in protective factors available. As a neighborhood-level example, future-oriented plans and policies for urban renewal may be associated with short-term strategies such as condemning and bulldozing block upon block of neighborhood housing. The resulting interim state of social devastation presents significant risk. That is, the immediate implications (e.g., health, safety, feelings of social isolation) for youth continually navigating the interim "urban renewal and social fabric removal" of physical and psychological space are often under- or unexamined. Similarly, the consequences of accumulated and unchanged dust levels or the lack of green space and recreational opportunities for developing youth living in the peripheral and central corridors of such contexts continue to be ignored.

More specifically, and as illustrated in Figure 1.1, an identity-focused cultural ecological perspective on the process of human development in a sociocultural context has been described as a phenomenological variant of ecological system theory (referred to as the acronym PVEST and pronounced "P-VEST") (see Spencer, 1995, 2006, 2008b; Spencer, Dupree, & Hartmann, 1997; Spencer, Harpalani, et al., 2006). The framework suggests that even with the heightened risks described, bundled and adequate resources such as one's faith, available mentors, close-knit families, community partnering schools, responsibility-linked monetary incentive structures, and well-trained and sensitive teaching staffs can be internalized as foundational supports. Such options offset the cumulative risks described and, alternatively, increase the probability for *obtaining resiliency* (i.e., good outcomes achieved even under conditions of high risk) (Spencer, 2005; Spencer, Noll, & Cassidy, 2005).

1.3. **RESILIENCY: OBTAINING GOOD OUTCOMES INDEPENDENT OF RISK LEVEL**

We surmise that everyone is vulnerable and that the specific character or level of vulnerability has to do with the balance between the level of risks confronted and available protective factor attributes (refer back to Figure 1.1). The unique combination of and degree of balance evident between these attributes matter (e.g., protective factors may include significant relational support, economic resources, a good education, as well as the presence of risks [e.g., having significant disabilities, few economic resources, no health care, or limited social or cultural exposure]). Certainly for youth described as Millennials, the degree and character of exposure to technology may serve both as a protective factor for some or risk factor (i.e., dependency and overexposure) for others. The level of vulnerability has implications for the attainment of positive life-course trajectories and resiliency (i.e., obtaining good outcomes in the face of significant challenge) (see Anthony, 1974).

Undoubtedly, having a variety of protective factors which are translated into and experienced as diverse supports is helpful. As suggested, they are useful as broad sources of assistance as individuals confront the normal human developmental tasks of the particular developmental period (e.g., the toddler's acquisition of sphincter control and the adolescent's exploration of social roles) (see Havighurst, 1953), as well as less traditional tasks (e.g., the need to work to assist one's family economic stability; adjusting to dual and independent parenting efforts). Thus, protective factors experienced as supports are needed to diminish the adverse impact of risk.

However, supports may not always function as protective factors and be experienced as supportive (or protective). For example, frequently there are problems associated with particular "delivery systems," which are purportedly designed to support and protect and, in addition, are paid for with

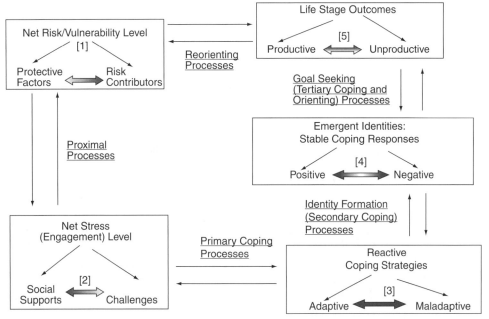

■ **FIGURE 1.1** Spencer's (1995) Phenomenological Variant of Ecological Systems Theory (PVEST). (Modified from Spencer & Harpalani (2004).)

tax dollars. Very visible examples of inadequacies for many citizens include services provided by the educational, health, social services, and criminal justice systems. Unfortunately, instead of providing support, services may cause injuries to specific groups: the lack of fit between need and service quality may result in unintentional systems harm (Spencer, 2008a).

However, there are many types of protective factors and manifested supports frequently underexplored in the literature and unacknowledged relative to practice. Recognizing the types and degree of protection available translates into diverse coping expressions, helpful modeling, and experiences of support—all of which may translate into broad opportunities for good outcomes and youth resiliency. All are critically needed as young people engage in activities and navigate settings where they are faced with a wide assortment of traditional and nontraditional challenges for which a wide spectrum of protective factors and support types are required.

Of course, there may be inattentiveness to particular challenges, such as persistent inequality and intergenerationally transmitted poverty, in addition to the many assumptions about earned conspicuous privilege, race and color biases, and first language use (refer to Spencer, 2008a). A lack of familiarity with cultural traditions and obvious resiliency outcomes and opportunities may result in overlooking opportunities, strategies, and policies to enhance potential supports. Opportunities may be wasted or culturally significant insights may go unacknowledged if particular protective factors and supports are not recognized (e.g., cultural identity and cultural socialization parental strategies) (see Lee et al., 2003).

There are exemplar remedies or supports which are linked with specific risks due to group membership, such as race, gender, political party, religiosity, and level of economic impoverishment. Context-specific remedies are often ignored because of the implicit messages communicated about life in a democratic society and assumptions concerning everyone's access to unique opportunities. They are included in this volume since they have demonstrated efficacy as sources of youth resiliency. Published examples demonstrating efficacy include cultural socialization practices (see Hughes et al., 2006). The transmission of cultural beliefs concerning group membership varies broadly (see Spencer, 1983, 1990). For example, *youths' perceptions of parental monitoring*, reinforced identity processes, and monetary incentives have significant implications for high academic performance (e.g., Swanson, Spencer, Dell'Angleo, Harpalani, & Spencer, 2002; Swanson, Spencer, & Petersen, 1998; Spencer, Noll, & Cassidy, 2005). Although each type is responsive to the needs of particular groups (e.g., as a function of race, ethnicity, gender, and poverty), there are also other sources of group exceptionality associated with historical time.

1.4. CONTEMPORARY ADOLESCENTS' UNIQUE CHALLENGES AND OPPORTUNITIES

Consistent with all stages of the life course, adolescence unfolds in contexts influenced by the particular historical moment, physical place, sociocultural traditions, and the distinctive interactions among them (e.g., the nation's election of its first President of color). As an example, advances in communication technology made the fact of Barack Obama's election and global reactions to it instantly observable to a technologically linked "global community." Unfortunately, negative media depictions of youth too frequently frame news reports without concomitant acknowledgment of the rapid changes and unique and additional challenges which accompany some youths' coping efforts to prepare for adulthood status (Howe & Strauss, 2000).

On the one hand, and as a part of their efforts to attain adulthood status, adolescents strive to attain progressively abstract academic and career-linked competencies as well as socially and emotionally relevant relationship skills (see Chapter 11, this volume). As suggested, their efforts may occur in generally underacknowledged and broadly diverse contexts relative to support level. Nonetheless, and at the same time, universal expectations for the character of youth outcomes are broadly disseminated by media, which also aid their reinforcement and maintenance. Thus, the socially constructed or historically linked variations in support level are frequently overlooked or not recognized in media portrayals of "difference or gap outcomes" (i.e., social portrayals), more generally.

Human processes and subsequent outcomes, as we have suggested, are influenced by multiple factors and, too, are sensitive to time and place. Accordingly, we posit that the historical moment, in and of itself, matters, as aptly demonstrated by Elder in his classic work, *Children of the Great Depression* (see Elder, 1974). As reported by Howe and Strauss, youth born in or following 1982 are seen as virtually matchless in their uniqueness and, in fact, are described as totally unlike previous generations and are often referred to as Millennials. Described as the progeny of periods framed by slogans such as "Babies on Board" or "Have You Hugged Your Child Today?" the Howe and Strauss analysis describes the group's greater affluence, improved educational status, and broader exposure to significant ethnic diversity relative to other cohorts of adolescents. Equally important, media messages about adolescents assume that the group has uniformly benefited from unambiguous and evident protective factors, as well. Specifically, the perspective refers to noted protective factors and positive attitudes about children, along with the enthusiastic use of reproductive options and their availability by way of sophisticated fertility-enhancing technology clinics as "illustrative data." It has been hypothesized that the pattern suggests a "child friendly" American context (see Howe & Strauss, 2000). In general, and at the same time, along with assumptions about the greater valuing of children, there are multiple and easily documented examples of youth exposure to unprecedented events.

Life-changing events such as sociopolitical and adolescence-sensitive contexts include America's military engagement in sequential wars and conflicts, which are closely followed in the media. Likewise, dozens of mass killings in middle and secondary schools, in addition to assault episodes on college campuses, continue episodically as media events. Other dramatic and broadly shared life-course events include the "9/11" terrorist attacks in New York City and at the Pentagon, as well as the broad correlates of the nation's "economic meltdown." Specific illustrations include the well-publicized (although underanalyzed) reports of individual and corporate greed, significant levels of unemployment across social and class lines, and nationally experienced housing foreclosures, suicides, and family homelessness. All have been unavoidably and cumulatively witnessed by youth through significantly enhanced media exposure. In addition, for many young people, their own direct experiences with various types of loss and hardship continue to be witnessed in solo and processed at a very personal level. The degree of challenge exposure experienced by youth, considered overall, has not been seen previously given the exacerbating role of technology. Thus young people are exposed to quite significant life challenges in addition to the normal and expected tasks associated with their specific life-course position (e.g., the tasks of infancy, toddlerhood, early and late adulthood tasks) (see Havighurst, 1953).

In fact, on the one hand and as introduced previously, as an aspect of normal everyday experience, life transitions and traditional developmental tasks are confronted as challenges and are coped with on a daily basis; thus, coping processes continue unabated and are experienced by all youth (i.e., independent of unique protective factor accessibility or the availability of supports). However and also unique, in general, Millennials have been exposed to an unprecedented level of racial and ethnic diversity; thus, it appears important to explore whether the inherent benefits and psychohistorical risks of innovations such as technology and educational opportunities have been experienced in equivalent ways by the nation's diverse young people as each prepares for adult efficacy and "across the board" expectations for life-course success.

More specifically, as young people confront a litany of normative developmental tasks and social challenges, high protective factor presence maximizes youths' *healthy behavior and outcomes, which support their positive transition into adulthood.* However, as described elsewhere, support proffered may not necessarily be perceived or experienced more generally by young people as supportive of well-being and mental health (see Spencer, 2006, 2008b).

Further, although generally underacknowledged and analyzed, positive adulthood transitions may be influenced and determined by youths' identification of, and access to, *culturally strategic supports* (i.e., sources of assistance which recognize and respect the diversity of human traditions and identifications). Risk factors are experienced by youth as diverse challenges. They include the need to address normal human developmental tasks, such as achieving an identity, as well as to engage in experimentation with a variety of roles without significant risk or life-changing consequences (e.g., work roles, social roles, personal roles [such as providers of support to others as in civic engagement]). However, the normative becomes extraordinary if it occurs during rapid social change or when challenging contexts and conditions are in place or traditional supports are either unavailable or inaccessible. The situation exaggerates risks and attendant challenges; thus, the inherent "traditional character" of the so-called "normative developmental tasks confronted" change and appear more dire (refer to Havighurst, 1953). Accordingly, situations involving unequal risk factors or available supports matter for obtaining positive youth development and resiliency as outcomes. They have consequences for enacted behaviors and achieved outcomes as well as significance for transitioning into and navigating across the long period of adult development.

The degree to which societal supports such as schooling opportunities or health care delivery systems show cultural (i.e., continuity) consonance, respect, and connectedness with youths' own valued traditions is important. In fact, if present, they improve the relevant outcomes (e.g., academic achievement trajectories as well as health and well-being). That is, the context features and character of *intended youth supports* (e.g., the organization of schools and pedagogy) and their fit, given early cultural socialization traditions, are important. During the adolescent transition, the features of intended support can undermine the utility and foundational salience of early and middle childhood experiences. That is, the effects of early exposure to *protective factors, supports, and cultural capital can be undermined, and thus have implications for successful adulthood outcomes.* The former (i.e., early) resources and supports referenced are associated with the cultural capital of family, community, and societal investments (e.g., as widely supported pre-K programs and philanthropic innovations). On the other hand, if dissonance-producing traditions prevail following an intended policy change (e.g., inferior schooling conditions for Black youth after *Brown v. Board of Education*, 1954), then positive change may be encumbered and good outcomes compromised.

Thus, under *informed* system reform efforts (i.e., when socially constructed practices are acknowledged as challenges and responsibility and resources for change are confronted and addressed), good outcomes are possible. That is, when the socially structured character of conditions are candidly unpacked and confronted, resiliency is possible (i.e., good outcomes are obtained in the face of challenging conditions). As a consequence, changes in context features of support provide enormous opportunities for scaffolding youth into healthy adulthood status.

1.5. **THEORY-DRIVEN VOLUME ORGANIZATION**

As illustrated and presented in Figure 1.1 and referred to previously, the approach taken in organizing the chapter topics and their order of presentation represents a specific perspective and theoretical framework for explaining human development. Phenomenological Variant of Ecological Systems Theory (PVEST; Spencer, 1995, 2006, 2008b) affords a particular approach for interpreting human development, which includes sensitivity to the individual's interpretive frame of reference or meaning-making. As suggested throughout, a traditional definition of phenomenology refers to it as a philosophy or method of inquiry based on the premise that reality consists of objects and events as they are perceived or understood in human consciousness and not of anything independent of human consciousness. Spencer's variation on this view is informed by Bronfenbrenner (1992), as well as the early ecological psychologists. Thus, PVEST includes the specification of context character and represents what she refers to as an Identity-focused Cultural Ecological (ICE) perspective. The conceptual orientation makes several undergirding assumptions about human development processes (see Spencer). Influenced by Erikson's trail-blazing work on life-course ego identity processes, PVEST assumes that identity feats represent the unfolding life-course task. Its resolution is informed by Havighurst's (1953) notions, which have implications for how developmental tasks are confronted, coped with, and their final character as outcomes obtained.

Accordingly, as described, PVEST takes the position that human vulnerability is consistent for all humans, although the level of vulnerability will vary because of differences in the balance between risk level and protective factor presence. That is, like Piagetian views concerning human equilibration, which is always represented by the balance between "the known" and the "unknown" (i.e., assimilation vs. accommodation needs), human vulnerability is conceptualized in similar ways. In keeping with the views of Anthony (1974), vulnerability level represents the balance (or imbalance) between one's "risk burden" versus the "protective factor privilege" that is available and accessible. The character of the "balance" may represent significant variations (Spencer, 2006, 2008a) (see Figure 1.2).

The degree of context association and structured balance achieved is critical as an individual or group (i.e., in this case adolescents) confronts normative life-course-specific developmental responsibilities (see Havighurst, 1953). For example, there are specific tasks for the first 2 years of life; they are cumulatively important but quite different from the manifested tasks specific to the adolescent years. There are parallel similarities for the young

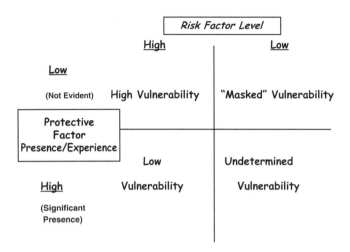

■ **FIGURE 1.2** PVEST-linked Vulnerability Status and Resiliency Prediction Dual Axis Model (adapted from Anthony, 1974).

adult since the sets of responsibilities across the life course mirror the important themes in need of addressing at the various points of the life course (i.e., situations navigated and tasks requiring confrontation vary by stage).

Accordingly, and as seen in Figures 1.1 and 1.2, human vulnerability (i.e., risk burden vs. protective factor privilege) can be influenced by race or ethnicity status as well as one's prior history of academic performance. One's awareness of these linkages and the societal acknowledgment of same also contribute to the sociopolitical aspect of context character.

Accordingly, and as one example, as one pursues the particular age-graded expectations for achieving a productive and positive adolescence, challenges abound. Of course, those incurred might be due to one's *perceptions* and/or *beliefs* concerning teachers' negative views about the self. On the other hand, the degree of supportiveness inferred by a teen may be enhanced by feelings that a school's climate communicates a commitment to learning, physical and psychological safety, and cultural pluralism. The latter, cultural pluralism, denotes a view that one's own cultural or social niche and the cultural traditions of others are equally valued and accepted. That is, independent of whether enacted policies actually intend for a noted outcome (e.g., the desegregation of America intended by the *Brown Decision 1954*), people's perceptions are what matter most.

In other words, it is the individual's *inferred sense of the fact* which actually matters regarding what he or she actually does in the relevant contexts *and in the moment*. Thus, as illustrated as component three in Figure 1.1, how a teen responds to and copes with the expectation of school engagement, both as a developmental task and valued schooling purpose, in fact depends on the inferences made about school climate. Youths' feelings about the degree of connectedness or inferred support thus influence their reactive or immediate coping response. Accordingly, it is youths' perceptual inferences which matter most relative to coping processes used. This is different than a focus on exo-level-determined social policies (e.g., desegregation orders or school funding legislation).

That said, youths' actual responses to contextual expectations and academic performance outcomes, phenomenological contributions, or the meanings they make of the situation, contribute to either adaptive responses or maladaptive patterns of behavior as reactive coping (e.g., see component three in Figures 1.1 and 1.2). For example, under parallel conditions, do males and females within or between groups respond in similar (or different) ways to the same developmental tasks while residing and learning in the same objective settings such as neighborhoods and classrooms? In similar fashion, especially given the 1954 Brown decision, do members of diverse ethnic enclaves interpret offered "opportunities" in the same or similar ways. (i.e., Are the academic tasks provided actually perceived and thus responded to in parallel ways?) Are the teaching and administrative resources and assumed supports actually experienced by diverse youth as equally supportive? Even within the same cultural niche, do youths who share group status but manifest different physiognomic characteristics such as skin tone, linguistic competencies (e.g., English as a second language skill set), or physical maturation precocity (e.g., physically large, early maturing Black males) engage in different meaning-making processes concerning their valued status, evaluative judgments concerning "perceptions of threat," and their accessibility to supports? Consistent with Figure 1.1, differences in outcomes are inevitable when young people reactively cope "in the moment" in response to what they perceive as variations in the evaluative judgments or meanings made about themselves or their group membership. That is, youths' inferences about the context have behavioral consequences. Adolescents' reactions to perceived context character are important (i.e., both the behavior of others within the context, such as teachers or the nature of the context itself [e.g., poor quality neighborhoods, inadequately trained teachers and administrators, and under-resourced schools]). Each either potentially facilitates adaptive responses to the developmental tasks at hand (e.g., student learning and academic engagement) or not. For the latter, negative perceptions and meaning-making inadvertently contribute to maladaptive responses to inferred insult (e.g., by focusing on issues of ego threat, joining negative peer groups such as gangs, retreating to web-based relationships, or by overly identifying with stereotypes of masculinity [bravado or hypermasculinity] as a reactive coping mechanism (refer to Figure 1.1) (see Spencer, 2006; Spencer, Fegley, et al., 2004). The strategy functions to protect the ego while maintaining—especially in the short term given long-term developmental adulthood tasks like stable employment—mental and physical health status and general well-being. The analytic approach pursued is very similar and, in fact, is informed by Erikson's (1968) analysis of youths' negative identity. That is, many highly vulnerable youths see negative identity to be better than a position requiring a period of exploration before arriving at a healthy identity. Undoubtedly, the latter requires that youth perceive the environment as safe and responsive enough to engage in psychologically "unprotected" exploratory exercises to be had in safe environments.

Considered together, the volume's chapter contributors provide ample illustrations both of sources of unaddressed risk as well as opportunities for exploiting the varied and much needed array of supports. The combination should provide policy makers, practitioners, and trainers with a host of adolescent sensibilities and sensitivities for maximizing the contexts for all youths' developmental transition into productive adulthood status.

1.6. CONCEPTUAL INTENT, PURPOSE, AND ORGANIZATION OF THE VOLUME

Accordingly, this book provides a strong basis for understanding developmental processes during adolescence that, on the one hand, acknowledges and encompasses youths' *unavoidable cognitive, biological, and psychosocial transitions and, on the other hand, examines contexts, challenges, and resiliency-facilitating supports.*

Unit One examines biological processes for diverse youth (see Chapter 2), as well as emphasizing the power and role of cognitive processes (see Chapter 3). Given that the character of coping is manifested as youths' patterned psychosocial processes, the latter perspective is emphasized under the rubric of psychosocial processes (see Chapter 4) and, as such, the three chapters considered together provide the organizing and framing of the volume's first unit. Given the opening overview of foundational developmental transitions governed by biological, cognitive, and psychosocial processes, this unit serves as a reminder of youths' unavoidable perceptual processes. That is, as an acknowledgment of context features, youths' perceptions and subsequent meaning-making and coping responses are linked to the noted foundational processes. The associations make evident how youths' efforts to make sense of the world take place in the diverse settings in which development unfolds.

That is, as adolescents navigate broadly varying socializing contexts, it is critical to take into account their "meaning-making" and responsive coping mechanisms (i.e., in response to the assumed wide range of policy-determined "contextual opportunities"). When considered along with youths' exposure to technology and media-communicated "equal opportunities" having to do with social, economic, and educational prospects, the sociopolitical implications are obvious. It is evident that discerning whether or not youths' exposure to academic presentations of the nation's "democratic ideals" in fact represent their actual experience of democracy in everyday life in their communities is important (i.e., Do they experience policy-based supports as, indeed, supportive?). Given media-disseminated assessments and stereotypes concerning outcome differences, it is important to consider youths' unavoidable awareness of societal enacted and disseminated ideals about equity versus youths' unavoidable exposure and analysis of their actual experiences. Thus, in addition to textbook exposure to the democratic ideals espoused under citizenship topics reviewed in their respective academic settings, research questions and interpretations of youth outcomes should consider how youth actually feel about available supports to engage in discussions of perceived differences. Their progressive familiarity with democracy allows for questioning about the equity of experiences between and within groups, as well as opportunities afforded across settings. The following question is illustrative of the dilemma. Given consistent academic performance expectations for youth overall, are there in fact equal options for identity-relevant apprenticeship work opportunities as well as postsecondary educational options?

In Unit Two, we take the position that to understand the developmental processes noted and their equal relevance as perceived by youth more generally, one needs to understand the obviously discernible coping processes and quite disparate outcomes evident across diverse groups. It is, in essence, critical to unpack and analyze when and why developmental processes and outcomes appear distinct for a particular adolescent as a function of group membership and the group's placement in society. As such, we need to ascertain whether the *actual contexts of socialization* are experienced in the same manner for ethnically diverse American youth.

Thus, in support of the needed insight, the chapters in Unit Two explore the experiences and socialization processes of youth in a variety of developmental contexts. A historical perspective is provided (see Chapter 5), as well as attention to leisure and technological influences (see Chapter 6). Youths' experiences in educational contexts (see Chapter 7), as well as those deemed as foundational sources of faith, are examined (see Chapter 8). Both conceptual orientations are intended as sources of support given the developmental tasks and accomplishments needed for successful adulthood transition.

Remindful that contemporary adolescents have experienced more ethnic diversity than prior groups, understanding its potential impact on self, racial, and ethnic identity processes appears critical (see Chapter 9). Similarly, understanding the role of immigration for well-being is critical and addresses youths' significantly more diverse world experience as well (see Chapter 8). Of course, family and peer relationships continue to be significant socializing contexts (see Chapter 10), as do other influences and challenges which have critical implications for the maintenance of physical health status and healthy lifestyles (see Chapter 12).

Given contemporary life and the level of social needs confronted as challenges by particular subgroups of American youth (i.e., all members of one of the wealthiest nations on earth), a particular perspective and approach to positive youth development is needed. Since diverse outcomes between and within groups remain the "elephant in the living room" dilemma, it is thus critical to address the sociopolitical and pyschohistorical factors within the U.S. that impact the settings in which development takes place for diverse youngsters. In general, there has been little focus on the salience of issues such as immigration and technological shifts that influence the climate and opportunities that are available and accessible to developing adolescents. Thus, this text addresses these issues in recursively and reciprocally exploring interactions between sociological and political influences with physiological and psychological processes. Physiological processes, for example, fueled by nutritional status variations and stress (e.g., maturational rate differences such as early physical precocity) can influence the experience of stress as youth transition across spaces occupied with, perhaps, hypervigilant socializing agents, including police officers or wary school personnel (teachers and security guards as well). Further, the dilemma is approached as a function of factors which are differentially influenced by gender and membership in diverse cultural groups. That is to say that different cultural groups and genders enjoy both similar and different risk factors and challenges and differentially benefit from protective factor level and supports.

Unit Three expounds on the impact of supports in maximizing developmental outcomes. Without adequate supports or possessing more than expected economic, social, and cultural capital, youths' experiences with normative developmental tasks as well as unique and heightened challenges (e.g., unsafe neighborhoods) result in different coping outcomes. Accordingly, in Unit Three, the authors tackle themes such as civic and family support responsibilities (see Chapter 13), school engagement needs (see Chapter 14), and spirituality resources (see Chapter 15) and assets.

Thus, from a phenomenological perspective which focuses on the perceptual processes and meaning-making invoked by an individual's human processes (refer to Figure 1.1), decisions are made as youths' developmental tasks take them across quite varied places and spaces. Individuals, groups, or systems make meaning of the normative and unique challenges and resources available and accessible; they then cope with the particular "in the moment" dilemma or challenge in particular ways. Equally relevant, and as illustrated in Figure 1.1, over time, youth engage in identity formation processes which suggest sustained strategies that are available and used as each youth navigates varied settings. Thus systems designed to provide wherewithal or support take particular forms to handle or cope with specific challenges or tasks.

Unit Four explores the structuring and facilitating character of supportive systems designed to aid the nation's diverse adolescent experiences. Accordingly, in examining what happens when we move from research to practice (see Chapter 16), the approach taken allows for an examination of intended youth-supporting systems and their actual impacts. Not surprisingly, decisions which support the character of systems intended to support are linked to policy decisions that require careful examination (see Chapter 17). The issue is critical since, as previously alluded to, all intended supportive systems do not provide support but instead impose what we have called unintended systems injury (see Spencer, 2006, 2008b). The injury has to do with the use of research and policy decisions as the foundation for the character of training those committed to youth development (see Chapter 18). If the training is based upon faulty "meaning-making" at the research, practice, or policy levels, the systems *re-create their inadequacies* and thus inadvertently contribute to unintentional systems injury and a loss of human capital and opportunity.

To summarize, this text on adolescence considers and integrates the domains of human development and analyzes their impact as youth navigate both within and between the broad cultural contexts which are foundational aspects of their growth and development. The previous is especially relevant given the abstract cognitive capacities associated with youths' reasoning abilities and cognitive maturation and their sensitivity to inequalities. A primary focus of this volume is on unpacking the reasons for the broad and variable outcomes.

REFERENCES

Anthony, E. J. (1974). The syndrome of the psychologically invulnerable child. In E. J. Anthony & C. Koupernik (Eds.), *The child in his family: Vol. 3. Children at psychiatric risk* (pp. 529–544). New York, NY: Wiley.

Baltes, P. B. (1987). Theoretical propositions of life-span developmental psychology: On the dynamics between growth and decline. *Developmental Psychology, 23*(5), 611–626.

Bernstein, R., & Edwards, T. (2008). *An older and more diverse nation by midcentury.* Washington, DC: U.S. Census Bureau.

Blum, R. W. (2003). Positive youth development: A strategy for improving health. In F. Jacobs, D. Wertlieb, & R. M. Lerner (Eds.), *Enhancing the life chances of youth and families: Public service systems and public policy perspectives: Vol. 2. Handbook of applied developmental science: Promoting positive child, adolescent, and family development through research, policies, and programs* (pp. 237–252). Thousand Oaks, CA: Sage.

Bronfenbrenner, U. (1992). Ecological system theory. In R. Vasta (Ed.), *Six theories of child development: Revised formulations and current issues* (pp. 187–249). London: Jessica Kingsley.

California Secretary of State. (1998). *California Voter Information: Proposition 227. Text of Proposed Law.*

Camarota, S. A. (2007). Immigrants in the United States, 2007: A profile of America's foreign-born population. *Backgrounder*, 1–43. (Center for Immigration Studies, Washington, DC).

Chestang, L. W. (1972). *Character development in a hostile environment* (Occasional Paper No. 3, pp. 1–12). Chicago, IL: University of Chicago Press.

Cooney, L. L. (2007–2008). Giving Millennials a leg-up: How to avoid the "If I knew then what I know now" syndrome. *Kentucky Law Journal, 96*(4), 505.

Damon, W. (2004). What is positive youth development? *The ANNALS of the American Academy of Political and Social Science, 591*, 13–24.

Dell'Angelo, T. (2009). *Teacher trust and perceived obstacles as mediators of student achievement in Philadelphia high schools.* (Dissertation). Philadelphia, PA: University of Pennsylvania.

Elder, G. H. (1974). *Children of the great depression: Social change in life experience.* Chicago, IL: Chicago University Press.

Erikson, E. H. (1964). *Insight and responsibility.* New York, NY: Norton.

Erikson, E. H. (1968). *Identity: Youth and crisis.* New York, NY: Norton.

Frand, J. (2000). The information age mindset: Changes in students and implications for higher education. *EDUCAUSE Review, 35*(5), 15–24.

Havighurst, R. J. (1953). *Human development and education.* New York, NY: McKay.

Howe, N., & Strauss, B. (2000). *Millennials rising: The next great generation.* New York, NY: Vintage Books.

Hughes, D., Rodriguez, J., Smith, E. P., Johnson, D. J., Stevenson, H. C., & Spicer, P. (2006). Parents' ethnic-racial socialization practices: A review of research and directions for future study. *Developmental Psychology, 42*(5), 747–770.

James, W. (1902). *The varieties of religious experience*. London: Longmans, Green.

Lee, C., Spencer, M. B., & Harpalani, V. (2003). Every shut eye ain't sleep: Studying how people live culturally. *Educational Researcher Journal*, *32*(5), 6–13.

Lerner, R. M., Theokas, C., & Bobek, D. L. (2005). Concepts and theories of human development: Historical and contemporary dimensions. In M. H. Bornstein & M. E. Lamb (Eds.), *Developmental science: An advanced textbook* (5th ed., pp. 3–43). Mahwah, NJ: Erlbaum.

Luthar, S. S., & Latendresse, S. J. (2002). Adolescent risk: The costs of affluence. In G. Noam, C. S. Taylor, R. M. Lerner, & A. von Eye (Eds.), *New directions for youth development: Theory, practice and research: Vol. 95. Pathways to positive development among diverse youth* (pp. 101–121). San Francisco: Jossey-Bass.

McIntosh, P. (1989). White privilege: Unpacking the invisible knapsack. *Peace and Freedom*.

Spencer, M. B (1983). Children's cultural values and parental child rearing strategies. *Developmental Review*, *3*, 351–370.

Spencer, M. B. (1990). Parental values transmission: Implications for the development of African-American children. In J. B. Stewart & H. Cheathan (Eds.), *Interdisciplinary perspectives on Black families* (pp. 111–130). Atlanta, GA: Transactions.

Spencer, M. B. (1995). Old issues and new theorizing about African American youth: A phenomenological variant of ecological systems theory. In R. L. Taylor (Ed.), *Black youth: Perspectives on their status in the United States* (pp. 37–69). Westport, CT: Praeger.

Spencer, M. B. (1999). Social and cultural influences on school adjustment: The application of an identity-focused cultural ecological perspective. *Educational Psychologist*, *34*(1), 43–57.

Spencer, M. B. (2001a). Resiliency and fragility factors associated with the contextual experiences of low resource urban African American male youth and families. In A. Booth & A. Crouter (Eds.), *Does it take a village?: Community effects in children, adolescents and families* (pp. 51–77). Mahwah, NJ: Erlbaum.

Spencer, M. B. (2001b). Identity, achievement orientation and race: "Lessons learned" about the normative developmental experiences of African American males. In W. Watkins, et al. (Eds.), *Race and education* (pp. 100–127). Needham Heights, MA: Allyn & Bacon.

Spencer, M. B. (2005). Crafting identities and accessing opportunity post Brown. *American Psychologist*, *60*(8), 821–830.

Spencer, M. B. (2006). Phenomenology and ecological systems theory: Development of diverse groups. In W. Damon & R. Lerner (Eds.), *Handbook of child psychology: Vol. 1. Theory* (6th ed., pp. 829–893). New York, NY: Wiley.

Spencer, M. B., Harpalani, V., Cassidy, E., Jacobs, C., Donde, S., Goss, T., et al. (2006). Understanding vulnerability and resilience from a normative development perspective: Implications for racially and ethnically diverse youth (Chap. 16). In D. Chicchetti, & E. Cohen (Eds.), *Handbook of developmental psychopathology* (Vol. 1, pp. 627–672). Hoboken, NJ: Wiley.

Spencer, M. B. (2008a). Lessons learned and opportunities ignored post-Brown v. Board of Education: Youth development and the myth of a colorblind society. *Educational Researcher, 37*(5), 253–266.

Spencer, M. B. (2008b). Phenomenology and ecological systems theory: Development of diverse groups. In W. Damon & R. Lerner (Eds.), *Child and adolescent development: An Advanced course* (chap. 19, pp. 696–735). New York, NY: Wiley.

Spencer, M. B., Dupree, D., & Hartmann, T. (1997). A phenomenological variant of ecological systems theory (PVEST): A self-organization perspective in context. *Development and Psychopathology, 9*, 817–833.

Spencer, M. B., Dupree, D., Swanson, D. P., & Cunningham, M. (1996). Parental monitoring and adolescents' sense of responsibility for their own learning: An examination of sex differences. *Journal of Negro Education, 65*(1), 30–43.

Spencer, M. B., Fegley, S. G., Harpalani, V., & Seaton, G. (2004). Understanding hypermasculinity in context: A theory-driven analysis of urban adolescent males' coping responses. *Research in Human Development, 1*(4), 229–257.

Spencer, M. B., Noll, E., & Cassidy, E. (2005). Monetary incentives in support of academic achievement: Results of a randomized field trial involving high-achieving, low-resource, ethnically diverse urban adolescents. *Evaluation Research, 29*(3), 199–222.

Stevenson, H. C. (2003). *Playing with anger: Teaching coping skills to African American boys through athletics and culture.* Westport, CT: Praeger Press.

Swanson, D., Cunningham, M., & Spencer, M. B. (2003). Black males' structural conditions, achievement patterns, normative needs, and "opportunities". *Urban Education, 38*, 608–633.

Swanson, D., Cunningham, M., & Spencer, M. B. (2005). Black males' structural conditions, achievement patterns, normative needs, and opportunities. In O. Fashola (Ed.), *Educating African American males* (reprinted pp. 229–254). Thousand Oaks, CA: Corwin Press.

Swanson, D. P., Spencer, M. B., Dell'Angleo, T., Harpalani, V., & Spencer, T. (2002). Identity processes and the positive youth development of African Americans: An explanatory framework. In C. S. Taylor, R. M. Lerner, & A. von Eye (Eds.), *Pathways to positive youth development among gang and non-gang youth* (pp. 73–99). New directions for youth development, No. 95 (Gnoam, Series Ed.) San Francisco: Josey-Bass .

Swanson, D. P., Spencer, M. B., & Petersen, A. (1998). Identity formation in adolescence. In K. Borman & B. Schneider (Eds.), *The adolescent years: Social influences and educational challenges, ninety-seventh Yearbook of the National Society for the Study of Education—Part 1* (pp. 18–41). Chicago, IL: University of Chicago Press.

Tinsley, B., Wilson S., & Spencer M.B. (in press). Commentary: Hip-hop culture, youth creativity, and the generational crossroads from a human development perspective *Jean Piaget Society Volume: Arts and Human Development.*

White, R. (1959). Motivation reconsidered: The concept of competence. *Psychological Review, 66*, 297–333.

White, R. (1960). Competence and psychosexual development. In M. R. Riley (Ed.), *Nebraska symposium on motivation* (pp. 3–32). Lincoln: University of Nebraska Press.

Developmental transitions

Chapter 2

Physiological activity during adolescence

Camara Jules P. Harrell
Department of Psychology, Howard University, Washington, DC

Enrique Neblett
Department of Psychology, The University of North Carolina, Chapel Hill, NC

Ikechukwu Onyewuenyi
Department of Psychology, The University of Pittsburgh, Pittsburgh, PA

In Toni Cade Bambara's short story, *The Hammer Man*, an African American girl at the doorstep of puberty narrates an account of adolescent life in the inner city. The central character is a Black boy that Bambara (1981) named Manny, probably to alert us to the fact that he will never see manhood. Almost casually, her narrator tells us that "Manny was supposed to be crazy. That was his story." He was also poor and desperately searching for options. When confronted by the police, while innocently shooting baskets on a neighborhood court, he stands "...waiting there with his hands in a time-out and there being no one to stop the clock." The narrator, who at the same time torments, fears, and loves Manny, refuses to sit impassively as agents of a hostile society crush what is left of his world. She senses that larger forces are operating here as she asserts "...none of my teachers, from kindergarten on up, none of them knew what they were taking about.... Dick and Jane was full of crap from the get go."

It is difficult to write about adolescent development without thinking about the Mannys in modern society. The trek to adulthood is perilous, even in lands where wealth and opportunity abound, and many young lives are derailed early. This is especially true for children of color. While focusing on the physiological dimensions of adolescent development, this chapter follows Bambara's lead and maps the convergence of developmental forces residing within and outside of the individual.

Adolescence: Development During a Global Era

Initially, this chapter presents a general perspective that will guide the examination of psychophysiological processes. We have derived this framework from work in the health and behavioral sciences that did not focus chiefly on adolescence but has major implications for the study of human development. The subsequent sections of the chapter provide examples of the complex interplay between biological and psychosocial processes during the course of development. Under separate headings we discuss genetic processes and behavior, prenatal influences on health and behavior, studies of psychophysiological activity in adolescents, and forces that impact adolescent resilience.

2.1. **THE RISE OF BIOPSYCHOSOCIAL MODELS**

In psychological research, physiological processes have served as independent, dependent, and moderator variables in the clinical (Tomarken, 1999), personality (Diamond & Otter-Henderson, 2007), developmental (Fox, Schmidt, & Henderson, 2000), and social areas (Gardner, Gabriel, & Diekman, 2000). Today, theories advanced in many branches of psychology are *multilevel* in that they analyze situational or contextual, psychological, and biological factors (see Pole, 2007; Schmader, Johns, & Forbes, 2008). Two distinct classes of multilevel approaches cooled some of the controversy that once surrounded the relative importance of biological and psychosocial factors in development. One set, the *outside in* models, begins by analyzing environmental forces and social and psychological factors that shape the individual. These theories show how various aspects of the environment and the individual's cognitive representation of them are integrated into biological structures and functions. The point of departure for the *inside out* conceptualizations is the design and regulation of biological systems, beginning with the nervous system. These models consider how physiological systems reflect the external environment organisms have encountered. They conclude that through evolutionary processes, challenges to survival sculpted physiology.

2.1.1. **Outside in models**

The writings of Fanon and Allport reveal multilevel thinking where biological factors are considered within social frameworks. Allport's (1937) writings mark the beginning of modern personality psychology. He appreciated the interaction between biogenetic and situational forces as well as the multiple levels of environmental influences. Allport devoted several passages to the interaction between genes and the environment and argued that "the two causal factors are not added together, but are related as multiplier and multiplicand (p. 68)." Later, in *The Nature of Prejudice*, All-port (1954) constructed a multilevel model of prejudice and attitude forma-tion. He linked prejudice to historical, cultural, immediate situational, personality, and phenomenological forces. Madhere, Harrell, and Royal (2009) followed Allport's lead in proposing that biogenetic forces interact with an array of situational influences, including culture and history.

Fanon (1967) discussed the roots of psychopathology among people living under colonialism. He made important observations about the influence of the family and the larger society (he called it the nation) on the develop-ment of Black and White children. Fanon argued that for children growing up under the heel of oppression, there exists a conflict between socializing forces emanating from the family and those whose source is the nation. He held provocatively that the "normal Negro child having grown up within a normal family, will become abnormal upon the slightest contact with the white world" (p. 143). Fanon was a psychiatrist, and his theoretical work always considered biological events. Notably, in the *Wretched of the Earth* (Fanon, 1968) his case studies of psychopathology included a separate section devoted to the physiological manifestations of toxic environments that take the form of psychosomatic disorders.

Today in the study of human development, there is general acceptance of Bronfenbrenner's (1977) conceptualization of a series of nested situational influences on development. These begin with microsystems, which encompass activities in the immediate social environment and directly contact the developing child. The most distal influences are macrosystems, which include structures and ideologies that inform interactions and pro-cesses within the other systems. Multilevel analyses that anticipated Bronfenbrenner's were implicit in traditional hybrid fields of study that were placed under the heading biological psychology (see Sternbach, 1966) and psychosomatic medicine (Dunbar, 1935). These older research areas matured and spawned new subdisciplines that reflect their multilevel roots. Cacioppo (1994) used the term *social neuroscience* to identify an emerging field that integrates biological and psychological factors in the study of higher social and cognitive functions. This was not the case with the earlier physiological psychology approaches, which tended to focus much more on basic activities related to perception and motivation. They often neglected complex cognitive activity like attitude formation or the regulation of human emotions (see Leukel, 1976; Thompson, 1967). Cacioppo and Bernston (2002) prefaced the weighty book, *Social Neuroscience*, with a reminder that social forces were prominent among the selection factors that governed the evolution of the mammalian ner-vous system. Cacioppo, Berntson, Sheridan, and McClintock (2002) noted that findings in several areas encourage cross-disciplinary perspectives that include biological and psychological views. These exciting studies have shown that social factors influence genetic constitutions and genetic expression, social variables impact the cardiovascular and immune system, and social factors contribute to the onset of physical illnesses.

Consistent with the multilevel analysis, Anderson (1998) asserted that health outcomes, a crucial marker of developmental processes, emerge from the interaction among molecular, cellular, organ system, psycho-behavioral, and social environmental influences. Both Anderson and Cacioppo et al. (2002) emphasize reciprocal influences between domains. Biology affects the psychological outcomes, and the psychological events affect biological processes. As Allport had done more than a half a century before, these authors warned against approaching the causes as simply additive. Rather, where interactions take place, not only do we account for the sum of several causes that produce an outcome, we recognize that the presence of one cause can alter the impact of other causes.

2.1.2. **Inside out models**

The multilevel approaches of the inside out perspectives grow out of the progress that has been made in understanding structural and functional aspects of the human nervous system. An astounding array of synaptic connections comprises the circuitry of the nervous system. These form the basis of our memories, cognitive schema, and behavioral patterns. Two competing views of how neural circuits develop agree in principle that environment plays a role as these networks are formed. Edleman (1987) and Piattelli-Palmarini (1989) argued that experience *selects* from and activates preexisting neural networks. In this view, genetic processes govern the setting up of the neuropathways. Experience activates pathways, and continued activation of these circuits renders the paths more likely to propagate impulses. This is consistent with Hebb's (1949) idea that repeated activation of neural circuits strengthens their connections. Elman, Bates, Johnson, and Parisi (1997) advanced an alternative position. They proposed a more active and *constructive* role for the environment. Experiments in many laboratories have shown that environmental stimulation results in structural changes in neurons and enhances new paths (see Pascual-Leone, Amedi, Fregni, & Merabet, 2005). Plasticity within the circuits of the brain indicates stimulation itself constructs rather than selects neural pathways.

LeDoux (2002) counseled that the processes advanced by selectivistic and constructionistic views "probably work together to shape the final connections of most neuro-circuits" (p. 89). Thus the debate with respect to the role of the environment is not whether it plays a part in developing neural circuitry but the kind and quality of the interaction between the genetic blueprint for neural networks and environmental stimulation.

Two relatively recent theories have provided frameworks for understanding the relationships between networks of neurons in the brain and peripheral nervous system and behavioral adaptations in a complex social world. The first is Porges's polyvagal theory (Porges, 1995, 2007). Porges called attention to similarities and differences in autonomic branches of the nervous system in mammals and reptiles. The central and peripheral nervous systems change in complexity across species, allowing simple approach and avoidance behaviors in reptiles to emerge as complex human activities of love and caring.

The vagus nerve is part of the parasympathetic branch of the autonomic system and has myelinated and unmyelinated components. The unmyelinated branch—the only branch found in reptiles—controls digestion and other "vegetative" functions. Under extremely stressful environmental conditions this part of the vagus reduces metabolic activity. Porges (1995, 2007) linked its activation with the very primitive responses of freezing and immobilization. The myelinated vagus, a feature of mammalian physiology, controls the heart, lungs, and pharynx. Porges (2001) noted that this part of the vagus shares neural origin circuits that control facial, head, and neck muscles, comprising a "social nervous system." In safe social contexts, the myelinated vagus works in concert with other cranial nerves to facilitate interactions with others. It inhibits autonomic arousal and aids social communication.

Studies of the heart rate responses of infants as well as adults during sustained attention, orienting, and defensive responding spawned the early tenets of the polyvagal theory (Porges, 1973). The theory has contributed to an interest in how beat-by-beat changes in heart rate, commonly designated heart rate variability (HRV), reflect changes in behavior. The vagus nerve is one cause of HRV, and vagal functioning has been linked to cardiovascular disease, as well as anxiety, depression, and death (Thayer & Lane, 2007). Polyvagal theory has added new measures to those traditionally used by psychophysiologists and has changed the manner in which scientists view the development of human social interactions.

The second theory is based on a century of research with animals and humans that has identified neural circuits that control cognitive, emotional, and autonomic system responses (Cannon, 1929; Damasio, 1998; LeDoux, 1996). Thayer and Friedman (2004) synthesized this research into a neurovisceral integration model (NIM). The circuits they discussed reside in cortical, midbrain, medullary, and autonomic structures of the nervous system. The NIM maintains that there is a rich and dynamic interplay among these circuits and, when functioning optimally, they permit "maximal organism flexibility in accommodating rapidly changing environmental demands" (p. 575). These networks can integrate responding to the environment through multiple excitatory and inhibitory pathways. They are responsive to input from both sensory and immune systems.

One remarkable feature of the NIM is a bold and detailed incorporation of psychological and social elements. Thayer and Friedman (2004) proposed that perseverative thinking and worry are particularly toxic to optimal emotional and physiological functioning. They suggested that chronic stress (including noxious events that would characterize environments fraught with social inequities and racism) promotes cognitive and emotional states that interrupt optimal autonomic levels and adjustments. Indeed, all developmental psychologists do not agree that adolescence is a period of "storm and stress" (Arnett, 1999). Still, NIM is useful when considering this period because the model identifies neural circuits that may be involved as developing individuals come to grips with changes in themselves and in those with whom they interact. Thayer and Friedman would concur with the polyvagal theory that HRV may be a useful marker of adolescent maturation and the integration of cognitive and emotional processes.

2.1.3. **A working model**

In summary, independent lines of theory and research have recognized that forces in the biological and psychological domains interact during the process of human development (Allport, 1937; Bronfenbrenner, 1977). The interplay of causal forces between and within domains is complex, sometimes conflicting (Fanon, 1967) and reciprocal (Anderson, 1998; Cacioppo et al., 2002). Environmental stimuli operate at the fundamental level of the structuring of neural networks that will contain memories and behavioral predispositions. However, the details of how the environment influences genetic blueprints for neural networks are still being debated (LeDoux, 2002). Neural circuits and systems that reside in the cortical levels in the brain, as well as those that contribute to the autonomic nervous system, favor flexible adaptation to social environments (Porges, 1995; Thayer and Friedman, 2004). Thus the demands involved in interacting with other human beings played a critical role in the development and architecture of our nervous system.

Epidemiologist Krieger (1994) argued that to understand the nature of disease outcomes, it is not sufficient for theories to be multilevel and proposed "webs" of causation. A spider, or organizing theme, must also be specified. Her analysis can be applied to the consideration of developmental outcomes. The approach she favored conceptualized no cleavage between biological and psychosocial factors at each level of analysis. For example, when investigators study molecular genetics, Krieger urged that they remember that psychosocial factors are at work. Similarly, social science researchers should bear in mind that genetic factors influence their findings. She used the metaphor of a fractal to represent causes that take the form of an "intertwining ensemble . . . at every level, subcellular to societal, repeating indefinitely" (p. 896).

Krieger's ecosocial model of health outcomes can be applied to the domain of adolescent development. In this application, researchers would construct a tree of developmental influences selected from biological, psychological, and social domains. When an investigator conducts research at a particular level, it is presumed that the other processes represented on the tree impact the selected domain. The influences are bidirectional, with psychosocial factors influencing biological outcomes and biological processes influencing psychosocial outcomes.

This model frames our approach to four topics related to physiological processes and adolescent development. Just as epidemiology and biological and developmental psychology are the source of the model, the subsequent sections sample diverse literatures. The present discussions of genetic and prenatal influences draw on some theory and research outside of developmental psychology. The literature cited in the sections on psychophysiology and resilience focus more particularly on studies of diverse adolescent populations.

2.2. **GENETICS AND DEVELOPMENT**

Significant increases in body size and rapid changes in secondary sexual characteristics are numbered among the more remarkable features of the adolescent period. Adolescence also brings important changes in neural circuitry in various parts of the brain. Clearly, genetic instructions partially underpin the structural and functional changes associated with the adolescent period. But what perspective provides the best view of these developmental processes? When viewing developmental outcomes across nations and continents, it would be most unfortunate to retreat to "hereditarian" models (see Rushton & Jensen, 2005). We will argue that estimates of the heritability of traits are often misleading. Our knowledge of genes and their actions increases daily. However, overestimating their role in determining traits will certainly lead to inaccurate views of the world's diverse populations (Cooper, 2004; Gould, 1981; Graves, 2001).

Moore's *The Dependent Gene* (2001) argued that nature and nurture are "shot through" with influences of each other (p. 11). Based on human and animal research, Moore concluded that the environment modulates all genetic signals, even those related to the determination of sex and the intensity of the expression of later sexual behavior. From Moore's "developmental systems" perspective, no traits, including the timing of the menstrual cycle, the size of the adolescent growth spurt, and the endpoints of cognitive development, are subject to exclusive genetic control.

The developmental systems approach is consistent with earlier insightful writings on the nature versus nurture controversy. Bronfenbrenner and Ceci (1994) cautioned against additive estimates of genetic and environmental influences. They argued that configurations of biological and environmental events, called *proximal processes*, converge to open the door for the expression of genetic potential. In the absence of these interactions or when they occur at less than optimal levels, the heritability estimate for a given trait is inaccurate and reflects unrealized potential. An environmental contribution to a proximal process that Bronfenbrenner and Ceci cited is the impact of parental monitoring of adolescent schoolwork on school achievement. They noted that parental education and family structure moderates the impact of parental monitoring. Thus, a two-pronged research challenge is to identify the proximal processes for a given genotype and to locate the environmental context, social and physical, that may moderate the impact of proximal processes.

Gottlieb (1998) urged adoption of a theoretical departure from "genetic dogma" that extended Bronfenbrenner and Ceci's cautions. He noted that original genetic formulations of the late 1950s (not including a later revision by Crick, 1970) set forth as unidirectional processes transcriptions from DNA to RNA and translations from RNA to protein synthesis. Phenotypes, that is, the traits we see, are based on protein synthesis. In contrast, Gottlieb's probabilistic epigenetic theory proposed that bidirectional causal paths exist among genetic, neurological, behavioral, and environmental factors. Gottlieb provided a table of examples of environmental influences on genetic expression. It included studies showing that incubation temperature determines sex in some reptiles and that maternal grooming influences the genetic unfolding of immune functions in rats.

Johnston and Edwards (2002) proposed that three major forces—genetic, sensory stimulation, and physical input—are responsible for the development of behavior. They placed under physical input environmental factors that do not operate primarily through the senses. Gravity, diet, and movement-related stress on the body are examples. Building on Gottlieb's model, Johnston and Edwards provided a detailed analysis of how all three factors operate. Within each domain, complicated processes occur, and each of these is subject to multiple influences. Physical input affects the development of bones and muscles, while genes influence the synthesis of proteins and the operation of the cell itself. The processes that genes and physical changes influence will eventually shape neural growth and the connections between neurons. Johnson and Edwards called special attention to the role of a class of genes called *immediate-early genes*. Sensory experience appears to stimulate these genes to set about their work of organizing the nervous system. For example, early experiences with sound arouse the genes that set in motion the organizing of the neurons in the ear and auditory pathways. Johnston and Edwards encouraged us to think of genes as affecting a cascade of molecular events and not directly influencing behaviors. Recognizing that genetic actions initiate these complex cellular actions reduces the tendency to speak of direct genetic causes of behavior.

Thus, emerging developmental perspectives speak to factors that affect the manner and extent to which genes will be expressed, that is, processes that are *epigenetic*. Jaenisch and Bird (2003) defined epigenetic events as "stable alterations in gene expression potential that arise during development and cell proliferation" (p. 245). Nutrition, aging, as well as the presence of other genes, can result in epigenetic modifications. Jaenisch and Bird showed, for example, that in genetically identical rats, diets in which methyl is experimentally increased or withheld change the color of the animal's coat. Surprisingly, the offspring of the affected animal can be altered by the change in the diet of the grandparent. Activating or silencing regions of the genome occurs at levels very close to DNA itself through the modification (methylation) of proteins. Jaenisch and Bird concluded that epigenetic mechanisms point to flexibility within the genome that facilitates adaptation.

Sequencing the human genome was a momentous undertaking, and an eager public awaits pronouncements of the functions of each of the 30,000 genes. On one research frontier, knowledge of the genome is being paired with another significant scientific breakthrough—the measurement of brain functioning using imaging techniques. This research is resulting in remarkable advances in the understanding of the genetic contributions to the neural networks that are activated as we behave (De Geus, Goldberg, Boomsma, & Posthuma, 2008). For example, the anterior cingulate cortex is known to be involved in the regulation of emotion and cognitive activity. Since adolescence presents challenges that require self-monitoring and judgment, these functions are of particular interest to developmental psychologists. Fossella et al. (2008) reviewed recent studies that are on the path to linking specific genes to brain activity in the anterior cingulate. They noted that "while heritable factors influence behavior, the developmental outcome of genetic variation can be influenced by environmental context" (p. 4). Thus, even work in this very refined area reminds us that the most revealing research on the genetic contributions to behavior will analyze the biological and environmental factors that impact the expression of genes.

2.3. **FETAL PROGRAMMING**

In 1944, World War II, through the actions of the German Army, brought a famine to Holland that many years later was linked to elevated lipid profiles, increased rates of heart disease, glucose intolerance, and poor general health status. The ailments were diagnosed in those who were fetuses during the famine, not in the Dutch who were adults. Thus, the Army's severe food restrictions had a delayed impact of increasing the adult vulnerability for the ravages of these diseases. During the famine the diets of pregnant women had been reduced from 1400 to 800 calories daily (Roseboom et al., 2001). The fetal programming, or fetal origins, hypothesis was formulated based on epidemiological evidence of this kind. It proposed that a compromised intrauterine environment may partially account for the onset of disease in adulthood (Barker, 1998, 2002).

Laboratory and field studies have tested and refined the hypothesis, and it has been useful in explaining rates of hypertension (Barker, Shiell, Barker, & Law, 2000; Walker, McConnachie, Noon, Webb, & Wyatt, 1998), heart disease (Barker, 2002), obesity (Breir, Vickers, Ikenasio, Chan, & Wong, 2001), kidney disease (Moritz, Dodic, & Wintour, 2003), and diabetes (Hales, 1997; Hales & Barker, 1992). Candidate mediators of the intrauterine effects include low birth weight and rapid postnatal weight gain (Barker, 2002; Brier, Vickers, Ikenasio, Chan, & Wong, 2001); however, there is evidence of programming effects in the absence of low birth weight (see Roseboom et al., 2001). Drake and Walker (2004) reviewed intriguing findings that suggest programming can extend beyond the initially affected offspring to the subsequent generation.

Medical and psychological sciences have long recognized the importance of the uterine environment, and in this respect, the fetal programming hypothesis represents a variation on an old theme (see Plagemann, 2005; Santrock, 2008). The recent findings with respect to prenatal effects on disease outcomes reveal an impact more subtle, delayed, and indirect than those that common teratogens, including alcohol or drugs, produce. However, some of the disorders that have been the focus of the fetal programming research, including obesity, hypertension, and hypercholesterolemia, are becoming increasingly problematic among adolescents (Daniels, Greer, & the National Committee, 2008; Muntner, He, Cutler, Widman, & Whelton, 2004). Physicians have called for earlier and more aggressive treatment of these life-threatening conditions.

Healthy psychological development depends on an environment that from conception nurtures the growth and unfolding of exceedingly complex neural networks. The fetal programming hypothesis is relevant to this delicate sculpting of human neural networks. Accordingly, mounting evidence from human and animal research confirms notions that maternal stress and anxiety lead to deficits in learning and attention and increased anxiety and depression in offspring (Weinstock, 2008). Moderators of these effects include the gender of the offspring and the timing of the stressful events.

Indeed, acute changes in the social climate have been shown to affect birth outcomes. Lauderdale (2006) reported an increase in low birth weight among children with Arabic names born in California during the 6 months following the assault on the World Trade Center in New York. However, where long-standing oppressive social systems and structural inequalities exist, the uterine environment may be affected indirectly. Inferior prenatal care, environmental toxins, and poorer health habits surface often in historically oppressed communities (Paradies, 2006; Semmes, 1996). The effects of these may be extensive and possibly cloaked. A recent neuroimaging study of 294 French Canadian adolescents (Paus et al., 2008) revealed that alterations in the corpus callosum (a network of fibers connecting the two hemispheres of the brain) were associated with maternal smoking, a known health-related behavior. The posterior portions of the corpus callosum were smaller among the female offspring of smoking mothers.

The impact of suboptimal early environments need not be evident at birth or even during the early years of life. Sophisticated and long-term studies of the impact of poor health care and environmental toxins on the nervous systems of children in the developing world are urgently needed. The promise of these studies, some of which will employ expensive brain-imaging technologies, is to identify, at earlier stages, subtle and less apparent neural effects of suboptimal prenatal environments. Though limited previous technology left these effects veiled at birth, as is the case with disease, they may surface during the adolescent or adult periods. Of course, early identification increases markedly the available therapeutic options (Plagemann, 2005).

2.4. **PSYCHOPHYSIOLOGICAL STUDIES**

In order to better understand how behavior and physiology change with age, researchers have obtained measures of hormonal and nervous system activity in adolescents. Some of the studies have used physiological variables as markers of the contours of normal human development. For example, investigators study heart rate patterns as indicators of children's increasing ability to pay selective attention to significant events in the environment as they get older (Richards, 1998). Other investigations have employed physiological processes to predict either physiological or behavioral outcomes that will occur during adolescence or adulthood. We will examine some of the studies that sought to predict conduct disorders and depression in adolescents on the basis of physiological processes.

Psychophysiological experimenters are particularly concerned with exercising strict control over the physical and social context in which the physiological measures are obtained. When they wish to obtain indices of resting or baseline activity, participants often sit quietly in comfortable chairs and read or listen to soft music. To measure the responses or reactivity of physiological systems, experimenters use tests, challenges, or brief social encounters to stimulate physiological changes.

Thus, in the study of human development, psychophysiological studies employ physiological measures to either chart normal changes that occur with age or to predict future outcomes. Some studies measure levels of physiological activity at rest, while others study reactions to carefully controlled stimuli. Figure 2.1 shows four quadrants that represent the types of studies in this field. The top two quadrants designate research that focuses on levels of resting physiological activity. The resting measures are used to mark normal processes or to predict future behavioral or physiological outcomes. The lower quadrants specify studies that measured physiological reactions to tasks as markers of processes or predictors of later outcomes. We will review examples of studies from each quadrant presently.

2.4.1. **Markers of adolescent development: Physiological levels**

Changes in the levels of several sets of hormones signal the onset of puberty. Just prior to puberty, androgens released by the adrenal cortex increase the rate of bone maturation and growth and stimulate the

Developmental psychophysiological paradigms

	Markers of normal development	Predictors of physiological or behavioral outcomes
Baseline or resting levels		
Reactions to tasks or challenges		

■ **FIGURE 2.1** Psychophysiological studies are designed to obtain measures of the levels of activity in a particular system at rest or to determine how that system changes when a person performs a task or encounters a change in environmental demands or stimulation. Studies of resting activity fall into the top quadrants. Studies in psychophysiology also differ with respect to their purpose. Some employ the physiological measures as markers of the behavioral processes that are expected to change as humans age. In other instances, the physiological measures forecast clinically important behavioral or physiological outcomes that will occur later in life. Research that searches for predictors of later developmental outcomes reside in the two quadrants on the right. Therefore, developmental psychophysiological research can be classified in terms of method (studies of resting activity or reactivity) and purpose (charting normal processes or predicting future outcomes).

appearance of pubic hair. Subsequently, increased levels of growth and gonadal hormones (estrogen and testosterone) result in marked physical changes. Spear (2000), in a remarkably thorough review of the physiology of this period, noted that the gonadal hormones are, in fact, reinstated during adolescence. Shortly after birth the high levels of gonadal hormones are suppressed only to be "reawakened" later. The gonadal hormones are responsible for the development of sexual organs and secondary sexual characteristics, while the growth hormones stimulate significant increases in height and weight.

Clearly, complex interactions among biological and psychosocial factors influence adolescent hormonal changes. The percent of body fat influences the onset of puberty (Frisch, 1991). Extreme exercise that reduces body fat often delays puberty. Leptin secretion is one possible mechanism involved in the relationship between body fat and puberty. Leptin, a product of fat cells, regulates food intake and has been shown to stimulate growth hormone. Additionally, Spear (2000) described the hypothalamic-pituitary-gonadal (HPG) axis, along which neural messages from the hypothalamus stimulate the pituitary gland to release chemical messages that activate the gonads. These complex pathways seem to open a gate for the impact of a host of systems on these important hormones. For example, activity in the branch of stress responses known as the hypothalamic-pituitary-adrenal cortical (HPA) axis inhibits activity in the HPG axis as well as the output of growth hormone. In humans, the glucocorticoid cortisol is released as part of the HPA reactions to stressful environments. Cortisol is thought to be primarily responsible for the effects of stress on growth and HPG activity. Thus, the reliable hormonal markers of adolescent development are the product of the interplay among psychophysiological forces.

The adolescent period also features major changes in levels of nervous system activity. A portion of the billions of nerve cells in the brain do not survive, and the number of synaptic connections between neurons declines significantly by early adulthood. This extensive "pruning" of neural connections takes place during adolescence (Rakik, Bourgeois, & Goldman-Rakik, 1994). In fact, in some respects, the nervous system appears to be refining itself through subtraction.

Spear (2000) noted that the brain's prefrontal cortex and limbic areas undergo major alterations during adolescence. Using magnetic resonance imaging (MRI), Jernigan, Trauner, Hesselink, and Tallal (1991) found that gray matter (unmylenated portions of the cortex) in the frontal regions of the brain declined across adolescence, particularly in the frontal regions. As the volume and number of synaptic connections in the frontal lobes decline, adolescents continue to improve on neuropsychological measures of performance related to these regions.

Researchers have proposed that as the brain develops, it becomes more organized and complex. Studies have assessed brain complexity by applying nonlinear time series analyses to measures of the electrical activity of the brain (EEG). An international group of researchers from Russia, Germany, and the United States led by Andre Anokhin has studied the emerging complexity of the EEG as children age. They have shown that adolescence is marked by increased complexity in brain activity as the participants rested comfortably (Anokhin, Birbaumer, Lutzenberger, Nikoleav, & Vogel 1996; Anokhin, Lutzenberger, Nikoleav, & Birbaumer, 2000). Thus, resting EEG activity may provide a useful way of marking the refinement of brain functioning as its physical characteristics change with age.

2.4.2. **Markers of adolescent development: Physiological reactions**

The behavioral changes adolescence brings can also be mapped by studying how young people respond to psychological tests. Age-related changes are reflected in how well the younger individuals perform these tasks and the magnitude and quality of their physiological responses to them. Again, researchers have been particularly interested in the functions associated with the frontal lobes. For example, van der Molen, Somsen, and Jennings (2000) tested selective attention abilities by requiring participants to count the number of rare tones presented to one ear over headphones while ignoring all tones presented to the other ear. Individuals from 7 to 20 years of age were recruited for this study. Paying attention to external stimuli is normally accompanied by a slowing of the heart rate. Van der Molen et al. found that older individuals (ages 12-20) in this study made fewer errors on the task and had progressively greater decreases in heart rate as they ignored the irrelevant tones and listened for the rare tones.

EEG activity that occurs as psychological tasks are performed changes during adolescence. Friedman, Brown, Vaughn, Cornblatt, and Erlenmeyer-Kimling (1984) instructed participants, ages 12-17, to lift a finger when they heard a specified (rare) tone that was embedded in a sequence of tones. They measured cortical evoked potentials, which are based on averages of the EEG and reflect timing of changes in brain activation as stimuli are received and processed. Earlier components of the evoked potential reflect the registration of stimuli, while the later components are related to more elaborate processing, including attention and memory. Friedman et al. found that the later components of evoked potentials in the frontal lobes were affected by the age of the adolescents. The frontal lobes control executive cognitive functioning, including the regulation of attention and working memory. The findings of Friedman et al. reveal that components of the evoked potentials related to higher order thinking in this region of the brain are particularly sensitive to developmental changes. In another study, children, adolescents, and adults were shown pictures of objects and instructed to rate them as being the same or different on various dimensions (Friedman, Putman, Ritter, Hamberger, & Berman, 1992). The later components of the evoked potentials in the frontal lobes decreased in amplitude with age. The authors suggested that this change might reflect increases in the speed of processing in the older participants. Finally, Anokhin's team reported that brain complexity increased from the ages of 7-16 years in frontal but not occipital areas when participants engaged in both verbal and spatial visualization tasks (Anokhin et al., 2000). Evidence from these studies suggests, therefore, that the continuing maturation of the frontal lobes during adolescence is evident in physiological responses to tasks involving selective attention and complex mental work.

2.4.3. **Physiological levels as harbingers**

As knowledge of psychological and physiological processes grows, often it becomes possible to use physiological measures as predictors of clinically significant outcomes. Several personality theorists (Eysenck, 1967; Gray, 1964; Zuckerman, 1994) suggest that physiological arousal levels have optimal set points, and individuals who are "under-aroused" search for stimulating situations. Among adolescents, a tendency to gravitate toward exciting situations may be expressed in terms of risk-taking behavior and conduct disorders. Cortisol, a useful measure of the level of activation of the HPA axis, is released when humans are stressed or threatened. Several studies have attempted to predict future disruptive behavior based on levels of cortisol sampled at an earlier time. Three of the larger studies suggest that a relationship may exist under certain conditions. Shoal, Giancolo, and Kirillova (2003) tested 300 boys in the United States and found low levels of cortisol were associated with aggressive behaviors 5 years later. Conduct disorders in 194 Dutch boys 14-16 years of age were related to higher cortisol levels when they were 13 years old (Van Bokhoven et al., 2005). In the largest of the longitudinal studies, Sondeijker et al. (2008) assessed cortisol and, 2 years later, obtained reports from parents of disruptive behavior in 1399 Dutch boys and girls. They found lower cortisol levels in boys with conduct problems but not in girls. Because levels of cortisol fluctuate during the day, these researchers sampled cortisol three times. They found the reported association between behavioral outcomes and cortisol levels in measurements taken during the evening.

It seems reasonable to link physiological arousal to adolescent tendencies to take risks and seek stimulation, however, research using numerous physiological variables to measure arousal show consistently low correlations. Moreover, people differ with respect to the physiological system or the measure that best reflects their state of arousal (Cacioppo et al., 1992). Indeed cortisol is a particularly complicated measure, as it may be elevated in response to acute stress, but reduced to low levels in those experiencing chronic stress (Diamond & Otter-Henderson, 2007). Thus, though the findings relating cortisol levels to behavior problems are interesting, more research is needed to clarify the relationship between arousal and adolescent behavioral problems.

Researchers have also attempted to predict the onset and course of depression in adolescence using levels of EEG activity. Davidson (1995, 1998) proposed that a *frontal asymmetry* consisting of lower levels of arousal in the left frontal lobes relative to levels in the right frontal lobes predisposes one to depression.

The left frontal lobes are activated during positive emotions, while the right frontal lobes appear to mediate negative emotional states. Davidson's model predicted that depression may occur when individuals whose right frontal lobes are more activated encounter negative life circumstances. The model has received strong empirical support (Davidson, 2004).

Here again, longitudinal studies provide the best test of the impact of frontal asymmetries on depression. Possel, Lo, Fritz, and Seeman (2008) assessed EEG activity in 80 German adolescents (ages 13-15) and measured depressive as well as anxiety symptoms twice over a 12-month period. They found that the frontal as well as a parietal EEG asymmetry predicted depressive symptoms 1 year later, as did an EEG in the parietal lobes. Possel et al. noted that parietal asymmetries are associated with anxiety and that often depression and anxiety occur simultaneously among adolescents. Thus, EEG patterns may assist in predicting the onset of depression, but mixed psychological symptoms will be predicted by overlapping asymmetries.

2.4.4. **Physiological reactions as harbingers**

An increasingly efficient ability to regulate behavior in social situations helps young people clear life's social hurdles and obstacles (Porges, 2001). Conversely, difficulties in controlling social behaviors can lead to disruptive behavior disorders (DBD). Extending polyvagal theory (Porges, 1995) and using variations on the NIM (Thayer and Friedman, 2004), investigators have studied the underlying neural activity in DBD in terms of autonomic nervous system reactions. Beauchaine, Gatzke-Kopp, and Mead (2007) examined the cardiac pre-ejection period (PEP) and HRV changes in middle school children in two experimental conditions. PEP measures cardiac sympathetic activity, and its duration shortens under stress. The participants, 17 with attention deficit hyperactivity disorder, 20 with conduct disorder, and 22 controls, watched a film clip that showed an escalating interpersonal conflict. In a separate condition, they were paid to match numbers presented on a screen with those on a key pad. Beauchaine et al. reported reduced resting HRV in the conduct disorder group; this activity continued to decline as they watched the film. Those with conduct disorder evidenced less shortening of the PEP than controls during the incentive task, suggesting sympathetic underarousal in response to a motivational task. Marsh, Beauchaine, and Williams (2008) found that boys with DBD, ranging in age from 9 to 13 years, showed dissociations between autonomic measures (HRV, PEP, and skin conductance) and facial expressions during an emotional film. In contrast to boys in the control group, when boys with DBD showed sad facial expressions during the film, their autonomic systems did not reflect the experiencing of emotions.

Reduced or dissociated autonomic responding may be a marker or eventually a predictor of DBD. Still it is important to bear the working model discussed in Section 2.1.3 in mind when viewing these findings. As Beauchaine et al. (2007) noted, the pattern of autonomic activity shown by a child with DBD will be influenced by genetic as well as social events. Accordingly, Katz (2007) had children with conduct disorders listen to a tape of a belligerent child with whom they were anticipating a future interaction. They found that the children who had witnessed more domestic violence in the home showed increased HRV, indicating parasympathetic activation when they listened to the tape.

Thus differences in cardiac reactions exist within adolescents with DBD as well as between those with DBD and normal children. These are likely to result from a reciprocal interplay between unfolding genetic instructions and psychological events. Indeed social inequities produce structural forces, including unemployment and economic disparities, that will influence psychological and physiological determinants of autonomic activity.

In many low- and middle-income nations and in the United States, cardiovascular diseases are a leading cause of death (Salim et al., 2004). Early detection might prevent a portion of the deaths due to cardiovascular disease. Nearly 30 years ago, psychophysiologists began to revive attempts to predict the onset of heart disease based on the cardiovascular responses to laboratory stressors (Krantz & Manuck, 1984; Obrist, 1981). They hypothesized that those with exaggerated responses would be more inclined to develop disease. Because hypertension and other cardiovascular diseases ravage the Black community in the United States, often African American youth were recruited for these reactivity studies.

The inclusion of a diverse sample in these studies was refreshing, though some researchers expressed concern about the racial comparative nature of the designs (Harrell, Merrit, & Kalu, 1998; Krieger et al., 1993). The emerging body of research sometimes studied the relationship between reactivity and disease simultaneously with questions related to racial difference in responses to stressors. Unfortunately, when differences in cardiovascular responses between participants classified as Black and White were found, investigators often proposed that they were the source of racial differences in disease. Because race was viewed in biological terms, the causes of the reactivity differences and disease disparities were linked to genetics (see Dimsdale, 2000; Grim & Robinson, 1996). Early findings suggested that Black participants responded primarily with vascular versus cardiac sympathetic nervous system responses to stressors, providing some support for notions of genetic differences in cardiovascular control (Anderson, 1989). More recent studies often failed to replicate findings of racial differences in sympathetic responses to tasks (see Allen & Matthews, 1997; Salomon, Matthews, & Allen, 2000).

Trieber et al. (2003) concluded that the reactivity hypothesis has been supported by a growing body of longitudinal evidence. They reviewed studies of the relationship between reactions to stressors in the laboratory and the onset and progression of hypertension and heart disease. Positive findings have been reported in studies that included children and adolescents of Somoan (Newman, McGarvey, & Steele, 1999), Asian American (Matthews, Woodall, & Allen, 1993), and African American (Trieber, Musante, Kapuku, Davis, Litaker, & Davis, 2001) backgrounds. Matthews, Salomon, Brady, and Allen (2003) derived a composite score of cardiac reactivity by summing responses to mirror tracing, reaction time, a stress interview, and cold to the forehead. In a sample of White and African American children and adolescents, the composite measures predicted blood pressure levels taken during a follow-up period 3 years later. Trieber et al. (2003) noted that research in this area is moving at a rapid pace and predicted continued progress as investigators control for genetic differences, chronic stressors, and preexisting diseases.

Two avenues of research may refine the prediction of diseases based on measures of reactivity taken during adolescence. Cardiovascular responses vary according to the nature of the task used to elicit reactions. The reactions to certain tasks may show a relationship with disease, while reactions to others may not. Ewart has studied the responses of adolescents to a social competence interview that directs them to discuss, in detail, reoccurring life stressors (Ewart, Jorgenson, Suchday, Chen, & Matthews, 2002). He has shown that this interview taps different psychophysiological mechanisms than other laboratory stressors, including exposure to heat or cold, mental arithmetic, and mirror tracing. Ewart and Kolodner (1994) reported that in Black and White adolescent participants, the social competence interview predicted blood pressure measures taken at school even after the relationship between blood pressure and other reactions to laboratory stressors were controlled. Ewart, Jorgenson, Schroder, Suchday, and Sherwood (2004) provided evidence that the social competence interview brings about a form of vigilance that repeated stressors would be expected to elicit. In contrast to other stressors, vigilance leads to strong vascular changes and reduced cardiac responses, and this pattern may be associated with later diseases.

A second avenue of research that may lead to better predictions of illnesses is to focus on differences between people in the configuration of autonomic system reactions to stressors. Commonly, the branches of the autonomic nervous system are thought to act in a reciprocal fashion: as one increases in strength, the other decreases. Bernstson, Cacioppo, and Quigley (1991) showed that in some instances the systems can be activated simultaneously or coactivated, and in other instances, the systems are coinhibited. Salomon et al. (2000) found that during a reaction time task, a stress interview, and mirror tracing task, adolescents tend to show characteristic autonomic patterns, with the majority responding with reciprocal sympathetic arousal, that is, increased sympathetic and decreased parasympathetic activity. Berntson, Norma, Hawkley, and Cacioppo (2008) employed cardiac sympathetic (PEP) and parasympathetic (HRV) indices to compute measures of the balance between the systems and the tendency of the systems to be coactivated. Certainly, in the near future, longitudinal studies of children and adolescents of the kind reported by Matthews et al. (2003) will determine if the configuration or pattern of autonomic activity at rest and when challenged are related to cardiovascular diseases in adulthood.

2.4.5. **Physiological activity and cognitive efficiency**

Aristotle thought cognitive functions were orchestrated by the heart and that the brain cooled the heart and blood. Hippocrates disagreed and posited the brain was the seat of intelligence and mediated bodily sensations. Galen's animal and human studies corroborated this view. As implausible as Aristotle's "cardiocentric" view seems today, for more than 40 years, cardiovascular psychophysiologists have reported evidence that a two-way channel of causal communication exist between the cardiovascular system and the brain (Lacey & Lacey, 1978).

The brain controls the vagus nerve through neural circuitry designated the central autonomic network (Benarroch, 1993, 1997). This region shares anatomical structures with the anterior executive region (Devinsky, Morrell, & Vogt, 1995) of the brain, an area that facilitates executive functions and goal-directed behavior. Thayer (2007) summarized several studies that used HRV to measure the functioning of the vagus nerve while adult participants were given tests of executive cognitive functions. Individuals with low HRV, indicating low levels of vagal control, showed impaired performance on working memory tasks. In one study, Thayer's team actually reduced the HRV by instructing a group of participants not to stop engaging in regular exercise. This "mild de-training" not only affected HRV, it impacted cognitive performance. The group that continued to exercise showed improvements in performance when retested on working memory and executive functioning tasks, while the detrained participants failed to improve (Hansen, Johnsen, Sollers, Stenvik, & Thayer, 2004).

Researchers have found that impaired cognitive performance is one of the early consequences of even mildly elevated blood pressure or hypertension (Waldstein, Manuck, Ryan, & Muldoon, 1991). Lande, Kaczorowski, Aunger, Schwartz, and Weitzman (2003) analyzed blood pressure and cognitive performance data taken from the Third National Health and Nutrition Study (NHANES III), which included 5398 children between the ages of 6 and 16 years. Scores on tests of digit span—the capacity to hold a series of numbers in working memory—were lower in individuals in the top 90th percentile of the sample. Among those children with the highest blood pressure levels, systolic blood pressure predicted poorer performance even when the effects of socioeconomic status, race, and heart rate were controlled.

Thus, there is reason to suspect that the cognitive performance of young people may be affected by the status of their cardiovascular systems. Blood pressure levels and HRV are modifiable through changes in weight and aerobic fitness. It is time to acknowledge that Aristotle was on the right track and rank cardiovascular variables among factors that impact the cognitive performance of adolescents.

2.4.6. **Resilience and resistance**

In an attempt to understand positive adaptation despite the adversity adolescence might bring, many researchers have adopted a risk and resilience approach to the study of adolescent development. This approach posits that not everyone who is exposed to the same level of risk will experience the same degree of harm as a result of that exposure. Resilience theory suggests that compensatory and protective factors such as dispositional attributes, characteristics of the family milieu, and other developmental competencies counteract and protect adolescents against the deleterious effects of adversity and trauma (Garmezy, Masten, & Tellegen, 1984). A dynamic interplay between multiple levels of the individual and hierarchical developmental contexts over time determines the extent to which adolescents are able to resist successive threats to adaptation and development.

Research literature reveals no shortage of risk or resilience factors or contexts that have been foci of the study of adolescent development. Examples of risk factors include child maltreatment, parental psychopathology, marital conflict, poverty, violence, racism and discrimination, and even material wealth, to name a few. These elements constitute significant adversity or trauma and place adolescents at increased risk for negative developmental outcomes. The list of resilience factors is even longer and includes factors such as attachment status, quality parenting, positive familial relationships, positive relationships with teachers, peers, and mentors, the capacity to regulate emotions, religious affiliation, parental social support, neighborhood cohesion, intelligence, internal locus of control, identity, and so on (for a detailed review, see Luthar, 2006). These factors operate at the level of the individual, family, and wider social contexts, with significant interactions across the three (Luthar). For the most part, the preponderance of resilience studies has focused on behavioral and psychosocial correlates of resilience (Curtis & Cicchetti, 2003); however, interest in biological contributors to resilience has changed as the cultural Zeitgeist has shifted to be more inclusive of biopsychosocial approaches and as researchers have become more interested in not only identifying associations, but also understanding underlying mechanisms in risk and resilience pathways.

The emerging body of literature examining resilience and physiological processes is relatively small. Even smaller is the number of studies to examine these processes in diverse adolescent populations. Nevertheless, the available studies examining biological contributors to resilience pave the road for an exciting new direction in the study of resilience and physiological processes in adolescent development. One of the most compelling aspects of resilience factors and processes is the focus (although not exclusive) on relationships. Several of the risk factors noted above can be linked with disruptions in relationships, while many of the resilience factors are associated with positive relationships with others. Not surprisingly, Luthar (2006) notes: "resilience rests, fundamentally, on relationships. The desire to belong is a human need, and positive connections with others lie at the very core of psychological development; strong supportive relationships are critical for achieving and sustaining resilient adaptation" (p. 780). Consistent with this observation, Ryff and Singer (2002) found that adults with positive prior relationships with their parents and positive, current relationships with their spouses, were significantly less likely to show high allostatic load (i.e., compromised metabolic, cardiovascular, HPA axis, and sympathetic nervous system physiological systems). Positive relationships also buffered the negative effects of economic risk on allostatic load so that only 22% of individuals with positive relationships showed high allostatic load in the presence of economic risk, compared with 69% of those with negative prior relationships with parents and current relationships with spouses. Luthar interpreted this data as suggestive of "a type of biopsychosocial pathway of resilience" (p. 758).

In addition to physiological processes implicated in positive relation-ships, physiological mechanisms have been implicated in resistance and resilience across several physiological domains. In the area of neu-ral plasticity, for example, there is evidence to suggest that the human brain is highly sensitive to environmental conditions, with exposure to various contexts carrying implications for the development of psychopa-thology (Curtis & Cicchetti, 2003). One possibility is that resilient and nonresilient children might demonstrate divergent patterns of brain structure and functioning (Luthar, 2006) as a function of differential exposure to diverse developmental contexts associated with protection and/or risk early in development. In studies of emotion regulation—a critical component in the development of psychopathology—there is evidence to suggest that resistance to adversity might be manifested by the ability to recover quickly from negative events. Physiological studies have examined startle response (Grillon, Dieker, & Merikangas, 1997, 1998) and reactivity of the HPA axis following a stressor as indices of emotion regulatory processes. Grillon et al., for example, reported ele-vated baseline startle magnitude and startle response to a threat condi-tion in children of parents with anxiety disorders, compared to control children. These data suggest that exposure to an environmental context infused with parental anxiety over time might compromise physiologi-cally mediated emotion regulatory processes and place children at risk for subsequent developmental challenges. With regard to the activation of the HPA axis, exposure to risk factors and contexts may result in elevated levels of cortisol, thus carrying implications for neuron synthe-sis, neurotransmitter reuptake, sensitivity of neuronal receptors (Luthar), and long-term effects on subsequent regulatory processes. Resistance to adversity may be compromised with the disruption of critical component tasks necessary for regulatory processes necessary to fend off maladap-tation. Finally, work by Anokhin et al. (2000) in the area of cortical complexity (reviewed earlier in the chapter) may eventually shed light on individual differences in intelligence as a protective factor and in higher level brain functioning in children and adolescents who resist adversity despite the odds. Recent evidence linking *emotional* intelli-gence in adulthood to relatively low cortisol levels and blood pressure responses to acute stressors (Salovey, Stround, Woolery, & Epel, 2002) may also reveal important clues regarding underlying physiologi-cal processes in a specific domain of intelligence as it pertains to adoles-cent resilience. Together, these studies provide preliminary evidence of biological processes that may play a role in adolescent development and resilience.

The study of physiologically mediated resilience processes in adolescent development is yet in its infancy. However, the available studies provide an important foundation on which future research can build. First and foremost, it will be necessary to conduct studies investigating these processes in diverse adolescent populations. To date, many of the studies examining physiological contributors to resilience have been conducted solely with adults. Second, in light of the emphasis on relationships and emotion regulatory processes in resilience, the so-called "social nervous system" may be a worthy candidate for focus in subsequent studies of resistance and resilience in adolescent populations. Future research should examine variations in vagal tone and/or reactivity to various stressors across developmental contexts. Prospective studies of HRV, in particular, may provide important clues regarding not only the role of the autonomic nervous system in resilience pathways, but also the context-mediated interplay between the brain and the peripheral nervous system as influences on positive adolescent developmental outcomes. Third, the study of physiological processes involved in resistance and resilience is not inconsistent with examining these mechanisms in persons other than the adolescent. In fact, given what we know about the hierarchical, interacting, mutually influential nature of social systems, future research efforts should, where possible, examine *in vivo* reactivity of multiple physiological systems across multiple ecological settings. Recent technological advances will allow such work to take place.

2.5. **CONCLUSION**

The research literature sampled here reveals that the changes associated with adolescence reach far beyond sexual development and obvious increases in height and weight. In response to genetic instructions and input from the external world, modifications in networks of neurons in the brain take place at a dizzying pace. In the best instances, neural changes mediate increased attentional and behavioral control, more complex information processing abilities, as well as a capacity for deeper reflection on the ramifications of one's actions. Additionally, the social environment radically changes its posture toward the evolving young person. To varying degrees, in most cultures the adolescent encounters higher expectations for ethical conduct, new responsibilities to both younger and older members of society, and more severe consequences for transgressions. Neither the changes associated with the adolescent period nor their causes should be viewed parochially. Each set of evolving influences and outcomes, from those biological to those in societal domains, is to some extent a product of events within other causal realms. Adolescents—those who make it to the national spelling bee, play raucous games on city playgrounds, or like Bambara's Manny, are hustled away in hand-cuffs by the authorities—are the product of a staggering array of factors that begin to interact the moment after conception. Our awe in the face of the complexity of these converging forces should be matched by the strength of our commitment to optimize the factors that nurture productive and healthy adolescent development.

REFERENCES

Allen, M. T., & Matthews, K. A. (1997). Hemodynamic responses to laboratory stressors in children and adolescents: The influence of age, race, and gender. *Psychophysiology, 34*, 329–339.

Allport, G. (1937). *Personality: A psychological interpretation.* New York, NY: Henry Holt.

Allport, G. (1954). *The nature of prejudice.* Reading, MA: Addison-Wesley.

Anderson, N. B. (1989). Racial differences in stress-induced cardiovascular reactivity and hypertension: Current status and substantive issues. *Psychological Bulletin, 105*, 89–105.

Anderson, N. B. (1998). Levels of analysis in health science: A framework for integrating sociobehavioral and biomedical research. *Annals of the New York Academy of Sciences, 840*, 563–576.

Anokhin, A. P., Birbaumer, N., Lutzenberger, W., Nikoleav, A., & Vogel, F. (1996). Age increases brain complexity. *Electroencephalography and Clinical Neurophysiology, 99*, 63–68.

Anokhin, A. P., Lutzenberger, W., Nikoleav, A., & Birbaumer, N. (2000). Complexity of electrocortical dynamics in children: Developmental aspects. *Developmental Psychobiology, 99*, 63–68.

Arnett, J. (1999). The "storm and stress" of adolescence reconsidered. *American Psychologist, 54*, 317–326.

Bambara, T. C. (1981). The hammer man. In T. C. Bambara (Ed.), *Gorilla, my love.* New York, NY: Vintage Press.

Barker, D. J. P. (1998). *Mothers, babies and health in later life* (2nd ed.). Edinburgh: Churchill Livingstone.

Barker, D. J. P. (2002). Fetal programming in coronary heart disease. *Trends in Endocrinology and Metabolism, 13*, 364–368.

Barker, D. J. P., Shiell, A. W., Barker, M. E., & Law, C. M. (2000). Growth *in utero* and blood pressure levels in the next generation. *Journal of Hypertension, 18*, 843–846.

Beauchaine, T. P., Gatzke-Kopp, L., & Mead, H. K. (2007). Polyvagal theory and developmental psychopathology: Emotion dysregulation and conduct problems from preschool to adolescence. *Biological Psychology, 74*, 174–184.

Benarroch, E. E. (1993). The central autonomic network: Functional organization, dysfunction, and perspective. *Mayo Clinic Proceedings, 68*, 988–1001.

Benarroch, E. E. (1997). The central autonomic network. In P. A. Low (Ed.), *Clinical autonomic disorders* (2nd ed., pp. 17–23). Philadelphia, PA: Lippincott-Raven.

Bernstson, G. G., Cacioppo, J. T., & Quigley, K. S. (1991). Autonomic determinism: The modes of autonomic control, the doctrine of autonomic space, and the laws of autonomic constraint. *Psychological Review, 98*, 459–487.

Berntson, G. G., Norman, G. B., Hawkley, L. C., & Cacioppo, J. T. (2008). Cardiac autonomic balance versus cardiac regulatory capacity. *Psychophysiology, 45*, 643–652.

Brier, B. H., Vickers, M. H., Ikenasio, B. A., Chan, K. Y., & Wong, W. P. S. (2001). Fetal programming of appetite and obesity. *Molecular and Cellular Endocrinology, 185*, 73–79.

Bronfenbrenner, U. (1977). Toward and experimental ecology of human development. *American Psychologist*, 513–531.

Bronfenbrenner, U., & Ceci, S. J. (1994). Nature-nurture reconceptualized in developmental perspective: A bioecological model. *Psychological Review, 101*, 568–586.

Cacioppo, J. T. (1994). Social neuroscience: Autonomic, neuroendocrine, and immune responses to stress. *Psychophysiology, 31*, 113–128.

Cacioppo, J. T., & Berntson, G. G. (2002). Social neuroscience. In J. T. Cacioppo, G. G. Bernson, R. Adolphs, C. S. Carter, R. J. Davidson, M. K. McClintock, B. S. McEwen, M. J. Meaney, D. L. Schacter, E. M. Sternberg, S. S. Soumi, & S. E. Taylor (Eds.), *Foundations in social neuroscience* (pp. 3–10). Cambridge, MA: MIT Press.

Cacioppo, J. T., Berntson, G. G., Sheridan, J. F., & McClintock, M. K. (2002). Multilevel integrative analyses of human behavior. Social neuroscience and the complementing nature of social and biological approaches. In J. T. Cacioppo, G. G. Bernson, R. Adolphs, C. S. Carter, R. J. Davidson, M. K. McClintock, B. S. McEwen, M. J. Meaney, D. L. Schacter, E. M. Sternberg, S. S. Soumi, & S. E. Taylor (Eds.), *Foundations in social neuroscience* (pp. 21–46). Cambridge, MA: MIT Press.

Cacioppo, J. T., Uchino, B. N., Crites, S. L., Snydersmith, M. A., Smith, G., Berntson, G. G., et al. (1992). Relationship between facial expressiveness and sympathetic activation in emotion: A critical review, with emphasis on modeling underlying mechanisms and individual differences. *Journal of Personality and Social Psychology, 62*, 110–128.

Cannon, W. B. (1929). *Bodily changes in pain, hunger, fear, and rage*. New York, NY: Appleton.

Cooper, R. S. (2004). Genetic factors in ethnic disparities in health. In N. B. Anderson, R. A. Bulatao, & B. Cohen (Eds.), *Critical perspectives on racial and ethnic differences in health in late life* (pp. 269–309). Washington, DC: The National Academies Press.

Crick, F. (1970). Central dogma of molecular biology. *Nature, 227*, 561–563.

Curtis, W. J., & Cicchetti, D. (2003). Moving research on resilience into the 21st century: Theoretical and methodological considerations in examining the biological contributors to resilience. *Development and Psychopathology, 15*, 773–810.

Damasio, A. R. (1998). Emotions in the perspective of an integrated nervous system. *Brain Research Reviews, 26*, 83–86.

Daniels, S. R., & Greer, F. R., & The National Committtee. (2008). Lipid screening and cardiovascular health. *Pediatrics, 122*, 198–208.

Davidson, R. J. (1995). Cerebral asymmetry, emotion, and affective style. In R. J. Davidson & K. Hughdal (Eds.), *Brain asymmetry* (pp. 361–387). Cambridge, MA: MIT Press.

Davidson, R. J. (1998). Anterior electrophysiological asymmetries, emotion, and depression: Conceptual and methodological conundrums. *Psychophysiology, 35*, 607–614.

Davidson, R. J. (2004). What does the prefrontal cortex "do" in affect: Perspectives on frontal EEG asymmetry research. *Biological Psychology, 67*, 219–233.

De Geus, E., Goldberg, T., Boomsma, D. I., & Posthuma, D. (2008). Imaging the genetics of brain structure and function. *Biological Psychology, 79*, 1–8.

Devinsky, O., Morrell, M. J., & Vogt, B. A. (1995). Contributions of the anterior cingulated cortex to behavior. *Brain, 118*, 279–306.

Diamond, L. M., & Otter-Henderson, K. D. (2007). Physiological measures. In R. W. Robins, R. C. Fraley, & R. F. Krueger (Eds.), *Handbook of research methods in personality psychology* (pp. 370–388). New York, NY: The Guilford Press.

Dimsdale, J. E. (2000). Stalked by the past: The influence of ethnicity on health. *Psychosomatic Medicine, 62*, 161–170.

Drake, A. J., & Walker, B. R. (2004). The intergenerational effects of fetal programming; nongenomic mechanisms for the inheritance of low birth weight and cardiovascular risk. *Journal of Endocrinology, 180*, 1–16.

Dunbar, F. (1935). *Emotions and bodily changes*. New York, NY: Columbia University Press.

Edleman, G. (1987). *Neural Darwinism*. New York, NY: Basic Books.

Elman, J., Bates, E. A., Johnson, M. H., & Parisi, D. (1997). *Rethinking Innateness: A Connectionist perspective on development*. Cambridge, MA: MIT Press.

Ewart, C. K., Jorgenson, R. S., Schroder, K. E., Suchday, S., & Sherwood, A. (2004). Vigilance to persistent personal threat: Unmasking cardiovascular consequences in adolescents with the Social Competence Interview. *Psychophysiology, 41*, 799–804.

Ewart, C. K., Jorgenson, R. S., Suchday, S., Chen, E., & Matthews, K. A. (2002). Measuring stress resilience and coping in vulnerable youth: The Social Competence Interview. *Psychological Assessment, 14*, 339–352.

Ewart, C. K., & Kolodner, K. B. (1994). Negative affect, gender, and expressive style predict ambulatory blood pressure in adolescents. *Journal of Personality and Social Psychology, 66*, 596–605.

Eysenck, H. J. (1967). *The biological basis of personality*. Springfield, IL: Charles C. Thomas.

Fanon, F. (1967). *Black skin white masks*. New York, NY: Grove Press.

Fanon, F. (1968). *The wretched of the earth*. New York, NY: Grove Press.

Fossella, J., Fan, J., Liu, X., Guise, K., Brocki, K., Hof, P. R., et al. (2008). Provisional hypotheses for the molecular genetic of cognitive development: Imaging genetic pathways in the anterior cingulated cortex. *Biological Psychology, 79*, 23–29.

Fox, N. A., Schmidt, L. A., & Henderson, H. A. (2000). Developmental psychophysiology: Conceptual and methodological perspectives. In

J. T. Cacioppo, L. G. Tassinary, & G. G. Berntson (Eds.), *Handbook of psychophysiology* (pp. 665–686). New York, NY: Cambridge University Press.

Friedman, D., Brown, C., Vaughn, H. G., Cornblatt, B., & Erlenmeyer-Kimling, L. (1984). Cognitive brain potential components in adolescents. *Psychophysiology, 21*, 83–96.

Friedman, D., Putman, L., Ritter, W., Hamberger, M., & Berman, S. (1992). A developmental event-potential study of picture matching in children, adolescence, and young adults: A replication and extension. *Psychophysiology, 29*, 593–610.

Frisch, R. E. (1991). Puberty and body fat. In R. M. Lerner, A. C. Petersen, & J. Brooks-Gunn (Eds.), *Encyclopedia of adolescence* (pp. 884–892). New York, NY: Garland Publishing.

Gardner, W. L., Gabriel, S., & Diekman, A. B. (2000). Interpersonal processes. In J. T. Cacioppo, L. G. Tassinary, & G. G. Berntson (Eds.), *Handbook of psychophysiology*. New York, NY: Cambridge University Press.

Garmezy, N., Masten, A. S., & Tellegen, A. (1984). The study of stress and competence in children: A building block for developmental psychopathology. *Child Development, 55*, 97–111.

Gottlieb, G. (1998). Normally occurring environmental and behavioral influences on gene activity: From central dogma to probabilistic epigenesis. *Psychological Review, 105*, 792–802.

Gould, S. J. (1981). *The mismeasure of man.* New York, NY: W. W. Norton.

Graves, J. L. (2001). *The Emperor's new clothes: Biological theories of race at the millennium.* New Brunswick, NJ: Rutgers University Press.

Gray, J. A. (1964). Strength of the nervous system as a dimension of personality in man. In J. A. Gray (Ed.), *Pavlov's typology.* New York, NY: Macmillan.

Grillon, C., Derker, L., & Merikangas, K. R. (1998). Fear-potentiated startle in adolescent offspring of parents with anxiety disorder. *Biological Psychiatry, 44*, 990–997.

Grillon, C., Dierker, L., & Merikangas, K. R. (1997). Startle modulation in children at risk for anxiety disorders and/or alcoholism. *Journal of the American Academy of Child & Adolescent Psychiatry, 36*, 925–932.

Grim, C. E., & Robinson, M. (1996). Blood pressure variations in Blacks: Genetic Factors. *Seminars in Nephrology, 16*, 83–93.

Hales, C. N. (1997). Metabolic consequences of intrauterine growth retardation. *Acta Paedriatrica Supplment, 423*, 184–187.

Hales, C. N., & Barker, D. J. P. (1992). Type 2 (non-insulin-dependent) diabetes mellitus; the thrifty phenotype hypothesis. *Diabetologia, 35*, 595–601.

Hansen, A. L., Johnsen, B. B., Sollers, J. J., Stenvik, K., & Thayer, J. F. (2004). Heart rate variability and its relation to prefrontal cognitive function: The effect of training and detraining. *European Journal of Applied Physiology, 93*, 263–272.

Harrell, J., Merritt, M. M., & Kalu, J. (1998). Racism, stress, and disease. In R. Jones (Ed.), *African American mental health: Theory research and intervention.* Hampton, VA: Cobb and Henry Publishers.

Hebb, D. O. (1949). *The organization of behavior.* New York, NY: Wiley.

Jaenisch, R., & Bird, A. (2003). Epigenetic regulation of gene expression: How the genome integrates intrinsic and environmental signals. *Nature Genetics Supplement, 33*, 245–254.

Jernigan, T. L., Trauner, D. A., Hesselink, J. R., & Tallal, P. A. (1991). Maturation of human cerebrum observed *in vivo* during adolescence. *Brain, 114*, 2037–2049.

Johnston, T. D., & Edwards, L. (2002). Genes, interactions and the development of behavior. *Psychological Review, 109*, 26–34.

Katz, L. F. (2007). Domestic violence and vagal reactivity to peer provocation. *Biological Psychology, 74*, 154–164.

Krantz, D. C., & Manuck, S. B. (1984). Acute psychophysiological reactivity and the risk for disease: A review and methodological critique. *Psychological Bulletin, 96*, 435–464.

Krieger, N. (1994). Epidemiology and the web of causation: Has anyone seen the spider. *Social Science Medicine, 39*, 887–903.

Krieger, N., Rowley, D. L., Herman, A. A., Avery, K., Rowley, H., Avery, B., et al. (1993). Racism, sexism, and social class: Implications for the study of health, disease, and well-being. *American Journal of Preventive Medicine, 9*, 82–122.

Lacey, B. C., & Lacey, J. I. (1978). Two-way communication between the heart and the brain. *American Psychologist, 33*, 99–113.

Lande, M. B., Kaczorowski, J. M., Aunger, P., Schwartz, G. J., & Weitzman, M. (2003). Elevated blood pressure and decreased cognitive function among school-aged children and adolescents in the United States. *Journal of Pediatrics, 143*, 720–724.

Lauderdale, D. S. (2006). Birth outcomes for Arabic-named women before and after September 11. *Demography, 43*, 185–201.

LeDoux, J. (1996). *The emotional brain*. New York, NY: Simon and Schuster.

LeDoux, J. (2002). *Synaptic self: How our brains become who we are*. New York, NY: Penguin Books.

Leukel, F. (1976). *Introduction to physiological psychology*. Saint Louis: C. V. Mosby Company.

Luthar, S. S. (2006). Resilience in development: A synthesis of research across five decades. In D. Cicchetti & D. J. Cohen (Eds.), *Developmental psychopathology: Vol. 3. Risk, disorder, and adaptation* (2nd ed., pp. 739–795). New York, NY: Wiley.

Madhere, S., Harrell, J. P., & Royal, C. (2009). Social ecology, genomics, and African American health: A nonlinear dynamical perspective. *Journal of Black Psychology, 35*, 154–179.

Marsh, P., Beauchaine, T. P., & Williams, B. (2008). Dissociation of sad facial expressions and autonomic nervous system responding in boys with disruptive behavior disorders. *Psychophysiology, 45*, 100–110.

Matthews, K. A., Salomon, K., Brady, S. S., & Allen, M. T. (2003). Cardiovascular reactivity to stress predicts future blood pressure in adolescence. *Psychosomatic Medicine, 65*, 410–415.

Matthews, K. A., Woodall, K. L., & Allen, M. T. (1993). Cardiovascular reactivity to stress predicts future blood pressure status. *Hypertension, 22*, 479–485.

Moore, D. S. (2001). *The dependent gene: The fallacy of nature vs. nurture*. New York, NY: Henry Holt and Company.

Moritz, M. D., Dodic, M., & Wintour, E. M. (2003). Kidney development and the fetal programming of adult disease. *BioEssays, 25*, 212–220.

Muntner, P., He, J., Cutler, J. A., Widman, R. P., & Whelton, P. K. (2004). Trends in blood pressure among children and adolescents. *Journal of the American Medical Association, 291*, 2107–2113.

Newman, J. D., McGarvey, S. T., & Steele, M. S. (1999). Longitudinal association of cardiovascular reactivity and blood pressure in Samoan adolescents. *Psychosomatic Medicine, 61*, 243–249.

Obrist, P. (1981). *Cardiovascular psychophysiology: A perspective.* New York, NY: Plenum.

Paradies, Y. (2006). Defining, conceptualizing, and characterizing racism in research. *Critical Public Health, 16*, 143–157.

Pascual-Leone, A., Amedi, A., Fregni, F., & Merabet, L. B. (2005). The plastic human brain cortex. *Annual Review of Neuroscience, 28*, 377–401.

Paus, T., Nawazkhan, I., Leonard, G., Perron, M., Pike, M., Pitiot, G. B., et al. (2008). Corpus callosum in adolescent offspring exposed prenatally to maternal cigarette smoking. *NeuroImage, 40*, 435–441.

Piattelli-Palmarini, M. (1989). Evolution, selection and cognition: From "learning" to parameter setting in biology and in the study of language. *Cognition, 31*, 1–44.

Plagemann, A. (2005). Perinatal programming and functional teratogenesis: Impact on body weight regulation and obesity. *Physiology and Behavior, 86*, 661–668.

Pole, N. (2007). The psychophysiology of post traumatic stress disorder: A meta analysis. *Psychological Bulletin, 133*, 725–746.

Porges, S. W. (1973). Heart rate variability: An autonomic index of reaction time performance. *Bulletin of the Psychonomic Society, 1*, 270–272.

Porges, S. W. (1995). Orienting in a defensive world: Mammalian modifications of our evolutionary heritage: A polyvagal theory. *Psychophysiology, 32*, 301–318.

Porges, S. W. (2001). Polyvagal theory: Phylogenetic substance of a social nervous system. *International Journal of Psychophysiology, 42*, 123–146.

Porges, S. W. (2007). The polyvagal perspective. *Biological Psychology, 74*, 116–143.

Possel, P., Lo, H., Fritz, A., & Seeman, S. (2008). A longitudinal study of cortical EEG activity in adolescents. *Biological Psychology, 78*, 173–178.

Rakik, P., Bourgeois, J. P., & Goldman-Rakik, P. S. (1994). Synaptic development in the cerebral cortex for learning, memory, and mental illness. In J. van Pelt, M. S. Corner, H. B. M. Ulings, & F. H. de Silva (Eds.), *Progress in brain research, the self organizing brain: From growth cones to functioning neural networks* (Vol. 102). Amsterdam: Elsevier.

Richards, J. E. (Ed.) (1998). *The cognitive neuroscience of attention: A developmental perspective.* London: Erlbaum.

Roseboom, T. J., van der Meulen, J. H. P., Ravelli, A. C. J., Osmond, C., Barker, D. J. P., & Bleker, O. P. (2001). Effects of prenatal exposure to the Dutch famine on adult disease in later life: An overview. *Molecular and Cellular Endocrinology, 185*, 93–98.

Rushton, J. P., & Jensen, A. R. (2005). Thirty years of research on race differences in cognitive ability. *Psychology, Public Policy and Law, 11*, 235–294.

Ryff, C. D., & Singer, B. (2002). From social structure to biology: Integrative science in pursuit of human health and well-being. In C. R. Snyder & S. J. Lopez (Eds.), *Positive psychological assessment: A handbook of models and measures* (pp. 541–554). Washington, DC: American Psychological Association.

Salim, Y., Hawken, S., Ounpuu, S., Dans, T., Avezum, A., Lanas, F., et al. (2004). Effects of potentially modifiable risks factors associated with myocardial infarction in 52 countries (the INTERHEART study) case-control study. *Lancet, 364,* 937–952.

Salomon, K., Matthews, K. A., & Allen, M. T. (2000). Patterns of sympathetic and parasympathetic reactivity in a sample of children and adolescents. *Psychophysiology, 37,* 842–849.

Salovey, P., Stroud, L. R., Woolery, A., & Epel, E. S. (2002). Perceived emotional intelligence, stress reactivity, and symptom reports: Further explorations using the trait meta-mood scale. *Psychology and Health, 17,* 611–627.

Santrock, J. W. (2008). *Life-span development* (11th ed.). Boston, MA: McGraw Hill.

Schmader, T., Johns, M., & Forbes, C. (2008). An integrated process model of stereotype threat effects on performance. *Psychological Review, 115,* 336–356.

Semmes, C. E. (1996). *Racism. Health and post-industrialism: A theory of African-American health.* Westport, CN: Praeger.

Shoal, G. D., Giancola, P. R., & Kirillova, G. P. (2003). Salivary cortisol, personality, and aggressive behavior in adolescent boys: A 5-year longitudinal study. *Journal of the American Academy of Child and Adolescent Psychiatry, 42,* 1101–1107.

Sondeijker, F. E. P. L., Ferdinand, R. F., Oldehinkel, A. J., Tiemeier, H., Ormel, J., & Verhulst, F. C. (2008). *Psychophysiology, 45,* 398–404.

Spear, L. P. (2000). The adolescent brain and age-related behavioral manifestations. *Neuroscience and Behavioral Reviews, 24,* 417–463.

Sternbach, R. A. (1966). *Principles of psychophysiology.* New York, NY: Academic Press.

Thayer, J. F. (2007). What the heart says to the brain (and vice versa) and why we should listen. *Psychological Topics, 16,* 241–250.

Thayer, J. F., & Friedman, B. H. (2004). A neurovisceral integration model of health disparities in aging. In N. B. Anderson, R. A. Bulatao, & B. Cohen (Eds.), *Critical perspectives on racial and ethnic differences in health in late life* (pp. 567–603). Washington, DC: The National Academies Press.

Thayer, J. F., & Lane, R. D. (2007). The role of vagal function in the risk of cardiovascular disease and death. *Biological Psychology, 74,* 224–242.

Thompson, R. F. (1967). *Foundations of physiological psychology.* New York, NY: Harper and Row Publishers.

Tomarken, A. (1999). Methodological issues in psychophysiological research. In P. C. Kendall, J. N. Butcher, & G. N. Holmbeck (Eds.), *Handbook of research methods in clinical psychology.* (2nd ed.). New York, NY: Wiley.

Trieber, F. A., Kamarck, T., Schneiderman, N., Sheffield, D., Kapuku, G., & Taylor, T. (2003). Cardiovascular reactivity and development of preclinical and clinical disease states. *Psychosomatic Medicine, 65,* 46–62.

Trieber, F. A., Musante, L., Kapuku, G., Davis, C., Litaker, M., & Davis, H. (2001). Cardiovascular (CV) responsivity and recovery to acute stress and future CV functioning in youth with family histories of CV disease: A 4-year longitudinal study. *International Journal of Psychophysiology, 41*, 65–74.

Van Bokhoven, I., Van Goozen, S. H. M., Van Engeland, H., Schall, B., Arseneault, L., & Seguin, J. L. (2005). Salivary cortisol and aggression in a population-based longitudinal study of adolescent males. *Journal of Neural Transmission, 112*, 1083–1096.

Van der Molen, M. W., Somsen, R. J. M., & Jennings, J. R. (2000). Developmental changes in auditory selective attention as reflected by phasic heart rate changes. *Psychophysiology, 37*, 626–633.

Waldstein, S. R., Manuck, S. B., Ryan, C. M., & Muldoon, M. F. (1991). Neuropsychological correlates of hypertension: Review and methodological considerations. *Psychological Bulletin, 110*, 451–468.

Walker, B. R., McConnachie, A., Noon, J. P., Webb, D. J., & Wyatt, G. C. (1998). Contributions of parental blood pressures to association between low birth weight and adult high blood pressure: Cross sectional study. *British Medical Journal, 316*, 834–837.

Weinstock, M. (2008). The long-term behavioral consequences of prenatal stress. *Neurosciences and Behavioral Reviews, 32*, 1073–1086.

Zuckerman, M. (1994). *Behavioral expressions and biosocial bases of sensations seeking*. New York, NY: Cambridge University Press.

Chapter 3

Cognitive development for adolescents in a global era: A social justice issue?

Davido Dupree

University of Pennsylvania, Philadelphia, USA

Cognitive development encompasses life-course changes in a range of behaviors related to cognitive processes, including but not limited to, language and thought, learning and memory, decision making and problem solving. It encompasses patterns and processes by which individuals experience changes in their understanding and use of language, how they learn and what they are capable of comprehending, and how they make meaning of and respond to their daily experiences.

During adolescence, cognitive development takes on special importance because adolescents are also experiencing a number of other critical changes: changes in hormonal activity (Yurgelun-Todd, 2007), changes in body size and shape (Mendle, Turkheimer, & Emery, 2007), as well as changes in social contexts and peer groups (Collins & Laursen, 2004; Zimmer-Gimbeck, 2002). Thus, the developing adolescent must learn to adapt to all these various changes whether they occur sequentially or simultaneously. The very need to adapt to these changes serves as catalyst for further cognitive development. It is their cognitive developmental status that determines how adolescents make meaning of their experiences and make decisions while navigating the different contexts in which they live and function. Yet the global era offers a new "virtual" (i.e., Internet-based) context in which development can take place. The goal of this chapter is to consider ways in which normative cognitive developmental processes are

Adolescence: Development During a Global Era

impacted in a technologically global era. More specifically, this chapter will consider the ways in which access to new technologies—ushered in by the global era—can influence the processes of cognitive development for adolescents. In support of this goal, there is a need to establish a useful point of reference for understanding normative cognitive development among adolescents. The theoretical perspectives of Piaget and Vygotsky are described below to provide that necessary point of reference.

3.1. **PIAGET'S CONSTRUCTIVIST PERSPECTIVE**

Piaget's theoretical contributions to our understanding of cognitive development reflect both stage-independent processes—processes assumed to be a factor regardless of the stage of development—and stage-dependent processes—processes that are specific to discrete stages of development (e.g., Muuss, 1996). Central to Piaget's perspective is the assumption that cognitive development is an active process by which children actively *construct* knowledge through their interactions with the environment. In other words, cognitive development is a function of active exploration. It is through this active exploration that developing individuals generate schema to guide their subsequent explorations. This active exploration results in the ongoing development and revision of cognitive structures through which individuals make meaning of their experiences and observations. Piaget employed the concept of schemas to represent different kinds of exploration strategies. Specifically, schemas are combinations of actions that individuals use to explore their environments using their senses of taste, touch, sight, smell, and hearing. In a related fashion, structures represent the knowledge resulting from the different schemata that have been enacted by the individual. For example, an adolescent may engage in a series of exploratory behaviors (schemata) to determine whether a new classmate is a potential friend or foe. The adolescent's friendship "structure" may include characteristics of other individuals he or she has befriended in the past (e.g., physical characteristics, personality characteristics, behaviors and activities, etc.). Accordingly, the adolescent may engage in a series of exploratory behaviors (schemata) to determine whether a new classmate shares characteristics with current friends and engages in the same types of "friendly" behavior as they do. Such schema might include looking at the classmate's clothes, listening to how the classmate talks and what he or she talks about, extending a hand as a gesture of friendship to establish a physical connection, etc.

It is important to note that such schemata and structures can continue to evolve (e.g., Fox & Riconscente, 2008). That is, from Piaget's perspective, schemata and structures can persevere only as long as they are effective in helping the individual make sense of his or her experiences and observations. Once the individual encounters experiences or makes observations that do not fit within their existing schemata or structures, adaptation must take place. Adaptation is the result of ongoing processes of assimilation and accommodation. Assimilation refers to new experiences that fit with current schemata and structures and are simply assimilated into these preexisting schemata and structures. They represent additional examples or "illustrations" for the existing knowledge structures, and they reinforce existing schemata. However, if new experiences do not fit with existing schemata or structures then accommodation must take place. Existing schemata and structures must be adapted to accommodate these new experiences. If an adolescent, for example, ends up befriending a classmate who does not "fit the profile" of current friends, then the adolescent must modify his or her friendship "structure" to account for a broader range of physical characteristics, personality characteristics, behaviors, and actions. Likewise, the adolescent may also revise schemata to include looking for different types of dress and behavior, listening for different types of conversation, and engaging in additional types of "friendly" behavior.

Piaget's theorizing includes stages of development that roughly correspond to infancy, early childhood, middle childhood, and adolescence (Thomas, 2001). For Piaget, structures in each stage are qualitatively different from those in other stages. Progression through these stages represents advancement toward more logical thinking. It is important to note, however, that research suggests that the manifestations of these stage-specific levels of functioning may not be as distinct as Piaget originally theorized. That is, some research demonstrates that, depending on context and the character of the developmental tasks to be performed, the developing individual can act in ways that reflect earlier stages of development in spite of having already achieved a more advanced stage of development. Likewise, under the right contextual conditions, a developing individual can complete a task in a way that reflects a more advanced stage of development. Such observations may be explained in part by Piaget's assumption that development reflects qualitative changes in the interactions between the individual and the environment. These changes in the quality of interaction occur because the developing child is experiencing physical and physiological changes as a function of "in-wired" development—that is, the types of changes that all humans experience in sequential fashion, although at different rates of change. These "in-wired" changes—such as improvement in motor skills, increases in height and weight, development of synaptic connections in the brain—lead to changes in how the developing child is able to interact within and act upon his or her environment. It would follow then that competencies developed are a function of qualitative changes in the abilities of the individual to explore his or her environment, as well as qualitative differences in the actual character of the different environments in which the individual lives and functions. In a nutshell, developing individuals may be more likely to express competence within contexts that are familiar to them and in response to tasks that are also familiar to them.

In terms of his proposed stages of cognitive development, Piaget's *formal operations stage* is most closely aligned with the period of adolescence (Muuss, 1996). The formal operations stage is characterized by increases in abstract thought, hypothetical thinking (e.g., considering possibilities), thinking about one's own thinking (i.e., metacognition), and more relativistic views of truth (i.e., they no longer think of truth in absolute terms, recognizing that what may be true in one context may not be true in another). Piaget's theory offers an explanation of progression toward more logical thinking. With that in mind, it is also important to note that formal operational thinking is not necessarily optimized during adolescence. Adolescents may engage in formal operations as described above, but their engagement in such behaviors may not be as consistent or proficient as it would be for adults, who have the benefit of time and life experiences. Furthermore, research suggests that optimization of the formal operations stage is associated with more formal schooling (see Muuss). Thus, one should expect a diversity of behaviors and abilities to be reflected within this stage as a function of differences in such factors as language skills and memory capacity, the richness of the environments in which developing adolescents have lived and functioned, and the extent to which they do, or are allowed to, actively explore their environments.

The formal operational stage reflects both changes in how adolescents think and the focus of their thoughts: themselves (e.g., Fox & Riconscente, 2008). Adolescents are more likely to think about themselves in both concrete (e.g., their physical characteristics, activities they engage in) and abstract terms (e.g., the values they espouse, their perceived mental capacities). They are able to think about and imagine potential outcomes for experiences they have not yet engaged in. They become more self-reflective and self-conscious. Fairly or not, adolescents are assumed to be much more egocentric compared to those in other stages of development. From a Piagetian perspective, there is potentially some manifestation of egocentrism at every stage of development (Muuss, 1996). Adolescent egocentrism is simply manifested differently (i.e., imaginary audience, personal fable) (Elkind, 1978). They not only have the capacity to think abstractly about themselves but can now consider the possibility that others are also thinking about them in abstract or hypothetical terms too! They may develop an "imaginary audience," reflecting their assumptions that their every move is being monitored by others.

Regarding their ability to think more logically, adolescents may still experience deficits in their ability to accurately predict outcomes of their actions by taking into account relevant variables. In keeping with such a perspective, adolescents may create "personal fables" in which they dismiss or minimize the likelihood of experiencing negative outcomes for their actions despite the actual prevalence of those same negative outcomes among peers and others. Nevertheless, it is important to note that research suggests that adolescents are actually more likely to overestimate rather than underestimate the risk of certain negative outcomes (Reyna & Farley, 2006). Thus, the assumed existence of "personal fables" may actually be the result of inferences made by outside observers that adolescents are behaving as if they do not believe there are consequences for their actions. Consequently, the assumption of "personal fables" may not be a reflection of the adolescents' own decision-making processes (e.g., Boyer & Byrnes, 2009) but of conclusions drawn by outside observers.

3.2. **VYGOTSKY'S SOCIOCULTURAL PERSPECTIVE**

While Vygotsky's theoretical perspective does not isolate adolescence as a unique stage of development (Thomas, 2001), it does offer insight into the processes by which cognitive development can be stimulated by social interaction. This is particularly important to consider in light of the fact that adolescence can be characterized in terms of changes or expansion of social networks (e.g., Collins & Laursen, 2004; Zimmer-Gimbeck, 2002). Vygotsky's perspective can help us understand the processes by which the different social networks with which the developing adolescent may interact can influence cognitive development.

For Vygotsky, cognitive development depends on interaction with (1) the people in the developing child's world and (2) the tools that the culture provides to support thinking (e.g., books, toys, video games) (Thomas, 2001). From this perspective, culture shapes cognitive development by determining *how* and *what* one learns. Culture determines what a developing child is exposed to and how the developing child is expected to interact within and upon the cultural environment.

In terms of specific mechanisms for development, Vygotsky asserts that language is essential for cognitive development (e.g., Wertsch, 2008).

For example, developing children engage in private speech (e.g., talk to themselves) for the purpose of "thinking out loud" (see Jones, 2009, for critique). They are essentially labeling what they experience and observe in their environments and "codifying" their thoughts with the words of their native language. Furthermore, language allows children to interact with knowledgeable others. Though it should go without saying, the developing child and knowledgeable others should be speaking the same language. More specifically, it is possible for two individuals to use and perceive the same words but attribute different meanings and connotations to those same words. In such instances, there is inadvertent miscommunication. Thus, it is important to understand the cultural points of reference that contribute to oral and written communications.

Perhaps most relevant to this discussion is Vygotsky's notion of the Zone of Proximal Development (ZPD). The ZPD encompasses the difference between what a developing child can do on his or her own and what that same child can accomplish with scaffolding from an adult or more sophisticated peer (e.g., Wertsch, 2008). In terms of learning, scaffolding is not simply giving a developing child the answer to a question or the solution to a challenge. Rather, scaffolding refers to strategies for probing (e.g., asking questions), guiding (e.g., coaching, encouraging), or directing the attention of a developing child in ways that allow him or her to initiate the process of discovering the answer or solution for himself or herself. Valsiner elaborates on the ZPD positing that there are three interrelated zones (Thomas, 2001):

- *Zone of Free Movement*: The environment and objects present and available to influence a person's actions within a particular setting at a given time.
- *Zone of Promoted Action*: The modes of action that caregivers encourage or demand within the zone of free movement.
- *Zone of Proximal Development*: Within ZFMs and ZPAs, children can acquire more advanced modes of thought before they discover them on their own.

Valsiner's elaboration identifies the units of analysis by which we should assess the potential effects of any social context in which adolescents may find themselves.

3.3. **COGNITIVE DEVELOPMENT IN CONTEXT**

Both Piaget's and Vygotsky's perspectives take into account interactions between individual and environment. However, Piaget emphasizes the individual's active exploration of the environment, while Vygotsky emphasizes reciprocal social interactions. Considered together, their perspectives provide critical points of reference for considering cognitive development in context. When considering cognitive development in context, the developing individual is also a part of the context. Accordingly both intra- and interindividual interactions can influence development.

In terms of interindividual interactions, the presence of developmentally instigative characteristics is important (Bronfenbrenner, 1993). These are individual characteristics that elicit responses from other individuals within the different environments in which a developing adolescent lives and functions. For instance, adolescent females who experience early maturation (i.e., the development of breasts, the broadening of hips) may be perceived by others as chronologically older and, in some instances, more sexually experienced than they actually are (e.g., Mendle et al., 2007). As a result, older males, in particular, may respond to and interact with them as if they are older and cognitively mature.

In intraindividual interactions, however, development is uneven. As development takes place along a number of dimensions (i.e., physical, social, emotional, cognitive, etc.) these different dimensions do not necessarily progress in "lock-step" fashion. In many instances, it is this unevenness (i.e., interactions among uneven levels of development) that can be the catalyst for cognitive development. In using the previous example of an early maturing adolescent female, the unevenness between her physical and cognitive development creates a degree of cognitive dissonance that requires adaptation—in the Piagetian sense—to accommodate these new experiences. In the absence of responsible scaffolding to help them anticipate and effectively make meaning of and cope with unsolicited romantic interest, these early maturing females may develop schemata (e.g., look for friends that are similar in physical maturation) and structures (e.g., mistakenly believe that, because they are more physically mature they are also more cognitively mature) that place them on negative trajectories associated with early sexual activity.

In addition to acknowledging that the developing individual is a part of the context and can "contribute" to his or her own cognitive development, it is also important to acknowledge that "virtual" spaces (e.g., cyberspace, Internet) also constitute contexts for development. While not existing in a physical space in which one can walk and touch and otherwise physically inhabit, virtual spaces still provide the context and opportunity for the exercise of different cognitive processes and social interactions that can promote cognitive development. The remainder of this chapter considers cognitive development for adolescents in the context of technological advances. In this consideration, Piagetian perspectives are relevant to the extent that they highlight the ways in which "exploration" in cyberspace or on the Internet can facilitate cognitive development. Likewise, Vygotskyian perspectives are relevant to the extent that they highlight the ways in which new technologies can be seen as cultural tools as well as scaffolding strategies and relationships.

3.4. NEW TECHNOLOGY TRANSFORMS COGNITIVE ABILITY

In this global era, technological advances have expanded what we can do and how we do what we do. With the greater independence typically afforded to youth during adolescence, technology provides adolescents with greater access to more diverse information and images from around the world. Adolescents can communicate with people from around the corner or around the world—friends, family, and strangers alike. New technologies even allow adolescents new ways of experimenting with identities (e.g., Valkenburg, Schouten, & Peter, 2005). With the relative anonymity provided by some technologies, adolescents can create virtual identities that may or may not be a reflection of who they are. The relative social distance allows adolescents to assert themselves in ways they might not behave in face-to-face interactions.

Within the framing of this chapter, technology refers to technological innovations that increase the frequency and diversity of global access to people, information, and images. These include but are not limited to the Internet, videoconference monitors, smartphones, and camera phones. The specific functions afforded by these global devices are person-to-person communications, text messaging, Internet searching, bulletin board dialoguing, "blogging," online chatting, videoconferencing, and online gaming. New technologies may not necessarily be used to gain global access. It is the fact that they allow for global access that makes them representative of the global era. In terms of adolescent development, it is the local uses of global technologies that are most relevant. While global technologies can expand human abilities, the processes that drive cognitive development remain the same. Accordingly, while narrowing the gap in terms of access to information resources globally, these new technologies have the potential to widen gaps in cognitive development locally.

Expanded ability through technology would appear on the surface to bring a long sought after equity in access to and use of information resources. The potential pedagogical uses of new technologies are intuitively appealing in that they offer the opportunity for self-paced, self-motivated, and self-evaluated exploration and learning. However, the social and economic inequities that exist for some youth (see Chapter 1), and which are evident in their daily experiences, also exist and may be further exacerbated in cyberspace. To be clear, the inequity addressed in this chapter is not in access to the technologies, but rather the potential inequity in how the technologies are used and, consequently, influence cognitive development. The greater global access ushered in by newer and more sophisticated technologies has simultaneously closed gaps and created new gaps in terms of "how" the availability and access to the technological and human resources can stimulate cognitive development for adolescents. Gaps in how adolescents gain access to information (i.e., procedural knowledge) and what types of information they access (i.e., declarative knowledge) may be closing, while gaps in how adolescents make meaning of and use that information (i.e., conceptual knowledge) may be widening. The effects of this global era on cognitive development for adolescents may become a social justice concern.

In an oral presentation at Emory University in the early 1990s, George Lakoff offered that technology transforms human ability. As an example, he offered that with the introduction of the handheld calculator, developing individuals did not necessarily have to learn how to perform arithmetic calculations in their heads. With the introduction of the calculator as a new "cultural tool," individuals have the ability to perform more frequent and more complex arithmetic calculations than they would in the absence of the calculator...without having the conceptual understanding typically necessary to perform those same calculations "by hand" or "in their heads." From a functional standpoint, the individual's capabilities have been expanded; yet, from a developmental standpoint, cognitive development has been hindered. Their development of mathematical knowledge (e.g., understanding numbers as symbols, units of measurement, and the reversibility of arithmetic functions) has been hindered if they do not have sufficient opportunities to practice performing these same arithmetic functions by hand or in their heads.

The types of technology that have made global communication increasingly more accessible likely have also transformed the abilities of adolescents. Essentially, technology in this global era allows adolescents the ability to perform functions that they would not necessarily be able to perform in the absence of such technology. Procedurally, they are able to perform functions that they might not yet understand conceptually. With this in mind, using technological tools, the adolescents' cognitive abilities may be transformed in ways that are functional and adaptive in the short term but maladaptive due to conceptual limits in the long term.

It is possible that adolescents will learn to do new things using technological tools (i.e., they develop procedural knowledge) without understanding the conceptual processes (i.e., they do not develop the conceptual understanding that will optimize the application of their procedural knowledge). Examples include but are not limited to constructing and transmitting written communications without having mastered the rules of grammar or spelling; accessing information on novel topics without having the experiential knowledge necessary to determine the credibility of the sources or the accuracy of the information; and constructing a base of knowledge about a topic or concern using information accessed through a variety of global technologies without having the conceptual knowledge necessary to ensure that information is used in appropriate ways and appropriate inferences are drawn.

3.5. IMPLICIT LEARNING AND ITS IMPLICATIONS FOR THE GLOBAL ERA

The introduction of new technologies has the potential to widen the gaps in conceptual understanding that maximize the use of accessible information. Conceptual knowledge is often developed implicitly—through implicit learning (e.g., learning how to spell through texting, learning "scientific thinking" through conducting Internet searches, etc.). Implicit learning refers to learning that takes place as a function of engaging in specific activities that result in knowledge that is not necessarily available for conscious recall (Schacter, Chiu, & Ochsner, 1993; see Gee, 2003 for discussion of the skills and knowledge implicitly learned through video game play). Individuals may not be able to consciously recall the conditions under which they have "learned" new information or procedures but still behave in ways consistent with learned knowledge. Implicit learning is normative. The remainder of this section describes three different examples of implicit learning. The purpose is to illustrate the ways in which implicit learning—a normative cognitive developmental process— can influence other dimensions of cognitive and social development. The very act of using new technologies thus provides the context and opportunity for implicit learning.

3.5.1. The implicit learning of spelling strategies

Using spelling as an example, some research suggests that, in the absence of direct instruction, spelling is learned as a function of implicit cognition (Steffler, 2001). That is, we "unconsciously" pick up patterns of language (e.g., consistencies in how words sound or are spelled). Many of the communications afforded by global technologies are text-based (i.e., websites, text messages, bulletin boards, chat rooms, etc.). Exposure to correct or incorrect spellings of words can affect later spelling performance (i.e., priming) (Steffler). Interestingly, research suggests that both good and poor spellers are affected equally by prior exposure. The critical difference is that good spellers perform better on words that require "abstract morphophonemic" knowledge (i.e., what word units mean and from where they originate). The cognitive development gap is widened as better educated youth with preexisting declarative and conceptual spelling knowledge maintain an advantage over their more poorly educated counterparts because they have the critical point of reference provided by their morphophonemic knowledge in terms of the development of their spelling strategies.

Most relevant to adolescent development, in particular, there also appears to be a developmental trajectory. Specifically, spellers will make analogies to known words when attempting to spell words (Steffler, 2001). That is, if two words sound alike, the speller will use the spelling of the known word as a reference for how to spell the unknown word (e.g., using "sanity" to spell "vanity" results in a correct spelling; using "robin" to spell "bobbin" as "bobin" results in an incorrect spelling). Marsh and colleagues (cited in Steffler, 2001) found that in middle childhood, 7-year-olds don't use analogies to spell and that one-third of 10-year-olds used analogies to spell. However, over half of college students use analogies to spell. Through adolescence, there is an increase in the use of analogies to known words—words to which one has been exposed—as a spelling strategy. If we consider Internet-based resources or technology-driven communications as contexts for learning or practicing literacy, then we must consider the potential effects on academic skills for adolescents already matriculating through poor educational systems or who have been disfranchised from local educational systems.

3.5.2. **The implicit learning of stereotypes**

Implicit cognition is not limited to academic knowledge. Implicit cognition is also reflected in self-knowledge and social perceptions (e.g., stereotypes). Implicit or unconscious learning can be observed in contexts in which technological advances are not present. Yet the possibilities for implicit learning are increased with the greater access to information and images provided by global technologies. As an illustration, this possibility is demonstrated in the development of stereotype consciousness.

From a developmental perspective, color consciousness and attitudes about color emerge at an early age. Over 60 years ago, well before the public introduction of the technological advances that have ushered in this global era, Clark and Clark (1939, 1940) found that Black children as young as 3 years old had knowledge of skin color connotations and could appropriately self-identify themselves based on their skin color. In a later experiment, Clark and Clark (1947) found that when children were given a Black and a White doll and asked questions such as which one they would "like to play with" or which one is the "nice doll?" the majority of the children indicated the White dolls in response to positive attributes. The Clarks interpreted these findings as an indication of Black children's internalization of color connotations or stereotypes that resulted in low self-esteem or self-hatred. Follow-up studies have yielded similar findings that Black children displayed a preference for lighter skin (i.e., White people) more frequently than they displayed a preference for darker skin (i.e., Black people) (e.g., Gopaul-McNicol, 1988; Porter, 1991; Williams & Roberson, 1967). If the awareness of color connotations could be observed over 60 years ago in the absence of access to the range of information and images now available, how much more likely is it that children and youth will encounter information and images that stimulate the development of and reinforce implicitly or unconsciously learned color connotations? That is, the content of cyberspace or Internet-based contexts arguably reflects the same social biases that are present in physical or face-to-face interactions. Accordingly, the content of cyberspace or Internet-based content exponentially increases the opportunities and risks inherent in unexamined implicit learning processes.

Additional research suggests that, for younger children who are still cognitively egocentric, there is no link between their understanding of color connotations and their personal self-esteem. Specifically, subsequent research, also conducted with Black children, has shown that despite having a preference for the color white (for dolls, pictures, or other objects), Black children display high self-esteem and positive self-concept (Banks, 1984; McAdoo, 1985; Spencer, 1984). These researchers maintain that Black children's personal self-esteem is independent from racial self-esteem; these color connotations or stereotypes have not been internalized. For instance, Spencer conducted research with a sample 130 Black preschool children between the ages of 4 and 6 years and found that 80% of the sample had positive self-concept scores, even though they demonstrated pro-White biased cultural values. She concluded that these children separated personal identity (i.e., self-concept) from knowledge of race and color connotations. Spencer's (1999) later studies examined children's pro-White or Eurocentric response patterns and found that Black children demonstrate Eurocentric attitudes, preferences, and color connotations regardless of age. Older children, however, demonstrate a marked shift in their attitudes and preferences as they begin to gain an understanding of their own attitudes about skin color, society's attitudes toward skin color, and stereotypes about color (e.g., Dupree, Spencer, & Bell, 1997).

As they get older and experience more advanced cognitive development (e.g., can take into account multiple concrete and abstract factors in making meaning of their experiences), youth are less able to ignore any dissonance created by their understanding of their own and society's attitudes toward skin color. For example, as adolescents become more cognitively sophisticated they are more likely to experience cognitive dissonance when they encounter or recognize differences between themselves and others in terms of treatment in day-to-day interactions, experience of privilege, access to resources, and so forth. These dissonance-generating encounters increase the likelihood that members of disfavored racial or ethnic groups will actively explore their own racial or ethnic identities as a result (e.g., French, Seidman, Allen, & Aber, 2006).

In the absence of direct instruction or scaffolding such as racial or ethnic socialization (see Hughes et al., 2006, for more detailed discussion), children are able to perceive color connotations or stereotypes. Furthermore, research suggests that children who are members of disfavored racial or ethnic groups develop stereotype consciousness earlier than children who are members of favored racial or ethnic groups (e.g., McKown & Weinstein, 2003). The implication is that the prejudice or discrimination they may encounter directly (i.e., personal experiences or direct observations of biased treatment toward members of their particular racial or ethnic group) or indirectly (e.g., the differential representation of members of their particular racial or ethnic group in the media) serve to stimulate the development of stereotype consciousness of children of disfavored racial or ethnic groups. This stereotype consciousness is established around 10 years of age, just prior to early adolescence. Essentially, they enter adolescence with cognitive schemes that are likely to be further reinforced by their subsequent experiences in the absence of racial or ethnic socialization that can instill racial pride or prepare youth to address racial or ethnic bias in adaptive ways (Hughes et al., 2006).

Self-paced, self-motivated, and self-evaluated exploration using new global technologies allows for more frequent exposure to information and images that will essentially serve the purpose of reinforcing preexisting schemes or stereotypes. The greater access to information and images afforded by new technologies increases the likelihood that adolescents will encounter information and images that have implications for their identity exploration without the scaffolding that can provide alternative interpretations, reducing potentially negative effects on identity development (i.e., internalization of negative racial stereotypes). In other words, implicit learning processes can stimulate or reinforce the acquisition of cognitive schemas that facilitate the development of stereotype consciousness which—in the absence of constructive scaffolding in the Vygotskian sense—can negatively affect identity development.

3.5.3. Implicit learning of behavior schemes: The example of exposure to violence

Though not necessarily discussed in terms of cognitive development or learning, exposure to violence is associated with cognitive symptoms and arguably has implications for the development of cognitive schemes that influence how youth make meaning and respond to subsequent exposure to violence. There is, in essence, implicit learning involved in action or behavior schemes (Schacter et al., 1993).

Violent media have been associated with engagement in violent behavior (e.g., Boxer, Rowell Huesmann, Bushman, O'Brien, & Moceri, 2009). Violent media may include a fight between students or a teacher, a student's attack on a teacher that is video-recorded by students using a camera phone and subsequently uploaded to the Internet to be viewed by others, the filming and web posting of videos of hate crimes, or video games and movies. However, it is important to clarify that research suggests that it is not necessarily exposure to violent media that predicts violent behavior (e.g., Savage & Yancey, 2008), but rather it is a preference for violent media that further predicts engagement in violent behavior (e.g., Boxer et al.). In terms of technology, such findings offer that the ability to actively seek out and access violent media can reinforce and/or further develop knowledge structures for making meaning of violent experiences, both directly experienced and observed.

While there may be multiple perspectives about both its causes and effects, violence arguably has effects on child and adolescent development. Research suggests that different types of exposure to violence may elicit different effects on individuals. For instance, some studies indicate that, in response to personal victimization, adolescents will manifest posttraumatic stress disorder (PTSD) symptoms such as intrusive thoughts, sleep disorders, avoidant behavior, and difficulty concentrating (Bell & Jenkins, 1991; Pynoos & Nader, 1990). Pynoos and Nader (1988) offer that, in response to violent experiences, some adolescents may manifest development-specific responses: self-consciousness about their fears, a sense of vulnerability, or a fear of being labeled abnormal. Pynoos and Nader further indicate that adolescents may make a premature entrance into adulthood (e.g., leaving school), make radical changes in life attitudes that influence identity formation, or show detachment, shame, and guilt much like adult responses. Cognitive schemes can focus on action or behavior sequences. Accordingly, through experiences with violence, adolescents can implicitly develop schemas for responding to exposure to violence. Interestingly, prior exposure to violence increases the likelihood that an individual will re-experience PTSD-like symptoms (e.g., American Psychiatric Association, 1994; Spencer et al., 2003). Essentially, this re-experiencing of symptoms may reflect the existence of schemas for how to respond to exposure to violence. Again, from a Piagetian perspective, schemas and corresponding knowledge structures can continue to evolve as subsequent experiences either fit into or represent significant departures from existing schemata and structures. Experiences that fit can be assimilated, allowing for the development of more articulated knowledge structures. The developing adolescent acquires more diverse exemplars or illustrative experiences that reinforce and further define their existing knowledge. On the other hand, novel experiences require accommodation to explain or support observations that cannot be explained or accounted for by existing structures. Related to the experience of violence, in particular, there can be implicit lessons communicated by adults' responses, or lack thereof, to adolescents' exposure to and experience with violence. For example, a lack of response from responsible adults to adolescents' exposure and responses to community violence can signal to the youth that both their exposure and responses—adaptive or maladaptive—to such violence should be considered normative and acceptable.

If we further consider the effects of exposure to violence in the absence of direct instruction or scaffolding related to coping with such experiences, the effects of violence on school engagement and academic performance can often go unnoticed when students are in communities where there are few systemic responses beyond police intervention. The problem is that, in many instances, the criminal aspects of violent experiences are addressed while possible developmental effects can go unacknowledged or misattributed. This belief is supported, in part, by the fact that many studies documenting exposure to violence have been conducted on nonclinical samples (e.g., Bell & Jenkins, 1991, Spencer et al., 2003). That is, youth who have not received clinical counseling—a form of scaffolding—for exposure to violence are reporting symptoms typically associated with it.

The processes by which youth make meaning of their experiences (i.e., phenomenology) help determine the ultimate effects of exposure to violence. In particular, experiences with violence can affect cognitive functions that are necessary for learning: difficulty concentrating (i.e., paying attention), hypervigilance, memory or recall difficulty, or sleep problems (Pynoos & Nader, 1988, 1990). Each of these symptoms relates to learning processes. Memory and recall are primary indicators of learning. That is, it is assumed that one has successfully learned new information or skills if information previously taught can be recalled or applied in specific and appropriate ways. However, attention is a necessary prerequisite of memory and learning. A student cannot learn information or skills to which they have not attended (i.e., seen, heard, touched, smelled, tasted). While they are not the only factors that influence learning, attention and memory are critical components of the learning process. Even when one cannot explicitly recall information or procedures, tests of the speed with which one relearns information or procedures are an indication of the "fluency of re-processing" (Schacter et al., 1993). Whether one recalls information or procedures explicitly or implicitly, attention is a necessary prerequisite. Any factor that hinders a student's ability to pay attention will hinder that student's ability to learn.

Experience with violence can lead to difficulty concentrating or remaining focused on classroom-relevant materials and activities. Accordingly, academic performance is compromised. Yet, attention can, as a result of exposure to violence, become more attuned to violent stimuli (e.g., May, 1986). For instance, when May presented study participants who had and had not been involved in violent activities with pairs of tachistoscopic images (i.e., visual stimuli presented for an extremely brief period) of benign and violent themes, the participants who had experience with violence were more likely to identify violent themes. These images were presented at speeds that allowed the participants to see the images but not enough time for them to focus on any aspect of the images. Again, consider the effects on cognitive development when learning (1) takes place using new technologies, (2) is self-paced, self-motivated, and self-evaluated, and (3) is absent direct instruction or scaffolding. Experiences with violence frame the interpretation of subsequent experiences, making certain violent information and images more salient than others. With these implicit learning effects of exposure to violence, it is reasonable to expect that selective attention effects will also be a factor as adolescents access information and images with violent themes through different global technologies. Direct instruction and scaffolding are required to assist developing adolescents to make meaning of such images when encountered.

3.6. **COGNITIVE DEVELOPMENT AND ADOLESCENTS IN A GLOBAL ERA**

As illustrated in the prior section, implicit learning takes place in a variety of contexts. There are lessons drawn from our everyday experiences. These lessons are learned with no conscious regard for the intentionality of the learning experience nor the accuracy of the "lesson." We use whatever knowledge or understanding we have to make sense of our experiences whether they are sufficient or not. The normative use, or application, of insufficient experiential knowledge is demonstrated in the simplest Piagetian experiments, in which sequential patterns were found in the types of mistakes children make as they attempt to solve specific developmental tasks (e.g., Flavell, Miller, & Miller, 2001). From a Piagetian perspective, these sequential patterns reflect transformations in how children perceive and use information in their development toward more sophisticated and logical thinking.

The patterns in cognitive development that Piaget identified are probably similar to the patterns in the development of knowledge and understanding that any individual will follow in mastering any new topic. For instance, in solving conservation tasks, children are initially unable to coordinate the use of multiple pieces of information to help them recognize that when an equal amount of liquid is successfully poured from one vessel into another, the volume of the liquid remains the same regardless of varying vessel shapes (e.g., Flavell et al., 2001). Children do not successfully solve the conservation task because, developmentally speaking, they will only focus on one piece of information that is salient for them (i.e., the height of the vessel) to the exclusion of other relevant pieces of information.

This simple example is focused on childhood cognition but arguably describes a process that lays the foundation for adolescent cognition. The example is further distinguished from adolescent development in that it is focused on concrete experiences wherein adolescent cognition is characterized by the increasing ability to think on an abstract level and consider hypothetical situations (Steinberg, 2005; Yurgelun-Todd, 2007). However, Case (Case & Okamoto, 1996; Flavell, Miller, & Miller, 2001) offers that there are information-processing efficiency substages for all periods of cognitive development. This perspective opens up the possibility that adolescents will make similar types of errors, though the focus of their cognitions may be different. Case's substages include:

- Operational consolidation—integrating milestones already achieved.
- Unifocal coordination—focusing on one factor at a time to solve a problem.

■ Bifocal coordination—greater neural maturation; more experience increases ability to pay attention to two factors to solve a problem.

■ Elaborated coordination—coordinating two or more factors in complex ways to solve problems (Case & Okamoto, 1996; Flavell, Miller, & Miller, 2001).

As previously asserted, new technologies offer greater opportunities for self-paced, self-motivated, and self-evaluated exploration. Additionally, in the absence of direct instruction or scaffolding around how to use information to effective advantage, individuals will focus on elements of information resources or images that are most salient for them to the exclusion of other relevant information. Such processes can ultimately lead to the erroneous use of specific elements of information resources and images in ways that create or sustain gaps in cognitive development. We will continue to observe gaps in the types of cognitive skills acquired. From a Piagetian perspective, the underlying assumption is that differences in the acquisition of cognitive skills result from differences in the availability of opportunities for exploration, scaffolding, and direct instruction that generates cognitive disequilibration (or cognitive dissonance). It is these experiences of cognitive dissonance that prompt individuals to develop or acquire more advanced cognitive skills. The impact of these developmental gaps then becomes a matter of social justice.

3.6.1. The development of scientific thinking skills in the global era

In self-directed experimentation (SDE), learners explore and learn scientific thinking skills (i.e., multivariable cause and effect systems) through activities that are self-initiated (for detailed discussion, see Zimmerman, 2007). In the spirit of this chapter, the phrase "scientific thinking skills" does not refer to the development of one's skills as a scientist but, instead, to the development of one's ability to effectively identify cause-and-effect relationships in daily experiences. Transformations in knowledge are associated with the use of valid experimentation and inference strategies, yet it takes appropriate knowledge to select appropriate experimentation strategies. In turn, systematic and valid experimentation strategies support the development of more accurate and complete knowledge (Schauble, 1996, cited in Zimmerman). There are reciprocal relationships between knowledge and experimentation, and increasing sophistication of scientific thinking involves both strategy changes and the development of knowledge (Zimmerman).

So what might self-directed experimentation look like in the global era? Consider adolescents' searches for technologically transmitted health-related information and perspectives. A study by Borzekowski and Rickert (2001a) found that 49% of participating adolescents used the Internet to access health-related information. Another study by Borzekowski and Rickert (2001b) indicated that there is socioeconomic and ethnic diversity among the youth who use the Internet to access health-related information, although there are differences in how often and from where they gained access to Internet-based health information. Health information is potentially available through a variety of sources: personal communications using a variety of technologies, online bulletin boards, chat rooms, weblogs, personal websites, health organization websites, health advocacy websites, etc. Using increasingly sophisticated technologies to access information (procedural knowledge), an adolescent may encounter multiple sources of health-related information. In actuality, the sources themselves could range from informal (e.g., personal accounts) (e.g., Wiemann, DuBois, & Berenson, 1998) to formal (e.g., Web-based health information clearinghouses).

In a study by Gray, Klein, Cantrill, and Noyce (2002) focusing on female adolescents, participants asserted that one advantage of the Internet was the volume of information immediately accessible to the user from any computer. At the same time, some expressed concern about their ability to manage the high volume of information available. Interestingly, another study by Gray, Klein, Noyce, Sesselberg, and Cantrill (2005), including both male and female adolescents, indicated not only that most of the adolescents in their study used the Internet to access health-related information but that they also employed different strategies for assigning credibility to Internet sources. For instance, Internet-based information from an academic institution was deemed more credible than other less formal sources. They recognized the need to get accurate information and were concerned about misdiagnosis.

As noted earlier, the social and economic inequities present in the daily experiences of adolescents are no less relevant in cyberspace. Accordingly, we must understand how the normative processes by which adolescents make decisions influence how they use their "health-related knowledge" to address their own health challenges—in the absence of direct instruction or scaffolding from a health professional.

Gray, Cantrill, and Noyce (2002) conducted a study exploring the schema used by adolescents to make health-related decisions. Their findings suggested that the adolescents participating in their study had initially assimilated information during childhood and adolescence related to the medicines preferred by their mother. However, over time, many of their repertories evolved to include medical consultation and prescription therapies, such as antibiotics, in their schemas to manage longer term symptoms they may have experienced. Likewise, focus group and case study data showed that the likelihood of information being incorporated into specific minor ailment schemas was dependent upon its saliency (i.e., the relevance of that information to the individual's situation). The authors suggest that adolescents manage common ailments by compiling a series of "health repertory" schemas based on personal experience— direct or observed—as well as more formal sources. In keeping with the ability to think more hypothetically, they offer that adolescents may also combine schemas to enable them to manage new minor ailments experienced.

Disparities in educational achievement also become a consideration when adolescents conduct online searches for health information. In their investigation of adolescents' use of the Internet to find health-related information, Gray, Klein, Sesselberg, Cantrill, and Noyce (2002a) found that adolescents felt challenged by difficulties in spelling medical terms and constructing questions for searches. In keeping with what is known about learning how to spell through implicit cognition, adolescents do not generally experience high exposure to medical terminology. In the absence of the necessary morphophonemic knowledge about how to correctly spell medical terms, they are more likely to use misspelled words in search engines and thus are vulnerable to finding less relevant information, no relevant information or, at worst, irrelevant information. By their own self-reports, they believed that "scaffolding" through interactive online consultations and "frequently asked questions" sections on sites would help them confront such challenges.

These adolescents also recognized the challenge of managing the high volume of information available and judging its quality (Gray, Klein, Sesselberg, Cantrill, & Noyce, 2002b). There was diversity in the self-assessments of their ability to judge the Internet-based health information (e.g., critical, gullible). The adolescents who self-identified themselves as "critical" noted that they often developed their assessment skills through "trial and error." Only rarely they had received direct instruction through health education or scaffolding through other guidance at school or at home. Study participants from the United States who were successful in judging the quality of the information used strategies such as checking information consistency across multiple sites and using a "trusted brand" encyclopedia site.

Adolescents may "diagnose" themselves based on the saliency of the health information (e.g., the degree to which they recall their symptoms matching with those mentioned in personal accounts of others or descriptions of particular ailments described in online health information clearinghouses) (Gray et al., 2002). Accordingly, they not only need to know how to spell relevant medical or physiological terms, but also how to effectively determine cause-and-effect relationships: They need to have developed effective scientific thinking skills. In terms of pinpointing cause and effect, there are common errors that individuals can make (e.g., Flavell, Miller, & Miller, 2001; Zimmerman, 2007). These errors include but are not limited to (1) failing to distinguish between what one thinks is a cause-effect relationship and what is evidence of a cause-effect relationship, (2) considering possible explanations that are not mutually exclusive (e.g., the adolescent may focus on the symptoms shared by the flu or stomach virus and the symptoms that distinguish them), and (3) not exhausting possible contributing factors for the symptoms (e.g., the adolescent may not recognize the potential relevance of experiencing their specific symptoms after having eaten a new dish at a restaurant).

An adolescent may construct "health knowledge" through a variety of communications facilitated by global technologies. In the absence of appropriate spelling and scientific thinking skills, adolescents need the scaffolding of knowledgeable others, such as a health professional specifically trained to diagnose such symptoms as they relate to one's individual experience. It is these direct personal interactions, involving a mutual exchange of information and perspectives, that allow greater insight into the meaning and significance of the symptoms as well as potential causes. A health professional will ask scaffolding questions intended to elicit not only a list of symptoms but the timing, duration, severity, and qualitative character of the symptoms, the presence or absence of risk factors known to increase the likelihood of those symptoms, the broader health history of the individual, and how these symptoms may or may not relate to one's current experience.

The use of the aforementioned medical analogy is not intended to suggest that social and economic disparities in health care did not exist prior to the introduction of global technologies. The implication is that preexisting gaps in access to adequate health care (e.g., Fox et al., 2007; Mayberry, Mili, & Ofili, 2000) can result in limited health knowledge as a result of insufficient schemes for how to use health information communicated through global technologies. This illustration demonstrates how new gaps can emerge as a result of greater access to once privileged knowledge without the requisite conceptual understanding to make such declarative knowledge most useful. There is a difference between having the knowledge of how to access health information and having the knowledge of how to properly apply such information to troubleshoot one's own health problems. The new technologies that have helped to usher in this global era increase the likelihood that such distinctions are obscured.

This disparity between acquisition of procedural knowledge and acquisition of conceptual knowledge now becomes a social justice issue. Instead of considering errors in the interpretation of information as unfortunate mistakes, it is important to develop conceptual and pedagogical frameworks that formally acknowledge nontraditional contexts that can stimulate cognitive development. Importantly, nontraditional learning contexts may yield knowledge and insights that compete with the type of lessons and insights that could potentially be stimulated through direct instruction or scaffolding in traditional educational contexts.

3.7. **NORMATIVE COGNITIVE PROCESSES TRANSFORMED BY NEW TECHNOLOGY**

As noted earlier, the major premise of this chapter is that technology transforms cognitive ability, but the types of cognitive processes or mechanisms that drive cognitive development remain the same. The underlying assumption is that we see transformations in human ability not because there has been a change in what cognitive processes are considered normative but rather because cognitive processes are subject to different types and/or amounts of cognitive stimuli. If we consider the Piagetian notion that cognitive development is stimulated by exploration (e.g., Flavell, Miller, & Miller, 2001), then the greater global access provided by technology represents new modes of exploration. Internet connections, PDAs, smartphones, and camera phones provide access to more information about and images of what is going on around the world. This increased access expands the types of events and issues adolescents need to be able to accurately interpret and respond to. The unmonitored ability to transmit information and images around the world very quickly undoubtedly has an impact on cognitive developmental outcomes. Consider the images and initial reporting about such events as Hurricane Katrina, the Indian Ocean tsunami, and the 2008 earthquake in China. Unavoidably, adolescents will draw inferences and make meaning of the images used to depict these events and the words used to discuss them based on their prior experiences and respective stages of cognitive development.

If we further consider Piaget's notion of adaptation in response to disequilibration (e.g., Flavell, Miller, & Miller, 2001), then greater global access affords opportunities for more frequent experiences of disequilibration or cognitive dissonance as developing individuals have an increased likelihood of encountering ideas, attitudes, beliefs, and perspectives that run counter to their own. Consider the initial images and reporting in the aftermath of the 9/11 terrorist attacks as well as the sustained war on Iraq. How might developing youth make meaning of (1) images that run counter to what they would normally expect (e.g., images of individuals reported to be celebrating the 9/11 attacks when one would expect mourning) or (2) images and information that are real but which are typically seen in media designed for entertainment (e.g., images of airliners flying into a skyscraper may be expected in a feature length movie but not during a network news broadcast). These are events that are replete with clashes of divergent worldviews that are implicit in the language used to talk about these issues as well as the images used to reinforce these differing worldviews.

Likewise, if we consider the Vygotskian notion that cognitive development is stimulated by social interaction (e.g., Flavell, Miller, & Miller, 2001), then the greater opportunities for interaction with others around the world provided by technology represent additional and, possibly, more varied opportunities for social interaction. On one hand, the "cultural tools" of Internet connections, videoconference monitors, smartphones, and camera phones afford opportunities for cross-cultural global interactions that can provide contexts and opportunities for the same types of interactions that stimulate cognitive development in direct, face-to-face interactions. However, there is the possibility that such interactions can take place with a broader range of individuals representing a broader range of demographics than those with whom one might effectively engage during daily experiences. For example, the type of scaffolding that might take place between family and friends can also take place with an Internet blogger, in a chat room, or on a discussion board. The information and opinions offered and exchanged through these Internet-based mechanisms can essentially provide the scaffolding that individuals may use to make meaning of their own experiences and perceptions. These same cultural tools can be used to facilitate the types of interactions that may not otherwise take place in daily interactions where there is an increased possibility of monitoring and scaffolding by parents and other concerned peers or adults.

3.7.1. Moving toward a socially conscious theory of cognitive development

A socially conscious approach to cognitive development in the global era must be sensitive to the social and economic inequities that contribute to differential outcomes for youth (e.g., Coll et al., 1996). In addressing cultural differences, for example, Ladson-Billings' (1995) work on culturally relevant pedagogy suggests that cultural relevance is characterized by high regard for others, high expectations for all students, and an emphasis on "pulling out" knowledge from within a child. These characteristics describe the cognitive and affective nature of interactions between students and teachers. In different ways, each characteristic reflects a positive interaction: value placed on a student as a person, a belief in the student's ability to perform at high levels, and the belief that the student already has knowledge and skills that have value and can be brought to bear as they learn new information, skills, and procedures.

In the absence of these culturally relevant characteristics or conditions, students often experience feelings of disfranchisement for formal educational contexts (see Chapter 14). But disfranchisement from formal educational contexts should not suggest that there is no longer a motivation to learn. In contrast, it may lead one to search for alternative sources of knowledge, alternatives to traditional curricula, or experiences that evoke more positive affect (i.e., activities they like, are inspired by, receive positive feedback from). With this in mind, it is important to acknowledge the important role of positive affect in any potential educational context— inside or outside of formal educational contexts.

Positive affect can result from supportive relationships with adults and peers or from pleasant experiences. Such relationships and experiences can create the context and opportunity for positive learning experiences. Accordingly, there are lessons to be learned from our understanding of cultural mismatches that facilitate our understanding of the gaps exacerbated by greater global access to information and images. Matches between culturally relevant experiences and traditional educational experiences facilitate cognitive transfer or transfer of learning (e.g., Holyoak & Spellman, 1993; Holyoak & Thagard, 1997).

Information, skills, and procedures learned within specific cultural contexts may become internalized because of the positive affect that a learner, implicitly or explicitly, associates with them. However, such information, skills, or procedures are more likely to be transferred to more traditional academic learning tasks when learners recognize commonalities among such aspects of the cognitive experiences: (1) similarities in the conditions under which specific information, skills, or procedures are or should be applied or (2) similarities in the concepts, beliefs, or perspectives that underlie specific types of information, skills, or procedures (e.g., Holyoak & Spellman, 1993; Holyoak & Thagard, 1997). For example, playing a game of online poker requires a player to estimate the likelihood that the other players have cards of certain suits based on the cards that have already been played and the cards remaining in his or her own hand. While this type of recreational play is analogous to determining probability, there can only be a transfer of learning if the individual explicitly recognizes the similarities in the ways in which they determine probability in the context of an online poker game and the ways in which they are being taught to determine probability in a more traditional academic setting.

The description above exemplifies transfer of learning—one's thoughts about the similarities between the ways that information is used in activities that appear to be fundamentally different (e.g., Holyoak & Spellman, 1993; Holyoak & Thagard, 1997). This type of metacognition among adolescents does not typically happen unless such relationships are explicitly identified by another more sophisticated peer or adult. Yet it should not be assumed that in the absence of this metacognitive scaffolding, individuals have no metacognitive knowledge. They may simply develop metacognitive strategies that are less well informed than might be possible. Consequently, there is a need to more formally study the ways in which youth implicitly acquire new knowledge by their participation in informal technological learning contexts.

3.8. **CONCLUSION**

There should be a more purposeful consideration of the potential effects of global technologies on the cognitive development of adolescents from both low-resource and high-resource communities. There is open access to the Internet, but there are no regulated stipulations about how cyberspace-based information and images should be used or interpreted. From that perspective, the challenges described in this chapter would seem impossible to manage.

However, the major premise of the chapter is that preexisting social and economic inequities directly and indirectly influence how adolescents will use information resources accessed through global technologies. There are already gaps in metacognitive development and conceptual understanding. Differences in performance on a variety of school-related tasks can be attributed to differences in the knowledge and application of metacognitive strategies and conceptual understanding. This is no less relevant when using global technologies. There is a wide diversity of inputs that should be counted as information–ranging from informal, unvetted personal communications to formally certified, web-based information clearinghouses. The implication is that there are many sources of influence on how adolescents think. Again, it is probably close to impossible to regulate all these sources. But if we better understand and acknowledge the processes by which these diverse sources can exercise their influence on cognitive development in this global era, we will be better positioned to recognize and develop responses to contexts that compete with more traditional educational systems and may further complicate the educational process.

A ready application of insights offered in this chapter is to adapt current primary and secondary school curricula to include formal opportunities to use these global technologies in ways that provide the context for increasing students' awareness of their own implicit cognition or learning processes. Essentially, educators should create opportunities that build the metacognitive understanding of adolescents. Specifically, critical awareness of development should be increased as it relates to their learning processes in informal learning contexts inadvertently created by global technologies (e.g., implicit processes by which we learn how to spell, skin color connotations and stereotypes, cause-and-effect relationships). Many websites, for example, have the sole purpose of educating their viewers. Such websites may include not only factual information but also include suggested instructional strategies for teachers or self-teaching activities for potential learners. In those instances, the purposes of the Internet-based information resources have been made explicit. However, there are many more instances in which unvetted information and images are communicated in ways that allow them to have an implicit and unconscious effect on learning that can only be countered or at least recognized in the light of competing factual declarative or conceptual knowledge.

Adolescents develop the ability to apply critical thinking skills in ways that will allow them to determine the credibility of sources and the validity of information. Theory and research, however, suggest that they have not yet accumulated the experiences that would actually lead them to make such judgments. This reality increases the need for direct instruction and scaffolding from knowledgeable, caring adults and cognitively sophisticated peers. Social and economic inequities are already major problems limiting many youths' access to needed resources. There must be a concerted effort to ensure that new global technologies do not create false confidence about equitable global access to information and images, obscuring a widening gap in the metacognitive development and conceptual understanding of our adolescents.

REFERENCES

American Psychiatric Association. (1994). *Diagnostic and statistical manual of mental disorders* (4th ed.). Washington, DC: Author.

Banks, J. A. (1984). Black youths in predominantly White suburbs: An exploratory study of their attitudes and self-concepts. *Journal of Negro Education, 53*(1), 3–17.

Bell, C. C., & Jenkins, E. J. (1991). Traumatic stress and children. *Journal of Health Care for the Poor and Underserved, 2*(1), 175–185.

Borzekowski, D. L., & Rickert, V. I. (2001a). Adolescent cybersurfing for health information: A new resource that crosses barriers. *Archives of Pediatric Adolescent Medicine, 155*, 813–817.

Borzekowski, D. L., & Rickert, V. I. (2001b). Adolescents, the Internet, and health: Issues of access and content. *Applied Developmental Psychology, 22*, 49–59.

Boxer, P., Rowell Huesmann, L., Bushman, B. J., O'Brien, M., & Moceri, B. (2009). The role of violent media preference in cumulative developmental risk for violence and general aggression. *Journal of Youth and Adolescence, 38*, 417–428.

Boyer, T. W., & Byrnes, J. P. (2009). Adolescent risk-taking: Integrating personal, cognitive, and social aspects of judgment. *Journal of Applied Developmental Psychology, 30*, 23–33.

Bronfenbrenner, U. (1993). The ecology of cognitive development: Research models and fugitive findings. In R. H. Wozniak & K. W. Fischer (Eds.), *Development in context* (pp. 3–44). Hillsdale, NJ: Erlbaum Associates.

Case, R., & Okamoto, Y. (1996). The role of central conceptual structures in the development of children's thought. *Monographs of the Society for Research in Child Development, 61*(1–2), 1–265.

Clark, K. B., & Clark, M. K. (1939). The development of consciousness of self and the emergence of racial identification in Negro preschool children. *Journal of Social Psychology, 10*, 591–599.

Clark, K. B., & Clark, M. K. (1940). Skin color as a factor in racial identification of Negro preschool children. *Journal of Social Psychology, 11*, 159–169.

Clark, K. B., & Clark, M. P. (1947). Racial identification and preference in Negro children. In T. M. Newcomb & E. L. Hartley (Eds.), *Reading in social psychology*. New York, NY: Holt, Rinehart & Winston.

Coll, G., Lamberty, G., Jenkins, R., McAdoo, H. P., Crnic, K., Wasik, B. H., et al. (1996). An integrative model for the study of developmental competencies in minority children. *Child Development, 67*, 1891–1914.

Collins, W. A., & Laursen, B. (2004). Changing relationships, changing youth: Interpersonal contexts of adolescent development. *Journal of Early Adolescence, 24*(1), 55–62.

Dupree, D., Spencer, M. B., & Bell, S. (1997). The ecology of African-American child development: Normative and non-normative outcomes. In G. Johnson-Powell & Y. Yamamoto (Eds.), *Transcultural child psychiatry: A portrait of America's children* (pp. 237–268). New York, NY: Wiley.

Elkind, D. (1978). Understanding the young adolescent. *Adolescence, 13*, 1025–1034.

Flavell, J. H., Miller, P. H., & Miller, S. A. (2001). *Cognitive development* (4th ed.). Englewood Cliffs, NJ: Prentice Hall.

Fox, E., & Riconscente, M. (2008). Metacognition and self-regulation in James, Piaget, and Vygotsky. *Educational Psychology Review, 20*, 373–389.

Fox, H. B., McManus, M. A., Zarit, M., Fairbrother, G., Cassedy, A. E., Bethell, C. D., et al. (2007). *Racial and ethnic disparities in adolescent health and access to care*. Washington, DC: Incenter Strategies.

French, S. E., Seidman, E., Allen, L., & Aber, J. L. (2006). The development of ethnic identity during adolescence. *Developmental Psychology*, *42*(1), 1–10.

Gee, J. P. (2003). *What video games have to teach us about learning and literacy*. New York, NY: Palgrave Macmillan.

Gopaul-McNicol, S. (1988). Racial identification and racial preference of Black preschool children in New York and Trinidad. *Journal of Black Psychology*, *14*(2), 65–68.

Gray, N. J., Cantrill, J. A., & Noyce, P. R. (2002). 'Health repertories': An understanding of lay management of minor ailments. *Patient Education and Counseling*, *47*, 237–244.

Gray, N., Klein, J., Cantrill, J., & Noyce, P. (2002). How do you spell gonorrhea? Adolescents' health literacy and the Internet. *Abstracts of the Academy for Health Services Research and Health Policy Meeting*, *19*, 21.

Gray, N. J., Klein, J. D., Noyce, P. R., Sesselberg, T. S., & Cantrill, J. A. (2005). Health information-seeking behaviour in adolescence: The place of the Internet. *Social Science and Medicine*, *60*, 1467–1478.

Gray, N. J., Klein, J. D., Sesselberg, T. S., Cantrill, J. A., & Noyce, P. R. (2002a). Adolescents' health literacy and the internet. *Journal of Adolescent Health*, *32*(2), 124.

Gray, N. J., Klein, J. D., Sesselberg, T. S., Cantrill, J. A., & Noyce, P. R. (2002b). Adolescent girls' use of the Internet for health information: Issues beyond access. *Journal of Medical Systems*, *26*(6), 545–553.

Holyoak, K. J., & Spellman, B. A. (1993). Thinking. *Annual Review of Psychology*, *44*, 265–315.

Holyoak, K. J., & Thagard, P. (1997). The analogical mind. *American Psychologist*, *52*(1), 35–44.

Hughes, D., Rodriguez, J., Smith, E. P., Johnson, D. J., Stevenson, H., & Spicer, P. (2006). Parents' ethnic–racial socialization practices: A review of research and directions for future study. *Developmental Psychology*, *42*(5), 747–770.

Jones, P. E. (2009). From 'external speech' to 'inner speech' in Vygotsky: A critical appraisal and fresh perspectives. *Language and Communication*, *29*, 166–181.

Ladson-Billings, G. (1995). Toward a theory of culturally relevant pedagogy. *American Educational Research Journal*, *32*(3), 465–491.

May, J. M. (1986). Cognitive processes and violent behavior in young people. *Journal of Adolescence*, *9*, 17–27.

Mayberry, R. M., Mili, F., & Ofili, E. (2000). Racial and ethnic differences in access to medical care. *Medical Care Research and Review*, *57*(Suppl. 1), 108–145.

McAdoo, H. P. (1985). Racial attitudes and self-concept of young Black children over time. In H. P. McAdoo & J. L McAdoo (Eds.), *Black children: Social, educational, and parental environments* (sage focus editions, Vol. 72, pp. 213–242). Thousand Oaks, CA: Sage Publications, Inc.

McKown, C., & Weinstein, R. S. (2003). The development and consequences of stereotype consciousness in middle childhood. *Child Development*, *74*(2), 498–515.

Mendle, J., Turkheimer, E., & Emery, R. E. (2007). Detrimental psychological outcomes associated with early pubertal timing in adolescent girls. *Developmental Review*, *27*, 151–171.

Muuss, R. E. (1996). *Theories of adolescence*. New York, NY: The McGraw-Hill Companies.

Porter, C. P. (1991). Social reasons for skin tone preferences of Black school-age children. *American Journal of Orthopsychiatry*, *61*, 149–154.

Pynoos, R. S., & Nader, K. (1988). Psychological first aid treatment approach to children exposed to community violence: Research implications. *Journal of Traumatic Stress*, *1*(4), 445–472.

Pynoos, R. S., & Nader, K. (1990). Children's exposure to violence and traumatic death. *Psychiatric Annals*, *20*(6), 334–344.

Reyna, V. F., & Farley, F. (2006). Risk and rationality in adolescent decisión making: Implications for theory, practice, and public policy. *Psychological Science in the Public Interest*, *7*(1), 1–44.

Savage, J., & Yancey, C. (2008). The effects of media violence exposure on criminal aggression: A meta-analysis. *Criminal Justice and Behavior*, *35*, 772–791.

Schacter, D., Chiu, C. Y. P., & Ochsner, K. N. (1993). Implicit memory: A selective review. *Annual Review of Neuroscience*, *6*, 159–182.

Schauble, L. (1996). The development of scientific reasoning in knowledge-rich contexts. *Developmental Psychology*, *32*(1), 102–119.

Spencer, M. B. (1984). Black children's race awareness, racial attitudes and self-concept: A reinterpretation. *Journal of Child Psychology and Psychiatry*, *25*(3), 433–441.

Spencer, M. B. (1999). Social and cultural influences on school adjustment: The application of an identity-focused cultural ecological perspective. *Educational Psychologist. Special Issue: Social Influences on School Adjustment: Families, Peers, Neighborhoods, and Culture*, *34*(1), 43–57.

Spencer, M. B., Dupree, D., Cunningham, M., Harpalani, V., & Munoz-Miller, M. (2003). Vulnerability to violence: A contextually-sensitive, developmental perspective on African American adolescents. *Journal of Social Issues*, *59*(1), 33–49.

Steffler, D. J. (2001). Implicit cognition and spelling. *Developmental Review*, *21*, 168–204.

Steinberg, L. (2005). Cognitive and affective development in adolescence. *Trends in Cognitive Sciences*, *9*(2), 69–74.

Thomas, R. M. (2001). *Recent theories of human development*. Thousand Oaks, CA: Sage Publications, Inc.

Valkenburg, P. M., Schouten, A. P., & Peter, J. (2005). Adolescents' identity experiments on the internet. *New Media and Society*, *7*(3), 383–402.

Wertsch, J. V. (2008). From social interaction to higher psychological processes: A clarification and application of Vygotsky's theory. *Human Development*, *51*, 66–79.

Wiemann, C. M., DuBois, J. C., & Benerson, A. B. (1998). Racial/ethnic differences in the decision to breastfeed among adolescent mothers. *Pediatrics*, *101*(6), 1–8.

Williams, J. E., & Roberson, J. K. (1967). A method for assessing racial attitudes in preschool children. *Educational and Psychological Measurement, 27*(3), 671–689.

Yurgelun-Todd, D. (2007). Emotional and cognitive changes during adolescence. *Current Opinion in Neurobiology, 17,* 251–257.

Zimmer-Gembeck, M. J. (2002). The development of romantic relationships and adaptations in the system of peer relationships. *Journal of Adolescent Health, 31,* 216–225.

Zimmerman, C. (2007). The development of scientific thinking skills in elementary and middle school. *Developmental Review, 27,* 172–223.

Chapter 4

Adolescent psychosocial processes: Identity, stress, and competence

Dena Phillips Swanson

Warner School of Education and Human Development, University of Rochester, Rochester, New York, USA

The developmental progression through adolescence involves shifts in expected behaviors, changes in social networks, and forming an identity. It is a period of rapid change, physiologically, psychologically, and socially (see Feldman & Elliot, 1990). Interactions with the outside world increase, allowing further integration of cognitive skills, social skills (i.e., behavior), and emotions. Erikson (1968), in offering a developmental/life-span approach to psychological health, emphasized the role of social and cultural factors on development and analyzes their impact on personality development throughout the life course. Adolescents are confronted with a range of biological changes (e.g., puberty), psychosocial tasks (e.g., identity formation), and environmental shifts (e.g., school transitions). Adapting to these normative developmental demands requires balancing aspects of the self (e.g., problem-solving skills or self-esteem) with the social environment (e.g., the availability of social support) (Swanson, Spencer, & Petersen, 1999). The breadth of competing demands on these processes during adolescence greatly contributed to a long history of the period being characterized as one of storm and stress (Arnett, 1999). Although youth encounter various stressors and experience periods of uncertainty, contemporary developmental framing conceptualizes adolescence as one of exploration and opportunities influential in developmental outcomes and the transition into adulthood.

This chapter explores aspects of psychosocial development of youth across racial and ethnic groups. This representation is an approach encompassing a "diverse" perspective which includes White youth. In taking this approach, the tendency toward normalizing Whiteness is minimized but incorporates their experiences as one of many diverse groups (see McIntosh, 2007). Although the stressors and basic developmental challenges faced by all youth are comparable, the normalization of Whiteness assumes cultural consonance across school, family, and neighborhood settings is also comparable, contributing to systematic and institutionalized practices resulting in the subordination and devaluation of minority groups and their experiences. The consequences of this are twofold (see Spencer et al., 2006). First, instances of success and competence displayed by minority youth, in spite of adverse or compromising conditions, can go unnoticed (i.e., the capacity to negotiate cultural dissonance and racial stereotyping), thus denying youth a sense of success and validation (Cunningham, 1999). Second, the unquestioned assumptions regarding privilege for White youth contribute to their unacknowledged risks. Notwithstanding the marginalized experiences of some White youth (i.e., gay and lesbian), the limited opportunities to experience and obtain successful resolution to challenges limits their coping options when experiencing stress. Greater exploration of potential risks associated with compromising outcomes enhances an understanding of the common risks for all youth. A lack of understanding of cultural context leads to a misinterpretation of behavior and development. Understanding developmental processes, contributing factors, and related consequences is crucial to promoting an understanding of intrapersonal, interpersonal, and contextual influences on adolescent development.

Research regarding adolescent development shows the influences of cultural beliefs and practices as socially and economically mediated (Swanson, Cunningham, & Spencer, 2003). This chapter presents information on diverse adolescent psychosocial processes using the following framework, proposed by Cocking (1994, p. 402), as a guide. These criteria were suggested as necessary for incorporating the experiences of diverse youth in a field historically reflecting ethnocentric models of development:

1. Articulating the developmental processes and levels of variable functioning in ways that cut across cultures and subcultures.
2. Accounting for inconsistent findings within a framework of developmental continuities and discontinuities.
3. Going beyond variables function toward a model of how the variables influence one another in predicting developmental trajectories.
4. Accounting for normative trends and their variations within cultural and individual differences parameters.

5. Separating enduring from transitory effects and accounting for transitory behaviors as part of the developmental cycle.
6. Specifying patterns of relationships in cognitive and social influences on development.
7. Specifying vulnerabilities and resiliencies to account for cultural and contextual features that protect or place youth at risk.

The chapter is organized with an initial overview of developmental tasks during adolescence. Using this foundation, self-development and identity processes are discussed. The impact of these processes is subsequently explored as foundational for understanding adolescent stress and competence. The chapter concludes with a discussion of future directions for examining the psychosocial processes for diverse youth.

4.1. FRAMING NORMATIVE DEVELOPMENT

Baltes (1987) presents a trifactor model of age-graded, history-graded, and nonnormative influences in organizing the complexities of life-course developmental influences. These three influences, and their effects over time, collectively contribute to individual development (see Chapter 1). This section focuses on psychosocial processes associated with age-graded influences (i.e., interindividual similarity) in providing a foundation for examining the impact of nonnormative influences on developmental outcomes. The latter form of influences are not related to a dimension of developmental time and do not follow a general or predictable course. A primary consideration is the reconceptualizing of ethnocentrically framed interpretations of normative processes. An overview of developmental tasks and major psychosocial processes is presented.

4.1.1. Havighurst and Erikson

Adolescence is treated as a distinct time of development, theoretically and conceptually, that is globally (Brown, Larson, & Saraswathi, 2002). While representing the timing and expectations of this transitional period are defined by societal expectations regarding the attributes necessary for adult functioning. Developmental goals are culturally shared and negotiated among members of the cultural group. Among groups valuing autonomy and independence, individual rights are... and opportunities for personal choice are maximized. Among groups valuing collective responsibility, interdependence and social responsibilities are prioritized over individual choice. The former stresses individuation as a developmental goal while the latter emphasizes conformity to established social norms (see Greenfield, Keller, Fuligni, & Maynard, 2003).

The basis for understanding adolescence as a unique period of development in Western societies grew, in part, out of the need to respond to shifts in social and economic demands and youths' behaviors that were inconsistent with socially approved norms (see Arnett, 1999; Lerner & Steinberg, 2009). This provided the foundation utilized in promoting a compulsory education agenda and rehabilitative behavior efforts (i.e., juvenile justice) toward citizenship and socialization (see Chapter 17). Over time, efforts to provide effective intervention responses or to identify factors contributing to problem behaviors required a frame for differentiating normal from problem behaviors. Havighurst (1973), in delineating specific tasks associated with periods of development, identified several tasks for adolescence (see Table 4.1).

Table 4.1 Descriptions and concepts associated with developmental tasks during adolescence

Developmental tasks	General description	Concepts
Achieving new and more mature relations with others, both boys and girls, in their age group	Adolescents learn about reciprocity and relationship trust through interactions with others	Peer affiliations
Achieving a masculine or feminine social role	Adolescents develop an understanding of what it means to be male or female given sex role expectations	Gender identity
Accepting one's physique	Adolescents are able to accept their physical attributes, particularly given the physiological changes during early adolescence, which continue through adolescence (weight, muscle, height)	Pubertal timing
Achieving emotional independence from parents and other adults	Adolescents examine and become responsible for their decisions	Emerging adulthood
Preparing for marriage and family life	Adolescents learn how to establish close relationships in preparation for building and maintaining long-term adult relationships	Intimacy
Preparing for an economic career	Adult status is associated with the ability to financially support oneself with career objectives and marketable skills helping prepare younger adolescents for the transition	Educational attainment
Acquiring a set of values and an ethical system as a guide to behavior—developing an ideology	Adolescents can think abstractly and hypothetically, developing the capacity for committing to a personal set of values and beliefs	Spirituality
Desiring and achieving socially responsible behavior	Status within the community, beyond that of family is important as adolescents become financially and emotionally independent from parents	Civic engagement

While taken at face value, some developmental tasks have undergone revised conceptualizations over time that are consistent with shifts in social perspectives. Developing a gendered social role, for example, would seemingly be less salient than originally conceptualized given changes in social expectations and the broadened access to opportunities, particularly for females. The literature on adolescence and emerging adulthood, however, highlights many of these characteristics, including expectations regarding instrumentality for males (see Swanson, Spencer, & Petersen, 1999) and attributes of femininity for females (Krane, Choi, Baird, Aimar, & Kauer, 2004). As such, the original interpretations of these tasks could be perceived as dated according to contemporary attitudes regarding equity, but the primary tasks have remained fairly unchange Table 4.1 presents constructs comparable to developmental tasks outlined by Havighurst. The concepts have been further delineated for both expanding an understanding of adolescent development and facilitating empirical investigations examining the processes and interactions. Achieving new and more mature relations with others in their age group, for example, shapes adolescents' knowledge about reciprocity and relationship trust through interactions with others. This developmental task is examined theoretically and empirically based on characteristics of adolescents' interactions with peers, where acquiring a set of values incorporates not only moral development but also spirituality. The concept examples are not presented as exclusively representing any one developmental task but emphasize the continued relevance of the developmental tasks.

Achieving emotional maturity, establishing committed values, and forming a career trajectory are progressively achieved from early through late adolescence. The emphasis, as well as the expectations, associated with these is dependent upon the context in which they are needed (Steinberg & Morris, 2001). The developmental processes during adolescence are espoused to ultimately result in a member of society who no longer requires full support of family members for care and survival, and is able to take on adult-like roles, contributing to the well-being and survival of others. A balance between "autonomy and relatedness" or "individuation and connectedness" appears to be necessary for adolescent adjustment, in that it provides children the opportunity to develop the ability to think and act independently within the context of supportive relationships (e.g., Grotevant & Cooper, 1986). Although most youth will experience a process comparable to autonomy and relatedness, there is variability in the extent to which each dimension is "emphasized, expected, and granted during adolescence across different societies, different ethnic groups with the same society, and different socioeconomic conditions, as well as under conditions of social change" (Greenfield, Keller, Fuligni, & Maynard, 2003, p. 479). If autonomy were reconceptualized as the expression of culturally defined responsibilities, the concept would imply less individuation associated with the transition to adulthood and thus represent one's accountability to society or their cultural group, hence providing greater cultural breadth than the general concept of autonomy.

Complementing Havighurst's developmental tasks, Erikson's (1968) primary task of identity formation during adolescence captures youths' consolidation of the developmental tasks consistent with life course perspective theorizing. Identity formation from an Eriksonian framing, however, is subsequently shaped by the resolution of the preceding developmental tasks from infancy through late childhood. Resolutions of trust, autonomy, and industry provide the foundation for identity and intimacy associated with adolescent and early adulthood development. When these have been negatively resolved, the result compromises future development relevant to exploration (i.e., role experimentation) and commitment (Marcia, 1987).

Identity formation processes are based on interactions between human biological potentialities and environmental conditions such that the processes represent the capacity to adapt to different environmental conditions and constraints—conceptually similar to competence formation (see Greenfield et al., 2003). Attention to individualism (i.e., personal responsibility, freedom of choice) versus collectivism (i.e., mutual obligations toward a common good), as part of differential experiences impacting youth outcomes, is historically presented within developmental psychology as culturally dichotomized (Oyserman, Coon, & Kemmelmeier, 2002). In contrast, however, cultural groups emphasize socialization practices that represent their cultural values. As such, groups identified as collective recognize individuals as having unique strengths and abilities, but they are shaped and directed to benefit the group.

4.1.2. **Developmental tasks and assets**

The early pathology-based perspective of adolescence was challenged by heightened attention to understanding risk that contributed to negative outcomes *and* the resilience expressed by youth encountering risk but exhibiting positive outcomes. This conceptual shift toward normative developmental framing of adolescence contributed to efforts in identifying factors associated with positive outcomes. The positive youth development

(PYD) perspective introduced a strength-based conception of adolescent development, prevention, and intervention. Derived from developmental systems theory, the perspective stresses the potential plasticity of human development as aligned with developmental assets (see Lerner, Almerigi, Theokas, & Lerner, 2005). It has demonstrated usefulness for all youth, particularly racial and ethnically diverse youth, with implications for community programs and social policies (see Edwards, Mumford, & Serra-Roldan, 2007). Based on prevention and resiliency research, The Search Institute identified variables contributing to healthy development and positive outcomes for adolescents. The result was a set of environmental and intrapersonal strengths characterized as 40 developmental assets for adolescents (Benson, 2003). Categorized as internal and external assets, internal assets are represented by commitment to learning, positive values that shape choices, social competencies (necessary for establishing and maintaining relationships), and positive identity. External assets represent perceived supports, boundaries and expectations, and constructive use of time. The assets, for example, highlight the important roles of schools and school personnel in shaping students' school engagement and success. They represent available social and psychological resources that form a system of supports relevant to enhanced opportunities and provide a foundation for negotiating developmental tasks throughout adolescence and the transition into adulthood (Seligman & Csikszentmihalyi, 2000; Sesma, Mannes, & Scales, 2005; Theokas et al., 2005). The developmental assets framework is one PYD model that reduces students' poor decision making, adverse school experiences, and negative life outcomes (Benson, Leffert, Scales, & Blyth, 1998; Edwards et al., 2007).

Cross-cultural and multiethnic research has shown that children who encounter adversities (i.e., risks) and demonstrate resilience share similar external and internal developmental assets (Benson, 2007). The more external and internal assets students exhibit, the less they participate in various high-risk personal behaviors mentioned previously (Sesma et al., 2005; Benson et al., 1998). Children with multiple developmental assets engage more frequently in behaviors that facilitate positive outcomes. They demonstrate leadership skills, maintain good peer and parental relationships (Leffert et al., 1998), and actively participate in extracurricular activities, youth programs, and sports (Scales, Benson, Leffert, & Blyth, 2000). Furthermore, these students demonstrate academic competence, engagement in school, and overall satisfactory school functioning. Scales, Benson, and Mannes (2006), based on a five-year longitudinal study, found community involvement was related to youths increased engagement with nonfamily adults, empowerment, boundary setting, fewer risk behaviors and higher levels of thriving.

To examine individual and ecological assets, Taylor et al. (2004) interviewed African American adolescent males affiliated with a gang or in community-based organizations from the same community. Youth in the community-based organizations (selected for their focus on promoting positive youth development) had higher levels of internal and external assets. However, they also found that some gang youth reported assets equivalent to or higher than their peers in community-based organizations. In turn, the asset scores for the former group were more likely to be correlated than among the latter group. By their third wave of data collection (Taylor et al., 2005) both groups had comparable stability across high and low asset levels over the three waves. Their findings support the assertion that all youth utilize available assets to thrive and highlight the relevance of these processes for developing programs that facilitate positive youth outcomes.

Schwartz, Pantin, Coatsworth, and Szapocznik (2007) present a framework utilizing the risk-protection approach and applied developmental science perspectives. Their model proposes an integration of protective factors and developmental assets, as well as the complementarity of the intrapersonal mechanisms proposed within the two perspectives. Given the effects of contextual factors on intrapersonal processes and functioning, they assert that it is essential to consider self and context as they interact to "produce developmental trajectories" (p. 134). The following sections examine self-development and interpersonal processes.

4.2. **SELF-DEVELOPMENT AND IDENTITY FORMATION**

Developmentally, children's opportunities for enhancing and expanding skills provide a supportive foundation for positive self-esteem. In the absence of these opportunities, establishing a foundation for positive outcomes can be compromised. Prior research has consistently demonstrated a decline in children's school related or academic self-esteem beginning in second grade followed by another significant decline in fourth grade (Compas et al., 2001) which places children at greater risk for later school disengagement (see Swanson, Cunningham, Youngblood, & Spencer, 2009). The early decline in academic self-esteem corresponds with children's increased social cognitive abilities, representing their capacity for making social comparisons and recognizing others' perspective about personal attributes in their academic setting. Attributes associated with self development beyond school experiences include sex, race, ethnicity, name, physical stature, and temperament (see Swanson et al., 2009; Swanson & Spencer, 1998) which provide children with information about the self and the value that others associate with the relevant attribute. One's given name, surname, or tribal name, for example, holds great significance among Native and Asian American families (see Spencer, Swanson, & Cunningham, 1991). It connects youth with a collective history and family values which are central to their self-appraisal processes.

Appraisal processes are based on the social cognitive abilities of youth to interpret information from external sources about self characteristics (see Spencer, 1995). In examining the effect of the Internet on adolescent identity development, Zhao (2005) found, for example, that Internet relationships constitute a distinctive "looking glass" that produces a "digital self" different from the self represented offline. Consistent with youth's exploration, this type of activity allows an online self-presentation that is an integral part of the self development process. As such, "intimate strangers" or "anonymous friends" on the Internet play an important role in affecting their appraisal processes and ultimately their self-development.

As a foundational component of the Phenomenological Variant of Ecological Systems Theories (PVEST; Spencer, 1995), self-appraisal processes, as noted in Figure 4.1, shape adolescents' perceptions of personal strengths, challenges, and available supports. They are inexplicably linked to

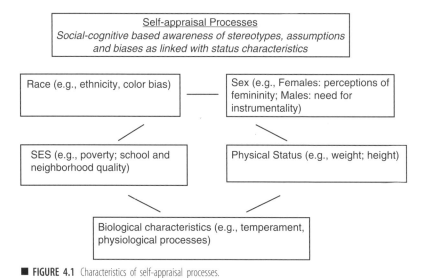

■ **FIGURE 4.1** Characteristics of self-appraisal processes.

social-cognitive abilities that provide the framework for interpreting external information. Adolescents, having been exposed to societal assumptions since early childhood, develop the cognitive capacity to interpret these assumptions and biases about what it means to be, for example, middle class, male, or overweight (see Swanson et al., 2009). In essence, with cognitive maturation, the capacity to internalize biases increases unless there is active (and consistent) intervention to minimize the influence. Given the interpretative framing of self-appraisal processes, supportive adults are relationally positioned to offer alternative interpretations and coping strategies relevant for any youth facing marginalization due to self attributes (e.g., gender stereotypes, physical abilities, etc.). Similarly, Markus et al. (1997) purport that these processes, referred to as selfways, occur within specific sociocultural contexts that shape their meaning.

> *Selfways are patterns or orientations, including ways of thinking, feeling, wanting, and doing, that arise from living one's life in a particular sociocultural context structure... according to some specific, substantive set of cultural understandings (goals, values, pictures of the world). Selfways thus include important cultural ideas, values, and understandings of what it means to be a self and how to be a good self...manifest[ed] in everyday behavior, language practices, patterns of caretaking, schooling, religion, work, the media, and social episodes, both formal and informal.... The notion of selfways implies that every sense of self will be grounded in some shared meanings and customary practices and ... to act, live, or function well in a given culture means practicing the underlying cultural views of how to be (Shweder et al., 2006, pp. 754-755).*

Identity formation incorporates personal identity, social identity, and collective identity. As a psychosocial construct, it influences their decisions, actions, and ability to establish realistic goals and expectations, serving as a foundation for later adult development and interpersonal relationships (Scales, Blyth, Berkas, & Kielsmeier, 2000; Steinberg & Caufman, 1996; Swanson, Spencer, et al., 2003). The need to belong, be valued, and have a purpose reflects identity development processes relevant for all youth (Swanson, Spencer, & Petersen, 1999).

Research efforts to identify protective factors and processes in children's lives define these factors as characteristics that mitigate the development of psychopathology despite the existence of risk factors (i.e., resilience). Protective factors are considered to manifest an effect only in the presence of risk (Anthony, 1987; Rutter, 1987) conceptually distinguishing them from developmental assets that are not dependent on manifested risk. Latent vulnerabilities are proposed to emerge in conjunction with the numerous and rapid changes of early adolescence. Such changes as those experienced in school transitions, familial and peer relationships, physiological changes and increasing responsibilities, can instigate or expose vulnerabilities. Adolescence is considered one of the greatest periods of vulnerability in development, second to early childhood, due to the multiplicity of changes occurring. The effects, therefore, of earlier risks as well as the "buffering" effects of protective factors are behaviorally or emotionally expressed during adolescence (see Swanson, 2009), shaping experiences that impact identity formation.

Individual attributes develop as a function of behaviors or beliefs that reflect an active, selective, structuring orientation toward the environment (Compas, 1987). The ability to modify, select, and reconstruct the environment, however, depends on conditions that enable or empower youth to engage in behavior that influences the environment (i.e., competence). Social structures and conditions, such as expectations at home and school, provide relevant experiences that interact with psychological processes to encourage or discourage certain behaviors. Many adolescents exhibiting problem behaviors are likely to be among those with limited supportive opportunities or inadequate educational experiences contributing to appraisals of "disempowerment." Existing research underscores the significance of positive academic experiences and competencies for producing positive, and preventing negative outcomes (Swanson, Spencer, et al., 2003). Examinations, for example, of stress exposure to school-based competence show that youth with less positive family support were less competent and more likely to be disruptive at high stress levels (Weist, Freedman, Paskewitz, Proescher, & Flaherty, 1995). Males appear to be less protected by positive family supports when stress is high. Irrespective of gender, adolescents with positive self-efficacy and a sense of competence demonstrate a more active adaptation to stress.

4.2.1. **Racial and ethnic identity**

Although decades of research has focused on the need for African American youths' ability to identify with Black culture, several theories acknowledge that ethnic and racial minority youth must successfully negotiate identification with *both* their ethnic culture and the dominant White culture (LaFromboise, Coleman, & Gerton, 1993; see Chapter 9 for a detailed theoretical overview). Along similar lines, Cross' (1971) initial stages of psychological Nigrescence for Black Americans consist of two dimensions, which Cross argued were in direct conflict with each other: (1) individuals' orientation toward Black culture and (2) individuals' orientation toward mainstream White society. As such, positive Black identity has been assumed to have a direct negative relationship with Eurocentric values. Research has consistently shown that both of these dimensions, also associated racial centrality, regard, and ideology, are important for youths' sense of self and mental health (Caldwell, Zimmerman, Bernat, Sellers, & Notaro, 2002; Scottham, Sellers, & Nguyen, 2008). Caldwell, Sellers, Bernat, and Zimmerman (2004) examined racial identity and parental support in predicting alcohol use among African American adolescents. They found private regard (i.e., the extent to which one feels positively about Black people) and racial centrality were among factors associated with less self-reported alcohol use.

Similar studies have examined the extent to which the protective nature of racial identity differentially influences the well-being of males and females, and other minority groups. For instance, the impact of African American youth's positive racial identity is particularly beneficial for girls; racial identity may buffer the negative perceptions of normal physical development by providing a positive reference group for appraising ideal body types (see Vasquez & de las Fuentes, 1999). In contrast, stronger racial identification may be detrimental for young adolescent males, as it potentially contributes to greater internalization of negative attitudes and stereotypes regarding their social status leading to poor mental health or behavioral expressions of exaggerated masculinity (Cunningham, 1999). Such outcomes are particularly heightened in the absence of supportive adults that acknowledge the challenges and provide alternative coping options (Stevenson, 2004). Strength of racial identity may thus act as a protective factor for young adolescent African American girls, but may not for young African American males.

There have been similar findings of the association between ethnic identity and well-being among ethnic minority youth. Rhee and Shrake (2004) found fewer behavior problems among Korean adolescents with strong ethnic identity and satisfactory academic performance. Martinez & Dukes (1997) found that a strong ethnic identity was predictive of higher self-esteem, purpose in life, and self confidence. Among their sample, Whites and Native Americans had lower ethnic identity, and African American and Latinos had higher ethnic identity. Asian Americans and respondents of mixed ethnicity had intermediate levels of ethnic identity. Lysne and Levy (1997) examined the influence of contextualized minority status on ethnic identity. They found that Native American high-school students attending a school with a predominantly Native American student body reported significantly greater ethnic identity exploration and commitment than students from high schools with a predominantly White student body. While White American youth can experience ethnic identity development (see Hardiman, 2001), it has little salience on their personal and social identity development due to the relinquishing of cultural affiliations as part of their history as European immigrants (Waters, 2006).

Amiot, de la Sablonniere, Terry, and Smith (2007) present a model of social identity development and integration in the self. Relying on inter-group models and developmental frameworks, they propose a four-stage model explaining the specific processes by which multiple social identities develop intraindividually and become integrated within the self over time: anticipatory categorization, categorization, compartmentalization, and integration. Transitioning from the least differentiated to an integration of a coherent identity across "multiple and distinct social identities" (p. 375), they propose that perceived threats along with status and power incongruence hinder identity development. This perspective is consistent with that of Chestang (1972), who maintained that societal inconsistencies contributed to individual impotence. Amiot et al. conceptually validates adaptation and social support as factors that facilitate these identity change processes. Research on racial/ethnic identity processes and adolescent well-being suggest the significance of self development (e.g., self-esteem) on identity processes and the impact of context in shaping them.

4.2.2. **Identity and interpersonal processes**

As children enter adolescence, they experience changes in the quality of close relationships with peers and adults. They develop emotionally close relationships with peers as a result of their increased time together (Buhrmester, 1990; Marsh, Allen, Ho, Porter, & McFarland, 2006). "Friendships are closer and more intense in early adolescence than in any other phase of the life span" and represent the development of emotional intimacy (Berndt, 1982, p. 1447). These relationships enhance an adolescent's sense of self-worth and identity as they negotiate social structures and opportunities (Henrich, Kuperminc, Sack, Blatt, & Leadbeater, 2000). Developing self-worth and identity are central to socio-emotional adjustment and a sense of belonging among friends (Bauminger, Finzi-Dottan, & Har-Evan, 2008).

Through peer interactions, youth experience social support and learn skills necessary for establishing and maintaining interpersonal relationships (Buhrmester, 1990). Friendships experienced particularly during adolescence are central in providing a foundation for confidence in later relationships (Arndorfer & Stormshak, 2008; Berndt, 1982). Building a foundation of basic intimacy skills is necessary for the progression of more romantic relationships, which typically occur in late adolescence (Romig & Bakken, 1992).

Erikson proposed the necessity of establishing a secure identity in healthy development as preceding intimacy as a task associated with young adult-hood (see Shulman, Laursen, Kalman, & Karpovsky, 1997). Historically, intimacy was more closely aligned with marriage and establishing a family than with close relationships which were more family-oriented than peer-oriented. The expected age for establishing a family has extended over time to account for the increased years in post high-school educational aspirations; romantic interests have accordingly become more integrated with identity development than theoretically suggested. Generally from middle to late adolescence, romantic interests become a central focus in providing acceptance, worth, and validation for many youth (Taradesh, Connolly, Pepler, Craig, & Costa, 2001). These early relationships, how-ever, not only affect future relationships but also youths' values regarding intimacy, sexuality, and romance.

Gender identity development influences adolescents' expectations of rela-tionships and are associated with behaviors regarding sexuality (Josselson, 1994). Most intervention programs targeting adolescent sexuality, how-ever, either neglect the role of intimate relationships and their etiology as a normative aspect of development (Pedlow, & Carey, 2004) or the syn-ergistic influences of relational expectations with racial/ethnic identity and gender role expectations (Swanson, Spencer, & Petersen, 1999). While adolescents' relationships with parents and peers provide a foundation for autonomy (i.e., culturally defined responsibilities), intimate relation-ships are distinct from familial or peer relationships (Furman & Shaffer, 1999). Additionally, each is developmentally significant from childhood through adolescence (Lobel, Nov-Krispin & Schiller, 2004) with varied gender differences (Wichstrom, 1999; Galambos, Almeida, & Petersen, 1990). Defining intimacy as emotionally close relationships, in contrast to caring relationships or romantic interests, acknowledged the role of inti-macy in friendships and was instrumental in expanding the interpretation of differential gender findings (Shulman et al., 1997). Girls' empirically documented interest in relationships involving intimacy (i.e., caring) was in contrast to boys interest in independence and valuing of assertiveness and logic (Lacombe & Gay, 1998; Romig & Bakken, 1992). These find-ings suggested that intimacy was less significant in the development of males than for females. Studies examining intimacy among males, that have included ethnically diverse youth, note the significance of intimacy on their well-being. Way and Chu (2004) identified intimacy themes expressed by their diverse group of male participants as sharing secrets, sharing money, providing physical and emotional protection and having connections with family and friends. The participants, African American, Latino, and Asian American boys from poor and working-class families, discussed their loyalty, desire to share "everything," and their trust in close male friends. They also shared experiences of deceit, issues of distrust, and fears of betrayal that were barriers to establishing new friendships. While physically engaged activities (i.e., video gaming or basketball) represented how they spent time together, the reported themes were important in understanding how boys define, shape, and maintain relationships. Familial connections were particularly significant for the African American and Latino boys' friendships throughout adolescence.

As youth experience changes in the quality of their relationship with adults, maintaining strong relationships is essential to healthy development. Adult mentors, formal and informal, provide additional opportunities for establishing close and trusting relationships. These relationships are forged and solidified through engagement in shared activities, trust and mutual respect, and role modeling (Liang, Spencer, Brogan, & Corral, 2008; Spencer, 2007). Longevity of a relationship was found to be a significant factor associated with positive health outcomes (i.e., mental, physical, and emotional) for 18-26 year olds (DuBois & Silverthorn, 2005). With an average of 9 years, the findings from their study emphasize the significance of close supportive adult relationships during early to middle adolescence contributing to increased perceptions of efficacy and empowerment (see Liang et al, 2008).

4.3. **STRESS AND COMPETENCE**

Adolescents are confronted with numerous events that are normative (i.e., puberty, school transitions) but differentially experience many that are non-normative (i.e., community violence). The incongruence between environmental or contextual demands and youths' ability to effectively manage them constitutes stress (Lazarus & Folkman, 1984). The extent to which a stressful experience is chronic or uncontrollable impacts the ability to manage the event or the effect it creates. Extensive conceptual perspectives and research are provided in the literature on stress, coping, and competence (see Compas, Connor-Smith, Saltzman, Thomsen, and Wadsworth, 2001; Moos, 2002 for an overview). Some of the key concepts and considerations are reviewed here as a foundation for illustrating conceptual perspectives and challenges on psychosocial development for diverse adolescents.

The environmental context in which a potentially stressful event occurs is a significant factor in the meaning ascribed to it and an individual response (Compas, Connor-Smith, Saltzman, Thomsen & Wadsworth, 2001). There are numerous environmental stressors for youth living in urban (i.e., densely populated) communities that are exacerbated by chronic, uncontrollable stressors if living in low-income communities (Allison et al., 1999). Similarly, youth in rural communities face multiple stressors associated with poverty that is further exacerbated by geographic isolation from formal support systems (Wadsworth & Compas, 2002). In addition, immigrant youth and their families in rural communities have few informal support systems along with the additional challenges of language acquisition (see Stone & Meyler, 2007). Wadsworth et al. (2008) confirmed an indirect effect of poverty on a range of youths' functioning using a multiethnic sample. Although there were differential findings by ethnicity, youth were negatively effected by stressors related to poverty (i.e., economic strain, violence, and discrimination).

As noted, responses to stressful events are affected by the appraisal of the event and youths' coping resources but also by resources provided and sanctioned by the culture and reactions of others. Cultural influences on stress and coping occurs through (1) framing the types of stressors an individual is likely to experience, (2) shaping the appraisal of a specific event, (3) defining coping strategy options, and (4) sanctioning types of coping (Aldwin, 2007). For example, dating is a normative experience during adolescence but with variation in cultural expectations regarding appropriate ages and activities. Romantic relationships for some ethnic minority youth are sources of conflict due to tensions created between youths' desires and expectations and their parent's beliefs and values. Given different expectations of males and females in many cultures, gendered expectations pose additional stressors exacerbated by the cultural dissonance (see Spencer et al., 2006).

Youth that develop strategies for coping with stressful experiences acquire a set of coping responses for facing future stressors. These strategies can result in positive resolutions which contribute to the development of an effective repertoire of responses. Some youth, however, will acquire strategies responsive to their short term needs (e.g., avoidant strategies) but counterproductive for future successes (Cunningham, 1999; Seiffge-Krenke & Klessinger, 2000). In the absence of effective strategies, the transition into adolescence occurs with limited internal resources for negotiating compromising external demands. Seaton (2007) found, for example, hypermasculinity among young African American males was attributed to their heightened sense of fear. Adaptive strategies are important independent of the developmental period; however, the possible negative or problematic consequences are particularly relevant during adolescence as the implications for mental and physical health extend into adulthood.

The extent to which youth experience competence in their efforts to change their circumstances is critical for establishing a foundational framework for future challenges. Numerous definitions of competence exist and although most earlier definitions were not developmentally oriented, they have contributed to theoretical perspectives applied to child and adolescent development. Pearlin and Schooler (1978) defined competence as a psychological resource in which an individual regards life changes as being within their control in contrast to being fatalistically controlled. Other definitions over the last few decades include having a sense of control over important circumstances in life, and the extent to which an individual feels capable of acting effectively on the environment to meet personal needs (see Master & Coatsworth, 1998).

Theoretical foundations of competence have been described under the label of personal agency beliefs (Ford, 1985), self-efficacy expectations (Bandura, 1982), locus of control (Rotter, 1966), or personal causation (deCharms, 1968). A common theme across many definitions and theories of competence is the reference "to a person's capacity to handle environmental demands and opportunities in an active and effective way" (van Aken, 1992, pp. 267-268). *As such, the basis and precondition for competence formation is the development of abilities and skills that permit an individual to effectively interact with the environment.* This highlights a common thread or underlying philosophy of competence as having both cognitive and behavioral components. Another underlying philosophy is that the process involving both the individual and the environment, whether the process is attained through interaction, interfacing, or negotiating. These conceptual considerations highlight the need for understanding not only psychosocial influences on outcomes, but also the context in which these influences occur.

In negotiating developmental tasks, adolescents' increased capacity for formal cognitive processing (see Chapter 3) would suggest they possess a range of appropriate and effective responses. As suggested, however, relevant factors in this process include prior opportunities to implement and generalize effective strategies, cultural influences, and contextually supportive conditions. These factors are also relevant in the central developmental task of identity formation. As suggested by competence theories (see Spencer, Swanson, & Cunningham, 1991), an established or manifested identity is associated with either adverse or productive life-course experiences. Conceptualizing the role of competence in identity processes understanding academic and behavioral outcomes. The framework accounts for the impact of diverse experiences and shifts in developmental expectations and demands.

4.3.1. **Youth vulnerability and adaptation**

Negative behaviors, depression, poor academic performance, and anxiety are a few significant correlates of stress during adolescence. Two most frequently cited predictors of adaptation and resilience for diverse youth are relationships with safe, supportive adults and good intellectual functioning (Masten & Coatsworth, 1998). Ethnic identity is an additional predictor of well-being for racial and ethnic youth (Spencer et al., 2006). This section highlights the impact of stressful experiences on youths' psychosocial outcomes.

As previously noted, diversity is a key issue with regard to immigration status, exposure to stressful events, and psychological coping strategies. Perceptions and experiences of discrimination are frequently associated with negative outcomes (i.e., aggression, substance use) for ethnic minority youth. Differences in experiences of discrimination are attributed to differential stereotypes encountered. For example, Asian Americans are frequently perceived as academically competent (i.e., model minority) while African Americans and Latinos are frequently cited in concerns regarding academic achievement gaps. Additionally, negative behavior is attributable to a history of poor academic performance that increases disenfranchised from the schooling process (see Spencer et al., 2006). Feelings of alienation, perceptions of low emotional support, and contextual hassles (i.e., gang-related turf wars) are factors associated with increased reactivity (i.e., hypermasculinity).

For youth living in environments in which exploration and mistakes can occur without long-term repercussions, this time of exploration provides optimum opportunities for well-being. There is considerable variability in available supports impacting adaptation across diverse youth in the U.S., particularly given variations in their group history and experience (see Chapter 10 for a detailed overview). Three contextualized areas of significance in youths' negotiation of developmental demands and their well-being are (1) social supports and mentoring relationships, (2) apprenticeship opportunities, and (3) high-school completion (see Masten & Coatsworth, 1998; Swanson, Spencer, & Petersen, 1999).

In differentiating between coping, competence, and resilience, Compas et al. (2001) denote coping as a process of adaptation, with competence representing characteristics and resources needed for successful adaptation, and resilience as the outcome of effectively utilizing competence and coping in response to stressful experiences. Rutter (1987) found that while most children recovered from a major stressful event, vulnerability for poor long-term outcomes increased when there were multiple events or when an event was compounded by a chronic stressor (i.e., economic strain).

Table 4.2 compares attributes associated with adolescents' level of risk and available supports (based on Spencer's 2006 model of vulnerability). Phelan, Davidson, and Cao (1991), Spencer et al. (2006), and (Benson, 2003) each present developmentally based perspectives useful in understanding the impact of stressors on adolescent outcomes.

Phelan et al. (1991) identified four patterns youth use in "negotiating boundaries" between three contextual domains: home, school, and peers. The boundaries represent congruency in values, beliefs, and expectations across these contexts. As previously noted, cultural dissonance is a stressor for many diverse youth due to conflicting value and belief systems. The patterns are based on the level of consistency in values, beliefs, and expectations across the boundaries or domains and the degree of psychological difficulty in navigating them. In *congruent world/smooth transitions*, there are shared values, beliefs, and expectations across the domains, resulting in smooth transitions and minimal distress. There is, in essence, low vulnerability (i.e., risk) to youths' functioning irrespective of available protective factors. In *different worlds/boundary crossing managed*, differences may exist between two of the domains (e.g., home and school), but the differences are not unduly taxing, allowing the adolescent to effectively interact in each. Although the risk is modestly high, protective factors are available to mitigate their impact. In *different worlds/boundary crossings hazardous*, there are distinct differences in values and expectations requiring divergent rather than integrated social identities. The effort required to consistently maintain distinct identities for the purpose of

Table 4.2 Conceptual comparisons of vulnerability status for youth

Vulnerability status	Phelan et al.	Spencer et al.	Benson
High risk/low protective	Impenetrable/insurmountable — Different/hazardous	High vulnerability	0-10
High risk/high protective	Different/managed	Low vulnerability	11-20
Low risk/high protective	Congruent/smooth	Undetermined	21-30
Low risk/low protective	Congruent/smooth	Masked	31-40

adaptation heightens the degree of vulnerability and psychological distress. The final category, *borders impenetrable/boundary crossings insurmountable*, represents those youth facing contexts that are so distinct that they are unable to effectively negotiate them. This heightened level of risk, in conjunction with limited supports, contributes to negative outcomes with long-term implications (e.g., runaways, school failure, or peer rejection). A major external factor in the degree to which adolescents are able to negotiate incongruent boundaries is the level of perceived available support.

In determining youths' level of vulnerability, Spencer et al. (2006) categorizes youth into four quadrants based on level of risk and level of protective factors. Those who are the most vulnerable have multiple risks (e.g., social class, temperament, or chronic illness) with the fewest protective factors (e.g., parental monitoring, socializing adults, adaptive skills). Those identified as truly resilient (i.e., habitually demonstrating productive outcomes despite persistent challenges) are those with high risks but significant protective factors. The two low risk groups are hypothesized to be those with masked vulnerability because of their inordinately high degree of privilege and absence of clear challenges or those with undetermined vulnerability due to their connectedness to others even with minimal challenges. Given the limited empirical documentation, the masked vulnerability group is of particular concern as their afforded privileges suggest limited opportunities to develop effective adaptive strategies necessary during and following the transition into adulthood.

According to Phelan's typology any incongruence in one's world requires negotiation strategies. Spencer's typology suggests that all youth are vulnerable and their outcomes are dependent on the degree of vulnerability and level of perceived available supports. As previously discussed, the greater number of developmental assets available to youth corresponds to positive developmental outcomes associated with low or mitigated risks.

These models, to varying degrees, associate risk with forms of stress recently compared to traumatic stress. Some stressors are adolescent-dependent, in that they are events unique to adolescence (i.e., pubertal changes, school transitions). Most normative stress adolescents encounter is inevitable and uncontrollable: they are encountered by most youth and include day-to-day hassles in different social environments. Examples of these are shown in Table 4.3, such as changing schools and establishing new relationships. Normative stressful events, however, will differ from traumatic forms of stress (i.e., chronic and acute). As elaborated on earlier,

Table 4.3 Sources of normative stressful events, traumatic experiences, and adolescent reactions

Normative events	Traumatic events	Youth-based reactions
Change schools	Death of a loved one	Intense and chronically upset
Academic challenges	Maltreatment	Depression
Break up with boy/girlfriend	Abandonment	Anxiety
Make a new friend	Out of home placements	Aggression M
Close friendship ends	Physical and sexual abuse	Difficulties at school
Physical changes	Automobile accidents	Problems in relationships
Dating	Hospitalization	Difficulty eating and sleeping
Obtain driver's license	Migration/acculturation	Somatic symptoms (aches, pains)
Working	Community violence	Withdrawal/Avoidance
Move to new home	Emotional abuse	Substance use/abuse
Arguments with parents	Domestic violence	Risk-taking behaviors
Join a group or club	Parental substance abuse	Unhealthy sexual activity
Increased responsibilities	Natural disasters	

the extent to which a stressful experience is chronic or uncontrollable will impact a youth's ability to effectively manage it. Chronic stress is consistent, although varying at times in intensity, such as dealing with a depressed or alcoholic mother. Acute stress is associated with a specific event of temporary duration, referred to as situational—for example, hospitalization.

Youth who encounter traumatic stress have frequently been exposed to one or more over the course of their lives and develop reactions that persist and affect their functioning, often long after the traumatic events have ended (Pynoos, Steinberg, & Wraith, 1995). When symptoms associated with stress exposure persists, or when they are extreme, post traumatic stress disorder (PTSD), depression and anxiety disorders may result. Types of traumatic experiences encountered by youth and possible reactions are noted in Table 4.3. The experiences range from those that are direct and proximal (i.e., loss of a loved one, abuse) to those that are shared (i.e., community violence, natural disasters).

The normative events are consistent with the developmental demands of adolescence. Individual attributes and contextual supports facilitate identity development and competence formation. They are compromised by increased exposure to traumatic stressors with few protective factors. The subsequent reactions, while possible for normative and traumatic events, are vastly exaggerated for the latter. Based on the presented models of assets and vulnerability, structural and organizational supports also provide opportunities for mitigating the impact of stress and negative or debilitating responses of youth.

4.4. **FUTURE DIRECTIONS**

As identity formation begins during the transition from late childhood to early adolescence, feelings of positive self-esteem established during childhood are challenged and contribute to the development of positive efficacy. Positive experiences and social competence are associated with youths' ability to adapt to change. During a time when peer relations become significantly more relevant to an adolescent's self-esteem, the role of adults in ensuring continued positive efficacy is expected to provide a sustaining impact.

In establishing a future research agenda, two of the framing criteria for this chapter remain relevant for the continuation of an expanded representation in understanding psychosocial processes for all diverse youth: (1) accounting for normative trends and their variations within cultural and individual differences parameters and (2) separating enduring from transitory effects and accounting for transitory behaviors as part of normative development. There remain significant gaps in the current literature on these processes, for example, on Arab immigrants youth. There is a need to examine behavioral outcomes against psychological demands and cultural expectations, examine areas of discontinuity in domains of competence (i.e., academic performance and intimacy relationships), and explore the role of trauma and protective factors.

Additionally, there remains a need for youth to receive active and consistent support in appraising individual attributes and interpreting life events during this developmental period. The support, however, should be conducted in a manner consistent with the developmental needs and contextual experiences given the long term implications of responses to stress. The relevance of these issues are fully comprehended when considering the coping patterns found in adulthood are frequently learned and incorporated into one's identity during adolescence. In essence, a primary thesis of the chapter was to facilitate an understanding of the developmental needs of diverse youth, given changing social contexts and demands.

4.5. **CONCLUSION**

As identity formation begins during the transition from late childhood to early adolescence, feelings of positive self-esteem established during childhood are challenged and contribute to the development of positive efficacy. Positive academic experiences and social competence are associated with adolescents' ability to adapt. During a time when peer relations become significantly more relevant to an adolescent's self-esteem, the role of adults in ensuring continued positive efficacy is expected to provide a sustaining impact.

Adolescence, as a time of normal exploration and unavoidable cognitive transformations, provides opportunities for further growth and positive development that can be facilitated through parenting strategies and integrated services and programs directed toward youth. Among diverse youth, positive identity formation, safe interpersonal relationships, and development of skills and interpersonal competencies in conjunction with available supports are vital for experiencing and transitioning the adolescent years.

REFERENCES

Aldwin, C. M. (2007). *Stress, coping, and development: An integrative perspective* (2nd ed.). New York: Guilford Press.

Allison, K. W., Burton, L., Marshall, S., Perez-Febles, A., Yarrington, J., Kirsh, L. B., et al. (1999). Life experiences among urban adolescents: Examining the role of context. *Child Development, 70,* 1017–1029.

Amiot, C. E., de la Sablonniere, R., Terry, D. J., & Smith, J. R. (2007). Integration of social identities in the self: Toward a cognitive-developmental model. *Personality and Social Psychology Review, 11*(4), 364–388.

Anthony, E. J. (1987). Risk, vulnerability, and resilience: An overview. In E. J. Anthony & B. J. Cohler (Eds.), *The invulnerable child* (pp. 3–48). New York, NY: Guilford Press.

Arndorfer, C. L., & Stormshak, E. A. (2008). Same-sex versus other-sex best friendship in early adolescence: Longitudinal predictors of antisocial behavior throughout adolescence. *Journal of Youth and Adolesecence, 37,* 1059–1070.

Arnett, J. J. (1999). Adolescent storm and stress, reconsidered. *American Psychologist, 54*(5), 317–326.

Baltes, P. B. (1987). Theoretical propositions of life-span developmental psychology: On the dynamics between growth and decline. *Developmental Psychology, 23*(5), 611–626.

Bandura, A. (1982). Self-efficacy mechanism in human agency. *American Psychologist, 37*(2), 122–147.

Bauminger, N., Finzi-Dottan, C. S., & Har-Evan, D. (2008). Intimacy in adolescent friendship: The roles of attachment, coherence, and self-disclosure. *Journal of Social and Personal Relationships, 25,* 409–428.

Benson, P. L. (2003). Developmental assets and asset-building community: Conceptual and empirical foundations. In R. M. Lerner & P. L. Benson (Eds.), *Developmental assets and asset-building communities: Implications for research, policy, and practice* (pp. 19–43). New York: Kluwer Academic/Plenum.

Benson, P. L. (2007). Developmental assets: An overview of theory, research, and practice. In R. K. Silbereisen & R. M. Lerner (Eds.), *Approaches to positive youth development* (pp. 33–58). Thousand Oaks, CA: Sage.

Benson, P. L., Leffert, N., Scales, P. C., & Blyth, D. A. (1998). Beyond the "Village" rhetoric: Creating healthy communities for children and adolescents. *Applied Developmental Science*, 2(3), 138–159.

Berndt, T. J. (1982). The features and effects of friendship in early adolescence. *Child Development*, 53(6), 1447–1460.

Brown, B. B., Larson, R. W., & Saraswathi, T. S. (Eds.) (2002). *The world's youth: Adolescence in eight regions of the globe.* New York, NY: Cambridge University Press.

Buhrmester, D. (1990). Intimacy of friendship, interpersonal competence, and adjustment during preadolescence and adolescence. *Child Development*, 61(4), 1101–1111.

Caldwell, C. H., Sellers, R. M., Bernat, D. H., & Zimmerman, M. A. (2004). Racial identity, parental support, and alcohol use in a sample of academically at-risk African American high school students. *American Journal of Community Psychology*, 34(1-2), 71–82.

Caldwell, C. H., Zimmerman, M. A., Bernat, D. H., Sellers, R. M., & Notaro, P. C. (2002). Racial identity, maternal support, and psychological distress among African American adolescents. *Child Development*, 73(4), 1322–1336.

Chestang, L. (1972). *Character development in a hostile environment.* Occasional Paper No. 3. Chicago, IL: University of Chicago.

Cocking, R. R. (1994). Ecologically valid frameworks for development: Accounting for continuities and discontinuities across contexts. In P. M. Greenfield & R. R. Cocking (Eds.), *Cross-cultural roots of child development* (pp. 393–409). Hillsdale, NJ: Lawrence Erlbaum Associates.

Compas, B. E. (1987). Stress and life events during childhood and adolescence. *Clinical Psychological Review*, 7, 275–302.

Compas, B. E., Connor-Smith, J. K., Saltzman, H., Thomsen, A. H., & Wadsworth, M. E. (2001). Coping with stress during childhood and adolescence: Problems, progress, and potential in theory and research. *Psychological Bulletin*, 127(1), 87–127.

Cross, W. E. Jr., (1971). The Negro-to-Black conversion experience. *Black World*, 20, 13–27.

Cunningham, M. (1999). African American adolescent males' perceptions of community resources and constraints: A longitudinal analysis. *Journal of Community Psychology*, 27(5), 569–588.

deCharms, R. (1968). *Personal causation: The internal affective determinants of behavior.* New York: Academic Press.

DuBois, D. L., & Silverthorn, N. (2005). Natural mentoring relationships and adolescent health: Evidence from a national study. *American Journal of Public Health*, 95(3), 518–524.

Edwards, O. W., Mumford, V. E., & Serra-Roldan, R. (2007). A positive youth development model for students considered at-risk. *School Psychology International*, *28*(1), 29–45.

Erikson, E. (1968). *Identity, youth, and crisis.* New York, NY: Norton.

Ford, M. E. (1985). The concept of competence: Themes and variations. In H. A. Marlowe & R. B. Weinberg (Eds.), *Competence development: Theory and practice in special populations* (pp. 3–49). Springfield, IL: C.G. Thomas.

Furman, W., & Shaffer, L. A. (1999). A story of adolescence: The emergence of other-sex relationships. *Journal of Youth and Adolescence*, *28*(4), 513–523.

Galambos, N. L., Almeida, D. M., & Petersen, A. C. (1990). Masculinity, femininity, and sex role attitudes in early adolescence: Exploring gender intensification. *Child Development*, *61*, 1905–1914.

Greenfield, P. A., Keller, H., Fuligni, A., & Maynard, A. (2003). Cultural pathways through universal development. *Annual Review of Psychology*, *54*, 461–490.

Grotevant, H., & Cooper, C. (1986). Individuation in family relationships: A perspective on individual differences in the development of identity and role-taking skill in adolescence. *Human Development*, *29*(2), 82–100.

Hardiman, R. (2001). Reflections on White identity development theory. In C. L. Wijeyesinghe & B. W. Jackson III (Eds.), *New perspectives on racial identity development: A theoretical and practical anthology* (pp. 108–128). New York, NY: New York University Press.

Havighurst, R. J. (1973). History of developmental psychology: Socialization and personality development through the life span. In P. B. Baltes & K. W. Schaie (Eds.), *Life-span developmental psychology: Personality and socialization* (pp. 3–24). New York, NY: Academic Press.

Henrich, C. C., Kuperminc, G. P., Sack, A., Blatt, J., & Leadbeater, B. J. (2000). Characteristics and homogeneity of early adolescent friendship groups: A comparison of male and female clique and nonclique members. *Applied Developmental Science*, *4*(1), 15–26.

Josselson, R. (1994). Identity and relatedness in the life cycle. In H. A. Bosma, T. L. G. Graafsma, H. D. Grotevant, & D. J. de Levita (Eds.), *Identity and development: An interdisciplinary approach* (pp. 81–102, 185–195). Thousand Oaks, CA: Sage.

Krane, V., Choi, P. Y., Baird, S. M., Aimar, C. M., & Kauer, K. J. (2004). Living the paradox: Female athletes negotiate femininity and muscularity. *Sex Roles*, *50*(5-6), 315–329.

Lacombe, A. C., & Gay, J. (1998). The role of gender in adolescent identity and intimacy decisions. *Journal of Youth and Adolescence*, *27*(6), 795–802.

LaFromboise, T., Coleman, H. L., & Gerton, J. (1993). Psychological impact of biculturalism: Evidence and theory. *Psychological Bulletin*, *114*(3), 395–412.

Lazarus, R. S., & Folkman, S. (1984). *Stress, appraisal, and coping.* New York, NY: Springer.

Leffert, N., Benson, P. L., Scales, P. C., Sharma, A. R., Drake, D. R., & Blyth, D. A. (1998). Developmental assets: Measurement and prediction of risk behaviors among adolescents. *Applied Developmental Science*, *2*(4), 209–230.

Lerner, R. M., Almerigi, J. B., Theokas, C., & Lerner, J. V. (2005). Positive youth development a view of the issues. *The Journal of Early Adolescence*, *25*(1), 10–16.

Lerner, R. M., & Steinberg, L. (2009). The scientific study of adolescent development: Historical and contemporary perspectives. In R. M. Lerner & L. Steinberg (Eds.), *Handbook of adolescent psychology, Vol. 1: Individual bases of adolescent development* (3rd ed., pp. 3–14). Hoboken, NJ: Wiley.

Liang, B., Spencer, R., Brogan, D., & Corral, M. (2008). Mentoring relationships from early adolescence through emerging adulthood: A qualitative analysis. *Journal of Vocational Behavior, 72*, 168–182.

Lobel, T. E., Nov-Krispin, N., & Schiller, D. (2004). Gender discriminatory behavior during adolescence and young adulthood: A developmental analysis. *Journal of Youth and Adolescence, 33*(6), 535–546.

Lysne, M., & Levy, G. D. (1997). Differences in ethnic identity in Native American adolescents as a function of school context. *Journal of Adolescent Research, 12*(3), 372–388.

Marcia, J. E. (1987). The identity status approach to the study of ego identity development. In T. Honess & K. Yardley (Eds.), *Self and identity: Perspectives across the lifespan* (pp. 161–171). New York, NY: Routledge.

Markus, H. R., Mullally, P. R., & Kitayama, S. (1997). Selfways: Diversity in modes of cultural participation. In U. Neisser & D. A. Jopling (Eds.), *The conceptual self in context: Culture, experience, self-understanding* (pp. 13–61). New York, NY: Cambridge University.

Marsh, P., Allen, J. P., Ho, M., Porter, M., & McFarland, C. (2006). The changing nature of adolescent friendships: Longitudinal links with early adolescent ego development. *Journal of Early Adolescence, 26*(4), 414–431.

Martinez, R. O., & Dukes, R. L. (1997). The effects of ethnic identity, ethnicity, and gender on adolescent well-being. *Journal of Youth and Adolescence, 26*(5), 503–516.

Masten, A. S., & Coatsworth, J. D. (1998). The development of competence in favorable and unfavorable environments: Lessons from research on successful children. *American Psychologist, 53*(2), 205–220.

McIntosh, P. (2007). White privilege and male privilege: Unpacking the invisible knapsack. In M. L. Andersen & P. H. Collins (Eds.), *Race, class, and gender: An anthology* (pp. 98–102). Belmont, CA: Thomson Wadsworth.

Moos, R. H. (2002). The mystery of human context and coping: An unraveling of clues. *American Journal of Community Psychology, 30*(1), 67–88.

Oyserman, D., Coon, H. M., & Kemmelmeier, M. (2002). Rethinking individualism and collectivism: Evaluation of theoretical assumptions and meta-analyses. *Psychological Bulletin, 128*(1), 3–72.

Pearlin, L. I., & Schooler, C. (1978). The structure of coping. *Journal of Health and Social Behavior, 22*, 337–356.

Pedlow, C. T., & Carey, M. P. (2004). Developmentally appropriate sexual risk reduction interventions for adolescents: Rationale, review of interventions, and recommendations for research and practice. *Annals of Behavioral Medicine, 27*(3), 172–184.

Phelan, P., Davidson, A. L., & Cao, H. T. (1991). Students' multiple worlds: Negotiating the boundaries of family, peer, and school cultures. *Anthropology & Education Quarterly, 22*(3), 224–250.

Pynoos, R. S., Steinberg, A. M., & Wraith, R. (1995). A developmental model of childhood traumatic stress. In D. Cicchetti & D. J. Cohen (Eds.), *Developmental Psychopathology, vol. 2: Risk, Disorder, and Adaptation* (pp. 72–95). New York, NY: Wiley.

Rhee, S., & Shrake, E. K. (2004). Ethnic identity as a predictor of problem behaviors among Korean American adolescents. *Adolescence, 39*, 601–622.

Romig, C., & Bakken, L. (1992). Intimacy development in middle adolescence: Its relationship to gender and family cohesion and adaptability. *Journal of Youth and Adolescence, 21*(3), 325–338.

Rotter, J. B. (1966). Generalized expectancies for internal versus external control of reinforcement. *Psychological Monographs: General & Applied, 80*(1), 1–28.

Rutter, M. (1987). Psychosocial resilience and protective mechanisms. *American Journal of Orthopsychiatry, 57*(3), 316–331.

Scales, P. C., Benson, P. L., Leffert, N., & Blyth, D. A. (2000). Contribution of developmental assets to the prediction of thriving among adolescents. *Applied Developmental Science, 4*, 27–46.

Scales, P. C., Benson, P. L., & Mannes, M. (2006). The contribution to adolescent well-being made by nonfamily adults: An examination of developmental assets as contexts and processes. *Journal of Community Psychology, 34*(4), 401–413.

Scales, P. C., Blyth, D. A., Berkas, T. H., & Kielsmeier, J. C. (2000). The effects of service-learning on middle school students' social responsibility and academic success. *The Journal of Early Adolescence, 20*(3), 332–359.

Schwartz, S. J., Pantin, H., Coatsworth, J. D., & Szapocznik, J. (2007). Addressing the challenges and opportunities for today's youth: Toward an integrative model and its implications for research and intervention. *Journal of Primary Prevention, 28*(2), 117–144.

Scottham, K. M., Sellers, R. M., & Nguyen, H. X. (2008). A measure of racial identity in African American adolescents: The development of the Multidimensional Inventory of Black Identity-Teen. *Cultural Diversity and Ethnic Minority Psychology, 14*(4), 297–306.

Seaton, G. (2007). Toward a theoretical understanding of hypermasculine coping among urban Black adolescent males. *Journal of Human Behavior in the Social Environment, 15*(2–3), 367–390.

Seligman, M. E. P., & Csikszentmihalyi, M. (2000). Positive psychology: An introduction. *American Psychologist, 55*(1), 5–14.

Seiffge-Krenke, I., & Klessinger, N. (2000). Long-term effects of avoidant coping on adolescents' depressive symptoms. *Journal of Youth and Adolescence, 29* (6), 617–630.

Sesma, A., Mannes, M., & Scales, P. C. (2005). Positive adaptation, resilience and the developmental asset framework. In S. Goldstein & R. B. Brooks (Eds.), *Resilience in children* (pp. 281–296). New York, NY: Kluwer Academic/Plenum.

Shulman, S., Laursen, B., Kalman, Z., & Karpovsky, S. (1997). Adolescent intimacy revisited. *Journal of Youth and Adolescence, 26*(5), 597–617.

Shweder, R. A., Goodnow, J. J., Hatano, G., LeVine, R. A., Markus, H. R., & Miller, P. J. (2006). The cultural psychology of development: One mind, many mentalities. In R. M. Lerner & W. Damon (Eds.), *Handbook of child psychology, vol. 1: Theoretical models of human development* (6th ed., pp. 716–792). Hoboken, NJ: Wiley.

Spencer, M. B. (1995). Old issues and new theorizing about African American youth: A phenomenological variant of ecological systems theory. In R. L. Taylor (Ed.), Black youth: Perspectives on their status in the United States (pp. 37–69). Westport, CT: Praeger.

Spencer, M. B., Harpalani, V., Cassidy, E., Jacobs, C. Y., Donde, S., Goss, T. N., et al. (2006). Understanding vulnerability and resilience from a normative developmental perspective: Implications for racially and ethnically diverse youth. In D. Cicchetti, D. J. Cohen, & J. Donald (Eds.), *Developmental psychopathology, Vol. 1: Theory and method* (2nd ed., pp. 627–672). Hoboken, NJ: Wiley.

Spencer, R. (2007). "I just feel safe with him": Emotional closeness in male youth mentoring relationships. *Psychology of Men and Masculinity, 8*(3), 185–198.

Spencer, M. B., Swanson, D. P., & Cunningham, M. (1991). Ethnicity, ethnic identity, and competence formation: Adolescent transition and cultural transformation. *Journal of Negro Education, 60*(3), 366–387.

Steinberg, L., & Cauffman, E. (1996). Maturity of judgment in adolescence: Psychosocial factors in adolescent decision making. *Law and Human Behavior, 20,* 249–272.

Steinberg, L., & Morris, A. S. (2001). Adolescent development. *Annual Review of Psychology, 52,* 83–110.

Stevenson, H. C. (2004). Boys in men's clothing: Racial socialization and neighborhood safety as buffers to hypervulnerability in African American adolescent males. In N. Way & J. Y. Chu (Eds.), *Adolescent boys: Exploring diverse cultures of boyhood* (pp. 59–77). New York, NY: New York University Press.

Stone, R. A. T., & Meyler, D. (2007). Identifying potential risk and protective factors among non-metropolitan Latino youth: Cultural implications for substance use research. *Journal of Immigrant and Minority Health, 9*(2), 95–107.

Swanson, D. P., Cunningham, M., Youngblood, J., & Spencer, M. B. (2009). Racial identity development during childhood. In H. A. Neville, B. M. Tynes & S. O. Utsey (Eds.), *Handbook of African American psychology* (pp. 269–281). Thousand Oaks, CA: Sage.

Swanson, D. P., Cunningham, M., & Spencer, M. B. (2003). Black males' structural conditions, achievement patterns, normative needs, and "opportunities." *Urban Education Journal, 38,* 608–633.

Swanson, D. P., & Spencer, M. B. (1998). Developmental and cultural context considerations for research on African American adolescents. In H. E. Fitzgerald, B. M. Lester, & B. Zuckerman (Eds.), *Children of color: Research, health, and public policy issues* (pp. 53–72). Chicago: University of Chicago Press.

Swanson, D. P., Spencer, M. B., Dupree, D., Harpalani, V., Noll, E., Seaton, G., et al. (2003). Psychosocial development in diverse groups: Conceptual and methodological challenges in the 21st century. *Development and Psychopathology, 15,* 743–771.

Swanson, D. P., Spencer, M. B., & Petersen, A. (1999). Adolescent identity formation: 21st century issues and opportunities. In K. M. Borman &

B. Schneider (Eds.), *Youth experiences and development: Social influences and educational challenges (National Society for the Study of Education Yearbook)* (pp. 18–41). Chicago: University of Chicago Press.

Taradesh, A., Connolly, J., Pepler, D., Craig, W., & Costa, M. (2001). The interpersonal context of romantic autonomy in adolescence. *Journal of Adolescence, 24*, 365–377.

Taylor, C. S., Lerner, R. M., von Eye, A., Bobek, D. L., Balsano, A. B., Dowling, E. M., et al. (2004). Internal and external developmental assets among African American male gang members. *Journal of Adolescent Research, 19*(3), 303–322.

Taylor, C. S., Smith, P. R., Taylor, V. A., von Eye, A., Lerner, R. M., Balsano, P. M., et al. (2005). Individual and ecological assets and thriving among African American adolescent male gang and community-based organization members—A report from wave 3 of the "overcoming the odds" study. *The Journal of Early Adolescence, 25*(1), 72–93.

Theokas, C., Almerigi, J. B., Lerner, R. M., Dowling, E. M., Benson, P. L., Scales, P. C., et al. (2005). Conceptualizing and modeling individual and ecological asset components of thriving in early adolescence. *The Journal of Early Adolescence, 25*(1), 113–143.

van Aken, M. A. G. (1992). The development of general competence and domain-specific competencies. *European Journal of Personality, 6*, 267–282.

Vasquez, M. J. T., & de las Fuentes, C. (1999). American-born Asian, African, Latina, and American Indian adolescent girls: Challenges and strengths. In N. G. Johnson, M. C. Roberts, & J. Worell (Eds.), *Beyond appearance: A new look at adolescent girls* (pp. 151–173). Washington, DC: American Psychological Association.

Wadsworth, M. E., & Compas, B. E. (2002). Coping with economic strain and family conflict: The adolescent perspective. *Journal of Research on Adolescence, 12*, 243–274.

Wadsworth, M. E., Raviv, T., Reinhard, C., Wolff, B., Santiago, C. D., & Einhorn, L. (2008). An indirect effects model of the association between poverty and child functioning: The role of children's poverty-related stress. *Journal of Loss and Trauma, 13*(2–3), 156–185.

Waters, M. C. (2006). Optional ethnicities: For Whites only. In T. E. Ore (Ed.), *The social construction of difference and inequality: Race, class, gender, and sexuality* (pp. 29–41). New York, NY: McGraw-Hill.

Way, N., & Chu, J. Y. (2004). Intimacy, desire, and distrust in the friendships of adolescent boys. In N. Way & J. Y. Chu (Eds.), *Adolescent boys: Exploring diverse cultures of boyhood* (pp. 167–196). New York, NY: New York University Press.

Weist, M. D., Freedman, A. H., Paskewitz, D. A., Proescher, E. J., & Flaherty, L. T. (1995). Urban youth under stress: Empirical identification of protective factors. *Journal of Youth and Adolescence, 24*(6), 705–721.

Wichstrom, L. (1999). The emergence of gender difference in depressed mood during adolescence: The role of intensified gender socialization. *Developmental Psychology, 35*(1), 232–245.

Zhao, S. (2005). The digital self: Through the looking glass of telecopresent others. *Symbolic Interaction, 28*(3), 387–405.

Contexts of development: socialization process

A contemporary history of the church, hip hop, and technology: Their influence on African American youth development

Marybeth Gasman and Edward M. Epstein

University of Pennsylvania, Philadelphia

Over the past 40 years, the societal influences on African American young people have changed significantly. Hip-hop culture and electronic communications technology (e.g., computers, video, and television) have had a substantial impact on youth, providing venues for self-expression and empowerment, while simultaneously distracting some adolescents from the traditional learning process. At the same time, one long-standing influence in the lives of Black youth, the Church, has seen its sway erode in recent years (Lincoln & Mamiya, 1990). This chapter focuses on the relationship between these three societal forces, showing how throughout history the Church has earned a venerable status in African American society as a provider and a mentor for youth—and how modernity has thrown this institution a curve ball. Comparisons with youth of other racial and ethnic backgrounds are offered throughout the chapter.

5.1. THE BLACK CHURCH

Since its creation, the Black church has served as a means by which African Americans have weathered the often-turbulent storms they have faced in American society. Historians and sociologists emphasize that it was the mixture of social needs, response to White racism, and Black initiative that spurred the foundation of the Black church (Frazier, 1974; Lincoln, 1974; Lincoln & Mamiya, 1990; Woodson, 1921). The

Adolescence: Development During a Global Era

first Black churches took root in the Northern states. Among them was the African Methodist Episcopal (AME) Church, which was established in Philadelphia in 1816 by a group of Black Methodists who were unhappy with the treatment they received in the White churches of that denomination. By 1846 the AME Church had 17,375 congregants who met in 206 member institutions, led by 176 clergymen. Also founded in the Northeast was the African Methodist Episcopal Zion Church, which grew from six congregations in 1821 to 132 congregations in 1864 with 113 clergy and 13,702 members (Frazier; Lincoln; Lincoln & Mamiya; Woodson).

According to Jones (1982), "The largest ingathering of blacks into the Christian church occurred in the first half of the nineteenth century when many [Blacks] were converted during the extended "great awakening" (pp. 1801-1858). The majority of the congregants were located in the South and belonged to either the Methodist or Baptist denomination. Jones further notes, "As the nineteenth century drew to a close, black Christianity had achieved a fair degree of institutionalization and stability" (Jones, p. 9). Consequently, the AME Church had expanded its membership to include 494,777 persons, while the AME Zion Church reported a membership of 184,542. In addition, The Colored Methodist Church had increased its membership to 172,996.

Much has been written about the socially repressive culture at some Black churches up to the period before the Civil Rights Movement (Frazier, 1957, 1974). According to critics, the institutions tended to reinforce class distinctions and promote a kind of internalized racism in which lighter skin color imparted status (Green, 1982). Nevertheless, the Black church came to be one of the most effective mechanisms for advocating and promoting the social needs of Blacks in America (Adams, 1985). Jones (1982) indicates, "In point of fact, no institution or organization seeking to make an impact in black communities could do so without the support and cooperation of the churches" (p. 9). How then, did the Black church come to acquire the level of respect and prestige that it now has among the larger Black community? Has this level of respect changed among youth cultures?

A key test of the church's true character was its response to the Civil Rights Movement. The Black church's fight against racial injustice entered the national consciousness in 1955 in Montgomery, Alabama. On December 1 of that year, a Black seamstress named Rosa Parks refused to relinquish her seat on a segregated bus and was subsequently jailed. This event in turn started a social movement that would rock the foundation of America, and the Black church served as the movement's catalyst. The resulting bus boycott was organized largely out of the Dexter Avenue Baptist Church. Harris (1994) states, "An important lesson the black church should remember from the Civil Rights Movement is that while the movement served as a prophetic criticism of American society, it demanded prophetic self-criticism and internal transformation of the black church as well" (p. 2). Of note, African American youth were instrumental in the movement, but they were not always appreciated. Church leaders involved in the Southern Christian Leadership Conference (SCLC) enlisted the support of mainly adults and controlled the focus of the movement's efforts. Eventually young people, mainly from historically Black colleges and universities, grew frustrated and formed the Student Nonviolent Coordinating Committee (SNCC). SNCC had a profound influence on the movement and brought considerable attention to inequities at the local level throughout the South (Garrow, 1987).

In a call to promote the racial equality of Black Americans, the Black church rose to the occasion. Consequently, during the mid-twentieth century the Black church became an institution that was both prepared and willing to serve as an active agent in the liberation of its congregants from social injustice and oppression. Whereas the Black Church served, in some capacity, as a liberator of Black Americans from social plights prior to 1955, the Civil Rights Movement allowed the Black Church to escalate that liberation to a level that was witnessed throughout the world (Lincoln, 1974; Lincoln & Mamiya, 1990). In the wake of the Civil Rights Movement, Black church membership—still largely composed of Baptist and Methodist denominations—continues to expand with nearly three million members making up the Black Baptist and Methodist churches (Lincoln & Mamiya).

Within a segregated society, the Black church was one of a few cohesive institutions, providing ample services and solace to the Black community at large. According to Lincoln and Mamiya (1990),

> *At the beginning of the last decade of the twentieth century the black churches are, on the whole, still healthy and vibrant institutions. While there has been some chipping away at the edges, particularly among unchurched underclass black youth and some college educated, middle-class young adults, black churches still remain the central institutional sector in most black communities (p. 382).*

Scholars contend that the influence and popularity of the Black church has been diminished in recent years due to a bounty of opportunities such as sports and entertainment and influences such as hip hop and technology-based social networking stimulating youth culture (Billingsley, 1999; Lincoln & Mamiya, 1990). In addition, desegregation and secularization in the post-Civil Rights era have led to a weaker role for the church. Scholars also attribute the lack of participation among African American youth in the church to the dominance of church elders who want to maintain the status quo rather than change with the times (Lincoln & Mamiya).

Throughout American history, Black churches have provided ample opportunity to young African Americans, helping them to develop their talent and leadership skills. In fact, many young people have used the church to launch professional careers in education, politics, music, and entertainment (Lincoln & Mamiya, 1990). The success that the Black church has with young people is linked to the church's "holistic ministry" and emphasis on humans as "not only spiritual, but also physical and social creatures" (Lincoln & Mamiya, p. 400). In recent years, Black churches have turned their attention to bolstering the self-esteem and racial and cultural identity of African American youth. Research shows that church role models, both clerical and lay, play a significant part in the lives of those youth active in the Black church (Johnson, Jang, Spencer, & Larson, 2000). Of note, the church is also of great significance in the lives of Latino youth, with research showing that involvement leads to higher grades, less trouble with delinquency in school, and higher self-esteem. Moreover, Latino churchgoers "engage more in activities with their children"—activities that enhance the family learning environment (Sikkink & Hernandez, 2003, p. 13).

According to Johnson et al. (2000), church-going inner city youth are more resilient and able to "escape from the world of poverty, drug use, and crime" at greater rates than their non-churchgoing counterparts (p. 481). This resiliency is often fostered by church-affiliated mentors "who are involved in young people's lives and who help them make important decisions." (Cook, 2000, p. 719). Moreover, research by Freeman (1986) shows that Black and Latino males living in high poverty areas of Philadelphia, Boston, and Chicago who attend church are significantly less likely to participate in criminal activities. Churches instill faith in individuals and provide much needed structural supports in many communities. These individuals were more likely to stay in school, have an after-school job, and less likely to behave in ways termed "socially deviant" (Cook; Freeman; Sikkink & Hernandez, 2003). In particular, Latino youth who attended church were more likely to feel close to their peers at school and more likely to get along with their teachers (Edwards, Fehring, Jarrett, & Haglund, 2008; Sikkink & Hernandez). Interestingly, Johnson et al.

found that African American youth living in high-crime neighborhoods that were active in the church were less likely to become involved in criminal activity than those non-church-going young people living in low-crime areas. This relationship, in the words of Johnson et al., could be attributed to what Stark (1996) calls a moral community or, in other words, a community in which the vast majority of individuals are connected to a religious institution and active in their connectedness. According to Sikkink and Hernandez, the church and religion in general are "sometimes the only form of social support in inner city areas" for Black and Latino youth (p. 20).

In addition to helping young people avoid a life of crime, there is some evidence that youth involvement in the church is highly correlated with these individuals having "a better chance of moving out of poverty conditions than those [youth] condemned to the anonymity of poverty" (Edwards et al., 2008; Lincoln & Mamiya, 1990, p. 403; Sikkink & Hernandez, 2003). Some churches have been quite purposeful in their attempts to change the life of young African Americans, feeling that the church is "the only institution capable of turning their lives around" (Billingsley, 1999, p. 102). For example, many churches provide support services for young, pregnant Black and Latino women, including child rearing, financial management, and counseling classes. Other churches have directed their attention to crises in the Black and Latino male youth community, creating programs that empower young Black and Latino men. These programs provide Black and Latino male role models for young people who do not have a stable father figure in their lives. According to the minister at Atlanta's Antioch Baptist Church, for example, "The presence of men attracts other men. It signifies that the men of Antioch are respected and empowered" and this message has a significant impact on Black, male youth (*Christian Century*, 1994, p. 1). And research shows that church-going African American youth are more likely to have mentors than their non-church-going counterparts (Cook, 2000). Many times these mentors help their mentees make important decisions about family and career.

In recent years, Black mega churches (large nondenominational churches that offer religion as well as a variety of social services) have been established throughout the country. Supporters of the Black mega church movement claim that during this time of disengagement among youth, these churches are playing a disproportionate role in educating and mentoring young African Americans, especially the urban poor (*Christian Century*, 1994). Unfortunately, in the minds of Black church leaders, Black youth are not engaging with the Black church at the same levels as in the past.

When Frazier wrote his classic *The Negro Church in America* a generation ago, over 80% of African American youth participated in the Church or Sunday school (*Christian Century*; Frazier, 1974). However, today, some researchers estimate that almost 60% of Black youth have no contact at all with the church (*Christian Century*). According to a recent article in *Christian Century*, the reasons for the lack of engagement are many:

> *Some are children of those drawn to Islam by the preaching of Malcolm X. Others find the turn-the-other-cheek Christian pacifism that was a hallmark of the civil rights era irrelevant. Some, turned off by images of a white Jesus, reject Christianity as a faith imposed on slaves that replaced their original beliefs in animism or Islam. Others simply fall victim to the temptations of a consumerist popular culture or the violent ethos of the street* (Christian Century, 1994, p. 2).

Other scholars, including Bachman, Johnston, and O'Malley (2005) found the situation to be less dire for the Black church, with 56% of African American high-school seniors believing in the importance of religion and 45% regularly attending religious services.

In the words of one scholar, "Being a faithful, moral person is against the odds and weight of the entire [inner city] culture" and it is here in the inner city where most of the drop-in African American (as well as Latino) youth engagement has taken place (Franklin in *Christian Century*, 1994, p. 2). The inner city culture to which the author refers includes a strong dose of hip hop—rap music, dancing, and visual art.

According to Cone (1990), Herndon, (2003), McAdoo (1993), and Sikkink and Hernandez (2003), whereas Blacks and Latinos traditionally and typically "embrace the value of religion, its liberating power, the reliance on a higher power, and the practical application of spiritual principles in life," Whites tend to view religion as something more abstract or intellectual (Herndon, p. 76). These researchers attribute this difference to issues of race, social conditions, class, and stress, noting that African Americans, Latinos, and some Asian American groups may use religion as a coping mechanism for the stress in their lives (Chau, 2006; Cone; Edwards et al., 2008; Herndon; McAdoo; Sikkink & Hernandez). Of course, Whites may also use religion to address issues of stress but less often. Some researchers have focused on the impact of faith on the lives of young African Americans and Latinos, noting that faith serves as the "ultimate support when the other things they depend on in their lives collapse around them" (Sikkink & Hernandez; Stewart, 2002, p. 581). Many young African Americans and Latinos who have participated in studies pertaining to the Black church and resilience have noted that their ability to pray, attend church, and read scripture has helped them during times of personal turmoil (Sikkink & Hernandez). According to research by Herndon, African American church-going youth "believed that these acts [church attendance and praying] assisted in shouldering the stresses and strains of life and caused them to excel in the face of academic and social adversities" (p. 78).

Still, some researchers have found that an affiliation with the church provides mentoring, fosters comfort with public discussion and disagreement, and enables young African American men and women to view each other as equals or peers, which in turn helps to build a strong nuclear African American family unit (Franklin in *Christian Century*, 1994). Other researchers have found that churches offer several other mechanisms for supporting resilience among African American youth. These include assisting Black teenagers to "develop self-regulatory abilities, fostering identity development … and offering a relationship with a powerful and loving Other" (Cook, 2000, p. 3). Self-regulatory abilities are particularly important, as these skills help young people to modify their behavior when necessary. The Black church's assistance with identity formation is also vitally important in that "if young people are willing to negotiate life within the context of the church rather than a gang, they have a better chance of avoiding prison, early pregnancy, and the numerous other negative outcomes that limit their ability to achieve health and happiness" (Cook).

According to researchers, the Black church, like all religion, has the ability to provide a sense of structure that is sought by youth in general and inner city African American youth in particular (Ianni, 1989). African American youth involved in the church are offered "a standard for behavior" and taught right and wrong (Cook, 2000, p. 8). Many of these young people, when confronted with a potentially negative or dangerous situation, report hearing the voice of their pastor or youth minister telling them not to make the wrong decision (Cook). Moreover, these young people credit the Black church with providing a sense of purpose and direction in their lives, labeling their spirituality their "inner core" or "peace of mind" (Herdnon, 2003, p. 79). This crediting of the Black church is particularly poignant when students are in college; the church serves as a home away from home, an extended family, and a venue for exploring their spirituality.

In addition, congregants of the Black church have the potential to act as a close-knit web of support for young African Americans. Though it sounds simplistic, when youth are kept busy, they tend to stay out of trouble.

Of greater importance, they participate in activities that have a positive impact on their lives. According to Cook (2000), "the church provides youths with a place to go and things to do, instead of watching television all afternoon or hanging out with friends, a situation in which trouble easily develops" (p. 9). Although church is often thought of as a Sunday-only event, most Black churches and especially megachurches offer young people "youth groups, Bible classes, sports events, or after-school tutoring programs" throughout the week (Cook, p. 9). However, researchers also note that young people may not be spiritually mature enough to actually reap the benefits that the Black church has to offer until later in life (Stewart, 2002).

5.2. **HIP HOP**

The Black church, for the most part, has been seen throughout American history as a positive influence on African American youth development. On the other hand, hip hop is often viewed as a negative factor in the lives of young Blacks as well as Latinos and some Asian American groups, labeled as nihilistic and destructive by a host of scholars, journalists and leaders, Black and White, from across the political spectrum (McWhorter, 2003). Hip hop, with roots in the U.S. Black, Caribbean, and African traditions, came into being on the streets of the Bronx, New York, during the 1970s; beginning as a local movement, it quickly spread nationally and internationally (Chang, 2005; Hill, in press; Petchauer, 2009; Rose, 1994). Kitwana claims that those Blacks born between 1965 and 1984 represent the "hip hop generation" and are influenced by a particular set of values and attitudes that play a role in their learning process (2003). In effect, the hip hop movement introduced a culture, lifestyle and musical genre into society. According to Hill (in press),

> From the i-Pods of suburban American teens to revolutionary movements of the Global South, the sites, sounds, and spectacles of hip-hop have become a central feature of an increasingly globalized cultural landscape (p. 1).

For contemporary youth, hip hop *is* culture. They have grown up in a world where styles of music and dance pioneered by the hip-hop generation are all-pervasive. These styles are as well known to White suburbanites as Black inner city dwellers.

Of significance is the fact that hip-hop culture first appeared as the Civil Rights Movement waned. After nonviolent civil disobedience had given way to rioting in the inner cities; after "urban renewal" had eviscerated cities' physical and social infrastructure; and as the mostly white suburb was entrenched as a convenient replacement for legalized segregation—at this moment, a group of creative individuals fashioned what we now know as hip hop. Although they did not experience the Civil Rights struggle directly, hip-hop pioneers like Kool Herc and Afrika Bambaataa would have seen the confrontations unfolding on television. This partially explains the distinct political consciousness present in much rap music. However, most hip-hop pioneers grew up with a very different world view than the civil rights protesters. Hip hop's epicenter was the Bronx, one of the areas hardest hit by urban decline—and also a melting pot of West Indian and Latino immigrants. Consequently, the ideological leanings of hip-hop innovators were a mixed bag as well. DJ Kool Herc, for example, came from Jamaica and would have been aware of freedom struggles there as well as in the United States. Afrika Bambaataa's Zulu Nation too was inspired by worldwide anticolonial movements (Chang, 2005; Rose, 1994). It would not be accurate, then, to say that hip hop's social consciousness was a product of the Black Church's protest tradition.

For many Americans, hip hop is synonymous with rap music; the words "hip hop" and "rap" are often used interchangeably. Those more knowledgeable about the movement identify four pillars—rapping, DJing, graffiti, and break dancing—as the primary forms of expression the movement spawned (Chang, 2005). But hip hop also encompasses fashion, advertising, linguistic characteristics, postures, and more recently, various forms of activism (Petchauer, 2009). Chang (2005) claims that "Hip-hop offers a generational worldview that encompasses the shoes you choose to whether you're inclined to vote or not to how you understand the issues of race" (p. 1). Because hip-hop culture includes elements of material culture, Kitwana (2003) asserts that the hip-hop generation is more career-oriented and material-based than previous generations of African Americans, who were more focused on gaining their legal rights. Specifically, he notes:

> *For many, the American Dream means not just living comfortably but becoming an overnight millionaire while still young. Many of us can't imagine waiting until we are forty, or even thirty-five, for that matter. This desire for wealth is accompanied by a sense of entitlement. That a handful of widely celebrated hip-hop generationers have achieved the dream makes the possibility real, despite the odds. And this desire to achieve not simply financial security but millionaire status is the driving force of our generation's work ethic (Kitwana, 2003, p. 46).*

In this sense, hip hop picks up where the Civil Rights Movement left off: pursuing the yet unfulfilled promise of economic equality that should rightly follow legal equality.

According to Morrel and Duncan-Andrade (2002), hip hop also "represents a resistant voice of urban youth through its articulation of problems that this generation and all Americans face on a daily basis" (p. 88). And, hip hop is the "representative voice of urban youth, since the genre was created by and for them" (p. 88). It reflects the hopes, dreams, aspirations, and concerns of urban youth of all racial and ethnic backgrounds; every issue and aspect of life in the inner city is the subject of interpretation (Powell, 1991 and Rose, 1991). Hip-hop culture is a "multiracial, multiethnic phenomenon" (McFarland, 2008, p. 173). Hip hop emerged as an alternative source of identity development and social status for youth at a moment when "economic and social disparity left the traditional support pillars of the church, school, and neighborhood—literally and figuratively—crumbling" (Petchauer, 2009, p. 28). The identity formed by the hip-hop generation and its descendents is highly different from those reared during the Civil Rights Movement. As Petchauer (2007) explains,

> *The old racial politics and definitions . . . are rigid constructions of race, ethnicity, and cultural ownership – the kind from which many accusations of cultural thievery are posited (e.g., Elvis and rock and roll). Hip-Hop is frequently perceived as a participatory culture, one that operates upon notions of civic (rather than primordial) membership and challenges the older notion that Black culture is only available to individuals who are phenotypically Black (p. 31).*

An explanation for the more fluid identity of the hip-hop generation's members rests in the art forms themselves, which, moreso than previous African American art forms, rely on recycling. Hip hop's earliest originators were DJs, individuals like Kool Herc and Grandmaster Flash, whose main contribution was to refashion prerecorded sounds to create new beats. The break beat—the kernel of rhythm these DJs sampled and repeated to generate a hip-hop groove—often came from a funk track such as James Brown's "Funky Drummer" or the Winstons' "Amen, Brother." But they would add to that a rich palette of sounds that included pop, rock and roll, disco, voice overlays, and raw noise. Consider this description by hip-hop critic Nelson George (1999) of a Grand Master Flash performance:

> *It begins with "you say one for the trouble," the opening phrase of Spoonie Gee's "Monster Jam," broken down to "you say" repeated seven times, setting the tone for a record that uses the*

music and vocals of Queen's "Another One Bites the Dust," the Sugar Hill Gang's "8th Wonder," and Chic's "Good Times" as musical pawns that Flash manipulates at whim. He repeats "Flash is bad" from Blondie's "Rapture" three times, turning singer Deborah Harry's dispassion into total adoration. While playing "Another One Bites the Dust," Flash places a second record on the turntable, then shoves the needle and the record against each other. The result is a rumbling, gruff imitation of the song's bass line. As guitar feedback on "Dust" builds, so does Flash's rumble, until we're grooving on "Good Times."

As hip hop was multilayered, so were the people who made it. Many break dance innovators were Latino (e.g., Richie "Crazy Legs" Colon), as were graffiti writers (Lee "LEE" Quinones). Kool Herc himself was Jamaican-born, and many of his stylistic innovations paralleled Jamaican forms such as dub (Chang, 2005). According to McFarland (2008),

Rap music and hip-hop have most commonly been understood as black American phenomena. While it is undoubtedly true that black American youth have been the driving force in the creation of hip-hop, numerous other cultures and peoples have contributed to it. Jamaican music, dance, and oral tradition, Asian martial arts and philosophy, Italian gangster fantasy, Japanese technology, Chicano dress and style, Islam, Euro-American capitalist ideology, and Puerto Rican dance and music all played a role in the early development of hip-hop culture and music (pp. 173-174).

Given the mixed provenience of this genre, it is not surprising that hip hop-influenced African American youth construct race and ethnicity differently from previous generations of Black Americans.

According to some researchers, hip-hop artists consider themselves to be educators, seeking to promote "consciousness within their communities" (Morrell & Duncan-Andrade, 2002, p. 89). These researchers consider hip hop to be "prophetic and empowering" (Petchauer, 2009, p. 3). Although the primary discussion in this chapter focuses on African Americans, it should be noted that the influence of hip hop transcends race and as mentioned above, young people from various ethnic and racial backgrounds have been strongly influenced by hip-hop culture (Morrel & Duncan-Andrade). While hip hop began in the African American community, 70% of compact discs have been purchased by White youth; more recently, song downloads have also been mainly consumed by White youth although there is less of a gap. And, it should be noted that African American and hip-hop cultures are "neither identical nor completely separate entities" (Petchauer, p. 21). According to Petchauer,

> *Although hip-hop in many ways is a subset of Black culture – exhibiting many characteristics of African American culture, maintaining some of the ideological underpinnings of the civil rights and Black power movements, and having been assembled by marginalized African American and Latino youth – participation and cultural membership in hip-hop in the Twenty First century is not limited to individuals who are phenotypically Black (p. 21).*

Petchauer (2007) claims that hip hop lacks the clear components of a social movement, including "grievance, common goals, [and a] communication network," which is fundamentally different from the Civil Rights Movement (Petchaur, p. 30). Lang (2000) describes hip hop as even more apolitical, noting that young African Americans engaged in hip-hop culture tend to:

> *View cultural expression as resistance in and of itself, ignoring the importance of organized, state-directed activity around material conditions. Thus, one hears often references to hip-hop being a social movement in the same vein as civil rights and Black Power. Yet hip-hop, like all forms of art and culture, has no fixed political character (p. 127).*

Hill (in press) as well at Petchauer (2009) contend that hip-hop music and culture shape youth identity, including the identity of African Americans, Latinos, Asian Americans, and Whites. In Petchauer's opinion, "The magnitude of hip-hop's cultural influence upon youth and young adults is much greater than the literal meanings of commercial, mainstream rap music" (p. 28). And in fact, both scholars advocate for a curriculum in schools that uses hip hop to engage students in meaningful ways. Hip hop, according to some, can be used to bridge the world of the street with academics (Morrel & Duncan-Andrade, 2002). For example, some scholars suggest that juxtaposing hip-hop lyrics with "traditional" poets can help African American and Latino youth to understand how people of different generations view and comment on their "rapidly deteriorating societies." (Morrell & Duncan-Andrade, p. 91; Pulido, 2009). Of course, according to critics, this kind of curriculum is controversial given the sexual and misogynistic lyrics of many hip-hop songs and the culture in general (Giroux, 1996; McWhorter, 2003). Moreover, scholars argue that some young people have constructed a "generational identity of being more morally corrupt compared to previous generations" (Petchauer, p. 18) and this could hold back these individuals' potential. But, those who support the incorporation of hip hop into curricula, according to Morrel and Duncan-Andrade, think that "the knowledge reflected in these lyrics could engender discussions of esteem, power, place, and purpose or encourage students to further their own knowledge of urban sociology and politics" (p. 89). According to some scholars, historic images from the Civil Rights Movement or of Martin Luther King Jr. are too far removed from the lives of young people to be a strong influence (Petchauer, 2007). Instead, other scholars claim that "constructing a myth that Tupac survived his fatal 1996 shooting helped students transcend feelings of vulnerability in their local spaces" (Petchauer, 2009, pp. 17 and 18). Perhaps the best way to describe the influence of hip hop on African American youth culture is to quote Petchauer (2007) when he says "Hip-hop, now integrated into the fabric of American culture, is both a cause and effect of these shifting and more open constructions of ethnicity among young adults" (p. 31).

5.3. **TECHNOLOGY**

A rat done bit my sister Nell
And Whitey's on the moon
Her face and arms began to swell
With Whitey on the moon
The revolution will not be brought to you by the
Schaefer Award Theatre and will not star Natalie
Woods and Steve McQueen or Bullwinkle and Julia.
The revolution will not give your mouth sex appeal.
The revolution will not get rid of the nubs.
The revolution will not make you look five pounds
thinner, because the revolution will not be televised, Brother.
—Gil Scott Heron (1971)

Previous generations of African Americans viewed technology with a certain mistrust. Scientific innovations—whether in space, medicine, or communications—were seen by some African Americans as at best a distraction from the real problems of life, and at worst a conspiracy, part of a racist apparatus that kept them down. These suspicions were borne out in certain baneful incidents in U.S. history, such as the Tuskegee experiment in which African Americans were used as lab rats to test the effects of syphilis contagion (Gray, 1998; Jones, 1981). Yet the hip-hop generation was different. This is a generation whose point of reference is television and video games. An irony of the above quoted

"Revolution will not be Televised" from Gil Scott Heron is that while it certainly takes aim at the deadening effects of television, it inadvertently tells us that he's been watching quite a bit of it. Heron's music, which predates hip hop by a few years, points the way toward rap—a music that often makes sly, ironic jabs at electronic culture, but also presumes a knowledge of it.

Perhaps one reason for hip hop's embrace of technology is that it is woven into the fabric of the music. It was a profound achievement of the early hip-hop innovators that, using analog sound equipment, they were able to build tapestries of sound rich enough to put today's digital technicians to shame. Kool Herc's claim to fame was his speaker system ("the Herculords"), which he carried proudly from one party to the next. Grand Master Flash was particularly adept with the use of electricity and electronics. When power was lacking, his crew famously wired the system to a street-light pole. Flash also added a toggle to his headphone jack in order to monitor two turntables and seamlessly switch from one to the other. This innovation, along with techniques like the "backspin" and the "cut," made it possible to loop sound on the fly, using only vinyl records (Hager, 1984). From the beginning, hip hop DJing displayed virtuosity in the use of technology, rather than in singing or playing an instrument.

Today's youth, and African American youth in particular, spend more time with various forms of electronic media than any other activity with the exception of sleeping (Roberts & Foehr, 2008). The average 8- to 18-year old, for example, uses technology (television, computers, video games, Ipods, etc.) more than 6 h a day (Fazzaro, 1999; Roberts & Foehr). And, according to a recent study by Roberts and Foehr, youth have become astute at media multitasking—or using several media concurrently—which increases their use to approximately 8.5 h a day. Televisions are in 99% of American households, and 95% of these same households have at least five other forms of technology available to family members. Of note, according to the Kaiser Foundation, "68 percent of U.S. eight- to eighteen-year-olds and 33 percent of children from birth to age six had a TV in their bedroom (19 percent of children under age one roomed with a TV set)" (Roberts & Foehr, p. 15). Also of note, as of 2005, 45% of teens owned their own cell phones, and the number is on the increase with access to phone service lowering in cost (Roberts & Foehr). Although young people are benefiting from their technological skills, they are being hindered by fewer hours of adult interaction and face-to-face social interaction in general.

Interestingly, Carver predicted in 1999 that African Americans and Latinos would fall on the wrong side of the digital divide. He is correct on some fronts; most African American and Latino communities do not have access to technology in the same ways as their White counterparts. Public schools and libraries have antiquated equipment and many African American and Latino homes do not have access to the internet. However, in certain respects, African American and Latino youth are well connected to technology. Most have access to cell phones, iPods, video games, and televisions (Mason & Dodds, 2005; Roberts & Foehr, 2008). In a report for the Kaiser Foundation, Rideout and Hamel (2006) found that African American adolescents had more media exposure than Hispanics and Whites, with 10, 9, and 8 h, respectively. In fact, African Americans spend double the amount of time in front of a television than their White counterparts. They also use video games more often, averaging 65 min per day (Rideout & Hamel).

Unfortunately, their use of computers is significantly lower than Whites. When Carver began his study in 1999, African American and Latino youth had 20% less access to computers than their White counterparts, and when they had access in schools or in their homes, it was typically access to 3- to 4-year-old equipment (Carver, 1999; Mason & Dodds, 2005). And, African American and Latino youth received and continue to receive inadequate training on computers—typically the focus is on remedial skill development rather than advanced technologies (Carver; Mason & Dodds; Roberts & Foehr, 2008). However, this access to technology has increased slowly over the past 10 years (U.S. Department of Commerce, 2002). Closing the digital divide has become the focus of a great deal of investment by foundations and universities, leading to such projects as the Microsoft School of the Future in Philadelphia, where students from an impoverished neighborhood learn on laptop computers. As a result, computer usage by African Americans and Latinos is up to about with about 33% of Latino's and 40% of African American's having Internet access at home (Fairlie, 2003).

5.4. **CONCLUSION**

When we look at young African Americans' interests (as well as Latinos and Asian Americans in some cases)—their embrace of the electronic media, their love of the sound wizardry found in hip-hop music—we begin to see why many are alienated from Church culture. As noted earlier in this chapter, Black churches are still led by an older generation that is suspicious of technology. Moreover, the church remains an essentially segregated institution. In fact, Martin Luther King Jr. once said that "Sunday is the most segregated day in America." This is true because White churches have traditionally been unfriendly toward Blacks, but also because Black churches have long fulfilled a spiritual need that the White ones do not address. Black churches have different music, preach different sermons, and voice a different perspective than the rest of America. They assume the same rigid constructions of race, ethnicity, and cultural ownership that Petchauer (2009) notes have been rejected by the hip-hop generation. Hip-hop youth do acknowledge the depth of racial inequality in America—rap music, for example, often exposes police brutality—yet their take on race is fundamentally different from that of the previous generation. Will the Black church (and other churches for that matter) adapt to the changing attitudes of these young people? It would seem that to do so would require more than just installing a pair of turntables in place of the church organ. With its embrace of the worldly—material success and the mastery of life's challenges through man-made technology—hip hop represents a marked departure from the church's emphasis on the other-worldly.

REFERENCES

Adams, J. H. (1985). Stewardship and the black church. *Urban League Review*, 9(1), 17–27.

Bachman, J. G., Johnston, L. D., & O'Malley, P. M. (2005). *Monitoring the future: A continuing study of American youth (8th, 10th, and 12th-grade surveys), 1976-2003 [Computer files].* Conducted by University of Michigan, Survey Research Center, Ann Arbor.

Billingsley, A. (1999). *Mighty like a river. The black church and social reform.* New York, NY: Oxford University Press.

Carver, B. A. (1999). The information rage: Computers and young African American males. In V. C. Polite & J. E. Davis (Eds.), *African American males in school and society: Practices and policies for effective education.* New York, NY: Teachers College Press.

Chang, J. (2005). *Can't stop won't stop: A history of the hip hop generation.* New York, NY: St. Martin's Press.

Chau, W. W. (2006). The relationship between acculturative stress and spirituality among Chinese immigrant college students in the United States. Unpublished Thesis. ERIC Online submission: ED491387.

Christian Century. (1994). Young black men and church. *Christian Century*, 111(14), 439–441.

Cone, J. H. (1990). God is black. In S. B. Thistlethwaite & M. P. Engel (Eds.), *Life every voice: Constructing Christian theologies from the underside.* San Francisco: Harper Collins Publishers.

Cook, K. V. (2000). 'You have to have somebody watching your back, and if that's God, then that's mighty big': The church's role in the resilience of inner city youth. *Adolescence*, 35(140), 717–730.

Edwards, L. M., Fehring, R. J., Jarrett, K. M., & Haglund, K. A. (2008). The influence of religiosity, gender, and language preference acculturation on sexual activity among Latino/a adolescents. *Hispanic Journal of Behavioral Sciences*, 30(4), 447–462.

Fairlie, R. W. (2003). *Is there a digital divide? Ethnic and racial differences in access to technology and possible explanations*. Final Report to the University of California, Latino Policy Institute and California Policy Research Center U.C. Santa Cruz.

Fazarro, D. E. (1999). Motivating African-American youth in technology education. *Tech Directions*, *59*(1), 25–29.

Frazier, E. F. (1957). *Black bourgeoisie*. New York, NY: Free Press.

Frazier, E. F. (1974). *The Negro church in America*. New York, NY: Schoken Books.

Freeman, R. B. (1986). Who escapes? The relation of churchgoing and other background factors to the socioeconomic performance of black male youth from inner-city tracts. In R. B. Freeman & H. J. Holzer (Eds.), *The black youth employment crisis*. Chicago, IL: University of Chicago Press.

Garrow, D. (1987). *Martin Luther King Jr. and the Southern Christian leadership conference*. New York, NY: HarperCollins.

George, N. (1999). *Hip hop America*. New York, NY: Penguin Books.

Giroux, H. (1996). *Fugitive cultures: Race, violence, and youth*. New York, NY: Routledge.

Gray, F. D. (1998). *The Tuskegee syphilis study: The real story and beyond*. New York, NY: River City Publications.

Green, R. L. (1982). Growing up black, urban, and in the church. *The Crisis*, *89*(9), 13–19.

Hager, S. (1984). *Hip hop: The illustrated history of break dancing, rap music, and Graffiti*. New York, NY: St. Martins Press.

Harris, F. C. (1994). Something within: Religion as a mobilizer of African American political activism. *The Journal of Politics*, *56*(1), 42–68.

Herndon, M. K. (2003). Expressions of spirituality among African American college males. *Journal of Men's Studies*, *12*(1), 75–83.

Heron, G. S. (1971). *Pieces of man*. Record Album.

Hill, M. L. (in press). 'Stakes is high': Towards an anthropology of hip-hop based education. In M. L. Hill (Ed.), *Beats, rhymes, and classroom Life: Hip-Hop, pedagogy, and the politics of identity*. New York, NY: Teachers College Press.

Ianni, F. A. J. (1989). *The search for structure: A report on American youth today*. New York, NY: Free Press.

Johnson, B. R., Jang, S. J., Spencer, D. L., & Larson, D. (2000). The 'invisible institution' and black youth crime: The church as an agency of local social control. *Journal of Youth and Adolescence*, *29*(4), 47–64.

Jones, J. H. (1981). *Bad blood: The Tuskegee syphilis experiment*. New York, NY: Free Press.

Jones, L. H. (1982). The black churches in historical perspectives. *The Crisis*, *89*(9), 16–21.

Kitwana, B. (2003). *The hip-hop generation: Young Blacks and the crisis of African American culture*. New York, NY: Basic Civitas Books.

Lang, C. (2000). The new global and urban order: Legacies for the 'hip-hop generation. *Race and Society*, *3*, 111–142.

Lincoln, C. E. (1974). *The black church since Frazier*. New York: Schoken Books.

Lincoln, C. E., & Mamiya, L. H. (1990). *The black church in the African American experience*. Durham, North Carolina: Duke University Press.

Mason, C. Y., & Dodds, R. (2005). Bridge the digital divide for educational equity. *The Education Digest*, 25–27.

McAdoo, H. P. (Ed.). (1993). *Family ethnicity: Strength in diversity*. Newbury Park: Sage Publications.

McFarland, P. (2008). Chicano hip-hop as interethnic contact zone. *Aztlán: A Journal of Chicano Studies*, *33*(1), 173–183.

McWhorter, J. H. (2003). How hip-hop holds Blacks back. *City Journal*, *13*, 3 Retrieved September 10, 2008, from http://www.city-journal.org/html/13_3_how_hip_hop.html

Morrell, E., & Duncan-Andrade, J. M. R. (2002). Promoting academic literacy with urban youth through engaging hip-hop culture. *English Journal*, 88–92.

Petchauer, E. M. (2007). African American and hip-hop cultural influences. In A. P. Robai, L. B. Gallien, Jr., & H. R. Stiff-Williams (Eds.), *Closing the African American achievement gap in higher education*. New York, NY: Teachers College Press.

Petchauer, E. M. (2009). Framing and reviewing hip-hop education research. *Review of Educational Research*, *79*(2), 946–978.

Powell, C. T. (1991). Rap music: An education with a beat from the street. *Journal of Negro Education*, *60*(3), 245–259.

Pulido, I. (2009). "Music fit for us minorities": Latinas/os' use of hip hop as pedagogy and interpretive framework to negotiate and challenge racism. *Equity and Excellence in Education*, *42*(1), 67–85.

Rideout, V. J., & Hamel, E. (2006). *The media family: Electronic media in the lives of infants, toddlers, preschoolers, and their parents*. Menlo Park, CA: Kaiser Family Foundation.

Roberts, D. F., & Foehr, U. G. (2008). Trends in media use. *The Future of Children*, *18*(1), 11–37.

Rose, T. (1991). "Fear of a black planet": Rap music and black cultural politics in the 1990s. *Jounral of Negio Education*, *60*(3), 276–290.

Rose, T. (1994). *Black Noise: Rap and Black Culture in Contemporary America*. Hanover, NH: Wesleyan University Press.

Sikkink, D., & Hernandez, E. I. (2003). *Religion matters: Predicting schooling success among Latino youth*. Notre Dame: University of Notre Dame, Institute for Latino Studies.

Stark, R. (1996). Religion as context. Hellfire and delinquency one more time. *Social Relations*, *57*, 163–173.

Stewart, D. (2002). The role of faith in the development of an integrated identity: A qualitative study of black students at a white college. *Journal of College Student Development*, *43*(4), 579–596.

U.S. Department of Commerce. (2002). *A nation online: How Americans are expanding their use of the internet*. Washington, DC: U.S.G.P.O.

Woodson, C. G. (1921). *The history of the Negro church*. Washington, DC: The Associated Publishers.

Leisure and technological influences

Lisa Bouillion Diaz

University of Illinois, Urbana-Champaign, Illinois

Carol Cuthbertson Thompson

Rowan University, Glassboro, New Jersey

Donna DeGennaro

UMass Boston, Boston, Massachusetts

Adolescence is a pivotal period in which young people are developing expectations, experiences, and competencies that they will draw upon as they enter adulthood. In the United States, as in other postindustrial countries, this framework of experience is increasingly constructed within leisure activities (Larson & Richards, 1989; Larson & Verma, 1999; Wartella and Mazzarella, 1990). Youth engage in a wide range of activities in their free time, including interacting with friends, listening to music, watching various media, reading, drawing, and playing sports and video games. These activities occur in structured and unstructured spaces, including time spent alone, with peers and with adults.

This spectrum of youth practice within leisure or out-of-school time is increasingly mediated by new communication technologies, including cell phones, personal digital assistants (PDAs), computers, iPods, MP3 players, video cameras, game players, and the Internet. Research from the PEW Internet and American Life Project (Lenhart & Madden, 2007; Lenhart, Madden, & Hitlin, 2005; Lenhart, Madden, Macgill, & Smith, 2007; Lenhart, Rainie, & Lewis, 2001; Lenhart et al., 2008) has found that 93% of U.S. teens use the Internet, and more of them than ever are using sites like Facebook, YouTube, MySpace, MyBlog, and MUVEs[1] to construct a virtual identity for themselves, meet new friends, and create content to share with others. Fifty-five percent of online teens aged 12-17 have created

---

[1]Multi-User Virtual Environments, such as Second Life.

Adolescence: Development During a Global Era

profiles on social network sites, and 64% have participated in one or more content-creating activities on the Internet. Those online creations include artwork, photos, stories, videos, webpages, and blogs.

This rapid increase in youth involvement online has sparked the interest of parents, educators, and media alike. Just how radically is the Internet transforming the experiences of childhood and adolescence? This question provided the platform for a January 2008 Frontline Report, Growing Up Online.[2] The youth interviewed for this documentary describe their lives as so infused with online activity that they wouldn't know what to do without their Internet connection. "*Everyone* is online," they say, "the geeks, the nerds, the popular people—just all sorts of people."

There is concern that this increasing ubiquity of technology creates new opportunities for youth activity that extends beyond the purview of adults (Jordan, Singer, & Singer, 2001). Rideout, Foehr, Roberts, and Brodie (1999) of a nationally representative sample of 2014 children ages 8-18 reveals that bedrooms are an important site of technology access and practice. According to this report, 94% of older youth have a radio in their bedroom, 89% have a tape player, 88% have a CD player, 64% have a TV, 41% have a video game player, 19% have a computer, and 12% have Internet access. Close to half of teens (45%) have a cell phone allowing them to interact with friends anywhere, anytime (Lenhart, Madden, & Hitlin, 2005). Eighty-four percent of youth report having at least one personal media device (e.g., computer, cell phone, or personal digital device such as Sidekicks or Blackberries), and 44% say they have two or more of these devices (ibid, p. 9).

Use of mobile and online technologies has been referred to as the greatest generational divide since rock-n-roll *(Frontline).* "While some see 'digital kids' as our best hope for the future, others worry that new media are part of a generational rift and a dangerous turn away from existing standards for knowledge, literacy, and civic engagement" (Ito et al., 2008, p. ix). Studies of adolescent practice with technology reflect dual frameworks of "youth at risk" and "youth empowered" (Buckingham, 2008). This debate is further troubled by evidence that low-income, ethnic and language minority youth have unequal access to these technologies (Lenhart et al., 2005), placing them at risk of exclusion from an important site of information exchange and community participation that intersects all arenas of public life.

---

[2]What We Learned: The producers of *Growing Up Online* discuss the making of this report and what they learned about—and from—the Internet generation. http://www.pbs.org/wgbh/pages/frontline/kidsonline/etc/notebook.html.

This chapter seeks to inform our understanding of leisure time as an important context for adolescent development, with special attention to how those leisure activities are increasingly mediated by digital and communication technologies. We start with a discussion of studies that examine adolescent development within structured youth programs. Since there are several existing literature reviews on this broader topic, we point readers to some of the seminal works and limit a more in-depth analysis to studies of program structures designed to intentionally connect youth to adult worlds of practice. Following this discussion, we examine how technology is increasingly utilized within camps and community-based programs as a tool for supporting this developmental transition. Next, we examine leisure activities that are conducted within more informal, peer-centered spaces, including media viewing/production, social networking, and gaming. As in the first section, we highlight research that sheds light on how new technologies mediate opportunities for adolescent development, particularly in relation to preparation for entry into adult worlds of practice. In our conclusion we identify areas for future study and argue the need to better understand the role of emerging technologies in mediating opportunities for adolescent development in leisure activities.

6.1. **STRUCTURED LEISURE TIME ACTIVITIES**

The last 30 years have seen a growing number of programs designed to constructively engage youth during out-of-school hours. As distinct from other types of leisure activities, structured activities are defined as those that are "generally voluntary, have regular and scheduled meetings, maintain developmentally based expectations and rules for participants in the activity setting (and sometimes beyond it), involve several participants in the activity setting (and sometimes beyond it), involve several participants, offer supervision and guidance from adults, and are organized around developing particular skills and achieving goals" (Mahoney, Larson, & Eccles, 2005, p. 4)

These include after-school programs, community programs, and extracurricular activities. Some focus on academics while others focus on arts, sports, technology, or other skill development areas. They are offered by a wide range of organizations, including school districts, park and recreation departments, community centers, faith-based institutions, universities, museums, and nationwide organizations such as 4-H and Girl Scouts.

The benefits of structured leisure activity have been well documented, identifying conditions associated with positive changes in school attendance, school grades, self-efficacy, attitudes, life skills, leadership, social adjustment and development, resilience, independence, friendship skills, competence, emotional intelligence, and improved health outcomes (see extensive literature reviews in Harvard Family Research Project Research and Evaluation Database; Mahoney et al., 2005; National Research Council and Institute of Medicine, 2002). In-depth studies have been conducted around specific models of youth programs such as Boys and Girls Clubs (Hirsch, 2005) and 4-H (Lerner et al., 2008). Other studies have examined programs with particular content foci, such as the arts (e.g., Heath, 2001) and competitive sports (e.g., Danish, Taylor, & Fazio, 2008; Eccles, Barber, Stone, & Hunt, 2003; Scanlan, Babkes, & Scanlan, 2005).

National Research Council and Institute of Medicine (2002) is a synthesis of research and findings developed over 2 years by a 15-member Committee on Community-Level Programs for Youth as part of the National Research Council and the Institute of Medicine. This report identifies eight features of adolescents' everyday experiences that are known to promote positive youth development. Those features include (1) physical and psychological safety, (2) clear and consistent structure and appropriate adult supervision, (3) supportive relationships with adults, (4) opportunities to belong, (5) positive social norms, (6) support for efficacy and mattering, (7) opportunities for skill building, and (8) integration of family, school, and community efforts (p. 87).

In our review of the literature, we understand these features to unfold within the complex web of day-to-day interactions between youth and adults (For elaboration of a sociocultural view of development, see Bronfenbrenner, 1979; Rogoff, 1991; Vadebonncoer, 2006; Vygotsky, 1980; Wertsch, 1993). Further, these interactions are mediated by the participation structures and practices of local activity systems (McLaughlin, 1987), responding to diverse clientele and different constraints, resources, and goals (National Research Council and Institute of Medicine, 2002). In the following section, we use the example of camps as a structured youth program space in which the mission of adolescent development is enacted through long-standing use of youth leadership and apprenticeship structures. We will follow this review with an examination of how technology is used within a broader spectrum of structured youth programs (e.g., camps, after-school programs, community-based programs) as both a target knowledge base (i.e., learning *about* technology) and as a tool for connecting youth to adult worlds of practice (i.e., learning *with* technology).

6.1.1. **Camps as a mediating space between youth-adult worlds**

Summer camps have a long and venerable tradition—one that reflects the societal conceptions of youth and leisure over the last century and a quarter. From the beginning, as Smith (2002) and Paris (2001) point out, camps have taken as their mission adolescent development, citizenship, the effects of industrialization and technology, concerns about gender, and the amelioration of socioeconomic difficulties. These missions have remained stable over time, although camps have made several interesting reversals in how they address them. The nineteenth-century issue of child labor, for example, gave rise to the notion of camp as respite from labor; now camps, like many programs for adolescents, are concerned to offer entry points into adult worlds, including those of work. In the nineteenth century camps looked to natural settings as refuges from the machine age; beginning in the last quarter of the twentieth century there has been a growing interest in camps that provide access to the new "machinery" of computer technologies. Although many camps retain a focus of nature and outdoors activities, there is a growing focus on urban youth and technology camps. The changes in summer camp experiences for children over the last 100 years offer a glimpse at our changing notions of childhood, class, and biopsychological and cultural issues. These effects of summer camp experiences on children have been theorized for nearly 80 years; the newest work reflects the continual use of camp as a transformative experience, but one with many new foci.

Three publications in particular are useful starting points for understanding how camp experiences reflect the larger tensions in American society over the past century. In "The Adventures of Peanut and Bo: Summer Camps and Early Twentieth-Century American Girlhood" Leslie Paris (2001) outlines some of the missions of recreation and summer camp in the nineteenth and early twentieth centuries. Among others, these missions included "artificial leisure" meant to "teach[...] social acculturation and good citizenship" (p. 48). These missions, however, were subject to concerns about class, race, and gender. Although camps were initially available only for upper class Protestant white boys, early in the twentieth century settlement houses began to establish camps for working class and immigrant boys, and scouting organizations and the YMCA began to provide camping experiences for middle class boys. Although a few girls' camps were established in the nineteenth century, they were not widespread until decades later than those for boys. Like boys' camps, Paris argues, they were largely segregated along similar class lines. The poorest girls attended charity camps for free, and settlement house camps had modest fees; middle and upper class girls' families paid rates that were 25 times higher. By 1932, Paris notes, camps for middle and upper class girls some to provide "opportunities for exploration and personal transformation" to girls whose homes "are a little more conservative than the modern girl, who is more or less aware of a new freedom" (p. 49).

If, as this quote indicates, camps sometimes provided opportunities to subvert gendered social norms, Paris argues that they also "inculcat[ed]" girls into gendered identities through the "transformative ritual spaces" that camp and recreation for girls required (p. 49). As Paris notes, however, this transformational experience did not include diversity. Both the settlement house camps for the working class immigrant girls and the Scouts preferred separate camps for African American youth.

Paris also offers a lengthy analysis of how the changing understanding of childhood affected recreation opportunities generally and the summer camp movement in particular. As she notes, childhood in the late nineteenth and early twentieth century became a separate landscape from adulthood as children increasingly were kept out of the labor market and sent to school. This cordoning off of a developmental stage gave rise to an interest in "children's recreation, which was aimed particularly toward middle and upper class children and their parents; and the rise of social service associations devoted to aiding (and regulating) working class children..." (p. 52). These same tensions can be seen in the kinds of camp experiences currently offered to different socioeconomic strata today, where the middle and upper classes can attend expensive sleepaway camps, but urban youth may find their choices limited to city-run local day camps.

Smith's *And They Say We'll Have Some Fun When It Stops Raining: A History of Summer Camp in America* (2002) is a comprehensive look at the foci of summer camp over a century, and it contains an invaluable list of resources. In tracing the development of summer camp he demonstrates how camps have responded first to nineteenth-century industrialization, then to world wars, and more recently toward specialized concerns, including that of the environment. From the beginning, Smith argues, summer camp has been a counter to the perceived stresses of modern urban life. Smith (2006) terms the position of summer camp to the surrounding world as "countermodern, exalting something more 'natural' and more 'real' as a means to being modern in a different way." This emphasis continues today in camps run by, among others, the YMCA/YWCA (since 1884) and the Scouts. Camps took as their putative missions offering alternatives to the "evils wrought by modernity," though, as Smith argues, what constituted evil changed regularly over time. The out-of-doors was conceptualized as a site for helping children return to a more natural, more real, state of being. Nature, as Smith 2006 documents here, later reappears as a camp mission in 1960s as the burgeoning environmental movement exerted a powerful influence on many social institutions.

That influence was, however, in tension with the new emphases of specialty camps, which took advantage of two other influences, on the self and on specialized interests. Although special interest camps had existed for decades, they had initially concentrated on activities such as sailing and horseback riding for the wealthy. Those continue, but camps that began in the 1970s and 1980s renewed their appeal to the interests of a wider public.

Smith notes an interesting counterpoint to Paris's observation that a century earlier, removal from labor was seen as protective of childhood, and leisure was a prized practice of the middle and upper classes. With the removal from labor, childhood became a time of innocence. However, by the latter part of the twentieth century the conception of "childhood [changed once again] from a time of innocence and sheltered living to a time of explicit preparation for adulthood" (p. 192). This change in conceptions of adolescence saw the institution of subject matter camps such as space, computer, foreign language, and other camps with specialized concerns. It is a hallmark of much youth development literature today that apprenticeship into adult worlds is prized, and very much a part of middle and upper class practice. For many poor rural and urban youth, however, access to adult worlds, particularly technological ones, is limited.

The concerns and tensions outlined by both Paris and Smith above continue to be evident in the most recent literature. Most camps have overlapping aims. On the one hand, they emphasize the mastery of some kind of skill, such as learning a new technology like geocaching. At the same time, camps are by their very nature about development and roles—usually movement into an adult world or leadership of some kind—so that even a camp for children with health concerns may also have an apprenticeship focus. The following sources reflect the interest in job-related/adult world skills versus the kinds of traditional "artificial" leisure activities that Paris mentions outlines. As did camps 80 years ago, contemporary ones also reflect the industrial shifts and social interests that surround them, so there are an increasing number of camps that focus on a variety of technologies. We will look next at camps that focus on technology before moving to a discussion of opportunities for youth leadership.

Camps and technology

Science and technology camps have been a staple since the 1970s. The NASA camp (Hoff, 2003) is the most famous, but there are a variety of residential and day camps for students at universities, local museums, hospitals, and governmental venues, and 4-H organizations, among others (see Mlester, 2004, for a partial list; Cavanagh, 2007, notes the number of academic camps for girls is on the rise). Some science camps run by universities require campers to collect, analyze, and present their data to faculty in large group sessions. Some programs have clear missions of apprenticeship and initiation into adult worlds, and they frequently depend on teaching youth to think like scientists by immersion in activity. In a similar way, other camps allow adolescents to gain experience in health careers; held in hospitals, they allow youth both hands-on and discursive experience (Gibbs, 2005). Crombie, Walsh, and Trinneer (2003) look at how science and technology camps more generally affect confidence and career intentions.

Sterling, Matkins, Frazier and Logerwell (2007) look at a variation on this theme. The science camp program they discuss presumed attendance for two summers and was targeted toward younger adolescents still in middle school. As a learning community it is an interesting model for a university/ urban school partnership with the explicit goals of being a transformative experience for all stakeholders, including parents and preservice teachers. The campers used a problem-based curriculum that required teachers and students alike to rethink their roles. Not only did the camp prevent the informational losses that students often experience over the summer, it also helped both students and parents familiarize themselves with the kinds of thinking that students do in college.

Finally, Bers and Chau (2006) link a summer camp experience to civic engagement, noting that "a growing amount of research on virtual environments concentrates on technical and social characteristics that foster the development of community" (p. 749). The development of Zora, "a multi-user virtual environment," allowed Bers and Chau to study the ways in which youth (aged 11-15) learned to use, "design and inhabit a virtual city." (p. 750). The goal was to understand the kinds of civic engagements that participants would create in a program piloted at a summer day camp; the authors note that this kind of environment could also be used in a variety of settings.

Camps and leadership

Most camps have an apprenticeship structure in which campers may eventually take on junior and then senior counselor roles. 4-H camps are excellent examples, and there is substantial literature on them because they are numerous, national, and longstanding. Ferrari, McNeely, and Nestor (2007) examine the developmental trajectories of 4-H counselors at residential and day camps in Ohio, finding, not unexpectedly, that years of experience correlated significantly with leadership. What that experience contributes, Garton, Miltenberger, and Pruett (2007) found, was in the activities themselves; the largest impacts of 4-H camp activities were on "responsible citizenship, accepting differences, and the marketable skills of accepting responsibility and contributing as a member of a team." Carter and Kotrlik's (2007) study uses a Positive Youth Development perspective to investigate developmental progress in 288 adolescent 4-H counselors in Louisiana. On measures of identity and initiative, they found, among other things, that Black counselors had more experiences than did White counselors in developing identity, skill, relationships, and teamwork, though all counselors reported significant gains in problem solving and a variety of social and relational issues. The authors note that, "As participation in 4-H leadership and life skill development opportunities increases, so do experiences with Positive Relationships" (p. 25). And, in looking at another specific population, sports campers, Magyar et al. (2007) examine the relation between "caring" interactional structures and positive youth development. They find that leadership can be more effective if leaders are given feedback that encourages their self-regulation, noting that "leaders who were more confident in their ability to teach and who felt they were quite capable in assessing and regulating their own personal emotions and understanding the emotions of others were also more likely to perceive the climate they created to be caring" (p. 316). These studies all point to the value of camps as apprenticeship organizations that help youth connect to others while learning valuable skills. Camps, however, usually offer short-term experiences for youth. In the next section, we examine out-of-school youth organizations that use technologies as activities through which youth can develop relationships with the adult worlds around them.

6.1.2. **Out-of-school organizations for youth**

Out-of-school youth organizations have frequently been ideal places for youth to learn both old and new technologies. In fact, those organizations that feature technologies are often quite attractive to youth, for whom there is an undeniable "coolness factor" in being able to use valued cultural tools. This is especially true when those tools allow youth voices to be heard in communities. Frequently the organizations that help youth learn to use technological tools have been the primary sites where digital divides are bridged, partly because they can function flexibly within their communities in a way schools frequently cannot (Hall, 2006). For underserved youth, after-school organizations provide opportunities to learn basic Internet skills and to connect with their communities in new ways (Ba, Culp, Green, Henriquez, & Honey, 2001; Penuel & Kim, 2000). In general, most youth programs that focus on technologies do so in one of two fashions: by teaching technological literacies and other literacies in combination (i.e., learning *about* technology), or by using media-related technological tools to promote deep community connections (i.e., learning *with* technology). There is often considerable overlap between these two approaches, but for the sake of illustration, we provide the following examples to illuminate some of the particularities of these agendas in practice.

There are two groups of organizations that have linked technological and print literacies in quite innovative ways. One of the most influential programs, Michael Cole's *Fifth Dimension*, is devoted to combining literacy, technology, and problem solving. Older adolescents from universities and communities participate with the younger adolescents in problem solving in an atmosphere of play, in which there are elements of magic and wizardry. Activities include computer games and educational activities (e.g., chess, origami) that require socially constructed problem solving. Although age 14 is the upper limit in most *Fifth Dimension* programs the model has been adapted in a variety of community programs, and there are a number of *Fifth Dimension* sites. Rather than situating the older university students as teachers, and the youth as students, the program's central tenet is that community, university, and younger youth collaborate (see Cole, 2006; Nocon & Cole, 2008, for an extensive look at the history of *Fifth Dimension* programs; see also Cole, 1996, for a close explanation of their activities).

A second organization combining technological and print literacies innovatively is DUSTY (Digital Underground Storytelling for Youth), developed by Glynda Hull and her colleagues at UC Berkeley. Like the *Fifth Dimension*, it is a university-community partnership that involves students from both areas in problem solving with technology. Hull and her colleagues have used Digital Storytelling, originally developed by Lambert (2002), as a project space in which urban youth from Oakland, California, can develop narratives about themselves and their communities. Once recorded, these narratives are imported into digital editing programs to which image and music tracks are added; completed digital stories are shown to a public audience. DUSTY uses the digital editing technologies to help urban elementary and middle school students expand both their literacy skills and their technological fluency. Hull and her colleagues have written extensively about the results of their work (Hull, 2003; Hull & Katz, 2006; Hull & Nelson, 2005; Nelson, Hull, & Roche-Smith, 2008), noting the powerful effect of the story-making process on identity formation. They argue that the kinds of opportunities afforded by the "social world" of the DUSTY program help participants develop "agentive selves" that they can "enact...in relation to new skills, technologies, knowledge, relationships, and practice that we see at the center of development for both children and adults" (Hull & Katz, 2006, p. 71). Ware and Warschauer (2006) have analyzed how this kind of hybrid space can work to bridge in-school and out-of-school literacy practices (see also Thompson, Bouillion, & DeGennaro, 2007, for similar use of Digital Storytelling in an East Coast community setting).

Although *Fifth-Dimension* and DUSTY programs link youth, community, and university, their structures of participation keep the focus on youth roles within the organization. However, a number of other organizations interested in technology have programs that allow youth to play adult roles within their communities. In cases where youth are researchers or consultants to their communities they step outside their more customary roles as students. Organizations with this kind of participation structure use technologies ranging from radio to Geographic Information Systems (GIS) mapping, web design, and Internet chat rooms.

The older technology of radio can be used in dynamic ways. Youth Radio, widely known for its broadcasts on National Public Radio, has listeners numbering in the millions. As is the case with many of the other youth organizations with a technological focus, it is a partnership, but unlike most it differs because of its multiple connections to world and national audiences. Its apprenticeship structure allows urban youth from the San Francisco Bay area to enter through the CORE class, where they learn journalistic fundamentals, including those of image making. Classes at intermediate and advanced levels help youth solidify skills, and there are subsequent opportunities for internships. Chavez and Soep's (2005) article in the Harvard Educational Review analyzes the ways in which the participants at Youth Radio progress through the program in a partnership with the adult staff, whose aim is to enable democratic participation. Chavez and Soep are at pains to stress that rather than simple job training, their use of the "pedagogy of collegiality" at Youth Radio is an opportunity for youth to form intellectual partnerships with adults and connections to communities. (A somewhat similar organization in Australia is the Student Youth Network [SYN], one of the largest youth projects in Australia. It emphasizes peer-to-peer learning of radio, television, and digital broadcasting and claims a radio audience of listenership of 124,000 per week; 5000 students have participated since it was founded in 2000.) Both of these organizations for youth, like the others discussed here, are examples of the powerful ways in which youth can begin to participate in adult worlds through partnerships with more expert others.

Civic engagement

A different kind of civic engagement is evident in the venerable and even larger 4-H organization, which has roots in every state through its links to land grant universities; currently there are 6.5 million members. 4-H, originally an organization for youth interested in agriculture, now has a large and varied technology focus. Its clubs are facilitated by adult volunteers and provide learning opportunities for youth to explore a wide range of topics through experiential-based projects. Community mapping with GIS is one of several new 4-H curriculum offerings using technology to intentionally support youth development and at the same time position youth as a resource within their communities. 4-H youth are further tied to communities through partnerships with varied adult organizations that have an investment in and use for the data they are collecting (Bouillion Diaz, in press).

There are, of course, much smaller organizations with close ties to their communities. Computer Clubhouse, which began as a single after-school club, now has 100 locations all over the world, many dispersed throughout the United States. Originally founded in a partnership between The Computer Museum and the MIT MediaLab, it has an apprenticeship mission, collaborates with Boys and Girls Clubs, and helps youth make the transition to college (see Kafai, Peppler, & Chapman (2009), which looks at the Computer Clubhouse from a constructionist perspective.) There are also smaller organizations with single sites. DeGennaro's (2008) study of one such organization examines the tensions between social class of the suburban youth who teach the urban "learners" in an organizational context that attempts to bridge not only a digital divide but also an economic one. In another example, Hopeworks, in Camden, New Jersey, combines multiple technologies from website design to GIS mapping, digital storytelling, and sales technologies in an apprenticeship structure that emphasizes leadership. Youth who achieve training goals move into production jobs and are paid for their work with local and national clients. Youth also facilitate training workshops for community partners, and they present their work to national audiences of adult professionals (Thompson, 2006).

Some youth organizations have an explicit focus on the use of technology to further civic engagement. Yablon (2007) examines the use of a temporary after-school program for Arab and Israeli youth designed to facilitate "peace encounters." The participants received training prior to participation, and because of the difficulties involved in bringing them together, they met physically only at the beginning and end of the program. Their encounters took place primarily through IM, the Internet, and chat rooms.

Sandoval and Latorre (2008) provide the example of the Social and Public Art Resource Center (SPARC) in which large-scale digitally generated murals, educational DVDs, animations, community archives, and digital art are created by youth of color in collaboration with Chicana artist and activist, Judy Baca. Intergenerational productions from this program are displayed in the streets of Los Angeles as well the cyber domain of SPARC's website (www.sparcmurals.org). Sandoval and Latorre's inquiry into this program reveals ways in which digital technology allow for a merging of "distinct forms of aesthetic consciousness to converge, namely, those of the adults and of the children in the project" (p. 99). "The converging and diverging nature of these digital social movements thus allows for collectivity and autonomy to take place the same time, something that greatly facilitated the collaborative forum of digital activism taking place between children and adults" (p. 100).

6.1.3. **Summary**

Structured youth programs continue to wrestle with the idea of how best to address the developmental needs of adolescents through various skill building and social experiences. The concerns about citizenship of 100 years ago are present today in conversations such as Bers and Chau's (2006) about civic engagement. Preparation for taking one's place in adult worlds has become a goal instead of a preoccupation from which to seek respite. As reviewed in this section, out-of-school youth programs have become important sites for trying out new kinds of participation patterns to facilitate this youth-adult transition. While an increasing number of programs are responding to a call for youth and every citizen to know more about technology and related literacies (National Academy of Engineering, 2002), others are leveraging the affordances of these technologies to connect youth to their neighborhoods and to engage them as active contributors to real world issues previously constrained to the purview of adults.

While there is an emerging body of research on skill development outcomes in technology-focused programs (Hall & Israel, 2004; Harvard Family Research Project, 2006; Valdez et al., 2000) the broader impact and potential for adolescent development is still largely in question. The goals of youth organizations employing technologies are often complex (Vadebonncoer, 2006), and there is, as the examples above indicate, tremendous variety in out-of-school programs for youth. However, Stroble, Kirshner, O'Donoghue, and McLaughlin (2008) found, even with variety, "youth want to do more than just dabble" (p. 1697). The issue then becomes how to provide sites of possibility without using after-school programs that merely replicate school-like activities. As Nocon and Cole (2006) have noted: "As flexible sites of informal education, after-school programs have allowed low-income and immigrant children access to safe places and flexible, responsive programming as well as contact with diverse perspectives. The choice and 'looseness' that characterize these programs provide opportunities for participation in problem-solving, self-regulation, and learning that goes beyond rigid standards and limited basic content. Informal and potentially limitless education in adult-organized after-school programs is a necessary complement to the formal and limited education provided by schools. We believe that the value of after-school programs is located in their traditionally open, informal, and tenuously institutionalized nature" (pp. 117-118). As programs struggle with their perceived charge to meet both the intellectual and social needs of the youth they serve, they will have to take account of what distinguishes after-school from school, and why that distinction is important.

And although youth across racial lines report wanting more options for structured activities outside school (Charles Stewart Mott Foundation, 1998; Quinn, 1999), research by Newman, Smith, and Murphy (1999) indicates that already more than 11 million youth are left without access to after-school programming. Other research estimates that as much as 25% (14.3 million) of youth care for themselves in the hours after school (Afterschool Alliance, 2004), and 36% of youth spend time home alone after school at least once a week (Duffett & Johnson, 2004). Across most types of programs, Latino youth are underrepresented, White youth are overrepresented, and Black youth are somewhere in between (Bouffard et al., 2006). Barriers to participation for low- to moderate-income working families include financial and transportation constraints (Newman et al., 1999; Villarruel, Montero Sieburth, Dunbar, & Outlay, 2005). Additional barriers to participation for ethnic minority youth include peer pressure in the form of negative opinions about the youth program and constraints on participation by parents or guardians with concerns about child safety (Borden, Perkins, Villarruel, & Stone, 2005).

6.2. INFORMAL LEISURE TIME ACTIVITIES

As previously noted, the contexts of adolescent development are increasingly characterized by a ubiquity of computing technologies. An edited volume by Cope and Kalantzis (in press) argues that these technologies create unprecedented opportunities for anytime, anywhere learning and development. As we seek to adjust existing patterns of education, workplace practice and daily life in light of these changes, there has been a call to look for insight from those who have grown up with these technologies. The argument is that as adults, we are essentially second language learners, foreigners struggling to navigate a new culture. As "digital natives" (Prensky, 2001), today's adolescents are framed as fluent in the practices, norms, and expectations of a technology-infused world. Others have drawn attention to conditions of persistent inequity that constrain low-income and minority youth from full participation in this "culture of power" (Delpit, 1995; see Everett, 2008, for discussion of race and ethnicity for youth and digital media).

A 1999 Kaiser Family Foundation report by Roberts et al. described the homes of youth ages 8-18 as "media rich"; 99% of kids' homes had a TV, 87% a VCR, 90% a CD player, 74% cable or satellite, 70% a game player, 69% a computer, and 45% Internet access. In their 2004 follow-up report, Roberts et al. found that many technologies, such as TVs, VCRs, and CD players hit a ceiling of saturation in which these devices could be found in nearly every home, often in duplicates (Rideout, Roberts, & Foehr, 2005). At the time of this study, nearly three-quarters of US kids lived in homes that contained three or more TV sets (14% contain five or more), and roughly two-thirds reported more than three radios and three CD/tape players. In this study, race and ethnicity were not associated with differences in the likelihood of living in a household with these technologies but did relate to ownership of a personal computer. Ninety percent of White children had one or more computers in the home as compared to 78% for Black children and 80% for Hispanic children. A Pew/Internet Study by Lenhart et al. (2005) found a similar pattern of racial inequity in home access to personal computers but reports that 84% of youth report having a device that can be connected to the Internet, including desktop computers, laptop computers, cell phones, and personal digital devices such as Sidekicks or Blackberries. Forty-four percent said they have two or more of these devices, while 12% had three and 2% reported having all four.

In this section of the chapter, we review available literature to understand how youth are using technology in leisure time spent outside the context of structured youth programs. The impact of these leisure activities for cognitive, social, and physical well-being is a topic of great concern, particularly as communication technologies create opportunities for youth to interact with others during leisure time in ways never before possible. In our analysis, we consider findings that point to both developmental risks and benefits. We first examine the research related to online communication technologies such as IM, Internet chats, and social networking sites. Next, we discuss the current research on adolescent use of video games.

6.2.1. **Online communication technologies: IM, Internet chats, and social networking sites**

According to studies by the PEW Internet and American Life Project, the majority of youth spend at least some portion of their leisure time on the Internet. Their 2005 report (Lenhart & Madden, 2007; Lenhert, Madden, & Hilton) indicated that 85% of male adolescents and 88% of female adolescents were online. Of those surveyed across racial groups, African American teens are the least likely be online, representing only 77% of African American youth compared to 87% of Whites and 89% of English-speaking Hispanics. At the same time, there is evidence that youth participation online continues to grow, up to 93% of all youth surveyed just 2 years later (Lenhart, Madden, Macgill, & Smith, 2007).

When teens use their leisure time for online activities, they are most often developing relationships with friends that they have in their offline worlds. To do this, teens are using e-mail, instant messaging, Twitter, text messaging, social networking, and online chat sites. While e-mail remains a means by which youth communicate, IM is increasingly popular with 75% of teens reporting using it at least once a day (Lenhart et al., 2005). IM is a technology that allows for instant communications with buddies (those friends listed in a user's contacts). Text messaging between cell phones is also growing in popularity among teens. Lenhart et al. found that close to half of all teens (45%) own their own cell phone, with older teens being more likely to have their own phone; 57% of teens aged 15-17 as compared to 32% of teens aged 12-14. Cell phone text messaging is not typically included in discussions of "online" activity, although more recent technological advances that are connecting web-based social networking sites to cell phones are quickly blurring this definition. The 2005 study by Lenhart et al. identifies the primary use of these tools is to support and cultivate current relationships that exist offline (See also Grinter & Eldridge, 2001, 2003).

Similarly, social networking sites are used to connect with established friends. Briefly, "a social networking site is an online location where a user can create a profile and build a personal network that connects him or her to other users" (Lenhart et al., 2007, p. 1). The most popular social networking sites include MySpace and FaceBook. Fifty-five percent of adolescents participate in online social network sites (SNSs). Of this group, 70% of girls and 57% of boys reported creating personal profiles for others to view online. Those who use SNSs describe it as a way to manage friends and make plans. However, teens are known to expand their "friend" networks through this medium as well as develop romantic relationships. Some teens report having anywhere between 150 and 300 friends connected to an online social network. (see history of SNS practices by Boyd & Ellison, 2008.).

Another form of Internet communications is online chats. Online chats are spaces where teens can talk with friends or strangers. These sites are often places where teens go to talk about issues, find emotional support, or ask health questions. As we review in the following sections, researchers have identified that regardless of whether these technologies are used to connect with friends or strangers, there are both positive and negative associations with these forms of leisure activity.

6.2.2. **Opportunities for positive development within online leisure activities**

Internet communication technologies have provided adolescents with many opportunities to develop new roles, skills, and forms of communication. A major function of these tools for adolescents is to connect with others and reinforce friendships (Grinter & Eldridge, 2001, 2003; Gross, 2004). For example, many teenage girls use IM to form alliances, discuss and solve problems, and make plans that later influence social positions and interactions within face-to-face settings (Jacobs, 2003). Teens find that discussion skills and fostered connections developed within IM and FaceBook help them to shift social standings (Lewis & Fabos, 2005) and to negotiate entrance into cliques that were once out of reach in the real world, redefining friendships to include friends of friends (Subrahmanyam & Greenfield, 2008).

A growing body of research reveals how adolescents are using online technology to experiment with emerging identities and navigate membership within different communities. In a study by Boneva, Quinn, Kraut, Kiesler, and Shklovski (2006), youth ages 12-17 report that online communications are not as psychologically satisfying as in-person connections, but that these tools help them peer group networks that formerly seemed impossible. Turkle's research highlights the affordances of online spaces for experimentation with how one's public identity is projected to others. When creating an online profile, it is possible to choose a different race, gender, age, and overall persona. This affordance has led to a phenomenon that Nakamura (2002) calls "cyber tourism," exemplified by White users playing Asian characters in online games.

At the same time, there is evidence that interactions within social networking sites intersect with and inform interactions in "real" offline communities (Byrnes, 2008; Ignacio, 2006; Subrahmanyam, Greenfield, & Tynes, 2004).

Byrne describes these online community forums as "vital public spaces for (re)thinking and (re)producing social knowledge" (p. 19; see also Everett, 2008; Rheingold, 1993; Turkle, 1995). Through discursive exchanges, participants "shape online communities to sometimes reflect, refine, reject, and reproduce social knowledge as informed by their offline experiences" (Byrne, p. 20).

These sites can be "useful vehicles for strengthening their cultural identities, for teaching them how to navigate both public and private dimensions of their racial lives, and for providing them access to a more globalized yet unfixed conversation about their community histories" (Byrne, p. 33). This study echoes a larger body of research that shows the importance of intragroup cultural networks for minority youth (e.g., Rotheram-Borus, Lightfoot, Moraes, Dopkins, & LaCour, 1998; Spencer, Fegley, & Harpalani, 2003).

In addition to using Internet technologies to strengthen existing (and make new) friendship ties, adolescents are also using these tools to seek romantic relationships. There is evidence that these different uses of the technology are gendered. Males report using social networking sites to not only make new friends, but also flirt with potential romantic interests, while females report still using them to reinforce existing relationships (Lenhart et al., 2007). For both genders, text messaging with peers is a way to make connections with romantic interests (Grinter & Eldridge, 2001). IM has been used by both genders to ask people out (Lenhart, Lee, & Lewis, 2001), whereas individuals use FaceBook to find someone to date (Lampe, Ellison, & Stienfield, 2006).

Teens see technology-mediated communications as a safe place to try out dating and identity exploration (Russell, Franz, & Driscoll, 2001). Specifically, they feel that they are safe from in-person harassment and prejudice that go along with, for example, being gay, lesbian, or bisexual. Technology-mediated peer activities in this arena have given youth the opportunity to safely explore this aspect of their life. "Hiding" behind the screens protects youth from embarrassment and ridicule that is often felt in face-to-face encounters. Like in the development of friend relationships, youth are practicing communication skills of how to act in the real world. Increasingly, researchers are seeing a connection between the virtual and the real; a pattern in which online interactions inform ways of acting in person (see Byrnes, 2008). As we will see in the next section, however, this kind of communication in particular does not come without its concerns.

Extending from this idea of safety and practice connecting with others, technology-mediated interactions also create opportunities for social and academic support. A study by Grinter and Eldridge (2001) describes a growing trend in which teens are using online mediums to support their social activities and to find homework help. This research suggests that online communication allows teens feeling disconnected from their peers or fearing ridicule to reach out for assistance. The anonymity of many online interactions facilitates a sense of safety and security for teens, eliminating the embarrassment or inhibitions of talking to someone in person. More specifically to learning, adolescents value the informality and immediacy of online communication tools. For example, they indicate that IM affords simple access to teachers, which then results in quick responses from them (Jeong, 2002). IM's ease of use also facilitated academic communication between students (Nicholson, 2002). Further, IM also helped to develop strong student-instructor bonds, which in turn fostered positive attitudes toward their own learning (Rau, Gao, & Wu, 2008). From a youth perspective, IM communications afford opportunities for students to employ social strategies for learning and provide more occasions to be part of a conversation (Beach & Lundell, 1998).

Research suggests that online communication technologies also create opportunities for improved youth health impacts. One of the fastest growing uses of the Internet among youth is to obtain health information, growing by 47% between 2000 and 2005 (Lenhart et al., 2005). According to an extension review of the literature by Lazarus and Wainer (2005), almost 20% of all young adults ages 18-25 use the Internet to search for health information. Both reports suggest that the Internet offers teenagers and young adults a safe way to learn about sensitive subjects like birth control, pregnancy, and AIDS and that this has been shown to lead young people to make better choices about healthy behavior. According to Lenhart et al., older girls aged 15-17 are much more likely than any other group to seek out sensitive health information online; 34% of older girls compared to 18% of boys in the same age group. In their report, 19% of online girls and 18% of online boys aged 12-14 reported that they use the Internet to find sensitive health information. At the same time, Lazarus and Wainer's report identifies the rate at which Asian American and White young adults ages 18-25 use the Internet to search for health information (23% and 22%) as almost double that of Native Americans, African Americans, and Latinos (13%, 12%, and 11%, respectively), even though these ethnic minorities have disproportionate prevalence of certain conditions like AIDS and hypertension. Dutta, Bodie, and Basu (2008) argue that this gap in health benefits for minority youth are reflective of preexisting, offline health disparities in access to quality health care. This gap is furthered by a continued digital divide in terms of which youth have access to a computer and the Internet at home (Lenhart et al., 2005, 2007).

In summary, there are many ways in which Internet communication technologies create opportunities for positive adolescent development. In practicing ways of communicating with peers, navigating relationships, setting boundaries, and establishing rules of participation, youth are developing self-esteem. They are strengthening friendships, finding skills to communicate effectively offline, and are more likely to speak their minds and stand up for themselves outside of the virtual world (Lenhart, Rainie, & Lewis, 2001). In addition, they are forming new codes and modes of communication (Greenfield & Subrahmanyam, 2003). Finally, they are practicing community development as they create the rules for participation within their own fields of communication (see Prensky, 2001, 2006; Tapscott, 1998).

Developmental concerns within online leisure activities

Despite the many opportunities for positive youth development within the online activities previously described, there are many rising concerns. For example, teens are experiencing forms of discrimination and harassment through online communications. Reports by adolescents indicate that 47% of bullying or some form of harassment takes place on instant messaging, followed by 13% through e-mail, 11% through chat rooms, and only 3% through blogs (Wolak, Mitchell, & Finkelhor, 2006). Along similar lines, research by Daniels (2008) suggests that many forms of racial hostility and negative stereotypes that exist offline are reified online.

Through discursive exchanges online, youth are found to both affirm and silence the contributions of others. In one example, Byrne analyzes a thread of conversation in BlackPlanet where a debate is sparked by one participant's post expressing that he has very little sympathy for (White) Americans over the 9/11 attacks, describing the event as "poetic justice" in making the White male now the target of profiling that Black men and women have long experienced. One respondent argues back "they don't care about Black [people] at all…they hate America…and as far as they are concerned we are part of America…they didn't send out a memo for all the Black people to stay home so that only whites get killed…they attacked our country and they are the enemy…period" (Byrne, p. 23). In another example, a participant in BlackPlanet who posted messages in Arabic was "shouted" out (using a big font) and told to leave the discussion because he had "no business speaking where you don't belong" (p. 21). Byrne cites these and other examples to argue that youth participating in online social communities learn which attitudes they must subscribe to in order to be accepted. Byrne also notes that while conversations among youth in these online communities tackle issues of institutional racism and hegemonic controls, in over 3000 threaded forum messages these discussions never moved to talk of what to do about it.

Another issue of concern is the formation of romantic relationships with strangers. As previously discussed, online interactions have the benefit of providing a low-risk space for adolescents to try out dating and explore different expressions of self within those interactions (Russell, Franz, & Driscoll, 2001). While the weakened function of social censoring and peer pressure in these cases may lead to positive outcomes, there is also research to suggest related risks. For instance, there is research to suggest that a growing number of adolescents use online communication technologies as a means of connecting with strangers in search of casual sex (Wolak et al., 2006). MySpace is more open than FaceBook and therefore many teens report being contacted for relationships by adults through this venue (Annenberg Public Policy Center, 2006). Easy access to and between an adolescent and a stranger means that youth could potentially become involved in situations they are not yet ready to deal with. The occurrences of these kinds of relationships are often found with troubled adolescents (Beebe, Asche, Harrison, & Quinlan, 2004), but more specifically with girls who have significant conflict with parents and with boys who have no one with whom to communicate (Wolak, Mitchell, & Finkelhor, 2003). The more severe the conflict, the more likely it is that these youth will form close relationships with strangers (Wolak et al.). Although this form of communication has significant concern, there are underlying benefits. For example, youth with these connections are more likely to talk to or reach out to strangers (Gross, Juvonen, & Gable, 2002). As a result, adolescents connecting with "safe adults" are more likely to find support and thus experience recovery from social exclusion (Gross, 2004).

Perhaps the concern voiced most often is lack of parental control in how youth are using these online technologies. Researchers indicate that the more time adolescents spend online, the more they become disconnected from family and adult life (Subrahmanyam & Greenfield, 2008). In fact technology-mediated peer activities are changing the nature of communications with adults and relatives (Ochs, Graesch, Mittmann, Bradbury, & Repetti, 2007). For example, youth use online tools to talk directly with their friends. There is virtually no adult filtering or monitoring from parents or members in the household. What research has found is that adolescents have control over whom they speak with and find space to discuss thoughts and ideas that might not be accepted as the social norm (Ling & Yttri, 2006). Thus the intercommunications that bind these peers are available only to members of the community; thus parents have no entry point (Ling & Yttri). In this way, youth can more readily evade parent rules and boundaries. One example of this is when youth avoid homework guidelines set by parents. While at the computer and appearing as if they are focused on a homework task, youth can escape with a silent click of a mouse to be in touch with a prohibited friend or boyfriend or create a party plan that far exceed what mom or dad agreed to (Rosen, 2007). Similarly, adolescents are also able to easily alter priorities without parents' awareness. Parents may not know who their children talk with or what they post on their social network spaces (Rosen, Cheever, & Carrier, 2007). This is partially a result of the lack of knowledge that parents have about their sons' and daughters' technology-mediated communications. Without taking an active role in or finding a means by which to become part of this aspect of their children's lives, the distance will likely increase.

Yet another risk of Internet communication technologies relates to the previously identified trend of adolescents seeking health and other information online. As described, the Internet has the advantage of letting adolescents seek sensitive information without risking the embarrassment of asking someone in person. The Internet may also become an important gateway to information that would not otherwise be available through existing networks. The risk is that adolescents may access and use information without the skills to discern the reliability and credibility of the information source (Eysenbach, 2008).

6.2.3. **Gaming**

As in the case of online communication activities, video game playing is a prevalent activity within adolescents' leisure time. For clarity, we define video games to include games played on televisions, portable and handheld devices, or computers. These games are being played both individually and with others. According to current research, 99% of boys and 94% of girls play video games (Lenhart et al., 2008). A report by the Kaiser Family Foundation suggests that game players spend an average of at least 1 h a day in this activity (Roberts, Foehr, & Rideout, 2005). According to the same report, use of games among different racial groups is nearly equal across race: 82% of Whites, 86% of Blacks, and 81% of Hispanics. Boys, however, are playing more often. About 65% of boys say they play everyday, while only 35% of girls play daily. About 86% of reported game players use game boxes such as Xbox, PlayStation, and the Wii. In addition, 73% of game players play games on desktop computers, 60% on portable devices, and 48% play on cell phones.

While game playing is seen across gender and racial categories, research suggests that this activity varies in terms of which game genres they prefer.

A Pew/Internet & American Life study (Lenhart et al., 2008) identifies several genres of games with which youth engage. These include racing, puzzles, sports, action, adventure, rhythm, simulation, fighting, first-person shooters, role playing, survival horror, MMOGs (massive multiplayer online games), and Virtual Worlds. According to the same report, boys tend to play a wider variety of genres than do girls. Regardless of the type of game or which youth are playing them, research points to both benefits and concerns related to adolescent learning and development.

6.2.4. **Opportunities for positive development within gaming**

Current research identifies several features of gaming that create opportunities for positive adolescent learning and development. For example, gaming is seen as a constructive social experience. Although many game players report playing video games in isolation, youth play games with friends more often than not. This can mean that adolescents play video games while their friends are in the room or they engage with others through the Internet. These and other findings are elaborated in the 2008 report by the Pew/Internet & American Life project, Teens, Video Games & Civics (Lenhart et al., 2008). When playing games through the Internet, 47% of teens report playing with friends they associate with offline. Only 27% of teens say that they play with someone they met online. Interestingly, about 23% of these youth say that they play with both known friends and with strangers. In any case, the social experience of gaming often results in interactions that embody encouragement, helpfulness, and generosity. Further, adolescents see gaming experiences as opportunities to negotiate roles and rules of play as well as distribute expertise across players. An overwhelming 85% of adolescents report positive social experiences when gaming with others.

In addition to positive social experiences, researchers are seeing a connection between game playing and increased participation in civic life. Here civic life includes raising money for charity, committing to civic participation, establishing an interest and performing research in politics, volunteering, participating in demonstrations (Lenhart et al., 2008). While there is no direct link between the amount of time spent playing games and increased civic engagement, reports indicate that those who play games with contextualized civic components (moral, social, or societal issues) are more likely to engage in civic life in the real world. It is important to note also that a greater correlation exists when games are played with others in face-to-face settings rather than in virtual ones. When adolescents play in person with others, they are more likely to be guiding, assisting, and engaging in collective decision making. These are skills that are transferrable to civic participation.

Many learning potentials are attributed to playing video games as well. For example, researchers assert that games promote situated learning opportunities (Gee, 2003; Shaffer, Squire, Halverson, & Gee, 2005). That is, learning is directly tied to content, and meaningful activities are embedded. Learning then is not just about facts or isolated skills, but embodies particular social practices. They, in turn, argue that video games make it possible for players to participate in valued communities of practice and as a result develop the ways of thinking that organize those practices (Shaffer et al.). In these communities of practice, gamers try out and try on different identities. Through practices in games, adolescents develop roles to negotiate and create shared goals and develop social and cultural norms for their community. In the process of game playing they are also seeking out new sites to help them play their games, reading and writing FAQs, participating in discussions, and becoming critical consumers and creators of information. In essence, adolescents are thinking and acting in similar ways that professionals might act, but in their own communities of practice (Shaffer et al.).

Researchers also indicate an increase in sustainment of youth's attention (Malone & Lepper, 1987), particularly in students with ADHD (Schmidt & Vandewater, 2008). Their assumption is that this is due to engaging players in fantasy or imaginary worlds. The participation in these worlds not only connects youth to purposeful movement through activities, it also allows for freedom of participation without repercussion or inhibitions (Thomas & Macredie, 1994). In general, games seem to increase activity and arousal as well as stimulate the neural reward systems. Researchers believe that playing these games causes the brain to release dopamine, which is often associated with learning and positive reinforcement (Koepp et al., 1998). Regardless of the user, research suggests that video games enhance visual and spatial skills (Brooks-Gunn & Donahue, 2008) as well as problem solving, inference making, recall, attention, and navigation of reading environments (Schmidt & Vandewater). Specifically researchers see improvement in visual tracking, mental rotation, and target localization (Schmidt & Vandewater).

In summary, games are helping to form new communities and new ways of learning. For example, Jenkins (2006) sees games as developing a "new participatory culture." He sees game playing as a positive pathway to opportunities for civic participation and debates, roles in leadership, and an ability to alter one's self-perception and perception with others.

As more users find opportunities to connect with their fellow citizens, they are engaging in opportunities of open worldviews (Steinkuehler & Williams, 2006). In terms of learning, there are situational and contextual emphases that are helping youth make more connections between facts and real world situations. In each area, teens are developing skills and trying new roles that prepare them for their future roles in life.

Developmental concerns with gaming

Although the most recent research is pointing to more positive outcomes related to gaming than negative ones, there are still concerns about the use of video games in adolescent's crucial stage of development. In terms of social participation, there are numerous themes that are cited as worrisome. For example, researchers warn that video games can foster social isolation (National Institute on Media and the Family, 2008), aggressive behavior (Anderson, Gentile, & Buckley, 2007), and gender bias (Brenick, Henning, Killen, O'Connor, & Collins, 2007). Further, and not unlike other technology-mediated peer communication, video gamers experience social exclusion through means of racial and ethnic derogatory remarks. Research indicates that 49% of adolescents have received some form of hate statements related to race or ethnicity, and 63% have been the recipient of aggressive behavior (Lenhart et al., 2008).

It is not surprising then, that a great deal of the video game research relates a possible relationship between gaming and risky behavior. One form of risky behavior that receives much attention is violence and aggression. Evidence suggests that violent media, Grand Theft Auto and Halo, for example, increases the likelihood of both immediate and long-term aggressive and violent behavior (Anderson et al., 2007; Bushman & Anderson, 2001). Specifically, studies show a positive correlation between violent video exposure and aggression such as violent behavior and violent crimes, as much as 40% higher for those who play violent games as compared to those who did not (Anderson et al.). Additional studies have also linked violent video games to a host of additional aggression-related cognitive, emotional, and behavioral outcomes. Outcomes include more positive attitudes toward violence, increased use of aggressive words or solutions to hypothetical problems, quicker recognition of facial anger, intensified self-perception as being aggressive, enhanced feelings of anger and revenge motives, decreased sensitivity to scenes and images of real violence, and changes in brain function associated with lower executive control and heightened emotion (Swing & Anderson, 2007). More studies in this area deserve attention as researchers are beginning to question the validity of this research. Researchers questioning these findings cite exaggeration and strong ideological ideas about learning as influencing the outcomes (Kutner & Olson, 2007).

Obesity is another negative outcome that studies associate with playing video games. For example, a study by Escobar-Chaves and Anderson (2008) finds elevated weight gain in girls who play games. Further, this study suggests that there is a particular risk for weight gain for Mexican American and African American game players. Although there are increased levels of energy, which are expired during game playing, these energies are more stress related than physically aspiring. Being sedentary has particular consequences for health as well. In another study (Subrahmanyam, Kraut, Greenfield, & Gross, 2000), researchers have seen a relationship between video games and increased seizures in patients with epilepsy. This is attributed to the frequency of flashing images on standard television screens. One positive aspect of newer interactive game systems such as Wii and Dance Dance Revolution is that they require adolescents to be more physically active while playing video games. As more of these become popular with youth, new research in this area will be necessary.

A final negative outcome of video game use relates to learning. Some researchers argue that the video game culture distracts youth from reading (Bauerlein, 2008). It is believed that reading will ultimately be more important for our youth's future academic success. The concern comes as studies illustrate that in addition to playing several hours of video games on the computer, the average teen spends 49 min a day playing console or handheld games (Kaiser Family Foundation) and only 43 min a day reading magazines, books, or newspapers (Rideout, Roberts, & Foehr, 2005). Despite this, studies show that games can be important ways for youth to increase their ability to read text and images in context with each other, as well as follow several images at the same time (Subrahmanyam et al., 2000). These are skills that new literacies researchers argue are important for the future expectations facing our young today (Gee, 2003; Leu, Kinzer, Coiro, & Cammack, 2004; Shaffer et al., 2005). Until researchers further investigate the relationship between emerging literacies and emerging learning practices, it is too soon to be overtly pessimistic about the correlation between video game use and learning practices.

Summary
Adolescents' informal leisure activities are increasingly mediated by and connected to use of digital technologies. Our literature review suggests that these activities represent both opportunities and concerns for adolescent development. A key challenge is that these technologies are rapidly changing, making it difficult to capture, let alone project, their impact

on development (Subrahmanyam & Greenfield, 2008). One example of this rapid development is the ability of many social network sites to send and receive information from mobile devices such as cell phones. It is possible, therefore, to alter one's online presence and communicate with anyone logged into the Internet from the privacy of a cell phone at any location. Despite the difficulties with anticipating the role and influence of these new technologies in pathways of adolescent development, the research suggests increased adult understanding about these tools and activities will help to reconnect adults with youth.

6.3. UBIQUITOUS COMPUTING AND THE NEGOTIATION OF BORDERS BETWEEN YOUTH AND ADULT WORLDS

This chapter examines the importance of leisure time as a context for adolescent development. We organized our review of the literature to examine activities within structured youth programs as well as informal, more peer-centered activities. Across both types of activities, we discuss the varied ways in which leisure time for youth is increasingly mediated by computing technologies. Findings from this body of research identify both opportunities and risks for adolescent development and learning. In summary, we turn our focus now to the ways in which the infusion of digital technologies in our lives is challenging us to rethink the borders of youth and adult worlds. We argue that this blurring of borders has important implications for our understanding of the developmental moves needed to prepare adolescents for full participation within adult worlds.

Computing and Internet technologies can be found nearly everywhere–reshaping how we work, learn, shop, follow news, communicate with others, find directions when we travel, and many other daily activities. Burbules (in press) outlines six dimensions to how computing technology has permeated our lives: spatial ubiquity (anywhere access), temporal ubiquity (anytime access), portability (personalized technologies that are always with you), interconnectedness (distributed information networks), practical ubiquity (connecting previously distinct spheres of life such as work/play; public/private), and ubiquity in the sense of globalized and transnational networks.

Cope and Kalantzis (in press) outline seven moves that characterize learning within this context of ubiquitous computing: (1) blurring the traditional institutional, spatial, and temporal boundaries of education, (2) shifting the balance of agency to move beyond traditional teacher-learner roles, (3) recognizing learner differences and using them as a productive resource, (4) broadening the range and mix of representational modes, (5) developing conceptualizing capacities, (6) connecting one's own thinking into the social mind of distributed cognition and collective intelligence, and (7) building collaborative knowledge cultures. Haythornthwaite (in press) argues that this ubiquity of new communication technology is giving rise to a "new relational order" in which we are challenged to rethink our notions of expertise, related roles for learners and teachers, and valued literacies for information retrieval and contribution.

We propose that opportunities for adolescent development may be similarly explored within this framework. That is, ubiquitous computing creates opportunities for youth to learn anytime and anywhere, to develop roles as both media consumers and producers, to leverage multiple media forms and literacies (e.g., New London Group) in pursuit of goals for skill building and community membership, to connect to diverse and distributed knowledge networks and sometimes contribute as equals to adults. Development thus has the potential to occur within what Burbules (in press) describes as an "extensible intelligence" in which "one's knowledge, memory, and processing power are enhanced by constantly available devices that can supplement and support what we are able to do in our own heads. Socially, one is perpetually in contact with others who may know things or be able to do things that we cannot do ourselves" (p. 26).

Opportunities for adolescent development within this framework of ubiquity have been proposed as both "youth empowered" and "youth at risk" (Buckingham & Willet, 2006). While some have emphasized the potential for the Internet to realize a democratic vision in which everyone has the potential to participate fully in society (e.g., Brown & Duguid, 2002; Jenkins, 2006), others have revealed ways in which existing mechanisms of racism and exclusion may be amplified by these same technologies (see example of Daniels' 2008 study of hate speech online). Byrne's study (2008) of racially dedicated social network sites (e.g., AsianAvenue.com, BlackPlanet.com, MiGente.com) highlights this tension. On the one hand, youth who participate in these forums are active producers of their content and exert a sense of ownership over these online spaces. On the other hand, they are susceptible to the influence of peers in which "members learn the importance of consensus, as both a measure of collective reasoning and as a mechanism for silencing or ignoring those opinions that are out of favor with the majority" (p. 31). Drawing upon the work of Adam Banks, Byrne argues that "literacy skills alone cannot guarantee material, function, experiential, and critical access that is needed for young users of color to see themselves as 'users, producers, and even transformers' (Banks, 2005) of the varying technologies informing their day-to-day lives" (p. 32). Byrne suggests young people of color may need help in seeing these social networking sites as vehicles for collective social change and are currently at risk of internalizing the immobilizing rhetoric of a digital divide in which they are considered peripheral and underrepresented members of the overall online society.

Although supportive relationships with adults are identified as a key feature for positive youth development (Hirsch, 2005; Jarrett, Sullivan, & Watkins, 2005; McLaughlin, Irby, Langman, 2001; National Research Council and Institute of Medicine, 2002), our literature review reveals the ways in which computing technologies increasingly consume adolescents' attention within leisure activities that may fall outside the purview of adults. It could be argued that there have always been portions of youth time that are unsupervised by adults, well before the infusion of computers and the Internet in our lives. These activities have included time spent hanging out with friends, talking on the phone, watching TV, reading books, and so on. A key difference, we argue, is that the Internet and mobile technologies make it possible for youth to engage with an infinite range of people, information, and ideas when engaged in these activities. These computing technologies also provide the means through which youth are able to assume roles of producers and agents of change in ways previously constrained to the realm of adult worlds.

The role of structured youth organizations and related youth-adult relationships take on new importance as computing ubiquity challenges us to rethink the developmental moves needed for full participation in adult worlds. Youth-adult collaborations with technology for civic engagement (Bouillion Diaz, in press; DeGennaro, 2008; Thompson, Putthoff, & Figueroa, 2006) become an important site in which to examine related questions of development. Thompson et al. describe how collaborative youth-adult work in web design and GIS mapping projects create opportunities for youth to take up varied roles such as tool modifier, project leader, friend, colleague, mentor to a younger youth, researcher, and conference presenter. Their study demonstrates how these roles create opportunities for youth to connect with different audiences and different communities of practice in ways that are supported by relationships with adults.

Further study is needed to understand the different constellations of participation structures in these programs that are associated with positive outcomes for youth. A fruitful starting point can be found in studies of non-technology-focused youth programs, which illuminate the supportive role of adult program leaders (e.g., Jarrett et al., 2005; Larson & Hansen 2005; Larson, Hansen, & Walker, 2005; Larson, Walker, & Pearce, 2005;

McLaughlin, 1993). This research illuminates the ways in which adult leaders assist youth in gaining insights into the functioning of adult networks and workplaces and support youth engagement in those worlds. Larson, Walker, and Pearce comparison of youth-driven and adult-driven activities in structured youth programs provides further insight. This study found that while youth-driven activities are associated with opportunities for youth empowerment and development of leadership and strategic planning skills, adult-driven activities are associated with opportunities for sharing knowledge and social capital related to participation in adult worlds. A study by Bouillion (in press) suggests that technology-centered collaborations have the potential to serve as a "third space," bringing together the diverse expertise and contributions of both youth and adults. In this case, community mapping with Geographic Information Systems (GIS) serve as a focal activity that brings together youth knowledge of their community and adult knowledge of GIS technology. This hybridity of contribution is found to foster mutuality and reciprocity in youth-adult relationships. Certain genres of video games provide similar opportunities for collaboration between youth and family members at home (Lenhart et al., 2008). These and other features of technology-focused youth activities (both structured and informal) need further investigation to more fully understand the opportunities for adolescent development during leisure time.

REFERENCES

Afterschool Alliance. (2004). *Working families and afterschool. A special report from America after 3PM*. Retrieved from www.afterschoolalliance.org/press_archives/Working_Families_Rpt.pdf

Anderson, C., Gentile, D., & Buckley, K. (2007). *Violent video game effects on children and adolescents: Theory, research, and public policy*. New York, NY: Oxford University Press.

Annenberg Public Policy Center. (2006, September). *Stranger contact in adolescent online social networks*. Annenberg Public Policy Center Report. Philadelphia, PA: University of Pennsylvania.

Ba, H., Culp, K. M., Green, L., Henriquez, A., & Honey, M. (2001). *Effective technology use in low-income communities: Research review for the American Connects Consortium*. Newton, MA: America Connects Consortium.

Banks, A. (2005). *Race, rhetoric, and technology: Searching for higher ground*. Mahwah, NJ: Erlbaum.

Bauerlein, M. (2008). *The dumbest generation: How the digital age stupefies young Americans and jeopardizes our future (or, don't trust anyone under 30)*. New York, NY: Penguin Group.

Beach, R., & Lundell, D. (1998). Early adolescents' use of computer-mediated-communication in writing and reading. In D. Reinking, M. McKennay, L. Labbo, & R. Kieffer (Eds.), *Handbook of literacy and technology: Transformations in a post-typographic world* (pp. 93–114). Mahwah, NJ: Erlbaum.

Beebe, T. J., Asche, S. E., Harrison, P. A., & Quinlan, K. B. (2004). Heightened vulnerability and increased risk-taking among adolescent chat room users: Results from a statewide school survey. *Journal of Adolescent Health, 35*(2), 116–123.

Bers, M. (2006). The role of new technologies to foster positive youth development. *Applied Developmental Science, 10*(4), 200–219.

Bers, M., & Chau, C. (2006). Fostering civic engagement by building a virtual city. *Journal of Computer-Mediated Communication, 11*, 748–770.

Boneva, B., Quinn, A., Kraut, R., Kiesler, S., & Shklovski, I. (2006). Teenage communication in the instant messaging era. In R. Kraut, M. Brynin, & S. Kiesler (Eds.), *Computers, phones and the internet: Domesticating information technology* (pp. 201–218). New York, NY: Oxford University Press.

Borden, L. M., Perkins, D. F., Villarruel, F. A., & Stone, M. (2005). To participate or not to participate: That is the question. *New Directions for Youth Development, 105*, 33–49.

Bouffard, S. M., Wimer, C., Caronongan, P., Little, P., Dearing, E., & Simpkins, S. (2006). Demographic differences in patterns of youth out-of-school time activity participation. *Journal of Youth Development: Bridging Research and Practice, 1*(1), 24–39.

Bouillion Diaz, L. (in press). Creating opportunities for ubiquitous learning with geospatial technologies: Negotiating roles at the borders of youth and adult practice, In B. Cope, & M. Kalantzis, (Eds.), *Ubiquitous learning*. Champaign, IL: University of Illinois Press.

Boyd, D. M., & Ellison, N. B. (2008). Social network sites: Definition, history, and scholarship. *Journal of Computer-Mediated Communication, 13*, 210–230.

Brenick, A., Henning, A., Killen, M., O'Connor, A., & Collins, M. (2007). Social evaluations of stereotypic images in video games. *Youth and Society, 38*(4), 395–419.

Bronfenbrenner, U. (1979). *The ecology of human development: Experiments by nature and design*. Cambridge, MA: Harvard University Press.

Brooks-Gunn, J., & Donahue, E. H. (2008). Introducing the issue. *Future of Children, 18*(1), 3–10.

Brown, J. S., & Duguid, P. (2002). *The social life of information*. Cambridge, MA: Harvard Business School Press.

Buckingham, D., & Willett, R. (Eds.) (2006). *Digital generations: Children, young people and new media*. Mahwah, NJ: Erlbaum.

Buckingham, D. (2008). Introducing identity. In D. Buckingham (Ed.), *Youth, identity, and digital media*. The John D. and Catherine T. MacArthur Foundation Series on Digital Media and Learning (pp. 1–24). Cambridge, MA: The MIT Press, doi: 10.1162/dmal.9780262524834.001. Retrieved 11/15/08 from: http://www.mitpressjournals.org/toc/dmal/-/6

Burbules, N. (in press). Meanings of "ubiquitous learning." In B. Cope, & M. Kalantzis, (Eds.), *Ubiquitous learning*. Champaign, IL: University of Illinois Press.

Bushman, B. J., & Anderson, C. A. (2001). Media violence and the American public: Scientific facts versus media misinformation. *American Psychologist, 56*(6–7), 477–489.

Byrne, D. (2008). Public discourse, community concerns, and civic engagement: Exploring Black social networking traditions on BlackPlanet.com *Journal of Computer-Mediated Communication*, *13*, 319–340.

Byrnes, D. N. (2008). The future of (the) "race": Identity, discourse, and the rise of computer-mediated public spheres. In A. Everett (Ed.), *Learning race and ethnicity: Youth and digital media* (pp. 15–38). Cambridge, MA: The MIT Press.

Carter, D. N., & Kotrlik, J. W. (2007). *Factors related to the developmental experiences of youth serving as Louisiana 4-H camp counselors. Proceedings of the 2007 AAAE Research Conference 34*. Minneapolis: American Association of Agricultural Education.

Cavanagh, S. (2007). Science camp just for the girls. *Education Week*, *26*(45), 26–28.

Charles Stewart Mott Foundation. (1998). *Press release: Poll finds overwhelming support for after-school enrichment programs to keep kids safe and smart.* Flint, MI: Charles Stewart Mott Foundation.

Chavez, V., & Soep, E. (2005). Youth radio and the pedagogy of collegiality. *Harvard Educational Review*, *75*(4), 409–434.

Cole, M. (1996). *Cultural psychology: The once and future discipline.* Cambridge, MA: Belknap Press of Harvard University Press.

Cole, M. (2006). *The Fifth Dimension: An after-school program built on diversity.* New York, NY: Russell Sage Foundation Pub.

Crombie, G., Walsh, J., & Trinneer, A. (2003). Positive effects of science and technology summer camps on confidence, values, and future intentions. *Canadian Journal of Counselling*, *37*(4), 256–269.

Daniels, J. (2008). Race, civil rights, and hate speech in the digital era. In A. Everett (Ed.), *Learning race and ethnicity: Youth and digital media* (pp. 129–154). Cambridge, MA: The MIT Press.

Danish, S. J., Taylor, T. E., & Fazio, R. J. (2008). Enhancing adolescent development through sports and leisure. In G. R. Adams & M. D. Berzonsky (Eds.), *Handbook of adolescence* (pp. 92–108). Malden, MA: Blackwell.

DeGennaro, D. (2008). Learning designs: Tapping technology fluency of the Net Generation. *Journal of Research on Technology in Education 40*(1), 81–100.

DeGennaro, D. (2008). Sociotechnical cultural activity: Expanding an understanding of emergent technology practices. *Journal of Curriculum Studies*, *40*(3), 329–351.

Delpit, L. (1995). *Other people's children: Cultural conflict in the classroom.* New York, NY: New Press.

Duffett, A., & Johnson, J. (2004). *All work and no play? Listening to what kids and parents really want from out-of-school time.* New York, NY: Public Agenda.

Dutta, M. J., Bodie, G. D., & Basu, A. (2008). Health disparity and the racial divide among the nation's youth: Internet as a site for change? In A. Everett (Ed.), *Learning race and ethnicity: Youth and digital media* (pp. 175–197). Cambridge, MA: The MIT Press.

Eccles, J. S., Barber, B., Stone, M., & Hunt, J. (2003). Extracurricular activities and adolescent development. *Journal of Social Issues*, *59*(4), 865–889.

Escobar-Chaves, S. L., & Anderson, C. A. (2008). Media and risky behaviors. *Future of Children*, *18*(1), 147–180.

Everett, A. (Ed.) (2008). *Learning race and ethnicity: Youth and digital media*. The John D. and Catherine T. MacArthur Foundation Series on Digital Media and Learning. Cambridge, MA: The MIT Press.

Eysenbach, G. (2008). Credibility of health information and digital media: New perspectives and implications for youth. In M. J. Metzger, & A. J., Flanagin, (Eds.), *Digital media, youth, and credibility* (pp. 123–154). The John D. and Catherine T. MacArthur Foundation Serieson Digital Media and Learning. Cambridge, MA: The MIT Press.

Ferrari, T. M., & McNeely, N. N. (2007). Positive youth development: What's camp counseling got to do with it? Findings from a study of Ohio 4-H camp counselors. *Journal of Extension (ASCII Edition)*, *45*(2). Retrieved from http://www.joe.org/joe/2007april/rb7.php

Garton, M., Miltenberger, M., & Pruett, B. (2007). Does 4-H camp influence life skill and leadership development? *Journal of Extension (ASCII Edition)*, *45*(4). Retrieved from http://www.joe.org/joe/2007august/a4.php

Gee, J. P. (2003). *What video games have to teach us about learning and literacy*. New York, NY: Palgrave Macmillan.

Gibbs, H. (2005). The epidemic growth of career camps. *Techniques*, *80*(8), 38–41.

Greenfield, P. M., & Subrahmanyam, K. (2003). Online discourse in a teen chat room: New codes and new modes of coherence in a visual medium. *Journal of Applied Developmental Psychology*, *24*, 713–738.

Grinter, R. E., & Eldridge, M. A. (2001). y do tngrs luv 2 txt msg? In W. Prinz, M. Jarke, Y. Rogers, K. Schmidt, & V. Wulf (Eds.), *Proceedings of the Seventh European Conference on Computer Supported Cooperative Work, September 16–20, 2001, Bonn, Germany* (pp. 219–238). Dordrecht, Netherlands: Kluwer Academic Publishers.

Grinter, R. E., & Eldridge, M. A. (2003). Wan2tlk?: Everyday text messaging. *Proceedings of the SIGCHI conference on human factors in computing systems* (pp. 441–448). New York, NY: ACM Press. Retrieved from http://delivery.acm.org/10.1145/650000/642688/p441-grinter.pdf

Gross, E. F. (2004). Adolescent internet use: What we expect, what teens report. *Journal of Applied Developmental Psychology*, *25*(6), 633–649.

Gross, E. F., Juvonen, J., & Gable, S. (2002). Internet use and well-being in adolescence. *Journal of Social Issues*, *58*(1), 75–90.

Hall, G. (2006). Teens and technology: Preparing for the future. *New Directions for Youth Development*, *111*, 41–52.

Hall, G., & Israel, L. (2004). *Using technology to support academic achievement for high school-age youth during the out-of-school time hours: A review of the current literature and research*. A report for America Connects Consortium of the U.S. Department of Education. Wellesley, MA: National Institute on Out-of-School Time.

Harvard Family Research Project (2006). *Harnessing technology in out-of-school-time settings*. Cambridge, MA: Harvard Family Research Project Database of Evaluations on Health and Sports/Recreation Programs. Retrieved from http://www.hfrp.org/publications-resources/browse-our-publications/health-and-sports-recreation-program-evaluations

Heath, S. B. (2001). Three's not a crowd: Plans, roles, and focus in the arts. *Educational Researchers*, *30*(7), 10–17.

Hirsch, B. (2005). *A place to call home: After-school programs for urban youth.* Washington, DC: American Psychological Association and New York, NY: Teachers College.

Hoff, D. (2003). Rocket kids. *Education Week, 22*(36), 26–30.

Hull, G. (2003). Youth culture and digital media: New literacies for new times. *Research in the Teaching of English, 38*(2), 229–233.

Hull, G., & Katz, M. L. (2006). Crafting an agentive self. *Research in the Teaching of English, 41*(1), 43–81.

Hull, G., & Nelson, M. (2005). Locating the semiotic power of multimodality. *Written Communication, 22*(2), 224–262.

Ignacio, E. N. (2006). E-scaping boundaries: Bridging cyberspace and diaspora studies through nethnography. In D. Silver & A. Massanari (Eds.), *Critical cyberculture studies* (pp. 186–187). New York, NY: New York University Press.

Ito, M., & Series Editors. (2008). Foreword. In W. L. Bennett (Ed.), *Civic life online: Learning how digital media can engage youth* (pp. vii-ix). The MacArthur Foundation Series on Digital Media and Learning. Cambridge, MA: The MIT Press.

Jacobs, G. (2003). *Breaking down virtual walls: Understanding the real space/ cyberspace connections of language and literacy in adolescents' use of instant messaging.* Paper presented at the annual meeting of the American Educational Research Association, Chicago, IL.

Jarrett, R. L., Sullivan, P. J., & Watkins, N. D. (2005). Developing social capital through participation in organized youth programs: Qualitative insights from three program. *Journal of Community Psychology, 33*, 41–55.

Jenkins, H. (2006). *Confronting the challenges of participatory culture: Media education for the 21st Century.* Chicago, IL: MacArthur Foundation.

Jeong, W. (2002). *The impact of instant messenger services in class settings, including distance learning.* Paper presented at the meeting of the Association for Library and Information Science Education, New Orleans, LA.

Jordan, A., Singer, D., & Singer, J. (2001). Public policy and private practice: Government regulations and parental control of children's television use in the home. In A. Jordan, D. Singer, & J. Singer, (Eds.), *Handbook of children and the media* (pp. 651–662). Thousand Oaks, CA: Sage.

Kafai, Y., Peppler, K., & Chapman, R. (2009). *The computer clubhouse: Constructionism and creativity in youth communities.* New York, NY: Teachers College Press.

Koepp, M. J., Gunn, R. N., Lawrence, A. D., Cunningham, V. J., Dagher, A., Jones, T., et al. (1998). Evidence for striatal dopamine release during a video game. *Nature, 393*, 266–268.

Kutner, L., & Olson, C. (2008). *Grand theft childhood.* New York, NY: Simon & Schuster.

Lambert, J. (2002). *Digital storytelling: Capturing lives, creating community.* Berkeley, CA: Digital Diner Press.

Lampe, C., Ellison, N., & Steinfeld, C. (2006). *A face(book) in the crowd: Social searching vs. social browsing.* Proceedings of the 20th Anniversary Conference on Computer Supported Cooperative Work (pp. 167–170). New York, NY: ACM Press.

Larson, R., & Hansen, D. (2005). The development of strategic thinking: learning to impact human systems in a youth activism program. *Human development, 48*, 327–349.

Larson, R., Hansen, D., & Walker, K. (2005). Everybody's gotta give: Adolescents' development of initiative within a youth program. In J. Mahoney, R. Larson, & Eccles J. (Eds.), *Organized activities as contexts of development: Extracurricular activities, after-school and community programs* (pp. 159–184). Hillsdale, NJ: Erlbaum.

Larson, R., & Richards, M. (Eds.). (1989). The changing life space of early adolescence [special issue]. *Journal of youth and adolescence, 18*(6), 501–626.

Larson, R., & Verma, S. (1999). How children and adolescents around the world spend time: Work, play, and developmental opportunities. *Psychological Bulletin, 125*, 701–736.

Larson, R., Walker, K., & Pearce, N. (2005). A comparison of youth-driven and adult-driven youth programs: Balancing inputs from youth and adults. *Journal of Community Psychology, 33*(1), 57–74.

Lazarus, W., Wainer, A., & Lipper, L. (2005, June). *Impacts of technology on outcomes for youth: A 2005 review*. Washington, DC: The Children's Partnership. Retrieved at http://www.childrenspartnership.org/AM/Template. cfm?Section=Home&Template=/CM/ContentDisplay.cfm&ContentID=7931

Lenhart, A., Kahne, J., Middaugh, E., Rankin, A., Evans, C., & Vitak, J. (2008). *Teens, video games, and civics: Teens' gaming experiences are diverse and include significant social interaction and civic engagement*. Washington, DC: Pew Internet and American Life Project.

Lenhart, A., & Madden, M. (2007). *Social networking websites and teens: An overview*. Washington, DC: Pew Internet and American Life Project.

Lenhart, A., Lee, R., & Lewis, O. (2001). *Teenage life online: The rise of the instant-message generation and the Internet's impact on friendships and family relationships*. Washington, DC: Pew Internet and American Life Project. Retrieved from http://www.pewinternet.org/reports/pdfs/PIP_Teens_Report.pdf

Lenhart, A., Madden, M., & Hitlin, P. (2005). *Teens and technology: Youth are leading the transition to a fully wired and mobile nation*. Washington, DC: Pew Internet and American Life Project.

Lenhart, A., Madden, M., Macgill, A. R., & Smith, A. (2007). *Teens and social media*. Washington, DC: Pew Internet and American Life Project.

Lenhart, A., Rainie, L., & Lewis, O. (2001). *Teenage life online: The rise of the instant-message generation and the internet's impact on friendships and family relationships*. Washington, DC: Pew Internet and American Life Project.

Lerner, R. M., Lerner, J. V., Phelps, E., & Colleagues (2008). *Report of the findings from the first four years of the 4-H study of positive youth development*. Institute for Applied Research in Youth Development: Tufts University. Retrieved from http://ase.tufts.edu/iaryd/documents/ 4HStudyFindings2008.pdf

Leu, D. J., Kinzer, C. K., Coiro, J., & Cammack, D. W. (2004). Toward a theory of new literacies emerging from the internet and other information and communication technologies. In R. B. Ruddell & N. J. Unrau (Eds.),

Theoretical models and processes of reading (pp. 1570–1613). Newark, DE: International Reading Association.

Ling, R., & Yttri, B. (2006). Control, emancipation, and status: The mobile telephone in teens' parental and peer relationships. In R. Kraut, M. Brynin, & S. Kiesler (Eds.), *Computers, phones, and the internet: Domesticating information technology* (pp. 219–234). New York, NY: Oxford University Press.

Magyar, T., Guivernau, M. R., Gano-Overway, L. A., Newton, M., Kim, M., Watson, D., et al. (2007). The influence of leader efficacy and emotional intelligence on personal caring in physical activity. *Journal of Teaching in Physical Education, 26*(3), 310–319.

Mahoney, J., Larson, R., & Eccles, J. (Eds.) (2005). *Organized activities as contexts of development: Extracurricular activities, after-school and community programs*. Hillsdale, NJ: Erlbaum.

Malone, T. W., & Lepper, M. R. (1987). Making learning fun: A taxonomy of intrinsic motivations for learning. In R. E. Snow & M. J. Farr (Eds.), *Aptitude, learning and instruction - Vol. 3: Cognitive and affective process analyses* (pp. 223–253). Hillsdale, NJ: Erlbaum.

McLaughlin, M. W. (1987). Learning from experience: Lessons from policy implementation. *Educational Evaluation and Policy Analysis, 9*(2), 171–178.

McLaughlin, M. W. (1993). Embedded identities: Enabling balance in urban contexts. In S. B. Heath & M. W. McLaughlin (Eds.), *Identity and inner city youth: Beyond ethnicity and gender*. New York, NY: Teachers College Press.

McLaughlin, M. W., Irby, M. A., & Langman, J. (2001). *Urban sanctuaries: Neighborhood organizations in the lives and futures of inner city youth*. San Francisco, CA: Jossey-Bass.

Mlester, S. (2004). High-tech summer camps. *Technology and Learning, 24*(9), 38–39.

Nakamura, L. (2002). *Cybertypes: Race, ethnicity, and identity on the internet*. New York, NY: Routledge.

National Institute on Media and the Family (2008). *Fact sheet—Effects of video game playing on children*. Retrieved from http://www.mediafamily.org/facts/facts_effect.shtml

National Research Council and Institute of Medicine. (2002). Community programs to promote youth development. In J. Eccles & J. A. Gootman (Eds.), *For the Board on Children, Youth, and Families, Division of Behavioral and Social Sciences and Education (Committee on Community-Level Programs for Youth)*. Washington, DC: National Academy Press.

National Research Council and Institute of Medicine. (2002). *Community programs to promote youth development*. In J. Eccles & J. Gootman (Eds.), *Committee on Community-Level Programs for Youth*. Washington, DC: National Academy Press.

National Academy of Engineering. (2002). *Technically speaking: Why all Americans need to know more about technology*. Washington, DC: National Academy Press.

Nelson, M. E., Hull, G., & Roche-Smith, J. (2008). Challenges of multimedia self-presentation: Taking, and mistaking, the show on the road. *Written Communication, 25*, 415–440.

Newman, R., Smith, S., & Murphy, R. (1999). *The cost of youth development - A matter of money: The cost and financing of youth development.* Washington, DC: Academy for Educational Development.

Nicholson, S. (2002). Socialization in the "virtual hallway": Instant messaging in the asynchronous Web-based distance education classroom. *Internet and Higher Education, 5,* 363–372.

Nocon, H., & Cole, M. (2006). School's invasion of "after-school": Colonization, rationalization, or expansion of access? In Z. Bekerman, N. Burbules, & D. Silberman (Eds.), *Learning in places: The informal education reader.* New York, NY: Peter Lang Publishing.

Ochs, E., Graesch, A. P., Mittmann, A., Bradbury, T., & Repetti, R. (2007). *Video ethnography and ethnoarcheological tracking.* Los Angeles, CA: University of California.

Paris, L. (2001). The adventures of Peanut and Bo: Summer camps and early-twentieth-century American girlhood. *Journal of Women's History, 12*(4), 47–76.

Penuel, W. R., & Kim, D. (2000). *Promising practices and organizational challenges in community technology centers.* Menlo Park, CA: SRI International.

Prensky, M. (2001). Digital natives, digital immigrants. *On the Horizon, 9*(5). Retrieved from http://www.marcprensky.com/writing/

Prensky, M. (2006). *Don't bother me mom, I'm learning.* St. Paul, Minnesota: Paragon House.

Quinn, J. (1999). Where need meets opportunity: Youth development programs for early teens. In R. Behrman (Ed.), *The future of children: When school is out* (pp. 96–116). Washington, DC: The David and Lucile Packard Foundation.

Rau, P. P., Gao, Q., & Wu, L. (2008). Using mobile communication technology in high school education: Motivation, pressure, and learning performance. *Computers and Education, 50*(1), 1–22.

Rheingold, H. (1993). *The virtual community: Homesteading on the electronic frontier.* Reading, MA: Addison.

Rideout, V., Foehr, U. G., Roberts, D., & Brodie, M. (1999, November). *Kids media @ the new millennium.* A Kaiser Family Foundation Report. Retrieved at http://www.kff.org/entmedia/1535-index.cfm

Rideout, V., Roberts, D. F., & Foehr, U. G. (2005). *Generation M: Media in the lives of 8–18 year-olds.* Menlo Park, CA: The Henry J. Kaiser Family Foundation.

Roberts, D. F., Foehr, U. G., Rideout, V., & Brodie, M. (1999). *Kids and media @ the new millennium.* Menlo Park, CA: The Henry J. Kaiser Family Foundation.

Rogoff, B. (1991). *Apprenticeship in thinking: Cognitive development in social context.* New York, NY: Oxford University Press.

Rosen, L. (2007). *Me, MySpace, and I: Parenting the net generation.* New York, NY: Palgrave Macmillan.

Rosen, L., Cheever, N. A., & Carrier, L. M. (2007). *The impact of parental attachment style, limit setting, and monitoring on teen MySpace behavior.* California State University, Dominguez Hills. Retrieved from http://www.csudh.edu/psych/The%20Impact%20of%20Parental%20Attachment%20Style%20Rosen-Cheever-Ca.pdf

Rotheram-Borus, M. J., Lightfoot, M., Moraes, A., Dopkins, S., & LaCour, J. (1998). Developmental, ethnic and gender differences in ethnic identity among adolescents. *Journal of Adolescent Research, 13*(4), 487–507.

Russell, S. T., Franz, B. T., & Driscoll, A. K. (2001). Same-sex romantic attraction and experiences of violence in adolescence. *American Journal of Public Health, 91*(6), 903–906.

Sandoval, C., & Latorre, G. (2008). Chicana/o artivism: Judy Baca's digital work with youth of color. In A. Everett (Ed.), *Learning race and ethnicity: Youth and digital media* (pp. 81–108). The MacArthur Foundation Series on Digital Media and Learning. Cambridge, MA: The MIT Press.

Scanlan, T. K., Babkes, M. L., & Scanlan, L. A. (2005). *Participation in sport: A developmental glimpse at emotion.* In J. L. Mahoney, J. S. Eccles & R. Larson (Eds.), Organized activities as contexts of development: Extracurricular activities, after school and community programs (pp. 275–309). Mahwah, NJ: Erlbaum.

Schmidt, M. E., & Vandewater, E. A. (2008). Media and attention, cognition, and school achievement. *Future of Children, 18*(1), 63–85.

Shaffer, D. W., Squire, K. R., Halverson, R., & Gee, J. P. (2005). Video games and the future of learning. *Phi Delta Kappan, 87*(2), 104–111.

Smith, M. (2002). *And they say we'll have some fun when it stops raining: A history of summer camp in America.* Unpublished dissertation. Indiana University.

Smith, M. (2006). The ego ideal of the 'good camper' and the nature of summer camp. *Environmental History, 11*(1), 70–101.

Spencer, M. B., Fegley, S., & Harpalani, V. (2003). A theory and empirical examination of identity as coping: Linking coping resources to the self processes of African American youth. *Journal of Applied Developmental Science, 7*(3), 180–187.

Steinkuehler, C., & Williams, D. (2006). Where everybody knows your (screen) name: Online games as "Third Places." *Journal of Computer-Mediated Communication, 11*, 885–909.

Sterling, S., Matkins, J., Frazier, W., & Logerwell, M. G. (2007). Science camp as a transformative experience for students, parents, and teachers in the urban setting. *School Science and Mathematics, 107*(4), 134–148.

Stroble, K., Kirshner, B., O'Donoghue, J., & McLaughlin, M. (2008). Qualities that attract urban youth to after-school settings and promote continued participation. *Teachers College Record, 110*(8), 1677–1705.

Subrahmanyam, K., Greenfield, P. M., & Tynes, B. (2004). Constructing sexuality and identity in an online teen chatroom. *Journal of Applied Developmental Psychology, 25*(6), 651–666.

Subrahmanyam, K., & Greenfield, P. (2008). Online communication and adolescent relationships. *Future of Children, 18*(1), 120–146.

Subrahmanyam, K., Kraut, R. E., Greenfield, P. M., & Gross, E. (2000). The impact of home computer use on children's activities and development. *The Future of Children, Children and Computer Technology, 10*(2), 123–144.

Swing, E. L., & Anderson, C. A. (2007). The unintended negative consequences of exposure to violent video games. *Cognitive Technology, 12*, 3–13.

Tapscott, D. (1998). *Growing up digital. The rise of the net generation.* New York, NY: McGraw Hill.

Thomas, P., & Macredie, R. (1994). Games and the design of human-computer interfaces. *Educational Technology, 31,* 134–142.

Thompson, C. (2006). Hopeworks: Youth identity, youth organization, and technology. In D. Buckingham & R. Willett (Eds.), *Digital Generations: Children, young people and the new media.* Mahwah, NJ: Erlbaum.

Thompson, C., Putthoff, J., & Figueroa, E. (2006). Hopeworks: Youth identity and technology. In D. Buckingham & R. Willett (Eds.), *Digital generations: Children, young people, and the new media.* Mahwah, NJ: Erlbaum.

Thompson, C., Bouillion, L., & DeGennaro, D. (2007). Tapping youth as tech leaders: A discussion of expertise, learning, & mutual benefit within collaborative IT initiatives. In C. Montgomecie & J. Seale (Eds.), *Proceedings of World Conference on Educational Multimedia, Hypermedia and Telecommunications 2007* (pp. 1991–1996). Chesapeake, VA: AACE.

Turkle, S. (1995). *Life on the screen: Identity in the age of the Internet.* New York, NY: Simon and Schuster.

Vadebonncoer, J. (2006). Engaging young people: Learning in informal contexts. *Review of Research in Education, 30,* 239–278.

Valdez, G., McNabb, M. L., Foertsch, M., Anderson, J., Hawkes, M., & Raack, L. (2000). *Computer-based technology and learning: Evolving uses and expectations.* Oak Brook, IL: North Central Regional Educational Library.

Villarruel, R. A., Montero Sieburth, M., Dunbar, C., & Outlay, C. W. (2005). Dorothy, there is no yellow brick road: The paradox of community youth development approaches for Latino and African American urban youth. In J. Mahoney, J. Eccles, & R. Larson (Eds.), *Organized activities as contexts of development: Extracurricular activities, after-school and community programs* (pp. 111–130). Mahwah, NJ: Erlbaum.

Vygotsky, L. S. (1980). *Mind in society: Development of higher psychological processes.* Cambridge, MA: Harvard University Press.

Ware, P. D., & Warschauer, M. (2005). Hybrid literacy texts and practices in technology-intensive environments. *International Journal of Educational Research, 43*(7–8), 432–445.

Wartella, E., & Mazzarella, S. (1990). A historical comparison of children's use of leisure time. In R. Butsch (Ed.), *For fun and profit* (pp. 173–194). Philadelphia, PA: Temple University Press.

Wertsch, J. (1993). *Voices of the mind: A sociocultural approach to mediated action.* Cambridge, MA: Harvard University Press.

Wolak, J., Mitchell, K. J., & Finkelhor, D. (2003). Escaping or connecting? Characteristics of youth who form close online relationships. *Journal of Adolescence, 26*(1), 105–119.

Wolak, J., Mitchell, K. J., & Finkelhor, D. (2006). *Online victimization of youth: Five years later. National Center for Missing and Exploited Children Bulletin.* Retrieved from http://www.unh.edu/ccrc/pdf/CV138.pdf

Yablon, Y. (2007). Feeling close from a distance: Peace encounters via Internet technology. *New Directions for Youth Development, 116,* 99–107.

Adolescents and schooling: Differences by race, ethnicity, and immigrant status

Grace Kao

Department of Sociology, University of Pennsylvania, Philadelphia, PA

Kristin Turney

School of Public Health, University of Michigan, Ann Arbor, MI

There is little debate that educational experiences and outcomes during adolescence lay the foundation for one's social, economic, and psychological well-being during adulthood (Dornbusch, 1989). For adolescents, school integration, strong friendships, high levels of self-esteem, positive educational outcomes, and high aspirations are independently associated with future socioeconomic (SES) outcomes, and researchers also find these domains to be inextricably linked to each other. Adolescents who have friends at school, for example, are more likely to feel they belong at school, and they earn higher test scores and grades (Corsaro & Eder, 1990; Ryan, 2000, 2001).

However, much of what social scientists know about the educational experiences of adolescents is based on studies of White native-born youth. Mostly because of data limitations, it is not entirely clear how school experiences of racial, ethnic, and immigrant adolescents may differ from those experiences of White native-born youth. This is particularly important because minorities, as well as immigrants and children of immigrants, comprise an increasingly large demographic in the United States. Currently, more than one-third of the school-age population in the United States is African American, Hispanic, or Asian American. Further, the Census Bureau estimates that the percentage of school-aged children in

Adolescence: Development During a Global Era

the United States who are racial and ethnic minorities will grow to 62% by 2050 (U.S. Census Bureau, 2008). In addition, nationally, almost one in four children is an immigrant or child of an immigrant (O'Hare, 2004). In diverse cities such as New York, immigrant children already account for almost half of the student body (Suarez-Orozco & Suarez-Orozco, 2001). Immigrant status is especially important for minorities, as approximately 60% of Hispanic and 90% of Asian American youth have at least one immigrant parent. Among immigrant adolescents, compared with adolescents from native-born families, structural opportunities and cultural preferences may interact to produce very different experiences and outcomes.

This chapter presents a broad overview of sociological and psychological research on the educational experiences of adolescents and how these experiences are related to the transition to adulthood, a distinct period in the life course where one becomes emotionally and, often, financially independent from one's family of origin (Arnett, 2000). We begin by reviewing how parental SES translates into differences in educational opportunities for youth. In particular, we examine how differences in parental SES and race may work together to affect adolescents' educational opportunities. We then move to explore the direct influence of schools in shaping educational opportunities for adolescents. Next, we examine both the academic and social experiences of youth in school and specifically examine peer relations, students' sense of belonging at school, self-esteem, self-concept, and, importantly, academic achievement. With respect to academic performance, we review the literature on variation in educational aspirations, educational achievement in terms of test scores and grades, and, finally, the odds of transitioning to postsecondary education. Throughout the chapter, we closely examine how these experiences may vary by race, ethnicity, and foreign-born status. Some of our discussion is based on newer empirical work, although much of the time, we rely on theoretical hypotheses simply because these populations are still relatively understudied.

7.1. DEFINITIONS OF RACE, ETHNICITY, AND IMMIGRANT STATUS

Throughout this chapter, we refer mainly to Whites, African Americans (or Blacks), Hispanics, and Asian Americans. Although race and ethnicity are complex and overlapping concepts, brevity requires that we rely on their normative definitions in social science research. It is important to note that the U.S. Census does not consider Hispanics to comprise a separate racial group; Hispanics can be of any race (White, Black, Asian, or other race). Hence, when we refer to Whites, we are actually referring to non-Hispanic Whites. Likewise, African Americans, or Blacks, refer to non-Hispanic African Americans or Blacks, and Asian Americans refer to non-Hispanic Asians.

In addition, the panethnic categories of White, African American, Hispanic, and Asian American encompass a wide variety of ethnic groups. Because Whites are predominately native-born and ethnic differences within this broad category have mostly dissipated (and are usually not measured), ethnic demarcations are not noted (Alba, 1990). African Americans are predominately (94%) native-born. The remaining 6% of the African American population, who are foreign-born, largely come to the United States from the Caribbean (60% of foreign-born African Americans) and Africa (24% of foreign-born African Americans) (U.S. Census Bureau, 2005). Due to the small sizes of immigrant populations, many large-scale studies do not differentiate by ethnicity or national origin of African Americans.

As noted earlier, though Hispanics can be of any race, they are also composed of many diverse national-origin and ethnic groups. Most typically, they include Mexicans, Puerto Ricans, Cubans, Dominicans, Central Americans (e.g., Costa Rican, Guatemalan, Honduran), South Americans (e.g., Argentinean, Bolivian, Colombian), Spaniards, and other Hispanics (U.S. Census Bureau, 2004a,b). Mexicans are by far the largest Hispanic ethnic group, accounting for 60% of Hispanics in 2000. In comparison, about 10% of Hispanics are Puerto Rican, 4% are Cubans, 5% are Central Americans, 4% are South Americans, 2% are Dominicans, and 16% are other Hispanics (U.S. Census Bureau, 2004b, Figure 1).

Asian Americans are an even more complex population. Approximately 4.2% of the U.S. population (11.9 million people) reported that they were Asian in the 2000 Census. This figure includes those who chose more than one racial group. The 11 largest Asian groups are Chinese (23.8%), Filipino (18.3%), Asian Indian (16.2%), Vietnamese (10.9%), Korean (10.5%), Japanese (7.8%), Cambodian (1.8%), Hmong (1.7%), Laotian (1.6%), Pakistani (1.5%), and Thai (1.1%). The remaining groups (Malaysian, Burmese, etc.) comprise 4.7% of the Asian population (U.S. Census Bureau, 2004a, Figure 1). Often, Southeast Asians are considered together, as they share the experience of entry to the United States as refugees and migrated to the United States primarily after the fall of Saigon in 1975.

Immigrants are individuals who were born outside of the United States and migrated to the United States. Because this chapter examines youth, we often use the phrase immigrant youth to refer to individuals who have immigrant parents regardless of whether they themselves were born in the United States. Although some of these youth are native-born and others are foreign-born, household dynamics and parent-child interactions are driven by parental characteristics (see Zhou, 1997). Individuals who are foreign-born and migrate to the United States are known as first-generation immigrants, their native-born children are considered second-generation immigrants, and so forth. Some researchers use the term 1.5 generation for those who are foreign-born but migrated as children. Following this terminology, some scholars use 1.75 generation for those who migrated as very young children, or 1.25 generation for those who migrated near the end of adolescence.

7.2. **RACE, ETHNIC, AND IMMIGRANT DIFFERENCES IN PARENTAL BACKGROUND**

Although popular portrayals of educational experiences tend to focus on how differences in school quality produce unequal opportunities for children, children come from vastly different parental backgrounds. Recent research, for example, shows that children enter the school system with extremely different social and material resources (Farkas, 2003; Lee & Burkam, 2002). Their parents' SES—which often includes by educational attainment, income, occupational prestige, and wealth—lays the groundwork for future patterns of educational stratification. What further complicates matters is that race, ethnicity, and immigrant status are correlated with SES. Thus, part of the race differences in educational outcomes can be accounted for by SES differences. Still, in most cases, differences in SES do not completely account for racial disparities in educational outcomes (Cosa & Alexander, 2007).

From sociological research, we know that there is probably no greater single predictor of one's future education and career trajectories than parental SES (Campbell, 1983; Hallinan, 1988; Kao & Thompson, 2003; Sewell, Haller, & Portes, 1969; Sewell & Shah, 1968). Parental SES is associated with educational differences starting in early childhood, and these early differences generally increase over time (Duncan, Yeung, Brooks-Gunn, & Smith, 1998; Entwisle, Alexander, & Olson, 1997; Lee & Burkam, 2002). By adolescence, youth with highly educated parents have schooling experiences that are in alarming contrast to their counterparts with less educated parents. Children from more advantaged backgrounds not only have the opportunity to attend schools with more resources, but also their parents have greater knowledge about how to successfully navigate their children through the schooling process. High-SES youth are also more likely to have friends who stay in school and plan to attend college.

When thinking about racial, ethnic, and immigrant minority children, it is crucial to keep in mind that these demographic factors are strongly correlated with SES. In social science research, differences attributable to social class are often described as *structural*. In other words, these are differences that result from class stratification in U.S. society and exist outside of individuals and families. African American, Hispanic, and Asian American parents have different educational profiles relative to their White native-born counterparts. On average, Asian American parents have higher educational attainment than White parents, and African American and Hispanic parents have lower educational attainment. In 1990, among individuals aged 25 and older, 37% of Asian Americans, 22% of Whites, 11% of Blacks, and 9% of Hispanics had a Bachelor's degree or higher (National Center for Education Statistics, 1997). According to the 2000 Census, the percentage of individuals aged 25 and older who had a Bachelor's degree or higher was 44% for Asians, 26% for Whites, 14% for Blacks, and 10% for Hispanics (U.S. Census Bureau, 2004c).[1] Thus, the educational differences among parents account for some of the racial and ethnic disparities in educational outcomes of youth.

For Hispanics and Asian Americans, broad panethnic categorizations mask the great ethnic diversity in parental SES. For instance, approximately 70% of Indians, 67% of Taiwanese, more than 40% of Chinese, and 36% of Filipino immigrants aged 25 and above had a college degree in 2000 (Portes & Rumbaut, 2006). However, only 10% of Cambodian and 8% of Laotian foreign-born over the age of 25 had at least a college degree. Still, these percentages far surpass those of Mexican immigrants, of whom only 4% had at least a college degree (Portes & Rumbaut, 2006). Approximately 33% of Brazilian, 22% of Colombian, and 19% of Cuban immigrants aged 25 and older had at least a Bachelor's degree.

Because of the stark variation in parental educational attainment by race, ethnicity, and immigrant status, youth begin schooling with very different levels of parental SES and social and cultural capital. Moreover, these class differences somewhat overlap with their race and ethnic backgrounds. Overall, Asian American youth are advantaged because their parents are largely foreign-born, and those Asians who are able to immigrate are disproportionately from more advantaged backgrounds.

---

[1]Note that the numbers are not directly comparable as individuals were allowed to choose more than one race in the 2000 Census. The numbers we report above are for single-race individuals. Twenty percent of multiracials aged 25 and over had at least a Bachelor's degree.

The barriers to entry to the United States are high for immigrants, and this is especially true of those coming from countries that are geographically distant from the United States. Immigration laws favor skilled workers. In addition, the financial costs associated with immigration to the United States from outside North America are extremely high. In contrast, because most Mexicans migrate to work in agricultural or other low-skilled jobs, these parents are much less likely to have high levels of education.

It is clear that these differences may account for race and ethnic disparities in educational outcomes (i.e., structural explanations), but some researchers have also argued that *cultural* preferences may be important predictors of these disparities. The cultural explanation is most often used to explain the higher educational performance of Asian Americans, who are often seen as the model minority (Kao, 1995; Lee, 1996). For instance, Caplan, Choy, and Whitmore's (1997) study of Vietnamese youth found that because older children were expected to tutor their younger siblings, this reinforced the importance of learning and helped them review basic skills. Zhou and Bankston (1998), in their study of Vietnamese youth in New Orleans, argued that youth whose cultural tastes were more similar to their parents were less likely to be delinquent. Similarly, Valenzuela and Dornbusch (1994) reported that youth who valued close ties to their family also had higher grades in school. And, in a study of nearly 400 recently arrived children of immigrants, Suarez-Orozco and Suarez-Orozco (2001) found that immigrant children face a distinct set of challenges in adapting to life in the United States. These children often had to deal with leaving family members behind in their home country, learning a new language, and the tension inherent in adapting to a new culture more quickly than their parents.

In some ways, the arguments supporting the positive influences of proximity to parents' cultural values are in direct contrast and opposition to notions of the *culture of poverty* (Lewis, 1966). The phrase *culture of poverty* was coined by Oscar Lewis in *Five Families: Mexican Case Studies in the Culture of Poverty* (1959) and *La Vida: A Puerto Rican Family in the Culture of Poverty* (1966). In essence, Lewis argued that, along with poverty over many generations, comes a pathology of values that work to keep individuals in poverty. Among other things, the culture of poverty includes feelings of helplessness and the inability to defer gratification. In other words, to bring individuals out of poverty, one must not only provide them with financial resources but also reorient their values. Anthropologist John Ogbu later noted that some minorities were better equipped for attaining socioeconomic success due to the paths through which they migrated to the United States (Ogbu, 1991). He differentiated between *voluntary* (sometimes he called them immigrant) minorities and *involuntary* minorities, those who did not choose to come to the United States. Most notably, his description of involuntary minorities suited his early studies of African American youth in school (Ogbu, 1978), while the notion of immigrant minorities helped to explain the relative educational success of Asian Americans. He argued that immigrant and involuntary minorities differ in five ways: (1) frame or reference for evaluating their status and future possibilities; (2) folk theory of how to attain socioeconomic mobility; (3) sense of collective identity; (4) cultural frame for judging their own behavior and affirming their group membership; and (5) the extent to which, as members of their group, they can trust the dominant groups and institutions (Ogbu, 1991). Simply put, involuntary minorities compare themselves to the dominant group (Whites), and immigrants have lower expectations, for their own SES attainment because they compare themselves to people in their country of origin. Moreover, immigrant minorities are more likely to believe that any discrimination they face stems from their immigrant status (lack of English proficiency, less knowledge of U.S. cultural norms, etc.) rather than their racial status. Hence, they feel their children will overcome these obstacles and be treated fairly (Kao & Tienda, 1995). Because immigrant minorities believe in the American Dream, they are more likely to believe that academic achievement leads to socioeconomic mobility; moreover, they would not equate their own success to somehow becoming a sell-out or as a sign of disloyalty to their group. Ogbu argued that involuntary minorities (i.e., Blacks) did not believe that mainstream institutions would treat them fairly; thus, Black students perceive fewer occupational returns to school success. Moreover, he argued elsewhere that *acting Black* was associated with not doing well in school because it was defined in opposition to *acting White* (Fordham & Ogbu, 1986). Black students therefore resist traditional markers of academic success and are sanctioned by their peers if they experience such success. In other words, being Black is an *oppositional identity* to being White.

Although theoretically appealing to some researchers, other scholars have argued against Ogbu's thesis, with many finding no empirical evidence for his hypotheses (Ainsworth-Darnell & Downey, 1998; Carter, 2005; Cook & Ludwig, 1998; Tyson, Darity, & Castellino, 2005). Ainsworth-Darnell and Downey (1998), for example, examined these hypotheses with a longitudinal and nationally representative sample of adolescents. They found that Black students were actually more optimistic about their career prospects and held more positive views of school than White students. They also discovered that these attitudes and beliefs cannot explain racial differences in school performance. Thus, the authors found no support for the idea that Black students achieve at lower levels than White students because of a resistant cultural orientation. Similarly, Tyson et al. (2005) found no evidence of oppositional culture among Black high school students in North Carolina; instead, these students generally embraced academic achievement, although the school context played an important role in students' attitudes toward schooling. They found that Black oppositional culture only exists when there are distinct class differences between Black and White students within a single school and that, in other contexts, economically disadvantaged White youth can also experience an oppositional culture. Moreover, others criticize Ogbu's argument as a variant of theories that blame the victims for their outcomes (Gould, 2002).

Alternatively, individuals can internalize perceived stereotypes of their own group. Research from psychologist Claude Steele and his colleagues suggests that test subjects perform less well when they are given negative feedback about individual performance that is consistent with stereotypes (Steele, 1997; Steele & Aronson, 1995). In other words, if one is a member of a group that is stereotyped to be less skilled in a particular activity, with the right prompt, that individual will also score lower on a test of that activity. Stereotype threat might be particularly detrimental to the outcomes of high-achieving Black youth, as those who strongly identify with achievement and have invested in schooling may be more likely to be influenced by stereotypical beliefs about themselves (Steele & Aronson, 1998).

7.3. **THE ROLE OF PARENTS IN AFFECTING EDUCATIONAL TRAJECTORIES**

Although popular literature portrays adolescence as a time when youth move away from their parents, there is considerable evidence that parents play a crucial role during this period (Dornbusch, 1989; Giordano, 2003; Vandell, 2000). Furthermore, though adolescence is typically associated with rebelliousness (think of the films *Rebel Without a Cause* or *American Graffiti*, which today has spawned an entire genre of teen films, or even prominent sociologist James Coleman's landmark study in *The Adolescent Society*, 1961), research consistently finds that peers and parents jointly influence students and, that more often than not, peers reinforce a similar set of norms as parents (Brown, 1990; Dornbusch, 1989). Space limitations prevent us from a thorough discussion of the consequences of parenting for educational outcomes, but it is important to highlight some of this literature. For the purposes of this chapter, we summarize research on parenting styles and parent-school interactions.

Bronfenbrenner (1979) was an early advocate of understanding the process of adolescent development in context, encouraging both psychologists and sociologists to think jointly about this key period of the life course. His conceptual model emphasized not only interpersonal relationships but also the role of families and schools in influencing adolescent development (Bronfenbrenner, 1979; Dornbusch, 1989). The period in which he worked also marked the movement away from the emphasis on the biological changes that come with adolescence but instead toward the pathways through which societal norms and the expectations of others influence youth (Bronfenbrenner & Morris, 1998).

Sociologists emphasize the importance of the home environment (which we address below), but also the influence of historical circumstances. The concepts of age, cohort, and period that are major underpinnings of demographic research argue for the interaction between age and historical period (i.e., cohort effects). For example, teenagers born in the 1950s and the 1990s may share some similar experiences due to their age (age effects), but they are situated in very different historical circumstances (period effects); together, these age and period influences form cohort effects. Thus, social pathways are age-graded; timing of events, beginning early in one's development, have lasting implications on subsequent development (Elder, Johnson, & Crosnoe, 2003). In the developmental literature, this is more commonly known as the *life course* perspective. This approach is widely credited to Elder's landmark study of the children born during the Great Depression (Elder, 1974). Another guiding principle of life course theory is the concept of linked lives, the idea that individuals live their lives interdependently of one another. Thus, in accordance with life course theory, parents' attitudes and behaviors influence children's outcomes from early childhood through adulthood.

Researchers in the 1970s also emphasized that though adolescence marked a period during which friends take a more central position in the lives of youth, parents continue to have a strong influence on youth. Studies beginning in the late 1960s found that *authoritative* parenting (where parents and children share in decision-making processes) led to more positive child outcomes (such as grades) than either *permissive* (where children have considerable decision-making power) or *authoritarian* (where parents unequivocally make decisions for their children) decision-making styles (Dornbusch, 1989; Kao & Thompson, 2003). Some researchers maintain that these styles of decision making, correlated with parental social class, are much more important than parental SES in determining children's educational outcomes. This perspective is exemplified by Clark's (1983) landmark study of poor African American children who were successful despite the odds against them. He found that these parents had warm and close relationships with their children, and consistently monitored them. In other words, social class may be an important predictor of educational outcomes, but disadvantages can be overcome through parenting behavior. These arguments are convincing because though social class accounts for some disparities in educational outcomes, it by no means determines one's life chances.

Sociologists have always maintained that parents are crucial determinants of children's educational and social psychological outcomes. Beginning with the Wisconsin School, sociologists emphasized the transmission of class advantage from parents to children in a model also known as *status attainment*. Sewell and his colleagues (e.g., see Campbell, 1983; Sewell, Haller, & Portes, 1969; Sewell & Shah, 1968) argued that parents' educational attainment leads to their occupational status and these jointly affect children's educational aspirations, educational attainment, and future occupational status. Part of the process focused on modeling behavior, but they also argued for the social psychological benefits of college plans that stem from parental SES.

Though there is no doubt that educational aspirations in high school are highly correlated with later educational attainment, it is not clear whether aspirations actually represent the level of motivation children have toward future outcomes or if they simply reflect future plans. Recent empirical evidence further suggests that the vast majority of high school sophomores expect to graduate from college. In fact, only 8% of high school sophomores expected to receive a high school diploma or less. On the other hand, 72% of students expected to receive a Bachelor's degree or higher (36% of students reported expecting to graduate from a 4-year college program, 20% expected to receive a Master's degree, and 16% expected to receive an advanced or doctoral degree such as a Ph.D. or an M.D.). Of course, it is important to note that many youth drop out before their sophomore year and thus are not represented in these reports on educational expectations. Though differences in expectations vary slightly among race and class lines, the majority of students report high expectations (NCES, 2002).

However, we know that even among adults aged 25-29 in 2005, only 28% attained at least a Bachelor's degree (NCES, 2007a). The discrepancy between aspirations and attainment suggests that some youth have higher expectations than they achieve. The discrepancy also suggests that some youth may answer questions about educational aspirations with socially desirable responses. According to the National Center for Education Statistics (NCES), in 2004, 60.3% of Asians, 41.7% of Whites, 31.8% of Blacks, and 24.7% of Hispanics aged 18-24 were enrolled in colleges and universities (NCES, 2007a). Hence, it is likely that there is substantial variation in the meaning of aspirations among respondents.

Sociologists also emphasize other pathways through which parents transmit their class advantages to their children. For example, Baker and Stevenson (1986) found that highly educated mothers, compared to their counterparts with less education, were more likely to manage their high school children's academic careers. Additionally, in her study of young children, Lareau (2000) argued that mothers with more education are more likely to feel empowered to challenge their children's teachers and to more actively engage in educational activities at school. In another study, Lareau found the relationship between upper middle-class parents and their children's schools to be one of *interconnectedness*, where parents see themselves as responsible for their children's education. The relationship between working-class parents and their children's schools, on the other hand, is one of *separateness*, where the parents are more inclined to put responsibility of their children's education in the hands of the schools. Thus, socioeconomic advantage provides different cultural resources, which include symbolic access to the world of educated people, social status, confidence, income and other material resources, work relationships that mirror teachers' preferred school-family relations, and social networks that provide more access to educators and general information about schooling (Lareau, 2003).

Additionally, research finds that parents' SES is positively associated with parental involvement in school. Parental involvement in school is usually measured, among other things, by participation in Parent-Teacher Organizations, parental attendance at school events, and parental conversations with teachers. Parents with higher income and greater educational attainment are more involved than parents with lower SES (Baker & Stevenson, 1986; Crosnoe, 2001; Desimone, 1999; Hoover-Dempsey, Bassler, & Brissie, 1987; Lareau, 2000; for contradictory findings, see Sui-Chi & Willms, 1996). Class differences in parental involvement are particularly important, as parental involvement is linked to academic success across the life course (Domina, 2005; Englund, Luckner, Whaley, & Egeland, 2004; Falbo, Lein, & Amador, 2001; Hoover-Dempsey & Sandler, 1995; Jeynes, 2007; Muller, 1993; Sui-Chi & Willms, 1996). Elsewhere, we found that minority immigrant parents face particular challenges (such as a lack of English language proficiency or the inability to take time off from work) in getting involved with their children's schools (Turney & Kao, 2009a).

It is important to note that many examinations of parental influence are based on predominately White samples or predominantly White and African American samples. We know much less about how parents influence Asian, Hispanic, and immigrant children, though the research that does exist suggests that parent-child interactions may be different in these households. For instance, Dornbusch and his colleagues (Dornbusch, Ritter, Leiderman, Roberts, & Fraleigh, 1987; Steinberg, Lamborn, Dornbusch, & Darling, 1992) and Kao (1999) found that for Asian youth, *authoritarian* parenting style is associated with better educational outcomes than either *authoritative* or *permissive* styles; this is in direct contrast to the findings for White children.

Similarly, there are race and immigrant status differences in parental involvement, and some evidence that the consequences of this involvement vary by race and immigrant group (McNeal, 1999). For example, Black and Hispanic parents are more likely to be involved with Parent-Teacher Organizations than White parents, and Asian parents are less likely to be involved (Muller & Kerbow, 1993). More recent research, however, found that race differences in parental involvement are mediated by students' academic performance (Crosnoe, 2001). According to Crosnoe (2001), White parents are more likely to reduce their involvement as their children experience better outcomes. Black parents with children in the remedial track have higher participation rates than their White counterparts; however, they are more likely to reduce their level of participation if their children persistently achieve at lower levels. Additionally, immigrant parents may be less involved in their children's elementary and high school experiences (Kao, 2004; Nord & Griffin, 1999), perhaps because they face unique barriers, such as language barriers, to such involvement (Turney & Kao, 2009a). Immigrant families also face additional challenges, as parents sometimes have difficulty keeping up with their children, who have assimilated more quickly to American culture. Additionally, language barriers often force these parents to be dependent on their children, which affects parental authority, and immigrant families often lack social support from extended kin members (Tse, 1996; Turney & Kao, 2009b; Zhou, 1997).

7.4. **SCHOOL EXPERIENCES**

7.4.1. **School segregation and other structural differences**

In addition to the home environment, youth spend a considerable amount of time at school. However, schools vary not only in their organizational styles, but also in terms of the composition of their student bodies.

Because the vast majority of public schools in the United States are linked to residential neighborhoods and because neighborhoods tend to be segregated by race and class, schools mirror and sometimes further intensify neighborhood segregation (Charles, 2003; Massey & Denton, 1993). Holding their parents' income constant, White children are more likely to grow up in affluent neighborhoods with substantial resources and good schools, and Black and Hispanic children are likely to grow up in socioeconomically disadvantaged neighborhoods and attend overcrowded schools with limited and strained resources (Charles, 2003). Although racial segregation among Blacks declined slightly from 1980 to 2000, segregation among Hispanics and Asians increased during this time (Charles, 2003). Neighborhoods, and the resources associated with place of residence, may play a crucial role in both child and adolescent development. Having affluent neighbors, as opposed to disadvantaged neighbors, is strongly related to developmental outcomes. Although both White and Black youth benefit from affluent neighbors, White adolescents tend to benefit more than their Black adolescent counterparts. Specifically, the positive effect of neighborhood SES on a youth's odds of dropping out of high school only persists for White youth and not for Black youth (Brooks-Gunn, Duncan, Klebanov, & Sealand, 1993). However, methodological pitfalls characterize much research on neighborhood effects. Most importantly, it is difficult to estimate the causal effect of neighborhood characteristics on individual outcomes as families have some degree of choice in choosing a neighborhood and how long to stay there (Duncan & Raudenbush, 1999; Sampson, Morenoff, & Gannon-Rowley, 2002).

According to NCES, in 2004, 65% of Whites attended schools that were less than 25% minority, compared to 9% of Blacks, 8% of Hispanics, and 20% of Asians. On the other end of the spectrum, 3% of Whites, 52% of Blacks, 58% of Hispanics, and 34% of Asians attended schools that were at least 75% minority (NCES, 2007a). In addition, minority children are more likely to attend schools where many of their peers live in poverty. For instance, in 2005, 5% of Whites, 48% of Blacks, 49% of Hispanics, and 16% of Asians attended school where more than 75% of children received free lunch (NCES, 2007a).

Approximately 4% of all public schools are designated as charter schools, schools that parents can choose and that are usually governed by a group or organization under a charter or contract from the state. They are exempt from some local and state regulations, although they are regularly reviewed and must meet basic accountability standards (NCES, 2007c). Charter schools, compared to their public school counterparts, are more likely to enroll minority children. Although charter schools have been touted by some as a way to improve public schools, their effects on academic performance are somewhat mixed. The average math and reading test scores of fourth graders in charter and conventional public schools in 2003, for example, were no different from one another. However, given that minority children, on average, have lower test scores, this might be seen as evidence that charter schools are more effective. It is nevertheless difficult to disentangle the effects of charter schools versus the effects of selection into charter schools, as parents who choose to place their children in charter schools are likely to be different from parents of children in regular public schools (Goldhaber, 1999).

Studies also suggest that the opportunities and experiences of students vastly differ between public and private schools. Coleman and his colleagues (Coleman & Hoffer, 1987; Hallinan, 1988), for example, found that students in private schools had higher educational gains in test scores compared with their counterparts in public schools. Moreover, empirical evidence suggests that religious and secular private schools may also offer different educational experiences in addition to differences that stem from socioeconomic disparities. Hallinan, in her 1988 review, calls this the *value climate* perspective (Hallinan, 1988). For example, Bryk, Lee, and Holland (1993) argued that Catholic schools emphasize values of community and personal responsibility as well as a general curriculum for all students, all of which lead to higher test scores. They argued that this orientation is particularly important because Catholic schools increasingly serve a minority and lower-SES student population, yet students who attend these schools maintain high academic achievement.

Prep schools and boarding schools may also offer unique experiences for students. Cookson and Persell (1985), in their study of elite preparatory schools, argued that these schools teach and reinforce values that maintain the elite status of their students. Boarding schools, in particular, serve as total institutions so that they can better regulate norms and prevent contact with lower socioeconomic groups. These authors argued that schools teach children that life is difficult and that winning is essential for survival. Prep schools regulate the daily schedules of their students and thus help to prepare youth for their future membership in the power elite. Prep schools also give all students a common identity and outlook. Of course, they also work to build friendship networks that are essential as individuals enter the workforce.

7.4.2. **Peer relations at school**

Psychologists and sociologists have also examined friendships and peer relationships at school. Adolescents, like adults, have friends who are similar in terms of race, ethnicity, class, and interests (Clark & Ayers, 1992; Crosnoe,

2001; Giordano, 2003; McPherson, Smith-Lovin, & Cool, 2001). Part of the sorting that comes with friendship formation is a result of choice, but what is often overlooked is how the opportunity to interact with different groups may influence who becomes friends with whom (Joyner & Kao, 2000). Beginning with Coleman's (1961) study, earlier work by sociologists focused on the negative influence of peers. These studies, for example, find that youth whose friends use illegal drugs are also more likely to use drugs themselves (Cook, Deng, & Morgano, 2007; Kandel, 1978). Additionally, friends' delinquency is an important predictor of one's own delinquency (Haynie, 2001; Kandel, 1978, 1980). However, psychologists argue for the positive influences of peers and friendships. At a most fundamental level, youth who are able to forge meaningful and deep relationships are better equipped to do so later in life (Giordano, 2003). Early relationships can serve as a testing ground for learning how to interact with others. Moreover, friends can provide important psychological support to youth.

Students' educational aspirations and orientations toward schooling are also influenced by peers (Duncan, Haller, & Portes, 1968; Kandel, 1978). Specifically, Ryan (2001) found that peers are associated with students' liking and enjoyment of school and their achievement over the school year. However, peers do not influence students' beliefs about the importance of school or their expectations for academic success (Ryan, 2001). Additionally, others have found that adolescents' peers play an important role in their course selection during high school (Crosnoe, Riegle-Crumb, Frank, Field, & Muller, 2008). It is clear that friends and peers can provide either positive or negative influences on youth and it is likely that the influence of friends is mostly intensely felt during adolescence. Research shows that adolescent peer groups are often homophilous with respect to race, though the development of interracial friendships may be influenced by school or neighborhood context (Joyner & Kao, 2000; Moody, 2001). Additionally, some have found that the positive influence of peers on academic performance may not vary by race (Crosnoe, Cavanaugh, & Elder, 2003; Giordano, 2003), though other contextual characteristics such as school composition might matter (Crosnoe et al., 2003). Among Vietnamese immigrants in New Orleans, variation in friendship networks led to variation in delinquency, though this study lacks a comparison to other race groups or nonimmigrant children (Zhou & Bankston, 1998). Aside from these few studies, discussions of how the influence of peers may vary by race, ethnicity, and immigrant status are largely absent from the literature (Giordano, 2003).

Gender is also an important stratifying characteristic in developing peer relationships during adolescence. Although same-sex peer groups are more common in childhood and early adolescence, later adolescence is marked with more mixed-sex peer groups and the development of adolescent romantic relationships (Adler & Adler, 1998; Giordano, 2003; Joyner & Laumann, 2000). In fact, experiences with peers and romantic partners are linked. According to one study, having social networks with more opposite-sex friends is associated with an increased likelihood of being in a romantic relationship. Additionally, the quality of one's friendship network is associated with the quality of one's romantic relationship (Connolly, Furman, & Konarski, 2000). Gender is also important in determining the nature of friendship. Girls are more emotionally close to their friends, and boys are more likely to spend time with large groups of friends (Dornbusch, 1989).

7.5. **OUTCOMES IN ADOLESCENCE**

7.5.1. **Educational outcomes**

Because educational outcomes (such as grades and test scores) serve as a gate-keeper of future postsecondary educational and occupational attainment, those who study youth in schools are particularly interested in these outcomes. Studies consistently find large and persistent racial disparities in test scores throughout the life course, with Asians and Whites at the top and Blacks and Hispanics at the bottom (Kao & Thompson, 2003). Differences in SAT scores in the 2005-2006 academic year exemplify test score differences by race and ethnicity. In SAT-Critical Reading, the average score for Whites was 527, compared to 434 for Blacks, 458 for Hispanics, and 510 for Asians. Asians earned higher scores than other groups in SAT-Mathematics, with an average score of 578, compared with 536 for Whites, 429 for Blacks, and 463 for Hispanics (NCES, 2007a).[2] These differences are even more apparent at the highest achievement levels. Among high school graduates in 2005, 24.6% of Asians, 10.1% of Whites, 2.9% of Blacks, and 5.0% of Hispanics had taken AP Calculus, and the figures for AP Chemistry, Physics, and Biology reveal the same pattern (NCES, 2007b).

Though grades may be arguably a less standard measure of performance than standardized test scores, due to vast differences in criteria across teachers, classes, and schools, they are important because they provide consistent and primary feedback to students and parents about their educational progress (DiMaggio, 1982; Kao & Thompson, 2003). Grades are correlated with test scores, but they are also more susceptible to student

---

[2]These numbers exclude Mexicans and Puerto Ricans. The means of these groups are no more than 5 points different from those of Hispanics, but because the source does not provide sample sizes, the authors are unable to compute an overall average for Hispanics.

input. Not surprisingly, race and ethnic disparities in grades mirror race and ethnic disparities in test scores (e.g., see Fuligni, 1997; Kao, 1995).

Educational outcomes are particularly important for immigrant children, as education is a crucial step toward adaptation to the United States (Zhou, 1997). There are also important differences in educational outcomes by immigrant status. Children of immigrants generally follow a pattern of segmented assimilation. Segmented assimilation directly challenges the traditional concept of assimilation often used to describe the process of the first wave of immigrants' incorporation into American society (i.e., Gordon, 1964). Instead, assimilation is not a linear process, and outcomes vary across immigrant minorities; upward mobility and assimilation into the American mainstream is just one possibility experienced by second and subsequent generations. Thus, some groups, on average, have better educational outcomes than their native-born White counterparts, and other groups fare much worse (Portes & Rumbaut, 2001). Cubans, for example, have relative success in school, though Mexican children tend to have worse outcomes than their White or Cuban counterparts (Rumbaut & Portes, 2001). Other work supports the idea that national origin plays an important role in adolescents' educational outcomes (Portes & MacLeod, 1996; Portes & Rumbaut, 2001; Rumbaut & Portes, 2001).

Other factors also play a role in how immigrant children do in terms of educational outcomes. Kao and Tienda (1995), for example, found that generation status is associated with middle school grades, standardized math and reading test scores, and aspirations to graduate from college among eighth graders. First-generation immigrants, compared with their native-born counterparts, have better educational outcomes, but second-generation immigrants and native-born adolescents have similar outcomes. They also found that ethnicity is important; parental nativity is most crucial for Asians and less crucial for Hispanics (Kao & Tienda, 1995). Additionally, Glick and White (2003) found that generational status is more important for academic performance (test scores) than academic trajectories (the probability of dropping out of high school), with first-generation students doing worse than third-generation students in 1980 and better in 1990. When looking at academic performance, generational status is more important for later cohorts than for earlier cohorts.

7.5.2. **Social and emotional outcomes**

Another important dimension of adolescent well-being includes social and emotional adjustment, both in school and out of school. Self-efficacy, generally regarded as the sense of control one has over planning and implementing life options, is an outcome that matters for adolescents (Gecas, 1989). On a related note, students with higher self-esteem generally perform better in school than their counterparts with low self-esteem (D'Amico & Cardaci, 2003; Ross & Broh, 2000). Emotional adjustment of adolescents is also associated with stronger friendship networks, less delinquency, and robust ties to the labor market (Rosenberg, Schooler, & Schoenbach, 1989).

Similar to measures of educational attainment and achievement, adolescent social and emotional well-being varies by race and immigrant status. This variation in social and emotional outcomes, however, does not follow the same pattern as differences in educational outcomes. For example, Asian American youth have comparable or higher academic outcomes than White, Black, or Hispanic youth, but they have lower levels of self-esteem and self-efficacy (Kao, 1999). Moreover, though African American students have lower levels of academic performance than their White counterparts, studies consistently show them as having relatively high levels of self-esteem.

There are few examinations of differences in well-being between native- and foreign-born adolescents, though research on adults finds that immigrants have lower levels of psychological functioning than their native-born counterparts, and existing theoretical frameworks and empirical analyses suggest that these findings are applicable to their children (Aronowitz, 1984; Kao, 1999). The experience of immigration itself can be challenging, particularly for those individuals without material or social resources (Suarez-Orozco & Suarez-Orozco, 2001). National origin and generation status may also matter in predicting adolescent well-being. Filipino adolescents who come to the United States, for example, are especially likely to suffer from depression (Rumbaut & Portes, 2001). Additionally, first-generation immigrants may experience lower levels of depression and more positive well-being than their native-born counterparts, but second-generation immigrants and native-born adolescents experience similar levels of positive well-being (Harker, 2001). These findings suggest that schools should more closely examine the particular mental health challenges that face immigrant youth, especially in light of cultural norms that prevent discussing these problems with outsiders.

7.6. **THE TRANSITION TO ADULTHOOD**

Similar to other outcomes discussed, SES plays a particularly important role in the transition to adulthood, a process within one's life course that is associated with the following transitions: leaving school, starting a full-time job, leaving the home of origin, getting married, and becoming a parent (Shanahan, 2000). The timing and sequencing of these five markers have changed over time, mostly as a result of the major demographic transitions of the past 50 years, and many scholars suggest that the transition to adulthood today is more prolonged than it has been in the past (Arnett, 2000; Buchmann, 1989; Shanahan, 2000). Individuals now take more time to transition to adult status, and these transition years are characterized by change and exploration of possible life directions. Recently, research suggests that the transition to adulthood is less marked by these five transitions mentioned above, but is instead subjective and more related to psychological factors such as how much independence and autonomy one feels over one's life. The more sense of independence a youth has, the more likely he or she is to feel like an adult (Arnett, 2000).

Not surprisingly, there is substantial heterogeneity in how individuals experience these years of their lives (Arnett, 2000). The transition to adulthood may be particularly prolonged for individuals from high-SES families, as these families may have the resources to pay for not only a college education but often education beyond college such as medical school or graduate school. On the other hand, those from lower-SES families may have a more difficult transition (Furstenberg, 2008; Osgood, Foster, Flanagan, & Ruth, 2005). One study, for example, found that the process of transitioning into adulthood varies across social groups. The most vulnerable populations—for example, those with mental health issues or experience with the criminal justice system—face a particularly difficult transition to adulthood (Osgood et al., 2005). Research on race, ethnic, and immigrant differences in the transition to adulthood is particularly scarce. Mostly due to data limitations, researchers know very little about how different non-White groups experience the transition to adulthood and the various challenges that each group faces (Osgood et al., 2005; Shanahan, 2000). There are several exceptions. Some research, for example, finds that Blacks and Asians are less likely to leave home than Whites, though the mechanisms underlying these differences are less understood (White, 1994). Additionally, Blacks and foreign-born individuals are less likely to be employed than native-born Whites, though this gap has decreased over time (Fussell & Furstenberg, 2007).

What these patterns suggest is that youth who directly transition to a 4-year university straight out of high school do not need to depend on the educational system to help them make the transition to adulthood. These youth are more likely to receive continued assistance from their parents and are not seen by others (and do not see themselves) as independent adults. They are also most likely to delay marriage, childbearing, and full-time employment. Youth who transition from high school to work (or to childbearing or other markers of adulthood) need the most help from high schools to successfully make the transition to adulthood, but these youth are often those who are the least integrated into the school environment. Along with education, marriage is one aspect of the transition to adulthood that has been studied more extensively among non-White groups (though research in this domain is still relatively scant). A majority of men and women do end up marrying, but individuals are approaching the institution with greater hesitancy and delaying marriage (Cherlin, 1992; Coontz, 2005; Goldscheider & Waite, 1991; Spain & Bianchi, 1996; Wu & Li, 2005). In the past, marriage and school attendance were seen as mutually exclusive; thus, adults who stay in school are likely to delay marriage. Although marriage rates have declined across the board, Blacks and lower-SES individuals are much less likely than their White and higher-SES counterparts to marry (Ellwood & Jencks, 2004). These disparities, along with the SES differences in educational attainment and achievement, ultimately end up reproducing class stratification.

7.7. **CONCLUSION**

Educational achievement (often measured as grades or test scores), educational attainment, and social and behavioral outcomes are not equally distributed across the population, with minority and immigrant groups generally having less favorable outcomes than their native-born White counterparts. Though the educational disadvantages faced by minority immigrant adolescents can be traced to many factors, parental SES plays a key role in the intergenerational transmission of disadvantage. When families have few economic resources, for example, parents are less likely to get involved in their children's schools, children are more likely to live in resource-poor neighborhoods and attend disadvantaged schools. In addition to the influence of families and schools in predicting outcomes in adolescence, youth's peers are also linked to their success or failure in the educational system.

Taken together, the literature reviewed in this chapter suggests that minority and immigrant adolescents experience the U.S. educational system very differently from their native-born White counterparts. Although research that considers race, ethnic, and immigrant status variation in educational experiences and outcomes has been increasing in recent years, there are at least two noteworthy gaps in this literature. First, very little research examines the schooling experiences of minority and immigrant adolescents. This is mostly a result of data limitations, as it is difficult to obtain a large, representative sample of adolescents who migrated from a particular country. Additionally, there is very little research that looks at how the transition to adulthood may be different for minority and immigrant youth, as compared to White youth. It is particularly important to understand the mechanisms underlying these divergent trajectories, as educational experiences in adolescence lay an important foundation for how individuals experience the transition to adulthood. These educational experiences, as well as how individuals make the transition to adulthood, have crucial implications for social, economic, and psychological well-being during adulthood.

REFERENCES

Adler, P., & Adler, P. (1998). *Peer power: Preadolescent culture and identity*. New Brunswick, NJ: Rutgers University Press.

Ainsworth-Darnell, J. M., & Downey, D. B. (1998). Assessing the oppositional culture explanation for racial/ethnic eifferences in school performance. *American Sociological Review*, *63*, 536–553.

Alba, R. D. (1990). *Ethnic identity: The transformation of white America*. New Haven, CT: Yale University Press.

Arnett, J. J. (2000). Emerging adulthood: A theory of development from the late teens through the twenties. *American Psychologist*, *55*(5), 469–480.

Aronowitz, M. (1984). The social and emotional adjustment of immigrant children: A review of the literature. *International Migration Review*, *18*(2), 237–257.

Baker, D. P., & Stevenson, D. L. (1986). Mothers' strategies for children's school achievement: Managing the transition to high school. *Sociology of Education*, *59*, 156–166.

Bronfenbrenner, U. (1979). *The ecology of human development: Experiments by nature and designs*. Cambridge, MA: Harvard University Press.

Bronfenbrenner, U., & Morris, P. A. (1998). The ecology of developmental processes. In W. Damon & R. M. Lerner (Eds.), *Handbook of child psychology, Vol. 1: Theoretical models of human development* (pp. 993–1028). New York, NY: Wiley.

Brooks-Gunn, J., Duncan, G. J., Klebanov, P. K., & Sealand, N. (1993). Do neighborhoods influence child and adolescent development? *American Journal of Sociology*, *99*(2), 353–395.

Brown, B. B. (1990). Peer groups and peer cultures. In S. S. Feldman & G. R. Elliott (Eds.), *At the threshold: The developing adolescent* (pp. 171–196). Cambridge, MA: Harvard University Press.

Bryk, A., Lee, V. E., & Holland, P. B. (1993). *Catholic high schools and the common good*. Cambridge, MA: Harvard University Press.

Buchmann, M. (1989). *The script of life in modern society: Entry into adulthood in a changing World*. Chicago, IL: University of Chicago Press.

Campbell, R. T. (1983). Status attainment research: End of the beginning or beginning of the end? *Sociology of Education*, *56*, 47–62.

Caplan, N., Choy, M. H., & Whitmore, J. K. (1997). *Children of the boat people: A study of educational success*. Ann Arbor, MI: University of Michigan Press.

Carter, P. (2005). *Keepin' it real: School success beyond black and white*. Oxford: Oxford University Press.

Charles, C. Z. (2003). The dynamics of racial residential segregation. *Annual Review of Sociology, 29*, 167–207.

Cherlin, A. J. (1992). *Marriage, divorce, remarriage*. Cambridge, MA: Harvard University Press.

Clark, M. L., & Ayers, M. (1992). Friendship similarity during early adolescence: Gender and racial patterns. *Journal of Psychology, 126*(4), 393–405.

Clark, R. (1983). *Family life and school achievement: Why poor black children succeed or fail*. Chicago, IL: The University of Chicago Press.

Coleman, J. S. (1961). *The adolescent society: The social life of the teenager and its impact on education*. New York, NY: The Free Press.

Coleman, J. S., & Hoffer, T. (1987). *Public and private high schools*. New York, NY: Basic Books.

Connolly, J., Furman, W., & Konarski, R. (2000). The role of peers in the emergence of heterosexual romantic relationships in adolescence. *Child Development, 71*(5), 1395–1408.

Cook, P. J., & Ludwig, J. (1998). The burden of 'Acting White': Do black adolescents disparage academic achievement? In C. Jencks & M. Phillips (Eds.), *The black-white test score gap* (pp. 375–400). Washington, DC: Brookings University Press.

Cook, T. S., Deng, Y., & Morgano, E. (2007). Friendship influences in early adolescence: The special role of friends' grade point average. *Journal of Research on Adolescence, 17*(2), 325–356.

Cookson, P., & Persell, C. (1985). *Preparing for power: America's Elite Boarding Schools*. New York, NY: Basic Books.

Coontz, S. (2005). *Marriage, a history: From obedience to intimacy, or how love conquered marriage*. New York, NY: Viking Press.

Corsaro, W. A., & Eder, D. (1990). Children's peer cultures. *Annual Review of Sociology, 16*, 197–220.

Cosa, T. L., & Alexander, K. L. (2007). (Dis)Advantage and the educational prospects of better off African American youth: How race still matters. *Teachers College Record, 109*(2), 285–321.

Crosnoe, R. (2001). Academic orientation and parental involvement in education during high school. *Sociology of Education, 74*, 210–230.

Crosnoe, R., Cavanaugh, S., & Elder, G. H. (2003). Adolescent friendships as academic resources: The intersection of friendship, race, and school disadvantage. *Sociological Perspectives, 46*(3), 331–352.

Crosnoe, R., Riegle-Crumb, C., Frank, K., & Muller, C. (2008). Peer group contexts of girls' and boys' academic experiences. *Child Development, 79*(1), 139–155.

D'Amico, A., & Cardaci, M. (2003). Relations among perceived self-efficacy, self-esteem, and school achievement. *Psychological Reports, 92*(1), 745–754.

Desimone, L. (1999). Linking parent involvement with student achievement: Do race and income matter? *The Journal of Educational Research, 93*, 11–30.

DiMaggio, P. (1982). Cultural capital and school success: The impact of status culture participation on the grades of U.S. high school students. *American Sociological Review, 47*, 189–201.

Domina, T. (2005). Leveling the home advantage: Assessing the effectiveness of parental involvement in elementary school. *Sociology of Education, 78*, 233–249.

Dornbusch, S. M. (1989). The sociology of adolescence. *Annual Review of Sociology, 15*, 233–259.

Dornbusch, S. M., Ritter, P. L., Leiderman, P. H., Roberts, D. F., & Fraleigh, M. F. (1987). The relation of parenting style to adolescent school performance. *Child Development, 58*(5), 1244–1257.

Duncan, G. J., & Raudenbush, S. W. (1999). Assessing the effects of context in studies of children and youth. *Educational Psychologist, 34*(1), 29–41.

Duncan, G. J., Yeung, W. J., Brooks-Gunn, J., & Smith, J. R. (1998). How much does childhood poverty affect the life chances of children? *American Sociological Review, 63*(3), 406–423.

Duncan, O. D., Haller, A. O., & Portes, A. (1968). Peer influences on aspirations: A reinterpretation. *American Journal of Sociology, 74*(2), 119–137.

Elder, G. (1974). *Children of the great depression: Social change in life experience*. Chicago, IL: The University of Chicago Press.

Elder, G. H., Jr., Johnson, M. K., & Crosnoe, R. (2003). The emergence and development of life course theory. In J. Mortimer & M. J. Shanahan (Eds.), *Handbook of the life course* (pp. 3–19). New York, NY: Kluwer Academic/Plenum Publishers.

Ellwood, D. T., & Jencks, C. (2004). The spread of single-parent families in the United States since 1960. In D. P. Moynihan, T. M. Smeeding, & L. Rainwater (Eds.), *The future of the family* (pp. 25–65). New York, NY: Russell Sage Foundation.

Englund, M. M., Luckner, A. E., Whaley, G. J. L., & Egeland, B. (2004). Children's achievement in early elementary school: Longitudinal effects of parental involvement, expectations, and quality of assistance. *Journal of Educational Psychology, 96*, 723–730.

Entwisle, D. R., Alexander, K. L., & Olson, L. S. (1997). *Children, schools, and inequality*. Boulder, CO: Westview Press.

Falbo, T., Lein, L., & Amador, N. A. (2001). Parental involvement during the transition to high school. *Journal of Adolescent Research, 16*, 511–529.

Farkas, G. (2003). Cognitive skills and noncognitive traits and behaviors in the stratification process. *Annual Review of Sociology, 29*, 541–562.

Fordham, S., & Ogbu, J. U. (1986). Black students' school success: Coping with the burden of 'Acting White'. *Urban Review, 18*, 176–206.

Fuligni, A. (1997). The academic achievement of adolescents from immigrant families: The roles of family background, attitudes and behavior. *Child Development, 68*, 351–363.

Furstenberg, F. F. (2008). The intersections of social class and the transition to adulthood. *New Directions for Child and Adolescent Development, 119*, 1–10.

Fussell, E., & Furstenberg, F. F. (2007). The transition to adulthood during the twentieth century: Race, nativity, and gender. In R. A. Settersten Jr.,

F. F. Furstenberg, & R. G. Rumbaut (Eds.), *On the frontier of adulthood: Theory, research and public policy* (pp. 29–75). Chicago, IL: University of Chicago Press.

Gecas, V. (1989). The social psychology of self-efficacy. *Annual Review of Sociology, 15*, 291–316.

Giordano, P. C. (2003). Relationships in adolescence. *Annual Review of Sociology, 29*, 257–281.

Glick, J. E., & White, M. J. (2003). The academic trajectories of immigrant youths: Analysis within and across cohorts. *Demography, 40*(4), 589–603.

Goldhaber, D. (1999). School choice: An examination of the empirical evidence on achievement, parental decision making, and equity. *Educational Researcher, 28*(9), 16–25.

Goldscheider, F. K., & Waite, L. J. (1991). *New families, no families? The transformation of the American home.* Berkeley, CA: University of California Press.

Gordon, M. M. (1964). *Assimilation in American life: The role of race, religion, and national origins.* New York, NY: Oxford University Press.

Gould, M. (2002). Race and theory: Culture, poverty, and adaptation to discrimination in Wilson and Ogbu. *Sociological Theory, 17*(2), 171–200.

Hallinan, M. T. (1988). Equality of educational opportunity. *Annual Review of Sociology, 14*, 249–268.

Harker, K. (2001). Immigrant generation, assimilation, and the adolescent psychological well-being. *Social Forces, 79*(3), 969–1004.

Haynie, D. L. (2001). Delinquent peers revisited: Does network structure matter? *American Journal of Sociology, 106*(4), 1013–1057.

Hoover-Dempsey, K. V., Bassler, O. C., & Brissie, J. S. (1987). Parent involvement: Contributions of teacher efficacy, school socioeconomic status, and other school characteristics. *American Educational Research Journal, 24*, 417–435.

Hoover-Dempsey, K. V., & Sandler, H. M. (1995). Parental involvement in children's education: Why does it make a difference? *Teacher's College Record, 97*, 310–331.

Jeynes, W. H. (2007). The relationship between parental involvement and urban secondary school student academic achievement: A meta-analysis. *Urban Education, 42*, 82–110.

Joyner, K., & Kao, G. (2000). School racial composition and adolescent racial homophily. *Social Science Quarterly, 81*(3), 810–825.

Joyner, K., & Laumann, E. O. (2000). Teenage sex and the sexual revolution. In O. Laumann & R. T. Michael (Eds.), *Sex, love, and health in America: Private choices and public policy* (pp. 41–71). Chicago, IL: University of Chicago Press.

Kandel, D. B. (1978). Homophily, selection, and socialization in adolescent friendships. *American Journal of Sociology, 84*(2), 427–436.

Kandel, D. B. (1980). Drug and drinking behavior among youth. *Annual Review of Sociology, 6*, 235–285.

Kao, G. (1995). Asian-Americans as model minorities? A Look at their academic performance. *American Journal of Education, 103*, 121–159.

Kao, G. (1999). Psychological well-being and educational achievement among immigrant youth. In D. J. Hernandez (Ed.), *Children of immigrants: Health, adjustment, and public assistance* (pp. 410–477). Washington, DC: National Academy Press.

Kao, G. (2004). Parental influences on the educational outcomes of immigrant youth. *International Migration Review, 38,* 427–450.

Kao, G., & Thompson, J. (2003). Race and ethnic stratification in educational achievement and attainment. *Annual Review of Sociology, 29,* 417–442.

Kao, G., & Tienda, M. (1995). Optimism and achievement: The educational performance of immigrant youth. *Social Science Quarterly, 76*(1), 1–19.

Lareau, A. (2000). *Home advantage: Social class and parental intervention in elementary education* (updated ed.). Lanham, MD: Rowan and Littlefield.

Lareau, A. (2003). *Unequal childhoods: Class, race, and family life.* Berkeley, CA: University of California Press.

Lee, S. J. (1996). *Unraveling the model minority stereotype: Listening to Asian American youth.* New York, NY: Teachers College Press.

Lee, V. E., & Burkam, D. T. (2002). *Inequality at the starting gate: Social background differences in achievement as children begin school.* Washington, DC: Economic Policy Institute.

Lewis, O. (1966). The culture of poverty. *Scientific American, 215,* 19–25.

Massey, D. S., & Denton, N. A. (1993). *American apartheid: Segregation and the making of the underclass.* Cambridge, MA: Harvard University Press.

McNeal, R. B., Jr, (1999). Parental involvement as social capital: Differential effectiveness on science achievement, truancy, and dropping out. *Social Forces, 78,* 117–144.

McPherson, M., Smith-Lovin, L., & Cool, J. M. (2001). Birds of a feather: Homophily in social networks. *Annual Review of Sociology, 27,* 415–444.

Moody, J. (2001). Race, school integration, and friendship segregation in America. *American Journal of Sociology, 107*(3), 679–716.

Muller, C. (1993). Parental involvement and academic achievement: An analysis of family resources available to the child. In B. Schneider & J. S. Coleman (Eds.), *Parents, their children, and schools* (pp. 77–131). Boulder, CO: Westview Press.

Muller, C., & Kerbow, D. (1993). Parent involvement in the home, school, and community. In B. Schneider & J. S. Coleman (Eds.), *Parents, their children, and schools.* Boulder, CO: Westview Press.

National Center for Education Statistics. (1997). *Digest of education statistics.* Washington, DC: Office of Educational Research and Improvement, U.S. Department of Education.

National Center for Education Statistics. (2002). *A profile of the American high school sophomore in 2002: Initial results from the base year of the education longitudinal study of 2002.* Washington, DC: U.S. Department of Education. http://nces.ed.gov/pubs2005/2005338.pdf

National Center for Education Statistics. (2007a). *Status and trends in the education of racial and ethnic minorities.* Washington, DC: U.S. Department of Education. http://nces.ed.gov/pubsearch/pubsinfo.asp?pubid=2007039

National Center for Education Statistics. (2007b). *The condition of education: 2007.* http://nces.ed.gov/fastfacts/display.asp?id=97

National Center for Education Statistics. (2007c). *America's charter schools: Results from the NAEP study.* http://nces.ed.gov/nationsreportcard/studies/charter/2005456.asp

Nord, C. W., & Griffin, J. A. (1999). Educational profile of 3- to 8-year-old children of immigrants. In D. J. Hernandez (Ed.), *Children of immigrants: Health, adjustment, and public assistance.* Washington, DC: National Academy Press.

O'Hare, W. (2004). *Trends in the well-being of America's children.* New York, NY/Washington, DC: Russell Sage Foundation/Population Reference Bureau.

Ogbu, J. U. (1978). *Minority education and caste: The American system in cross-cultural perspective.* New York, NY: Academic Press.

Ogbu, J. U. (1991). Immigrant and involuntary minorities in comparative perspective. In *Minority status and schooling: A comparative study of immigrant and involuntary minorities* (Chap. 1). NewYork, NY: Garland.

Osgood, D. W., Foster, E. M., Flanagan, C., & Ruth, G. R. (2005). *On your own without a net: The transition to adulthood for vulnerable populations.* Chicago, IL: University of Chicago Press.

Portes, A., & MacLeod, D. (1996). Educational progress of children of immigrants: The roles of class, ethnicity, and social context. *Sociology of Education, 69*(4), 255–275.

Portes, A., & Rumbaut, R. (2001). *Legacies: The story of the immigrant second generation.* Berkeley, CA: University of California Press.

Portes, A., & Rumbaut, R. (2006). *Immigrant America: A portrait* (3rd ed.). Berkeley, CA: University of California Press.

Rosenberg, M., Schooler, C., & Schoenbach, C. (1989). Self-esteem and adolescent problems: Modeling reciprocal effects. *American Sociological Review, 54*(6), 1004–1018.

Ross, C. E., & Broh, B. A. (2000). The roles of self-esteem and the sense of personal control in the academic achievement process. *Sociology of Education, 73*(4), 270–284.

Rumbaut, R. G., & Portes, A. (2001). *Ethnicities: Children of immigrants in America.* Berkeley, CA: University of California Press.

Ryan, A. M. (2000). Peer groups as a context for the socialization of adolescents' motivation, engagement, and achievement. *Educational Psychologist, 35,* 101–113.

Ryan, A. M. (2001). The peer group as a context for the development of young adolescent motivation and achievement. *Child Development, 72*(4), 1135–1150.

Sampson, R. J., Morenoff, J. D., & Gannon-Rowley, T. (2002). Assessing 'neighborhood effects': Social processes and new directions in research. *Annual Review of Sociology, 28,* 443–478.

Sewell, W. H., Haller, A. O., & Portes, A. (1969). The educational and early occupational attainment process. *American Sociological Review, 34,* 82–92.

Sewell, W. H., & Shah, V. P. (1968). Social class, parental encouragement, and educational aspirations. *American Journal of Sociology, 73,* 559–572.

Shanahan, M. J. (2000). Pathways to adulthood in changing societies: Variability and mechanisms in life course perspective. *Annual Review of Sociology, 26,* 667–692.

Spain, D., & Bianchi, S. M. (1996). *Balancing act: Motherhood, marriage, and employment among American women.* New York, NY: Russell Sage Foundation.

Steele, C. M. (1997). A threat in the air: How stereotypes shape intellectual identity and performance. *American Psychologist, 52,* 613–629.

Steele, C. M., & Aronson, J. (1995). Stereotype threat and the intellectual test performance of African Americans. *Journal of Psychology and Social Psychology, 69,* 797–811.

Steele, C. M., & Aronson, J. (1998). Stereotype threat and the test performance of academically successful African Americans. In C. Jencks & M. Phillips (Eds.), *The black-white test score gap* (pp. 375–400). Washington, DC: Brookings University Press.

Steinberg, L., Lamborn, S., Dornbusch, S., & Darling, N. (1992). Impact of parenting practices on adolescent achievement: Authoritative parenting, school involvement, and encouragement to succeed. *Child Development, 63*(5), 1266–1281.

Suarez-Orozco, C., & Suarez-Orozco, M. M. (2001). *Children of immigration.* Cambridge, MA: Harvard University Press.

Sui-Chi, E. H., & Willms, J. D. (1996). Effects of parental involvement on eighth-grade achievement. *Sociology of Education, 69,* 126–147.

Tse, L. (1996). Language brokering among Latino adolescents: Prevalence, attitudes, and school performance. *Hispanic Journal of Behavioral Sciences, 17,* 180–194.

Turney, K., & Kao, G. (2009a). Barriers to school involvement: Are immigrant parents disadvantaged? *The Journal of Educational Research, 102,* 257–271.

Turney, K., & Kao, G. (2009b). Assessing the private safety net: Social support among minority immigrant parents. *The Sociological Quarterly, 50*(4), 666–692.

Tyson, K., Darity, W., Jr., & Castellino, D. R. (2005). It's not 'A Black Thing': Understanding the burden of acting white and other dilemmas of high achievement. *American Sociological Review, 70*(4), 582–605.

U.S. Census Bureau. (2004a). *We the people: Asians in the United States: Census 2000 Special Reports.* Washington, DC: U.S. Census Bureau.

U.S. Census Bureau. (2004b). *We the people: Hispanics in the United States: Census 2000 Special Reports.*

U.S. Census Bureau. (2004c). *Educational attainment: 2000: Census 2000 brief.*

U.S. Census Bureau. (2005). *We the people: Blacks in the United States: Census 2000 Special Reports.*

U.S. Census Bureau. (2008). *An older and more diverse nation by midcentury.* http://www.census.gov/Press-Release/www/releases/archives/population/012496.html

Valenzuela, A., & Dornbusch, S. (1994). Familism and social capital in the academic achievement of Mexican origin and Anglo adolescents. *Social Science Quarterly, 75,* 18–36.

Vandell, D. L. (2000). Parents, peers, and other socializing influences. *Developmental Psychology, 36*(6), 699–710.

White, L. (1994). Coresidence and leaving home: Young adults and their parents. *Annual Review of Sociology, 20,* 81–102.

Wu, L. L., & Li, J. A. (2005). Marital and childbearing trajectories of American women: 50 years of social change (pp. 110–149). In R. A. Settersten, F. F. Furstenberg, & R. G. Rumbaut (Eds.), *On the frontier of adulthood: Theory, research, and public policy.* Chicago, IL: University of Chicago Press.

Zhou, M. (1997). Growing up American: The challenge confronting immigrant children and children of immigrants. *Annual Review of Sociology, 23,* 63–95.

Zhou, M., & Bankston, C.L., III (1998). *Growing up American: How Vietnamese children adapt to life in the United States.* New York, NY: Russell Sage Foundation.

Chapter 8

Foundations of faith

Lynn Bridgers
St. Norbert College, De Pere, WI

John Snarey
Emory University, Atlanta, GA

8.1. INTRODUCTION

Thus far, this unit on socialization processes has focused on contextual factors that enhance or impede positive outcomes during adolescence. The historical perspective has contributed to understanding the contemporary roles of technology, school, and church, along with providing a framework for understanding the impact of socialization processes on personal development. This chapter examines the role of faith and the impact of faith-based institutions as sources of support for adolescent development, in the broader context of the relationship between religious identity and culture. The chapter also looks at how institutionalized religion can serve as a source of support, a stressor in the process of adolescent development, or both. This examination begins with an exploration of how faith is defined and the role it plays in adolescent development. It then examines the array of faith-based institutions—from churches, mosques, and temples to religious schools and other religious organizations. When the paradoxical relationship of the adolescent to the faith-based institution is examined, it becomes clear that while religious institutions can and do provide unique venues for social and emotional support, many adolescents struggle with the confinement of religious doctrines in the stormy process of identity development. Finally this chapter explores selected social and cultural implications of the faith-based institution in adolescent development, including the interplay of religious identities in a diverse pluralistic landscape.

8.2. **ADOLESCENCE**

While the concept of adolescence as a distinct developmental period is widely accepted today, it is actually a fairly recent creation. As late as the nineteenth century, the human lifespan was simply divided into childhood and adulthood. The idea of an intervening stage of development is a relatively late arrival, most often associated with the work of psychologist G. Stanley Hall. Hall, sometimes called the "father of adolescence," influenced not only psychology and education through his extensive scholarly work, but also influenced popular American culture through public speaking and writing. As early as 1883, Hall was recognized as a leader in what was termed the "child-study" movement (Hall, 1883). Hall's exposure to Darwin's theory of evolution and the German physiological psychology of the time brought him to believe in a biologically based phylogenetic theory of human development. His two-volume work, *Adolescence: Its Psychology and Its Relations to Physiology, Anthropology, Sociology, Sex, Crime, Religion, and Education,* published in 1904, brought widespread recognition to the term adolescence and the corresponding concept of adolescence as a normal stage of development. Hall would further influence psychological thought in 1910, while serving as the president of Clark University, when he invited the then relatively unknown Sigmund Freud to present his theories of psychosexual development to the American public. Although introduced relatively recently, the concept of adolescence as a distinct stage in human development is now universally accepted.

Hall also influenced our understanding of the adolescent's relationship to faith-based institutions through the work of his student, Edwin D. Starbuck. While completing a master's degree at Harvard University, Starbuck worked with William James and became interested in religious experience, particularly conversion and the growth of religious commitment. Starbuck pursued his doctoral training at Clark University, where he worked with Hall. The results of his doctoral work at Clark, and his later work as a fellow in the same institution, were published in his 1899 book, *The Psychology of Religion.* Starbuck believed that conversion was largely an adolescent phenomenon and that incidents of conversion increased up to the age of 16, then became increasingly rare after 20 years of age. He also believed that conversion was related to the emotional turmoil believed to accompany the adolescent years. William James was greatly impressed by Starbuck's work. He included numerous references to Starbuck's studies in *The Varieties of Religious Experience,* and also wrote a preface for Starbuck's book (James, 1902; Starbuck, 1899). Subsequent scholarship has challenged whether conversion is solely an adolescent phenomena, but Starbuck's work is recognized as having made a substantial contribution to our understanding of religious experience in the lives of adolescents.

8.3. **DEFINING FAITH**

With the concept of adolescence widely accepted, an understanding of the role that faith and faith-based institutions play in the process of adolescent development requires a clear understanding of what one means by the nebulous term *faith*. For many people faith is synonymous with religious belief. For others it is a foundation for trust in a person or institution. For still others it is a reliance on positive outcomes, or unyielding belief in a providential future.

One of the researchers most strongly associated with studies of faith and development is James W. Fowler. In the early 1980s Fowler published *Stages of Faith*, in which he presented research that came to be known as Faith Development Theory (Fowler, 1981). In the introduction to that text Fowler asserts, "I believe faith is a human universal. We are endowed at birth with nascent capacities for faith. How these capacities are activated and grow depends to a large extent on how we are welcomed into the world and what kinds of environments we grow in" (Fowler, 1981, p. xiii). While influenced by the psychosocial developmental theory of Erik H. Erikson (1950) and, especially, the moral development theory of Lawrence Kohlberg (1984), Fowler's own theory gave greater attention to the role of the transcendent. Kohlberg and, especially, Erikson recognized the vital relevance of the sociocultural environment for an individual's development. Fowler also recognized the relevance of an individual's ultimate environment. "Faith," Fowler writes, "is interactive and social; it requires community, language, ritual and nurture. Faith is also shaped by the initiative from beyond us and other people, initiatives of spirit and grace. How these latter initiatives are recognized and imaged, or unperceived and ignored, powerfully affects the shape of faith in our lives" (1981, p. xiii).

Although well aware of the communal and social dimensions of faith, Fowler suggests that a working definition of faith must move beyond the simple equivalency of faith with religious belief. For Fowler, the faithful wrestle with "fidelities—and infidelities—to other persons and to the causes, institutions and transcending centers of value and power that constitute their lives' meanings" (1981, p. 16). Erikson also saw fidelity as an important component in both adolescent development and mature faith:

> *The specific strength emerging in adolescence—namely,* fidelity— *maintains a strong relation both to infantile trust and to mature faith. As it transfers the need for guidance from parental figures to mentors and leaders, fidelity eagerly accepts their ideological mediatorship—whether the ideology is one implicit in a "way of life" or a militantly explicit one (Erikson, 1998, p. 73).*

Fidelity, then, becomes foundational for mature faith and plays a critical role in the exploratory identifications of the adolescent. It is important to note that in Fowler's work, faith is not solely limited to religious belief, but is the fidelity one demonstrates to any chosen center of value and power. Given this perspective, faith still plays a critical role in the life of the individual, even one with no specific religious belief, if that individual remains committed to a specific social or political institution, or to a particular set of values. Similarly, as adolescent faith emerges from the matrix of a family's interpersonal dynamics and traditional religious belief, it can be directed to religion or redirected to social movements, peer values, or alternative spiritual perspectives.

8.4. **FAITH IN ADOLESCENT DEVELOPMENT**

Central to the developmental tasks of adolescence is the formation and integration of identity. In his psychosocial theory of development, Erikson framed the critical developmental challenge of adolescence as the achievement of ego identity versus role confusion (Erikson, 1950, p. 261). With the advent of genital maturity, in the midst of physiological changes and emotional transitions, the developing adolescent must achieve a stable form of ego identity, grounded in both individual and communal processes. First, as an individual, the adolescent must re-examine previously accepted identifications—retaining some and rejecting others as no longer viable. Second, the community must offer some form of recognition of the emerging identity of the adolescent, accepting that identity and indicating that it is worthy of communal trust.

The struggle of the adolescent to achieve a stable ego identity comes with significant risks. The opposite of identifying with a specific religious role or theological position is rejecting it or repudiating it. The adolescent must stubbornly resist any values which seem contrary to the self. This can manifest in a form of passive resistance or in outright defiance. Another danger is the adoption of a negative identity, when the adolescent consciously adopts roles, values, and ideologies that are socially unacceptable yet is determined to maintain them.

While identity is central in adolescent development, the relationship between identity and faith is complex. Fowler adopts a triadic structure first set forth by H. Richard Niebuhr to characterize the complexity of relationships between identity and faith (Fowler, 1981, pp. 19-23; Niebuhr, 1960). Niebuhr proposed the terms polytheism, henotheism, and radical monotheism to describe three faith-identity relationships. Polytheism suggests a diverse pattern of faith and identity, where no single center becomes the dominant belief. Henotheism, as Fowler describes it, characterizes "a pattern of faith and identity in which one invests deeply in a transcending center of value and power, finding in it a focal unity of personality and outlook, but this center is … not something of ultimate concern" (1981, p. 20). Finally, Fowler sees radical monotheism as "a type of faith-identity relation in which a person or group focuses its supreme trust and loyalty in a transcendental center of value and power, that is neither a conscious or unconscious extension of personal or group ego nor a finite cause or institution" (1981, p. 23).

Since the establishment of identity is commonly in flux during adolescent development, it may reflect all three of these faith-identity relationships. Without grounding in a specific faith tradition, the adolescent's exploration of religious possibilities can result in a transitional or permanent form of polytheism, in which the person shifts rapidly from one ideological identification to another. Henotheism can emerge in an entrenched fixation on a musical group, sporting activity, fashion, or a specific group of peers. At the same time, faith-based institutions will strive to produce a grounded form of radical monotheism in the adolescent who attends.

8.5. **DEFINING FAITH-BASED INSTITUTIONS**

With the establishment of the White House Office of Faith-Based and Community Initiatives and Centers for Faith-Based and Community, 11 federal agencies were directed to strengthen and expand the role of faith-based and community initiatives in providing social services in the United States. This public policy shift has brought the role of faith-based institutions that sponsor these initiatives into greater public awareness. In general, however, the public understanding of the term "faith" in this regard is not the inclusive one advocated by Fowler and described above. Rather, most Americans understand faith-based institutions as those clearly aligned with specific religious organizations—namely, religious congregations and the traditions, organizations, and beliefs they represent.

The tendency to equate faith-based institutions solely with religious congregations underestimates the breadth and diversity of faith-based institutions operating today. In addition to the different forms of common congregational worship—churches, mosques, meeting houses, and temples—faith-based institutions also include the governing bodies or organizational infrastructures of religious traditions (such as the diocesan structure and United States Conference of Catholic Bishops in the Roman Catholic tradition), the widespread prevalence of religious schools, and numerous other religious organizations, including volunteer groups and youth organizations, nonprofit organizations and agencies (such as Jewish Family Services or Catholic Charities), and religious media (including music, radio, publishing, and the Internet). With this understanding, the context for any evaluation of the impact of faith-based institutions on adolescent development extends beyond the role congregational communities play. Each of these groups—religious congregations, governing bodies, religious schools, and other organizations—can deeply affect adolescents during this formative period of their lives. A brief description of the forms each of these types of institutions take follows.

8.6. CHURCHES, MOSQUES, AND TEMPLES

The Association of Religion Data Archives reports the results of a national survey of the activities and finances of religious congregations. The survey was done to provide information about religious organizations as part of a larger national survey of the activities and finances of private, nonprofit, charitable organizations in the United States. The study found 257,648 such places of worship listed in telephone directories, including churches, congregations, synagogues, temples, and other places of formal religious worship (Independent Sector, 1993).

Religious congregations in the United States today represent a wide spectrum of world religions as well as Catholic and Protestant denominations. The U.S. Religious Landscape Survey, for instance, identified the four largest groups of religious affiliation as Evangelical Protestant Churches (26.3%), Roman Catholic (23.9%), Mainline Protestant Churches (18.1%), and Historically Black Churches (6.9%). Those with no religious affiliation also represent a sizeable group (16.1%). Buddhist, Hindu, Jewish, Jehovah's Witness, Mormon, and Russian and Greek Orthodox traditions each made a small but quite significant contribution to the religious landscape of the United States (Pew Forum on Religion & Public Life, 2008). These figures can be considered fairly representative of the diversity of adolescent engagement with religious congregational bodies as well.

Most of these congregations offer some form of religious education for adolescents. Often classes are offered before or after liturgical ceremonies that train children and adolescents in the formal doctrines of the faith tradition, its history, and its sacred texts. In addition, many religious congregations sponsor youth programs that are specifically designed to engage the adolescents in their community.

8.7. **GOVERNING BODIES**

The governing bodies or organizational infrastructures maintained by various denominational and religious groups are also important faith-based institutions, given their role in directing the religious education and formation of adolescents. One of the most visible of these is the diocesan structure of the Roman Catholic Church and its governing body, the United States Conference of Catholic Bishops (USCCB). The United States is home to 194 dioceses and archdioceses, which serve an estimated American Catholic population of 61 million persons. The USCCB directs religious education of adolescents not only through its formal programs of catechesis, but also through the promulgation of Catholic social teachings, publication of church documents, evangelization, and ministries specifically directed toward family life and teaching of sexual morality.

Another organizational infrastructure, the Southern Baptist Convention, now represents over 16 million members and has the largest number of churches in the country, 42,000. The Convention also directs a network of local associations, state conventions, and fellowships. In 2007 alone the North American Mission Board of the Southern Baptist Convention sent out 5081 missionaries, helped to start over 1700 new churches, and baptized 415,000 people as new members.

Similar organizational infrastructures exist for many of the mainline Protestant churches, including the General Conference of the United Methodist Church, the Lutheran Church–Missouri Synod, the General Convention of the Episcopal Church, and the General Assembly of the Presbyterian Church (USA).

8.8. **RELIGIOUS SCHOOLS**

Over 700 religious colleges and universities operate in the United States, and the number of Evangelical undergraduate institutions has risen dramatically in the last decade. Silverstein and Olsen, writing for the *Los Angeles Times*, report, "According to the Council for Christian Colleges & Universities, the nation's largest umbrella organization for evangelical undergraduate institutions, U.S. enrollment at its schools climbed 26.6 percent from 1997 to 2002, to 215,593" (2003).

In addition, many religious traditions operate elementary and secondary schools. The Catholic Church alone operates over 8000 such schools across the nation. "Approximately 85 percent of all private school students attend schools affiliated with religious organizations, and about 50 percent of all private school students attend Catholic schools" (Private Education in the

United States, 2009). Another 34% of students in private schools attend non-Catholic religious schools. Many of these are conservative Christian schools and are sometimes affiliated with a specific congregational body or church. Other Christian traditions—including the Seventh-Day Adventists, Baptists, Lutherans, Episcopalians, and Quakers—also have established a sizeable number of religious elementary or high schools.

While schools such as these are required to meet the standards of education set by the local educational authorities, religion is incorporated into the educational process and curriculum in a variety of ways. Some schools offer religious instruction on a daily basis, while others offer a more traditional curriculum that is enriched with religious study or participation. Many of the schools actively foster a specific religious identity, associated with the affiliated religious tradition, including specialized training of instructors for the school and information about the tradition's history and key figures are part of the curriculum. Almost all consider their approach and curriculum as a balance to the secular model that prevails in the nation's public schools and popular media.

8.9. OTHER RELIGIOUS ORGANIZATIONS

In addition to congregational communities, their governing bodies, and religious schools, religious traditions have an impact on adolescent development through volunteer groups and youth organizations, nonprofit organizations and agencies, and religious media. These added dimensions of faith-based institutions often target adolescents specifically and gear their efforts toward having a lasting impact on youth.

8.9.1. Volunteer groups and youth organizations

Many congregations sponsor volunteer group activities to encourage adolescents to give back to the needy or to the communities in which they live. These can be informal, one-time events or long-term programs, encouraging young people to live out religious virtues of charity and empathy for the plight of others. A team of sociologists at University of North Carolina in Chapel Hill found a strong positive correlation between students who attended religious services on a weekly basis and the amount of time spent volunteering in their communities. "In analyzing 1996 data from the Monitoring the Future (MTF) survey, a nationally representative survey of U.S. high school students, researchers found that nearly 17 percent of 12th graders who attend religious services weekly or more also volunteer their time in their communities weekly or more often. Only 7 percent of those who never attend church volunteer with the same frequency" (Smith, Smith, & Denton, 2005, p. 10). Since the amount of time spent in volunteer work was more than double for students who attended religious service over those who did not, it is clear that many congregational communities support volunteer work among adolescent members of their communities—whether explicitly through established programs or implicitly through living out the ideals of the religious tradition.

Additionally, many religious congregations and denominations have local or national youth organizations that specifically minister to adolescent members of their congregation and/or advocate for them in terms of denominational resources and further development of youth ministry programs. These include such diverse organizations as the National Federation of Catholic Youth Ministry, the Episcopal Ministries with Young People, the United Methodist National Youth Ministry Organization, the Presbyterian Youth Connection, the YouthScape ministry of the Southern Baptist Convention, the National Conference of Synagogue Youth, United Synagogue Youth, the Muslim Student Association, the Friends Youth (evangelical Quakers) and the Young Friends (liberal Quakers).

Some religious or denominational streams emphasize the provision of educational resources and resources for those actively involved in direct ministry to youth, while others use youth organizations as an opportunity for adolescents to come into direct contact with one another, focusing on the development of leadership and spiritual formation in the context of conferences for high school students, short-term missions, or fellowship-building activities.

8.9.2. **Nonprofit organizations and agencies**

Some denominational or religious traditions have established nonprofit organizations or agencies for their charitable activities. While a wide scope of services come under the umbrella of such organizations, many of the programs are specifically targeted toward the well-being of children and youth. Catholic Charities provides social support services, educational enrichment programs, socialization and neighborhood services, services for at-risk populations, as well as counseling and mental health services. Jewish Family Service provides services in support of children and families, including child abuse advocacy, counseling, divorce mediation, foster care and parenting as well as opportunities for volunteer work in a myriad of local programs. While such organizations may not be targeted exclusively toward adolescents or young people, tens of thousands of young people benefit from their activities each year through programs that address family, housing, immigration, legal advocacy, counseling, or other services. They also serve as a vital model for the spiritual values of compassion and charity in the face of dire need within specific communities, demonstrating to adolescents the need to do more than give lip service to the central tenets of religious belief.

8.9.3. **Religious media**

A final aspect of the influence of faith-based institutions on adolescent development can be found in religious media, including music, radio programming, publishing, and Internet services.

Religious music is not popular in all faith traditions, but Christian music has expanded dramatically in the last few years, and is now the sixth most popular form of music (Riley-Katz, 2006). Christian music has long been available in the form of gospel music, but now includes Christian contemporary music, Christian rock, and even Christian heavy metal. One popular Christian music artist, Carman, had an audience of 71,000 people attend a concert at Texas Stadium in Dallas, Texas (Saunders, 1997). Given the relative importance of music to adolescents, addressed below, it is clear that significant numbers of adolescents are absorbing religious values from listening to Christian music. The popularity of Christian music has expanded, in part, due to the dramatic increase in religious radio programming.

The National Religious Broadcasters, an international association of Christian communicators, reports that 46% of American adults listen to Christian radio broadcasts in a given month (Powers, 2008). Between 2000 and 2005 the number of Christian radio stations broadcasting in the country grew by 14% (Powers, 2008). Based on statistical data collected by Arbitron, Inc., those listening to Christian radio are 19% more likely to have children than the typical American, indicating that sizeable numbers of children and young adults are hearing Christian radio broadcasts in their homes.

Religious publishing has also grown considerably in the last decade. In 1996, publisher Werner Mark Linz estimated that the American public spent $2 billion a year on religious books, and religious books made up between 5% and 10% of the American book market (Linz, 1996). Since that time book sales have increased dramatically. Rick Warren's book *The Purpose Driven Life* has sold 16 million copies. The Book Industry Study Group (2005) reports "*Book Industry TRENDS 2005* estimates total publishers' net revenues in 2004 reached $28.6 billion, up 2.8 percent over the previous year [and] predicts that over the next five years total book industry revenues will increase 18.3 percent, paced by religious books with a 50 percent rise" (2005).

The number of these books read by adolescents is clearly a smaller percentage, but adolescents are affected not only by print reading but by the use of Internet resources with religious content. Almost a decade ago, Magnuson (1999) estimated that as many as two million children in American were being home schooled. Dozens of Internet companies have emerged that provide curricula for parents home schooling their children. More recently, researchers for the National Study of Youth and Religion (Smith, Pearce, Clark, & Longest, 2008a) found that 92% of Jewish teens and 91% of Protestant teens have access to the Internet. The number falls to 80% for both Black Protestant and Catholic teens. "There are no consistent parent and teen practices with regard to the Internet across the religious traditions analyzed," reports the lead investigator, Smith. "Mormon teens, for instance, have very high access to Internet but also high parental monitoring and low hourly use per week. But teens from other groups with relatively high parental monitoring also spend about the national average of time on the Internet" (Smith, Pearce, Clark, & Longest, 2008b). Research completed by Gardyn and Fetto (2000) indicated that 16% of teens said that the Internet would serve as a substitute for their current church-based religious experience in the next 5 years, with 31% of Black teens and 8% of White teens reporting this. Few studies are available, but these numbers have increased in the years since this demographic study was completed. As Lutz and Borgman (2002) conclude, "Given the finding that religious Websites are seeing more and more activity (although that activity is not broken down by age-group), one may reasonably infer that the number of teens who use the Internet to access religious information is increasing and will continue to do so" (p. 150).

8.10. FAITH-BASED INSTITUTIONS AS SUPPORT FOR ADOLESCENT DEVELOPMENT

To understand the role of the above faith-based institutions in supporting adolescent development, one must first recall the developmental needs of the adolescent. Adolescence is a time of transition, on multiple levels. The adolescent is between childhood and adulthood. Their bodies are changing with the onset of sexual maturity. Their sense of independence is increasing, as they begin to shift identifications from the family to the outside world. Their ability to conceptualize has changed dramatically with the onset of the cognitive ability to conceptualize and think abstractly rather than strictly relying on the concrete (Piaget, 1968).

Cognitive theorist Jean Piaget indicates that formal operational thought first becomes possible at the age of 11 or 12, when "logical operations begin to be transposed from the plane of concrete manipulation to the ideational plane" (Piaget, 1968, p. 62). This hypothetical deductive form of thought "permits one to draw conclusions from pure hypotheses and not merely from actual observations" (p. 63). So central is this shift in the ability to abstract that Piaget concludes "only after the inception of formal thought, at around eleven or twelve, can the mental systems that characterize adolescence be constructed" (p. 63). The ability to generate and consider a variety of theoretical possibilities, of course, also allows adolescents from religious families to think through and question the theological and behavioral doctrines of their inherited religious traditions.

The same changes in the ability to conceptualize—to think abstractly and explore different hypothetical perspectives—can also result in a shift in perspective taking. Fowler notes how "the adolescent shows both a marked improvement in taking the perspectives of others and a tendency to an overconfident distortion of others' perspectives through over-assimilation of them into his or her own" (1981, p. 71). As the capacity for abstraction increases, adolescents become aware not only of their own view of themselves, but increasingly build up ideas about how others view them and use these ideas to shape their own morality. As Fowler puts it, "I see you seeing me; I construct the me I think you see" (1981, p. 72). He associates this change in perspective with the third of his stages of faith development, which he terms Synthetic-Conventional faith. Synthetic-Conventional faith is characterized by "mutual interpersonal expectations, relationships and interpersonal conformity. In stage three moral actions are right if they conform to the expectations of one's 'significant others'" (p. 74).

Recognizing this shift in perspective taking helps one to understand the vital importance of peers and social interaction during adolescence. Adolescents, as Erikson notes, "are sometimes morbidly, often curiously, preoccupied with what they appear to be in the eyes of others as compared with what they feel they are, and with the question of how to connect the roles and skills cultivated earlier with the ideal prototypes of the day" (1968, p. 128).

This process of connection also demonstrates some of the vulnerabilities that adolescents have as they navigate the world between childhood and adulthood. In childhood they have lived in a world of imagination, imagining what they might become when they "grow up." Adolescence is marked instead by the growth of fidelity. The adolescent develops a "willingness to put his [or her] trust in those peers and leading, or misleading, elders who will give imaginative, if not illusory, scope to his [or her] aspirations. . ." (Erikson, 1968, p. 129).

By understanding the conceptual shift that comes with the advent of formal operational thought, the interpersonal conformity that characterizes Fowler's third stage and the fidelity that characterizes Erikson's fifth psychosexual stage, we can better understand the role faith-based institutions provide in support of adolescent development.

8.10.1. **Religious congregations**

As the adolescent moves into formal operational thought, he or she is better able to understand the doctrinal positions of the religious tradition in which the congregation is grounded. With an increased ability for abstract reflection and hypothetical positions, the adolescent moves beyond simply learning Bible stories—as in the second of Fowler's stages, the Mythic-Literal stage of faith. The adolescent now has the cognitive capacity to reflect on questions of morality, to formulate his or her own positions on religious subjects, and to consider diverse routes to salvation. While most congregations offer more sophisticated intellectual content in religious education for adolescents, perhaps the greatest contribution congregations have in support of adolescent development in church or temple is found in related social opportunities.

Religious educators have long recognized the importance of socialization for the adolescent on two levels. For personal identity to become integrated and for social perspective taking to develop, the adolescent needs relatively unstructured social opportunities to engage with others. This engagement also must take place on two levels—with adults and with peers. First, the adolescent must be offered adult role models on which to base his or her aspirations. These can come in the form of historical figures, such as the founders of religious traditions, or through interaction with older members of the same congregation—the pastor, rabbi, or the ministry staff. The majority of adolescents report having relationship with nonfamily adults in the context of religious participation. Jewish teenagers report the highest level of nonfamily relationships (92%), and Catholics report the lowest (62%) (Smith et al., 2005, p. 60). Although not all reported having such relations, the majority in all traditions said "they wish they did" (Smith et al., 2005, p. 61). The adults in such relationships not only provide role models for adolescents, but also become someone they can turn to when they are seeking aid, advice, or support. Drawing on the research on the National Study of Youth and Religion, scholars Smith and colleagues concluded that "religious organizations thus appear to help foster cross-generational ties for large numbers of U.S. teenagers, ties we would expect to help legitimize and reinforce the religious faith and practices of those teens" (p. 61).

The second type of needed social engagement involves opportunities to interact with peers. Youth groups can provide the best opportunity for such interaction. In fact, one researcher concluded of all the organized activities teens participate in, faith-based youth groups provide the highest proportion of personal and interpersonal growth experiences. After completing a study of 2280 11th-grade students, Reed W. Larson, Endowed Chair of Family Resiliency at the University of Illinois, concluded "Faith-based youth groups give teens rich opportunities for identity development, learning to regulate their emotions, and developing positive relationships with peers and meaningful connections with adults" (Larson, Hansen, & Moneta, 2006, p. 852). The growth experiences associated with religious youth groups included identity work, initiative development, emotional regulation, teamwork and social skills, positive relationships with peers, and positive relationships with adults, which they asserted was "because these groups—whether at church, synagogue, or mosque—provide a positive belief system that addresses the issues that teens struggle with" (p. 852). They further concluded that "Faith-based groups give teens the opportunity for self-exploration, discussing values, and figuring out where they fit in the world. This doesn't happen as often in other settings" (p. 852).

Youth groups are widely available and accessible to adolescents, although the structure and content of such groups vary widely among different religious traditions or denominations. Smith (Smith et al., 2005) reports "nearly 70 percent of all teens attend a religious congregation that also sponsors a youth group; fully 85 percent of teens who attend religious services belong to congregations with youth groups" (p. 52). Smith also reports that 69% of all teenagers are either currently members of a religious youth group or have been members at some time in the past (Smith et al., 2005, p. 52). The types of activities offered vary widely, but include icebreakers, study of sacred texts, recreational opportunities such as camping, discussion groups, and groups built around media or specific events.

8.10.2. **Governing bodies**

Many of the governing bodies or organizational infrastructures of religious traditions also contribute to meeting the developmental needs of adolescents. Some have published specific programs or guidelines to shape youth ministry within their congregations. One example of the same is a document published by the United States Conference of Catholic Bishops (1997), which names youth ministry a "top concern in our parish communities" (1997). Building on research by The Search Institute, the bishops frame their response through a process of developmental "asset building." They assert:

- Asset development begins at birth and needs to be sustained throughout childhood and adolescence.
- Asset building depends on building positive relationships with children and adolescents, and requires a highly consistent community in which they are exposed to clear messages about what is important.
- Families can and should be the most powerful generators of developmental assets.
- Assets are more likely to blossom if they are nurtured simultaneously by families, schools, youth organizations, neighborhoods, religious institutions, health care providers, and in the informal settings in which adults and youth interact.
- Everyone in a community has a role to play (USCCB, 1997).

Besides offering practical direction for ministry within the church, the bishops believe that ministry with adolescents needs to be more comprehensive and grounded in the larger community, again emphasizing the social dimensions of adolescent faith formation.

In addition to efforts by the bishops, Pope John Paul II emphasized the importance of supporting adolescent development through the establishment of World Youth Day in 1986. The most recent World Youth Day was billed as the "largest youth event in the world." Held in Sydney, Australia, in July of 2008, the event, which included a visit from Pope Benedict XVI, attracted 223,000 pilgrims, with representatives from 170 different nations.

The needs of Jewish youth have been met for over 80 years by the B'nai B'rith Youth Organization (BBYO). Founded in 1923, the BBYO helps adolescents to develop their leadership potential, foster a positive Jewish identity, and pursue personal development (B'nai B'rith, 2008). Their programs include religious services, interfaith activities, seminars, performing arts, and athletics. With approximately 20,000 members, it is one of the world's largest youth organizations. The organization implements a youth leadership model in which leadership for the program is drawn from its membership. Elections are held semiannually at the local, regional, and international levels. Those elected make decisions as to specific programming, but BBYO has consistently demonstrated a commitment to community service, social action, and a pluralistic approach to Jewish life.

Most Christian Protestant denominations have youth organizations, youth ministry programs, or both. Examples include the United Methodist Youth Organization, Adventist Youth Ministries, the Alliance Youth Fellowship, the Lutheran Youth Organization, the Baptist Youth Mission, and many others. These organizations and ministries support adolescent development by planning events for adolescents to meet one another, sponsoring service programs, and fostering religious identity in the given denominational tradition.

8.10.3. **Religious schools**

Research seems mixed on the benefits of attending a religious school during adolescence. Proponents of religious schools suggest that there are strong benefits. In addition to the religious or moral dimensions of the educations offered, they cite smaller school size, smaller class size, and greater attention from educators among the benefits of attending a private religious school. In addition many argue that religious schools provide a better quality of education and have higher graduation rates than public schools.

Given the number of students that attend religious schools, it is certain that parents perceive benefits, because, after all, parents are undertaking the additional cost of private schooling. The largest system of religious schools in the United States is the Catholic school system, which educates 2.5 million students in over 8000 schools (Donovan, 2003). The largest Protestant school system is run by the Seventh-Day Adventist Church, which has 1049 schools and 65,000 students in North America (Christian School, 2008). Millions of American parents clearly perceive some benefit from having children attend private religious schools.

Religious schools, as faith-based institutions, have a substantial impact on adolescent development and socialization when they provide a primary learning environment for particular adolescents. It is estimated that students spend half of their waking hours in a school environment. Thus a large part of their social interaction will take place in the context of a school. Depending on admission criteria for individual schools, students may encounter a more homogenous student population, which can influence identity formation. Given the extent to which peer groups influence adolescent development, it may help establish a certain framework of moral values and acceptable behaviors.

One study by Cohen-Zada (2006) of Ben-Gurion University indicated that the decision to send children to religious schools was often related to minority status. His study suggests that "when the share of the minority in the local population grows—and outside influences become less threatening—the demand for separate religious schooling among the members of the religious group decreases. This pattern implies concavity in this relationship between enrollment in private and religious schooling and the share of the religious group in the population" (p. 372). While parents often choose religious schools in an attempt to preserve ethnic or religious identity, interestingly other studies (Bertram-Troost, de Roos, & Miedema, 2006, p. 313; Sanders, 1998) suggest the strongest predictors of an adolescent's religious identification will be the beliefs of the parents themselves. If parents practice what they preach, that is, they will have less need to rely on a religious school. One such study, conducted in the Netherlands on the effects of schools and religious backgrounds of adolescents and their parents, found that differences in religious commitments and exploration among adolescents could be best explained by the worldview adopted by the students themselves and the importance of that worldview to their parents (Bertram-Troost et al., 2006, p. 313).

8.10.4. **Other organizations**

Another dimension of faith-based institutions supporting adolescent development includes volunteer groups and youth organizations, nonprofit organizations and agencies, and religious media.

Volunteer groups and youth organizations

Volunteer groups and youth organizations within different religious and denominational branches support adolescent development in a variety of ways, as they provide additional avenues of socialization in which adolescents can interact with one another in relatively unstructured environments. Working together on a service project, doing fund-raising for an event, or participating in religiously sponsored camping, retreats, or recreational activities gives adolescents an opportunity to make new friends, deepen existing relationships, and learn more about their communities and the needs of others in those communities.

Smith et al. (2005) found that "an average of about one half of all teens' five closest friends held religious beliefs similar to those of the teens" (p. 57). Smith et al. also found that one out of five of teens' closest friends were participating in the same religious groups as the teens themselves. These numbers were slightly higher for Mormon youth, Black youth, and conservative Protestant youth. They concluded, ". . .religious teenagers tend to make most of the best friendships with other religious teens, and nonreligious teenagers tend to make most of the friendships with nonreligious teens. Religious and nonreligious identities thus tend to cluster around and be reinforced by close friendship networks" (p. 58). Volunteer groups and youth organizations give adolescents the opportunity to spend time with other adolescents with similar religious backgrounds and assumptions, which supports not only the formation of religious identity but peer identity as well.

8.10.5. **Nonprofit organizations and agencies**

Faith-based nonprofit organizations and agencies also support adolescent development in a variety of ways. Many sponsor programs that are directly targeted toward adolescents or their families. Catholic Charities is the largest private network of social service organizations in many parts of the United States (Catholic Charities, 2008). The services offered by Catholic Charities vary from city to city, in response to local needs. Examples of programs for adolescents include the provision of counseling services for adolescents, services to support pregnant adolescents, housing for emotionally disturbed adolescents, and programs targeting at-risk youth. Similarly, Jewish Family Service offers clinical, psychological, and psychiatric services for troubled adolescents, programs for intervention in family violence, support for adolescent grief and illness, and programs for adolescents coping with divorce or eating disorders. Baptist Children's Services provides housing for pregnant teens, residential programs for abused, neglected and dependent teenagers, and services to at-risk adolescents.

The services offered to adolescents through faith-based nonprofits and agencies are particularly important, as in many communities they are the provider of last resort, serving those who could not otherwise afford legal representation, mental health services, housing, and health care. They also serve as an emergency safety net for adolescents in homes that are marred by violence or neglect.

8.10.6. **Religious media**

Religious media are playing an increasingly important role in adolescent development. One study, conducted by Donald Roberts and Peter Christianson found that "music is central to youth culture" (O'Toole, 1997). Christenson and Roberts found that music was more influential in the lives of teens than movies, television, or Internet usage, given the estimated 4-5 h a day that American teenagers listen to music or watch music videos. They conclude "Music matters to adolescents, and they cannot be understood without a serious consideration of how it fits into their lives" (O'Toole, 1997). In addition to emulating the models musicians provide, the researchers note, "adolescents also use music to gain information about the adult world, to withdraw from social contact (such as using a Walkman as a barrier, not unlike an adult hiding behind a newspaper at the breakfast table), to facilitate friendships and social settings, or to help them create a personal identity" (O'Toole, 1997).

With the expansion of the Christian music market, and in light of parental concerns about music's influence, an increasing number of teens are listening to music that deliberately avoids references to drugs, sexuality, or violence (Roberts, Christianson, & Gentile, 2003). Christian music markets are also becoming more tolerant of crossover musicians who operate in both contemporary pop and Christian markets. Christian radio networks have not failed to notice the popularity of Christian music among youth. Frank Breeden, former president of the Christian Music Trade Association, noted a shift in radio programming in 2001. "We have had to promote our albums through touring, personal appearances. But in the last year, two major Christian radio networks have aggressively acquired stations in major markets, and are beginning to program them with contemporary Christian music" (Morris, 2001). Those two networks added 30 new stations in an 18-month period. Thus adolescents are able to access Christian music through radio as well as other forms of music distribution, and the distinction between Christian and secular pop is becoming increasingly blurred.

The Pew Internet and American Life study reported that the number of teenagers using the Internet had risen 24% between 2000 and 2004 and that by 2004, 87% of those between the ages of 12 and 17 were using the Internet (Pew, 2007). Adolescents use the Internet for numerous purposes other than schoolwork or research, and some use it extensively. Pew reports, "There is a subset of teens who are super-communicators— teens who have a host of technology options for dealing with family and friends, including traditional landline phones, cell phones, texting, social network sites, instant messaging, and email. They represent about 28% of the entire teen population and they are more likely to be older girls" (Pew, 2007). Adolescent use of the Internet for socialization and communication not only fosters peer group association and identification, but also means adolescents are more comfortable with the media and more likely to use the Internet in their interactions with faith-based institutions as well.

Faith-based institutions foster adolescent development in numerous ways—through religious congregations and their governing bodies, through religious schools, through nonprofit organizations and agencies, and through the growing exposure to religious media. But faith-based institutions also have significant limitations in supporting the process of adolescent development.

8.11. **LIMITATIONS OF FAITH-BASED INSTITUTIONS**

Every parent who has heard an adolescent respond to a question with "whatever..." knows the frustrations involved in confronting adolescent apathy. Adolescent apathy can also impact the effectiveness of faith-based institutions in responding to adolescent development. Christian Smith, in a lecture at Brigham Young University, reminded his listeners that in terms of social structure religious faith is in a relatively weak position in American life today. Faith traditions were once central to community life. Today, however, they must compete for adolescent time and attention in the context of more immediate demands such as school, sports, interpersonal relationships, and media. Many "youth today have adopted a kind of religious apathy," says Smith. "American youth tend to assume an instrumental view of religion, with individual desire or wish being what drives 'what's going to be done with religion'" (Williams, 2008).

As the adolescent tries to figure out "what's going to be done with religion," he or she is still moving through the changing interior landscape of identity formation. Fowler suggests that most adolescents are in the third of his stages of faith, which he terms Synthetic-Conventional faith. At this stage, authority is usually externalized. Fowler writes:

> *For Stage 3, with its beginnings in adolescence, authority is located externally to the self. It resides in the interpersonally available 'they' or in the certified incumbents of leadership roles in institutions. This is not to deny that adolescents make choices or that they develop strong feelings and commitments regarding their values and behavioral norms. It is to say, however, that despite their genuine feelings of having made choices and commitments, a truer reading is that their values and self-images, mediated by significant others in their lives, have largely chosen them (1981, p. 154).*

This dependence on externalized authority can also bring resistance. The dependence created by this stage of development can be interpreted as what Parks called the "tyranny of the they" (1980). Resistant to their dependence on others, the adolescent's Synthetic-Conventional faith can become mired in ambivalence. "On the one hand there is an awareness of dependence and the paramount importance of connectedness. On the other hand, there is a usually unrecognized resentment of the fact of this dependence. . . ." (Fowler, 1987, p. 66). This resentment, whether consciously recognized or not, can lead the adolescent to adopt contrary stances toward external authorities, including the authority of religious tradition.

While the adolescent is seeking out values and commitments to which he or she can be loyal, developing a sense of Erikson's fidelity, this process is not always a smooth or easy one. Erikson reminds us that the opposite of fidelity is a form of rejection. The opposite of fidelity "is role repudiation: an active and selective drive separating roles and values that seem workable in the self from what must be resisted or fought as alien to the self. Role repudiation can appear in the form of diffidence covering a certain slowness and weakness in relation to any available identity potential or in the form of a systematic defiance" (Erikson & Erikson, 1997, p. 73).

This latter stance, which Erikson terms a "negative identity," can be directed toward the faith-based institution, its doctrinal teachings, or figures who represent religious authority.

In terms of pastoral care at the congregational level, then, it is important that the adolescent feel recognized as a person and feel a strong emotional connection to their youth minister or to the resident pastor, priest, or rabbi. Since their sense of self is dependent on their sense of connection to others, disagreement, tensions, or estrangement in important relationships imperil the sense of self and spill over into a sense of estrangement from God (Fowler, 1987). Thus the betrayal of trust by an all-too-human religious leader may become a traumatic event in the life of an adolescent. Religious participation of adolescents is also particularly at risk when other important human connections are severed—such as in the death of a parent, divorce, or breakup of a long-term relationship. Consistent communal support and affirmation of the adolescent are critical at such times if the adolescent is to remain connected to the congregation.

Just as a sense of emotional disconnection can affect the relationship of the adolescent with religious congregations or the Divine, other developmental processes can influence the adolescent's consideration and acceptance of religious doctrine. As the adolescent struggles to construct a sense of self, to achieve identity formation, an emphasis on the importance of grace, for example, which stresses the need for human reliance on the Divine, can undermine the newly emerging sense of autonomy. A doctrine such as predestination, which emphasizes the limits of human agency, can threaten to overwhelm the fragile sense of self. An overemphasis on the role of sin and damnation can threaten the sense of assurance and connectedness the adolescent needs to find in the religious community. Adolescent questioning of, or challenges to, such doctrines are sometimes viewed as act of defiance, or a rejection of a family's traditional religious faith. In a snowball effect, that perception can create further tension and an even greater sense of disconnection or estrangement.

One of the areas likely to create challenges in adolescent development and maturation are doctrines relating to sexuality and sexual mores. Adolescence is a time of emerging sexuality, as sexual maturation continues and the adolescent experiences the effects of hormonal drives and sexual curiosity. As their own level of sexual exploration and activity expands, many adolescents confront religious doctrines that advise abstinence, pursuit of sexual activity only in marriage, and the denunciation of both contraception and abortion. These positions stand in stark contrast to messages adolescents perceive in the larger secular world and in media.

Given that adolescents may offer considerable resistance to specific elements of religious teachings about sexuality, it is surprising that regular religious attendance still has a substantial impact on their sexual behavior. Ball, Armistead, and Austin conducted a study of 492 African American female adolescents, aged 12-19, to examine relationships between religiosity, sexual activity, self-esteem, and psychological functioning (2003). They found that the more often teens attended church services, the less likely they were to be sexually active, and that church attendance was the only variable in their study that had a significant effect for sexual behavior. This finding, they concluded, "may be reflective of the considerable number of messages that teens receive about sexual behavior." Nevertheless, "the impact of peers and the media on sexual behavior may overpower the impact of religiosity outside of the church context" (Ball, Armistead, & Austin, 2003, p. 443). While frequent church attendance had a limiting effect on sexual behavior, however, it had a paradoxical effect on self-esteem. Notably both those who never attended church and those who attended every day had lower levels of self-esteem and higher levels of psychological distress than those whose church attendance was reported as moderate. This suggests that moderate levels of church attendance may be supportive of adolescent development, but that never attending or attending everyday may actually inhibit development in crucial areas. One interpretation would be that adolescents who never attend religious services lack the community support created by such attendance and that those who require the adolescent to attend every day may actually evoke greater resistance on the part of the developing adolescent, both resulting in lower levels of self-esteem.

8.12. **SOCIALIZATION AND CULTURAL CONSIDERATIONS**

As has been addressed at several previous points, the communal dimensions of participation in faith-based institutions can clearly be supportive of the socialization process that is central to adolescent development. Attending religious services and participating in religious education classes or youth groups can provide important opportunities for the developing adolescent to engage with peers, make new friendships, and explore values and commitments. Additionally, such participation can provide the questioning youth with specific traditions, historical and contemporary role models, and cohesive systems of belief. But, of course, it must also be remembered that participation in faith-based communities or programs is only one element in the life of the contemporary adolescent. Socialization also occurs in peer interaction, school life, recreational activities, and, increasingly, through use of the Internet and modern communication devices.

That socialization also occurs in an emotional landscape that is far different from historic and traditional views of family. It has been estimated that more than 50% of children in the United States do not live with both biological parents (Boyd-Franklin & Franklin, 2000, p. 22). There are numerous causes for this—including death of a spouse, separation, divorce, and remarriage— but clearly these circumstances have an impact on adolescent development. Adolescents with divorced parents may be living in single-parent homes, with one parent and then the other on a rotating basis, or in blended families. Thus it is not surprising that contact with extended family has declined in many populations, and adolescent identities are formed in homes that may or may not provide adequate role models and meet their complex needs (Furstenberg & Cherlin, 1994, p. 91).

Today, we have a much better understanding, for example, of the role of fathers in development. Studies making use of repeated interviews with the same people over a long period of time, particularly the four-decade Glueck Longitudinal Study (Snarey, 1993), have shown that the quality of care fathers provide their children has consequences for the quality of their daughters' and sons' lives during high school, college, and beyond. Most notably, the fathers of successful adult children engaged their sons and daughters differently during the childhood and adolescent decades. These findings fit well with the developmental theories of Erik H. Erikson and James Fowler.

During childhood both sons and daughters need their fathers to help them negotiate the early stages of identity and faith development. For boys to do this, the early portion of the childhood decade requires them to separate from the mother and identify with the father, the same-sex parent, as part of the boy's gender identity development. Fathers' warm, close, guiding support of their sons' physical-athletic, intellectual, and social-emotional development promotes this transition. In contrast, daughters' primary identification remains with their mother. Fathers' friendly, but not extremely warm or tender, childcare is an important support that does not draw them away from their primary identification.

During the second decade of life, adolescence, sons and daughters need their fathers to change in terms of the nature of their interaction. Both sons and daughters are striving to establish their independence and distinctive identities, of course, but the type of fathering that will support their development is different for sons and daughters. For adolescent sons, their psychosocial task includes achieving a significant degree of separation from their fathers. Their fathers' support from the sidelines, for instance, promotes their ability to achieve such a significant degree of separation from them while also providing them with an ongoing bridge back to the family. For adolescent daughters, in contrast, fathers' active, close, energetic involvement can promote their ability to achieve a significant degree of separation from their mothers. A father's care supports his daughter's autonomous identity and faith development by providing opportunities for constructive, assertive interactions with males. John Snarey's four-decade study, for instance, found that daughters who had experienced a high level of one-to-one involvement with their fathers during adolescence, especially physical-athletic activity (e.g., playing basketball together) and social-emotional support (e.g., attending church together), were significantly more upwardly mobile in educational and occupational levels by early adulthood. The significance of fathers' physical-athletic care in raising daughters who will go on to become high achievers (e.g., pastors or other types of managers and leaders) suggests that the nature of the father-daughter relationship was more vigorously challenging and affirmed the daughters' ability to function autonomously and to transcend culturally determined gender roles. In contrast, women who recalled traditional fathers tended to show poorer levels of academic achievement but were depicted by their professors and peers as dependable, well- organized, and capable of maintaining interpersonal relationships (p. 159). Furthermore, women with traditional fathers who abstained from physical-athletic engagement with them had significantly lower levels of educational and occupational mobility than women with fathers who gave them physical-athletic support (p. 182).

Adolescent development is also affected by gender and gender stereotypes. Female adolescents face significant challenges in a culture that remains largely patriarchal in its assumptions, media images, and pay scale. Taylor, Gilligan, and Sullivan (1995), in a study of 26 "at-risk" adolescent females, found that many of these young women had experienced a "loss of voice" as they moved through adolescence. "Girls' descriptions of their increasing isolation and psychological distress, including their experience of having no effective voice, regularly preceded overt manifestations or symptoms of psychological trouble" (p. 3). While many of the girls in this study reported this "loss of voice," they paradoxically resisted the idea of stereotypes applied to themselves, believing they could accomplish whatever they set out to do. The girls seemed painfully unaware of social barriers that might impede their progress. The researchers concluded that the belief "that 'I can be anyone I want' can also be a dangerous one if it is not informed by a realistic appraisal of academic history, preparation and ability, as well as an awareness of opportunities in the job market and obstacles that may be specific to race, class and gender" (Taylor et al., 1995, p. 189). Finally, faith-based institutions based on androcentric theologies may fully support adolescent male development while not providing adequate parallel support for the adolescent girls in their faith traditions.

Like gender biases, racial divides in American culture also remain firmly entrenched, with detrimental effects on adolescents in specific racial-ethnic groups. When the perspectives of nonmajority adolescents are considered, vital new complexity is added to the understanding of adolescent development. Duncan (2004) has done some of the most creative scholarship on the identities or "voices" of African American adolescents. His research on Black adolescent culture and life draws on the concept of "biculturalism" to also expand and enrich our general understanding of the religious and moral identities of adolescents from nondominant racial-ethnic groups. Biculturalism, as Duncan (2004) explains, "is a process wherein individuals live in two distinct sociocultural milieus, their primary culture of origin and that of the dominant society" (p. 39). Biculturalism functions to help the adolescent both to adapt to and resist the control of alien customs and oppressive institutions (cf. Darder, 1995). Duncan identified and described several types of bicultural African voices that mediate the construction of self-identity and the ethical-religious experiences of contemporary Black adolescents. We will summarize two of them:

Unofficial-underground voices are used by Black adolescents, Duncan (2004) found, to explicitly "refute official versions of both past and present events" (p. 46). Unofficial information is communicated through the Black Church grapevine and other institutions unique to the Black community, such as Black-owned newspapers, magazines, and radio stations. These "alternative" texts openly refute any biased "spin" placed on events by traditional media. For instance, on the issue of whether the Black Panther Party is a terrorist organization or a positive force in Black communities, the view underneath the surface would be the latter. Psychologist Erik H. Erikson had a similar idea when he compared the Black Panthers and Mahatma Gandhi (Erikson & Newton, 1973). These unofficial voices become religious-like moral voices as they turn conventional "truth" on its head. These voices challenge the conventional White dominance as it has been carried out in U.S. society by providing different but valid interpretations of real situations. The primary institutional source of nurture for unofficial-underground voices is the traditional Black Church; this may seem somewhat contradictory (and for some modern Black churches it is), but the traditional Black Church continues to provide a venue where Blacks become aware of their voice and exercise it. And as with the Black Church, Duncan (2004) observed that the adolescents he studied "most often" called themselves "Black" and explicitly "rejected the *hyphenated* term African-American" (p. 47). One reason was that the hyphenated term was seen as an attempt by the dominant society to obscure the visibility of race, *involuntary* immigration, and the holocaust of slavery in the history of the United States. Others see the hyphenation as another example of imperialism and coercion whereby the dominant group assumes the power to "name" others. In sum, Black adolescents use unofficial-underground critiques of the larger society to dispute prevailing "mainstream" racism and to help free themselves, in defining themselves for themselves and within their own community.

Transgressive-profane voices are used by Black adolescents, according to Duncan's (2004) findings, to "respond indirectly to mainstream narrative discourses in history, religion, and culture and, given their reliance upon implicit and hidden metaphors, may or may not be comprehensible to most White Americans" (p. 50). Duncan identifies them as "transgressive" voices, since they go against the grain of dominant institutions (although they also take dominant institutions seriously enough to critique them). But he also identifies them as "profane" voices "because they critique these institutions with a considerable degree of contempt and outrage, as indicated by the strong, sometimes blasphemous, language that individuals use to make their point" (p. 50). For instance, some Black youth refer to themselves as "God" and to White people as "devils," which certainly challenges most Americans' conception of God and of themselves (cf. Duncan, 1996). Furthermore, this language is supported by faith and quasi-faith-based organizations that have marginal or even outlaw standing in the United States (e.g., The Nation of Islam, The Five Percent Nation of Poor, Righteous Teachers, The Universal Negro Improvement Association, The Black Panther Party for Self-Defense, and The New African Independent Movement). Such voices of resistance, however, are *not* owned by any of these intentionally unorthodox organizations. Most successfully and creatively, for instance, transgressive-profane voices have been used and widely distributed in the performances of rap and hip-hop artists. Furthermore, on a local level, Black teenagers develop their own voices of resistance to speak truth to specific experiences of disrespect that are found in their own local youth cultures.

Like other teenagers, of course, Black adolescents are experiencing an abundance of challenges. They are riding a biologically programmed transformation that is shared by all youth (Erikson & Newton, 1973).

They are confronting, to greater or lesser degrees, issues of gender identity. Those who are academically highly successful may also be confronting issues of social class migration. All teenagers who are identified as "lower" on anything (e.g., social class, cooperativeness, and IQ test scores) are at risk for dropping out, being pushed out, or flunking out of school (Garrod, Ward, Robinson, & Kilkenny, 1999). Black adolescents experience the same or similar metamorphosis of identity as other adolescents, but because this transformative process occurs within the framework of Black culture, these adolescents frame identity "in terms of resistance to oppression and a legacy of Black struggle for equality" (Duncan, 2004, p. 52). Duncan's research suggests that such identity formation was common among Black students with teachers who acknowledged their bicultural voices and affirmed their attempts "to challenge the institutional narratives and media images that misrepresent them" (p. 53). Such "bicultural affirmation" helps Black youth selectively to appropriate dominant cultural tools and to maintain linkages with their Black cultural heritage. Duncan does not mention other groups, but one could draw from his research that "bicultural affirmation" extends to other ethnic-racial groups and enclaves in the United States.

Cultural considerations have long played a role in our understanding of adolescent development. Erik H. Erikson (1950) explored the cultural landscapes and child-rearing practices of the Sioux in the Dakotas and the Yurok on the Pacific Coast (pp. 111-186), allowing Native Americans to expand our cross-cultural understanding of human development. In the cultural pluralism of America today, a high school student probably sits in a classroom with students of dramatically diverse cultural backgrounds. Many ethnic minorities have longstanding ties to specific faith traditions and their corresponding faith-based institutions. In many cases cultural assumptions are deeply embedded in family religiosity, traditions, and religious practices.

These cultural assumptions often developed in areas where religious belief and practice were fairly homogenous. The Roman Catholic belief of Ireland, Italy, and Spain; the Greek Orthodox tradition in Greece; the tradition of Judaism in Israel; or the Lutherans in Germany could all serve as examples. But historically, the American religious landscape is not monochromatic. Rather it is inherently interreligious, interdenominational, and multicultural and gives significant credence to religious experience (Bridgers, 2006). In the contemporary landscape of the United States, faith traditions and the believers they represent must come to terms with widely divergent belief systems and practices. The adolescent must find the means to develop a cultural identity, as well as a religious identity, in a world of difference.

8.13. **CONCLUSION**

Over the years, we have come to much greater understanding of the stormy process of adolescence first popularized by Hall and the religious dimensions of adolescent development first explored by Starbuck. Erikson's psychosocial development and Kohlberg's moral development theory have nuanced our understanding of the central issues of adolescent development. Fowler's faith development theory has challenged us to reconsider how we define faith and reminded us that adolescent faith development is forged in a matrix of individual, communal, social, and transcendent dimensions. While the central tasks of adolescent development—the formation and integration of identity—emerge, the complexity of the relationship between identity and faith is clear. Faith-based institutions—including religious congregations, governing bodies, religious schools, volunteer groups, nonprofit agencies, and religious media—all affect adolescent development. As adolescents utilize their newly acquired capacity for abstraction to conceptualize how they believe others see them, and use that understanding and available role models to shape their own morality, the limitations of faith-based support for adolescent development are also clear. Apathy, resistance, ambivalence, the struggle for independence, and emerging adolescent sexuality often inhibit the ability of faith-based institutions to foster healthy adolescent development. And faith-based institutions must operate in a complex cultural context in which other factors, including varieties in family structure, racial and gender stereotyping, peer interaction, school life, recreational activities, and the use of the Internet and modern communication devices exert competing influences. Yet faith-based institutions do affect the development of millions of adolescents as they negotiate the turbulent waters of growth. One may question their efficacy, but there is no doubt that faith-based institutions have provided critical resources and improved the quality of life of many adolescents today. For the most part, they have done so in a spirit of generosity and good will. Clearly, they will continue to do so for decades to come.

REFERENCES

B'nai B'rith Youth Organization. (2008). *Our mission*. Accessed August 5, 2008. http://bbyo.org/about/mission/

Ball, J., Armistead, L., & Austin, B.-J. (2003). The relationship between religiosity and adjustment among African-American, female, urban adolescents. *Journal of Adolescence*, *26*, 431–446.

Bertram-Troost, G. D., de Roos, S., & Miedema, S. (2006, December). Religious identity development of adolescents in religious affiliated schools. A theoretical foundation for empirical research. *Journal of Beliefs and Values*, *27*(3), 303–314.

Book Industry Study Group. (2005). *New study predicts robust growth in the religious and Elhi market segments*. Book Industry Study Group website. Accessed August 4, 2008. http://www.bisg.og/news/press.php?pressid=27

Boyd-Franklin, N., & Franklin, A. J. (2000). *Boys into men*. New York, NY: Dutton.

Bridgers, L. (2006). *The American religious experience*. Lanham, MD: Roman & Littlefield Publishers.

Catholic Charities. (2008). Accessed August 5, 2008. http://www. catholiccharitiesusa.org/NetCommunity/Page.aspx?pid=1174

Christian School. (2008). *Citizendia*. Accessed August 5, 2008. http://www. citizendia.org/Christian_school

Cohen-Zada, D. (2006, November). Preserving religious values through education: Economic analysis and evidence from the US. *Journal of Urban Economics*, *60*(3), 372–398.

Darder, A. (1995). *Culture and difference*. New York, NY: Bergin & Garvey.

Donovan, G. (2003, April 18). Enrollment down in nation's Catholic schools. *National Catholic Reporter*, *39*(24), 8.

Duncan, G. A. (1996). Space, place, and the problematic or race: Black adolescent discourse as mediated action. *Journal of Negro Education*, *65*, 133–150.

Duncan, G. A. (2004). The play of voices: Black adolescents constituting the self and morality. In V. Walker & J. Snarey (Eds.), *Race-ing moral formation: African American perspectives on care and justice* (pp. 38–54). New York, NY: Teachers College Press.

Erikson, E. H. (1950). *Childhood and society*. New York, NY: W. W. Norton & Company.

Erikson, E. H. (1968). *Identity youth and crisis*. New York, NY: W. W. Norton & Company.

Erikson, E. H., & Erikson, J. M. (1997). *The life cycle completed: Extended version*. New York, NY: W. W. Norton & Company.

Erikson, E. H., & Erikson, J. M. (1998). *The life cycle completed*. New York, NY: W. W. Norton & Company.

Erikson, E. H., & Newton, H. (1973). *In search of common ground: Conversations with Erik H. Erikson and Huey P. Newton*. New York, NY: W. W. Norton & Company.

Fowler, J. W. (1981). *Stages of faith*. San Francisco, CA: Harper & Row.

Fowler, J. W. (1987). *Faith development and pastoral care*. Philadelphia, PA: Fortress Press.

Furstenberg, F., & Cherlin, A. (1994). *Divided families: What happens to children when parents part*. Cambridge, MA: Harvard University Press.

Gardyn, R., & Fetto, J. (2000, April). Somebody say Amen! *American Demographics*, *22*, 72.

Garrod, A., Ward, J. V., Robinson, T., & Kilkenny, R. (1999). *Souls looking back: Life stores of growing up black*. New York, NY: Routledge.

Hall, G. S. (1883). The contents of children's minds. *Princeton Review*, *2*, 249–272.

Hall, G. S. (1904). *Adolescence: Its psychology and its relations to physiology, anthropology, sociology, sex, crime, religion, and education* (2 Vols). New York, NY: Appleton.

Independent Sector. (1992). *From belief to commitment: The community service activities and finances of religious congregations in the United States* (1993 ed.). Washington, DC: Independent Sector.

James, W. (1902). *The varieties of religious experience.* New York, NY: Longmans, Green and Co.

Kohlberg, L. (1984). *Essays on moral development (Vol. II): The psychology of moral development: The nature and validity of moral stages.* San Francisco, CA: Harper & Row.

Larson, R. W., Hansen, D. M., & Moneta, G. (2006, September). Differing profiles of developmental experiences across types of organized youth activities. *Developmental Psychology, 42*(5), 849–863.

Linz, W. M. (1996). A religious country reflected in its publishing industry. *Journal of the World Book Community, 7*(1), 6–11.

Lutz, A., & Bogman, D. (2002). Teenage spirituality and the Internet. *Cultic Studies Review, 1*(2), 137–150.

Magnuson, P. (1999, December). Working with the home-schooling community. *Communicator*, pp. 1–3.

Morris, J. (2001, November, 23). Mainstream movement benefits Christian music. *Nashville Business Journal, 17*(48), 1. Accessed August 2, 2008. http://www.bizjournals.com/nashville/stories/2001/11/26/story2.html

Niebuhr, H. R. (1960). *Radical monotheism and western culture.* New York, NY: Harper & Row.

O'Toole, K. (1997, November 12). Rock & Roll: Does it influence teens' behavior? *Stanford Report.* Accessed August 12, 2008. http://news-service.stanford.edu/news/1997/november12/teenmusic.html

Parks, S. (1980). *Faith development and imagination in the context of higher education.* Ph.D. Dissertation, Harvard Divinity School.

Pew Forum on Religion and Public Life. (2008). *U. S. religious landscape study.* Accessed August 1, 2008. http://religions.pewforum.org/affiliations

Pew Internet and American Life Project. (2007). *Family, friends and community.* Accessed August 12, 2008. http://www.perinternet.org

Piaget, J. (1968). *Six psychological studies.* New York, NY: Vintage Books.

Powers, R. (2008). Nearly half of all Americans listen to Christian radio. National Religious Broadcasters website. Accessed August 4, 2008. www.nrb.org

Private Education in the United States. (2009). *Microsoft® Encarta® Online Encyclopedia 2009.* Accessed August 2, 2008. http://encarta.msn.com © 1997-2009 Microsoft Corporation

Riley-Katz, A. (2006, May 1). Salem radio seeking Christian music stars. *Los Angeles Business Journal.* Accessed August 2, 2008. http://www.encyclopedia.com/doc/1G1-146175651.html

Roberts, D. F., Christianson, P., & Gentile, D. A. (2003). Chapter 8: The effects of violent music on children and adolescents. In D. A. Gentile (Ed.), *Media violence and children: A complete guide for parents and professionals* (pp. 153–170). Westport, CT: Praeger Press.

Sanders, J. L. (1998, November). Religious ego identity and its relationship to faith maturity. *The Journal of Psychology, 132*(6), 653.

Saunders, M. (1997, December 12). Young Messiah tour brings in new Christian sounds. *Boston Globe*. Accessed August 4, 2008. http://www.highbeam.com/doc/1P2-8446596.html

Silverstein, S., & Olsen, R. (2003, December 13). Evangelical schools gaining new status. *Los Angeles Times*. Accessed August 2, 2008. http://community.seattletimes.nwsource.com/archive/?date=20031213&slug=evangelical13

Smith, C., Pearce, L., Clark, T., & Longest, K. (2008a, August 2). National Study of Youth and Religion. http://www.youthandreligion.org/news/6-4-2002

Smith, C., Pearce, L., Clark, T., & Longest, K. (2008b, August 4). National Study of Youth and Religion. In *The Internet: More popular than god?* http://www.youthandreligion.org/news/2003-1112.html

Smith, C., Smith, C. S., & Denton, M. L. (2005). *Soul searching: The religious and spiritual lives of American teenagers*. New York, NY: Oxford University Press.

Snarey, J. (1993). *How fathers care for the next generation: A four-decade study*. Cambridge, MA: Harvard University Press.

Starbuck, E. D. (1899). *The psychology of religion*. New York, NY: Walter Scott.

Taylor, J. M., Gilligan, C., & Sullivan, A. M. (1995). *Between voice and silence*. Cambridge, MA: Harvard University Press.

United States Conference of Catholic Bishops. (1997). In Renewing the vision: A framework for Catholic Youth Ministry. *United States Conference of Catholic Bishops*. Washington, DC. Accessed August 4, 2008. http://www.usccb.org/laity/youth/renewingpart1.shtml

Williams, C. (2008). Marjorie Pay Hinckley lecture: Strengthening the religious teen. *Brigham Young University College of Family, Home and Social Issues Newsletter*. Accessed August 12, 2008. http://fhss.byu.edu/FHSSnewsletter/2008January/MarjoriePayHinckleyLecture.htm

Multicultural perspectives of self and racial/ethnic identity

Cherise A. Harris

Department of Sociology, Connecticut College, New London, CT

Kerry Ann Rockquemore

Department of African American Studies, University of Illinois at Chicago, Chicago, IL

While identities are often fluid, they carry a great deal of social significance (Christian, 2000). An individual's personal identity may encompass several dimensions, including physical and sexual identity, occupational goals, religious beliefs, and racial and/or ethnic background (Clarke & Justice, n.d.). Personal identity may also reflect "variables, traits, or dynamics that appear in evidence in all human beings regardless of social class, gender, race, or culture"[1] (Cross, 1991, p. 43). Additionally, identity may include a "reference group orientation," or "those aspects of the 'self' that are culture, class, and gender specific... [and seek] to discover differences in values, perspectives, group identities, lifestyles and worldview" (Cross, 1991, p. 45). According to Erikson (1963, 1968), the major goal of adolescence is developing a coherent identity and avoiding identity confusion, which may subsequently lead to isolation and other psychosocial difficulties. Adolescent identity development, in particular, involves two key steps: (1) letting go of childhood beliefs to explore various alternatives for identity in a particular area and (2) making a commitment to individual identity in that area (i.e., identity achievement) (Marcia, 1991).

---

[1]The term "culture" as it is used throughout this chapter refers to "a human group that shares certain cultural characteristics such as language or religion" (van de Berghe, 1967, p. 9; Yinger, 1985, p. 159; as cited in Jaret, 1995, p. 52).

Adolescence: Development During a Global Era

For all adolescents, achieving an identity is important because of its association with higher self-esteem, increased critical thinking, and advanced moral reasoning (Clarke & Justice, n.d.). However, adolescents of color must negotiate an additional challenge to identity development as they are forced to decide the degree to which their racial or cultural background will be part of their identity (Phinney & Kohatsu, 1997). For these adolescents, the ability to achieve a positive *ethnic* identity is associated with higher self-esteem, academic achievement, and better relationships with family and friends (Clarke & Justice, n.d.). It may also serve as a buffer from racism and act as motivation for achieving personal goals (Oyserman & Harrison, 1998). Moreover, for minority adolescents, a positive ethnic or racial identity is associated with feelings of competence and well-being (Carter, 1991; Phinney, 1990; Pyant & Yanico, 1991). As such, for both White and minority adolescents, identity development is a critical part of their experience.

For adolescents of color, forging a viable racial identity is difficult in the context of prejudice and discrimination, where Whiteness and White culture are positioned as the standard by which all other groups are measured. For White adolescents, developing a racial identity may be even more difficult in a world where Whites' majority group status exempts them from having to think of themselves in racial terms and where they are discouraged from examining the impact that Whiteness has both on their lives and the lives of others (Flagg, 1997; McIntosh, 2007). In this chapter, we explore the following questions: (1) How do adolescents forge a viable racial identity? (2) What are the difficulties involved in racial identity development for the various racial groups in the United States? and (3) How does ethnicity shape and inform identity processes? To explore these questions, we offer a critical review of the racial and ethnic identity development models proposed in previous research. Each of these models indicates that the processes of racial and ethnic identity development are both varied and complex and merit great consideration regarding their impact on the lives of today's adolescents.

9.1. WHITE RACIAL IDENTITY

Because Whites are the majority group in the United States, composed of over 211 million people and representing roughly 74% of the population (U.S. Bureau of the Census, 2006a), an examination of White racial identity development is of the utmost importance in understanding how White Americans perceive themselves and people of other races. In 1982, Rita Hardiman developed the first model of White racial identity development with the intent of "shift[ing] the focus to the dominant group,[2] the willing as well as the unknowing participants in a system of racial oppression" (Hardiman, 2001, p. 109). An additional goal of Hardiman's research was to explore whether it was possible for Whites to escape the effects of racist socialization and how such a process might happen. Her White Identity Development (WID) Model, originally constructed in 1982 and updated in 1992, describes and explains how White Americans arrive at a racial identity.

In the first stage, *naiveté*, the individual has no real understanding of the social meaning of race or the racial hierarchy as it exists in the United States. In other words, the individual has no social consciousness of race, racial inequalities, or racism. According to Hardiman (2001), this stage usually ends in early childhood and is followed by the *acceptance* stage in which White individuals begin to accept and/or internalize racism, while feeling him/herself superior to people of color. A sense of privilege, dominance, or entitlement occurs in this stage, although these feelings are often unconscious. The third stage, *resistance*, is characterized by questions about the dominant ideology and discourse about race and an emerging desire to resist and reject these ideologies. Psychologically, the individual may feel embarrassed by the unearned privileges of Whiteness, as well as guilt, shame, and an urge to distance him/herself from the White group. In the fourth stage, *redefinition*, "the White person begins to clarify his own self-interest in working against racism... [and takes] ownership of their Whiteness rather than trying to deny it or [embrace] another racial identity" (Hardiman, 2001, pp. 111-112). Finally, in the fifth stage, *internalization*, the individual integrates their new identity into all aspects of their life.

While Hardiman's research deserves much acclaim as the forerunner of future models of White racial identity development, her WID model is not without its limitations. Specifically, her model offers little understanding of how an individual progresses from one stage to the next, and like many other models of racial identity development, it suggests a linear progression through the proposed stages. Researchers following Hardiman suggest that individuals may move back and forth between various stages of racial identity (see Parham, 1989). Even Hardiman, when reflecting

---

[2]The term "dominant group" refers to the group with the "greatest power, most privileges, and highest social status" (Henslin, 2001, p. 209). In the U.S. that group is White Americans (see also Spencer, 1999, p. 45 for further discussion). To be consistent with other sociologists who study race, we use the term "dominant group" and the term "dominant culture" to refer to the "culture of the most powerful group in [a] society" (Andersen, Logio, & Taylor, 2009, p. 553).

back on her model in 2001 admitted that the model ignores and/or under-emphasizes how Whites identify *culturally* with their Whiteness. In other words, the WID model isn't about White identity in the conceptual sense, but is more about confronting one's personal racism. As such, it only discusses a small portion of Whites—those who are actively fighting against racism. Thus, the model is more of a prescription of what Hardiman believes Whites *need to do*, rather than a description of the common experience they actually experience in racial identity development. Essentially, the WID model wasn't developed through empirical research, which means that it has had "limited impact on the discourse of racial identity" (Hardiman, 2001, p. 112).

Unlike Hardiman's conceptual framework, Helms' widely cited White Racial Identity Development (WRID) model evolved directly from empirical research. Drawing on an analysis of interviews with Whites that explored their perceptions of their own racial consciousness, Helms (1984) argues that "all people regardless of race, go through a stage-wise process of developing racial consciousness wherein the final stage is an acceptance of race as a positive aspect of themselves and others" (p. 154). Like Hardiman, Helms' original model (published in 1984) consisted of "stages"; in 1995, she reframed these stages as "statuses"—a term that accounts for the fact that people can demonstrate attitudes, behaviors, and emotions that are suggestive of more than one stage. According to Helms (1995), a "stage" implies a static position that a person achieves at some point rather than a "dynamic interplay between cognitive and emotional processes" (pp. 182-183). For these reasons, "status" has become the preferable term among researchers. Nonetheless, the statuses suggest a sequence, and the basic model remains much the same.

In the first status of the WRID model, *contact*, the White individual is unaware of racism and their participation in it and may be comfortable with the racial status quo. However, this status is followed by *disintegration,* when a racial event occurs that provokes a moral dilemma forcing the person to choose between their in-group allegiance and humanism. In some cases, this can occur when the individual develops a close friendship or romantic relationship with a person of color (Tatum, 1997) that causes disorientation and anxiety. As such, the third status, *reintegration*, involves the resolution of whatever tension and conflicting feelings emerged in the previous status and the individual may revert back to an idealizing of Whites and negative feelings toward other races. According to Tatum (1997), the logic is: "If there is a problem with racism, then you people of color must have caused it and if you would just change your behavior, the problem would go away" (p. 101).

Helms (1995) claims that it is easy for many Whites to get "stuck" in this status and not progress to the latter statuses of identity. In part, this is because there is great pressure to ignore racism and accept socially sanctioned stereotypes; resting in this status relieves Whites of any responsibility for changing the societal status quo. The next status, *pseudoindependence*, is marked by an individual's "intellectualized commitment" to their own group and "deceptive tolerance" toward other groups (Helms, 1995, p. 185). Here, the individual might have a clear understanding of racism as a system of advantage but not know what to do about it (Tatum, 1997; see also Frankenberg, 1993). They may even try to interact with people of color, but experience Whiteness "as a source of shame rather than a source of pride" (Tatum, 1997, p. 107). These feelings mark an entrance into the fifth status, *immersion-emersion*, where there is an internal search to redefine Whiteness along with an understanding of racism and how the individual benefits from Whiteness. In the final status, called *autonomy*, the individual possesses the "capacity to relinquish the privileges of racism" (Helms, 1995, p. 185). This final status may bring positive feelings that renew the individual's commitment to confront racism and oppression in everyday life (Tatum, 1997).

Hardiman (2001) offers four critiques of Helms' WRID model. First, it closely mimics models of Black racial identity development, and scholars like Rowe, Bennett, and Atkinson (1994) argue that this is the wrong lens for trying to understand a majority group. Second, like Hardiman's WID model, it does not necessarily focus on White identity in the typical sense, but instead focuses on "how Whites develop different levels of sensitivity to and appreciation of other racial/ethnic groups" (Rowe et al., 1994, p. 131, cited in Hardiman, 2001). Third, the model cannot be considered "developmental" per se because Helms admits the possibility that individuals may skip some statuses and move backward and forward through the statuses. Finally, the WRID model appears to focus exclusively on White-Black relationships and as such does not account for Whites' interactions with other races.

Citing the limitations of the Helms' model, Rowe et al. (1994) propose their own model of White racial identity. The authors admittedly draw from Phinney's (1989) stages of ethnic identity and also from Marcia's (1980) ego identity statuses (both described in detail below). They simplify the developmental process by describing two statuses, "Unachieved" and "Achieved" White Racial Consciousness, each including a subset of possible attitudes. Generally speaking, Unachieved White Racial Consciousness includes attitudes that reflect an absence of racial concerns or analysis while individuals with an Achieved White Racial Consciousness express a dedication to exploring racial concerns and beliefs.

Unachieved White Racial Consciousness includes avoidant, dependent, and dissonant attitudes. The *avoidant* attitude is marked by a lack of consideration of one's own racial identity and avoiding the issues that are of concern for minority groups. Those in this category "ignore, minimize, or deny the existence or importance" (Rowe et al., 1994, p. 136) of racial issues. Those with the *dependent* orientation have not personally given thought to racial issues, but are instead reliant upon attitudes they have internalized from others. In the case of children and adolescents the racial attitudes of family members are particularly influential. Those with *dissonant* attitudes are ambivalent about their White racial consciousness and uncertain about issues of concern to minority groups. Unlike those with the dependent attitude, they are amenable to new information about racial issues because it might reduce their uncertainty. Still, they remain uncommitted to the ideas that they express. For some, this leads to a deeper search for information that will shape their future attitudes.

In contrast to the unachieved attitudes, Achieved White Racial Consciousness includes dominative, conflictive, reactive, and integrative attitudes. Individuals with a *dominative* attitude tend to hold extremely ethnocentric ideas that they use to justify majority dominance over racial minorities. This orientation is characterized by minimal knowledge of racial and ethnic groups, and no particular need for such information due to their extensive reliance on common negative stereotypes. These individuals feel entitled to the advantages conferred upon Whites and may engage in active expressions of their ethnocentrism (i.e., hostile overt behavior) or passive expressions (i.e., unwillingness to interact with members of minority groups, except in dominant/submissive roles). While those with dominative attitudes tend to express open hostility, those with *conflictive* attitudes are opposed to blatantly discriminatory practices. They are also opposed to ameliorative programs designed to reduce or eliminate discrimination. Conflictive attitudes are based on a principle of fairness, where individuals believe that all of the necessary legal and administrative measures have already been taken to eliminate discrimination, and any additional action would result in an unfair and undeserved advantage to minorities at the expense of Whites. Alternatively, individuals with a *reactive* attitude acknowledge the persistence of racial discrimination as a significant factor in American society and experience discomfort in the midst of this reality. They understand White privilege and endorse egalitarian values, while also feeling that they are connected with people from racial minority groups. They may also ignore the role of personal responsibility and rely heavily on structural explanations for problems facing minority groups. Finally, Whites with the *integrative* attitude are less reactive toward racial issues, and their behavior is "tempered by the reality of what will make a difference" (Rowe et al., 1994, p. 141). They have integrated their Whiteness with a regard for racial minorities and value a society built on cultural pluralism, while exhibiting a more nuanced understanding of sociopolitical factors affecting minority groups.

Each of the racial identity development models offers great insight into the process by which White people construct their racial identity. However, moving through these stages and statuses may sound easier than it actually is, particularly for adolescents. We know, for instance, that Whiteness is often the unexamined norm (Frankenberg, 1993; McIntosh, 2007; Perry, 2001), where Whites can easily reach adulthood without ever having given much thought to their racial identity (Tatum, 1997). Moreover, it is more difficult for White adolescents and adults to understand the role that race, ethnicity, and culture occupy in the lives of people of color because White history has shown that European immigrants essentially sacrificed their individual cultures in order to assimilate as White Anglos-Saxon Protestants (WASP) (Waters, 2006; see also Lieberson, 1981 for extended discussion). Moreover, as the majority group in America, Whites have the choice of which ethnic identity to adopt (if any) because White ethnicities no longer carry a social cost (Waters, 2007). Finally, great pressure exists in White families to silence discussions about race and ignore its sociological and psychological implications (Kenny, 2000; Tatum, 1997). As such, arriving at a positive and viable racial identity can prove extremely challenging for White adolescents.

The remaining models of racial identity pertain to adolescents of color. In general, these models follow a similar framework as has been outlined in the work of Phinney (1989, 1990). Phinney's model of adolescent ethnic identity development includes three general stages. In the first, *unexamined ethnic identity*, minorities may exhibit a preference for White culture or may simply not be interested in race or ethnicity and have not thought about it critically. In other words, race and ethnicity aren't salient for the individual. However, the second stage, *ethnic identity search*, is marked the individual's active search to define race and ethnicity for themselves and what it means to be a member of their own racial or ethnic group. Finally, in the third stage, *achieved ethnic identity*, the individual of color has found a "clear, positive sense of their racial or ethnic identity" (Tatum, 1997, p. 132). All of the remaining models follow this general pattern outlined by Phinney (1989).

9.2. **BLACK RACIAL IDENTITY**

Black Americans comprise 13.1% of the U.S. population (approximately 39 million people), making them the second-largest minority group (U.S. Bureau of the Census, 2006b). From slavery, through segregation, to the present age of modern institutional discrimination, Black Americans have faced a variety of obstacles in the pursuit of full equality in the United States, as well as having had to develop the "double consciousness" (described by DuBois, 1989) to navigate and negotiate life in both Black and White worlds. The pressures and stressors of assimilating to become successful in mainstream White society while also maintaining a healthy sense of Blackness can present significant challenges to a Black adolescent's racial identity development.

One of the first models of Black racial identity was offered by Marcia (1966). In an article entitled, "Development and Validation of Ego Identity Status" (1966), Marcia proposed four stages of racial identity for Black Americans. In the first stage, *diffuse*, the individual has not explored racial identity and expresses no psychological commitment to a racial identity. Stage two, *foreclosed*, is characterized by the individual's commitment to ideologies held by their parents, where they consider few or no alternatives to parental racial ideologies. In the third stage, *moratorium*, there is active exploration of roles and beliefs as they pertain to race, but no commitment to a racial identity. By the final *achieved* stage, the individual exhibits a strong personal commitment to a dimension of identity following the period of exploration. They are more certain in their racial self-definition and do not experience the anxiety inherent in some of the previous stages.

Introduced by Jackson (1976) and reconsidered by Jackson (2001), Black Identity Development (BID) theory proposes a five-stage theory of identity development for Black Americans. Occurring in early childhood (ages 0-4), the *naïve* stage is characterized by the absence of a social consciousness or identity. At this point, children are particularly susceptible to the ideologies of their socializing agents (e.g., parents, teachers, media, and significant others) (Jackson, 2001). As children begin to learn the dominant ideologies concerning Black Americans and the formal and informal social norms that manifest in differential treatment, they begin to enter the second stage, *acceptance*. This stage is marked by the internalization of Whites' stereotypical perceptions of Black people and culture and a perception that "White is right" (Jackson, 2001, p. 19). Individuals in this stage may subscribe to notions of meritocracy that suggest that if Blacks work hard, they will be judged by their merits and if a Black person doesn't become successful, it is through some failing of their own. At the exit point of this stage, individuals begin to ask more critical questions that continue with increasing fervor during the third stage, *resistance*. Here individuals experience a turning point where "one begins to understand and recognize racism in its complex and multiple manifestations" at the individual, institutional, attitudinal, behavioral, and policy levels (Jackson, 2001, p. 21). This stage includes the rejection of White culture's definition of—and value conferred upon—Black people and Black culture. The fourth stage, *redefinition,* is marked by "the renaming, reaffirming, and reclaiming of one's sense of Blackness, Black culture, and racial identity" (Jackson, 2001, p. 16). In this stage, the individual is intent on developing their contacts and interactions with other Blacks who are at the same level of consciousness and may even limit their interactions with other Black people. Jackson's final stage, *internalization*, represents the integration of the redefined racial identity into other aspects of the individual's self-concept. This stage reflects the convergence of knowledge and experience gleaned from the previous acceptance, resistance, and redefinition stages.

While both Marcia's and Jackson's models have proven useful in previous research, perhaps the most widely cited model of Black racial identity is Cross' *Nigrescence Theory*, originally proposed in 1971 (Cross, 1971). Referred to as "one of the most powerful interpretive lenses through which to view the historical reality of African-descent people in this country" (Parham, 2001, pp. 162-163), Cross offers five stages of Black identity development. In the first stage, *pre-encounter*, the Black person seeks White acceptance and will often uncritically accept negative Black stereotypes. The second stage, *encounter*, brings awareness that being a part of the White world is not a viable option and that a new identity must be constructed. During this stage, individuals may feel anxiety, anger, or hopelessness. In the *immersion/emersion* stage, the individual may withdraw into a Black world and may think, feel, and act in ways they believe are "authentically" Black. Additionally, they may judge and evaluate others by this criterion while in the immersion aspect of the stage. While in this state, it is possible for the individual to enter the emersion part of the stage, which consists of engaging in discussion and joining various political groups, developing a nonstereotypical Black view of the world, and acquiring the ability to sort out the strengths and weaknesses of Black culture. In the fourth stage, *internalization*, the individual forges a positive, personally relevant Black identity by beginning to negotiate their positions on Whites and no longer judges others by their group membership (Helms, 1993). In the final stage, *internalization-commitment*, the individual may devote more time to finding ways to transform their personal sense of Blackness into a plan of action or a general sense of commitment (Cross, 1991). In the internalization and internalization-commitment stages, a person is "willing to establish meaningful relationships across group boundaries with others, including Whites, who are respectful of this new self-definition" (Tatum, 1997, p. 76).

Researchers in psychology offer various criticisms of Cross' theory (1991). Parham (1989) notes several limitations of the Cross typology, including Cross' claim that the Nigrescence process starts in childhood. Parham argues that it does not occur until adolescence and early adulthood. He also challenges the idea that the process of psychological Nigrescence is not as linear or static as Cross' stages suggest. Parham maintains that individuals do not arrive at a stage and stay there, but that they "recycle" through the stages, depending on various events and circumstances (Parham, 1989, 2001) that occur throughout the life course. Despite these criticisms, Nigrescence theory is useful for understanding how Black people develop a positive racial identity. Still, as is the case for every racial/ethnic group, arriving at a positive racial identity comes with a host of challenges for Black adolescents, and there are a number of ways in which development through the stages may be slowed. Notable among these challenges is the pervasive nature of an oppositional culture that emphasizes that the essence of Blackness lies in stereotypical behaviors like speaking the Black English Vernacular (also known as "Ebonics"), avoiding academic achievement, listening to rap music, and being generally disrespectful and rude in one's disposition toward others (Fordham & Ogbu, 1986; Peterson-Lewis & Bratton, 2004). Adhering to these prescriptions may cause adolescents to get stuck in the immersion-emersion stage of identity, where they behave in ways they believe "authentically" Black persons should, without critical consideration as to the rigidity and limitations of such definitions of Blackness.

Another important criticism of previous theories of Black racial identity development comes from (Sellers, Chavous, & Cooke, 1998; Sellers, Smith, Shelton, Rowley, & Chavous, 1998), who argues that race may not be the most central aspect of self for Black Americans (Sellers, Chavous, et al., 1998, p. 11). Citing previous empirical research, they claim that aspects of identity like gender or religion may take precedence over racial identity. As an alternative to previous theories, Sellers, Chavous, et al. (1998) and Sellers, Smith, et al. (1998) propose a "Multidimensional Model of Racial Identity" (MMRI) that captures more of the complex nuances of racial identity. The MMRI addresses the significance of race in the individual's self-concept as well as the individual's subjective meaning as to what it means to be Black (Sellers, Chavous, et al., 1998,

p. 12). Specifically, the MMRI is based on four distinct dimensions: (1) *racial salience,* which reflects the extent to which race is a significant part of an individual's self-concept at a given moment in time; (2) *racial centrality,* which describes how the individual defines him/herself in terms of race; (3) *racial regard,* which refers to the judgments one forms about Blacks (i.e., "private regard") or their perception of others' view of Black Americans as a whole (i.e., "public regard"); and (4) *racial ideology,* which measures how an individual feels Blacks should behave (Sellers, Smith, et al., 1998). In these ways, the MMRI broadens our notions of Black identity by taking a more detailed and critical look at how Black Americans conceptualize members of their race, as well as how important race is to their personal identities.

In addition to the multidimensional nature of racial identity, the process of identity development remains influenced by a variety of other social statuses such as social class. As several researchers have documented (Cole & Omari, 2003; Collins, 2005; Lacy, 2007; Patterson, 1972), "authentic" Black culture and identity that emphasize stylized ways of talking, walking, acting and thinking as the root of Blackness ultimately came to be located among the lower class. Therefore, low-income adolescents are more likely to cling to these attitudes or behaviors as "authentic" expressions of Blackness. However, for upwardly mobile Black adolescents who live in a culture of mobility that stresses the opposite of these characteristics (Harris, 2009; see also Neckerman, Carter, & Lee, 1999), these types of attitudes and behaviors are discouraged and/or forbidden, leaving these young people without access to a particular type of "authentic" Blackness and maybe even leading them to reject any search for a positive Black identity, when they imagine that the only racial identity available is that of the oppositional culture.

For adolescents of Black Caribbean or African Immigrant heritage, ethnic and cultural differences between them and the larger Black American culture may present a different obstacle to Black racial identity development. Research by Waters (2007) documents how Black immigrants often see themselves as hardworking and ambitious, dedicated to education and family, and committed to their racial identities but not obsessed with race. However, they tend to view Black Americans as "lazy, disorganized, obsessed with racial slights and barriers, with a disorganized and laissez-faire attitude toward family life and child raising" (Waters, 2007, p. 519). As such, second-generation adolescents (and beyond) are forced to negotiate their ethnocultural immigrant heritage in the context of negative stereotypes of Black Americans proffered by their parents and notions of Black "authenticity" prescribed by the oppositional culture. For these adolescents, racial identity development can become extremely difficult due to the triple consciousness of having one foot in the Caribbean or African world, one in the Black American world, and yet another in the White world of the majority group.

A final but noteworthy challenge to the development of a healthy racial identity for Black adolescents is the politics of skin color (i.e., colorism) that exist in the Black community (and indeed, all communities of color). Colorism is a remnant of slavery and dictates that lighter-skinned Blacks are closer to the White-supremacist standard of beauty and are therefore more attractive and have more positive qualities than darker-skinned Blacks (Herring, Keith, & Horton, 2004; see also Collins, 2000; Graham, 1999; Russell, Wilson, & Hall, 1992). The ridicule directed at darker-skinned Black adolescents by family and peers (Boyd-Franklin, 2003; Tatum, 1997) may leave darker-skinned Black adolescents feeling uncomfortable around other Blacks and reluctant to forge a racial identity that includes attachments to a group from which they feel outcast and excluded. The same may also be said of lighter-skinned Black adolescents, who are sometimes perceived as "not Black enough" because of their light skin (Hunter, 2004) and any other Anglo features they may possess (e.g., long and/or straight hair, light-colored eyes, aquiline nose, etc.) These adolescents may also feel outcast and as if there is no community to which they belong. Alternatively, these types of features may make light-skinned adolescents feel as if they are superior to other Blacks and may therefore prompt them to distance themselves on these grounds (see Graham, 1999). In all of these ways, the politics of skin color can act as a substantial impediment to positive racial identity formation.

9.3. **NATIVE AMERICANS**

The term *Native American* refers to the indigenous people of the United States, including Alaskan Natives and Native Hawaiians. There is great diversity among the Native American population. In fact, the Federal Register (2007) reports 561 different tribes in the U.S. Each tribe sets its own criteria for membership (Tatum, 1997, p. 144), with some specifying a particular percentage of Indian ancestry and others specifying language fluency. As of 2000, the largest tribes in the U.S. population were Navajo, Cherokee, Choctaw, Sioux, Chippewa, Apache, Blackfeet, Iroquois, and Pueblo. According to a 2003 report from the Census Bureau, more than a third of the 2.8 million Native Americans in the United States live in three states: California, Arizona, and Oklahoma. Of the nearly 3 million Native Americans, almost 80% are now urbanized and living in the cities (Healey, 2007, pp. 144-145).

"[F]or the American Indian adolescent, "Indianness," or the outward display of tribal attitudes, beliefs, customs, values, and appearances, may be the most important aspect of personal identity development" (Red Horse, 1982, cited in Choney, Berryhill-Paapke, & Robbins, 1995). Despite this sentiment, no stage-wise racial identity development models exist for Native Americans like those we have described for other racial/ethnic groups. Previous researchers have attributed this to the great tribal diversity among Native Americans as a group and even the diversity within tribal membership (Choney et al., 1995; Johnson & Lashley, 1989; LaFromboise, Medoff, Lee, & Harris, 2007; LaFromboise, Trimble, & Mohatt, 1990; Spencer & Markstrom-Adams, 1990). Others point to the great cultural variation that exists between Natives who live on reservations versus those who live in urban areas (Choney et al., 1995). Conversely, the lack of developmental models may also be reflective of the relative invisibility that Native Americans face. Generally speaking, they are portrayed as "people of the past, not of the present or future" (Tatum, 1997, p. 150). Moreover, a good deal of Native American history is not taught in schools, which further contributes to the sense of invisibility and devaluation that Native American adolescents may feel.

Instead of linear identity models or theories, researchers have explored levels of cultural attachment to Native culture versus mainstream culture. LaFromboise et al. (1990) cite four different dispositions that indicate the level of cultural commitment among Native Americans: (1) traditional, (2) transitional, (3) bicultural, and (4) assimilated. Individuals with a *traditional* disposition speak and think in their native language and hold exclusively traditional values and beliefs. *Transitional* people speak both the native language and English, but don't fully accept either their tribal culture or mainstream culture. Some individuals maintain a *bicultural* disposition in which they are generally accepted by the mainstream society and are able to accept both mainstream *and* native values and beliefs. Finally, *assimilated* individuals are accepted by dominant society and subscribe only to mainstream, dominant culture.

Zitzow and Estes (1981; cited in Sue & Sue, 1999) propose two different and more specific typologies by which to conceptualize Native American acculturation and assimilation: Heritage Consistent Native Americans (HCNA) and Heritage Inconsistent Native Americans (HINA). For the *Heritage Consistent*, the primary orientation is tribal culture, so adolescents in this group may grow up and be educated on or near a reservation, may have an extended family orientation, are involved in tribal activities, primarily socialize with Native Americans, are knowledgeable or willing to learn about their culture, place low priority on materialism, and use shyness and silence as signs of respect. Accordingly, they may experience issues of insecurity when away from the reservation and extended family, difficulty with English, discomfort associating with non-Native people, diminished feelings of self-efficacy, and unfamiliarity with the norms of the dominant culture. For the *Heritage Inconsistent*, their behaviors and lifestyles reflect dominant, mainstream American culture. As such, they may face issues surrounding a lack of pride in being Native American (including negative feelings about the group as a whole), pressure to adopt mainstream cultural values, guilt over not knowing or participating in their culture, and a lack of a support and belief system (Sue & Sue, 1999, p. 278).

Like adolescents of all racial groups, Native American adolescents also experience obstacles to racial identity development. Using the work of various researchers, LaFromboise et al. (2007) describe several challenges Native American adolescents face that may impede their racial identity development. Chief among these is historical trauma, or the "trauma associated with colonial intrusion" (LaFromboise et al., 2007, p. 122). While this trauma may appear to be confined to the past, the past traumas of forced acculturation, genocide, and removal are passed on to present generations through narrative accounts (Struthers & Lowe, 2003). Furthermore, the stress of acculturation alone can result in feelings of marginality, alienation, and identity confusion as well as high levels of stress (Choney et al., 1995). Still, some researchers have found that Native youth are able to become bicultural without losing their Native identity or having to choose one culture over another (LaFromboise, Coleman, & Gerton, 1993). This does not exempt them from the overall stressors of acculturation. Enculturation, or learning about and identifying with one's culture, has proven to be a remedy for coping with the stressors of acculturation (Sunday, Eyles, & Upshur, 2001; Zimmerman, Ramirez-Valles, Washienko, Walter, & Dyer, 1996). As such, enculturation may prove crucial to the well-being of Native American adolescents.

For the most part, Native Americans have resisted acculturation into the mainstream more than any other group (Garrett & Garrett, 1994). However, in the twentieth century the movement of great numbers of Native Americans from reservations to urban areas in search of jobs means that the current population is highly urbanized. This may present another challenge to adolescent racial identity, where the migration has slowed the intergenerational transmission of tribal values. It has also created a cultural gap between Natives living on reservations and those living in the cities (Choney et al., 1995). Isolation in urban areas, without access to traditional values and culture, can, in and of itself, create significant challenges to racial identity development for Native American adolescents.

A third major challenge to Native adolescents' identity formation is the negative portrayals of Native Americans in the mass media (Spencer & Markstrom-Adams, 1990). Merskin's (2007) research offers numerous examples of the commercialized uses of Native American culture that can have a particularly damaging effect on racial identity development. From Jeep Cherokees to the Land O' Lakes Indian maiden and Crazy Horse Malt Liquor, Native peoples and cultures are used in company logos and brand names in a dehumanizing fashion. Meanwhile, movie representations portray Native Americans as alcoholics, bloodthirsty and lawless "savages," or as childlike, unsophisticated peoples requiring the paternalistic care of Whites. Perhaps even more dehumanizing are Native-themed mascots used for sports teams like the Atlanta Braves (complete with the crowd's "Tomahawk Chop"), the Cleveland Indians, the Fighting Illini, and the Florida Seminoles (Merskin, 2007; see also Churchill, 2007). Churchill argues that Native Americans remain the only racial group subject to intense and vitriolic public ridicule (2007). The impact on Native children is clear: "If, during the transition of adolescence, Native children internalize these representations that suggest that Indians are lazy, alcoholic by nature, and violent, this misinformation can have a life-long impact on perceptions of self and others" (Merskin, 2007, p. 454).

Due to past and present social inequalities and the pressures of acculturation and assimilation, forging a positive racial identity may prove particularly difficult for Native American adolescents. Indeed, some research indicates that many Native adolescents end up moving back and forth between a White identity and a tribal identity without the ability to integrate the two (Katz, 1981, cited in Spencer & Markstrom-Adams, 1990). Because of the unique pressures and stressors they face, native youth are particularly vulnerable to negative mental health outcomes such as alcoholism, depression, and suicide (Healey, 2007; see also Choney et al., 1995; LaFromboise et al., 2007). As a result, continued research on racial identity development among Native American adolescents is critical to future studies on racial identity development.

The remaining groups we describe each contain large immigrant populations. This reality may profoundly influence racial identity development among adolescents in each of these groups in ways that are distinct from other adolescents of color. For Hispanic and Asian American youth, key factors like the length of their family's tenure in America, maintenance of their native language, and forced acculturation play a significant role in the development of their racial identities.

9.4. **HISPANIC AMERICANS**

In 2004, Hispanics became the largest minority group in the United States, composed of 41 million people (Healey, 2007). Within this group, Mexican Americans are the largest ethnic group (approximately 8.7 million people). Other large groups include Puerto Ricans, Cubans, Salvadorans, as well as individuals from the Dominican Republic and various other countries located throughout Central and South America. Currently, 1 in every 10 Americans is Hispanic; by 2050, this ratio is expected to increase to 1 in 4 (Healey, 2007). The term *Hispanic* is used by the U.S. Census Bureau as an ethnic label rather than a racial label because "Hispanics are a racially mixed group, including combinations of European White, African Black, and indigenous American Indian" (Tatum, 1997, p. 136). Because the group generically labeled as "Hispanic" actually includes a diverse array of racial and cultural backgrounds, understanding racial identity development among adolescents differs from other racial groups.

Through his clinical work, Ruiz (1990; cited in Sue & Sue, 1999) identified five stages of racial identity development for Hispanic Americans. In the *causal* stage, messages from the larger society or significant others ignore or denigrate the individual's ethnic heritage. This may cause a failure to identify with Latino culture in any way, shape, or form. In the *cognitive* stage, the negative images are transformed into a belief system that associates Latinos with poverty and prejudice and identifies assimilation to White society as the only means of escaping this fate and becoming successful. In the third stage, *consequence*, the person may feel ashamed or embarrassed about ethnic markers such as their name, accent, or skin color and as a result may reject their culture. However, by the *working through* stage, two things happen to change the course of identity: (1) the individual becomes increasingly unable to deal with the psychological distress of the ethnic identity conflict, and (2) they can no longer pretend to identify with a culture other than their own. As a result of this, ethnic consciousness increases. Finally, by the aptly named *successful resolution* stage, individuals exhibit a greater acceptance of their own culture and ethnicity, thereby improving their self-esteem.

While stage models like Ruiz's offer insight into how Hispanic adolescents and adults may move through various stages of racial/ethnic identity, other models suggest just how difficult it is for them to reconcile Hispanic culture with White mainstream culture. Phinney, Lochner, and Murphy (1990) cite four possible outcomes for managing the cultural conflict that exists. The first possible outcome is *assimilation,* where Hispanic adolescents might attempt to blend into White culture as much as possible while distancing themselves from their own ethnic group. As part of this effort, a teenager might decide to reject the use of Spanish and advocate the speaking of English only. According to Tatum (1997), Hispanic teens often feel ashamed to be bilingual and will even avoid the use of Spanish in public, similar to the raceless strategy employed by Black teens. However, Hispanic teens eventually realize that abandoning their language does not give them access to the majority group and end up reclaiming their language as a result. A second outcome is *withdrawal*, where an individual clings to their ethnic culture while avoiding interactions with Whites. Tatum (1997) claims that this strategy is common in highly segregated communities (such as ethnic enclaves) where English is rarely spoken. A third strategy Hispanic adolescents use in order to negotiate the conflict between Hispanic and White culture is *biculturalism,* where they integrate aspects of both their own culture and the dominant culture (e.g., becoming bilingual). A fourth and final outcome is *marginalizatio*n, which brings alienation from both the Native and White worlds. In this status, Hispanic adolescents might rely on their peers for a sense of community, which may bring more negative outcomes, including gang membership (Tatum, 1997, p. 139).

Somewhat similar to Ruiz (1990), Ferdman and Gallegos (2001) employ a more nuanced and detailed model of Hispanic racial identity, where they describe six different orientations: *Latino-integrated*, *Latino-identified*, *subgroup-identified*, *Latino as other*, *undifferentiated/denial*, and *White-identified*. Each are depicted in Table 9.1, along with a description of the lens through which these individuals view the world, how they identify, their perception of Latinos, their perception of Whites, and their overall framing of race.

In the *Latino-integrated* orientation, an individual has the ability to understand and negotiate the complexity of Latino identity. Their Latino identity is fully integrated into their other social identities (i.e., gender, class, sexual orientation). Furthermore, they have a "both/and" philosophy, rather than an "either/or" philosophy reflective of dichotomous thinking. Latino-integrated individuals are able to see both the positives and negatives of Latinos (as a group) and are inclusive of all Latinos. Moreover, they are more likely to see Latinos as just one of many groups coexisting together in the United States.

Table 9.1 Ferdman and Gallegos' Model of Hispanic Racial Identity Orientations

Orientation	Lens	Identify as/Prefer	Latinos are Viewed	Whites are Viewed	Framing of Race
Latino-integrated	Wide	Individuals in a group context	Positively	Complex	Dynamic, contextual, socially constructed
Latino-identified (racial/raza)	Broad	Latinos	Very positively	Distinct; could be barriers or allies	Latino/not Latino
Subgroup-identified	Narrow	Own subgroup	My group OK, others maybe	Not central (could be barriers or blockers)	Not clear or central; secondary to nationality, ethnicity, culture
Latino as other	External	Not White	Generically, fuzzily	Negatively	White/not White
Undifferentiated/denial	Closed	People	"Who are Latinos?"	Supposed color-blind (accept dominant norms)	Denial, irrelevant, invisible
White-identified	Tinted	Whites	Negatively	Very positively	White/Black, either/or, one-drop or "mejorar la raza" (i.e., improve the race)

The *Latino-identified* orientation includes individuals with a pan-Latino identity that emphasizes Latino culture and history. They tend to reject the dichotomous nature of U.S. racial constructs and have a less rigid view of other groups than individuals in the remaining categories. However, those who are Latino-identified view Latinos as a distinct *racial* category and identify with the entire group, which they see through a positive lens. They also see Whites as a completely different race altogether and are likely to see institutional racism as a social problem and fight against discrimination. For them, culture is secondary to *la raza* (the race), because they see race as transcending cultural markers (such as ethnicity).

The *subgroup-identified* orientation includes Hispanics who think of themselves first and foremost as part of an *ethnic* group or *national-origin* group. They perceive themselves as distinct from Whites, and Whites are not central to their thinking. Individuals in this group do not necessarily identify with other Latinos or people of color. In other words, they tend to lack a broad pan-Latino perspective. They may even view other groups, including other Latino groups, as deficient or inferior. For individuals with this orientation, race is not a clear organizing concept, and they instead see nationality, ethnicity, and culture as more important.

Hispanics who fall in Ferdman and Gallegos' *Latino as other* category tend to be unaware of their specific Latino background, history, and culture. They simply do not distinguish themselves by ethnicity but instead see themselves as generic persons of color and may sometimes simply describe themselves as "a minority." Individuals in this category have an external lens whereby they are very concerned with how those outside the group view their own group. They do not follow Latino cultural values or norms, but do not identify with White cultural values or norms either. They see their skin color as something that connects them to other people of color generally and differentiates them from the majority group.

Individuals who hold an *undifferentiated* orientation are most likely to claim that they are "just people." They may also claim to be "color-blind" and promote this particular strategy, in part by not subscribing to racial categorizations. These individuals accept the dominant norms of society without challenging them and when they experience barriers to their inclusion, are more likely to attribute them to individual behavior rather than intergroup dynamics. In their daily life, they do not seek out any particular associations with other Latinos.

Finally, Latinos holding the *White-identified* orientation see themselves as racially White and as distinct from (and perhaps even superior to) people of color. They prefer most aspects of Whiteness and are disconnected from Latinos, or alternatively might feel connected to a particular Latino subgroup like Cuban refugees while denying or not seeing any connection to other ethnic groups. They may recognize that they are different from Whites, but still continue to prefer all aspects of Whiteness and consider that a primary part of their identity. The White-identified see Latinos as inferior to Whites and are more likely to view race as a White/Black proposition. Moreover, they see intermarriage with Whites as positive while marriage to darker groups is negatively viewed. They believe in *mejorar la raza*, meaning that they see intermarriage with Whites as a way of improving Latinos, while marrying Blacks or other people of color diminishes the group.

For Latino adolescents, several factors impact how much they identify with their racial or ethnic culture. Like all children of color, obtaining a positive outcome where racial/ethnic identity is concerned is complicated by prejudice and discrimination (Spencer & Markstrom-Adams, 1990). However, Latino adolescents deal with far more complicated factors. Most pressing is the issue of immigration and the length of one's tenure in the U.S. For example, those born outside of the U.S. who emigrated as children (sometimes referred to as the "1.5 generation") are more likely to identify with their parents' nationality. However, those born in the U.S. or those who acquired citizenship are less likely to adopt an immigrant self-identity and gravitate more toward an American identity. For second-generation adolescents, in particular, identity construction is complex because they feel simultaneously pulled in the direction of their native culture and the mainstream culture (Portes & Rumbaut, 2001). Ethnicity and social class may also play a role where Cubans are more likely than other groups to identify themselves as White (Portes & Rumbaut, 2001).

Language is a critical factor in the racial/ethnic identity development of Hispanic adolescents. According to Portes and Rumbaut (2001) "Through the use of the same language, individuals learn to identify each other as members of the same bounded cultural community. Common inflections and a common accent in the same language tightens this sense of 'we-ness' and links it firmly to a common historical past" (p. 113). However, mainstream culture often mandates language assimilation, where all are expected to use English to the exclusion of native languages like Spanish (Healey, 2007; Portes & Rumbaut, 2001; Rodriguez, 1981). Writer Rodriguez's (1981) essay "Aria: Memoir of a Bilingual Childhood" describes the connection between language and identity in the following way: "To hear its sounds was to feel myself specially recognized as one of the family, apart from *los otros* ... My parents would say something to me and I would feel embraced by the sounds of their words. Those sounds said: *I am speaking with ease in Spanish. I am addressing you in words I never use with* los gringos. *I recognize you as someone special, close, like no one outside. You belong with us. In the family. Ricardo*" (p. 28). Rodriguez illustrates the importance of language for many Hispanics and thus, the sense of loss that comes with having to relinquish it in the name of assimilation. When the nuns at the school that Rodriguez attends arrive at his parents' home and ask them to stop speaking Spanish at home, he feels a sense of mourning and that he lost a sense of closeness with his family. When his Spanish skills noticeably weaken, his relatives begin calling him *pocho*, meaning colorless or bland. They are filled with disdain for him because he no longer speaks *su propia idioma* (his native language). In these ways, retaining Spanish language can be integral to a sense of identity for Hispanic American adolescents and young adults.

Several additional factors shape racial identity development for Latino adolescents. First among them are the negative portrayals of Hispanics in the media (Spencer & Markstrom-Adams, 1990). Many images show Anglos as powerful and intellectually advanced while depicting groups like Mexican Americans as powerless, primitive, and in negative stereotypical ways (Mendelberg, 1986). Latino adolescents also face the hierarchy of color that exists in their community, much like it does for Black Americans. Those at the top of the hierarchy have Whiter features and those at the bottom are the most "Indian" in appearance (DeVos & Romanucci-Ross, 1982, cited in Spencer & Markstrom-Adams, 1990; see also Tatum, 1997). Similar to Black adolescents, Latino adolescents also may deal with an oppositional culture that emerges from the hopelessness engendered by a lack of job opportunities and racism in the job market (see Portes & Rumbaut, 2001). In this oppositional culture, academic achievement is perceived as "acting White" and being disloyal to one's group (Matute-Bianchi, 1986). A fourth factor that shapes racial/ethnic identity formation for Latino adolescents is the variation in racial backgrounds. Cubans, Brazilians, Dominicans, and Puerto Ricans each have a great deal of African ancestry and may appear phenotypically African American (Bailey, 2001; Portes & Rumbaut, 2001) as opposed to Hispanics who have European ancestry. One way that individuals may negotiate this is through language displays where they demonstrate their fluency in Spanish in intraethnic and interethnic interactions (Bailey, 2001).

In all of the aforementioned ways, forming a positive and viable racial/ethnic identity may be a challenge for Hispanic adolescents in ways that are similar to—and yet different from—other racial groups. However, as the largest and fastest growing American minority group, exploration of the racial/ethnic identities of Hispanic Americans is of the utmost importance. Not only is it important for psychosocial development, but it is also important because racial identity often carries political implications. Therefore, continued examination of the racial identities of Hispanic Americans may tell us a great deal about the power and direction of the Latino community in the future.

9.5. **ASIAN AMERICANS**

In 2006, the Census Bureau recorded 14.6 million people with either full or partial Asian heritage. This number represents approximately 5% of the U.S. population. The largest ethnic groups in this category are Chinese, Filipinos, Asian Indians, Vietnamese, Koreans, and Japanese. Like many racial/ethnic groups, Asian Americans began to reconsider their racial identity during the Civil Rights Movement and the rise of identity politics in the 1960s (Tatum, 1997). By the 1980s, researchers began to construct stage models of Asian American racial identity.

One of the forerunners in this area of research is Jean Kim, who originally developed the Asian American Identity Development (AAID) model in 1981. According to Kim (2001), there are three underlying assumptions of the model. First, the model assumes that racism is pervasive and therefore has a great impact on the way Asian Americans see themselves. Second, the model assumes that for Asian Americans, shedding their negative racial identity requires a conscious decision to unlearn negative messages they have received about themselves. The third assumption is that "the psychological well-being of Asian Americans is dependent on their ability to transform the negative racial identity they experience as a result of identity conflict" (Kim, 2001, p. 71) and form a positive racial identity in spite of this.

Kim's stage model (visually represented in Table 9.2) offers the caveat that even though the five stages may be sequential, the process of racial identity development is not necessarily linear or unidirectional. As such, it is possible to get stuck in a stage and not move to the next. Movement to the next stage is mostly dependent on the social environment, where various factors in the environment determine the length and quality of experiences in a particular stage. Kim (2001) admits that her theory focuses on racial identity development rather than ethnic identity development. While she acknowledges "the existence of real cultural diversity among Asian ethnic groups" (p. 81), her original conceptualization of the model was based on her belief that "much of what influences AAID is Asian Americans' status as a racial minority in the United States and the social and psychological consequences of this status" (Kim, 2001, p. 81). Moreover, based on research from other authors, it is clear that the various ethnic groups are perceived and treated from a similar set of racial stereotypes and prejudices that cast all Asian Americans (regardless of ethnicity) in the same way (Kim, 2001). In this way, Kim believes that "[i]t is their racial membership, not their ethnic membership, that impacts how Asian Americans feel about themselves in this country" (p. 82).

While Kim appears to be promoting a pan-Asian racial identity, other researchers focus on the diversity that exists within the Asian American populations and argue that these differences may necessitate a reconfiguration of AAID, as well as other more generic models like Helms' (1995; described below) and Phinney's (1989). All of these models begin with a stage in which the individual is either generally unaware of racism directed toward their group and/or the sociopolitical implications of their

Table 9.2 Kim's Model of Asian American Identity Development

Stage	Social Environment	Critical Factor	Self-Concept	Ego Identity	Primary Reference Group	Hallmark of the Stage
1. Ethnic Awareness	Mostly at home with family	Level of participation in Asian ethnic activities	Greater participation leads to positive self-concept; less leads to negative self-concept	Greater participation leads to clearer sense of Asian heritage; less participation yields less clear meaning about Asian heritage	Family	Discovery of ethnic heritage
2. White Identification	School and other public arenas	Increased contact with Whites, leading to acceptance of White values and standards	Negative self-image, particularly body image	Being different, not fitting in, inferior to White peers, feeling isolated and responsible for any negative treatment	White people and dominant society	Feelings of being different, alienation from self and other Asian Americans, inability to connect personal experiences with racism
3. Awakening to social political consciousness	Social political movements and/or campus politics	Greater political consciousness related to being a racial/political minority and awareness of White racism	Positive; identifies as a minority in the U.S.	Accepts minority status but resists White values and domination. Feels oppressed but not inferior to Whites	Those with similar social political philosophy and antiestablishment perspective	New political perspective and sociological imagination. Political alienation from Whites
4. Redirection to an Asian American consciousness	Asian American community	Immersion in Asian American experience	Positive; identifies as an Asian American	Proud of being Asian American; experience a sense of belonging	Asian Americans, particularly those at a similar stage of identity development	Focus on personal and Asian American experience. Feel anger about Whites' treatment of Asian Americans
5. Incorporation	General	Clear and firm Asian American identity	Positive as a person	Whole person with race as a part of their social identity	People in general	Blending of Asian American identity with their other identities

status. However, in their research on South Asians, specifically Indian and Pakastani Americans, Ibrahim, Ohnishi, and Sandhu (1997) counter that immigrants from these groups often have a very good understanding of the majority group's values and beliefs because they have already had the experience of being minorities in their own land through British colonization of these areas. Yet, for each successive generation, stages like *pre-encounter* or *conformity* (described in the Helms' model below) may exist, because the second generation (and beyond) are born in the United States and are thus born outside the context of colonization that the immigrant generation experienced. In these ways, Ibrahim et al. (1997) illustrate the variation among the "Asian American experience."

While this type of variation exists, most racial identity models do not take such diversity into account. For example, the most widely used model for Asian American racial identity is the *People of Color Racial Identity Model* (Chen, LePhuoc, Guzman, Rude, & Todd, 2006), originally proposed by Janet Helms in the mid-1990s and derived from Cross' original Nigrescence theory. The model consists of five different statuses all detailed by Helms (1995). In the first status, *conformity*, individuals may reject their own racial group and prefer members of the majority group as well as their ideologies. They may also be oblivious to the histories and backgrounds of racial groups in America. In the second status, *dissonance*, individuals may feel ambivalence or confusion about their personal racial group commitment and have a tentative attitude toward racial self-definition. The *immersion/emersion* status brings idealized notions of one's own group and denigration of all things White; dichotomous (i.e., either/or) thinking is employed. Individuals may also use external standards to define their racial identity. However, by the *internalization* status, a positive attitude and commitment to one's own group develops, and racial identity is internally defined. This stage is marked by more flexible and analytical thinking. Finally, in the *integrative awareness* status, individuals value their own racial identity as well as the similarities between their group and other oppressed groups. They have the ability to build coalitions with members of other groups and "may be motivated by globally humanistic self-expression" (Helms, 1995, p. 186).

Like all of the other racial/ethnic groups profiled in this chapter, Asian Americans also experience significant barriers to identity formation. Similar to Hispanics, their racial identities are impacted by the length of their tenure in America and language. The immigrant generation is more likely to feel a sense of belonging to their country of origin, whereas those of the second generation are more likely to struggle between their "Asianness" and "Americanness." However, second-generation adolescents often refuse to accept the dichotomous choice of being either Americans or foreigners. This may breed conflict between adolescents and parents, where the latter primarily see themselves as perpetual foreigners (Sodowsky, Kwan, & Pannu, 1995, p. 126). Indeed, Takaki (1993) indicates that regardless of how Asian Americans see themselves, they may often be regarded as perpetual foreigners, even if U.S. born (see also Wong, 1993). In this way, forging a personal racial identity may be superseded by the majority group's prejudices about Asians.

Despite the decrease in social distance between Asians and Whites (Sue & Sue, 1999), Asian Americans still experience racism at the hands of Whites, and this may also impact racial identity formation. To be sure, both historical and current experiences with racism have shaped the racial identities of individuals in this group. Sue and Sue (1999) point to historical traumas, like the Chinese Exclusion Act, categorizations of Asian Americans as "the Yellow Peril," and the internment of Japanese Americans during World War II. Still, despite these experiences with personal and institutional racism that are similar to other racial minority groups, Asian American adolescents often report feelings of invisibility in that they feel like their group does not merit attention and that minority groups like Blacks have more of a voice and presence in American culture (Tatum, 1997). In some part, this claim rings true, particularly when we consider some of the more blatantly racist portrayals of Asian Americans in the mass media. Asian American women are often portrayed as delicate "China dolls," evil "dragon ladies," or hypersexual geishas, while Asian American men are portrayed as either ineffectual and asexual (e.g., the Charlie Chan stereotype) or as "sinister Orientals" (e.g., the Fu Manchu stereotype) (Espiritu, 2007). That these images still exist suggests that perhaps Asian Americans have not been as politically successful in striking down negative images as Black Americans have been. Furthermore, the destructive nature of these images may ultimately contribute to the self-hatred that Asian American adolescents may feel (Tatum, 1997).

A third obstacle to positive racial identity formation among adolescents in this group is the model minority myth. Originating from a 1966 article by William Petersen entitled, "Success Story, Japanese-American Style," the myth claims that "superior" Asian cultural values have led the group to succeed despite various obstacles (cited in Tatum, 1997). It also claims that Asian Americans naturally excel in areas like math and science (Tan, 2000; Tatum, 1997). Regarding this particular claim, research shows that some Asian American adolescents are shuttled into these areas at the expense of other academic interests, while other research indicates that they may gravitate toward these disciplines because of insecurity over their writing and speaking ability (Tan, 2000; Tatum, 1997). In terms of the larger claim about Asian American success overall, many questions abound over whether or not Asian Americans are truly successful. Healey (2007) cites that on average, second-generation Chinese Americans earned less and had less favorable occupational profiles than comparably educated White Americans (see also Sue & Sue, 1999). This gap between qualifications and rewards reflects the persistent nature of racism and discrimination. Furthermore, Healey suggests that some ethnic groups, like Chinese Americans in particular, are "bipolar" in that they are concentrated at the very top and very bottom of the occupational structure. Moreover, the model minority myth obscures the large numbers of Asian Americans who experience rampant poverty, unemployment, and underemployment, whereas those who are successful may represent a small, highly visible minority (Woo, 2000). Despite these realities, the model minority myth prevails and becomes the standard to which many Asian American adolescents are held. As such, these adolescents may feel an incredible amount of pressure to become successful in order to prove their racial/ethnic identity while those who cannot or do not reach these expectations may feel as if they aren't "authentically" Asian.

Perhaps another challenge for racial identity among Asian Americans is the high rate of interracial marriage; Asian Americans are more likely than any other group to marry outside of their race (Kitano & Daniels, 1995, cited in Healey, 2007). As a result, Sodowsky et al. (1995) claim that the United States is in the midst of a biracial/interethnic baby boom. For Asian biracials, living between racial lines can cause difficulty in the context of the U.S.'s, rigid, uncompromising, and often dichotomous constructions of race. Sodowsky et al. cite difficulties for those in this group in terms of being forced to check a racial category on an application, dealing with racist or insensitive comments of Whites who may think that Asian-White biracial individuals in particular are "one of them," or the sense of having to prove their Blackness to other Blacks that exists for Asian-Black biracials. With the increase in multiracial families in the United States, examining biracial identity remains critical to future studies on racial identity development.

9.6. **MIXED-RACE AMERICANS**

Each of the racial identity development models we have presented assumes that individuals belong to one—and only one—racial group. Social scientists have long considered race to be a social construct, as opposed to a biological reality, yet the racial identity development of mixed-race adolescents has been largely ignored or understudied by researchers. As interracial unions and the visibility of multiracial children have increased in the years since the Civil Rights Movement, researchers are increasingly focusing attention on how racial identity development among this population is distinct from the monoracial identity models previously discussed.

Thornton and Wason (1995) describe the historical development of racial identity development theories for the multiracial population as following one of three approaches: (1) the problem approach, (2) the equivalent approach, and (3) the variant approach. Rockquemore, Brunsma, and Delgado (2009) expanded this framework to include a fourth distinct approach that has emerged in the last decade: the ecological approach. We discuss each of these approaches and the theories that illustrate them in turn.

The *problem approach* to racial identity assumes that being a mixed-race person in a racially divided world is an inherently tragic and problematic social position. As a result, researchers focused on the negative social and psychological outcomes that mixed-race people experience, such as inter-personal rejection, social isolation, and stigmatization by both majority and minority groups. For example, Park's (1928, 1937) *Marginal Man* theory emerged in the context of Jim Crow segregation when the color line was rigid and uncrossable, dooming mixed-race children (particularly those with Black ancestry) to a permanent state of crisis in which their lives would be marked by turmoil. Stonequist (1937) expanded on Park's general theory by arguing that multiracial people develop identification with both groups and an internalization of the social conflict between races. Stonequist outlined three predicable stages in the life cycle of the Marginal Man. In the initial introduction stage, the Marginal Man assimi-lates into the two cultures of his/her parents. This is followed by a crisis stage, where one or more defining incidents clarify the irreconcilable nature of the racial conflict that marks his existence. The crisis induces feelings of confusion, shock, disillusionment, and difference. Finally, individuals adjust to their racial status and develop a full understanding of their social location. In most cases, the adjustment is toward the majority group. However, in the case of Black/White multiracial people in the United States, adjustment toward the majority group (Whites) was impossible because of White supremacy, segregation, and the one-drop rule (that mandated anyone with "one drop" of "Black blood" was black). In this case, the Marginal Man was predicted to become either a leader among the subordinate group (Blacks) or withdraw into isolation.

Racial identity development theories for mixed-race people transitioned from the *problem approach* to an *equivalent approach* during the Civil Rights and Black Power Movements, wherein theorists reoriented their thinking about Blackness and the one-drop rule by assuming that (Black/White) mixed-race people were part of the Black population. Researchers reasoned that the vast majority of the Black population in the United States is racially mixed, so they found no reason to differentiate between those who were mixed by immediate parentage (children of interracial families) and those who were racially mixed over generations (most Black Americans). Given their equivalence to Blacks, mixed-race people with Black ancestry were expected to develop a positive sense of Black identity just like any other Black person (i.e., per Cross previously described Nigrescence theory).

By the mid-1980s and throughout the 1990s, a new generation of researchers emerged who focused on conceptualizing the mixed-race population as distinct from any single racial group. This new *variant approach* sought to explain psychologically, clinically, and developmentally how mixed-race people actively and consciously construct a "biracial" or "multiracial" identity and how they could maintain a healthy, integrated sense of their various racial ancestries, cultures, and social locations. This radical break from the equivalent tradition is best illustrated by Maria Root's groundbreaking anthology *Racially Mixed People in America* (1992), wherein an emergent group of mixed-race scholars and activists advanced the notion that the multiracial population is a distinct group worthy of study with unique, nonpathological experiences and identity development processes.

Poston's *Biracial Identity Development Model* (BIDM, 1990) is the most oft-cited theory within the variant approach. Poston asserts that models emerging out of the problem and equivalent approaches are fundamentally flawed because they force mixed-race people to choose one racial identity and fail to allow for even the possibility of an integrated racial identity that blends all aspects of their ancestry. While the BIDM takes the same shape of previous stage models, the racial identity development process culminates in an integrated "multiracial" identity. Poston's five stages of racial identity development begin with *personal identity* where mixed-race children's racial identity is constructed at a young age and is based on family and peer interactions. This is followed by *choice of group categorization* because individuals are forced to choose an identity, a process which induces crisis. The *enmeshment/denial* stage is one that is characterized by feelings of confusion and guilt that emerge when one aspect of the individual's racial ancestry is denied (as a result of forced choice). The *appreciation* stage occurs as an adolescent or young adult learns to appreciate the totality of their racial ancestry and broadens their reference group orientation. Finally, *integration* occurs when an individual achieves a sense of wholeness by constructing an integrated multiracial identity.

The most recent approach to racial identity development among the mixed-race population is the *ecological approach* that simultaneously challenges and builds upon *variant approaches*. Specifically ecological theorists challenge models like Poston's BIDM by arguing that they make the same mistake as the equivalent approaches by privileging one type of racial identity over another (i.e., "multiracial" over "Black"). Instead, empirical data suggest that mixed-race people vary in their racial identity so that some identify with one of their parent's races, others blend their ancestries into a multiracial identity, some shift their racial identity depending on where they are and who they are interacting with, and others refuse any racial identity and instead understand themselves as "human" (Rockquemore & Brunsma, 2001). In other words, mixed-race people construct different racial identities based on various contextually specific logics, and the process of identity development has no predictable linear process or end stages (Rockquemore & Lazloffy, 2005).

While the origins of the ecological approach lie with Bronfenbrenner (1979), Maria Root's theoretical modeling (1990, 1996) represents the original application of this framework to the multiracial population. For Root, the status of having parents of different races in a society that is organized by a mutually exclusive racial structure creates a social location in the borderlands. As a result, she describes a variety of ways that mixed-race individuals function in the five-race context and the ways they engage in "border crossing." She describes these as (1) having both feet in both groups so that one has the ability to "hold, merge, and respect multiple perspectives simultaneously," (2) shifting the foreground and background as an individual crosses between and among social contexts defined by race, (3) consciously choosing to sit on the border and experiencing hybridity and a border identity as a central reference point, and/or (4) creating a home in one "camp" while visiting other camps when necessary. Root (1997, 1998, 2003) has continually refined and expanded this model (now called the *Ecological Framework for Understanding Multiracial Identity*) by contextualizing the border crossings with consideration of regional and generational histories of race relations, sexual orientation, gender, class, community attitudes, racial socialization, family functioning, and individual personality traits and aptitudes.

9.7. **CONCLUSION**

Throughout this chapter, the various challenges adolescents face and must resolve in order to determine who they are (as individuals) and how they fit into their existing social world have been presented. While the construction of a racial identity is typically confined to discussions of people of color, we contend that *all* adolescents develop a racial identity. Whether White, Black, Native American, Asian American, Hispanic, or multiracial, all adolescents face the reality that their social world is stratified by race and ethnicity and must resolve their place in that hierarchy. While the typical development process differs among members of different racial groups, each racial identity theory shares an overarching process of individuals coming to terms with the uniquely American schema of race, racism, and racial group categorization. Once confronted with experiences that reveal the existing system of racial stratification and inequality, individuals respond in ways that either keep them stagnant or move them forward in a process of developing a sophisticated and complex personal racial identification and broader understanding of American race relations.

REFERENCES

Andersen, M. L., Logio, K. A., & Taylor, H. F. (2009). *Understanding society: An introductory reader*. Belmont, CA: Thomson Wadsworth.

Bailey, B. (2001). Dominican-American ethnic/racial identities and United States social categories. *International Migration Review, 35*(3), 677–708.

Boyd-Franklin, N. (2003). *Black families in therapy: An African-American experience*. New York, NY: Guilford Press.

Bronfenbrenner, U. (1979). *The ecology of human development*. Cambridge, MA: Harvard University Press.

Carter, K. (1991). Racial identity attitudes and psychological functioning. *Journal of Multicultural Counseling and Development, 19*, 105–114.

Chen, G. A., LePhuoc, P., Guzman, M. R., Rude, S. S., & Todd, B. G. (2006). Exploring Asian American racial identity. *Cultural Diversity and Ethnic Minority Psychology, 12*(3), 461–476.

Choney, S. K., Berryhill-Paapke, E., & Robbins, R. R. (1995). The acculturation of American Indians: Developing frameworks for research and practice. In J. G. Ponterotto, J. M. Casas, L. A. Suzuki, & C. M. Alexander (Eds.), *Handbook of multicultural counseling* (pp. 73–82). Thousand Oaks, CA: Sage Publications.

Christian, M. (2000). *Multiracial identity: An international perspective*. Hampshire, UK: MacMillan Press.

Churchill, W. (2007). Crimes against humanity. In M. L. Andersen & P. H. Collins (Eds.), *Race, class, and gender: An anthology* (pp. 376–383). Belmont, CA: Thomson Wadsworth.

Clarke, E. G., & Justice, E. M. (n.d.) Identity development: Aspects of identity. In *Child development reference* (Vol. 4). Retrieved from http://social.jrank.org/pages/322/Identity-Development.html

Cole, E. R., & Omari, S. R. (2003). Race, class and the dilemmas of upward mobility for African Americans. *Journal of Social Issues, 59*(4), 785–802.

Collins, P. H. (2000). *Black feminist thought: Knowledge, consciousness, and the politics of empowerment*. New York, NY: Routledge.

Collins, P. H. (2005). *Black sexual politics: African Americans, gender and the new racism*. New York, NY: Routledge.

Cross, W. E. (1971). The Negro-to-Black conversion experience. *Black World, 20*, 13–27.

Cross, W. E. (1991). *Shades of black: Diversity in African-American identity.* Philadelphia, PA: Temple University Press.

DeVos, G., & Romanucci-Ross, L. (1982). Ethnicity: Vessel of meaning and emblem of contrast. In G. Devos & L. Romanucci-Ross (Eds.), *Ethnic identity* (pp. 363–390). Chicago, IL: University of Chicago Press.

DuBois, W. E. B. (1989). *Souls of Black folk.* New York, NY: Penguin Books.

Erikson, E. H. (1963). *Childhood and society.* New York, NY: Norton.

Erikson, E. H. (1968). *Identity: Youth and crisis.* New York, NY: Norton.

Espiritu, Y. L. (2007). Ideological racism and cultural resistance: Constructing our own images. In M. L. Andersen & P. H. Collins (Eds.), *Race, class, and gender: An anthology* (pp. 156–165). Belmont, CA: Thomson Wadsworth.

Federal Register. (2007). *Indian entities recognized and eligible to receive services from the United States Bureau of Indian Affairs*, (Vol. 72).

Ferdman, B. M., & Gallegos, P. I. (2001). Racial identity development and Latinos in the United States. In C. L. Wijeyesinghe & B. W. Jackson III (Eds.), *New perspectives on racial identity development: A theoretical and practical anthology* (pp. 32–66). New York, NY: New York University Press.

Flagg, B. (1997). The transparency phenomenon, race-neutral decisionmaking, and discriminatory intent. In R. Delgado & J. Stefanic (Eds.), *Critical white studies: Looking behind the mirror* (pp. 220–224). Philadelphia, PA: Temple University Press.

Fordham, S., & Ogbu, J. U. (1986). Black students' school success: Coping with the burden of 'Acting White'. *The Urban Review, 18*(3), 176–206.

Frankenberg, R. (1993). *White women, race matters: The social construction of Whiteness.* Minneapolis, MN: University of Minnesota Press.

Garrett, J. T., & Garrett, M. W. (1994). The path of good medicine: Understanding and counseling Native American Indians. *Journal of Multicultural Counseling and Development, 22*, 3.

Graham, L. O. (1999). *Our kind of people: Inside America's Black upper class.* New York, NY: Harper Collins Publishers.

Hardiman, R. (2001). Reflections on White identity development theory. In C. L. Wijeyesinghe & B. W. Jackson III (Eds.), *New perspectives on racial identity development: A theoretical and practical anthology* (pp. 108–128). New York, NY: New York University Press.

Harris, C. A. (2009). *The costs of upward mobility: Growing up Black middle-class* (under review).

Healey, J. F. (2007). *Diversity and society: Race, ethnicity, and gender.* Thousand Oaks, CA: Sage Publications.

Helms, J. E. (1984). Toward a theoretical explanation of the effects of race on counseling: A Black/White model. *The Counseling Psychologist, 12*(4), 153–165.

Helms, J. E. (Ed.) (1993). *Black and White racial identity: Theory, research, and practice.* Westport, CT: Praeger.

Helms, J. E. (1995). An update of Helms' White and people of color racial identity models. In J. G. Ponterotto, J. M. Casas, L. A. Suzuki, & C. M. Alexander (Eds.), *Handbook of multicultural counseling* (pp. 181–198). Thousand Oaks, CA: Sage Publications.

Henslin, J. M. (2001). *Essentials of sociology: A down-to-earth approach*. Boston, MA: Allyn and Bacon.

Herring, C., Keith, V. M., & Horton, H. D.(Eds.) (2004). *Skin deep: How race and complexion matter in the 'colorblind' era*. Chicago, IL: Institute for Research on Race and Social Policy and University of Illinois Press.

Hunter, M. (2004). Light, bright, and almost white: The advantages and disadvantages of light skin. In C. Herring, V. M. Keith, & H. D. Horton (Eds.), *Skin deep: How race and complexion matter in the 'colorblind' era* (pp. 22–44). Chicago, IL: Institute for Research on Race and Social Policy and University of Illinois Press.

Ibrahim, F., Ohnishi, H. & Sandhu, D. S. (1997). Asian American identity development: A culture specific model for South Asian Americans. *Journal of Multicultural Counseling and Development, 25*(1), 34–50.

Jackson, B.W., III, (1976). Black identity development. In L. H. Golubchick & B. Persky (Eds.), *Urban, social, and educational issues* (pp. 158–164). Dubuque, IA: Kendall/Hunt Publishers.

Jackson, B.W., III, (2001). Black identity development: Further analysis and elaboration. In C. L. Wijeyesinghe & B. W. Jackson III (Eds.), *New perspectives on racial identity development: A theoretical and practical anthology* (pp. 8–31). New York, NY: New York University Press.

Jaret, C. (1995). *Contemporary racial and ethnic relations*. New York, NY: Harper Collins Publishers.

Johnson, M. E., & Lashley, K. H. (1989). Influence of Native Americans' cultural commitment on preferences for counselor ethnicity and expectations about counseling. *Journal of Multicultural Counseling and Development, 17*, 115–122.

Katz, P. (1981). Psychotherapy with Native Adolescents. *Canadian Journal of Psychiatry, 26*, 455–459.

Kenny, L. D. (2000). *Daughters of suburbia: Growing up White, middle-class, and female*. New Brunswick, NJ: Rutgers University Press.

Kim, J. (2001). Asian American identity development theory. In C. L. Wijeyesinghe & B. W. Jackson III (Eds.), *New perspectives on racial identity development: A theoretical and practical anthology* (pp. 67–90). New York, NY: New York University Press.

Kitano, H., & Daniels, R. (1995). *Asian Americans: Emerging minorities* (2nd ed.) Englewood Cliffs, NJ: Prentice Hall.

Lacy, K. R. (2007). *Blue chip black: Race, class and status in the new Black middle class*. Berkeley, CA: University of California Press.

LaFromboise, T., Coleman, H., & Gerton, J. (1993). Psychological aspects of bicultural competence: Evidence and theory. *Psychological Bulletin, 114*, 395–412.

LaFromboise, T. D., Medoff, L., Lee, C. C., & Harris, A. (2007). Psychosocial and cultural correlates of suicidal ideation among American Indian early adolescents on a northern plains reservation. *Research in Human Development, 4*(1-2), 119–143.

LaFromboise, T. D., Trimble, J. E., & Mohatt, G. V. (1990). Counseling intervention and American Indian tradition: An integrative approach. *The Counseling Psychologist, 18*, 628–654.

Lieberson, S. (1981). *A piece of the pie: Blacks and White immigrants Since 1880.* Berkeley, CA: University of California Press.

Marcia, J. E. (1966). Development and validation of ego identity status. *Journal of Personality and Social Psychology, 3*, 551–558.

Marcia, J. E. (1980). Identity in adolescence. In J. Adelson (Ed.), *Handbook of adolescent psychology* (pp. 159–187). New York, NY: Wiley.

Marcia, J. E. (1991). Identity and self-development. In R. M. Lerner, A. C. Peterson & J. Brooks-Gunn (Eds.), *Encyclopedia of adolescence* (Vol. 1, pp. 529–533). New York, NY: Garland.

Matute-Bianchi, M. E. (1986). Ethnic identities and patterns of school success and failure among Mexican-descent and Japanese American students in a California high School: An ethnographic analysis. *American Journal of Education, 95*, 233–255.

McIntosh, P. (2007). White privilege and male privilege: Unpacking the invisible knapsack. In M. L. Andersen & P. H. Collins (Eds.), *Race, class, and gender: An anthology* (pp. 98–102). Belmont, CA: Thomson Wadsworth.

Mendelberg, H. E. (1986). Identity conflict in Mexican-American adolescents. *Adolescence, 21*, 215–222.

Merskin, D. (2007). Winnebagos, Cherokees, Apaches, and Dakotas: The persistence of stereotyping of American Indians in American advertising brands. In C. A. Gallagher (Ed.), *Rethinking the color line: Readings in race and ethnicity* (pp. 446–455). New York, NY: McGraw-Hill Companies.

Neckerman, K. M., Carter, P., & Lee, J. (1999). Segmented assimilation and minority cultures of mobility. *Ethnic and Racial Studies, 22*(6), 945–965.

Oyserman, D., & Harrison, K. (1998). Implications of cultural context: African American identity and possible selves. In J. K. Swim & C. Stangor (Eds.), *Prejudice: The target's perspective* (pp. 281–300). San Diego, CA: Academic Press.

Parham, T. (1989). Cycles of psychological Nigrescence. *The Counseling Psychologist, 17*(2), 187–226.

Parham, T. (2001). Psychological Nigrescence revisited: A foreword. *Journal of Multicultural Counseling and Development, 29*, 162–164.

Park, R. (1928). Human migration and the marginal man. *American Journal of Sociology, 33*, 881–893.

Park, R. (1937). Introduction. In E. V. Stonequist (Ed.), *The marginal man: A study in personality and culture conflict* (p. xvii). New York, NY: Russell & Russell.

Patterson, O. (1972). Toward a future that has no past—Reflections on the fate of Blacks in the Americas. *Public Interest, 27*, 25–62.

Perry, P. (2001). White means never having to say you're ethnic: White youth and the construction of 'cultureless' identities. *Journal of Contemporary Ethnography, 30*(1), 56–91.

Peterson-Lewis, S., & Bratton, L. M. (2004). Perceptions of 'acting Black' among African American teens: Implications of racial dramaturgy for academic and social achievement. *The Urban Review, 36*(2), 81–100.

Phinney, J. S. (1989). Stages of ethnic identity development in minority group adolescents. *Journal of Early Adolescence, 9*, 163–173.

Phinney, J. S. (1990). Ethnic identity in adolescents and adults: A review of research. *Psychological Bulletin, 108*(3), 499–514.

Phinney, J. S., & Kohatsu, E. L. (1997). Ethnic and racial identity development and mental health. In J. Schulenberg, J. Maggs, & K. Hurrelmann (Eds.), *Health risks and developmental transitions during adolescence* (pp. 420–443). Cambridge: Cambridge University Press.

Phinney, J. S., Lochner, B. T., & Murphy, R. (1990). Ethnic identity development and psychological adjustment in adolescence. In A. R. Stiffman & L. E. Davis (Eds.), *Ethnic issues in adolescent mental health* (pp. 53–72). Newbury Park, CA: Sage Publications.

Portes, A., & Rumbaut, R. G. (2001). *Legacies: The story of the immigrant second generation*. Berkeley, CA: University of California Press.

Poston, C. (1990). The biracial identity development model: A needed addition. *Journal of Counseling and Development, 69*, 152–155.

Pyant, C. T., & Yanico, B. J. (1991). Relationship of racial identity and gender-role attitudes to Black women's psychological well-being. *Journal of Counseling Psychology, 38*, 315–322.

Red Horse, Y. (1982). A cultural network model: Perspectives for adolescent services and para-professional training. In S. M. Manson (Ed.), *New directions in prevention among American Indian and Alaska Native communities* (pp. 173–185). Portland, OR: Oregon Health Sciences University.

Rockquemore, K. A., & Brunsma, D. (2001). *Beyond Black: Biracial identity in America*. Thousand Oaks, CA: Sage Publications.

Rockquemore, K. A., Brunsma, D., & Delgado, D. (2009). Racing to theory or re-theorizing race? Understanding the struggle to build a multiracial identity theory. *Journal of Social Issues, 65*(1), 13–34.

Rockquemore, K. A., & Lazloffy, T. (2005). *Raising biracial children*. Lanham, MD: Altamira Press.

Rodriguez, R. (1981). Aria: A memoir of a bilingual childhood. *The American Scholar, 50*(1), 25–42.

Root, M. P. (1990). Resolving "other" status: Identity development of biracial individuals. *Women and Therapy, 9*, 185–205.

Root, M. P. (1996). The multiracial experience: Racial borders as significant frontier in race relations. In M. Root (Ed.), *The multiracial experience: Racial borders as the new frontier* (pp. xii–xxviii). Thousand Oaks, CA: Sage Publications.

Root, M. P. (1997). Mixed race women. In N. Zack (Ed.), *Race/sex: Their sameness, difference, and interplay* (pp. 157–174). New York, NY: Routledge.

Root, M. P. (1998). Experiences and processes affecting racial identity development: Preliminary results from the Biracial Sibling Project. *Cultural Diversity and Mental Health, 4*, 237–247.

Root, M. P. (2003). Racial identity development and persons of mixed race heritage. In M. P. P. Root & M. Kelly (Eds.), *The multiracial child resource book: Living complex identities* (pp. 34–41). Seattle, WA: Mavin Foundation.

Rowe, W., Bennett, S. K., & Atkinson, D. R. (1994). White racial identity models: A critique and alternative proposal. *The Counseling Psychologist, 22*(1), 129–146.

Ruiz, A. S. (1990). Ethnic identity: Crisis and resolution. *Journal of Multicultural Counseling and Development*, *18*, 29–40.

Russell, K. Y., Wilson, M., & Hall, R. (1992). *The color complex: The politics of skin color among African Americans*. New York, NY: Doubleday.

Sellers, R. M., Chavous, T. M., & Cooke, D. Y. (1998). Racial centrality as predictors of African American college students' academic performance. *Journal of Black Psychology*, *24*(1), 8–27.

Sellers, R. M., Smith, M., Shelton, J., Rowley, S., & Chavous, T. (1998). Multidimensional model of racial identity: A reconceptualization of African American racial identity. *Personality and Social Psychology Review*, *2*, 18–39.

Sodowsky, G. R., Kwan, K. K., & Pannu, R. (1995). Ethnic identity of Asians in the United States. In J. G. Ponterotto, J. M. Casas, L. A. Suzuki, & C. M. Alexander (Eds.), *Handbook of multicultural counseling* (pp. 123–154). Thousand Oaks, CA: Sage Publications.

Spencer, M. B. (1999). Social and cultural influences on school adjustment: The application of an identity-focused cultural ecological perspective. *Educational Psychologist*, *34*(1), 43–57.

Spencer, M. B., & Markstrom-Adams, C. (1990). Identity processes among racial and ethnic minority children in America. *Child Development*, *61*, 290–310.

Stonequist, E. (1937). *The marginal man: A study in personality and culture conflict*. New York, NY: Russell & Russell.

Struthers, R., & Lowe, J. (2003). Nursing in the Native American culture and historical trauma. *Issues in Mental Health and Nursing*, *24*, 257–272.

Sue, D. W., & Sue, D. (1999). *Counseling the culturally different: Theory and practice*. New York, NY: Wiley.

Sunday, J., Eyles, J., & Upshur, R. (2001). Applying Aristotle's doctrine of causation to Aboriginal and biomedical understandings of diabetes. *Culture, Medicine, and Psychiatry*, *25*, 63–85.

Takaki, R. (1993). *A different mirror: A history of multicultural America*. Boston, MA: Little, Brown & Co.

Tan, A. (2000). Mother tongue. In *The writer's presence: A pool of readings* (pp. 271–276). Boston, MA: Bedford/St. Martin Press.

Tatum, B. D. (1997). *Why are all the Black kids sitting together in the cafeteria? And other conversations about race*. New York, NY: Harper Collins Publishers.

Thornton, M., & Wason, S. (1995). Intermarriage. In D. Levinson (Ed.), *Encyclopedia of marriage and the family* (pp. 396–402). New York, NY: MacMillan Publishing.

U.S. Bureau of the Census. (2006a). *Race—Universe: Total population. Survey: 2006 American Community Survey*. www.factfinder.census.gov

U.S. Bureau of the Census. (2006b). *ACS demographic and housing estimates. Survey: 2006 American Community Survey*. www.factfinder.census.gov

van den Berghe, P. (1967). *Race and racism*. New York, NY: Wiley.

Waters, M. C. (2006). Optional ethnicities: For Whites only. In T. E. Ore (Ed.), *The social construction of difference and inequality: Race, class, gender, and sexuality* (pp. 29–41). New York, NY: McGraw-Hill Companies.

Waters, M. C. (2007). Ethnic and racial identities of second-generation Black immigrants in New York City. In C. A. Gallagher (Ed.), *Rethinking the color line: Readings in race and ethnicity* (pp. 518–534). New York, NY: McGraw-Hill Companies.

Wong, S. C. (1993). *Reading Asian American literature: From necessity to extravagance*. Princeton, NJ: Princeton University Press.

Woo, D. (2000). The gap between striving and achieving: The case of Asian American women. In M. Andersen & P. H. Collins (Eds.), *Race, class, and gender: An anthology* (pp. 243–251). Belmont, CA: Wadsworth.

Yinger, J. M. (1985). Assimilation in the United States: The Mexican Americans. In W. Connor (Ed.), *Mexican Americans in comparative perspective* (pp. 30–55). Washington, DC: Urban Institute Press.

Zimmerman, M. A., Ramirez-Valles, J., Washienko, K. M., Walter, B., & Dyer, S. (1996). The development of a measure of enculturation for Native American youth. *American Journal of Community Psychology*, 24, 295–310.

Zitzow, D., & Estes, G. (1981). The heritage consistency continuum in counseling Native American children. In *American Indian issues in higher education*. (pp. 133–139). Edited by Spring Conference on Contemporary American Issues.

10

Immigration and well-being

Cleopatra Y. Jacobs Johnson
University of Pennsylvania, Philadelphia, PA

Tirzah R. Spencer
University of North Carolina, Chapel Hill, NC

Michele Muñoz-Miller
University of Pennsylvania, Philadelphia, PA

Tyhesha Goss Elmore
University of Pennsylvania, Philadelphia, PA

Traditionally, migration to the United States is largely spurred by individuals' desire for increased freedom (e.g., political, religious, and social) and opportunity (e.g., educational and occupational; e.g., Suárez-Orozco, Suárez-Orozco, & Todorova, 2008). In the United States, immigrant parents often cite upward social mobility and educational opportunity as factors that influenced their decision to migrate to the United States with their children (Suárez-Orozco et al., 2008). Immigration to places such as Europe is also spurred by the desire for freedom and opportunity, but Europe's increasingly restrictive immigration policies, coupled with less restrictive immigration policies in the United States, have increased migration to the United Stattes (Halter, 2007). The *1965 Immigration Act* is generally regarded as a less restrictive immigration policy because it eliminated previous country-specific immigration quotas, which in turn ushered in the current era of increased immigration to the United States. In fact, there are more immigrants now living in the United States than at any other time in American history (Hernandez, Denton, & Macartney, 2007).

Unlike the immigration era of the first half of the twentieth century, post-1965, the largest number of immigrants did not come from Europe, but from Africa, Asia, the Caribbean, and Latin America, with the largest number of immigrants coming from Mexico followed by East and

Southeast Asia (Hernandez et al., 2007; Portes & Rumbaut, 2001). The diversity in immigrants' country of origin is contributing to greater cultural, linguistic, and racial/ethnic diversity in the United States and is increasing political and social debate about immigration policies and practices, particularly in relationship to the economic and social impact of immigration (e.g., Does increased immigration reduce job opportunities for American citizens, especially in the low-skilled labor market?). Debates centering on the economic and social impact of immigration are not unique to the United States. For example, the European Union is experiencing similar contention in its effort to create a common immigration policy (Guild, Carrera, & Eggenschwiler, 2009).

Recent population statistics estimate that one in five children in the United States is an immigrant or the child of immigrant parents, and the numbers are consistently rising (Hernandez et al., 2007). This has had two effects: First, among children in the United States, immigrant children[1] comprise the fastest growing segment of the population (Hernandez et al., 2007). Second, nationally, immigration accounts for practically all of the increase in public school enrollment over the past two decades (Camarota, 2007). Given the increase in the number of immigrant children, as well as adults, and the rapid rate with which they are entering educational, child welfare, and other social service systems designed to serve children and families, today's immigrant families pose a new and pressing challenge for a range of institutions. What is the continuum of issues and challenges faced by immigrant children and families as they adapt to their American lives? How do the complexities associated with being a newcomer in a strange land affect immigrant youth's development, specifically as it relates to multiple dimensions of their well-being?

This chapter presents a discussion of a particular set of challenges and experiences that immigrant children and families encounter in the process of building their lives in the United States. The specific foci of this chapter are the relationship between immigration and ethnic identity, physical health, and language brokering, along with the link between language, education, and policy. These issues are among the most pressing for immigrants, and a complete discussion of them is beyond the scope of this chapter; however, it is our hope that the reader will gain an increased understanding of some of the complexities related to being an immigrant child or adolescent in the United States. Immigration is

---

[1]The term "immigrant children" is commonly used when referring to both foreign-born children and U.S.-born children of immigrant parents.

contributing to a demographic shift toward racial and ethnic minorities, especially Latinos, becoming the new American majority (Hernandez et al., 2007), thus race and ethnicity are central to current discussions of immigration. Accordingly, Asian, Black, and Latino immigrant youth are the focus of this chapter.

10.1. **ETHNIC IDENTITY**

The United States' racial and ethnic diversity, coupled with its racial and ethnic hierarchies, can pose a challenge to immigrants. Immigrants from less racially and ethnically diverse nations may find themselves overwhelmed by the diversity found in the United States. In addition, immigrants who are classified as racial and ethnic minorities in the U.S., who are from nations in which their racial and ethnic group occupies the top of the social ladder, may also experience challenges with a new social hierarchy. In both instances, immigrants' struggle with the United States' racial and ethnic categories stems from their attempt to define themselves in a country that may be significantly culturally, socially, politically, and historically different from their homeland. For adolescent immigrants, the differences between their homeland and the United States may make the developmental task of identity development especially challenging as they define their racial and ethnic identity.

In a broader perspective, irrespective of the country that immigrants settle in, immigrant groups and individuals arrive in their new country with different attitudes related to the degree to which they can/will retain their native culture and integrate into the new society (Phinney, Horenczyk, Liebkind, & Vedder, 2001). From an interactional perspective, immigrants' attitudes toward retaining their native culture and integrating in the new society will correlate with (1) the actual and perceived acceptance of immigrants and (2) the official immigration policies (Phinney et al., 2001). Research specific to immigrant youth in the United States has yielded four categories of racial and ethnic identity: (1) national identity, (2) hyphenated American, (3) American, and (4) panethnic. A national identity (e.g., Chinese) reflects identification with the native country and hyphenated American identity (e.g., Chinese American) reflects a bicultural identity that incorporates features of the homeland and the United States. An American identity reflects a lack of connection with the native homeland, and a panethnic identity (e.g., Asian) refers to a denationalized identification with the United States' nonimmigrant racial and ethnic groups (Portes & Rumbaut, 2001; Rumbaut, 1994). Researchers have found that immigrant youths' ethnic identity choice is, in part, in response to the racial and ethnic climate in the United States.

Researchers have found that U.S. immigrant adolescents' racial and ethnic identities are influenced by or in response to their social context. Immigrant youth have been found to adopt the ethnic identity label of their peer group (Portes & Rumbaut, 2001; Rumbaut, 1994; Waters, 1994, 1996). For example, across national origin groups, youth attending inner-city schools with predominately nonimmigrant racial and ethnic minority students had an increased likelihood of identifying panethnically than immigrant youth who did not attend such schools (Portes & Rumbaut, 2001; Rumbaut, 1994). Similarly, Black immigrants attending school or living in predominately nonimmigrant Black neighborhoods were also more likely to identify panethnically (Rumbaut, 1994). In contrast, Haitian immigrants attending predominately nonimmigrant Black high schools were slightly more likely to identify themselves nationally (i.e., Haitian) or to use a hyphenated American identity (i.e., Haitian American; Stepick, Stepick, Eugene, Teed, & Labissiere, 2001). Further, Haitian youth attending predominately non-Black schools (i.e., predominately Latino schools) were somewhat more likely to identify as "mixed" or as African American.

Research on Black adolescent immigrants has found a link between their racial and ethnic identity and their experiences with and perceptions of Black Americans, racism, and discrimination. Specifically, Waters (1994, 1996) found that Black West Indian immigrant adolescents who chose a panethnic ethnic identity label (i.e., Black or Black American) expressed greater fondness for Black American culture than West Indian culture. In addition, the panethnically identified Black immigrant youth in Waters' studies viewed Black Americans and Black West Indians as being more socially, culturally, and historically similar than different.

In contrast, some Black West Indian immigrant adolescents reported reacting to racism and discrimination by making a conscious effort to distinguish themselves from Black Americans and did so by choosing either a national or hyphenated American identity (e.g., Antiguan or Antiguan American; Waters, 1994, 1996). The nationally identified or hyphenated American-identified youth's identity choices were largely due to their perception that White Americans treated Black West Indians better than Black Americans. In response to these perceptions, the Black West Indian immigrants sought to heighten the salience of their immigrant identity through both their ethnic identity label and other explicit behaviors (e.g., adopting an accent, displaying visual cues about one's country of origin such as flags), particularly when they encountered White Americans (Waters, 1994, 1996).

10.2. **ETHNIC IDENTITY AND PSYCHOLOGICAL WELL-BEING**

Researchers have long been interested in the link between psychological well-being and racial and ethnic identity (e.g., Cross, 1991; Phinney, 1990). Given that racism and discrimination can adversely affect racial and ethnic minorities' psychological health (e.g., Hammack, 2003; Williams, Neighbors, & Jackson, 2003) and the salience of discrimination and racism to Black immigrants' ethnic identity choices (e.g., Waters, 1994, 1996), the relationship between ethnic identity and psychological well-being among Black immigrant youth becomes important to examine.

In one study, Rumbaut (1994) found that the immigrant-identified Black West Indian adolescents had the highest self-esteem when compared to their peers in the other ethnic identity categories. Waters (1999) argues that Black West Indian immigrants' experience as the racial majority in their homeland gives them a "strong sense of personal efficacy and ambition" (p. 26). Foreign-born Black West Indian immigrant children who come to the United States at a young age or those who are born in the United States have little or no experience living in countries where Blacks are the racial majority. Their racial socialization primarily unfolds in the United States; however, they may still reap the benefits of their parents being socialized "back home" (Kasinitz, Battle, & Miyares, 2001). In the case of the immigrant-identified Black immigrant youth in Rumbaut's study, their identity may offer them psychological protection from the negative effects of discrimination and racism. Importantly, Kasinitz et al. (2001) did not find a difference in psychological well-being among Black West Indian adolescents as a function of ethnic identity type. Kasinitz et al. (2001) attributed their finding to the presence of positive images of Blacks in both African American and West Indian culture.

Although this discussion of immigration and ethnic identity centered on Black immigrant adolescents, undoubtedly the intersection between the two are not unique to this group. However, this discussion serves to highlight the role of socialization across contexts (e.g., home, neighborhood, country), discrimination, and racism in identity formation, particularly among racial and ethnic minority immigrant groups. Immigration and ethnic identity are important issues to continue pursuing, in part because, as demonstrated by previous research (e.g., Rumbaut, 1994; Stepick et al., 2001; Waters, 1994, 1996), immigrants have a range of choices for their ethnic identity. The ethnic identity choices immigrants make can provide some insight into their experiences in and their perceptions of their new home, which in turn can affect their psychological well-being.

10.3. **IMMIGRANT YOUTH AND PHYSICAL HEALTH: THE ROLE OF FAMILY, COMMUNITY, AND SOCIAL NETWORKS**

Studies suggest that relative to nonimmigrant youth, immigrant youth are in poorer physical health and have less access to healthcare, including dental care (Crosnoe, 2006; Huang, Yu, & Ledsky, 2006; Lessard & Ku, 2003; Sarmiento et al., 2005; Yu, Bellamy, Schwalberg, & Drum, 2001). A more nuanced perspective, however, suggests consideration should be given to variability within and across ethnic immigrant groups, as well as to the health outcomes that are under study. The Latino Health Paradox suggests that Latinos in the United States are healthier than the general population with similar demographic characteristics (Markides & Coreil, 1986). However, studies suggest that this comparison may be true only for health outcomes such as mental health and asthma, and not for overall health or obesity (Taningco, 2007). Additionally, this advantage may decrease the longer Latino immigrants remain in the United States (Lara, Gambo, Kahramanian, Morales, & Bautista, 2005).

Among Latinos in the United States, approximately 40% are foreign-born and experience a decline in their physical health the longer they live in the U.S., which contributes to higher rates of cervical cancer, sexually transmitted infections, teenage pregnancy, obesity, and diabetes, especially among Latinas (Bathum & Baumann, 2007). Other challenges specific to Latino immigrants, with health implications for youth, include experiences of discrimination and access to health insurance coverage and to a consistent health care provider who speaks Spanish. Furthermore, for all Latinos, regardless of immigrant status, obesity and overweight status are concerns (Taningco, 2007). Similar challenges are relevant for other immigrant populations as well, but this discussion utilizes research on Latino immigrant groups to highlight the salient issues related to physical health and immigration.

Critical areas to consider in the development of positive health outcomes and well-being among immigrant youth are challenges and supports specific to contexts within the family, community, and social networks. Immigrants experience multiple and varied stressors upon migrating to a new country, including stress related to familial separation and shifting family dynamics. These stressors and others have important implications for families, particularly women. Within immigrant families, women are often the central figure and have primary responsibilities for the production and preparation of food, along with being the primary point of family and community connections (Bathum & Baumann, 2007). For many newcomers the significance of family, community, and social networks are central aspects of their identity in their home country. However, as a consequence of migration, the loss or shift of these social structures exacerbates stress levels and affects the health status of families and youth (Bathum & Baumann, 2007). Thus, the roles of family, community, and social networks are important aspects to consider in public and scientific discussions of health outcomes among immigrant youth.

Among immigrant youth, maintaining a strong connection with family members from childhood through adolescence serves as a source of support in the presence of immigration-related challenges (Gallegos-Castillo, 2006; Guzmán, Arruda, & Feria, 2006). Compared with youth from other racial and ethnic groups, Latino youth, particularly girls, tend to report an emotionally closer relationship with their mothers than with their fathers during the transition through adolescence, although time spent with fathers is substantial and studies support positive relationships between Latino fathers and their daughters (Bronstein, 1999; Foster, 2004; Guzmán et al., 2006). Although Latino youth report closer relationships with their mothers than with their fathers, fathers nonetheless play a unique role in family dynamics and relationships. Being a father and a role model are important to Puerto Rican male identity (Foster, 2004). Among Mexican families, fathers of elementary school-aged children provided their children with greater encouragement and playfulness, as well as gender-specific socialization, than did mothers. In addition, fathers have been found to be gentler toward their daughters than to their sons and to be less demanding and critical (Bronstein, 1999). These types of developmentally specific father-daughter and mother-daughter interactions have implications for the development of positive health outcomes among youth (Gallegos-Castillo, 2006).

Familismo, a central cultural value within the Latino community, may have both positive and negative health implications for youth (Gallegos-Castillo, 2006). Informal and formal social networks within the family and community have the potential to promote positive health outcomes. Given the fluidity and significance placed on the extended family, Latinas tend to discuss issues that have potential health consequences for youth (such as sexual risk-taking behaviors) with nonparental others more often than do adolescent girls in other ethnic groups. In fact, Guzmán et al. (2006) report that girls talk about sex most often with their friends, followed by their sisters, aunts, and cousins, rather than with their mothers. Conversations with family members, in addition to religious activities, eating, chores, and parental modeling of behaviors, serve as opportunities to support positive health-related behaviors among youth (Ayala, 2006; Bronstein, 1999; Gallegos-Castillo, 2006). Additionally, family cohesion and obligation may also lead to friction between parents and their adolescents, particularly between mothers and daughters, as daughters challenge more traditional Latina roles (Zayas, Lester, Cabassa, & Fortuna, 2005).

Studies suggest that, in addition to the role of family in the health of immigrant youth, adolescents' perceptions of a "sense of community" and social networks are also important. Bathum and Baumann (2007) explored various aspects of community on the health status of Latina women by assessing the perceived sense of membership (or sense of belonging), influence, integration, and shared emotional connections within a community. Latina women in a focus group cited economic hardship and providing a better life for their children as the most common reasons for migrating. In addition, they identified community membership and perceived level of community integration as contributing to their decision to migrate to the United States.

Social networks within communities have also been found to influence adolescents' health. Shiao (2002) suggests that social networks refer not only to demographic characteristics such as size and the age of the community, but to ways in which individuals access and seek resources within their community. Examples of important factors to consider include coordination between community institutions and nonprofit organizations and access to city government offices and corporations, as well as community foundations, religious institutions, and grassroots efforts (Shiao, 2002).

Additional attention should be given to the unique and various ways in which immigrant youth and families experience family relationships, community, and social networks. The centrality and importance of these factors in the lives of immigrant adolescents suggest that they are important means for supporting efforts to address the significant health-related challenges adolescents face. Incorporating dimensions of family, community, and social networks will likely enhance efforts to promote adolescent immigrants' positive health outcomes.

10.4. **CHILD LANGUAGE BROKERING**

Immigrant families' ability to thrive in the United States is also impacted by the degree to which they are proficient in English. That is, where immigrants fall on the continuum of English language proficiency can either exacerbate or mitigate the challenges associated with immigration. Data from the 2000 Census indicated that among immigrant families with children between the ages of 5 and 17 years old, 74% of parents reported that their children speak English exclusively or very well, but only 58% parents reported that they speak English exclusively or very well (Hernandez et al., 2007). Given the difference between parents and children in English language proficiency, children from non-English-speaking families often find themselves serving as interpreters for their families in the predominately English-speaking United States (e.g., with doctors and medical personnel) as they become actively engaged in their families' day-to-day efforts to survive (de las Fuentes & Vasquez, 1999; Vasquez, Pease-Alvarez, & Shannon, 1994; Weisskirch, 2005, 2007). In this capacity, children in immigrant families become child language brokers.[2]

As language brokers, immigrant children are asked to translate and interpret for their parents during their interactions with English-speakers, thus creating connections between people from different cultures by enabling communication between linguistically different people (McQuillan & Tse, 1995). Tse (1995a,b) contends that child language brokers do not simply translate and interpret from one language to another. Rather, child language brokers *mediate* interactions between culturally and linguistically different people and have the power to "…influence the contents and nature of the messages they convey, and ultimately affect the perceptions and decisions of the agents for whom they act" (Tse, 1995b, p. 180). Child language brokers comprise a unique group of immigrant children whose work differs drastically from formal or professional translators and interpreters.

Language brokering is an informal practice that mainly takes place in the context of everyday activities (Halgunseth, 2003; Harris & Sherwood, 1978; McQuillan & Tse, 1995; Orellana, Reynolds, Dorner, & Meza, 2003; Tse & McQuillan, 1996), whereas formal or professional translators and interpreters mainly work in professional settings. Formal translators and interpreters also receive professional training, which is not the case for child language brokers (Harris & Sherwood, 1978). In fact, Harris and Sherwood (1978) argue that all bilingual people have a natural or innate ability to translate to the extent that they are proficient in both languages. Professional interpreters are also bound by rules that require them to be impartial or neutral to the parties involved, but child language brokers are not bound by such rules. Instead, child language brokers' efforts are solely on behalf of their parents and their interests (Valdes, 2003). In addition, child language brokers are in an unequal power relationship with the people for whom they broker, but this is not the case for formal translators and interpreters (Halgunseth, 2003; McQuillan & Tse, 1995).

A critical mass of research on child language brokering and brokers began to emerge in the mid-1990s (Morales & Hanson, 2005). Initial research on

---

[2]The use of the word "child" in the phrase "child language brokers" is intended to reflect status differences between parents and children, rather than chronological age.

language brokering was largely descriptive and included small study samples (Morales & Hanson, 2005), but there is a growing body of qualitative and quantitative research that offers insight into this common yet understudied reality for immigrant children who are more proficient in English than the adults in their household. To date, much of the research on language brokering focuses on Latino children and adolescents, with a small subset of studies on Vietnamese and Chinese populations (Morales & Hanson, 2005). Thus, the research findings may not adequately reflect the experiences of child language brokers from other regions or countries. Although child language brokering may be a common practice across immigrant groups irrespective of region or country of origin, some immigrant groups may find themselves relying more heavily on language brokering than others. For example, Spanish-speaking immigrants may more readily find that their linguistic needs are met due to the growth of the Latino population in the United States and the almost ubiquitous presence of Spanish language classes in public school. In contrast, Hmong immigrants and others from immigrant groups with small populations in the United States may have a different experience.

In many ways, child language brokers provide a critical service to their families as they become a day-to-day conduit for their parents' interactions with English-speaking individuals. Children's brokering skills are used in a variety of common settings for the purposes of home-school and medical provider-patient communications, completing business transactions, filling out government forms and job applications, reading and responding to mail, and communicating the messages in English-language newspapers and television programs (Harris & Sherwood, 1978; McQuillan & Tse, 1995; Orellana, 2001; Orellana, Reynolds, et al., 2003; Puig, 2002; Schieffelin & Cochran-Smith, 1984; Shannon, 1990; Tse, 1995b, 1996; Valenzuela, 1999; Weisskirch, 2005, 2007; Weisskirch & Alva, 2002; Worthy, 2006). As more attention is being drawn to the informal practice of child language brokering, questions are emerging surrounding the nature of the relationship between brokering and children's development.

10.5. EFFECTS OF CHILD LANGUAGE BROKERING

10.5.1. Academic performance and cognitive development

Research on the relationship between language brokering and academic performance has produced mixed results. In one of the earliest studies of language brokering, Latino adolescents' academic performance was not significantly related to language brokering (Tse, 1995b). In a later study of Latino adolescents, Acoach and Webb (2004) also found that language brokering and academic performance were unrelated. In contrast, Buriel, Perez, DeMent, Chavez, and Moran (1998) found that among Latino high school students, increased language brokering experience, particularly the number of places in which children brokered, was positively related to their academic grades. Later research with Latino early adolescents found that children who were actively engaged in language brokering activities had significantly higher standardized math and reading test scores than their non-language brokering peers (Orellana, 2003). The educational advantage associated with increased language brokering that Orellana reported persisted into the following academic year (Dorner, Orellana, & Li-Grining, 2007).

The cognitive benefits believed to be associated with language brokering are related to its effect on children's academic performance. For example, some have speculated that children's language skills and vocabulary are enriched by the variety of settings and documents to which they are exposed as they broker, which increases the likelihood that they will develop the linguistic skills necessary for educational success in school (Halgunseth, 2003; Heath, 1986). In addition, child language brokers are exposed to adult-level language and problem-solving tasks, thus requiring them to develop and use higher-order cognitive and decision-making skills (e.g., McQuillan & Tse, 1995; Morales & Hanson, 2005; Tse & McQuillan, 1996; Valdes, 2003; Weisskirch & Alva, 2002).

Child language brokering appears to have some educational benefits for children, but there are concerns that brokering places children at risk for poor educational outcomes. Specifically, Umaña-Taylor (2003) expressed concern that when schools and parents rely on children to serve as language brokers around issues related to school, children may assume their parents' role as decision makers. Furthermore, children's educational and occupational opportunities may be constrained by family obligations related to language brokering; for example, they may forgo a college scholarship to remain close to home (Umaña-Taylor, 2003). In examining this issue Sy (2006) found that among late adolescent Latina female college students, those who engaged in more language brokering activities for their parents reported higher levels of school-related stress related to graduation, maintaining grades, and balancing school demands with family responsibilities. In another group of studies, adolescent language brokers reported making school-related decisions for themselves and younger siblings without consulting their parents (Chu, 1999; McQuillan & Tse, 1995; Tse, 1995a,b; Valenzuela, 1999); in addition, parents' dependence on their children for language brokering along with their limited proficiency in English may hinder their efforts to remain involved in their children's education (Worthy, 2006).

10.5.2. **Parent-child relationships**

Arguably, one of the most contested areas in research and discussions about child language brokering centers on how it affects the parent-child relationship and family dynamics. Two conflicting schools of thought have emerged from research on child language brokering and family dynamics (Morales & Hanson, 2005). On one hand, the work child language brokers do is framed as being critical to their families' survival. Child language brokers can facilitate their parents' acculturation in the United States because they are often their parents' main source of information on American culture and norms (Halgunseth, 2003; McQuillan & Tse, 1995). Moreover, children's role as language brokers can have tangible and concrete benefits for their parents (e.g., parental employment; Orellana, Reynolds, et al., 2003; Valdes, 2003; Valenzuela, 1999). Children also reported using their role as a language broker to protect their parents from embarrassment and humiliation (Orellana, Reynolds, et al., 2003). In turn, helping their families accomplish everyday tasks and easing the burdens associated with a lack of English-language proficiency contribute to children taking pride in and enjoying being language brokers (Tse, 1995b, 1996; Valdes, 2003; Valenzuela, 1999; Worthy, 2006). Language brokering may also strengthen the parent-child bond (Love & Buriel, 2007), and the absence of family conflict also enhances adolescents' language brokering experiences (Weisskirch, 2007).

In contrast, others suggest that child language brokering can create an unhealthy role reversal for parents and children (e.g., Orellana, 2001; Umaña-Taylor, 2003; Worthy, 2006). Independence and maturity are paramount to adolescent development, but in their role as language brokers, children in immigrant families may assume or fulfill adult roles in their family (Morales & Hanson, 2005; Orellana, 2001; Puig, 2002). When children take on adult roles in their family, parents' authority diminishes, which can lead to parents becoming dependent on their children (Umaña-Taylor, 2003; Worthy, 2006). In one of the few child language brokering studies that includes parents, 78% of parents reported that language brokering gave their children the power within the family (Puig, 2002). As child language brokers, some youth find themselves engaged in activities, such as educational decisions, that would normally be under the purview of parents in English-speaking families (Hedges, 2000; Umaña-Taylor, 2003).

Child language brokers' increased power in the family coupled with parents' perceived dependence on children may heighten the stress that immigrant families, who are already vulnerable, experience (Umaña-Taylor, 2003; Worthy, 2006). Oftentimes, parents find themselves needing to share personal or private information with their children regarding financial and health-related matters, which can trigger parental resentment toward children (Umaña-Taylor, 2003). Similarly, youth report language brokering as being burdensome, stressful, and frustrating (McQuillan & Tse, 1995; Puig, 2002; Tse, 1995b, 1996; Worthy, 2006). Adolescents report their frustration with language brokering as largely stemming from the constant need to explain things to their parents (Puig, 2002; Worthy, 2006).

Child language brokers also reported that brokering embarrasses and humiliates them (McQuillan & Tse, 1995; Ng, 1998; Orellana, Dorner, & Pulido, 2003; Tse, 1995b, 1996; Valenzuela, 1999; Weisskirch, 2007). They are embarrassed by their parents' inability to speak English (McQuillan & Tse, 1995; Ng, 1998). Orellana, Dorner, et al. (2003) believe that brokering makes salient the families' identity as impoverished, working-class, and/or immigrant, particularly in settings in which the family is seeking assistance such as welfare benefits, which contributes to child language brokers' feelings of embarrassment, shame, and humiliation.

From the outside looking in, immigrant children serving as translators in settings such as a parent-teacher conference may seem unimportant or inconsequential. Yet that child is providing a critical service to his or her family. Beyond the importance of the activity to immigrant families, child language brokering appears to have a complex set of effects on the well-being of children and families. The impact of language brokering on youth and their families may be overlooked, misunderstood, or minimized by parents, service providers, teachers, and others utilizing child language brokers. Child language brokering is clearly an area that warrants additional research by those interested in child development, language, and immigration.

10.6. **LANGUAGE, EDUCATION, AND POLICY**

The increased presence of immigrant children in American public schools has raised concerns among some policy makers about the ability of public school systems to serve immigrant students. Most school-age immigrant children are concentrated in six states (California, Florida, Illinois,

New Jersey, New York, and Texas), with nearly half of California's school-age population being children of immigrants as of 2000 (Fix & Capps, 2005). The school districts in these states, along with districts in other states, report being overcrowded due to rising levels of immigration. Given these patterns and concerns, a significant question has arisen within education centers regarding the extent to which the public school system is responsible for immigrants' successful transitions into American society (National Clearinghouse for English Language Acquisition; NCELA, 2006). Some have argued that the overcrowding issue is putting undue strain on public school systems at the expense of "native" students. In an important move toward supporting immigrant families, the U.S. Supreme Court ruled it unconstitutional to deny an immigrant child access to public education regardless of their legal status (*Plyler v. Doe, 457, U.S. 202*, 1982).

Medical anthropologist and scholar of immigrant education Cortes (2008) argues that the issue of educating immigrant children is not simply the number of immigrant children in the nation's schools. Rather, it is the school system's inability to successfully integrate and educate them. The increasing diversity of the student body, especially in terms of the sheer number of languages spoken in a given school or classroom, offers considerable challenges. For many districts, the growing immigrant population has meant a significant increase in students requiring instruction in English as a Second Language (ESL). Indeed, more than half of the English language learners in U.S. schools are immigrants or children of immigrants (NCELA, 2006). Most of these children are living in "large urban areas, linguistically and culturally isolated, with principals and teachers lacking the skills to help them achieve"(Cortes, 2008). One unfortunate result of these difficulties is the high dropout rate among immigrants, particularly among Mexican immigrant adolescents (Schwarz, 2002), irrespective of their legal status.

How successful an individual immigrant student will be in school depends on numerous factors. Among these are age upon arrival, previous education, home language and literacy, family education, aspirations, and expectations, socioeconomic status, whether their immigration was voluntary or involuntary, and their current level of English language proficiency (NCELA, 2006). Recent research has also suggested that where a child goes to school is often linked to his or her English language proficiency. According to a 2005 study by The Urban Institute, nearly 70% of Limited English Proficiency (LEP) students are enrolled in merely 10% of elementary schools across the United States. More specifically, they are enrolled in the largest urban schools with the highest minority populations and poorest academic outcomes. Schools with higher LEP populations also tend to have less experienced principals and teachers, though they are more likely to engage in parental and community outreach than their lower LEP counterparts. There is a significant barrier, however, to the success of these parental outreach programs. Namely, many if not most parents of immigrant students have limited English proficiency as well, and necessarily rely on their children for language brokering.

While these differences are partially attributable to the demographic characteristics of their catchment areas (dense urban areas are more likely to have a larger immigrant population), it cannot be ignored that these disparate characteristics may be placing immigrant children at even greater risk than they would be otherwise. It is also possible, however, that this extreme polarity has enabled specific schools and districts to become more highly specialized in terms of offering ESL and other programs of great service to immigrant populations. It is certainly easier in most cases to argue for increased program funding when a large proportion of the student body would qualify for specialized services. Nevertheless, it is arguably detrimental to the acculturation of immigrant populations to be so segregated and isolated.

10.7. **CONCLUSION**

As mentioned at the outset, immigration to the United States has reached a record level and shows no sign of waning. Questions about immigrants' well-being have intensified as immigrants continue to transform the face of the United States by contributing to the growth of the nation's racial and ethnic minority population, which will eventually surpass the White non-Hispanic American population (Hernandez et al., 2007). Therefore, the issues this chapter has focused on in relation to immigrant adolescents' well-being—ethnic identity, physical health, child language brokering, and the intersection between language, education, and policy—will continue to persist. As noted, immigrant adolescents live in two worlds—that of their immigrant parents and American culture. The ways in which they incorporate both cultures have implications for their ethnic identity, physical health, and language use, including language brokering. Further, the educational policies related to language that immigrant youth encounter in school will affect the degree to which an American education, the impetus for many immigrants' migration to the United States, is available to them and, ultimately, their educational and long-term success.

How immigrant children are faring with respect to their psychological and physical health, education, family relationships, socioeconomic status, and other important social indicators of well-being is of particular concern to social scientists, policy makers, practitioners, human service agencies, and others (Arzubiaga, Noguerón, & Sullivan, 2009; Hernandez et al., 2007). Thus, behavioral and social scientists, along with educators, policy makers, and others focused on children and issues related to the multiple dimensions of their development and well-being, are challenged to attend to immigrant children and the diversity that they represent. This work must unfold within theoretical and conceptual frameworks [i.e., Phenomenological Variant of Ecological Systems Theory (PVEST; Spencer, 2006)] that can address the complex intersections between risk, resilience, context, and meaning-making during adolescence.

REFERENCES

Acoach, C. L., & Webb, L. M. (2004). The influence of language brokering on Hispanic teenagers acculturation, academic performance, and nonverbal decoding skills: A preliminary study. *The Howard Journal of Communications*, *15*, 1–19.

Arzubiaga, A. E., Noguerón, S. C., & Sullivan, A. L. (2009). The education of children in im/migrant families. *Review of Research in Education*, *33*, 246–271.

Ayala, J. (2006). Confianza, consejos, and contradictions: Gender and sexuality lessons between Latina adolescent daughters and mothers. In J. Denner & B. L. Guzmán (Eds.), *Latina Girls: Voices of adolescent strength in the United States* (pp. 29–43). New York, NY: New York University Press.

Bathum, M. E., & Baumann, L. C. (2007). A sense of community among immigrant Latinas. *Family and Community Health*, *30*(3), 167–177.

Bronstein, P. (1999). Differences in mothers' and fathers' behaviors toward children: A cross-cultural comparison. In L. A. Peplau, R. C. Venigas, & P. L. Taylor (Eds.), *Gender, culture, and ethnicity: Current research about women and men* (pp. 70–82). Mountain View, CA: Mayfield Publishing Company.

Buriel, R., Perez, W., DeMent, T. L., Chavez, D. V., & Moran, V. R. (1998). The relationship of language brokering to academic performance, biculturalism, and self-efficacy among Latino adolescents. *Hispanic Journal of Behavioral Sciences*, *20*, 283–297.

Camarota, S. A. (2007, November). *Immigrants in the United States, 2007: A profile of America's foreign-born population*. Retrieved from the Center for Immigration Studies Web site: http://www.cis.org/immigrants_profile_2007

Chu, C. M. (1999). *Immigrant children mediators (ICM): Bridging the literacy gap in immigrant communities*. Paper presented at the International Federation of Library Associations and Institutions (IFLA), Council and General Conference. Retrieved from http://www.ifla.org/IV/ifla65/papers/109-145e/htm

Cortes, J. D. (2008). *Educating America's immigrant children: Policies, challenges, and answers*. Retrieved June 30, 2008, from the University of Texas at Austin's K-16 Education Center Web site: http://www.utexas.edu/cee/dec/lucha/index.php?page=news

Cross, W. E., Jr. (1991). *Shades of black: Diversity in African American identity*. Philadelphia, PA: Temple University Press.

Crosnoe, R. (2006). Health and the education of children from racial/ethnic minority and immigrant families. *Journal of Health and Social Behavior*, *47*(1), 77–93.

de Las Fuentes, C., & Vasquez, M. J. T. (1999). Immigrant adolescent girls of color: Facing American challenges. In N. G. Johnson, M. C. Roberts, & J. Worell (Eds.), *Beyond adolescence: A new look at adolescent girls* (pp. 131–150). Washington, DC: American Psychological Association.

Dorner, L. M., Orellana, M. F., & Li-Grining C. P. (2007). "I helped my mom" and it helped me: Translating the skills of language brokers into improved standardized test scores. *American Journal of Education*, *113*, 451–478.

Fix, M., & Capps, R. (2005). *Immigrant children, urban schools, and the no child left behind act*. Washington, DC: Migration Policy Institute.

Foster, J. (2004). Fatherhood and the meaning of children: An ethnographic study among Puerto Rican partners of adolescent mothers. *Journal of Midwifery and Women's Health*, *49*, 118–125.

Gallegos-Castillo, A. (2006). La Casa: Negotiating family cultural practices, constructing identities. In J. Denner & B. L. Guzmán (Eds.), *Latina girls: Voices of adolescent strength in the United States* (pp. 44–58). New York, NY: New York University Press.

Guild, E., Carrera, S., & Eggenschwiler, A. (2009). *Informing the immigration debate*. Retrieved from the Centre for European Policy Studies Web site: http://www.ceps.eu/wAbout.php?article_id=576

Guzmán, B. L., Arruda, E., & Feria, A. L. (2006). Los papas, la familia y la sexualidad. In J. Denner & B. L. Guzmán (Eds.), *Latina girls: Voices of adolescent strength in the United States* (pp. 17–28). New York, NY: New York University Press.

Halgunseth, L. (2003). Language brokering: positive developmental outcomes. In M. Coleman & L. Ganong (Eds.), *Points and counterpoints: Controversial relationship and family issues in the 21st century: An anthology* (pp. 154–156). Los Angeles, CA: Roxbury Publishing Company.

Halter, M. (2007). Africa: West. In M. C. Waters & R. Ueda (Eds.), *The new Americans: A guide to immigration since 1965* (pp. 283–294). Cambridge, MA: Harvard University Press.

Hammack, P. L. (2003). Toward a unified theory of depression among urban African American youth: Integrating socioecologic, cognitive, family stress, and biopsychosocial perspectives. *Journal of Black Psychology*, *29*, 187–209.

Harris, B., & Sherwood, B. (1978). Translating as a natural skill. In D. Gerver & H. W. Sinaiko (Eds.), *Language interpretation and communication* (pp. 155–170). New York, NY: Plenum.

Heath, S. B. (1986). Sociocultural contexts of language development. In *Beyond language: Social and cultural factors in schooling language minority students* (pp. 143–186). Los Angeles, CA: California State University, Evaluation, Dissemination and Assessment Center.

Hedges, C. (2000, June 19). Translating America for parents and family. Children of immigrants assume difficult roles. *New York Times*. Retrieved from http://www.nytimes.com

Hernandez, D. J., Denton, N. A., & Macartney, S. E. (2007, April). *Children in immigrant families—The U.S. and 50 states*. Retrieved June 1, 2008, from the Child Trends Web site: http://www.childtrends.org/Files/Child_Trends-2007_04_01_RB_ChildrenImmigrant.pdf

Huang, Z. J., Yu, S. M., & Ledsky, R. (2006). Health status and health service access and use among children in U.S. immigrant families. *American Journal of Public Health*, 96(4), 634–640.

Kasinitz, P., Battle, J., & Miyares, I. (2001). Fade to Black?: The children of West Indian immigrants in Southern Florida. In R. Rumbaut & A. Portes (Eds.), *Ethnicities: Children of immigrants in America* (pp. 267–300). Berkeley, CA: University of California Press.

Lara, M., Gamboa, C., Kahramanian, M. I., Morales, L. S., & Bautista, D. E. H. (2005). Acculturation and Latino health in the United States: A review of the literature and its sociopolitical context. *Annual Review of Public Health*, 26, 367–397.

Lessard, G., & Ku, L. (2003). Gaps in coverage for children in immigrant families. *The Future of Children*, 13(1), 101–115.

Love, J. A., & Buriel, R. (2007). Language brokering, autonomy, parent-child bonding, biculturalism, and depression: A study of Mexican American adolescents from immigrant families. *Hispanic Journal of Behavioral Sciences*, 29, 472–491.

Markides, S., & Coreil, J. (1986). The health of Hispanics in the Southwestern United States: An epidemiologic paradox. *Public Health Reports*, 101(3), 253–265.

McQuillan, J., & Tse, L. (1995). Child language brokering in linguistic minority communities: Effects on cultural interaction, cognition, and literacy. *Language and Education*, 9, 195–215.

Morales, A., & Hanson, W. E. (2005). Language brokering: An integrative review of the literature. *Hispanic Journal of Behavioral Sciences*, 27, 471–503.

National Clearinghouse for English Language Acquisition. (2006). *Immigration and America's schools*. Retrieved April 12, 2008, from the National Clearinghouse for English Language Acquisition Web site: http://www.ncela.gwu.edu/resabout/immigration/intro/

Ng, J. (1998). From kitchen to classroom: Reflections of a language broker. *Voices from the Middle*, 6, 38–40.

Orellana, M. F. (2001). The work kids do: Mexican and Central American immigrant children's contributions to households and schools in California. *Harvard Educational Review*, 71(3), 366–389.

Orellana, M. F. (2003). Responsibilities of children in Latino immigrant homes. *New Directions for Youth Development*, 100, 25–39.

Orellana, M. F., Dorner, L., & Pulido, L. (2003). Accessing assets: Immigrant youth's work as family translators or "para-phrasers." *Social Problems*, 50, 505–524.

Orellana, M. F., Reynolds, J., Dorner, L., & Meza, M. (2003). In other words: Translating or "para-phrasing" as a family literacy practice in immigrant households. *Reading Research Quarterly*, 38, 12–34.

Phinney, J. S. (1990). Ethnic identity in adolescents and adults: Review of research. *Psychological Bulletin*, 108, 499–514.

Phinney, J. S., Horenczyk, G., Liebkind, K., & Vedder, P. (2001). Ethnic identity, immigration, and well-being: An interactional perspective. *Journal of Social Issue, 57*, 493–510.

Portes, A., & Rumbaut, R. G. (2001). Conclusion: The forging of a new America: Lessons for theory and practice. In R. Rumbaut & A. Portes (Eds.), *Ethnicities: Children of immigrants in America* (pp. 301–317). Berkeley, CA: University of California Press.

Puig, M. E. (2002). The adultification of refugee children: Implications for cross-cultural social work practice. *Journal of Human Behavior in the Social Environment, 5*, 85–95.

Rumbaut, R. G. (1994). The Crucible within: Ethnic identity, self-esteem, and segmented assimilation among children of immigrants. *International Migration Review, 28*, 748–794.

Sarmiento, O. L., Miller, W. C., Ford, C. A., Schoenbach, V. J., Adimora, A. A., & Viadro, C. I. et al. (2005). Routine physical examination and forgone health care among Latino adolescent immigrants in the United States. *Journal of Immigrant Health, 7*(4), 305–316.

Schieffelin, B. B., & Cochran-Smith, M. (1984). Learning to read culturally: Literacy before schooling. In H. Goelman, A. A. Oberg & F. Smith (Eds.), *Awakening to literacy: The University of Victoria symposium on children's response to a literate environment: Literacy before schooling* (pp. 3–23).

Schwarz, J. (2002, February 7). Mexican-born teens drop out at higher rate. *University Week*.

Shannon, S. M. (1990). English in the barrio: The quality of contact among immigrant children. *Hispanic Journal of Behavioral Sciences, 12*, 256–274.

Shiao, J. L. (2002). The political and philanthropic contexts for incorporating Asian American communities. In L. T. Vo & R. Bonus (Eds.), *Contemporary Asian American communities: Intersections and divergences* (pp. 216–228). Philadelphia, PA: Temple University Press.

Spencer, M. B. (2006). Phenomenology and ecological systems theory: Development of diverse groups. In W. Damon & R. Lerner (Eds.), *Handbook of child psychology, Vol. 1: Theoretical models of human development* (6th ed., pp. 829–893). New York, NY: Wiley.

Stepick, A., Stepick, C. D., Eugene, E., Teed, D., & Labissiere, Y. (2001). Shifting identities and intergenerational conflict: Growing up Haitian in Miami. In R. Rumbaut & A. Portes (Eds.), *Ethnicities: Children of immigrants in America* (pp. 229–266). Berkeley, CA: University of California Press.

Suárez-Orozco, C., Suárez-Orozco, M., & Todorova, I. (2008). *Learning a new land: Immigrant students in American Society*. Cambridge, MA: Harvard University Press.

Sy, S. R. (2006). Family and work influences on the transition to college among Latina adolescents. *Hispanic Journal of Behavioral Sciences, 28*, 368–386.

Taningco, M. T. V. (August, 2007). *Revisiting the Latino health paradox*. Retrieved from the Tomás Rivera Policy Institute (TRPI) Web site: http://www.trpi.org/PDFs/Latino%20Paradox%20Aug%202007%20PDF.pdf

Tse, L. (1995a, January-February). When students translate for parents: Effects of language brokering. *CABE Newsletter, 17*, 16–17.

Tse, L. (1995b). Language brokering among Latino adolescents: Prevalence, attitudes, and school performance. *Hispanic Journal of Behavioral Sciences, 17*, 180–193.

Tse, L. (1996). Language brokering in linguistic minority communities: The case of Chinese- and Vietnamese-American students. *The Bilingual Research Journal, 20*, 485–498.

Tse, L., & McQuillan, J. (1996). *Culture, language, and literacy: The effects of child brokering on language minority education.* Paper presented at the annual meeting of the American Educational Research Association, New York, NY.

Umaña-Taylor, A. J. (2003). Language brokering as a stressor for immigrant children and their families. In M. Coleman & L. Ganong (Eds.), *Points and counterpoints: Controversial relationship and family issues in the 21st century: An anthology* (pp. 157–159). Los Angeles, CA: Roxbury Publishing Company.

Valdes, G. (2003). *Expanding definitions of giftedness: The case of young interpreters from immigrant communities.* Mahwah, NJ: Lawrence Erlbaum Associates.

Valenzuela, A. (1999). Gender roles and settlement activities among children and their immigrant families. *American Behavioral Scientist, 42*, 720–742.

Vasquez, O. A., Pease-Alvarez, L., & Shannon, S. M. (1994). *Pushing boundaries: Language and culture in a Mexicano community.* Cambridge, MA: Cambridge University Press.

Waters, M. C. (1994). Ethnic and racial identities of second-generation Black immigrants in New York City. *International Migration Review, 28*, 795–820.

Waters, M. C. (1996). The intersection of gender, race, and ethnicity in identity development of Caribbean American teens. In B. J. Ross Leadbeater & N. Way (Eds.), *Urban girls: Resisting stereotypes, creating identities* (pp. 65–81). New York, NY: New York University Press.

Waters, M. C. (1999). *Black identities: West Indian immigrant dreams and American realities.* New York, NY/Cambridge, MA: Russell Sage Foundation/Harvard University Press.

Weisskirch, R. S. (2005). The relationship of language brokering to ethnic identity for Latino early adolescents. *Hispanic Journal of Behavioral Sciences, 27*, 286–299.

Weisskirch, R. S. (2007). Feelings about language brokering and family relations among Mexican American early adolescents. *Journal of Early Adolescence, 27*, 545–561.

Weisskirch, R. S., & Alva, S. A. (2002). Language brokering and the acculturation of Latino children. *Hispanic Journal of Behavioral Sciences, 24*, 369–378.

Williams, D. R., Neighbors, H. W., & Jackson, J. S. (2003). Racial/ethnic discrimination and health: Findings from community studies. *American Journal of Public Health, 93*, 200–208.

Worthy, J. (2006). Como si le falta un brazo: Latino immigrant parents and the costs of not knowing English. *Journal of Latinos and Education, 5*(2), 139–154.

Yu, S. M., Bellamy, H. A., Schwalberg, R. H., & Drum, M. A. (2001). Factors associated with use of preventive dental and health services among U.S. adolescents. *Journal of Adolescent Health, 29*(6), 395–405.

Zayas, L. H., Lester, R. J., Cabassa, L. J., & Fortuna, L. R. (2005). Why do so many Latina teens attempt suicide? A conceptual model for research. *American Journal of Orthopsychiatry, 75*(2), 275–287.

Chapter 11

Socializing relationships

Monica L. Rodriguez and Nicole J. Walden
University at Albany, State University of New York, Albany, NY

Socialization, the process by which people acquire the beliefs, norms, values, and behaviors of the social world they live in, is woven into the fabric of day-to-day lives of families, adolescents, and their peers. It is in the everyday interactions with family and peers where, explicitly or implicitly, societal norms are transmitted and adolescent cognitive, socio-emotional, and behavioral competencies are shaped (Arnett, 1995; Larson & Richards, 1994; Maccoby, 1992; Rogoff, 2003). According to ecological models of development, adolescents and their families intersect with multiple, interconnected contexts (e.g., school, neighborhood, communities, and culture) that influence, and are influenced by, changes in the family system during the adolescent transition (Bronfenbrenner, 1979; Garcia-Coll et al., 1996; McLoyd, 2006; Spencer, 2006). Parent-adolescent interactions reflect transformations that take place in the family as their socialization goals, beliefs, and practices are adapted to these multiple contexts. In times of rapid social change, families find novel solutions and display greater flexibility in their responses to cultural and societal pressures (Harrison, Wilson, Pine, Chan, & Buriel, 1990; McAdoo, 1993). As a result, youth become more influential in the forging of new family adaptations.

So far, most of the scientific knowledge about adolescent socialization has been based on Western, Eurocentric conceptions of families and youth, although the empirical evidence attesting to family diversity is increasing. Research on parenting has been devoted for several decades to the study of Western European models of parenting, using a "top-down" approach model of influences; that is, studies have been designed mostly to examine how different parenting styles affect adolescent development. In this chapter we will examine this typological model, as well as its application in cross-national and cross-cultural studies. We will

Adolescence: Development During a Global Era

also examine its application to ethnic minority families whose contextual influences diverge from those of the population on which this model was based.

Another area that has received much attention has been the parent-adolescent dilemma which defines the adolescent transition: granting more adolescent autonomy as the adolescent moves to an adult society while retaining parental control over certain domains. Parents and social scientists alike consider the two characteristic features of the adolescent period are (1) the negotiation of autonomy from parents, and (2) a significant increase in the amount of time spent with peers. Nevertheless, the view of adolescence as a transitional period where the adolescent task is to separate from the family to become a full individual member in a society of adult peers, is in great part a culturally dependent social construction determined by historical, social, and economic contextual forces. For example, Bangladeshi culture views a single transition from childhood to adulthood, effectively ignoring the adolescent period (Haq, 2007), and Indian and Arab adolescents continue to spend more time with their parents than with their peers without separating until marriage (Brown & Larson, 2002). A more global understanding of adolescence as a developmental period may be needed, one that can accommodate different cultural perspectives and a new social and cultural order that may result from changes such as an increasing life expectancy.

Indeed, in today's world, unprecedented changes are taking place due to globalization, technological advances, and immigration patterns. Many adolescents and their families are dealing with the demands of an increasingly fluctuating, interconnected, and complex world (Mortimer & Larson, 2002). Across nations, rises in migration, maternal employment, and mobility have resulted in smaller families organized into a wide array of family arrangements. Separation from grandparents and other extended family has meant a psychological and instrumental loss for many families. Yet for others, particularly in countries where significant family size reduction has occurred (Keijing & Myers-Walls, 2001), families report greater opportunity to invest economic and psychological resources in their adolescents (Gauthier, Smeedeng, & Furstenberg, 2004).

Despite rapid change, however, the family continues to function as the fundamental context that shapes adolescents' development into healthy and productive adults. Within their families, adolescents obtain the support they need to face new challenges and opportunities, as well as protection from possible risks, pressures, and perils. They connect to the personal narratives and shared memories that are necessary for continuity, stability, and the formation of a cohesive identity. Family connectedness, therefore, is valued both by adolescents and parents (Arnett, 2007). Perhaps this is why, despite the widely held view of adolescence as a period of parent-child conflict, the great majority of adolescents around the world report satisfaction in their relationships with parents. For example, Indian adolescents report that parents and family are at the center of their lives (Chaudhary & Sharma, 2005), Chilean adolescents consider their parents high in affection, communication, and understanding (Martinez, Cumsille, & Thinaut, 2007), Canadian adolescents value what their parents think of them (Sears, Simmering, & McNeil, 2007), and in Spain, 97% of adolescents report that they are satisfied with their families and consider family very important in their lives (DelBarrio, Moreno, & Linaza, 2007). There have been advances in theoretical and analytic models which will enable us to understand families in their diversity, representing the uniqueness of their particular ecologies as well as the variations represented in their interactions with specific contexts. This chapter will discuss ecological studies of families that have focused on variations within populations, and on the unique parenting strategies that have evolved in responses to specific contextual constraints and challenges.

In many cultures, as adolescents grow older they spend more time with their peers than with their parents or other adults (Csikszentmihalyi & Larson, 1984). Among European-American working-class and middle-class youth, the time spent with family drops from 35% of waking hours in 5th grade to 14% in 12th grade. This disengagement from family time, however, is not related to family conflict or to a decline in family cohesion; rather, it is associated with increased involvement in independent activities and with peers (Larson, Richards, Moneta, Holmbeck, & Duckett, 1996). Adolescents' relationships with peers also become closer, more intense and influential than those formed during childhood (Berndt, 1982; Furman & Buhrmester, 1985; Way, 1998). With the accelerated pace of advancement in communication and information technologies, the social landscape of adolescence is changing. Worldwide, adolescents have adopted the Internet as their own "social space" (Hellenga, 2002), connecting with their friends and with a wider group of peers. Recent increases in immigration also have expanded adolescents' communications to more diverse peers (Arnett, 2007). Thus, the interconnections among multiple contexts, cultures, and generations are ever increasing, creating a more intricate and complex network. In this time of rapid technological developments, for example, younger and older generations now learn about the world simultaneously (du Bois-Reymond, 1998). Families, in their diverse adaptations, are the crossroads where intergenerational and intercultural exchanges converge, and where new values, beliefs, and behaviors are instantiated. It is within families where parents connect the new generation to the past as much as adolescents and their peers connect parents to the future. As Flanagan (2001) points out, families are "engines for social change."

With a view of families and peers as the two primary socializing agents in the lives of adolescents, we will first review typological models of parenting and discussing their generalizability to families varying in ethnicity, culture, SES, minority and immigration status. Second, we will explore studies that take into account the influence that adolescents have on parenting styles and practices. Third, we will examine an ecological approach to the study of family socialization, one that incorporates population-specific constructs. In particular, we will address acculturation, family obligations, and ethnic-racial socialization, which are relevant to our understanding of socialization processes in ethnic minority families. Finally, we will examine the socializing influence of peers, focusing on adolescent friendships, peer conflict resolution, and peers as resources or drawbacks for adolescent school performance and achievement.

11.1. **PARENTAL SOCIALIZING INFLUENCES**

Much of the parenting research began as part of mainstream developmental science in the United States and, until fairly recently, was abstracted from cultural considerations (*Child Development*, Special Issue, 1996). One of the most researched perspectives on family socialization concentrated on a typological framework for characterizing parenting practices and its influences on adolescent development.

11.1.1. **Parenting styles**

Over the past several decades, Baumrind's (1971) tripartite typology of *authoritative*, *authoritarian*, and *permissive* parenting styles and its subsequent modification by Maccoby and Martin (1983) have dominated the study of family socialization. *Authoritative parenting* is characterized by warmth and acceptance, firmness and consistency in setting and enforcing rules, and open communication. In contrast, *authoritarian parenting* is characterized by high parental control, strictness in the enforcement of rules, criticism and negative emotionality. *Permissive (or neglectful) parenting* is characterized by low expectations and demands, a "laissez-faire" attitude toward unacceptable behaviors, and low involvement.

In families of *authoritative parents,* adolescents report high family satis-faction, and, as compared to adolescents with authoritarian or permissive parents, they show better psychosocial adjustment, higher academic achievement, better peer relations, and enhanced learning goals and well-being (Brown, Mounts, Lamborn, & Steinberg, 1993; Darling & Steinberg, 1993; Dornbusch, Ritter, Leiderman, Roberts, & Fraleigh, 1987; Fuligni & Eccles, 1993; Gonzalez, Doan Holbein, & Quilter, 2002; Gray & Steinberg, 1999; Wintre & Yaffe, 2000). Open communication and support, characteristic of authoritative parents, have been associated with self-protective sexual behaviors and decreased deviant behaviors (Kotchick, Dorsey, Miller, & Forehand, 1999). Parental high warmth and acceptance also correlate with a wide range of positive adolescent out-comes, including lower internalizing, externalizing, and substance use pro-blems, as well as higher psychosocial competence (see Steinberg, 2001 for a review). In a similar vein, authoritative parenting has been found to buffer adolescents from the detrimental effects of stressing circumstances such as economic hardship and chronic illness (Holmbeck & Hill, 1986; Murry et al., 2002; Wills & Cleary, 1996). Similar findings have been obtained in other parts of the world, including India (Carson, Chowdhury, Perry, & Pati, 1999), Korea (Mantzicopoulos & Oh-Hwang, 1998), Hong Kong (McBride-Chang & Chang, 1998), and Israel (Mayseless, Scharf, & Sholt, 2003).

In contrast, *authoritarian parenting practices,* such as the use of strict and punitive forms of control, have been associated with adolescents' lower self-esteem and higher vulnerability to internalizing problems (Barber, 1996; Barber & Harmon, 2002; Soenens et al., 2005). Hostile parenting and harsh discipline practices have also been consistently associated with adolescent conduct problems and antisocial behaviors (Ary, Duncan, Duncan, & Hops, 1999; Conger & Simons, 1997; Loukas, Fitzgerald, Zucker, & Eye, 2001; Patterson, DeBaryshe, & Ramsey, 1989). Addition-ally, adolescents from *permissive or neglectful* families, with lax or incon-sistent rules, have shown higher antisocial behavior, substance abuse and conduct problems, and lower social competencies (Lamborn, Mounts, Steinberg, & Dornbusch, 1991; Steinberg, Lamborn, Darling, Mounts, & Dornbusch, 1994).

Research on parenting styles among ethnic minority families in the U.S.

The associations between parenting styles and adolescent outcomes obtained in European-American families have differed from those observed among other ethnic, racial, and socioeconomically heterogeneous samples in the United States. In studies by Dornbusch, Steinberg, and colleagues (Dornbusch et al., 1987; Steinberg, Lamborn, Dornbusch, & Darling, 1992; Steinberg, Mounts, Lamborn, & Dornbusch, 1991), for example, an authoritative parenting style (e.g., an aggregate of high acceptance, supervision, and psychological autonomy granting), which had been associated with better school performance among European-American adolescents, was not associated with better school performance among African-American adolescents. Additionally, an authoritarian parenting style, which was found to be harmful for European-American adolescents' school performance, was not associated with lower school achievements in African-American youth (Steinberg, Dornbusch, & Brown, 1992).

Some researchers have hypothesized that the self-report methodology used in typological parenting studies may be the source of these divergent findings (McLoyd, Cauce, Takeuchi, & Wilson, 2000) and have suggested that, in contrast to self-reports, observational assessments of parent-adolescent interactions may facilitate the understanding of possible cultural variations in the meaning of behaviors (Cauce, Coronado, & Watson, 1998; Florsheim, Tolan, & Gorman-Smith, 1998; Gonzales, Cauce, & Mason, 1996; Gorman-Smith, Tolan, Henry, & Florsheim, 2000). Florsheim et al. (1998) conducted an observational study of parent-adolescent interactions in an inner-city African- and Latino-American sample and found that *nonauthoritative* (authoritarian) parenting was associated with less self-reported adolescent delinquency than authoritative parenting. These results are consistent with other research findings that suggest inner-city or ethnic minority parents may be more oriented toward the promotion of adolescent obedience and self-reliance (Kelley, Power, & Wimbush, 1992; McLoyd, 1990; Parke & Buriel, 1998). Arguably, strict and harsh authoritarian parental styles may be protective, given the exposure to potentially dangerous environments that inner-city youth may encounter in their daily lives (Furstenberg, Cook, Eccles, Elder, & Sameroff, 1999; Garcia-Coll et al., 1996; McLoyd, 1990). Many other investigators have concluded that assertive, authoritarian parenting may protect adolescents from harm and prevent engagement in antisocial activities when it occurs in disadvantaged socioeconomic contexts with greater risks and/or opportunities for engaging in adolescent problem behaviors (Brody & Flor, 1998; Dubrow & Garbarino, 1989).

The validity of applying Baumrind's parenting typology to Latino-American families has also been questioned. Latino families have been described as showing a combination of authoritarian, authoritative, and permissive styles (Fracasso & Busch-Rossnagel, 1992). While Latino parents display high levels of nurturance, warmth, and expressions of affect (characteristic of an authoritative style), they also use punitive parenting practices if their children show any sign of disobedience or disrespect (characteristic of authoritarian parenting). Latino families also impose few high demands on their children (characteristic of a permissive style). Therefore, it is possible to hypothesize that parental harshness may be experienced very differently by an adolescent if it occurs in the context of a nurturant, positive parent-child relationship rather than in the context of a hostile, conflictive parent-child relationship. Indeed, the findings on the negative effects of authoritarian parenting on adolescent outcomes has consistently not been found among Latino-American adolescents (Florsheim, Tolan, & Gorman-Smith, 1996; Gorman-Smith et al., 2000; Lindahl & Malik, 1999; Parke & Buriel, 1998). Some researchers have suggested that adolescents' differential perceptions of authoritarian parenting may explain these findings (Halgunseth, Ispa, & Rudy, 2006; Lindahl & Malik, 1999).

The global parenting typology has not effectively characterized parenting among Asian-American families, wherein findings also diverge from those obtained in European-American populations (Chao, 1994; Costigan, Bardina, Cauce, Kim, & Latendresse, 2006). Asian parents report high levels of control, and yet Asian-American adolescents demonstrate high levels of achievement (e.g., Dornbusch et al., 1987; Lamborn, Dornbusch, & Steinberg, 1996), frequently outperforming European-American youth (Chao, 1994; McLoyd et al., 2000; Nelson, Leibenluft, McClure, & Pine, 2005; Wu, Hoven, Tiet, Kovalenko, & Wicks, 2002; Yau & Smetana, 2003). Chao (1994) suggested that the subjective *meaning* of authoritarian parenting was not well captured with either Baumrind's authoritative or authoritarian typology. According to Chao (1994), Chinese-American parenting styles are more aligned with a concept akin to "training," which consists of providing clear and concrete guidelines for behavior. In a study of Chinese- and European-American parents' beliefs about child-rearing practices, Chao (1994) found that Chinese-American parents were much more likely to score higher on the concept of training than were European-American parents.

Inconsistent associations between parenting styles and adolescent adjustment have also been found in cross-national studies of youth. For example, studies examining Arab and Muslim adolescents' attitudes about parenting indicate that they consider rule enforcement to be the duty of a parent and view the use of punitive parenting practices as an acceptable form of control (Dwairy & Menshar, 2006; Kagitcibasi, 2005). Similarly, in a study of Korean youth, Rohner and Pettengill (1985) found that authoritarian parental styles were associated with parental warmth and low levels of neglect. Ethiopian adolescent immigrants in Israel report a sense of loss about their cultural values "back home," which dictated clear-cut rules and strict discipline (Goldblatt & Rosenblum, 2007).

Similar to Latino-American families, Asian-American families typically view authoritarian parenting as an indication of parents' high concern for their child's well-being and of their fulfilling the parental duty to teach children and adolescents socially appropriate behaviors (Chao & Sue, 1996). Thus, the meaning adolescents ascribe to authoritarian parental behaviors and parental negative affect appears to be a critical determinant of the manner in which control will influence adolescent outcomes. A qualitative study investigating the meaning of "good parenting" among Mexican-American adolescents supports this view (Crockett, Brown, Russell, & Shen, 2007). The following extract from their study illustrates how Mexican-American adolescents construe parental hostility in positive terms: "If they're yelling at you, that means they really love you because they're really concerned about you. There's not a day that goes by that she [my mother] doesn't say, 'Take care of yourself, be careful, don't do this, don't do that,' and that means she's really loving and she's concerned."

11.2. **ADOLESCENT INFLUENCES ON PARENTING**

Parenting adolescents is not a "top-down" process that occurs from the parent to the child, where the parent is a transmitter of family goals and values, rules, and decisions; rather, a two-way interactive, reciprocal process that occurs in context and unfolds over time. (Maccoby & Martin, 1983; Magnusson & Stattin, 1998; Stattin & Kerr, 2000). Such bidirectional influences can be understood by examining two important adolescent processes and their influence on parenting: adolescent disclosure and adolescent autonomy.

11.2.1. **Adolescent disclosure**

Parental monitoring has received special attention because of its negative association with adolescent antisocial behavior: Lower parental monitoring is consistently associated with higher adolescent engagement in delinquent activities. Studies have shown that when parents do not know where their adolescent children are, who they are with, or what they are doing, these adolescents are more likely to have deviant friends (Dishion, Capaldi, Spracklen, & Li, 1995), to associate with peers who approve of drug use (Chassin, Pillow, Curran, Molina, & Barrera, 1993), to increase their drug use over time and engage in more risky sexual activity (Fletcher, Darling, Steinberg, & Dornbusch, 1995; Metzler, Noell, Biglan,

Ary, & Smolkowski, 1994), and to drop out of school (McCluskey, Krohn, Lizotte, & Rodriguez, 2002). Cross-cultural findings are consistent with these results; that is, lower parental monitoring has been linked to adolescents' involvement in a variety of problem behaviors among adolescents from Australia, Hong Kong, and the United States (Feldman, Rosenthal, Mont-Reynaud, Leung, & Lau, 1991).

In a crucial study of parental monitoring, Kerr and Stattin (2000) and Stattin and Kerr (2000) argued that parental monitoring, rather than a set of behaviors initiated by parents or adults (as it is assumed in traditional parental monitoring assessments), is based on the knowledge that parents have about their adolescent's activities. This knowledge comes partly from the parents' own efforts to find out what their children are doing and partly from the adolescent's spontaneous disclosure of information. In a study of Swedish adolescents and their parents, Kerr and Stattin's (2000) results confirmed their hypothesis: parental knowledge about their adolescent's activities came mainly from *adolescent disclosure*, and adolescent disclosure was the best predictor of involvement in antisocial behavior. Therefore, parental monitoring reflects the adolescent's willingness to disclose, more than it reflects parental behaviors to solicit information.

Nearly all adolescents report that, at least occasionally, they do not disclose information to parents about their activities (Darling, Cumsille, Caldwell, & Dowdy, 2006) and that they use a variety of strategies for not disclosing information without lying. For example, they avoid bringing up issues, disclose information only when asked, disclose partial information, or omit important details. Youth who disclose more to parents about all issues have been found to have closer, more trusting relationships with parents and report greater obligations to aid and assist the family (Kerr & Stattin, 2000; Smetana, Villalobos, Tasopoulos-Chan, Gettman, & Campione-Barr, 2009; Soenens, Vansteenkiste, Luyckx, & Goossens, 2006; Stattin & Kerr, 2000).

In studies with middle adolescents from Mexican, Chinese, and European backgrounds, and of varied generational statuses, Smetana and her colleagues (Smetana, Metzger, Gettman, & Campione-Barr, 2006; Yau & Smetana, 1996), found that Chinese-American adolescents disclosed less to their parents than Mexican- or European-American adolescents. Moreover, second-generation Chinese-American youth used avoidance strategies more frequently. The use of avoidance was associated with depressed mood, problem behaviors, lower levels of family obligation, and less trust in parents. In contrast, first-generation Chinese-American youth used partial disclosure. This strategy was not significantly associated with any of the problems above, suggesting that the use of partial disclosure may be a way for adolescents to balance their autonomy while retaining parental trust. Parental monitoring, therefore, may conceptually have a stronger association with parental communication or warmth rather than with parental control. Adolescents who perceive their parents as warm and accepting are more likely to disclose information about their activities, as they may be more receptive to parental attempts to solicit information in the context of a close, trusting relationship (Stattin & Kerr, 2000).

11.2.2. **Adolescent autonomy**

The promotion of adolescent autonomy and its successful negotiation is reciprocally related to parental control (Lerner & Galambos, 1998; Williams, Holmbeck, & Greenley, 2002). Youth from all cultures desire more autonomy as they get older (Feldman & Rosenthal, 1991; Fuligni, 1998; Smetana et al., 2006). As American cultural views become more widespread through media and information technological advances, there is an increasing worldwide tendency toward endorsing adolescent autonomy (both by adolescents and their parents). Major social trends have shifted the balance of power between men and women and between younger and older generations, affecting family life substantially (Du Bois-Reymond, 2001; Flanagan, 2001). In contrast to former traditional family views, families today are shifting toward a more egalitarian views (Myers-Walls, Somlai, & Rapoport, 2001). The balancing of day-to-day duties and activities requires active negotiation between family members, and skills such as social competence, communication, planning, and frustration tolerance therefore become essential. This "negotiating family" framework is now massive, and fits with Western individualistic values, which even most collectivistic societies such as China are now accepting (Keijing & Myers-Walls, 2001). With this "negotiating" framework, adolescent autonomy refers to parent-adolescent agreement on who has the legitimate authority in the decision making of activities and situations in which the adolescent engages (Smetana & Turiel, 2003; Turiel & Smetana, 1984, 1998).

To better understand parent and adolescent views of authority and their effects on parent-adolescent relations, Smetana and Turiel (2003) have applied a social domain theory (Smetana, 2006; Turiel, 2006) that distinguishes between issues that should be socially regulated (such as moral issues and social conventions) and those that should be individually regulated (e.g., choices that are up to the individual and do not affect others). Smetana and colleagues (Smetana, 2000, 2002; Smetana & Daddis, 2002; Smetana, Daddis, & Chuang, 2003) have applied this theory to examine domains which are considered (by the adolescents or their parents) to be parent-regulated and those considered to be personally regulated. She and her colleagues have found that decision making regarding personal issues (e.g., recreation, clothes, hairstyles, music, and friends) is generally viewed as the legitimate territory of adolescents. However, adolescents and parents often disagree about where the boundaries of parental or personal authority should be drawn, which leads to conflict in their relationships.

In a cross-cultural study comparing adolescents in the United States, Chile, and the Philippines (Darling, Cumsille, & Pena-Alampay, 2005), it was found that adolescents and parents in all of these countries generally agree that activities related to moral and conventional domains, as well as "prudential" acts pertaining to health and safety, should be legitimately regulated by parents. However, adolescents often contest parents' legitimacy to control some of these activities as they consider them part of their personal domain. For example, they believe that for issues having to do with sexuality and safety, they should be able to make their own choices at earlier ages (Nucci, Hasebe, & Lins-Dyer, 2005; Smetana, 2002). Children and adolescents from Hong Kong (Yau & Smetana, 1996), China (Yau & Smetana, 2003), Japan (Hasebe, Nucci, & Nucci, 2004), Colombia (Ardila-Rey & Killen, 2001), and northeastern Brazil (Lins-Dyer & Nucci, 2007) report conflicts with parents regarding parental control over personal issues. In a Chilean sample, Darling, Cumsille, and Martinez (2008) found that adolescents were more likely to obey parents when they believed the issue in question was within the legitimate sphere of parental authority, in which case they felt obligated to obey, despite disagreement. These parent-adolescent "negotiations," are especially difficult when the societal rules known to parent and adolescents are in question, such as when families settle in a foreign land.

11.3. SOCIALIZATION IN THE CONTEXT OF ETHNICITY, RACE, IMMIGRATION, AND CULTURE

11.3.1. Research on parenting in immigrant families

Like indigenous minority populations, immigrant children and children of immigrants (first, second, and third generation) contend with stressors related to ethnic/racial minority status, such as discrimination and power imbalances. Relatively high percentages of youth in England, Germany, and Denmark hold negative attitudes toward immigrants (Boog, Donselaar, Houtzager, Rodrigues, & Schriemer, 2006; Torney-Purta, Lehmann, Oswald, & Schulz, 2001). Indeed, Suarez-Orozco and Suárez-Orozco (2001) have referred to immigration as "one of the most stressful events a family can undergo." Goldblatt and Rosenblum's (2007) qualitative study of immigrant Ethiopian youth in Israel indicates that, like many other immigrant youth, Ethiopian adolescents in Israel experience a sense of family disintegration, alienation from their Western Israeli school peers, and loss of a predictable world. Despite the difficult life conditions in Ethiopia, they miss the clear-cut rules and the respect younger generations have for their elders back home. An example extracted from Goldblatt and Rosenblum's (2007) study clearly depicts some of these experiences: "... I can't discuss my feelings or talk about school. They didn't study here, so they [parents] won't know what I'm talking about. They also have old-fashioned opinions.... My father used to help me, [with school] and would take me to school every day. He would help me with whatever was needed. He knew the language. Here, in Israel, he can't help. He knows nothing in Hebrew.... At weekends, we don't sit and talk with the family. Every-one eats when they feel like it. It was different in Ethiopia. We would sit together, do things together.... I feel bad about the way things have changed since our immigration. A family should stick together.... my father tries to understand and help me but he can't. He gives me money, though—he'll help with anything that depends on him. As for my mother, I confide in her and tell her about my friends. I help my parents—I go with them to the doctor, because they don't know the language. It's awful."

The migration experience destabilizes a family in many ways. One of the most significant socialization problems is the cultural intergenerational gap that is created as children become acculturated to the host mainstream culture at a faster pace than their parents. In the United States, immigrant parents are often more removed from the American culture, particularly if they work with coethnics, which is the case among many new immigrants (Suarez-Orozco & Suárez-Orozco, 2001). Children often pick up English and absorb the new culture sooner than their parents because they have regular contact with teachers and peers at school (Suarez-Orozco, Todorova, & Qin, 2006). For these adolescents, norms within their families and in the outside world are at odds, and as a result, immigrant and first-generation youth report being more dissatisfied in their relationships with their parents (Phinney & Ong, 2002). Immigrant parent-adolescent conflicts are exacerbated by the fact that adolescents' strivings for autonomy and independence are supported by mainstream American values of individualism (Buki, Ma, Strom, & Strom, 2003). Parents often feel they "lose" their children to the host culture. The stress generated by the acculturation process becomes a significant risk factor, increasing the risk for depression in parents and adolescents (Hovey & King, 1996) as well as adolescents' deviant behaviors. For example, compared to less-acculturated peers, more-acculturated Latinos display higher levels of alcohol, marijuana, and cocaine use, and increased levels of youth violence (Carvajal, Photiades, Evans, & Nash, 1997; Gil, Vega, & Dimas, 1994; Gonzales, Knight, Morgan-Lopez, Saenz, & Sirolli, 2002; Rogler, Cortes, & Malgady, 1991; Smokowski, David-Ferdon, & Stroupe, 2009).

Immigrant adolescents, however, often make clear distinctions between what they consider the "ideal characteristics" of good parent-child relationships and the reality of their own experience. For example, Mexican-American adolescents are aware of the cultural and intergenerational differences between themselves and their parents, and the fact that their parents' socialization goals, values, and parenting practices reflect how they grew up back home (Crockett et al., 2007). First-generation Asian-American immigrant adolescents often experience high levels of distress and socioemotional difficulties because of intergenerational and cultural differences with their Chinese-born parents (Weaver & Kim, 2008). Asian-American students tend to have higher level of anxiety and lower levels of self-esteem when compared to their European-American, Black, and Latino peers (Greene, Way, & Pahl, 2006; Rhee, Chang, & Rhee, 2003; Twenge & Crocker, 2002). Recent studies are offering a nuanced view of the acculturation process among Asian-American families. For example, Weaver and Kim (2008) showed that among Chinese families, parent-adolescent dyads constituted by a Chinese-oriented parent (e.g., did not speak much English and maintained Chinese cultural traditions and values without an interest in mainstream American values) and an American-oriented adolescent, parents were the least supportive and adolescents were the most depressed. In contrast, the optimal parent-adolescent relationship was found among parent-adolescent dyads in which the parent had a bicultural orientation (e.g., parent is relatively proficient in English, agrees with mainstream American values but protects Chinese cultural values and traditions), and the adolescent also had a bicultural orientation (e.g., relatively proficient in both languages and accepting of both cultures).

11.3.2. **Family obligations and filial responsibilities**

Latino and Asian values include a deep sense of familism (feelings of obligation, solidarity, and reciprocity within the family) and high family member interdependence. They value cooperation and family harmony over individual autonomy (Cauce & Domenech-Rodriguez, 2002; Chao & Tseng, 2002). Asian and Latino families who have immigrated to the United States tend to maintain these values. Since they may not endorse mainstream familial standards that emphasize autonomy, which would normalize adolescent defiance, immigrant parents tend to react more strongly to adolescent disagreements (Phinney & Ong, 2002). Familistic cultures emphasize closeness and mutually supportive behaviors among family members; families should stay close together, support each other, provide assistance, and respect their elders (Caplan, Choy, & Whitmore, 1991; Chao & Tseng, 2002; Garcia-Coll & Vazquez Garcia, 1995; Sabogal, Martin, Otero-Sabogal, Martin, & Perez-Stable, 1987). These values are endorsed more strongly by Latino- and Asian-American youth—as compared to European-American youth—across generation, gender, family composition and socioeconomic status (Freeberg & Stein, 1996; Fuligni, Tseng, & Lam, 1999). These values are also more strongly endorsed by youth from immigrant families, compared to their coethnic peers born in the U.S. (Fuligni, 1998).

Over the past two decades, researchers have examined the influence of family obligation on children's development. For adolescents, a sense of family obligation would compel them to respect elders, consult the family about important decisions, and provide support and assistance by helping with household chores, caring for siblings, and even contributing financially to the household (Kuperminc, Jurkovic, & Casey, 2009). Among Latino- and Asian-American immigrants, family obligation is associated with increased physical and emotional well-being, as well as greater academic motivation and achievement (Fuligni, 1997; Telzer & Fuligni, 2009). In fact, research has pointed to family obligation as one of the reasons why immigrant children tend to fare better than coethnic peers born in the U.S., physically, emotionally, and academically, even when controlling for socioeconomic status (Fuligni, 1998, 2001; Fuligni et al., 1999).

In addition to the ethnocultural origins of family obligation, economic hardship has also been associated with increased demands for adolescents to help their families. Adolescents whose families face economic crises have been found to provide greater family support (Elder, 1974; Elder & Conger, 2000), and adolescents from low-income families are expected to help care for siblings (Suarez-Orozco & Suárez-Orozco, 1995). Single-parent families may also require children to adopt duties and responsibilities typically shared by two parents (Suarez-Orozco & Suárez-Orozco, 1995). Within the context of such resource-driven demands for family obligation, Latino-, African-, and European-American adolescents have been found to report similarly high levels of family responsibilities (Walden, Rodriguez, & Bekar, 2009), regardless of ethnocultural origin. While these responsibilities may reflect increased burdens associated with economic hardship, there is evidence that greater family responsibility contributes to more positive outcomes among adolescents facing economic hardship. Specifically, in a study of economically disadvantaged

European-, African-, and Latino-American youth, greater family responsibility was found to mitigate the relation between negative life events and antisocial behavior across the three groups (Walden et al., 2009). Thus, family obligation may contribute to children's development and well-being in multiple contexts and across ethnic boundaries, both promoting normative outcomes and protecting against risk.

The effects of economic hardship, however, are not evenly distributed across all racial and ethnic groups. Minority families are especially likely to suffer economic problems, with significantly higher poverty rates for African- and Latino-American families than for White non-Latino families (Proctor & Dalaker, 2002). Among economically disadvantaged families, parents overwhelmed by life stressors are often depleted of psychological and material resources. Their interactions with their adolescent children are characterized by irritation and overtly hostile or disengaged behaviors (Conger & Donnellan, 2007; Leventhal & Brooks-Gunn, 2003), which are less propitious for the development of self-regulation and autonomy. The multiple, persistent stressors associated with poverty significantly jeopardize effective parenting. Forkel and Silbereisen (2001) reported that family climate (in terms of family cohesion and low conflict) mediated the relation between the family's economic hardship and adolescent depressed mood. Conger and colleagues (Conger et al., 2002) have developed and tested a family stress model that identified the quality of the parent-child relationship as a mediator of the link between family economic hardship and adolescents' adjustment. In the last several decades much research has been done that confirms this model of the negative impacts of economic problems on families and children (Conger & Elder, 1994; Conger, Rueter, & Conger, 2000; McLoyd, 1998). Intersecting with economic hardships and immigrant family acculturation processes and ethnicity is race, which plays a major role in the adolescent developmental experience. Teaching adolescents how to cope with racial issues is an important part of family socialization processes among families who are faced with discrimination.

11.3.3. **Ethnic-racial socialization**

An ecological perspective highlights the contextual embeddedness of individuals' experiences with ethnic-racial socialization, which is often conveyed through parental messages to children about race. In the case of family relationships, ethnic-racial socialization may vary relative to parental experiences of discrimination, to the social contexts in which these socialization strategies are used, and to the relational context of parent-adolescent interactions (e.g., Parke & Buriel, 1998). Due to all of these factors, similar experiences may have different implications for individuals in different settings (Bronfenbrenner & Crouter, 1983). While African-, Chinese-, Latino-, and Muslim-American youth all report considerable discrimination (Greene et al., 2006; Sirin & Fine, 2008), these experiences can differ in many ways, including the source of discrimination (e.g., teachers, peers, law enforcement), as well as the nature and history of stereotypes about their group. Compared to other minority groups in the United States, African Americans face the distinct challenges of a historical legacy of enslavement and segregation. African-American families are exposed to chronic experiences of blatant discrimination and negative stereotyping (e.g., Boykin & Toms, 1985; Garcia-Coll et al., 1996; McLoyd, 1990; Spencer, 2006), which affects the socialization process of children and adolescents. African-American adolescents report the most experiences with racial discrimination, with over 90% reporting experiences of discrimination in their lifetimes. Their understanding of racism includes greater awareness of socioprivilege and power differentials and a wider array of discrimination experiences (e.g., harassment from police, social exclusion, violence; McKown, 2004). Identity formation, a central process in the adolescent transition, may be compromised in African-American youth if buffering mechanisms to protect them from these deleterious contextual effects are not in place (Spencer, 2006). Indeed, studies have shown that African-American parents are more likely to talk with their adolescent children about racial and ethnic prejudice and how to handle it than other ethnic minority families, such as Mexican- and Japanese-American families (Phinney & Chavira, 1995).

To cope with negative stereotyping, bias, and discrimination, all of which adversely impact adolescents' physical and psychological well-being (Greene et al., 2006; Rumbaut, 1994; Sirin & Fine, 2008), parents convey specific sets of knowledge, skills, and behaviors for navigating race, culture, and social power differentials (Harrison et al., 1990; Hughes & Chen, 1999). Ethnic-racial socialization is a normative component of child rearing among ethnic and racial minority families. The content of parental messages about race and ethnicity has typically been classified into four general domains (Boykin & Toms, 1985; Demo & Hughes, 1990; Hughes & Chen, 1999; Hughes et al., 2006; Phinney & Chavira, 1995): (1) *cultural socialization*, aimed at promoting knowledge and pride about one's group; (2) *preparation for bias,* fostering awareness of discrimination and prejudice and providing coping strategies; (3) *promotion of mistrust,* teaching children to be wary of other ethnic-racial groups, or of the dominant mainstream group in particular; and (4) *egalitarianism*, stressing equality and the importance of individual characteristics over group membership.

Parents and children report that *cultural socialization* occurs most frequently and is necessary to protect children from negative experiences and messages from society and the media (Hughes, 2003; Hughes et al., 2006), as well as to compensate for the Eurocentric focus of education in mainstream schools. Among African-American youth, cultural socialization is associated with greater racial awareness and more pro-Black preferences (Branch & Newcombe, 1986). Similarly, among Mexican-American youth, cultural socialization is related to greater cultural awareness, increased Spanish/ethnic language use, and same-ethnic peer preference (Knight, Bernal, Garza, Cota, & Ocampo, 1993). Chinese-American adolescents whose parents engage in cultural socialization also show greater preference for co-ethnic peers (Ou & McAdoo, 1993). Across ethnic and racial groups, cultural socialization supports adolescent well-being and adjustment. For example, Chinese- and Mexican-American youth with higher regard for their ethnic group reported more happiness and less anxiety on a daily basis (Kiang, Yip, Gonzales-Backen, Witkow, & Fuligni, 2006).

Preparation for bias involves informing adolescents about barriers caused by racism and helping them to develop effective coping strategies. Parents may communicate to their adolescents when and how to ignore or confront discrimination and help them identify coping strategies such as drawing strength from religious faith and spirituality, becoming civically engaged, or affirming ethnic/racial identity. Parental messages may also include achievement-related communications about having to work harder and overcome barriers in order to attain equal success relative to members of more privileged groups. Research findings about how often preparation for bias occurs and what outcomes it predicts are mixed. Some studies suggest that this kind of message is highly prevalent (Hughes & Chen, 1997; Phinney & Chavira, 1995; Sanders-Thompson, 1994), while other studies suggest it is relatively uncommon (Bowman & Howard, 1985; Thornton, Chatters, Taylor, & Allen, 1990). Among racial-ethnic groups, African Americans report the highest preparation for bias, which has been associated with better academic adjustment in some studies of African- and Mexican-American adolescents (Bowman & Howard, 1985; Quintana & Vera, 1999; Sanders, 1997). In other research, however, it has been associated with lower self-esteem, poorer academic outcomes, and increased antisocial behavior (for a review, see Hughes et al., 2006; Hughes, Witherspoon, Rivas-Drake, & West-Bey, 2009). Other studies have found that cultural socialization, but not preparation for bias, predicts academic achievement and motivation among Mexican- and Chinese-American adolescents (Huynh & Fuligni, 2008). European-American families report the least preparation for bias (Hughes, 2003; Hughes & Chen, 1999; Huynh

& Fuligni, 2008; Rivas-Drake, Hughes, & Way, 2008). According to Steele (1997), when school contexts are unsupportive of African-American adolescents' academic self-concept, they seek other self-affirmation contexts. However, parental messages regarding the importance of education for future success, and encouragement to perform well at school, provide a powerful buffer.

Parents may also caution their children to be wary and distrusting of interethnic relationships or to avoid them altogether; this type of message is called *promotion of mistrust*. While preparation for bias may convey similar cautionary information in conjunction with strategies for coping with discrimination, promotion of mistrust does not convey any coping strategies (Hughes et al., 2006). A smaller percentage of families report engaging in this socialization strategy relative to the other strategies (Biafora, Taylor, Warheit, Zimmerman, & Vega, 1993; Hughes & Chen, 1997; Hughes & Johnson, 2001; Thornton et al., 1990). In some contexts, promotion of mistrust has been related to more deviant behavior and poorer academic adjustment (Huynh & Fuligni, 2008).

Messages of egalitarianism place the emphasis on individuals rather than on their group membership. For example, the emphasis that parents place on individual qualities, such as values of justice and personal integrity, a strong work ethic, and self-esteem, is a primary socialization strategy used by minority parents to instill egalitarianism in their children (see Hughes et al., 2006). Hamm (2001) has found that European-American parents in the southeastern United States promoted color blindness as an egalitarian strategy. While an emphasis on egalitarian values is laudable, a color-blind strategy may deny the relevance of the experiences associated with racial or ethnic minority status in a racially and ethnically stratified society. It is very different to be color-blind from a position of privilege than to be color-blind from a position of disadvantage.

11.4. **PEER SOCIALIZING INFLUENCES**

Peer relationships in adolescence become more intense, closer, and more influential, and the majority of adolescents' time is spent with peers. Parents, whose time with the adolescent is on the decline, are often concerned about their children's relationship with peers and the possible negative influence peers may exert on them. Peers have the potential to encourage problem behaviors; however, more often than generally believed, peers strengthen family values and beliefs (Azmitia & Cooper, 2001). During adolescence, friendships tend to be more complex, more exclusive, and more consistent than during earlier childhood. New types of relationships (e.g., opposite sex, romantic ties) and levels (e.g., best friends, cliques, and "crowds") emerge in this period.

11.4.1. **Peer groups**

Peer groups in adolescence can be thought of as a network of nested levels of interpersonal relationships as well as social contexts. At the most proximal level, peer interactions mostly occur among adolescent dyads and *cliques*, or small groups, which consist of five or six adolescents. Small groups are linked to *crowds,* a larger and more dispersed group of peers with whom small groups share common characteristics. Crowds are linked by the *youth culture,* a broader and more elusive group with its own system of norms, values, and rituals, often driven by the mass media.

Small groups and friendships

Particularly in early adolescence, peer groups are characterized by their members' similarity to one another. Adolescents in a group are typically of the same gender and ethnicity, share similar interests, and are drawn to a particular group based on their attraction to the group's norms, values, and activities. They are selected by the peer group for the same reason. Given the bidirectional nature of peer influences, the group reinforces the identity of its members, who in turn reinforce the identity of the group. Studies of peer group similarity have found peers within a group to be more similar to each other on characteristics such as their GPA (Urberg, Degirmencioglu, Tolson, & Halliday-Scher, 2000), college aspirations (Hallinan & Williams, 1990), and general engagement in schoolwork (Kindermann, 1993). Peers within a group are also similar to each other in their reported frequency of smoking, drinking, and drug use (Sussman, Dent, & McCullar, 2000; Urberg, Degirmencioglu, & Pilgrim, 1997).

Peers as resources and challenges

Peers offer an opportunity for adolescents to learn and practice social skills among their close friends and peer groups. In small groups, adolescents can express emotional closeness, develop intimate friendships, and solve conflicts. Studies have shown that positive peer relations enhance self-esteem (Azmitia & Cooper, 2001), social competence (La Greca, Prinstein, & Fetter, 2001), and leadership skills (Berndt, Hawkins, & Jiao, 1999). Friendships can also become a coping resource. For example, friendships have been found to buffer youth from the negative impact of family problems (Bolger, Patterson, & Kupersmidt, 1998) and to lessen the likelihood of experiencing peer victimization (Hodges, Boivin, Vitaro, & Bukowski, 1999).

Friendships can also provide opportunities to learn adaptive modes of conflict resolution. Adolescent friendships encompass positive relationship dimensions (e.g., intimacy, closeness, emotional support) as well as negative (e.g., conflict, negativity, distrust) relationship dimensions (Berndt, 1982; Furman & Buhrmester, 1985; Greene et al., 2006; Larson et al., 1996; Way & Greene, 2006). Adolescents experience significant conflict in their friendships (Furman & Buhrmester, 1992) and research has shown that the quality of their friendships largely depends on the adolescent's use of effective strategies for conflict resolution (Furman & Buhrmester, 1985). Indeed, Way and colleagues' (Way, Cowal, Gingold, Pahl, & Bissessar, 2001) research shows that adolescents who engage in positive friendships view an ideal friendship as one in which conflicts are not avoided but effectively solved without damaging the relationship. Solution-oriented strategies (e.g., negotiating compromise) are positively linked to intimacy and negatively associated with friendship negativity, whereas nonconfrontation (e.g., avoiding friends after disagreements) and control strategies (e.g., refusing to compromise one's opinion) are associated with greater relationship problems (Furman & Buhrmester, 1992). These types of strategies are affected by gender and ethnicity. For example, girls and Latino adolescents are more prone to using solution-oriented strategies (Azmitia & Cooper, 2001).

Crowds

In addition to cliques, most adolescents belong to crowds, a larger, looser group who share the same identity or reputation. In U.S. high schools, typical crowds tend to be organized across specific types of school activities (e.g., sports, performing arts, or prosocial activities) that characterize their identities. For example, athletes are more likely than those who do not play sports to be considered "jocks," and those who do well academically are more likely to be considered "nerds" (Barber, Eccles, & Stone, 2001; Eccles & Barber, 1999). Identification with the peer group facilitates the individual process of identity formation by providing a "provisional identity" (Silbereisen, 1995) by which peer groups norms and values are incorporated into an adolescent's own self-concept. The "prototype" group identity, generally associated with the peer group's activities, also becomes a powerful influence on the content of group members' identity. Indeed, peer statuses that have characterized many types of crowds formed in American high schools (e.g., the "jocks," the "populars," the "normals," the "brains," nerds," etc.) are also being "exported" to youths across Europe, the Middle East, and Africa. For instance, as in the United States, in the United Arab Emirates adolescent peer groups are labeling themselves as the "studious" (who wish to excel academically, follow school rules), the "cool" (who do not care about school or adults), the "wealthy" (who display material status symbols), and the "sporty" (Russell, Wadi, Klelifa, & Jendli, 2007). In line with broader traditional Islamic cultural norms, however, and distinct from their Western counterparts, the "cool" may not have obvious body marks such as tattoos or piercings, and the "sporty" are mostly boys. Thus, as other cultures adopt American modes of self-expression, including clothing, dance, and music, they also adopt new forms of social relations.

Belonging to a group is also an index of social acceptance or rejection. The social status of any of the groups they belong to can have a serious impact on its members' self-esteem (Crocker & Major, 1989). Also, peer relations can be a negative source of influence for youth's adjustment and functioning if it involves risky adolescent behaviors (Sussman et al., 2000). For example, while "brains" and their friends appear to engage in very low levels of health risk behaviors, such as unprotected sex, drinking, smoking, drug use, reckless driving, delinquency, and violence (Dishion et al., 1995; La Greca et al., 2001), "populars," who are more socially accepted than other groups, also show evidence of some selected areas of engagement in health risk behaviors.

Peer crowds and cliques can also have a profound influence on how adolescents adjust to a school setting. Steele (1992, 1997) has maintained that group membership can influence students' sense of commitment to the institution they attend and influence academic achievement (Ryan, 2000; Wentzel, Barry, & Caldwell, 2004). Schools may inadvertently reinforce social hierarchies if the groups that students belong to may have formed, in part, as a consequence of their class placements, which are determined by school teachers and school administrators (Brady, 2004). The grouping of students on the basis of perceived academic ability, for example, may affect the constitution of peer groups, as well as their relative positioning in the school's peer group hierarchy. For students placed in lower tracks, a sense of rejection from mainstream institution values may compromise their commitment to school.

11.4.2. **Mechanisms of peer group influence**

Longitudinal research shows that both selection and socialization processes are important mechanisms of peer influence that contribute to peer group homogeneity. Adolescents initially select friends whose attitudes, norms, and behaviors are similar to their own, but then the peer group reinforces the attitudes, norms, and behaviors that characterize them as a group.

Consequently, the likelihood that individual group members will behave similarly to each other increases (Downs, 1987; Ennett & Bauman, 1994; Kindermann, 1993; Urberg et al., 1997). In addition to the internalization of group norms (Eder & Nenga, 2003), processes such as modeling, information exchange, shared experience, and pressure to conform also contribute to the similarity of peer group members (Berndt et al., 1999; Brown, 2004).

While the pressure to follow group norms may be similar across most peer groups, the nature of this influence can vary widely between different groups (Clasen & Brown, 1985). For instance, students categorized as "jock-populars" in one study reported more peer pressure directed at school involvement, relative to students categorized as "druggie-toughs," who reported greater pressure to engage in misconduct (Clasen & Brown, 1985). Brown and colleagues (e.g., Brown, Clasen, & Eicher, 1986; Brown, Lohr, & McClenahan, 1986; Clasen & Brown, 1985) have identified five major areas of peer pressure: involvement with family, peers, and school, as well as peer norms and misconduct. Peer influence in these domains can be negative or positive, as pressures can promote or discourage misconduct, achievement, and supportive social relations, and group norms vary in the extent to which they are prosocial.

Much of peer influence operates indirectly. Among adolescents, humor, teasing, and gossip are common practices for both communicating and enforcing norms without addressing them directly (Eder & Sanford, 1986; Sanford & Eder, 1984). Theories of delinquent behavior propose that deviant peers positively reinforce antisocial behaviors (e.g., using jokes or humor), while they do not reinforce prosocial behavior. In a study designed to test this assumption, Dishion, Spracklen, Andrews, and Patterson (1996) observed delinquent and nondelinquent boy dyads involved in predetermined discussion topics. Observations focused on "rule-breaking talk," as well as the contingent reactions of the listener (laughing or pausing). Findings indicated that boys in nondelinquent dyads (both boys were nondelinquent) reacted positively to prosocial talk and used less contingent verbal positive reinforcement (e.g., laughing) at rule-breaking jokes. For the boys in the delinquent dyads (both boys had a history of delinquency, or one in the pair had a history of delinquency), it was just the opposite. They were more likely to react positively to rule-breaking topics and less likely to reinforce prosocial discussions. Furthermore, antisocial talk escalated as laughing led to more antisocial behavior talk. When examined longitudinally, this type of deviance "training," as labeled by Dishion et al. (1996), was predictive of higher engagement in serious antisocial behavior two years later, particularly among those boys who were low in antisocial behaviors at the initial assessment.

Contextual influences on friendships: Multiple intersections

Cultural and family influences shape the nature or quality of adolescents' friendships. For instance, while adolescents in North America and China find closeness and companionship to be the most salient elements of friendship, they differ in their perception of other important characteristics. Chinese adolescents emphasize "mutual understanding" (friends really "get" each other) and instrumental support (friends help each other learn and accomplish things), whereas adolescents in North America see friendship as a means of achieving individual goals of self-validation and self-esteem (e.g., friends think I am a good and unique person; Chen, Kaspar, Zhang, Wang, & Zheng, 2004). Among more traditionally authoritarian families, such as in Bangladesh (particularly when adolescents cannot talk to adults or their age cohort in extended family), friendships may be the primary trusting relationship for adolescents to confide personal problems. According to Way and Greene (2006), girls, particularly Latinas, report having more *ideal friendships*, characterized by feeling loved by their close friends and expressing love toward them, while Asian-American boys report having more *disengaged friendship*s, typically described as distant or dismissive of the importance of friendships. Presumably, cultural values promote these differences. Latina girls' engagement in *ideal friendships* may be influenced by high levels of *simpatia* ("niceness"), which are promoted by Latino families and by femininity ideals in mainstream American culture. Similarly, *disengaged friendships* among Asian-American boys may be influenced by strict parental rules and regulations regarding social interactions, and by American cultural norms which characterize close friendships as more typical of girls. Culture can also give rise to gender-based differences in friendship patterns. Way and colleagues' research (Way & Chen, 2000; Way & Greene, 2006) has also indicated that Asian-American adolescent girls reported the lowest levels of general friendship compared to African- and Latino-American adolescent girls. Across ethnic groups, adolescent girls report higher levels of close friendship support than do boys (Berndt, 1982; Caldwell & Peplau, 1982; Camarena, Sarigiani, & Petersen, 1990; Douvan, Douvan, & Adelson, 1966; Way & Chen, 2000). The pattern of findings obtained with Asian-American girls, according to Way and Chen (2000), may be a consequence of the lack of opportunities to engage in friendships, as Asian-American parents may approve less of the use of their leisure time with peers. In fact, other research has indicated that parents of Asian-American adolescents often impose strict regulations regarding peer interactions (Yu & Berryman, 1996). These regulations may particularly influence girls. Although such research has not indicated gender differences in the parental monitoring of peers, it is likely that girls are monitored more than boys because they are expected to help more at home (Yu & Berryman, 1996). Similar findings are reported for Muslim girls in the United States and girls in societies with strict gender norms. In Bangladesh, for example, boys can socialize and enhance their knowledge and skills, while girls are kept confined at home. Adolescent boys have access to more settings and activities, such as outdoor activities, the cinema, and neighborhood, while girls mostly remain in their own or a friend's house. Similarly, leisure time for girls in India and the United Arab Emirates is primarily home-based, while boys spend more outside activities such as playing sports, going to movies, or hanging out with friends (Russell et al., 2007; Verma & Sharma, 2003). Today, however, girls restricted to the home are increasingly able to connect with peers by using technologies such as mobile phones and the Internet (Russell et al., 2007).

Youth cultures

One way in which groups of adolescents consistently distinguish themselves is according to appearance (e.g., hairstyle, manner of dress, tattooing) and language (e.g., the kind of slang they use), which functions primarily to demarcate a clear distance between the world of adults and the world of youth. Adolescents' confidence in their physical and social appearance is an important predictor of self-esteem, higher than their confidence in cognitive or academic competencies. This tendency seems to be on the rise as the media targets youth products such as music and clothes, a trend that continues to expand and diversify (Arnett, 2007). As Western culture is transmitted through powerful U.S. media, including Hollywood, TV, and the multibillion dollar music industry, aspects of Western youth culture are being adopted by adolescents across the world. Youth around the world have become major consumers of products and images from global media that provide them with temporary sources of identification. The multiplicity of adolescent peer cultures and the different factors that influence each of them distinctly are creating new types of peer groups which are a fusion of traditional and modern influences. For example, in Austria and across Europe, groups form around a particular kind of music, such as house-techno, hard-core metal, straight edge, hip hop, or new wave (Haenfler, 2006). In Zambia (Mpofu, Jere, & Chemyu, 2007), these influences arrive through TV, newspaper, and radio stations; in Germany (Dreher & Zumkley, 2007) and Belgium (Goossens & Luyckx, 2007) peers mostly meet friends on the street or in parks, while in countries like Argentina (Facio & Resett, 2007), youth form similar groups though segregated by social class. As globalized peer groups multiply and diversify, the "youth culture" is being transformed into a more powerful "youth scene" (Grossegger, Heinzlmaier, & Zentner, 2001).

Peer relations and the Internet

The social ecology of adolescent peer networks is and continues to be radically transformed by the use of the Internet and technologically mediated communication. However, the most significant cultural and social transformation taking place worldwide is that technology-mediated interactions are mostly dominated by peer, youth-oriented models of social relations. That is, the social world of adults is changing to an adolescent-oriented peer system of communication. As an example, Facebook, a social networking website created by young adults for adolescent and young adult use, began as a college and high school social tool. Two-thirds of its 250 or more million active users today are over college age and 70% are outside the United States (Facebook, 2009). In this new social arena, families are adapting to their adolescents' use of the Internet, IM, cell phones, and text messaging and are following their pace. Adolescents use these modes of communication to interact with peers, having simultaneous access and constant accessibility to their entire social network. Parents believe that by knowing their adolescents' whereabouts, they will be able to keep track of peer influence. While in many families parents now can "microcoordinate" with their adolescent children the time and places of their activities with the use of cell phones, the potential lack of access to knowledge about their children's peer relations has never been greater. While adolescents may appear to be quietly focusing on homework or having dinner with the family, they most likely are simultaneously online, in intense interaction with multiple peers. According to Jones and Fox (2009), 93% of adolescents aged 12-17 currently go online, more than 70% talk to or text their friends on their cell phones daily.

In research on adolescent use of the Internet and technologically mediated tools for social interactions (cell phone, instant messaging, etc.), adolescents report using these tools almost exclusively to communicate with their peers offline, and report better relationship quality with their friends when compared to adolescents who do not use the Internet or cell phones (Valkenburg & Peter, 2007). In a qualitative study on adolescent girls' use of technology in social interactions at school and outside of school (Clark, 2005) it was indicated that the Internet has been a way to deepen relationships with friends in their offline life. Participants reported that by using the Internet, text messaging, or instant messaging, they could have control and privacy in their relations with peers while being with their parents at home or supervised by adults. Adolescents felt more autonomous and in control of their social lives, using various strategies to maintain relationships online and to work within the limits of parents' expectations.

According to Clark (2005), friendship maintenance now involves "hyper-coordination," which means that adolescents have to coordinate interactions with multiple friends simultaneously while fulfilling individual peers expectations. From these online interactions friends expect to receive truthful communication, expect to be kept aware of what is happening with the group, and to maintain confidentiality (violations of confidentiality can be made, for example, by cutting and pasting conversations that are sent to other friends). Being accessible to peers is a central part of building trust. In this, peers follow the group's norms for when to answer calls, for leaving messages, or for blocking calls. Rather than considering constant accessibility too demanding or stressful, adolescents consider receiving messages to be a confirmation of their group membership and status, as is their mastery in keeping up with many conversations at a time (also see Thiel, 2005). For parents, the response to adolescents' use of the Internet and technology-mediated communication is mixed. On the one hand, use of computers, the Internet and cell phones is an avenue for education and preparation for the future. On the other hand, parents perceive the continuous use of gadgets to be an interruption to homework and family interaction. For adolescents, it has represented a sense of mastery and control over their own lives.

11.5. **CONCLUSION**

In summary, the family and peer experiences of adolescents around the world are changing at an unprecedented pace. Increasing immigration, access to a global economy, and Internet-based communications have resulted in greater family diversity and a more youth-oriented culture. The research presented in this chapter underscores the value of using an ecological framework to understand the diverse socialization processes shaping adolescent development. Familial socialization takes place within specific contexts and circumstances that give meaning to parental and adolescent behaviors. For example, the parenting challenges faced by ethnic minority families in the U.S., such as protecting their children from the harmful effects of discrimination, have led parents to engage in adaptive racial and ethnic socialization practices that faster adolescents' healthy development. Investigating how socialization processes vary within and between different racial and ethnic groups may help us identify culturally specific processes as well as shared, fundamental experiences relating to social stratification. Despite the qualitative differences in their circumstances, different groups may share similar experiences of negative treatment, biases, and hardships generated by a system of cumulative privileges or disadvantages. Cross-cultural research of immigrant families in different regions of the world reveals factors that are common to the process of acculturation, and those that are more specific to unique individual circumstances. In the midst of a global upsurge of immigration, studying the socialization processes of immigrant families has practical worldwide applications.

The research on adolescent autonomy emphasizes the bidirectional nature of socialization processes. From the research on parental monitoring, one might conclude that adolescents require as much monitoring and supervision from parents as possible. However, parents' monitoring behaviors may be perceived as too controlling by their adolescent children, inhibiting their adolescents' willingness to disclose any information. Controlling parents, therefore, could end up knowing less about their adolescents' activities or friends. Thus, parents' efforts to improve communication, build a trusting relationship, and legitimize some areas in which their adolescent child can exert autonomy may be a better strategy. For parents who do not have the opportunity to closely monitor their adolescent children, such as a single mother working night shifts, or a father without breaks on the job, this may be welcome advice. Rather than having to make substantial personal changes in their own activities to monitor their children, parents may make efforts to listen to their adolescents' concerns, understand their points of view, and find common areas of agreement (Maccoby & Martin, 1983; Magnusson & Stattin, 1998). These strategies would likely improve adolescents' disclosure of their activities and may contribute to a mutual understanding of each others' expectations and worldviews.

Traditionally our society has perceived peer culture as a negative influence that often leads to adolescent problem behaviors. Alcohol abuse, drug use, truancy, and adolescent pregnancy are all attributed to a deviant youth culture. This characterization may sometimes lead parents to overlook the benefits of peers for their adolescents' positive development. Older generations' wariness of the younger generations goes far back. However, according to studies conducted by the William T. Grant Foundation to examine adults' conceptions of youth (2001), the gap between adults' perception of youth and youth behaviors is wider than ever. For example, when asked for words that come to mind when they think of adolescents nearly three-quarters of adults in their sample responded with negative descriptions, such as "rude," "wild," or "irresponsible." The overwhelming majority of adults in the U.S. believe that young people today do not have a strong sense of right or wrong; in as compared to the 1950s, when only a third of adults believed they did not. While adults have serious reservations about American youth, the adolescents reality is far from this adult picture; for example, most of high school students plan to attend a 4-year college, spend a fair amount of time thinking about their life after high school. The vast majority of adolescents place high value on honesty and hard work, and are thinking and planning seriously for the future. As we enter a new social era in which social relations may be fundamentally transformed, it may be time for adults to align their views with this reality. Our youth are not only our partners in this transformation, but they may be understated as a leading generation.

REFERENCES

Ardila-Rey, A., & Killen, M. (2001). Colombian preschool children's judgments about autonomy and conflict resolution in the classroom setting. *International Journal of Behavioral Development*, *25*, 246–255.

Arnett, J. J. (1995). Broad and narrow socialization: The family in the context of a cultural theory. *Journal of Marriage and the Family*, *57*(3), 617–628.

Arnett, J. J. (2007). *International encyclopedia of adolescence* (Vol. 1). New York, NY: Routledge.

Ary, D. V., Duncan, T. E., Duncan, S. C., & Hops, H. (1999). Adolescent problem behavior: The influence of parents and peers. *Behaviour Research and Therapy*, *37*(3), 217–230.

Azmitia, M., & Cooper, C. R. (2001). Good or bad? Peer influences on Latino and European American adolescents pathways through school. *Journal of Education for Students Placed at Risk (JESPAR)*, *6*(1), 45–71.

Barber, B. K. (1996). Parental psychological control: Revisiting a neglected construct. *Child Development*, *67*(6), 3296–3319.

Barber, B. K., & Harmon, E. L. (Eds.) (2002). *Violating the self: Parental psychological control of children and adolescents*. Washington DC: American Psychological Association.

Barber, B. L., Eccles, J. S., & Stone, M. R. (2001). Whatever happened to the jock, the brain, and the princess? Young adult pathways linked to adolescent activity involvement and social identity. *Journal of Adolescent Research*, *16*(5), 429–455.

Baumrind, D. (1971). Current patterns of parental authority. *Developmental Psychology*, *4*(1, Pt. 2), 1–103.

Berndt, T. J. (1982). The features and effects of friendship in early adolescence. *Child Development*, *53*(6), 1447–1460.

Berndt, T. J., Hawkins, J. A., & Jiao, Z. (1999). Influences of friends and friendships on adjustment to junior high school. *Merrill-Palmer Quarterly*, *45*(1), 13–41.

Biafora, F. A., Taylor, D. L., Warheit, G. J., Zimmerman, R. S., & Vega, W. A. (1993). Cultural mistrust and racial awareness among ethnically diverse Black adolescent boys. *Journal of Black Psychology*, *19*(3), 266–281.

Bolger, K. E., Patterson, C. J., & Kupersmidt, J. B. (1998). Peer relationships and self-esteem among children who have been maltreated. *Child Development*, *69*(4), 1171–1197.

Boog, I., Donselaar, J., Houtzager, D., Rodrigues, P., & Schriemer, R. (2006). *Monitor Rassendiscriminatie 2005 [Monitor race discrimination 2005].* Leiden, Netherlands: Universiteit van Leiden.

Bowman, P. J., & Howard, C. (1985). Race-related socialization, motivation, and academic achievement: A study of Black youths in three-generation families. *Journal of the American Academy of Child Psychiatry*, 24(2), 134–141.

Boykin, A. W., & Toms, F. D. (1985). Black child socialization: A conceptual framework. In H. P. McAdoo & J. L. McAdoo (Eds.), *Black children social, educational, and parental environment* (pp. 33–51). Thousand Oaks, CA: Sage Publications.

Brady, P. (2004). Jocks, teckers, and nerds: The role of the adolescent peer group in the formation and maintenance of secondary school institutional culture. *Discourse: Studies in the Cultural Politics of Education*, 25(3), 351–364.

Branch, C. W., & Newcombe, N. (1986). Racial attitude development among young Black children as a function of parental attitudes: A longitudinal and cross-sectional study. *Child Development*, 57(3), 712–721.

Brody, G. H., & Flor, D. L. (1998). Maternal resources, parenting practices, and child competence in rural, single-parent African American families. *Child Development*, 69(3), 803–816.

Bronfenbrenner, U. (1979). *The ecology of human development: Experiments by nature and design.* Cambridge, MA: Harvard University Press.

Bronfenbrenner, U., & Crouter, A. C. (1983). The evolution of environmental models in developmental research. In W. Kessen (Ed.), *Handbook of child psychology* (4th ed., Vol. 1, pp. 357–414). New York, NY: Wiley.

Brown, B. B. (2004). Adolescents'relationships with peers. *Handbook of Adolescent Psychology*, 2, 363–394.

Brown, B. B., Clasen, D. R., & Eicher, S. A. (1986). Perceptions of peer pressure, peer conformity dispositions, and self-reported behavior among adolescents. *Developmental Psychology*, 22(4), 521–530.

Brown, B. B., & Larson, R. W. (2002). The kaleidoscope of adolescence: Experiences of the world's youth at the beginning of the 21 st century. In B. B. Brown, R. W. Larson, & T. S. Saraswathi (Eds.), *The world's youth: Adolescence in eight regions of the globe* (pp. 1–20). New York, NY: Cambridge University Press.

Brown, B. B., Lohr, M. J., & McClenahan, E. L. (1986). Early adolescents' perceptions of peer pressure. *The Journal of Early Adolescence*, 6(2), 139.

Brown, B. B., Mounts, N., Lamborn, S. D., & Steinberg, L. (1993). Parenting practices and peer group affiliation in adolescence. *Child Development*, 64(2), 467–482.

Buki, L. P., Ma, T. C., Strom, R. D., & Strom, S. K. (2003). Chinese immigrant mothers of adolescents: Self-perceptions of acculturation effects on parenting. *Cultural Diversity and Ethnic Minority Psychology*, 9(2), 127–140.

Caldwell, M. A., & Peplau, L. A. (1982). Sex differences in same-sex friendship. *Sex Roles*, 8(7), 721–732.

Camarena, P. M., Sarigiani, P. A., & Petersen, A. C. (1990). Gender-specific pathways to intimacy in early adolescence. *Journal of Youth and Adolescence*, 19(1), 19–32.

Caplan, N. S., Choy, M. H., & Whitmore, J. K. (1991). *Children of the boat people: A study of educational success*. Ann Arbor, MI: University of Michigan Press.

Carson, D. K., Chowdhury, A., Perry, C. K., & Pati, C. (1999). Family characteristics and adolescent competence in India: Investigation of youth in southern Orissa. *Journal of Youth and Adolescence, 28*(2), 211–233.

Carvajal, S. C., Photiades, J. R., Evans, R. I., & Nash, S. G. (1997). Relating a social influence model to the role of acculturation in substance use among Latino adolescents 1. *Journal of Applied Social Psychology, 27*(18), 1617–1628.

Cauce, A. M., Coronado, N., & Watson, J. (1998). Conceptual, methodological, and statistical issues in culturally competent research. In M. Hernandez & M. R. Isaacs (Eds.), *Promoting cultural competence in children's mental health services* (pp. 305–329). Baltimore, MD: Paul H. Brookes Publishing.

Cauce, A. M., & Domenech-Rodriguez, M. (Eds.) (2002). *Latino families: Myths and realities*. Westport, CT: Praeger Publishers/Greenwood Publishing Group.

Chao, R., & Tseng, V. (Eds.) (2002). *Parenting of Asians*. Mahwah NJ: Lawrence Erlbaum Associates Publishers.

Chao, R. K. (1994). Beyond parental control and authoritarian parenting style: Understanding Chinese parenting through the cultural notion of training. *Child Development, 65*(4), 1111–1119.

Chao, R. K., & Sue, S. (1996). Chinese parental influence and their children's school success: A paradox in the literature on parenting styles. In S. Lau (Ed.), *Growing up the Chinese way: Chinese child and adolescent development* (pp. 93–120). Hong Kong: The Chinese University Press.

Chassin, L., Pillow, D. R., Curran, P. J., Molina, B. S. G., & Barrera, M. J. R. (1993). Relation of parental alcoholism to early adolescent substance use: A test of three mediating mechanisms. *Journal of Abnormal Psychology, 102*(1), 3–19.

Chaudhary, N., & Sharma, N. (2005). From home to school. In J. J. Arnett (Ed.), *International encyclopedia of adolescence* (Vol. 1, pp. 442–459). New York, NY: Routledge.

Chen, X., Kaspar, V., Zhang, Y., Wang, L., & Zheng, S. (Eds.) (2004). *Peer relationships among Chinese boys: A cross-cultural perspective*. New York NY: New York University Press.

Clark, L. S. (2005). The constant contact generation: Exploring teen friendship networks online. In S. Mazzarella (Ed.), *Girl wide web: Girls, the Internet, and the negotiation of identity* (pp. 203–221). New York, NY: Peter Lang Publishing.

Clasen, D. R., & Brown, B. (1985). The multidimensionality of peer pressure in adolescence. *Journal of Youth and Adolescence, 14*(6), 451–468.

Conger, K. J., Rueter, M. A., & Conger, R. D. (2000). The role of economic pressure in the lives of parents and their adolescents: The family stress model. In L. J. Crockett & R. K. Sibereisen (Eds.), *Negotiating adolescence in times of social change* (pp. 201–223). New York, NY: Cambridge University Press.

Conger, R. D., & Donnellan, M. B. (2007). An interactionist perspective on the socioeconomic context of human development. *Annual Review of Psychology, 58*, 175–199.

Conger, R. D., & Elder, G. H. (1994). *Families in troubled times: Adapting to change in rural America*. New York, NY: Walter de Gruyter.

Conger, R. D., & Simons, R. L. (1997). Life-course contingencies in the development of adolescent antisocial behavior: A matching law approach. In T. P. Thornberry (Ed.), *Developmental theories of crime and delinquency* (pp. 55–99). New Brunswick, NJ: Transaction Publishers.

Conger, R. D., Wallace, L. E., Sun, Y., Simons, R. L., McLoyd, V. C., & Brody, G. H. (2002). Economic pressure in African American families: A replication and extension of the family stress model. *Developmental Psychology*, *38*(2), 179–193.

Costigan, C. L., Bardina, P., Cauce, A. M., Kim, G. K., & Latendresse, S. J. (2006). Inter- and intra-group variability in perceptions of behavior among Asian Americans and European Americans. *Cultural Diversity and Ethnic Minority Psychology*, *12*(4), 710.

Crocker, J., & Major, B. (1989). Social stigma and self-esteem: The self-protective properties of stigma. *Psychological Review*, *96*(4), 608–630.

Crockett, L. J., Brown, J., Russell, S. T., & Shen, Y. L. (2007). The meaning of good parent-child relationships for Mexican American adolescents. *Journal of Research on Adolescence*, *17*(4), 639.

Csikszentmihalyi, M., & Larson, R. (1984). *Being adolescent: Conflict and growth in the teenage years*. New York, NY: Basic Books.

Darling, N., Cumsille, P., Caldwell, L. L., & Dowdy, B. (2006). Predictors of adolescents' disclosure to parents and perceived parental knowledge: Between- and within-person differences. *Journal of Youth and Adolescence*, *35*(4), 659–670.

Darling, N., Cumsille, P., & Martinez, M. L. (2008). Individual differences in adolescents' beliefs about the legitimacy of parental authority and their own obligation to obey: A longitudinal investigation. *Child Development*, *79*(4), 1103–1118.

Darling, N., Cumsille, P., & Pena-Alampay, L. (2005). Rules, legitimacy of parental authority, and obligation to obey in Chile, the Philippines, and the United States. *New Directions for Child and Adolescent Development*, *2005* (108), 47–60.

Darling, N., & Steinberg, L. (1993). Parenting styles context: An integrative model. *Psychological Bulletin*, *113*(3), 487–496.

DelBarrio, C., Moreno, A., & Linaza, J. L. (2007). Spain. In J. J. Arnett (Ed.), *International encyclopedia of adolescence* (Vol. 2, pp. 906–924). New York, NY: Routledge.

Demo, D. H., & Hughes, M. (1990). Socialization and racial identity among black Americans. *Social Psychology Quarterly*, *53*(4), 364–374.

Dishion, T. J., Capaldi, D., Spracklen, K. M., & Li, F. (1995). Peer ecology of male adolescent drug use. *Development and Psychopathology*, *7*, 803–824.

Dishion, T. J., Spracklen, K. M., Andrews, D. W., & Patterson, G. R. (1996). Deviancy training in male adolescent friendships. *Behavior Therapy*, *27*(3), 373–390.

Dornbusch, S. M., Ritter, P. L., Leiderman, P. H., Roberts, D. F., & Fraleigh, M. J. (1987). The relation of parenting style to adolescent school performance. *Child Development*, *58*(5), 1244–1257.

Douvan, E. A. M., Douvan, E., & Adelson, J. (1966). *The adolescent experience.* New York, NY: Wiley.

Downs, W. R. (1987). A panel study of normative structure, adolescent alcohol use and peer alcohol use. *Journal of Studies on Alcohol, 48*(2), 167–175.

Dreher, E., & Zumkley, H. (2007). Germany. In J. J. Arnett (Ed.), *International encyclopedia of adolescence* (Vol. 1, pp. 321–343). New York, NY: Routledge.

du Bois-Reymond, M. (1998). Negotiation strategies in modern families: What does it mean for global citizenship. In K. Matthijs (Ed.), *The family: Contemporary perspectives and challenges: Festschrift in honor of Wilfried Dumon* (pp. 57–72). Leuven, Belgium: Leuven University Press.

Du Bois-Reymond, M. (2001). Negotiation strategies in modern families. What does it mean for global citizenship? In J. A. Myers-Walls & P. Somlai (Eds.), *Families as educators for global citizenship* (pp. 55–68). Burlington, VT: Ashgate Publishing Company.

Dubrow, N. F., & Garbarino, J. (1989). Living in the war zone: Mothers and young children in a public housing development. *Child Welfare Journal, 68*(1), 3–20.

Dwairy, M., & Menshar, K. E. (2006). Parenting style, individuation, and mental health of Egyptian adolescents. *Journal of Adolescence, 29*(1), 103–117.

Eccles, J. S., & Barber, B. L. (1999). Student council, volunteering, basketball, or marching band: What kind of extracurricular involvement matters? *Journal of Adolescent Research, 14*(1), 10.

Eder, D., & Nenga, S. K. (2003). Socialization in adolescence. In J. Delamater (Ed.), *Handbook of social psychology* (pp. 157–182). New York, NY: Kluwer Academic.

Eder, D., & Sanford, S. (1986). The development and maintenance of interactional norms among early adolescents. *Sociological Studies of Child Development: A Research Annual, 1,* 283–300.

Elder, G. H. (1974). *Children ofthe Great Depression; social change in life experience.* Chicago, IL: University of Chicago Press.

Elder, G. H., & Conger, R. (2000). *Children of the land: Adversity and success in rural America.* Chicago, IL: University of Chicago Press.

Ennett, S. T., & Bauman, K. E. (1994). The contribution of influence and selection to adolescent peer group homogeneity: The case of adolescent cigarette smoking. *Journal of Personality and Social Psychology, 67,* 653–663.

Facebook. (2009). Facebook press room: Statistics, 2009, from http://www.facebook.com/press/info.php?factsheet#/press/info.php?statistics

Facio, A., & Resett, S. (2007). Argentina. In J. J. Arnett (Ed.), *International encyclopedia of adolescence* (Vol. 2, pp. 1–15). New York, NY: Routledge.

Feldman, S. S., & Rosenthal, D. A. (1991). Age expectations of behavioural autonomy in Hong Kong, Australian and American youth: The influence of family variables and adolescents' values. *International Journal of Psychology, 26*(1), 1–23.

Feldman, S. S., Rosenthal, D. A., Mont-Reynaud, R., Leung, K., & Lau, S. (1991). Ain t Misbehavin: Adolescent values and family environments as correlates of misconduct in Australia, Hong Kong, and the United States. *Journal of Research on Adolescence, 1*(2), 109–134.

Flanagan, C. A. (2001). Families and socialization: A new social contract and agenda for research. In J. A. Myers-Walls & P. Somlai (Eds.), *Families as educators for global citizenship*. Burlington, VT: Ashgate.

Fletcher, A. C., Darling, N. E., Steinberg, L., & Dornbusch, S. M. (1995). The company they keep: Relation of adolescents' adjustment and behavior to their friends' perceptions of authoritative parenting in the social network. *Developmental Psychology, 31*(2), 300–309.

Florsheim, P., Tolan, P., & Gorman-Smith, D. (1998). Family relationships, parenting practices, the availability of male family members, and the behavior of inner-city boys in single-mother and two-parent families. *Child Development, 69*, 1437–1447.

Florsheim, P., Tolan, P. H., & Gorman-Smith, D. (1996). Family processes and risk for externalizing behavior problems among African American and Hispanic boys. *Journal of Consulting and Clinical Psychology, 64*(6), 1222–1230.

Forkel, I., & Silbereisen, R. K. (2001). Family economic hardship and depressed mood among young adolescents from former East and West Germany. *American Behavioral Scientist, 44*(11), 1955.

Fracasso, M. P., & Busch-Rossnagel, N. A. (1992). Parents and children of Hispanic origin. In M. E. Procidano & C. B. Fisher (Eds.), *Contemporary families: A handbook for school professionals* (pp. 83–98). New York, NY: Teachers College Press.

Freeberg, A. L., & Stein, C. H. (1996). Felt obligation towards parents in Mexican-American and Anglo-American young adults. *Journal of Social and Personal Relationships, 13*(3), 457–471.

Fuligni, A. J. (1997). The academic achievement of adolescents from immigrant families: The roles of family background, attitudes, and behaviour. *Child Development, 68*(2), 351–363.

Fuligni, A. J. (1998). Authority, autonomy, and parent-adolescent conflict and cohesion: A study of adolescents from Mexican, Chinese, Filipino, and European backgrounds. *Developmental Psychology, 34*(4), 782–792.

Fuligni, A. J. (2001). A comparative longitudinal approach to acculturation among children from immigrant families. *Harvard Educational Review, 71*(3), 566–578.

Fuligni, A. J., & Eccles, J. S. (1993). Perceived parent-child relationships and early adolescents' orientation toward peers. *Developmental Psychology, 29*, 622–632.

Fuligni, A. J., Tseng, V., & Lam, M. (1999). Attitudes toward family obligations among American adolescents with Asian, Latin American, and European backgrounds. *Child Development, 70*, 1030–1044.

Furman, W., & Buhrmester, D. (1985). Children's perceptions of the personal relationships in their social networks. *Developmental Psychology, 21*(6), 1016–1024.

Furman, W., & Buhrmester, D. (1992). Age and sex differences in perceptions of networks of personal relationships. *Child Development, 63*, 103–115.

Furstenberg, F. F., Cook, T., Eccles, J., Elder, G. H., & Sameroff, A. (1999). *Managing to make it: Urban families in high-risk neighborhoods*. Chicago, IL: University of Chicago Press.

Garcia-Coll, C., Lamberty, G., Jenkins, R., McAdoo, H. P., Crnic, K., Wasik, B. H., et al. (1996). An integrative model for the study of developmental competencies in minority children. *Child Development, 67*(5), 1891–1914.

Garcia-Coll, C., & Vazquez Garcia, H. A. (1995). Hispanic children and their families: On a different track from the very beginning. In H. E. Fitzgerald, B. M. Lester & B. S. Zuckerman (Eds.), *Children of poverty: Research, health, and policy issues* (pp. 57–83). New York, NY: Garland.

Gauthier, A. H., Smeedeng, T. M., & Furstenberg, F. F. (2004). Are parents investing less time in children? Trends in selected industrialized countries. *Population and Development Review, 30*(4), 647–671.

Gil, A. G., Vega, W. A., & Dimas, J. M. (1994). Acculturative stress and personal adjustment among Hispanic adolescent boys. *Journal of Community Psychology, 22*(1), 43–54.

Goldblatt, H., & Rosenblum, S. (2007). Navigating among worlds: The experience of Ethiopian adolescents in Israel. *Journal of Adolescent Research, 22*(6), 585.

Gonzales, N. A., Cauce, A. M., & Mason, C. A. (1996). Interobserver agreement in the assessment of parental behavior and parent-adolescent conflict: African American mothers, daughters, and independent observers. *Child Development, 67*, 1483–1498.

Gonzales, N. A., Knight, G. P., Morgan-Lopez, A. A., Saenz, D., & Sirolli, A. (2002). Acculturation and the mental health of Latino youths: An integration and critique of the literature. In J. M. Contreras, K. A. Kerns, & A. M. Neal-Barnett (Eds.), *Latino children and families in the United States: Current research and future directions* (pp. 45–74). Westport, CT: Praeger.

Gonzalez, A. R., Doan Holbein, M. F., & Quilter, S. (2002). High school students' goal orientations and their relationship to perceived parenting styles. *Contemporary Educational Psychology, 27*(3), 450–470.

Goossens, L., & Luyckx, K. (2007). Belgium. In J. J. Arnett (Ed.), *International encyclopedia of adolescence* (Vol. 1, pp. 64–76). New York, NY: Routledge.

Gorman-Smith, D., Tolan, P. H., Henry, D. B., & Florsheim, P. (2000). Patterns of family functioning and adolescent outcomes among urban African American and Mexican American families. *Journal of Family Psychology, 14*(3), 436–457.

Gray, M. R., & Steinberg, L. (1999). Unpacking authoritative parenting: Reassessing a multidimensional construct. *Journal of Marriage and the Family, 61*, 574–587.

Greene, M. L., Way, N., & Pahl, K. (2006). Trajectories of perceived adult and peer discrimination among Black, Latino, and Asian American adolescents: Patterns and psychological correlates. *Developmental Psychology, 42*(2), 218–238.

Grossegger, B., Heinzlmaier, G., & Zentner, M. (2001). Youth scenes in Austria. In A. Furlong & I. Guidikova (Eds.), *Transitions of youth citizenship in Europe: Culture, subculture, and identity*. Strasbourg: Council of Europe Publishing.

Haenfler, R. (2006). *Straight-edge: Clean-living youth, hardcore punk, and social change*. New Brunswick, NJ: Rutgers University Press.

Halgunseth, L. C., Ispa, J. M., & Rudy, D. (2006). Parental control in Latino families: An integrated review of the literature. *Child Development*, *77*(5), 1282–1297.

Hallinan, M. T., & Williams, R. A. (1990). Students' characteristics and the peer-influence process. *Sociology of Education*, *63*(2), 122–132.

Hamm, J. V. (2001). Barriers and bridges to positive cross-ethnic relations: African American and White parent socialization beliefs and practices. *Youth and Society*, *33*(1), 62–98.

Haq, M. N. (2007). International encyclopedia of adolescence. In J. J. Arnett (Ed.), *International encyclopedia of adolescence* (Vol. 1, pp. 53–63). New York, NY: Routledge.

Harrison, A. O., Wilson, M. N., Pine, C. J., Chan, S. Q., & Buriel, R. (1990). Family ecologies of ethnic minority children. *Child Development*, *61*, 347–362.

Hasebe, Y., Nucci, L., & Nucci, M. S. (2004). Parental control of the personal domain and adolescent symptoms of psychopathology: A cross-national study in the United States and Japan. *Child Development*, *75*(3), 815–828.

Hellenga, K. (2002). Social space, the final frontier: Adolescents on the Internet. In J. T. Mortimer, & R. W. Larson (Eds.), *The changing adolescent experience: Societal trends and the transition to adulthood* (pp. 208–299). New York, NY: Cambridge University Press.

Hodges, E. V. E., Boivin, M., Vitaro, F., & Bukowski, W. M. (1999). The power of friendship: Protection against an escalating cycle of peer victimization. *Developmental Psychology*, *35*(1), 94–101.

Holmbeck, G. N., & Hill, J. P. (1986). A path-analytic approach to the relations between parental traits and acceptance and adolescent adjustment. *Sex Roles*, *14*(5-6), 315–334.

Hovey, J. D., & King, C. A. (1996). Acculturative stress, depression, and suicidal ideation among immigrant and second-generation Latino adolescents. *Journal of the American Academy of Child and Adolescent Psychiatry*, *35*(9), 1183–1192.

Hughes, D. (2003). Correlates of African American and Latino parents' messages to children about ethnicity and race: A comparative study of racial socialization. *American Journal of Community Psychology*, *31*(1-2), 15–33.

Hughes, D., & Chen, L. (1997). When and what parents tell children about race: An examination of race-related socialization among African American families. *Applied Developmental Science*, *1*(4), 200–214.

Hughes, D., & Chen, L. (1999). The nature of parents' race-related communications to children: A developmental perspective. In L. Balter, & C. S. Tamis–LeMonda (Eds.), *Child psychology: A handbook of contemporary issues* (pp. 467–490). New York, NY: Psychology Press.

Hughes, D., & Johnson, D. (2001, November). Correlates in children's experiences of parents' racial socialization behaviors. *Journal of Marriage and the Family*, *63*(4), 981–995.

Hughes, D., Rodriguez, J., Smith, E. P., Johnson, D. J., Stevenson, H. C., & Spicer, P. (2006). Parents' ethnic-racial socialization practices: A review of research and directions for future study. *Developmental Psychology*, *42*(5), 747–770.

Hughes, D., Witherspoon, D., Rivas-Drake, D., & West-Bey, N. (2009, April). Received ethnic-racial socialization messages and youths' academic and behavioral outcomes: Examining the mediating role of ethnic identity and self-esteem. *Cultural Diversity and Ethnic Minority Psychology, 15*(2), 112–124.

Huynh, V. W., & Fuligni, A. J. (2008). Ethnic socialization and the academic adjustment of adolescents from Mexican, Chinese, and European backgrounds. *Developmental Psychology, 44*(4), 1202–1208.

Jones, S., & Fox, S. (2009, January 28). Pew Internet and American life project: Generations. Online in 2009 Retrieved August 21, 2009, from http://www.pewinternet.org/(/media//Files/Reports/2009/PIP_Generations_2009.pdf

Kagitcibasi, C. (2005). Autonomy and relatedness in cultural context: Implications for self and family. *Journal of Cross-Cultural Psychology, 36*(4), 403–422.

Keijing, D., & Myers-Walls, J. A. (2001). The tradition and change of family education in mainland China. In J. A. Myers-Walls & P. Somlai (Eds.), *Families as educators for global citizenship*. Burlington, VT: Ashgate.

Kelley, M. L., Power, T. G., & Wimbush, D. D. (1992). Determinants of disciplinary practices in low-income Black mothers. *Child Development, 63*, 573–582.

Kerr, M., & Stattin, H. (2000). What parents know, how they know it, and several forms of adolescent adjustment: Further support for a reinterpretation of monitoring. *Developmental Psychology, 36*(3), 366–380.

Kiang, L., Yip, T., Gonzales-Backen, M., Witkow, M., & Fuligni, A. J. (2006). Ethnic identity and the daily psychological well-being of adolescents from Mexican and Chinese backgrounds. *Child Development, 77*(5), 1338–1350.

Kindermann, T. A. (1993). Natural peer groups as contexts for individual development: The case of children's motivation in school. *Developmental Psychology, 29*(6), 970–977.

Knight, G. P., Bernal, M. E., Garza, C. A., Cota, M. K., & Ocampo, K. A. (1993). Family socialization and the ethnic identity of Mexican-American children. *Journal of Cross Cultural Psychology, 24*(1), 99–114.

Kotchick, B. A., Dorsey, S., Miller, K. S., & Forehand, R. (1999). Adolescent sexual risk-taking behavior in single-parent ethnic minority families. *Journal of Family Psychology, 13*(1), 93–102.

Kuperminc, G., Jurkovic, G., & Casey, S. (2009). The relation of filial responsibility to the personal and social adjustment of Latino adolescents from immigrant families. *Journal of Family Psychology, 23*(1), 14–22.

La Greca, A. M., Prinstein, M. J., & Fetter, M. D. (2001). Adolescent peer crowd affiliation: Linkages with health-risk behaviors and close friendships. *Journal of Pediatric Psychology, 26*(3), 131–143.

Lamborn, S. D., Dornbusch, S. M., & Steinberg, L. (1996). Ethnicity and community context as moderators of the relations between family decision making and adolescent adjustment. *Child Development, 67*(2), 283–301.

Lamborn, S. D., Mounts, N. S., Steinberg, L., & Dornbusch, S. M. (1991). Patterns of competence and adjustment among adolescents from authoritative, authoritarian, indulgent, and neglectful families. *Child Development, 62*(5), 1049–1065.

Larson, R., & Richards, M. H. (1994). *Divergent realities: The emotional lives of mothers, fathers, and adolescents*. New York, NY: Basic Books.

Larson, R. W., Richards, M. H., Moneta, G., Holmbeck, G., & Duckett, E. (1996). Changes in adolescents' daily interactions with their families from ages 10 to 18: Disengagement and transformation. *Developmental Psychology, 32*(4), 744–754.

Lerner, R. M., & Galambos, N. L. (1998). Adolescent development: Challenges and opportunities for research, programs, and policies. *Annual Review of Psychology, 49*(1), 413–446.

Leventhal, T., & Brooks-Gunn, J. (Eds.) (2003). *Moving on up: Neighborhood effects on children and families.* Mahwah, NJ: Lawrence Erlbaum Associates Publishers.

Lindahl, K. M., & Malik, N. M. (1999). Observations of marital conflict and power: Relations with parenting in the triad. *Journal of Marriage and the Family, 61*, 320–330.

Lins-Dyer, M. T., & Nucci, L. (2007). The impact of social class and social cognitive domain on northeastern Brazilian mothers' and daughters' conceptions of parental control. *International Journal of Behavioral Development, 31*(2), 105.

Loukas, A., Fitzgerald, H. E., Zucker, R. A., & Eye, A. (2001). Parental alcoholism and co-occurring antisocial behavior: Prospective relationships to externalizing behavior problems in their young sons. *Journal of Abnormal Child Psychology, 29*(2), 91–106.

Maccoby, E. E. (1992). The role of parents in the socialization of children: An historical overview. *Developmental Psychology, 28*(6), 1006–1017.

Maccoby, E. E., & Martin, J. A. (1983). Socialization in the context of the family: Parent-child interaction. In P. H. Mussen & E. M. Hetherington (Eds.), *Handbook of child psychology* (Vol. 4, pp. 1–101). New York, NY: Wiley.

Magnusson, D., & Stattin, H. (Eds.) (1998). *Person-context interaction theories.* Hoboken, NJ: Wiley.

Mantzicopoulos, P. Y., & Oh-Hwang, Y. (1998). The relationship of psychosocial maturity to parenting quality and intellectual ability for American and Korean adolescents. *Contemporary Educational Psychology, 23*(2), 195–206.

Martinez, M. L., Cumsille, P., & Thinaut, C. (2007). Chile. In J. J. Arnett (Ed.), *International encyclopedia of adolescence* (Vol. 1, pp. 167–178). New York, NY: Routledge.

Mayseless, O., Scharf, M., & Sholt, M. (2003). From authoritative parenting practices to an authoritarian context: Exploring the person-environment fit. *Journal of Research on Adolescence, 13*(4), 427–456.

McAdoo, H. P. (1993). The social cultural contexts of ecological developmental family models. In P. Boss, W. Doherty, W. R. Schumm, & S. K. Steinmetz (Eds.), *Sourcebook of family theories and methods: A contextual approach* (pp. 298–301). New York, NY: Plenum.

McBride-Chang, C., & Chang, L. (1998). Adolescent-parent relations in Hong Kong: Parenting styles, emotional autonomy, and school achievement. *The Journal of Genetic Psychology, 159*(4), 421.

McCluskey, C. P., Krohn, M. D., Lizotte, A. J., & Rodriguez, M. L. (2002). Early substance use and school achievement: An examination of Latino, White, and African American youth. *Journal of Drug Issues, 32*(3), 921–944.

McKown, C. (2004). Age and ethnic variation in children's thinking about the nature of racism. *Journal of Applied Developmental Psychology, 25*(5), 597–617.

McLoyd, V. C. (1990). The impact of economic hardship on Black families and children: Psychological distress, parenting, and socioemotional development. *Child Development, 61*, 311–346.

McLoyd, V. C. (1998). Socioeconomic disadvantage and child development. *American Psychologist, 53*(2), 185–204.

McLoyd, V. C. (2006). The legacy of Child Development's 1990 special issue on minority children: An editorial retrospective. *Child Development, 77*(5), 1142–1148.

McLoyd, V. C., Cauce, A. M., Takeuchi, D., & Wilson, L. (2000). Marital processes and parental socialization in families of color: A decade review of research. *Journal of Marriage and the Family, 62*(4), 1070–1093.

Metzler, C. W., Noell, J., Biglan, A., Ary, D., & Smolkowski, K. (1994). The social context for risky sexual behavior among adolescents. *Journal of Behavioral Medicine, 17*(4), 419–438.

Mortimer, J. T., & Larson, R. W. (Eds.) (2002). *The changing adolescent experience: Societal trends and the transition to adulthood.* New York NY: Cambridge University Press.

Mpofu, E., Jere, J. P., & Chemyu, F. (2007). Zambia. In J. J. Arnett (Ed.), *International encyclopedia of adolescence* (Vol. 2, pp. 1095–1108). New York, NY: Routledge.

Murry, V. M. B., Brody, G. H., Brown, A., Wisenbaker, J., Cutrona, C. E., & Simons, R. L. (2002). Linking employment status, maternal psychological well-being, parenting, and children's attributions about poverty in families receiving government assistance. *Family Relations, 51*, 112–120.

Myers-Walls, J. A., Somlai, P., & Rapoport, R. N. (2001). *Families as educators for global citizenship.* Burlington, VT: Ashgate.

Nelson, E. E., Leibenluft, E., McClure, E. B., & Pine, D. S. (2005). The social re-orientation of adolescence: A neuroscience perspective on the process and its relation to psychopathology. *Psychological Medicine, 35*(02), 163–174.

Nucci, L., Hasebe, Y., & Lins-Dyer, M. T. (2005). Adolescent psychological well-being and parental control of the personal. *New Directions for Child and Adolescent Development, 108*, 17–30.

Ou, Y. S., & McAdoo, H. P. (1993). Socialization of Chinese American children. In H. P. McAdoo (Ed.), *Family ethnicity: Strength in diversity* (pp. 245–270), Thousand Oaks, CA: Sage Publishers.

Parke, R. D., & Buriel, R. (1998). Socialization in the family: Ethnic and ecological perspectives. In N. Eisenberg, W. Damon, & R. Lerner (Eds.), *Handbook of child psychology* (Vol. 3, pp. 463–552). Hoboken, NJ: Wiley.

Patterson, G. R., DeBaryshe, B. D., & Ramsey, E. (1989). A developmental perspective on antisocial behavior. *American Psychologist, 44*(2), 329–335.

Phinney, J. S., & Chavira, V. (1995). Parental ethnic socialization and adolescent coping with problems related to ethnicity. *Journal of Research on Adolescence, 5*(1), 31–53.

Phinney, J. S., & Ong, A. D. (2002). Adolescent-parent disagreements and life satisfaction in families from Vietnamese- and European-American backgrounds. *International Journal of Behavioral Development, 26*(6), 556–561.

Proctor, B. D., & Dalaker, J. (2002). *Poverty in the United States: 2001, Current Population Reports* (pp. 60–219). Washington, DC: U.S. Government Printing Office.

Quintana, S. M., & Vera, E. M. (1999). Mexican American children's ethnic identity, understanding of ethnic prejudice, and parental ethnic socialization. *Hispanic Journal of Behavioral Sciences, 21*(4), 387–404.

Rhee, S., Chang, J., & Rhee, J. (2003). Acculturation, communication patterns, and self-esteem among Asian and Caucasian American adolescents. *Adolescence, 38*(152), 749–768.

Rivas-Drake, D., Hughes, D., & Way, N. (2008). A closer look at peer discrimination, ethnic identity, and psychological well-being among urban Chinese American sixth graders. *Journal of Youth and Adolescence, 37*(1), 12–21.

Rogler, L. H., Cortes, D. E., & Malgady, R. G. (1991). Acculturation and mental health status among Hispanics. *American Psychologist, 46*(6), 585–597.

Rogoff, B. (2003). *The cultural nature of human development.* New York, NY: Oxford University Press.

Rohner, R. P., & Pettengill, S. M. (1985). Perceived parental acceptance-rejection and parental control among Korean adolescents. *Child Development, 56*(2), 524–528.

Rumbaut, R. G. (1994). The crucible within: Ethnic identity, self-esteem, and segmented assimilation among children of immigrants. *International Migration Review, 28*(4), 748–794.

Russell, A., Wadi, S., Klelifa, M., & Jendli, A. (2007). United Arab Emirates. In J. J. Arnett (Ed.), *International encyclopedia of adolescence* (Vol. 2, pp. 1037–1047). New York, NY: Routledge.

Ryan, A. M. (2000). Peer groups as a context for the socialization of adolescents motivation, engagement, and achievement in school. *Educational Psychologist, 35*(2), 101–111.

Sabogal, F., Marin, G., Otero-Sabogal, R., Marin, B. V., & Perez-Stable, E. J. (1987). Hispanic familism and acculturation: What changes and what doesn't? *Hispanic Journal of Behavioral Sciences, 9*(4), 397–412.

Sanders, M. G. (1997). Overcoming obstacles: Academic achievement as a response to racism and discrimination. *Journal of Negro Education, 66*(1), 83–93.

Sanders-Thompson, V. L. (1994). Socialization to race and its relationship to racial identification among African Americans. *Journal of Black Psychology, 20*(2), 175–188.

Sanford, S., & Eder, D. (1984). Adolescent humor during peer interaction. *Social Psychology Quarterly, 47*(3), 235–243.

Sears, H. A., Simmering, M. G., & McNeil, B. A. (2007). Canada. In J. J. Arnett (Ed.), *International encyclopedia of adolescence* (Vol. 1, pp. 140–156). New York, NY: Routledge.

Silbereisen, R. K. (1995). How parenting styles and crowd contexts interact in actualizing potentials for development: Commentary. In L. J. Crockett & A. C. Crouter (Eds.), *Pathways through adolescence: Individual development in relation to social contexts* (pp. 197–207). Mahwah, NJ: Lawrence Erlbaum Associates Publishers.

Sirin, S., & Fine, M. (2008). *Muslim American youth: Understanding hyphenated identities through multiple methods.* New York, NY: New York University Press.

Smetana, J. G. (2000). Middle-class African American adolescents' and parents' conceptions of parental authority and parenting practices: A longitudinal investigation. *Child Development, 71*(6), 1672–1686.

Smetana, J. G. (2002). Culture, autonomy, and personal jurisdiction in adolescent-parent relationships. *Advances in Child Development and Behavior, 29,* 51.

Smetana, J. G. (2006). Social-cognitive domain theory: Consistencies and variations in children's moral and social judgments. In M. Killen & J. G. Smetana (Eds.), *Handbook of Moral Development* (pp. 119–153). Mahwah, NJ: Lawrence Erlbaum Associates Publishers.

Smetana, J. G., & Daddis, C. (2002). Domain-specific antecedents of parental psychological control and monitoring: The role of parenting beliefs and practices. *Child Development, 73*(2), 563–580.

Smetana, J. G., Daddis, C., & Chuang, S. S. (2003). "Clean your room!" A longitudinal investigation of adolescent-parent conflict and conflict resolution in middle-class African American families. *Journal of Adolescent Research, 18*(6), 631–650.

Smetana, J. G., Metzger, A., Gettman, D. C., & Campione-Barr, N. (2006). Disclosure and secrecy in adolescent-parent relationships. *Child Development, 77*(1), 201–217.

Smetana, J. G., & Turiel, E. (Eds.) (2003). *Moral development during adolescence.* Malden MA: Blackwell Publishing.

Smetana, J. G., Villalobos, M., Tasopoulos-Chan, M., Gettman, D. C., & Campione-Barr, N. (2009). Early and middle adolescents' disclosure to parents about activities in different domains. *Journal of Adolescence, 32*(3), 693–713.

Smokowski, P. R., David-Ferdon, C., & Stroupe, N. (2009). Acculturation and violence in minority adolescents: A review of the empirical literature. *The Journal of Primary Prevention, 30*(3), 215–263.

Soenens, B., Elliot, A. J., Goossens, L., Vansteenkiste, M., Luyten, P., & Duriez, B. (2005). The intergenerational transmission of perfectionism: Parents' psychological control as an intervening variable. *Journal of Family Psychology, 19*(3), 358.

Soenens, B., Vansteenkiste, M., Luyckx, K., & Goossens, L. (2006). Parenting and adolescent problem behavior: An integrated model with adolescent self-disclosure and perceived parental knowledge as intervening variables. *Developmental Psychology, 42*(2), 14.

Spencer, M. B. (2006). Revisiting the 1990 special issue on minority children: An editorial perspective 15 years later. *Child Development, 77*(5), 1149–1154.

Stattin, H., & Kerr, M. (2000). Parental monitoring: A reinterpretation. *Child Development, 71*(4), 1072–1085.

Steele, C. M. (1992). Race and the schooling of black Americans. *Atlantic, 269*(4), 68–78.

Steele, C. M. (1997). A threat in the air: How stereotypes shape intellectual identity and performance. *American Psychologist, 52*(6), 613–629.

Steinberg, L. (2001). We know some things: Parent-adolescent relationships in retrospect and prospect. *Journal of Research on Adolescence, 11*(1), 1–19.

Steinberg, L., Dornbusch, S. M., & Brown, B. (1992). Ethnic differences in adolescent achievement: An ecological perspective. *American Psychologist, 47*(6), 723–729.

Steinberg, L., Lamborn, S. D., Darling, N., Mounts, N. S., & Dornbusch, S. M. (1994). Over-time changes in adjustment and competence among adolescents from authoritative, authoritarian, indulgent, and neglectful families. *Child Development, 65*, 754–770.

Steinberg, L., Lamborn, S. D., Dornbusch, S. M., & Darling, N. (1992). Impact of parenting practices on adolescent achievement: Authoritative parenting, school involvement, and encouragement to succeed. *Child Development, 63*(5), 1266–1281.

Steinberg, L., Mounts, N. S., Lamborn, S. D., & Dornbusch, S. M. (1991). Authoritative parenting and adolescent adjustment across varied ecological niches. *Journal of Research on Adolescence, 1*(1), 19–36.

Suarez-Orozco, C., & Suarez-Orozco, M. M. (1995). *Transformations: Immigration, family life, and achievement motivation among Latino adolescents*. Stanford, CA: Stanford University Press.

Suarez-Orozco, C., & Suárez-Orozco, M. M. (2001). *Children of immigrants*. Cambridge, MA: Harvard University Press.

Suarez-Orozco, C., Todorova, I., & Qin, D. B. (Eds.) (2006). *The well-being of immigrant adolescents: A longitudinal perspective on risk and protective factors*. Westport CT: Praeger Publishers/Greenwood Publishing Group.

Sussman, S., Dent, C. W., & McCullar, W. J. (2000). Group self-identification as a prospective predictor of drug use and violence in high-risk youth. *Psychology of Addictive Behaviors, 14*(2), 192–196.

Telzer, E. H., & Fuligni, A. J. (2009). Daily family assistance and the psychological well-being of adolescents from Latin American, Asian, and European backgrounds. *Developmental Psychology, 45*(4), 1177–1189.

Thiel, S. M. (2005). 'IM ME': Identity construction and gender negotiation in the world of adolescent girls and instant messaging. In S. R. Mazzarella (Ed.), *Girl wide web: Girls, the Internet and negotiation of identity* (pp. 179–201). New York, NY: Peter Lang.

Thornton, M. C., Chatters, L. M., Taylor, R. J., & Allen, W. R. (1990). Sociodemographic and environmental correlates of racial socialization by Black parents. *Child Development, 61*(2), 401–409.

Torney-Purta, J., Lehmann, R., Oswald, H., & Schulz, W. (2001). *Citizenship and education in twenty-eight countries: Civic knowledge and engagement at age 14*. Amsterdam: IEA (http://www.wam.umd.edu/iea).

Turiel, E. (2006). Thought, emotions, and social interactional processes in moral development. In M. Killen & J. G. Smetana (Eds.), *Handbook of moral development* (pp. 7–35). Mahwah, NJ: Lawrence Erlbaum Associates Publishers.

Turiel, E., & Smetana, J. G. (1984). Social knowledge and action: The coordination of domains. In J. L. Gewirtz & W. M. Kurtines (Eds.), *Morality, moral developmental, and moral behavior* (pp. 261–282). New York, NY: Wiley.

Turiel, E., & Smetana, J. G. (1998). Limiting the limits on domains: A commentary on Fowler and heteronomy. [Comment/Reply]. *Merrill-Palmer Quarterly, 44* (3), 293–312.

Twenge, J. M., & Crocker, J. (2002). Race and self-esteem: Meta-analyses comparing Whites, Blacks, Hispanics, Asians, and American Indians and comment on Gray-Little and Hafdahl (2000). [Comment/Reply]. *Psychological Bulletin, 128*(3), 371–408.

Urberg, K. A., Degirmencioglu, S. M., & Pilgrim, C. (1997). Close friend and group influence on adolescent cigarette smoking and alcohol use. *Developmental Psychology, 33*(5), 834–844.

Urberg, K. A., Degirmencioglu, S. M., Tolson, J. M., & Halliday-Scher, K. (2000). Adolescent social crowds: Measurement and relationship to friendship. *Journal of Adolescent Research, 15*(4), 427–445.

Valkenburg, P. M., & Peter, J. (2007). Preadolescents' and adolescents' online communication and their closeness to friends. *Developmental Psychology, 43* (2), 267–277.

Verma, S., & Sharma, D. (2003). Cultural continuity amid social change: Adolescents' use of free time in India. *New Directions for Child and Adolescent Development, 99*, 37–51.

Walden, N. J., Rodriguez, M. L., & Bekar, O. (2009). *The protection of family ties: Family responsibilites as a protective factor for at-risk youth.* Paper presented at the Society for Research in Child Development, Denver, CO.

Way, N. (1998). *Everyday courage: The lives and stories of urban teenagers.* New York, NY: New York University Press.

Way, N., & Chen, L. (2000). Close and general friendships among African American, Latino, and Asian American adolescents from low-income families. *Journal of Adolescent Research, 15*(2), 274.

Way, N., Cowal, K., Gingold, R., Pahl, K., & Bissessar, N. (2001). Friendship patterns among African American, Asian American, and Latino adolescents from low-income families. *Journal of Social and Personal Relationships, 18*(1), 29–53.

Way, N., & Greene, M. L. (2006). Trajectories of perceived friendship quality during adolescence: The patterns and contextual predictors. *Journal of Research on Adolescence, 16*(2), 293–320.

Weaver, S. R., & Kim, S. Y. (2008). A person-centered approach to studying the linkages among parent-child differences in cultural orientation, supportive parenting, and adolescent depressive symptoms in Chinese American families. *Journal of Youth and Adolescence, 37*(1), 36–49.

Wentzel, K. R., Barry, C. M. N., & Caldwell, K. A. (2004). Friendships in middle school: Influences on motivation and school adjustment. *Journal of Educational Psychology, 96*(2), 195–203.

Williams, P. G., Holmbeck, G. N., & Greenley, R. N. (2002). Adolescent health psychology. *Journal of Consulting and Clinical Psychology, 70*(3), 828–842.

Wills, T. A., & Cleary, S. D. (1996). How are social support effects mediated? A test with parental support and adolescent substance use. *Journal of Personality and Social Psychology, 71*, 937–952.

Wintre, M. G., & Yaffe, M. (2000). First-year students' adjustment to university life as a function of relationships with parents. *Journal of Adolescent Research, 15*(1), 9–37.

Wu, P., Hoven, C. W., Tiet, Q., Kovalenko, P., & Wicks, J. (2002). Factors associated with adolescent utilization of alcohol treatment services. *American Journal of Drug and Alcohol Abuse, 28*(2), 353–369.

Yau, J., & Smetana, J. (2003). Adolescent-parent conflict in Hong Kong and Shenzhen: A comparison of youth in two cultural contexts. *International Journal of Behavioral Development, 27*(3), 201–211.

Yau, J., & Smetana, J. G. (1996). Adolescent-parent conflict among Chinese adolescents in Hong Kong. *Child Development, 67*(3), 1262–1275.

Yu, P., & Berryman, D. L. (1996). The relationship among self-esteem, acculturation, and recreation participation of recently arrived Chinese immigrant adolescents. *Journal of Leisure Research, 28*(4), 251–273.

Critical health issues during adolescence

Mary Lou de Leon Siantz

Diversity and Cultural Affairs, The University of Pennsylvania School of Nursing, Philadelphia, PA

Tiffany Dovydaitis

Center for Health Equity Research, The University of Pennsylvania School of Nursing, Philadelphia, PA

12.1. **INTRODUCTION**

Adolescence in the twenty-first century is defined as the period from the onset of puberty to societal independence and includes developing sexual and psychosocial maturity (UNAIDS/WHO, 2006). Globally, there are an estimated 1.5 billion persons aged 12-24 years, the largest number of adolescents to date (2006). Adolescence harbors not only immense health risks but also vast opportunities for sustained well-being through health education and prevention. To provide a comprehensive view of adolescence, health and physical development cannot be overlooked. These two factors drive the developmental changes that are experienced during this vibrant period and the sustained consequences over time of health choices made. The purpose of this chapter is to introduce health issues critical to adolescents and potential areas of preventive intervention during this important period. In this exploration of the issues, the focus is on African-American adolescents.

Health is a state of complete physical, mental, and social well-being and not merely the absence of disease or infirmity (UNAIDS/WHO, 2006). It includes a complex interaction of biopsychosocial and cultural factors that interact not only during adolescence, but also across the human lifespan. These interactions underscore the interdisciplinary nature of adolescent health. Adolescence is unique because of the physical changes that occur and their effect on health and behavior.

Adolescent health concerns include risk for drug, tobacco, and alcohol misuse, among the affluent as well as the poor who seek to escape the

Adolescence: Development During a Global Era

341

social and/or economic poverty of their environments. In the United States in particular, over 17% of young people are considered overweight or obese, and the percentage of overweight adolescents has tripled since the 1970s. Among African-American adolescents, the risk and incidence are even higher (Wang et al., 2006). The long-term effects on future adult health include increased risk for diabetes and early signs of cardiovascular disease (Patel et al., 2007).

Many more adolescents risk contracting sexually transmitted infections, including HIV/AIDS. Over 10 million adolescents aged 15-24 years live with HIV/AIDS worldwide. An estimated 15.2 million children younger than 18 years of age have also lost one or both parents to AIDS (UNAIDS/WHO, 2006). Adolescent girls are especially vulnerable to living with the consequences of unplanned pregnancies. African-American adolescents are at highest risk for all of these health risks. About 1 million teenage African-American girls have unintended pregnancies every year, with nearly half ending in abortion (US Department of Health and Human Services, 2000).

12.1.1. **Pubertal transitions in health**

Human biological development occurs during two periods of rapid growth: (1) the prenatal period through the first 2 years of life and (2) adolescence. Inextricably linked to this physical growth are the physical and psychological changes that characterize differences between children and adults. Adolescent health depends on a fundamental understanding of the normal physical and psychosocial developmental—changes that occur during the transition from childhood to adulthood.

Puberty is initiated in late childhood through a surge of endocrine changes that lead to sexual maturation and reproductive capability. Human puberty is accompanied by major physical growth and substantial brain maturational changes (Jones, 1977; Spear, 2004). Variation in age of pubertal onset can range from 4 to 5 years among healthy individuals, even when living conditions are similar for all members of a group (Parent et al., 2003). Variation reflects genetics along with the effects of nutrition, psychological status, and socioeconomic conditions (Gluckman & Hanson, 2006; Kaplowitz, 2006; van den Berg et al., 2006). While physical maturation propels human beings into adolescence with peaks in strength, speed, and fitness, it also initiates emotional, cognitive, and behavioral changes. In the twenty-first century, these changes in youth underlie increased risk for mortality and morbidity from accidental and intentional injuries, suicide, mental disorders, substance abuse, sexually transmitted diseases, and eating disorders and are the foundation for future chronic health conditions endured as adults (Patton & Viner, 2007).

12.1.2. **Endocrinological changes**

Puberty begins with the poorly understood activation of a complex neuro-endocrine network that remains dormant from infancy (Delmarre-van de Wall, 2002). Sexual maturation (gonadarche) is initiated with the release of gonadotrophin-releasing hormone from a small number of specialized hypothalamic neurons that, in turn, lead to the pituitary release of folli-cle-stimulating hormone and luteinizing hormone. These two trophic hormones then stimulate production of gonadal hormones (testosterone and estrogen), which help induce puberty, along with other growth hormones (adrenal, thyroid). The resulting gonadal growth and production of gonadal sex steroids initiate the development of secondary sexual charac-teristics (Patton & Viner, 2007).

Preceding and independent of the hypothalmopituitary gonadal axis is the production of adrenal androgens, which increase from ages 6 to 8 years in a process known as *adrenarche*, which is unique to human beings and chimpanzees (Arlt et al., 2002). These androgens have a role in the devel-opment of axillary and pubic hair and contribute to the emergence of acne. The evolutionary significance of adrenarche is unclear, but evidence suggests that its timing may affect risk of physical and mental health problems (Goodyear et al., 2000).

12.1.3. **Linear growth**

Increased height for both boys and girls occurs during a 24- to 26-month span that is usually referred to as the "adolescent growth spurt" (Laitien et al., 2001; Sandhu et al., 2006). It is characterized by an accelerated linear growth, a peak period of growth, and then a sharp decline. While growth occurs in the same manner for both sexes, it usually occurs earlier among girls and in slightly less magnitude. Among girls, the onset of this growth spurt can occur as early as 9.5 years and as late as 14.5 years. In males, the onset can range from 10.5 to 16 years. By 18 years of age, 95% of growth has occurred (Cutler, 1997; Klein et al., 1996).

12.1.4. **Muscle and fat distribution**

In addition to linear growth, major changes also occur in the distribution and composition of body fat and muscle. Before puberty, both sexes have similar body composition. With the onset of the growth spurt, the rate of fat accumulation decreases for girls while boys have an absolute loss of fat. After the peak growth spurt, girls rapidly add fat while boys add it more slowly and in less quantity. The proportion of adipose tissue is a decisive factor in the menstrual activity of the female, with 17% body mass as fat needed for menstruation to occur and 22% to maintain a regular ovulatory cycle (Roemmich & Rogol, 1999). Boys accumulate greater lean body mass as muscle, with greater concentration in thighs, shoulders, and back. While these differences may be due to the effects of androgens, that assumption is far from conclusive (Nieves et al., 2005).

12.1.5. **Weight changes**

Adolescents increase body weight during puberty. The growth curves reflecting weight gain are similar to those showing linear growth. Weight accelerates with a period of peak weight gain followed by a decline. For females, weight gain occurs 6 months after her period of most rapid linear growth. On the other hand, among males, the periods of peak linear growth and weight gain coincide. In contrast to linear growth, where girls peak 2 years before males, girls peak weight gain which occurs 1.5 years before males (Kaplowitz, 2006; Stattin & Magnusson, 2003). In normal growth and development, patterns should be consistent so that when body mass index is plotted as a function of age, a smooth curve is obtained using standard graphs (Ogden et al., 2006; Tremblay & Frigon, 2005). The key to assessing "normalcy" of changes in height and weight is based on accurate records of an adolescent's growth curves with respect to both the onset of the growth spurt and progression through various stages (Tanner, 1962).

12.1.6. **Sexual maturation**

The hallmark of adolescence, excluding the growth spurt, is the development of secondary sexual characteristics, which for females includes the onset of menarche. A teenager during this period is constantly comparing himself or herself with peers. Misgivings or serious concerns about inadequacy or abnormality in its extreme are common occurrences (Herman-Giddings et al., 1997; Parent et al., 2003; van den Berg et al., 2006; Viner, 2002). To realistically help adolescents with their concerns, knowledge about the stages of normal sexual development and allowable degrees of variation is needed. Criteria describing the stages of sexual maturity indicators in boys and girls are well established (Marshall & Tanner, 1970; Tanner, 1962).

A maturational framework is available for basic understanding of sexual development based on Tanner's guidelines (Marshall & Tanner, 1969). Tanner's criteria provide a descriptive maturational framework for assessment of sexual growth and reassure the adolescent that development is proceeding normally.

Male puberty markers include genital and pubic hair development, which is assessed using the progressive Tanner (1962) staging scale. It is based on a scale of five progressive stages described and depicted by Marshall and Tanner (1970) in which stage 1 is prepubertal, stage 2 is onset, and stage 5 is adult (Tanner, 1962). These stages are based on observation alone, from a photograph, or in person by a trained professional, or self-assessment by the adolescent (Euling et al., 2008).

Recent national estimates concerning the timing of the sexual maturation and racial differences among U.S. children are based on Tanner stages. National estimates have reported that, while in general U.S. children complete their sexual development at about the same ages, ethnic differences exist. In a national sample of U.S. children to determine the degree of racial/ethnic differences in stages of sexual maturity, non-Hispanic Black girls had an earlier sexual development either by median age at entry for stage or for the mean age for a stage than did Mexican-American or non-Hispanic White girls (Sun et al., 2002). Among males, it was found that non-Hispanic Black boys also had earlier median and mean ages for sexual maturity stages than non-Hispanic White and Mexican-American boys (Sun et al., 2002). Familiarity with the Tanner stages should be a requirement for all professionals working in adolescent health education that targets the prevention of, and counseling about, sexually transmitted diseases, particularly when stage attainment, in comparison with peers, is a concern.

12.1.7. **Puberty and adolescent development**

Puberty was once considered the trigger to a biologically driven phase of inevitable emotional turmoil (Hall, 1905), with biology driving psychological and social development (Kestenberg, 1967). More recent research (Patton & Viner, 2007) has established that broader social processes define adolescence, with variance found across societies and cultures. Current concepts integrate the biological onset of puberty with a highly variable social transition that marks its completion. The biological processes initiated at puberty interact with the social context to affect an adolescent's emotional and social development (Brooks-Gunn & Warren, 1989; Gottlieb, 1976; Lerner, 1986). While in preindustrial societies adolescent transition to adult roles was defined by the onset of sexual activity, marriage, and parenthood, modern patterns of mature reproductive potential, including sexual activity, precede role transitions into parenthood and marriage (Furlong & Cartmel, 1997; Gluckman & Hanson, 2006).

In present society, prolonged education and the availability of effective contraception have meant that adolescence persists for more than 10 years (Gluckman & Hanson, 2006). More recently, the changing patterns in the number of premarital sexual partners have been associated with the increased incidence of sexually transmitted diseases.

While emotional turmoil is an inevitable consequence of puberty, research exists that supports the effect of puberty on early psychosocial development. Boys who attain puberty later than their peers are often less assertive and popular and are late to engage in sexual activity (Jones, 1950; Stattin & Magnusson, 2003). On the other hand, early puberty in females is associated with emotional and behavioral problems and earlier sexual activity (Ge et al., 2002, 2003).

12.1.8. **Psychosocial development**

The psychological and social tasks of adolescents are broken down into three stages: early adolescence (11-13), midadolescence (14-16) and late adolescence (17-24). In early adolescence, the child engages in concrete thinking, begins sexual identity development, and begins to focus on body image. This is a period characterized by separation from parents, stronger identification with peers, and increased risk-taking and experimental behavior. During midadolescence, thinking becomes more abstract, verbal abilities grow, and law and morality become more important. Socially, the adolescent continues to pull away from parents, form stronger bonds with peers, and is at increased risk for alcohol and drug use and sexual experimentation. Finally, during late adolescence, the youth is able to engage in complex abstract thinking, differentiate between law and morality, and further develop personal identity. The late adolescent becomes more socially autonomous, forms intimate and romantic relationships, begins development of vocational capability, and moves toward financial independence (Christie, 2005; McIntosh et al., 2003).

To better recognize the opportunities that exist to promote the health of adolescents, it is important to recognize the physical and cognitive development that occurs during this period (see Chapters 2 and 3, respectively, for detailed discussions). It is also necessary to understand associated factors that contribute to the health risks of African-American adolescents as a group with significant disparities across several health-monitored domains. Relevant factors include the social determinants of health and the child health disparities that exist.

12.2. **SOCIAL DETERMINANTS OF HEALTH**

According to the World Health Organization (2008), the social determinants of health are the circumstances into which people are born, develop, live, and work, including the health system. The distribution of money, power, global, national, and local resources, as well as public policies, converge to shape these circumstances. The social determinants of health are primarily responsible for health disparities and the unfair and avoidable differences that exist in the health status of vulnerable populations, especially among racial and ethnic minority groups. Health care can prolong life and promote the health of populations. However, critical to the health of all people are the social and economic conditions that contribute to their health (Donking et al., 2002).

Even among the most affluent countries like the United States, those who are less well off are more likely to have substantially shorter lifespans with more health problems than those who are wealthier. These health disparities have drawn attention not only to a social injustice, but also to determinants of health standards in modern society. Disadvantage has many forms and may include few family assets, a poorer education during adolescence, insecure employment, hazardous jobs, poor housing, and growing up in stressful social and economic circumstances. Such social and environmental inequities have led to a greater understanding of their impact on health (Bartley & Plewis, 2002).

The impact of the social determinants of health on adolescent health cannot be overlooked among African-American adolescents. Life contains a series of critical transitions that include emotional and material changes in early childhood, moving from primary to secondary education, and leaving home. Each of these transitions influences health by placing individuals in a more or less advantaged life course. Children disadvantaged in the past are at greatest risk in each subsequent transition (World Health Organization, 2003).

Recently, the National Children's Study has sought to explain the health disparities that exist among African-American children. For example, adolescent mortality rates are higher for African Americans than for any other ethnic group. African-American girls are among those at highest risk for overweight and obesity (Landrigan et al., 2006). Lack of physical activity is a major contributor to obesity. In a given week, African-American adolescents report no significant amount of physical activity. They are more likely to watch 3 or more hours of TV on a school day. They are more likely to be uninsured without a medical home and consistent source of health care (61%) with one or more emergency room visits in a given year (27%)

(Federal Interagency Forum on Child and Family Statisitcs, 2005). Race-associated differences in health outcomes are routinely documented in the United States but are generally poorly explained.

Although all racial and ethnic groups experience adolescence as a development process, the remainder of this chapter will focus on the experience of the African-American adolescent, including important changes in mental, physical, and psychosocial health.

12.3. **MENTAL HEALTH**

12.3.1. **Depression**

Current research on depression in African-American adolescents is inconclusive, with some studies showing higher rates of depression in this population (Brooks et al., 2002) and others showing lower rates (Saluja et al., 2004). Regardless, depression is a serious problem among all adolescents, especially females. Adolescent depression increases the risk for serious depression later in life (Lewinsohn et al., 1999) and is associated with poor health outcomes, such as risky sexual practices (Brady et al., 2009), pregnancy (Lee et al., 2009), violent behavior (Saluja et al., 2004), and suicide (CDC, 2008). The rates of death from suicide are much higher for boys (83%) than girls (17%), but girls are more likely to report attempting suicide than boys (CDC, 2008). One study found that almost half of African-American adolescents who attempted suicide did not meet all the criteria for a medical diagnosis of depression (Joe et al., 2009). These findings emphasize the importance of screening for suicidal ideation, even among those who have not been diagnosed with a psychiatric disorder. Also, there is a strong connection between bullying and depression, which includes both the perpetrator and the victim of bullying. Educators should consider untreated depression when confronting bullying, violent behaviors, and risky sexual practices. Recognizing depression in the adolescent could prevent further bullying, suicide, more severe depression later in life, and other serious negative outcomes.

12.3.2. **Identity development**

The primary developmental task of adolescence is establishing identity, which begins when the adolescent attempts to reconcile the identity imposed on them by family and society, with an alternate identity that gives the adolescent a feeling of satisfaction and competence (Erikson, 1968). In the past, little attention was given to the concept of *racial identity* during the adolescent period, but more scientists are beginning to recognize the importance of racial identity development during this stage of life (Caldwell et al., 2004; French et al., 2006; Kerpelman et al., 2008; Kiang & Fuligni, 2009; Schwartz, 2007). "Drawing on Eriksonian perspectives, ethnic identity involves elements of exploration with the ultimate goal of achieving a fully developed sense of self. Ethnic exploration involves an active search into what it means to be a member of one's ethnic group, including an examination of one's values, traditions and history" (Kiang & Fuligni, 2009; see also Chapter 9). Adolescents with intact ethnic identity are less likely to be involved in violent behavior (Caldwell et al., 2004), and more likely to have positive mental health functioning (Caldwell et al., 2002; Sellers et al., 2003) and positive academic outcomes (Kerpelman et al., 2008; Wong et al., 2003). Adolescents of mixed race are particularly vulnerable to dissonant feelings about their ethnicity, and have increased feelings of hopelessness and violent behavior (Bolland et al., 2007). As adolescents transition from elementary school to middle and then high school, the ethnic diversity in their education environments may change, catalyzing an exploration of ethnic identity (French et al., 2006). Educators should be cognizant of this developmental stage and encourage group esteem and ethnic exploration among students.

12.3.3. **Gay, lesbian, bisexual, and transgendered (LGBT) identity development**

There has been a recent increase in research on the normal developmental trajectories among sexual minorities, although much of it has focused on Caucasian populations. Regardless of race, LGBT adolescents generally go through a series of stages during their sexual identity development. Although there are certainly some individual differences, most youths go through the following stages: (1) initial awareness of same-sex attraction, (2) first sexual contact, and (3) disclosure (Maguen et al., 2002). It is not entirely clear if there are significant differences between races, although some literature suggests that African-American youth "come out" to their parents (Grov et al., 2006) and their peers (Eccles et al., 2004; Maguen et al., 2002) later than Caucasians. The delay in this important milestone may be due to fear of disconnection from social networks that support racial identity (Dube & Savin-Williams, 1999).

The relationship trajectory of LGBT adolescents has not been adequately studied, especially among lesbian and transgendered youth. For gay and bisexual males, the most common trajectory seems to be (1) youth enters gay/bisexual social environment; (2) youth meets male partner; (3) youth talks to partner over a period of weeks or months; (4) youth enters relationship and initiates sex; (5) couple experiences conflict over infidelity and breaks up; and (6) youth experiences low self-esteem, tries to get back with partner, and engages in revenge sex (Eyre et al., 2007). Among LGBT adolescents, approximately 93% of boys and 85% of girls report some type of sexual activity with a same-sex partner (Savin-Williams & Diamond, 2000).

LGBT youth experience high rates of bullying (Friedman et al., 2006), suicide (D'Augelli et al., 2005), discrimination, and violence (Ryan & Rivers, 2003). Since peer networks are extremely important during adolescence, the rejection of peers can be devastating to the LGBT youth. Acceptance of parents is equally important for normal psychosocial development (Maguen et al., 2002). Educators also play an important role in the disclosure process, as 72% of students will disclose their sexual orientation to their teachers, in addition to their friends (95%), mothers (84%), and siblings (79%) (Maguen et al., 2002). Many LGBT students feel judged by their school counselors and teachers and feel unsafe at school (Rutter & Leech, 2006). These fears are not unfounded, as sexual minority youths are at increased risk for extreme forms of violence (Russel et al., 2001). Gay and bisexual African-American boys, in particular, are at higher risk for substance abuse, bullying, suicide, depression, anxiety, discrimination, and violence because of both their racial and sexual minority status (Crawford et al., 2002; Richardson et al., 1997). This elevated risk is most likely due to heterosexism and racial discrimination experienced in combination (Crawford et al., 2002). As with racial identity, a developed sexual identity is linked with increases in self-esteem, stronger social support networks, greater levels of life satisfaction, and less psychosocial distress (Crawford et al., 2002).

12.4. **PHYSICAL HEALTH**

12.4.1. **Puberty**

African-American adolescents generally experience puberty earlier than their Caucasian counterparts (Herman-Giddings et al., 1997; Styne, 2004). The research at this time is unable to completely explain this phenomenon, but several studies have shown a link between high rates of obesity and early puberty (Styne, 2004). Regardless of race and ethnicity, early pubertal development in girls is associated with multiple behavioral and emotional problems (Ge et al., 2002, 2003), particularly the development of breasts, an attribute that can be seen by their peers (Carter et al., 2009). Girls who experience early development may feel victimized by their peers and exhibit more signs of depression and low self-worth (Nadeem & Graham, 2005). Also, girls who perceive their development as early are more likely to associate with older peers. Although their bodies appear developed, their cognitive and coping abilities are often still childlike and they are not prepared to navigate the social world of their older peers (Carter et al., 2009). Overall, African-American adolescent boys and girls have more positive body images at all stages of puberty than any other ethnic group (Siegel et al., 1999), yet the early development of sex characteristics in girls increases their self-surveillance and leads to greater body shame (Lindberg et al., 2007). Substance use is more likely among these girls as well (Ge et al., 2006). Interestingly, *late* pubertal development is also associated with poor psychosocial outcomes in African-American girls, but not their Caucasian peers (Carter et al., 2009).

In contrast, early pubertal development in African-American boys is associated with a decrease in developmental stress, while late development is associated with increases in stress (Cunningham et al., 2003). Early maturing boys across all ethnic groups have higher rates of violent and nonviolent delinquent behavior (Cota-Robles et al., 2002).

12.4.2. **Obesity**

Obesity is a major public health problem in the United States among all groups of people, but African Americans carry a greater health burden, due to the increased likelihood of developing comorbidities, like Type II diabetes (Nwobu & Johnson, 2007). Between the years of 1999 and 2004, 20% of African American, 19.2% of Mexican American, and 16.3% of Caucasian adolescents were classified as obese (Ogden et al., 2006). Obesity is the most important risk factor for developing Type II diabetes during childhood and adolescence, with the average age of onset at 13 (American Diabetes Association, 2000). Strongly correlated with adult obesity, adolescent obesity also puts the child at risk for early onset of hypertension, vascular disease, insulin resistance, and metabolic syndrome (Ogden et al., 2006). Despite these risks, the rates of inactivity among African-American adolescents are very high compared to other groups (Gordon-Larson et al., 1999; Wang et al., 2006). One study in Chicago found that only 26% of African-American children participated in physical activity for at least 20 min every day, while 73% spent 4 h or more watching TV, using the computer, or playing video games (Wang et al., 2006). The major risk factors that directly contribute to adolescent obesity are environmental and include poor availability of healthy foods (Powell et al., 2007), limited options for physical activity (dangerous neighborhoods, lack of green space), and culturally traditional high fat and high caloric diets (Ogden et al., 2006).

12.4.3. **Type II diabetes**

As a consequence of the high rates of obesity, many U.S. adolescents are beginning to suffer from diseases that have traditionally been diagnosed in adulthood. The average age of onset of Type II diabetes is currently 13 (American Diabetes Association, 2000), and minorities with the disease suffer greater rates of complications and early death than their Caucasian peers (National Institute of Diabetes and Digestive and Kidney Diseases, 1998). Type II diabetes occur when the body does not make enough insulin or does not adequately utilize the insulin that is produced (this is called *insulin resistance*). Type II diabetes increase the adolescents' risk for serious complications, including heart disease (cardiovascular disease), blindness (retinopathy), nerve damage (neuropathy), and kidney damage (nephropathy) (McCarren, 2004). Nonetheless, the risk of Type II diabetes can be cut by 58% simply by decreasing dietary saturated fat and engaging in at least 30 min of moderate to vigorous physical activity every day (McGinnis, 2002). Parents, educators, and public health officials need to find new ways to engage African-American youth in healthy lifestyles within their own cultural context.

12.5. **SEXUAL RISK**

A number of studies have found that African-American youth engage in sexual behaviors earlier than Caucasians, with significant sexual pressure beginning in the junior high years (Blum et al., 2000; Felton & Bartoces, 2002; Glenn & Wilson, 2008). African-American adolescents carry the highest burden of sexually transmitted infections (STIs) among their peers, with gonorrhea, chlamydia, and syphilis being the most prevalent (Newman & Berman, 2008). HIV rates are also highest among African Americans. Although African Americans only make up 15% of the adolescent population, they are the carriers of 61% of AIDS infection in the age group (Newman & Berman, 2008). In fact, the leading cause of death among 25- to 44-year-old African Americans is HIV/AIDS, much of which was very likely contracted during the adolescent years (Glenn & Wilson, 2008; Newman & Berman, 2008). The most frequently cited risk factors for sexual risk-taking behavior are early puberty (Liberman-Smith, 2001; Marin et al., 2000), early exposure to sexual pressure (Felton & Bartoces, 2002; Nahom et al., 2001), depression, low social support (Brady et al., 2009), and the absence of a father (Cochran, 1997; Glenn et al., 2008).

Abstinence, mutual monogamy, or consistent condom use are the best protections against STIs, HIV, and pregnancy, but the reasons that many adolescents do not use these methods are multifaceted. For example, an adolescent girl may have difficulty in condom negotiation if she is in an abusive relationship (Teitelman et al., 2008), has low self-efficacy or depression (Brown et al., 2006), or is significantly younger than her partner (Felton & Bartoces, 2002; Liberman-Smith, 2001; Marin et al., 2000). Also, adolescents are frequent users of the withdrawal method (*coitus interruptus*) in an effort to prevent pregnancy, but this does little to prevent STI transmission. The ability to withdraw during the sex act is often seen as a reflection of intimacy, familiarity, trust, and masculine skill and experience in the adolescent relationship (Horner et al., 2007).

12.6. **VIOLENCE**

12.6.1. **Neighborhood violence**

Levels of violence exposure have more to do with socioeconomic and neighborhood factors than race, but African-American adolescents and other minority groups are especially at risk for violence exposure due to a high percentage of the population living in urban poverty. Adolescent females are much more likely to respond to violence exposure with violence. "Minority females may also have lower thresholds for engaging in violent behavior as females react more violently to threats and/or perceived threats in an effort to prevent future instances of victimization" (Maher, 1997; Spano et al., 2009). Regardless, African-American adolescents who are exposed to violence are remarkably resilient. African Americans are often the majority in inner-city settings, which may partially explain their high levels of resiliency when exposed to violence (Bolland et al., 2007). Caucasians, which constitute a minority within this context, are at higher risk for the negative effects of violence exposure, while those of mixed race are at the highest risk (Bolland et al., 2007). Although all groups are living within the same environment, holding majority status seems to decrease some level of risk. As stated previously, an intact understanding of racial identity also provides protection against violent behavior in adolescents (Caldwell et al., 2004). Parenting practices and strong family ties are also mediators of violence risk and help explain why not all adolescents exposed to violence go on to become violent themselves (Spano et al., 2009).

12.6.2. **Bullying**

Approximately 30% of adolescence will experience some form of bullying in the school setting (Caryle & Steinman, 2007), which is associated with serious short- and long-term social-emotional problems (Gladstone et al.,

2006; Hawker & Boulton, 2000). Although males are more likely to report bullying behaviors, it is unclear if this is due to the female tendency to use more psychological forms of aggression, while males use more physical forms (Caryle & Steinman, 2007). Substance use is closely linked with perpetration, while depression is closely linked with victimization. While adolescents of all races experience bullying, African-American adolescents tend to underreport being victims of bullying (Sawyer et al., 2008).

12.6.3. **Dating violence**

According to the literature, the prevalence of dating violence in adolescents is anywhere from 9% to 40%, with the prevalence highest among African Americans (Raiford et al., 2007). In one qualitative study, male participants identified relationship violence as a way to maintain power, while females saw violence as a sign of commitment and reflection of love (Johnson et al., 2005). One should not assume that the perpetrators of violence are more often male, as there is a fairly high instance of adolescent female perpetration as well (Miller & White, 2003). Although unclear in the literature, there is some evidence that African-American females have higher rates of partner violence perpetration than their other female peers (O'Keefe, 1997). Although females are more likely to strike their partners, significant contextual factors in adolescent relationships include high rates of infidelity among boys, and a greater likelihood for girls to report verbal mistreatment (Miller & White, 2003). Partner violence is most often a result of gender inequalities. Often rooted in frustration over infidelity, sexual double standards or emotional detachment, female violence is interpreted as ineffectual and a consequence of their more emotional nature (Miller & White, 2003).

12.7. **SUBSTANCE USE**

African-American adolescents historically have had the lowest reported use of alcohol, cigarettes, and illicit drugs among all racial groups (Johnston et al., 2006). Paradoxically, African-American drug users suffer greater social and health consequences than the general public, and the population reports some of the highest risk for substance-related deaths (twice that of Caucasians) (Fothergill & Ensminger, 2006; Galea & Rudenstine, 2005; National Institute of Drug Abuse, 2003). For both males and females, educational attainment and parental encouragement in the academic arena are the most important factors in decreasing drug use in adolescence (Fothergill & Ensminger, 2006). Racial identity development, as discussed above, is also an important protective factor against multiple poor outcomes, including substance abuse (Caldwell et al., 2006).

Adolescents living in rural areas have higher rates of alcohol and drug use than those living in suburban or urban environments (Kogan et al., 2005).

Contrary to popular belief, low socioeconomic status in childhood does not predict future substance use, although low SES in adulthood is highly correlated with drug use (Fothergill & Ensminger, 2006). The factors that do place adolescents at risk for drug use are early childhood aggression and behavior problems (Fothergill & Ensminger, 2006) and exposure to peer and parental drug use (Jones et al., 2008).

Inhalant use (misuse of volatile substances) is a major problem among adolescents in the United States, but is most heavily concentrated within Caucasian communities (Edwards et al., 2007). Also called "huffing," inhalants are used to create a feeling of euphoria and are extremely dangerous, as the users can suffer cardiac arrest during first use (Edwards et al., 2007). Although there has been very little attention to inhalants within African-American communities, adolescents living in rural areas are at increased risk for inhalant use. Girls are particularly at risk, possibly because they already buy personal care products that can also be used as inhalants (nail polish remover, hair spray) (Edwards et al., 2007).

12.7.1. **Smoking**

African-American adolescents smoke less than their Caucasian peers, although this gap closes as they move into adulthood (Ellickson et al., 2004). Still, African Americans suffer higher rates of tobacco-related diseases, which may be due to the high percentage of African Americans who smoke menthol cigarettes, which are higher in nicotine, tar, carbon monoxide, and other carcinogenic compounds (Moolchan & Schroeder, 2004; Muilenburg & Legge, 2008). Antismoking education in schools should focus not only on the dangers of smoking, but also specifically on the increased risks involved with menthol cigarettes.

Exposure to peer and parental smoking increases the risks for early adolescent smoking among African Americans (Brook et al., 2006). In fact, one of the most important risk factors for early initiation of smoking is parental smoking (Key & Marsh, 2002). Additionally, African-American girls are at increased risk for early smoking initiation when exposed to high levels of racial discrimination (Guthrie et al., 2002) and daily stress (Guthrie et al., 2001). Regardless of race, smoking education programs should include family and peers within the curriculum. Educators should focus on building positive self-image, confidence, and racial identity, while reinforcing concerns about health problems and addiction (Kulbok et al., 2008).

12.8. **CONCLUSION**

This chapter has outlined the concept of social determinants of health, normal adolescent development, and special considerations for the African-American population. Although certainly not exhaustive in its scope, the information provided herein is a comprehensive overview of the topic and a valuable resource to educators working with this population. The more science understands about health, the more we recognize that it is the result of a complex interaction between genetics and environment. Therefore, adolescent health promotion requires an interdisciplinary approach involving not only health care providers, but also educators, families, and entire communities. A better understanding of how behavior affects health and heath affects behavior gives all of us a knowledge base from which to encourage health promotion and intervene with adolescents at risk.

REFERENCES

American Diabetes Association. (2000). Type 2 diabetes in children and adolescents. *Pediatrics, 105*, 671–680.

Arlt, W., Martens, J., Song, M., Wang, J. T., Auchus, R. J., & Miller, W. L. (2002). Molecular evolution of adrenarche: Structural and functional analysis of p450c17 from four primate species. *Endocrinology, 143*, 4665–4672.

Bartley, M., & Plewis, I. (2002). Accumulated labor market disadvantage and limiting long-term illness. *International Journal of Epidemiology, 31*, 336–341.

Blum, R., et al. (2000). The effects of race, ethnicity, income and family structure on adolescent risk. *American Journal of Public Health, 90*, 1879–1884.

Bolland, J., et al. (2007). Development and risk behavior among African American, Caucasian and Mixed-race adolescents living in high poverty inner-city neighborhoods. *American Journal of Community Psychology, 40*, 230–249.

Brady, S., et al. (2009). Supportive friendships moderate the association between stressful life events and sexual risk taking among African American adolescents. *Health Psychology, 28*, 238–248.

Brook, J., et al. (2006). Peer and parental influences on longitudinal trajectories of smoking among African Americans and Puerto Ricans. *Nicotine and Tobacco Research, 8*, 639–651.

Brooks, T., et al. (2002). Association of adolescent risk behaviors with mental health symptoms in high school students. *Journal of Adolescent Health, 31*, 240–246.

Brooks-Gunn, J., & Warren, M. (1989). Biological and social contributions to negative affect in young adolescent girls. *Child Development, 60*, 40–55.

Brown, L., et al. (2006). Depressive symptoms as a predictor of sexual risk among African American adolescents and young adults. *Journal of Adolescent Health, 39*, 444.e1–444.e8.

Caldwell, C., et al. (2002). Racial identity, maternal support and psychological distress among African Americans adolescents. *Child Development, 73*, 1322–1336.

Caldwell, C., et al. (2004). Racial discrimination and racial identity as risk or protective factors for violent behaviors in African American young adults. *American Journal of Community Psychology, 33*, 91–105.

Caldwell, C., et al. (2006). Racial identity, parental support and alcohol use in a sample of at-risk African American high school students. *American Journal of Community Psychology, 34*, 71–82.

Carter, R., et al. (2009). Pubertal timing and its link to behavioral and emotional problems among 'at risk' African American adolescent girls. *Journal of Adolescence, 32*, 467–481.

Caryle, K., & Steinman, K. (2007). Demographic differences in the prevalence, co-occurrence and correlates of adolescent bullying at school. *Journal of School Health, 77*, 623–629.

Center for Disease Control. (2008). National Center for Injury Prevention and Control, Division of Violence Prevention, August 4, 2008, Centers for Disease Control and Prevention, National Center for Injury Prevention and Control, http://www.cdc.gov/InjuryPublications/Vact Book?

Christie, D. (2005). Adolescent development. *British Medical Journal, 330*, 301–304.

Cochran, D. (1997). African American fathers: A decade review of the literature. *Families in Society, 78*, 340–351.

Cota-Robles, S., et al. (2002). The role of puberty in violent and nonviolent delinquency among Anglo American, Mexican American and African American boys. *Journal of Adolescent Research, 17*, 364–376.

Crawford, I., et al. (2002). The Influence of dual-identity development on the psychosocial functioning of African American gay and bisexual men. *The Journal of Sex Research, 39*, 179–189.

Cunningham, M., et al. (2003). The association of physical maturation with family hassles among African American adolescent males. *Cultural Diversity and Ethnic Minority Psychology, 9*, 276–288.

Cutler, G. (1997). The role of estrogen in bone growth and maturation during childhood and adolescence. *Journal of Steroid Biochemical Molecular Biology, 6*, 141–144.

D'Augelli, A., et al. (2005). Predicting the suicide attempts of lesbian, gay and bisexual youth. *Suicide and Life Threatening Behavior, 35*, 646–660.

Delmarre-van de Wall, H. A. (2002). Regulation of puberty. *Best Practices Research in Clinical Obstetrics and Gynecology, 16*, 1–12.

Donking, A., et al. (2002). Inequalities in life expectancy by social class 1972–1999. *Health Statistics Quarterly, 15*, 5–15.

Dube, E., & Savin-Williams, R. (1999). Sexual identity development among ethnic sexual minority male youths. *Developmental Psychology, 35*, 1389–1398.

Eccles, T., et al. (2004). More normal than not: A qualitative assessment of the developmental experiences of gay male youth. *Journal of Adolescent Health, 35*, 425.e11–425.e18.

Edwards, R., et al. (2007). Disparities in young adolescent inhalant use by rurality, gender and ethnicity. *Substance Use and Misuse, 42*, 643–670.

Ellickson, P., et al. (2004). From adolescence to young adulthood: Racial/ethnic disparities in smoking. *American Journal of Public Health, 94*, 293–299.

Erikson, E. (1968). *Identity, youth, and crisis*. New York, NY: Norton.

Euling, S., et al. (2008). Examination of US puberty-timing data from 1940–1994 for secular trends: Panel findings. *Pediatrics, 121*, S172–S191.

Eyre, S., et al. (2007). Romantic relationships trajectories of African American gay/bisexual adolescents. *Journal of Adolescent Research, 22*, 107–131.

Federal Interagency Forum on Child and Family Statistics. (2005). America's children: Key national indicators of well-being, 2005. In *FIFOCAF Statistics*. Washington, DC: US Government Printing Office.

Felton, G., & Bartoces, M. (2002). Predictors of initiation of early sex in Black and White adolescent females. *Public Health Nursing, 19*, 59–67.

Fothergill, K., & Ensminger, M. (2006). Childhood and adolescent antecedents of drug and alcohol problems: A longitudinal study. *Drug and Alcohol Dependence, 82*, 61–76.

French, S., et al. (2006). The development of ethnic identity during adolescence. *Developmental Psychology, 42*, 1–10.

Friedman, M., et al. (2006). The impact of gender role nonconforming behavior, bullying and social support on suicidality among gay male youth. *Journal of Adolescent Health, 38*, 621–623.

Furlong, A., & Cartmel, F. (1997). *Young people and social change: Individualization and risk in late modernity*. Maidenhead: Open University Press.

Galea, S., & Rudenstine, S. (2005). Challenges in understanding disparities in drug use and its consequences. *Journal of Urban Health, 82*, 5–12.

Ge, X., et al. (2002). Contextual amplification of pubertal transition effects on deviant peer affiliation and externalizing behavior among African American children. *Developmental Psychology, 39*, 430–439.

Ge, X., et al. (2003). It's about timing and change: Pubertal transition effects on symptoms of major depression among African American youths. *Developmental Psychology, 38*, 42–54.

Ge, X., et al. (2006). Pubertal maturation and early substance use risks among African American children. *Psychology of Addictive Behaviors, 20*, 404–414.

Gladstone, G., et al. (2006). Do bullied children become anxious and depressed adults? A cross-sectional investigation of the correlates of bullying and anxious depression. *Journal of Nervous and Mental Disease, 194*, 201–208.

Glenn, B., & Wilson, K. (2008). African American adolescent perceptions of vulnerability and resilience to HIV. *Journal of Transcultural Nursing, 19*, 259–265.

Glenn, B., et al. (2008). Father and adolescent son variables related to the son's HIV prevention. *Western Journal of Nursing Research, 30*, 73–89.

Gluckman, P., & Hanson, M. (2006). Evolution, development and timing of puberty trends. *Endocrinological Metabolism, 17*, 7–12.

Goodyear, J., et al. (2000). First episode major depression in adolescents: Affective, cognitive and endocrine characteristics of risk status and predictors of onset. *British Journal of Psychiatry, 176*, 142–149.

Gordon-Larson, P., et al. (1999). Adolescent physical activity and inactivity vary by ethnicity: The national longitudinal study of adolescent health. *Journal of Pediatrics, 135*, 301–306.

Gottlieb, G. (1976). The roles of experiences in the development of behavior and the nervous system. In G. Gottlieb (Ed.), *Neural and behavioral specificity:*

Studies on the development of behavior and the nervous system. New York, NY: Academic Press.

Grov, C., et al. (2006). Race, ethnicity, gender and generational factors associated with the coming-out process among gay, lesbian and bisexual individuals. *The Journal of Sex Research, 43,* 115–121.

Guthrie, B., et al. (2001). Dealing with daily hassles: Smoking and African-American adolescent girls. *Journal of Adolescent Health, 29,* 109–115.

Guthrie, B., et al. (2002). African American girls' smoking habits and day-to-day experiences with racial discrimination. *Nursing Research, 51,* 183–190.

Hall, G. (1905). *Adolescence: Its psychology and its relations to physiology, anthropology, sociology, sex, crime, religion, and education.* London: Sidney Appleton.

Hawker, D., & Boulton, M. (2000). Twenty years' research on peer victimization and psychosocial maladjustment: A meta-analytic review of cross sectional studies. *Journal of Child Psychiatry, 41,* 441–455.

Herman-Giddings, M., et al. (1997). Secondary sexual characteristics and menses in young girls seen in an office practice: A study from the pediatric research in office settings network. *Pediatrics, 99,* 505–512.

Horner, J., et al. (2007). Withdrawal (coitus interruptus) as a sexual risk reduction strategy: Perspectives from African-American adolescents. *Archives of Sexual Behavior, 38*(5), 779–787.

Joe, S., et al. (2009). 12-Month and lifetime prevalence of suicide attempts among black adolescents in the National Survey of American Life. *Journal of the American Academy of Child and Adolescent Psychiatry, 48,* 271–282.

Johnson, S., et al. (2005). "I know what love means." Gender-based violence in the lives of urban adolescents. *Journal of Women's Health, 14,* 172–179.

Johnston, L., et al. (2006). *Monitoring the future: National results on adolescent drug use. Overview of key findings, 2005.* Bethesda, MD: National Institute of Druge Abuse.

Jones, D., et al. (2008). Adolescent alcohol use in context: The role of parents and peers among African American and European American youth. *Cultural Diversity and Ethnic Minority Psychology, 14,* 266–273.

Jones, M. (1950). Physical maturing among boys as related to behavior. *Journal of Educational Psychology, 41,* 129–148.

Jones, R. (1977). Physical development. In M. L. D. L. Siantz (Ed.), *The nurse and the developmentally disabled adolescent* (pp. 49–60). Baltimore, MD: University Park Press.

Kaplowitz, P. (2006). Pubertal development in girls: Secular trends. *Current Opinions in Obstetrics and Gynecology, 18,* 487–491.

Kerpelman, J., et al. (2008). African American adolescents' future education orientation: Associations with self-efficacy, ethnic identity and perceived parental support. *Journal of Youth and Adolescence, 37,* 997–1008.

Kestenberg, J. (1967). Phases of adolescents with suggestions for a correlation of psychic and hormonal organization. Antecedents of adolescent organization in childhood. *Journal of the American Academy of Child Psychiatry, 6,* 426–463.

Key, J., & Marsh, L. (2002). Missed opportunities for prevention: Failure to identify smoking in the parents of adolescent patients. *Substance Abuse, 23,* 215–221.

Kiang, L., & Fuligni, A. (2009). Ethnic identity in context: Variations in ethnic exploration and belonging within parent, same-ethnic peer and different-ethnic peer relationships. *Journal of Youth and Adolescence, 38*, 732–743.

Klein, K., et al. (1996). A longitudinal assessment of hormonal and physical alterations during normal puberty in boys. Estrogen leels as determined by an ultra-sensitive bioassay. *Journal of Clinical Endocrinology Metabolism, 81*, 3203–3207.

Kogan, S., et al. (2005). Adolescent health brief: Metro status and African American adolescents' risk for substance use. *Journal of Adolescent Health, 38*, 454–457.

Kulbok, P., et al. (2008). Factors influencing adolescents' decision not to smoke. *Public Health Nursing, 25*, 505–515.

Laitien, J., et al. (2001). Family social class, maternal body mass index, childhood body mass index, and age at menarche as predictors of adult obesity. *American Journal of Clinical Nutrition, 74*, 287–294.

Landrigan, P., et al. (2006). The National children's study: A 21 year prospective study of 100,000 American children. *Pediatrics, 118*, 2173–2186.

Lee, S., et al. (2009). Relationships among depressive symptoms, sexually transmitted infections and pregnancy in African American adolescent girls. *Journal of Pediatric and Adolescent Gynecology, 22*, 19–23.

Lerner, R. (1986). *Concepts and theories of human development*. New York, NY: Random House.

Lewinsohn, P., et al. (1999). Natural course of adolescent major depressive disorder, I: Continuity into young adulthood. *Journal of the American Academy of Child and Adolescent Psychiatry, 38*, 56–63.

Liberman-Smith, J. (2001). Teenage relationship with an older partner may lead to early first sex. *Familiy Planning Perspectives, 33*, 1–2.

Lindberg, S., et al. (2007). Gender, pubertal development and peer sexual harassment predict objectified body consciousness in early adolescence. *Journal of Research on Adolescence, 17*, 723–742.

Maguen, S., et al. (2002). Developmental milestones and disclosure of sexual orientation among gay, lesbian and bisexual youths. *Applied Developmental Psychology, 23*, 219–233.

Maher, L. (1997). *Sexed work: Gender, race and resistance in a Brooklyn drug market*. Oxford: Claredon Press.

Marin, B., et al. (2000). Older boyfriends and girlfriends increase risk of sexual initiation in young adolescents. *Journal of Adolescent Health, 27*, 409–418.

Marshall, W., & Tanner, J. (1969). Variations in pattern of pubertal changes in girls. *Archives of Diseases of Childhood, 44*, 291–303.

Marshall, W., & Tanner, J. (1970). Variations in pattern of pubertal changes in boys. *Archives of Diseases in Childhood, 45*, 13–23.

McCarren, M. (2004). *A field guide to Type 2 diabetes*. Alexandria, VA: American Diabetes Association.

McGinnis, J. (2002). Diabetes and physical activity: Translating evidence into action. *American Journal of Preventative Medicine, 22*, 1–2.

McIntosh, N., et al. (Eds.) (2003). *Forfar and Arneil's textbook of paediatrics*. Edinburgh: Churchill Livingstone.

Miller, J., & White, N. (2003). Gender and adolescent relationship violence: A contextual examination. *Criminology, 41*, 1207–1248.

Moolchan, E., & Schroeder, J. (2004). Quit attempts among African American teenage smokers seeking treatment: Gender differences. *Preventative Medicine, 39*, 1180–1186.

Muilenburg, J., & Legge, J. (2008). African American adolescents and menthol cigarettes: Smoking behavior among secondary school students. *Journal of Adolescent Health, 43*, 570–575.

Nadeem, E., & Graham, S. (2005). Early puberty, peer victimization and internalizing symptoms in ethnic minority adolescents. *Journal of Early Adolescence, 5*, 197–223.

Nahom, D., et al. (2001). Differences by gender and sexual experience in adolescent sexual behavior: Implications for education and HIV prevention. *Journal of School Health, 71*, 153–158.

National Institute of Diabetes and Digestive and Kidney Diseases. (1998). Diabetes in African Americans. In National Institute of Diabetes and Kidney Disease (Eds.). *Diabetes in America*. Bethesda, MD: National Institute of Health.

National Institute of Drug Abuse. (2003). *Drug use among racial/ethnic minorities*. DHHS Pub. No. NIH 03-3888. Rockville, MD: National Institute on Drug Abuse.

Newman, L., & Berman, S. (2008). Epidemiology of STD disparities in African American Communitites. *Sexually Transmitted Diseases, 35*, S4–S12.

Nieves, J., et al. (2005). Males have larger skeletal size and bone mass than females, despite comparable body size. *Journal of Bone and Mineral Research, 20*, 529–535.

Nwobu, C., & Johnson, C. (2007). Targeting obesity to reduce the risk of type 2 diabetes and other co-morbidities in African American youth: A review of the literature and recommendations for prevention. *Diabetes and Vascular Disease Research, 4*, 311–319.

Ogden, C., et al. (2006). Prevalence of overweight and obesity in the United States, 1999–2004. *Journal of the American Medical Association, 295*, 1549–1555.

O'Keefe, M. (1997). Predictors of dating violence among high school students. *Journal of Interpersonal Violence, 12*, 546–568.

Parent, A., et al. (2003). The timing of normal puberty and the age limits of sexual precocity: Variations around the world, secular trends and changes after migration. *Endocrine Review, 24*, 668–693.

Patel, V., et al. (2007). Mental health of young people: A global public-health challenge. *Lancet, 369*, 1302–1313.

Patton, G., & Viner, R. (2007). Adolescent health 1: Pubertal transitions in health. *Lancet, 369*, 1130–1139.

Powell, L., et al. (2007). Associations between access to food stores and adolsecent body mass index. *American Journal of Preventative Medicine, 33*, S301–S307.

Raiford, J., et al. (2007). Prevalence, incidence and predictors of dating violence: A longitudinal study of African American female adolescents. *Journal of Women's Health, 16*, 822–832.

Richardson, M., et al. (1997). Substance use and psychopathology in African American men at risk for HIV infection. *Journal of Community Psychology, 25*, 353–370.

Roemmich, J., & Rogol, A. (1999). Hormonal changes during puberty and their relationship to fat distribution. *American Journal of Human Biology*, 2, 209–224.

Russel, S., et al. (2001). Same-sex romantic attraction and experiences of violence in adolescence. *American Journal of Public Health*, 91, 903–906.

Rutter, P., & Leech, N. (2006). Sexual minority youth perspectives on the school environment and suicide risk interventions: A qualitative study. *Journal of Gay and Lesbian Issues in Education*, 4, 77–91.

Ryan, C., & Rivers, I. (2003). Lesbian, gay, bisexual and transgender youth: Victimization and its correlates in the USA and UK. *Culture, Health and Sexuality*, 5, 103–119.

Saluja, G., et al. (2004). Prevalence of and risk factors for depressive symptoms among young adolescents. *Archives of Pediatric and Adolescent Medicine*, 158, 760–765.

Sandhu, J., et al. (2006). The impact of childhood body mass index on timing of puberty, adult stature and obesity: A follow up study based on adolescent anthropometry recorded at Christ's Hospital (1936–1964). *International Journal of Obesity*, 30, 14–22.

Savin-Williams, R., & Diamond, L. (2000). Sexual identity trajectories among sexual-minority youths: Gender comparisons. *Archives of Sexual Behavior*, 29, 607–627.

Sawyer, A., et al. (2008). Examining ethnic, gender, and developmental differences in the why children report being a victim of "bullying" on self-report measures. *Journal of Adolescent Health*, 43(2), 106–114.

Schwartz, A. (2007). "Caught" versus "Taught": Ethnic identity and the ethnic socialization experiences of African American adolescents in kinship and non-kinship foster placements. *Children and Youth Services Review*, 29, 1201–1219.

Sellers, R., et al. (2003). The role of racial identity and racial discrimination in the mental health of African American young adults. *Journal of Health and Social Behavior*, 44, 302–317.

Siegel, J., et al. (1999). Body image, perceived pubertal timing and adolescent mental health. *Journal of Adolescent Health*, 25, 155–165.

Spano, R., et al. (2009). Does parenting mediate the effects of exposure to violence on violent behavior? An ecological-transaction model of community violence. *Journal of Adolescence*, 32, 1321–1341.

Spear, L. (2004). Adolsecent brain development and animal models. *Annals of the New York Academy of Science*, 1021, 23–26.

Stattin, H., & Magnusson, D. (2003). *Pubertal maturation in female development*. Hillsdale, MI: Erlbaum.

Styne, D. (2004). Puberty, obesity and ethnicity. *Trends in Endocrinology and Metabolism*, 15, 472–478.

Sun, S., et al. (2002). National estimates of the timing of sexual maturation and racial differences among US children. *Pediatrics*, 110, 911–919.

Tanner, J. (1962). *Growth at adolescence*. Oxford, UK: Blackwell Scientific Publications.

Teitelman, A., et al. (2008). Sexual relationship power, intimate partner violence and condom use among minority urban girls. *Journal of Interpersonal Violence*, 23, 1694–1712.

Tremblay, L., & Frigon, J. (2005). The interaction role of obesity and pubertal timing on the psychosocial adjustment of adolescent girls: Longitudinal data. *International Journal of Obesity, 29*, 1204–1211.

UNAIDS/WHO. (2006). *AIDS epidemic update*. Geneva: UNAIDS & WHO.

US Department of Health and Human Services. (2000). *Healthy people 2010: Understanding and objectives for improving health* (2nd ed., Vols. 1–2). Washington, DC: US Goverment Printing Office.

van den Berg, S., et al. (2006). Individual differences in puberty onset in girls: Bayesian estimation of heritabilities and genetic correlations. *Behavioral Genetics, 36*, 1–10.

Viner, R. (2002). Splitting hairs: Is puberty getting earlier in girls? *Archives of Diseases in Children, 86*, 8–10.

Wang, Y., et al. (2006). Obesity prevention in low socioeconomic status urban African American adolescents design and preliminary findings of the HEALTH-KIDS study. *European Journal of Clincial Nutrition, 60*, 92–103.

Wong, C., et al. (2003). The influence of ethnic discrimination and ethnic identification on African American adolescents' school and socioemotional adjustment. *Journal of Personality, 71*, 1197–1232.

World Health Organization. (2003). The social gradient. In R. Wilkinson & M. Marmot (Eds.), *Social determinants of health: The solid facts*. Denmark: World Health Organization.

Confronting normative challenges: Risk, resilience, privilege, and coping

13

Rebirth: Civic engagement from adolescence to adulthood

Norman A. Newberg

Graduate School of Education, University of Pennsylvania, Philadelphia

This chapter introduces and underscores the salience of factors contributing to adolescent civic engagement and some of the challenges of engaging in civic activities for youth that provide support for their families. This overview asserts two different forms of responsibilities relevant to adolescents as emerging adults: family and society. While these responsibilities are generally complementary for most adolescents, they are difficult for others. Civic engagement is presented as a continuum of experience, opportunities and choices that allow adolescents to individuate and move into adulthood or remain within the family of origin as an adolescent caregiver and provider. The capacity to extend beyond one's family is discussed as necessary for learning productive citizenship, service learning, and experimenting with mature roles. For each of the four cases presented, details regarding their histories, their challenges in school and home, and their development (or lack of) toward civic engagement are discussed.

Up to the child's entry into adolescence, home, school, and neighborhood circumscribe his or her world. The particular skills needed to navigate within larger and more complex spheres of influence require the capacity to extend oneself beyond family, learning productive citizenship and trying on mature roles beyond self-interest. In highlighting the relevance of civic engagement, the American Psychological Association (APA Online, 2009) cites civic engagement as "...actions designed to identify and address issues of public concern... [that] can include efforts to directly address an issue, work with others in a community to solve a problem or interact with the institutions of representative democracy." Although there is no consensus regarding how civic engagement is defined, common attributes include activities that are mutually beneficial for the individual and the institution being supported. These range from volunteering with community organizations to voting and political participation. A basic premise of civic engagement is that individuals should have opportunities to function across different types of civic activities. For youth, several factors are associated with their socialization for civic engagement. Among them are family backgrounds, social groups, and school involvement (see Flanagan, 2003; Youniss et al., 2002).

One strategy used to expose and engage students in civic participation is service-learning opportunities integrated into their school curriculum or provided through school programs. Service learning is a method used to teach subject matter in schools but also to expose students to opportunities that develop these skills leading to greater civic engagement (Larson, 2000). In the example that follows, the topic under study is the quality of water and the impact of pollution. Embedded in the topic are social concerns demonstrating diverse levels of civic engagement.

The following service learning samples three learning opportunities in search of a definition:

- Picking up trash on a riverbank is service.
- Studying water samples under a microscope is learning.
- When students, under the guidance of a science teacher, collect and analyze water samples, document their results, and present findings to a local pollution control agency—that is service learning.

Service learning actively engages participants in meaningful and personally relevant service activities. Middle school and high school students learn to care about their water supply when they discover and demonstrate to adults that certain pollutants may be injurious to the community's health. In presenting their findings to the local pollution agency, students begin to understand the societal issues that emerged from their presentation. While their science appears objective, members of the agency may have vested interests in maintaining the status quo, funds may not be readily available, or funds may have been allocated for another community priority. Thus in presenting their findings, students learn the complexity of how communities make decisions and become aware of the range of perspectives that might influence the agency's decision making.

The teacher's role is to guide, facilitate, and coach students so that the service-learning processes demonstrate the behaviors and attitudes that introduce them to civic engagement. Young adolescents began to accept civic engagement by developing interest in a larger context than the confines of

their home. Consistent with most pedagogy, the benefits of this learning process is dependent on students' school attendance and engagement when present. They take incremental steps similar to the ones described in the care of
the water supply to repair and improve the quality of life in their community
and beyond. The service-learning example abstracts a process for learning
civic engagement. It does not show, however, how individual adolescents live
through restricting conditions of their lives to engage in broader social issues.
Many civic opportunities for youth, whether through schools or other institutions, assume youth have the time, energy, trust, and efficacy to focus
on community and society issues impacting their lives or others (Sherrod,
Flanagan, & Youniss, 2002; Woldoff, 2002). The following section addresses
these assumptions by presenting four case studies to illustrate how adolescents manage their growth and development in various situations.

13.1. **CHALLENGED LIVES**

The case study material for this chapter is drawn from adolescents
involved in a tuition guarantee program. Each student who graduated from
high school and gained admission to a college or university received a
grant for college tuition and room and board. The program, Say Yes to
Education (SYTE), began as students left elementary school and entered
junior high school. Most of these students were around 12 years old,
African American, and born into families with limited resources at the
program's start (for details see Newberg, 2006). The adolescents interviewed were 17 and 18 years old when first interviewed, with a second
interview being conducted when they were in their mid-20s. Civic
engagement for adolescents raised in poverty can potentially take a little
longer than for those with greater financial resources due to social impediments, some of which are also shared with their immigrant peers
(Balsano, 2005; Jensen, 2008). There are many youth, however, living
in impoverished communities who participate at different levels of
engagement and even serve as advocates in addressing community concerns (see Checkoway, 1998; Youniss et al., 2002). For others, however,
the energy needed to cope with family, school, and neighborhood stressors can impede their engagement. Additionally, adolescents raised in
poverty have fewer opportunities than their peers from middle- to
upper-income level communities to develop the efficacy or civic skills
to try on roles of civic engagement or may lack trust in others (Balsano,
2005; Flanagan, 2003). I divide the informants between two groups in
accordance with the framing statements of this chapter: those that
provided substantial direct support for their family of origin and those
who experienced sufficient stability at home to allow them to explore a

larger world beyond the confines of home. Michelle and Richard stand in for adolescents that take initial steps in civic engagement. Derrick and Tasha, who will be presented first, correspond to those adolescents required by circumstances to assume quasiparental responsibilities within their family of origin.

However, it should be noted that these are not static categories and could therefore be expanded to include the rich variation within each group. Of the four cases, Derrick, Tasha, and Michelle lived in single-parent households. None of their parents worked consistently and periodically required welfare assistance. Richard lived with his father and mother, who both worked. Nevertheless they lived in the same neighborhood as the other three families.

13.1.1. **Delayed engagement**

Surrogate parenting

Derrick was 14 and ready to enter 9th grade in high school when his parents divorced. Derrick is the oldest of four children. His "little brother" is 12 years younger than he is, while his sisters are 1 and 9 years his junior. His mother, who worked as a bar waitress, did not finish high school. His father completed high school and entered college on a football scholarship. After 1 year, he dropped out. None of his aunts or uncles completed high school. Derrick felt that he and his father might share an important status in the family: both would be high school graduates. Derrick held out the hope for himself that, one day, he would become a college graduate as well.

Growing up in a family with both parents employed, he felt he was "a spoilt child" who got everything he wanted. In addition to material gifts, he also managed to convince his mother when he would or would not attend school. He seemed to be making adult decisions before he was ready to understand the consequences of his behavior. His teachers praised him for his intelligence, but cautioned that he was missing too many days of class and often coming late to school.

When Derrick's parents separated, everything changed. He felt his world "crumble" around him. Bills didn't get paid. At one point the electricity was shut off. In the winter the gas was shut off. As Christmas neared, his father paid an outstanding gas bill of $2000 so they would have heat. The hard times reached a crisis when his mother started to drink heavily. When mortgage payments were not paid for months, they lost their house. Derrick pointed to the period between 9th and 10th grade as the most difficult time in his life.

Some teenagers do not have the luxury of a leisurely adolescence. Circumstances at home may require that students pick up adult responsibilities. Life circumstances shape or distort the way students experience high school. Derrick was a case in point. He explained that when his parents separated, his mother was often inebriated, leaving family responsibilities in his hands. He concluded that he was no longer the "spoilt child."

> *I worried how my little brothers and sisters were doing. My attention went to were they eating, being dressed properly, and going to school every day. After I got them all set, I felt tired. I didn't feel like going to school any more. If I didn't have to deal with my family, I would've been in school more often, and my grades would've been better, because I wouldn't have anything else to worry about. My head would've been in the books. I was fighting with myself saying to myself, 'Look, this would be a stupid opportunity for you to give up, a reference to the SYTE scholarship.' But I was also saying, 'I got to look out for my family.' Some days I didn't come to school. Then some days I came, but was late. And often I had teachers telling me:*
> *'We hear you're a very bright and intelligent man. So what's going wrong?' 'I tried to tell them. But they still didn't get the picture. And then I got frustrated.'*

Derrick's freshman and sophomore years in high school were full of upheaval, as his family moved from his father's to his grandmother's and finally to his aunt's house. His life was unstable, and he was expected to perform at school as if his home life were orderly. While he complained that teachers did not understand the magnitude of his situation, individual teachers tried to help him cope with his studies. He was allowed to make up tests, which helped him survive a challenging Elementary Functions class. One of his aunts rescued his family and gave them the shelter and structure that allowed Derrick to pay attention to his schoolwork. However, the damage to his self-concept during the 2 years where he was a surrogate parent to his younger siblings continued to have a negative affect that he found difficult to overcome.

Derrick had felt obligated to take care of his younger siblings and believed it would be unconscionable not to pick up the slack. And yet some of the negative effects of having adult-like discretion regarding school attendance and lateness had been seeded earlier in his life when he was a "spoilt child." Ironically, when his life became unstable it may have been that same discretion that gave him permission to largely abandon his studies. Once he assumed parental responsibilities, he did not have the psychic or physical energy to pick up his age/stage adolescent responsibilities.

Hidden aspirations

Tasha comes from a family of 10 children. When she turned 8 years old, her 24-year-old sister, Leslie, became her legal guardian. Tasha moved between her mother's and her older sister's houses, but increasingly spent more time at her sister's. "I wasn't getting what I wanted at my mom's house. I couldn't. Too many kids. It was dirty." Her mother didn't work, and she suffered from bouts of acute alcoholism that necessarily affected her ability to maintain a household. Leslie put more structure into Tasha's life. She had to clean her own room, do household chores, and be in bed by 9:30 p.m. However, the one area Leslie had limited influence over, because she lacked legal guardianship, was the irregularity of Tasha's school attendance. The chair of the special education department at the junior high school was particularly concerned with Tasha's poor attendance. "She's a really nice kid, pleasant and cooperative when she's in class. I think she has the ability to advance to Resource Room status, if she'd only come to school." Her reading and math scores placed her at a 4th-grade level entering 9th grade.

Tasha's mom moved into Leslie's house with her five children and Leslie's two. Her mom lost her own house because the rent collector was involved in a drug scam and never gave the money he received to the owner of the house. The crowded household increased tensions among family members that often exploded into violence. Tasha felt surrounded by violence: within her family, on the street, and in her high school. She was afraid to walk out the door for fear that something awful would happen to her. Her fears, while somewhat extreme, were not unfounded. The following example makes her point about the arbitrariness of violence: "You be hearing kids coming to school with guns. That scares me too, 'cause you don't know if you argue with somebody, if they're going to pull out a gun and shoot you." At a personal level she was robbed near her home. She related this harrowing experience:

> I was walking down the street, and a girl came up to me, a real big girl, put a knife to my neck and told me to give her all my stuff. She put this fear in me, 'I'm going to be looking, watching you and stuff, and you better not tell nobody.' So that had me scared, I just was nervous. My sister always talked to me and said, 'She's not gonna bother you, go out there and do what you have to do.' She always told me to go ahead and I'll take you to school.

These fears prevented her from attending school. She was terrified of being hurt and protected herself by staying at home. The street robbery gave her a reason to feel afraid of going to school. Leslie's offer to accompany her did not ease her worries. Whatever the reason for not attending school—real or imagined fears, or family circumstances—the juvenile court finally determined that Leslie had the legal engagement to insist that Tasha attend school. With more routine attendance, Tasha was able to improve some of her academic skills. Her consistent effort earned her the right to be moved out of special education into a regular English class. Unfortunately, these gains were short-lived as her attendance again deteriorated.

With the overcrowding tensions created in the household, Leslie and her husband Jake argued frequently. Jake became physically abusive, to which Leslie, during the peak of one altercation, reacted to by firing a bullet at him. Their marriage of 10 years ended with that shot: Jake was forbidden to enter the house by court order, and Leslie, for her part in the fight, faced a 4- to 8-month sentence at a correctional facility. Tasha's academic gains regressed following this time of bitter fighting between Leslie and Jake, and it became apparent to Tasha that Leslie needed help caring for her children.

In 11th grade, Tasha was in the process of dropping out. She'd go to school every other day, then skip a week; return to school for a couple of days, realize that she had fallen behind in her work, stay out for another week, then stop going entirely. She was upset with herself and felt conflicted: bored at home with childcare but provoked by fear and anxiety at school with thoughts of being harmed physically or psychologically. Even when she made some genuine progress in her studies, school was the place where she felt "stupid" and unsuccessful. She was subsequently retained in 11th grade and never returned to high school. Tasha had disengaged from school and was further removed from engaging in civic opportunities that schools support or encourage. Her home life created anxieties that limited a broader consciousness regarding civic concerns.

13.1.2. **Seeds of engagement**

Learning to trust

Michelle is the second of seven children. Her mother was 19 when Michelle was born. Neither parent finished high school, but her father did complete a General Education Degree (GED). Her parents separated when she was 7. Michelle said that, at her birth, her dad said to her mother that she was no longer his "first girl." That remark engendered jealousy and hostility between Michelle and her mother that persisted through her adolescence. She believed her mother hated her and wished that she were never born. She recounts that throughout her years growing up, until she turned 18, her mother beat her "…with ironing cords or whatever she could pick up."

Michelle's family moved several times in her early childhood, causing her to miss school. Between age 12 and 18 she lived with three different family units: her mother for 2 years, her father for 1 year, and her grandmother for 3 years. For short periods of time, she lived with an uncle and an aunt. Each of these households was crowded with younger cousins and various members of an extended family.

In reviewing her school records, the SYTE staff learned that she had performed below grade level in reading in 4th grade and was recommended for a special reading class that used programed instruction on a computer. As a reward for completing work successfully, she was allowed to play computer games for the remainder of the class period. Within 1 month, her reading teacher noticed that she was reading at grade level; therefore, she was no longer allowed to work on the computer. She reported that she "cried hard" when she lost that access.

Throughout middle school, Michelle's grades were below average, but passing. It was apparent to teachers and program staff that she had the ability to do better, but lacked motivation. When entering 9th grade, she announced her intentions to attend a vocational school to major in cosmetology. The SYTE staff tried repeatedly to convince her to attend a comprehensive high school so she could take college preparatory subjects. She refused to listen. By October of that year, she regretted her decision and transferred to a high school where she was able to study an academic track curriculum. None of her voc-ed courses were transferable; she spent the entire year catching up.

Even though she failed one subject the following year in 10th grade, she was recommended for a special program for students with potential to attend college, but were underachievers. The program was essentially a small school within her school, comprised faculty that worked with a cohort of students for 3 years. In such an intimate environment, students were seen and heard, and the anonymity of the larger school was significantly reduced. The smaller organization also made the SYTE staff's advocacy for Michelle simpler. That summer, SYTE staff found Michelle a paid internship in an office using a computer. She was elated. Her excellent performance earned her the opportunity to continue this work part-time during the school year. However, without much explanation, she did not return to work that fall.

Staff noted that "... Michelle got into frequent fist-fights with peers and seemed unperturbed if she was suspended. She looked angry. Her home situation continued to frustrate her, especially when her mother moved back into her grandmother's home." The staff decided to hire a therapist, who initially worked with a group of students, including Michelle, and eventually scheduled individual sessions with those students in greatest need. By winter of her 11th grade, Michelle accepted that she did have problems. Her academic performance was poor, and it was clear that she would be retained in grade. She wanted help. She also wanted to go to college. She said of the counselor: "It seemed like I was talking to my best friend. I could tell him anything, and he would help me out." Concurrently, her grades improved. Previously, she had achieved mostly Ds and Cs, and had at least one failure. Now she was consistently making As and Bs. In the summer of 1993, she took a college-level course in data processing and achieved a B as a final grade.

Michelle made some basic changes in her life and became more trusting of caring adults. Therapy helped change Michelle's attitude toward her brothers and sisters; previously she had used them as a target for her anger against her mother. She said:

> *It wasn't that I was angry at them. It's just that they was there at the time when I was angry, so I took it out on them. But now my attitude has changed towards them. I don't holler at them at all like I used to. But if I do, I always end up apologizing to them.*

Simultaneously, she no longer resisted academic learning. Her English teacher, Mr. Muller, got her interested in reading books. She admired him because he made her think. She appreciated the reach for excellence he demanded of students. "He pushes students to do the best that they can do," she remarked. "Then he pushes them to do better."

> *Most teachers are different: if you don't want to work, they leave you alone. But Mr. Muller, if he see that you don't want to work, he will find out what the problem is, why you don't want to work, and will try to help you out.*

Slowly, Michelle understood the value of supportive guidance and appreciated the pressure and expectations that motivated her to excel. She used writing as a way to make sense of her experience. Her English teacher encouraged her to write an essay for a contest on the importance of getting an education. She described how she came to believe that she could strive to compete:

> *And we had to write a paper about education and I just wrote how I felt because my teacher has taught me a lot, when my counselor wasn't around, I needed somebody to talk to. So I talked to my teacher; and he helped me out a lot. He was like a friend to me too. And he always pushed me to do better and kept telling me don't let*

this get you and don't let that get you. And I started taking his advice, and after that, my counselor's advice. And it changed the way I started thinking about things and that's what I wrote about in my paper.

Michelle won first place in the contest and received a plaque to commemorate the occasion.

Several times in high school, Michelle had been on the verge of dropping out and resisted being helped. Michelle had been hurt by her family's indifference and often seemed to be losing control over her life. SYTE staff understood that students move in and out of connection; the program did not give up on her. At some level, she had to learn the value of help and to trust the helper before she could accept it (Newberg and Sims, 1996). She began experiencing success and saw, by contrast, the consequences for some of her classmates who had dropped out and shook her head. Michelle was the first of her family to go to college. Aunts and uncles in her family "…graduated from high school but they went into the service or a trade school." Looking for role models who would inspire her to attain college, she would not find them in her family. But SYTE bridged this gap in Michelle's experience through visiting college campuses and by frequent contact with college tutors.

Michelle became goal-oriented. "Getting a high school diploma," to her, "means that I have reached my goal, done what I had to do and that's just my reward for finishing what I had to do." She was able to take her goal-directedness and project it into the future. Projecting 5 years after the interview, she imagined that she would have her "… own office, working in a big, big business building. Maybe become a manager. 'Cause I'm into computers." She allowed that she might have a child and marry. When I asked if anything could interfere with her attaining her goal she said emphatically: "No, nothing at all. I want to live. See, I'm not a party person, so I don't be out that much, so I just stay in the house and do whatever I have to do."

Business focused

Richard's mother had joined Jehovah's Witness when he was 6 years old. He accompanied his mother to Kingdom Hall regularly and gradually began to see himself serving within his religion. His father, who worked in a bank and had completed an accounting program in a community college, was opposed to the Jehovah's Witness religion. The family's divided religious allegiances resulted in household tensions that persisted throughout Richard's high school years.

In elementary school, Richard was one of two students identified in his class as mentally gifted (MG). His MG status gained him admission to an academically competitive middle school. Richard adjusted to an equally competitive high school without much difficulty, maintaining a B average. Between 9th and 10th grades he met his first girlfriend and fell in love. The relationship was consuming. His grades in school plummeted and, for the first time, Ds and Fs appeared on his report card. "I kinda forgot about religion and college, I was just focusing on her." His relationship with his girlfriend was part of a defense he constructed so that he would fail in a rigorous academic program. He asserted, "I wanted to do what I could to be certain that I didn't get into college."

He continued to sabotage his chances to be an exemplary student until a fellow student forced him to reevaluate his priorities. Richard attended the SYTE summer program between 10th and 11th grades. During a Geometry class, he faced a moment of truth that redirected his thinking about his studies. The math teacher asked a question that no one but Richard could answer. Derrick was also taking the same class; he observed that unique moment and was amazed at Richard's grasp of the subject. After class he approached Richard and said, "You really know that work. You must have straight As, or at least As and Bs. You must be on the honor roll." Richard felt embarrassed. He didn't tell his classmate that he was earning Ds, and even Fs.

That exchange with Derrick prompted a period of introspection. He wondered why he didn't earn more As. He probed more deeply and asked himself what was "bringing him down." He asked, "Did I really want to waste the gift I had?" I didn't want to be one of those people who in the future would say, "I could have done that. If I knew the work, why was I getting these bad grades?" The answer became clear to him, and so was the remedy. He broke off his relationship with his girlfriend, changed the way he acted at home, made up missing work at school, and maintained a regimen of studying after school, rather than playing basketball with friends in the neighborhood. Once he decided to change, Richard became goal oriented. He wanted to "dominate everyone else" with his academic prowess. With a sense of sadness he remarked, "Hurting people was the hardest thing I had to overcome. Letting them go. They didn't understand and thought that I was stuck up or something" He felt that his singleness of purpose was ". . . what changed me around." He asserted that he had hit his stride and was not going to stop. He sums up his mission this way: "If I try hard, I don't want to be second; I want to be first."

In the summer between 11th and 12th grades, SYTE organized paid internships so that students could get the feel of various work opportunities. Richard was given a job at a prominent center city bank. His superiors were so impressed with his work ethic that they invited him to work after school during his senior year and even suggested that he should consider a career in the bank after he completed college. It appeared that his father's career aspirations influenced his decision to attend college. His father had hoped to become a Certified Public Accountant, but he finished only 2 years of a 4-year college program and did not qualify to sit for the exam. But Richard had the potential to live out his father's dream.

Richard's refound success in academics and his work at the bank gave him confidence that he could succeed in business. He was accepted into one of the nation's most prestigious business schools. His interest in business provided him with the efficacy and exposure that contributed to his sense of civic responsibility. It would be unseemly to be in business only to make money; his religious upbringing would not allow such a utilitarian goal. "What I want to do in the future is start my own chain of businesses." His vision for the future spoke to his need to give back to his community. "Maybe daycare centers, or supermarkets, or something in the community to help the community out." His motive for wanting to start neighborhood businesses was motivated by his observation that the businessmen in his neighborhood were white or Asian. He felt exploited by the high prices they charged and their lack of commitment to his neighborhood.

For Richard self-discipline was a prerequisite to making a difference in a larger world. He had to reject the influence of the street, if he was to reach his goal of being able to help members of his community who might be less articulate or caught in anesthetizing their pain through selling and using drugs. Richard appeared to be an outlier among his peers. He had two parents who cared about education. Perhaps the strongest influence was his religion, which gave each day a sense of purpose and an orientation to his future. Richard admitted that while he lived in a poor neighborhood, he did not have nearly the challenges his peers faced. As he stated in an interview: "[My peers have] single parents on drugs. I have both my parents here. And they both loved and supported me" (Mezzaccappa, 1993). He also developed a sense of civic responsibility in observing other ethnic groups. Chinese and Korean businessmen, he noticed, were developed economically so that they were able to succeed in Black communities. His perception of price gouging by some business owners was considered exploitative and used to dominate the black customers they served. This appalled Richard and he sensed that if Blacks were able to own and manage their own businesses they might be fairer in the prices they charge. Further, he foresaw that Black business owners might develop concentrated shopping strips where they could assert power politically.

13.2. **DISCUSSION**

In the discussion section I provide a brief introduction of how each student evolved into "productive citizenship" and moved "beyond self-interest." Youniss, McLellan, and Yates (1997) suggest that direct contact with people in need or with issues of inequality and injustice is potentially important in making an impact on the civic development of participants. These types of experiences expose adolescents to social issues, challenge their ideologies, and help provide them with a sense of community (Fogel, 2004). Metz, McLellan, and Youniss (2003) propose that to achieve the greatest impact on youths' civic development, they should have direct contact with people in need or work on issues of social relevance. The youth highlighted in this chapter lacked these experiences as adolescents but as young adults began to evolve into productive citizenship and toward civic engagement. In examining the development of positive citizenship from adolescence to young adulthood, Zaff, Malanchuk, and Eccles (2008) found that social interactions, others' modeling of civic behaviors, and cultural factors cumulatively increased civic activities from adolescence into adulthood. As noted in these cases, their experiences provided them with greater exposure to positive adults and interactions that improved their trajectories (see Obradovic & Masten, 2007).

Being a surrogate parent exhausted and worried Derrick. His teachers tried to help him but he didn't believe they understood his situation. The help they offered was not enough to make a difference in his attitude toward school and he felt misunderstood and frustrated. He wondered if his scholarship was being frittered away by a situation he could not control. Life circumstances sometimes place children in adult roles. Some older children, like Derrick, seem overwhelmed by the enormity of the tasks and their inexperience in assuming conflicting roles of a developing adolescent and of a parental surrogate. Tasha was in a somewhat similar situation to Derrick, but with significant variations. She, too, was involved in providing childcare for some of her mother's children, her older sister's and her own children. Her living conditions seemed perpetually dire. Although focusing on parent's civic behaviors, Kelly (2006) also notes that providing caregiving skills potentially introduces skills that are later conducive to civic engagement.

By age 22, Tasha was the mother of two children of her own and with very few marketable skills. She not only realized the need for a less crowded and more orderly household to raise her children, but she also realized that she must take initiative. A growing maturity and work experiences motivated her to acquire behaviors that made the larger world more accessible. Equally impressive was her rationale that she was keeping a job so that she could model a strong work ethic for her children.

Michelle's persistent physical and psychological abuse by her mother contributed to her indiscriminately projecting internalized anger onto her siblings at home and toward classmates at school. Through her interactions with a therapist and an English teacher, she learned the value of guided attention and began to value academic instruction. As Michelle matured she thought she might be able to do things differently for the next generation. She wanted to be a change agent for kids and planned to work with youth who came from an environment similar to hers. One of her most formative college experiences was working as a receptionist while a student intern for the director of Multi-Cultural Affairs. She began talking with students about the problems they brought to the center and developed a reputation for being empathetic and pragmatic in the advice she offered. The director of the center encouraged her growth as a potential counselor and discussed career possibilities with her. At the Multi-Cultural office she was exposed to a spectrum of personal and social problems. Through this rich exposure she developed a deeper awareness of the needs of adolescent minority students. Her internship turned into a major experience in civic engagement that led her to choose a career in social work. Michelle completed her bachelor's degree and found a job as a counselor for young adults recently released from prison, advising them on how to reenter society. In addition to work, she and her husband share the childcare of their 2-year-old son and had saved enough money to make a down payment on a house.

Richard's adolescent life spoke most directly to the APA (2009) definition of civic engagement mentioned earlier. It's as if he awoke from a sleep of self-interest and became aware of the injustice African Americans experience in inner city communities. He saw other ethnic groups exploiting Blacks through price gouging. He questioned the status quo and imagined Blacks becoming the dominant group selling to fellow Blacks. He saw solutions of Blacks becoming business people who learn how to speak with a unified voice to legislators so that they could use the political process to achieve goals that would improve a lot of Blacks living in poverty. He did not have the skills or experience to organize to implement his vision. But he could articulate a problem in economic and political terms. Richard critiqued what may be wrong in his community and what should be done to solve the problem. A service-learning internship with an emphasis on community organizing might have offered some practical experience in translating ideas into action. He needed more time to consolidate his skills and establish a path in civic engagement.

13.2.1. **Resisting help**

Each of the case studies illustrates that these students had to learn how to receive help. They fought or avoided those adults who might be able to help them. The value of support and their own role in that process at times eluded them. Their circumstances and strategies for survival had compromised their ability to believe in and receive support offered by others (Flanagan, 2003; Fogel, 2004). Once each was able to comprehend the impact support would provide, they were able to begin the process of expanding their own contributions. Each of the cases exemplifies this point in varying degrees.

Derrick fought as an adolescent with the upheaval of his family, the drug dependency of his mother, and the additional responsibilities of caring for his younger siblings. Over time he graduated with a degree in Finance and pushing past what might otherwise have been expected, he used his broadened perception of self to mentor young black male adolescents in middle school. SYTE started a new chapter in Connecticut for middle school students and older students from Philadelphia attending the partner University in Connecticut were recruited to mentor the upcoming group. Derrick volunteered his time to show the new group the explicit steps needed to succeed in college and how to be educationally focused.

He often took his mentees on trips to his college campus. When they passed a basketball court and wanted to start a game, he intervened saying, "You have other opportunities to play basketball. While you're on this campus, I'd like you to get acquainted with the library and the computer lab." He seemed to demonstrate that getting ahead in life required focus, effort, and not succumbing to distractions. Derrick hoped that by engaging the next generation they would be better prepared than he was to achieve in school.

Tasha lived a life of frequent disruption and turmoil within her home. Her mother's alcohol addiction and instability meant that she could not rely on her for guidance. Her sister Leslie had some of the instincts that could lend structure and predictability to Tasha's life. But the violence inside and outside the house made Tasha fearful. As a young adult, Tasha believed her children needed to see her model the value of getting up in the morning to go to work. In following her grandmother's advice she succeeded in landing a job, established a record for timeliness and competence, and eventually realized the advantages to getting her General Equivalence Diploma (GED).

Michelle projected anger indiscriminately because of her sense of emotional abandonment from her family. Through the efforts of a therapist, an English teacher and the SYTE staff, Michelle discerned those people that were trustworthy. She learned that there were people that would not abandon her as her parents did. Gradually, she understood that she was the one who must be responsible for her life—through her direction and competence. Michelle was an example of an adolescent who learned how to be personally responsible (Felsman and Vallant, 1987). She struggled courageously to assert her independence from her family of origin so that she could take advantage of the resources through her high school's motivational program and the assistance provided by SYTE. Upon graduation from college, she became a counselor to men in their 20s that were newly released from prison and advised them on how to build productive lives.

Richard had been identified as a mentally gifted student in middle school. His academic achievement confirmed that he was talented. The summer after middle school graduation, SYTE sent Richard to a prestigious suburban prep school. Again he held his own. He distinguished himself in writing and in English, but showed that he could also achieve in science and math. The school was impressed and offered him a 4-year scholarship. He resisted taking the award and contended he would feel more comfortable attending a school in the city that had a majority of African American students.

After high school graduation, Richard entered a highly ranked School of Business expecting to fulfill his father's dream of becoming an accountant. However, by the end of his sophomore year he realized that he wanted to pursue his own dream. Like Michelle, he, too, had a transforming experience through therapy. His work with an African American therapist convinced him that he wanted to make his mark in a similar profession. After successful completion of a B.A. degree in Psychology, he married and moved south. The next few years he worked as a counselor treating delinquent adolescents. He developed a theory of how depression envelops inner-city lives where poverty and unemployment offer little hope of escape. He completed a master's degree in clinical psychology and began thinking about how he could combine his knowledge of Finance with his skills as a mental health therapist to address some of the problems of living in poverty.

13.2.2. **Separation-individuation**

What is in infancy [a desire to become individuated is] in adolescence the shedding of family dependencies ... to become a member of society at large, or simply, of the adult world (Blos, 1979).

While the concept of individuation reflects the egocentrism associated with many American youth and is the subject of scholarly debates, it does highlight the struggles of other youth that feel obligated to their families beyond what is a contribution to the collective good. For some youth, assisting family members or providing adult-like support during times of instability is an obligation and reflects their capacity for care, strength of character, and problem-solving abilities. The challenge comes when their development is compromised and they lack the maturity to know how to include themselves as a family member with needs that are being unaddressed. Youth that live through challenges, like those discussed here, can experience a rebirth that will allow them to comprehend how they can make a contribution even beyond the needs of their families.

At the start of this paper I presented a service-learning exercise illustrative of how it is possible to teach the intervening steps toward achieving civic engagement. The example described how a teacher helped junior high school students discover that the local water was polluted. Students saw the complexity of their work as they moved from a science activity in the classroom to figuring out how to convince an agency that they should require companies to desist from dumping polluted waste in the town's rivers and further authorize a company to reverse the damage so that the rivers may again serve the community's need for clean water. This was a difficult problem that started in science classroom. Students searched for reliable evidence in the field and then shifted to learning the political processes for persuading the agency to take action to prevent further water pollution. And, finally, concluded when students learned how to lobby a government agency to improve the quality of water through political action. The teacher modeled how to use science to provide reliable evidence that the pollution control agency must at least consider. The teacher took students through an experience that demonstrated how to participate in action that may lead to civic engagement. That experience produced a possible set of strategies that may be useful to those students when they face adult situations. Civic engagement can be learned in a variety of contexts. Some adolescents learn civic engagement from parents, others at school; still others may learn those skills from trusted friends. As previously noted, the trajectory may not only vary but may not even begin until beyond high school.

How did Derrick, Tasha, Michelle, and Richard begin to take on more adult roles through civic engagement?

After Derrick searched extensively for a job in his field, he was disappointed in not finding a job in Finance. And as a fallback position, he accepted working for his uncle selling memorabilia at sporting events. He was able to save money, and was planning to manage a fleet of vans that will provide transportation to elderly shut-ins so that they could make trips to the doctor or do their shopping. He had experience doing this type of service for a hospital. He had written a business plan and was looking for funding to purchase or rent the vans. Simultaneously, he continued to pursue a job in Finance. After a few false starts, he landed a job as budget officer for an emergency room of a large hospital. This job gave him the satisfaction of being able to use the skills he had learned as a college Finance major. In his leisure time he played a major role in planning and organizing an alumni celebration in honor of the 20th anniversary of the creation of the SYTE program, thus assuming a role in civic engagement. Tasha moved out of her sister's house, minimizing the crowded conditions and reducing the noise levels. She found a job and displayed a strong work ethic to model for her children the value of assuming adult behavior at home and at work. It was important that her children see her "...becoming a member of society at large, or simply, of the adult world." Tasha had lived in a narrow world constrained by poverty. But even within those constraints the potential existed for an adolescent to craft an identity separate from parents and family that allowed the emergence or rebirth of an individual into adulthood.

By the time Michelle was 17 her family appeared to have abandoned her and she learned that she must take care of herself and assume engagement for her life. She graduated from college, married a man who was also a college graduate, had two children with him, and accepted his two children as part of their blended family. At present she works as a counselor for newly released prisoners. All of those behaviors bespeak a person who is a member of the adult world and capable of assuming civic responsibilities.

Richard's vision encouraged Black community members to buy out a strip of stores so that they could serve their community responsibly by charging customers fare prices for services. Richard did not have the complex set of skills to manage this vision at age 18. However, by age 28 he had pursued a two pronged career path using some of the skills he learned in business school and the complementary degree in psychology that allowed him to work as a therapist. He believed that poor people rarely develop the skills that give them financial security. To that end he organized a financial advising company that offered consultation to working class families on how to save so that they might be able to invest a portion of their income. His goal continued to reflect the values he espoused when he was 18, but was tempered by a stronger knowledge base in Finance and a deeper understanding of how to motivate greater flexibility among low-income families.

During adolescence, a capacity for functioning in multiple roles develops. Being able to choose from several possible roles can lead to more autonomy and freedom (Markus & Nurius, 1986). To the degree that role options are less available to an adolescent, as in the case of Tasha, the possibility of functioning with a repertoire of roles in the larger adult world becomes reduced. When role options are limited, taking on the role of a civic engagement seems like a less possible or relevant choice. The four individuals described in the case studies, to varying degrees, have shed family dependencies. In each case study we see evidence of individuation—that is, finding ways to choose a particular path in life that is responsible in the adult world. What may be less obvious in reviewing the overview of their lives are the problem behaviors often reported of youth from similar backgrounds. What has been suggested, and certainly exemplified in these lives, is the support and models provided to them as adolescents were not only instrumental in their later transition, but minimized the further delays caused by issues such as drug and criminal activities (see Fogel, 2004). A common theme in each of their lives was the presence and support of SYTE. Even though they each had different experiences in utilizing the supports, it was always clear that the support was consistently available. Lerner (2004) notes that the most successful programs in contributing to youth's civic engagement are those that cultivate relationships, establish skill-building, and provide opportunities for youth participation and decision-making.

As adolescents are more successful in taking on multiple adult roles, they are also more able to become part of the larger world through civic engagement. The role of parents, educators, social workers, therapists, and teachers is to assist adolescents in finding resources and strategies that will launch them into a larger, more mature adult world.

13.3. **CONCLUSION**

Family and school contexts were highlighted in these cases because opportunities for civic engagement are most frequently provided within these contexts. Rare, although occasionally offered, are work sites that encourage employees to participate in an organized civic activity. Due to their part-time work status, adolescents are less likely to engage in work-sponsored civic activities but are potentially exposed to the issues being addressed and the impact of volunteering in service to others. For many youth, such opportunities are not available until beyond their high school years. Opportunities for self-efficacy, awareness of social issues, engaged social interactions, models of civic behaviors, and a sense of community continue to provide factors needed to support youth as they find their place in the broader society.

REFERENCES

American Psychological Association Online. (2009). Retrieved from the American Psychological Association website on Civic Engagement and Service Learning at http://www.apa.org/ed/slce/civicengagement.html

Balsano, A. B. (2005). Youth civic engagement in the United States: Understanding and addressing the impact of social impediments on positive youth and community development. *Applied Developmental Science*, *9*(4), 188–201.

Blos, P. (1979). *The adolescent passage: Developmental issues.* New York, NY: International Universities Press.

Checkoway, B. (1998). Involving young people in neighborhood development. *Children and Youth Services Review*, *20*, 765–795.

Felsman, J. K., & Vallant, G. E. (1987). Resilient children as adults: A 40-year study. In E. J. Anthony & B. J. Cohler (Eds.), *The invulnerable child.* New York, NY: The Guilford Press.

Flanagan, C. (2003). Trust, identity, and civic hope. *Applied Developmental Science*, *7*(3), 165–171.

Fogel, S. J. (2004). Risks and opportunities for success: Perceptions of urban youths in a distressed community and lessons for adults. *Families in Society*, *85*(3), 335–344.

Jensen, L. A. (2008). Immigrants' cultural identities as sources of civic engagement. *Applied Developmental Science*, *12*(2), 74–83.

Kelly, D. C. (2006). Parents' influence on youths' civic behaviors: The civic context of the caregiving environment. *Families in Society*, *87*(3), 447–455.

Larson, A. (2000). What is service learning? Retrieved from the National Youth Leadership Conference Website: www.nylc.org

Lerner, R. M. (2004). *Liberty: Thriving and civic engagement among America's youth.* Thousand Oaks, CA: Sage Publications.

Markus, H., & Nurius, P. (1986). Possible selves. *American Psychologist*, *41*(9), 954–969.

Metz, E., McLellan, J., & Youniss, J. (2003). Types of voluntary service and adolescents' civic development. *Journal of Adolescent Research*, *18*(2), 188–202.

Mezzaccappa, D. (1993). *A gift changed his life's path.* The Philadelphia Inquirer. January 17.

Newberg, N. (2006). *The gift of education: How a tuition guarantee program changed the lives of inner-city youth.* New York, NY: State University of New York Press.

Newberg, N., & Sims, R. (1996). Contexts that support success for inner-city students. *Urban Education*, *31*(2), 149–176.

Obradovic, J., & Masten, A. S. (2007). Developmental antecedents of young adult civic engagement. *Applied Developmental Science*, *11*(1), 2–19.

Sherrod, L. R., Flanagan, C., & Youniss, J. (2002). Dimensions of citizenship and opportunities for youth development: The what, why, when, where, and who of citizenship development. *Applied Developmental Science*, *6*(4), 264–272.

Shulman, L. (2009). *Promoting multiple identities.* Conference plenary address delivered at the Mendel Institute. Jerusalem, Israel. Unpublished paper.

Woldoff, R. A. (2002). The effects of local stressors on neighborhood attachment. *Social Forces, 81*(3), 87–116.

Youniss, J., Bales, S., Christmas-Best, V., Diversi, M., McLaughlin, M., & Silbereisen, R. (2002). Youth civic engagement in the twenty-first century. *Journal of Research on Adolescence, 12*(1), 121–148.

Youniss, J., McLellan, J. A., & Yates, M. (1997). What we know about engendering civic identity. *American Behavioral Scientist, 40*(5), 620–631.

Zaff, J. F., Malanchuk, O., & Eccles, J. S. (2008). Predicting positive citizenship from adolescence to young adulthood: The effects of a civic context. *Applied Developmental Science, 12*(1), 38–53.

Social contexts and adolescent school engagement

Ronald D. Taylor

Department of Psychology, Temple University, Philadelphia, PA

In the past nearly 30 years, many strides have been made in understanding the role of contextual factors in children's academic achievement. In research guided by Bronfenbrenner's (1979, 1986) ecological model of interconnected social contexts, a greater understanding of the complexity of mechanisms and processes explaining children's school achievement and psychological well-being has developed. This chapter examines the role of three important ecological contexts—family, classroom, and school—and their association with students' academic achievement and engagement. The conceptual model organizing the chapter is shown in Figure 14.1. Thus, three lines of research in the family literature, including parenting styles, parenting practices, and family social networks, will be examined, and the links to school engagement will be discussed. Adolescents' classroom as an important social environment will be discussed from the perspective of the role of teachers and their behavior, the social and academic climate of the classroom, and students' experiences in ethnically diverse classroom settings. Finally, the school as the larger social and organizational milieu governing students and teachers will be assessed. From the perspective of the school, academic orientation, use of academic tracking, and availability and impact of extracurricular activities will be assessed for their relation to students' achievement and engagement.

Also, in line with Bronfenbrenner's model, the developmental needs and capacities of adolescents have played an increasingly prominent role in the assessment of how social settings, particularly schools, are suited to promote or inhibit youngsters' academic achievement (Eccles & Midgley,

■ **FIGURE 14.1** Family-, classroom-, and school-based links to school engagement.

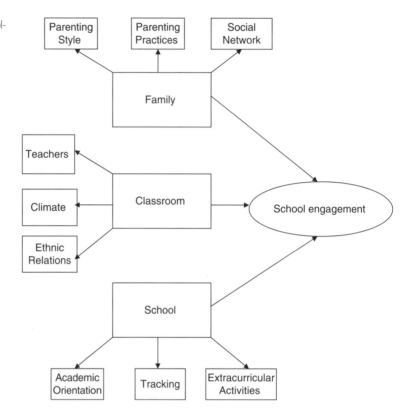

1989; Eccles et al., 1993). Therefore, work on the links between adolescents' developmental needs and adjustment and the nature of social settings will be emphasized. Finally, the academic performance of ethnic minority youngsters, especially the underachievement of some segments of the population, remains a vexing problem. Although continuously growing, the developmental literature on ethnic minority youngsters and families lags behind that of majority families. Thus, to the degree possible, the research on the school engagement of ethnic minority youngsters will be explicitly addressed.

14.1. **FAMILY ENVIRONMENT**

14.1.1. **Parenting styles**

Before youngsters enter school, important noninstructional factors in the home may influence their adjustment in ways that impact their engagement and achievement in the classroom. A substantial body of literature has examined the manner in which parents' socialization and child-rearing practices influence children's psychological adjustment (Baumrind, 1991; Maccoby & Martin, 1983). Much of the literature on parenting and academic achievement has focused on the links between parenting styles and child and adolescent outcomes. According to Darling and Steinberg (1993), parenting style is best characterized as a social contextual variable associated with parents' values and views of the developmental needs of their youngsters. Findings from research on parenting styles have shown that authoritative parenting, a style of parenting characterized by warmth and responsiveness and demandingness, was generally associated with better adjustment and school achievement for children and adolescents (Baumrind, 1991; Dornbusch, Ritter, Liederman, Roberts, & Fraleigh, 1987; Lamborn, Mounts, Steinberg, & Dornbusch, 1991; Steinberg, Dornbusch, & Brown, 1992; Steinberg, Lamborn, Dornbusch, & Darling, 1992; Steinberg, Mounts, Lamborn, & Dornbusch, 1991). When disaggregated across ethnicity, findings have shown that authoritative parenting was more prevalent among European American adolescents than among Asian, African American, or Hispanic adolescents (Dornbusch et al., 1987). Dornbusch et al. have also revealed that for European American adolescents, authoritative parenting was positively associated with school achievement, while authoritarian (high in demandingness, low in responsiveness) and permissive (high in responsiveness, low in demandingness) styles are negatively linked to school performance. For Asian American adolescents, authoritarian parenting was negatively associated with achievement. Among African American and Hispanic adolescents, parenting style was not associated with achievement. Additional work examined the effects of authoritative parenting across ecological niches based on ethnicity, social class, and family structure (e.g., White, working class, intact; Black, middle-class, nonintact; Steinberg et al., 1991). Findings revealed that there were positive effects on achievement and adjustment outcomes across contexts. For European American adolescents in all of the ecological niches considered, those in authoritative homes outperformed those in nonauthoritative homes in achievement. For African American, Asian, and Hispanic adolescents, those in authoritative versus nonauthoritative homes were higher in achievement in 50% (6 of 12) of the ecological contexts examined. Thus, African American adolescents in working-class, nonintact, and middle-class, intact, authoritative homes had higher achievement scores than those in nonauthoritative homes. Hispanic adolescents in middle-class, intact, and nonintact authoritative homes scored higher than those in nonauthoritative homes. Also, Asian adolescents in middle-class, intact, authoritative homes had higher achievement scores than those in nonauthoritative homes. Importantly, beyond achievement, the positive links of authoritative parenting to other aspects of adolescents' psychological adjustment (e.g., self-reliance, psychological distress, delinquency) were prevalent across all groups. Recent findings have shown that Mexican immigrant and Mexican American versus Mexican and Caucasian non-Hispanic mothers and fathers were more authoritarian (e.g., Varela et al., 2004). However, all groups were more authoritative than authoritarian in parenting and, as Darling and Steinberg (1993) note, parenting styles are typically stable and reflect parents' view of their childrens' and adolescents' developmental needs. An important question to be addressed later in the chapter is why the positive effects of authoritative parenting—on youngsters' adjustment and achievement in particular—are not universal for ethnic groups beyond European Americans.

Subsequent research has examined possible mechanisms through which the positive effects of authoritative parenting may be linked to adolescents' school achievement and engagement. Also, other work has assessed potential variables that moderate the association of authoritative parenting with achievement. In rationalizing the potential mediating processes underlying the association of authoritative parenting with better functioning, Durkin (1995) suggests that parents' behavior provides emotional security that promotes well-being, self-reliance and independence, and better school performance. He also suggests that authoritative parents' inclination to provide explanations and rationales for their decisions promotes adolescents awareness of their parents' values and aims. Adolescents' awareness and adoption of their parents' goals in turn has positive implications for their achievement. Finally, Durkin (1995) argues that the interpersonal skills and relations and school achievement of children of authoritative parents benefit from the joint (as opposed to unilateral) style of communication and decision-making characteristic of their homes. According to Durkin's discussion, mediating processes may exist in the realm of parents' values and behavior, adolescents' psychosocial functioning, or both domains.

Other findings have shown that parental involvement in schooling partially mediates the association of authoritative parenting with achievement (Steinberg, Lamborn, et al., 1992). Adolescents raised in authoritative homes were more likely to have parents who were more encouraging and involved in their schooling. Parenting involvement and encouragement in turn were positively associated with achievement. Other findings on mediating processes revealed that authoritative parenting was positively associated with adolescents' work orientation, which in turn was significantly related to school performance (Steinberg, Elmen, & Mounts, 1989). Also, Chao (2001) found that authoritative parenting promotes emotional closeness between adolescents and their parents, which in turn is associated with school performance. Additional research examined the possibility that the degree of authoritativeness experienced in the home may engender atttributional styles that either promote or inhibit school achievement. Results revealed that adolescents from nonauthoritative homes were more likely to make dysfunctional attributions (e.g., external causes, low ability) for achievement outcomes. Dysfunctional attributions in turn were associated with lower levels of classroom engagement and homework completion 1 year later (Glasgow, Dornbusch, Ritter, Troyer, & Steinberg, 1997).

In research on potential variables moderating the association of parenting styles with school achievement, ethnicity and community effects have been the primary focus of attention. Ethnicity has been a focus because, as noted earlier, authoritative parenting has not been shown to have the strong impact on the school achievement and adjustment of African American, Asian, or Hispanic adolescents that it does for European American youngsters (Dornbusch et al., 1987; Spera, 2005; Steinberg, Lamborn, et al., 1992). It has been suggested that the difference in the pattern of relations lies in differences in the qualities of ethnic groups' communities, differences in exposure to risks, access to resources, and cultural values and traditions (for a review see Spera, 2005). Empirical research examining the moderating effects of ethnicity and community composition has revealed that the positive effects of joint parent-adolescent decision making (a component of authoritative parenting) on adolescent functioning, including school competence, was apparent for European, Asian, and Hispanic American adolescents but not African American youngsters. Also, unilateral parental decision making (associated with authoritarian parenting) was positively associated with the adjustment (e.g., higher school competence and lower deviance) of African American youngsters living in predominantly white neighborhoods and unrelated to the functioning of Asian American and Hispanic American youth living in White or ethnically mixed neighborhoods (Lamborn et al., 1996). As Lamborn et al. note, the findings cast doubt on the supposition that authoritarian parenting practices among ethnic minority parents represent adaptive behaviors stemming from the dangers of living in ethnically isolated, risky neighborhoods (Baldwin, Baldwin, & Cole, 1990; Baumrind, 1991; Bronfenbrenner, 1986; Ogbu, 1985). However, it is possible that the restrictive parenting of African American parents across social contexts serves to protect their youngsters from potential risks involving racial and ethnic discrimination.

Research suggests that cultural forces and factors may in part explain the differences in the links between parenting styles and achievement for ethnic minority and European American children. Chao (1994, 2000, 2001) has argued that among Asian families, parents may engage in a style of parenting that is only partially captured in measures of parenting in the literature. Among Chinese families, parents typically engage in *chiao shun*, or training, "a disciplined style of teaching and inculcating children." *Chiao shun* involves intense familial investment in training children to be self-disciplined and hard working. Parents' concern and support is expressed through family-based control and parental involvement aimed at promoting obedience, excelling at school, and honoring the family. In empirical research, Chao (1994, 2001) has shown that Chinese mothers scored higher than European American mothers on measures of the training style of parenting. In other research, first- and second-generation Chinese youngsters reported experiencing a higher proportion of authoritarian parenting than did European American adolescents and also reported higher effort at school and higher grades (Chao, 2001). In relevant findings, Leung, Lau, and Lam (1998) found that authoritarian parenting was positively associated with academic achievement in Hong Kong and negatively related to school performance in the United States, Australia, and China. It is important to note that parents' education level moderates the association of country of origin, parenting style, and achievement, in that for parents with lower education in the United States and Australia, authoritarian parenting was positively associated with achievement.

Similar findings implicating cultural factors as potential reasons for the discrepant results for parenting style have been obtained for African American adolescents. Specifically, Mandara (Mandara, 2006; Mandara & Murray, 2002) suggests that for African American families, authoritative parenting has some elements of authoritarian parenting in that African American authoritative parents (distinguished from authoritarian parents in cluster analyses) tend to be "more demanding and less acquiescent to children's demands" than authoritative European American parents. African American boys raised in such families had higher self-esteem and self-control and were more generally well adjusted. Similarly, Gorman-Smith, Tolan, and Henry (2000) found that African American families with parents displaying the essential elements of authoritative parenting and greater control had adolescents with more positive views about schooling and fewer behavioral or emotional problems. Mandara's (2006) conceptualization of African American authoritative parenting appears similar to Brody and Flor's (1997) description of "no nonsense" parenting characteristic of rural African American parents in their research. No nonsense parenting combines high levels of parental control with warmth and affection. No nonsense parenting is aimed at preventing problem behavior and communicating parents' care, concern, and support. These findings highlight the fact that complex conceptual and methodological issues are challenges to be considered and addressed in research on parenting styles and achievement and engagement. Cultural values and structural factors are likely to shape parents' child-rearing practices in ways that have significant implications for adolescents' school achievement and engagement.

14.1.2. **Parenting practices**

According to Darling and Steinberg (1993), parenting practices are the behaviors through which parents' parenting goals and values and parenting style are linked to adolescents' academic outcomes. In this section, sets of parenting practices and the links to engagement and achievement will be considered.

Research has shown that the common domains of parenting practices, including emotional support, control and monitoring, and organization and routine, are positively associated with child and adolescent functioning (Amato & Fowler, 2002; Clark, 1983; McLoyd, Toyokawa, & Kaplan, in press; Taylor, 1996; Taylor & Lopez, 2005). Findings have shown that parents' emotional support was positively associated with adolescents' adjustment and academic performance (Gray & Steinberg, 1999; Gunnoe, Hetherington, & Reiss, 1999; Jackson, Henriksen, & Foshee, 1998; Kurdek & Fine, 1994). For example, Kurdek and Fine found that parental acceptance was positively associated with adolescents' psychosocial competence, including their school achievement. Similarly, Amato and Fowler found that support and acceptance were positively associated with adolescents' grades. Additionally, research has shown that parents' support is significantly associated with aspects of adolescents' adjustment and emotional well-being that are linked to school achievement and engagement. Thus, findings have revealed that emotional support is negatively associated with adolescents' psychological distress (Barber et al., 2005; Eccles, Early, Frasier, Belansky, & McCarthy, 1997), which is linked to their school engagement and performance.

Generally, research has shown that the positive association of parents' emotional support with achievement and adjustment does not vary across youngsters of different ethnic backgrounds. Amato and Fowler (2002) found, in examining White, Black, Mexican American, and other Hispanics, that support was positively associated with grades regardless of adolescents' ethnicity. Kerpelman, Eryigit, and Stephen (2008) found that mothers' support was significantly associated with African American adolescents' future orientation regarding their education. Also, among Mexican American adolescents, parental support was negatively associated with antisocial conduct (Davalos, Chavez, & Guardiola, 2005; Manongdo & Ramirez Garcia, 2007).

In the domain of behavioral control, which involves the provision of supervision, monitoring, and healthy restriction of behavior, findings have revealed positive links to adolescents' achievement and psychological functioning (Amato & Fowler, 2002; Bean, Barber, & Crane, 2006). As Amato and Fowler note, children and adolescents appear to function more adequately when their parents monitor their "behavior and expect them to follow rules." Indeed, research revealed that behavioral control was negatively associated with problem behavior (Bean et al., 2004; Bradford et al., 2003). Like the area of parental support, the association of behavioral control with better functioning appears to transcend ethnicity. Findings revealed that behavioral control was significantly associated with more positive values regarding school among African American adolescents (Pollock & Lamborn, 2006). Also, across European, African, and Mexican American adolescents, control and monitoring were negatively associated with deviance (Amato & Fowler, 2002). In addition, Mason, Cauce, Gonzales, and Hiraga (1996) found African American adolescents functioned best in terms of avoiding problem behavior when their mothers moderated their control and monitoring to match the quality of their youngster's peers (e.g., positive peers, less maternal control; negative peers, more maternal control).

The third domain of parenting reviewed here is that of organization and routine. Organization, structure, and routine have received comparatively less attention in the literature than support or control. Parental organization involves the provision of structure, routine, and regularity in the home. Family organization and routine create order and coherence in family life (Boyce, Jensen, James, & Peacock, 1983). Findings have revealed that organization and routine were positively associated with academic performance and school attendance (Guidubaldi, Cleminshaw, Perry, Nastasi, & Lightel, 1986). Clark (1983) found that family routine and organization were also characteristics of family life that distinguished high- and low-achieving, economically disadvantaged African American adolescents. Also, Taylor and Lopez (2005) found that family routine was positively associated with school achievement and engagement and negatively related to problem behavior among African American adolescents. Research has also shown that family routine and organization are linked to adolescents' functioning in areas that are relevant to school achievement and engagement. Thus, findings revealed that family routine was positively associated with the constructive use of time (i.e., reading, creative activities, etc.) among adolescents in mother-only households (Larson, Dworkin, & Gillman, 2001). Also, family routine was negatively associated with the externalizing and internalizing problems of African American preteens (McLoyd et al., in press). Additional evidence revealed that family routine moderated the negative effects of cumulative stressors (i.e., maternal distress, perceived financial strain, neighborhood problems) on externalizing behavior among Latino adolescent females (Loukas & Prelow, 2004).

Interestingly, research has shown that the general domains of parenting are linked to other parenting practices relevant to adolescents' school performance. Thus, Taylor (1996) found that family organization was positively associated with parental involvement in schooling. Parental involvement in schooling is an additional parenting variable that has been linked to adolescents' school engagement and achievement. Parental involvement considered here consists of either direct involvement through stimulating and helping, teaching or coaching, or through meeting and consulting with teachers regarding a youngster's achievement. Findings have revealed that stimulation of learning was associated with greater language competence and higher achievement test performance across age and ethnicity (Bradley, Corwyn, Burchnal, Pipes McAdoo, & Garcia Coll, 2001). Other research has shown that parents who engaged in more discussion concerning academic matters with their adolescents had teens who perceived themselves as more academically capable in 6th grade and had higher grades in 9th grade (Juang & Silbereisen, 2002). In contrast, findings have shown that over time, the less that parents and adolescents consulted about adolescents' schooling, the fewer math or science credits adolescents accumulated (Crosnoe & Huston, 2007). Math or science course taking is important because credits in these areas potentially influence future college entrance and academic and employment options. In terms of how parents' behavior and interactions in the school relate to students' academic performance, evidence has revealed positive links to achievement and engagement (Epstein & Becker, 1982; Fan, 2001; Grolnick & Slowiaczek, 1994). For example, Grolnick and Slowiaczek found that both mother's and father's involvement (e.g., parent-teacher conferences, participation in school events) was significantly associated with an adolescent's grades and academic competence. Also, Taylor found that both direct assistance and involvement through interactions in school were significantly associated with school achievement and engagement. Finally, collectively, and with a few notable exceptions (Ardelt & Eccles, 2001; Fan, 2001), results have shown that the positive links of parental involvement in school with achievement and engagement tend to transcend ethnicity (Jeynes, 2007).

It is important to note that reported findings on the impact of family relations (parenting styles, parenting practices) on education outcomes reflect the social contexts in which they occur (Bronfenbrenner, 1986). The association of parenting styles and practices and adolescents' achievement and adjustment may be mediated and moderated by social systems, including families' neighborhood and social support networks. Thus, Ceballo and McLoyd (2002) found that in neighborhoods characterized by low crime and high community involvement, parental support was higher and was enhanced by social support. In contrast, in lower quality neighborhoods (e.g., those with high crime and poverty, low involvement), parental nurturance was lower and was not enhanced by social support. Results also revealed that perceived neighborhood stress was positively associated with mothers' psychological distress, which in turn was linked to poorer parenting (Kotchick, Dorsey, & Heller, 2005). Also, findings have revealed that the positive association of social support and parental monitoring was more evident in neighborhoods perceived as dangerous (Jones, Forehand, O'Connell, Armistead, & Brody, 2005). Other research has shown that kin social support was positively associated with a mother's parenting (support and organization), which in turn was significantly linked to adolescent's achievement and engagement (Taylor, 1996; Taylor & Lopez, 2005; Taylor, Seaton, & Dominguez, 2008).

14.2. **CLASSROOM ENVIRONMENT**

14.2.1. **Teachers**

Beyond the home, adolescents spend a substantial amount of time in school with their peers and teachers. The following section examines the impact of teacher efficacy and expectations, classroom climate, and social and interpersonal relations on student achievement and engagement. Eccles et al. (1993) have noted that adolescents' beliefs about their academic abilities are significantly influenced by the beliefs of parents and teachers. For example, Midgley, Feldlaufer, and Eccles (1989) found that teacher effectiveness or efficacy had a significant association with students' academic self-perceptions. Students with low-efficacy teachers had lower perceptions of their math skills than those with high-efficacy teachers; the more that teachers had confidence in their abilities, the more likely students were to be confident in their own capacities and engaged in school (Aston, 1985). In contrast, evidence has shown that low teacher efficacy has been linked to lower student competence and disengagement from school (Lee & Smith, 2001). Eccles (2004) suggests that teachers with lower confidence in their teaching abilities may undermine students' school achievement and motivation by reinforcing "feelings of incompetence and alienation," thereby promoting emotional distress and "disengagement." Darling-Hammond (1997) has found that teacher quality variables are stronger predictors of student achievement than student demographic characteristics, which are themselves strong predictors of performance. Several scholars have noted that the preponderance of teachers with a low sense of teaching efficacy tends to serve schools with higher proportions of ethnic minority and low-income students (Darling-Hammond, 1997; Eccles, Wigfield, & Scheiefele, 1998).

In addition to the quality of teaching to which they are exposed, students are also met with the differing expectations teachers may have for their achievement. The work on teacher expectancy effects has sought to explain how teachers' high and low expectations for students are translated into differential classroom experiences and perceptions for students (Brophy, 1986; Eccles, 2004; Eccles & Wigfield, 1985; Rosenthal, 1969). Much of the work on teacher expectancy effects has focused on the potential role of expectancy effects in undermining the achievement of girls, ethnic minorities, or economically disadvantaged students. Thus, teachers' perceptions may create self-fulfilling prophecies that may operate through the quality and nature of the instructional practices and behaviors to which girls, ethnic minorities, and the poor are exposed. However, findings have shown that teachers' expectations affect students' achievements more because they are accurate than because they are self-fulfilling prophecies (Jussim, Eccles, & Madon, 1996). Thus, teachers' expectations tend to be an accurate reflection of students' past performance. Jussim et al. also note that expectancy effects tend to be relatively smaller than previously believed. However, they tend to be relatively stronger among African American students, girls, and poorer students. Jussim et al. reasoned that girls, African American, and poor students, given their greater likelihood of negative experiences in school, may have fewer "social and psychological resources for combating erroneous teacher expectations." They also speculate that for African American students and possibly girls and lower class students, stereotype threat (Steele, 1997) may be one factor that diminishes students' resources for resisting expectancy effects. Stereotype threat represents students' awareness that teachers and other adults may have negative views regarding their capacity for school work. According to Steele, this awareness may lead youngsters to disidentify with school in order to avoid stress and anxiety associated with school work.

14.2.2. **Climate**

The classroom climate, like the child-rearing environment created by parents, can be characterized in terms of key social and psychological dimensions, including support, control, and organization. Each of these aspects of school climate has been linked to students' engagement and achievement. For example, Roeser, Midgley, and Urdan (1996) found that supportive positive relations with teachers were positively linked to students' feeling of school belonging and, in turn, school belonging was positively associated with students' grades. Roeser et al. suggest that positive relations with teachers may promote adolescents' emotional security, which in turn may facilitate the development of academic competence and resilience. Also, Goodenow (1993) found that teacher support was positively associated with students' motivation. In addition, results have shown that decreases in adolescents' perceptions of teacher support have been associated with problems in students' adjustment (e.g., increased problem behavior and depression, decreased self-esteem; Way, Reddy, & Rhode, 2007).

In the area of classroom organization and structure, findings have shown that orderliness and routine were positively linked to students' engagement and achievement (Patrick, Turner, Meyer, & Midgley, 2003). These findings are similar to those reported earlier, revealing the importance of order and routine in the family for adolescents' functioning. Eccles (2004) has noted that student achievement is enhanced when teachers "establish smoothly running and efficient procedures" for managing assignments and organizing classroom work. Similarly, other research has shown that teachers' support and effective management of the classroom were factors which were positively associated with students' engagement and achievement (Walker, 2008). Walker found that teachers in classrooms who combined elements of authoritative parenting in their teaching style (e.g., emotional support, firm classroom management and structure, support for autonomy) had students who were the most academically and socially competent. Also, work has shown that by socializing students with respect to the organization and management of the classroom during the initial weeks of the school year, teachers were more likely to have students who were more engaged in the classroom and spent less time in off-task behavior (Emmer, Evertson, & Anderson, 1980; Evertson & Emmer, 1982).

In the area of control, research has examined how teachers manage the complex task of supporting adolescents' growing autonomy needs while also maintaining order and structure in the classroom. Findings have shown that students were more inclined to be engaged in their school work in classrooms in which autonomy and responsibility were promoted (McCaslin & Good, 1992; Patrick et al., 2003). For example, Patrick et al. found that teachers in supportive versus nonsupportive classrooms created environments in which students were expected to behave with maturity, self-control, and responsibility. Nonsupportive classrooms were characterized by a high degree of teacher control and little promotion of the development of student responsibility. Across race, class, and gender, students in supportive environments tended to be more engaged in their school work, while those in nonsupportive classrooms engaged in significantly more avoidance of their tasks. Similarly, McCaslin and Good argue that modern curricula in which autonomy, self-direction, and problem solving are stressed are significantly hampered by classroom management practices in which strict compliance and unquestioned obedience are expected.

Researchers have also examined the instructional/motivational climate of classrooms and the link to students' engagement. An important conceptual model for this work has been goal theory. Researchers interested in goal theory have identified two major goals into which teachers' practices in the classroom may fall. Teachers structuring their classroom practices under mastery-oriented goals stress learning and personal improvement, the development of effective problem solving, and task understanding. Those teachers stressing performance-oriented goals emphasize meeting external expectations and standards and comparative performance. Mastery-focused practices have consistently been associated with positive student outcomes, including engagement and achievement. For example, mastery goals have been linked to a variety of factors associated with school engagement, including time on task, persistence in the face of difficulty, search for effective problem-solving strategies, and enjoyment in learning (see Ames, 1992, for a review). Findings for performance goals have been mixed, with some evidence revealing significant links to avoidance behavior (Turner, Meyer, Midgley, & Patrick, 2003; Urdan, Midgley, & Anderson, 1998). Also, Midgley and Urdan (1995) found that students' perceptions that classrooms employed performance goals were associated with self-handicapping behaviors that diminished school engagement. Other research has revealed significant links to positive outcomes, including student affect (Ryan & Patrick, 2001) and engagement and academic progress (Bohn, Roehrig, & Pressley, 2004). Additional work has added to the understanding of the effects of mastery and performance goals by considering their effects in combination with individuals' desire to achieve, including their orientation to approach success or avoid failure (Elliot & Church, 1997; Midgley, Kaplan, & Middleton, 2001). Thus, performance-approach orientation (i.e., competitive classroom-achievement-oriented students) has been linked to positive academic outcomes (Witkow & Fuligni, 2007). Finally, few studies have examined ethnic group differences in goal orientation, and those few that have, have obtained mixed findings. For example, Elliot, Chirkov, Kim, and Sheldon

(2001) found that Asian students tended to have more avoidance goals than European American students. Also, Witkow and Fuligni found that Asian students had more performance-approach goals than either Latino or European American students. Also, the effects of goal orientation on achievement were similar across ethnic groups. For example, Midgley et al. found that the impact of performance-approach goals on achievement were similar for African American and European American adolescents. Also, Witkow and Fuligni found that the positive association of performance-approach and mastery-approach goals on achievement did not vary across Asian, Latino, or European American students.

14.2.3. Ethnic group relations

A growing body of recent research has also examined the links between students' ethnic group relations and their school engagement and achievement. School engagement and achievement may be more challenging for youngsters in the context of ethnic strife or hostility, and the formation of ethnic identity may represent an important developmental challenge. Given the growth in the ethnic diversity of the country and the changing distribution of the population, the need to understand intergroup relations will become ever more important. Research has shown that the more that adolescents anticipated that discrimination would impact their future social and economic opportunities, the less engaged they were in school (Fordham & Ogbu, 1986; Taylor, Casten, Flickinger, Roberts, & Fulmore, 1994). For example, Taylor and associates found that the more that African American adolescents perceived that a discriminatory job ceiling would limit their employment opportunities, the less importance they attached to schooling. Findings have also shown that racial discrimination from peers and teachers in daily experiences was associated with declines in school achievement and psychosocial adjustment (Wong, Eccles, & Sameroff, 2003). Wong and associates found that the more African American adolescents reported discrimination from peers and teachers, the less importance and value they attached to academic achievement, and the more they reported engaging in problem behavior. However, the *anticipation* of discrimination in the future was associated with increases in school engagement and achievement. Also, Brody et al. (2006) found that perceived discrimination was significantly associated with conduct problems and depressive symptoms. They also found, importantly, that this association was weaker for students who performed well in school. Research has also shown that discrimination in the classroom was negatively associated with the school achievement of African American boys for whom race was not central to their identity (Chavous, Rivas-Drake,

Smalls, Griffin, & Cogburn, 2008). Findings have also revealed the negative association of discrimination with the psychological adjustment of Asian and Latino students (e.g., Greene, Way, & Pahl, 2006; Rivas-Drake, Hughes, & Way, 2008). For example, Rivas-Drake et al. found that peer discrimination was significantly associated with Asian adolescents' self-esteem and depressive symptoms.

14.3. **SCHOOL ENVIRONMENT**

14.3.1. **Academic orientation**

With the advent and proliferation of charter schools there is renewed reason to be interested in the overarching mission and aims of schools and their translation in schools' academic and social climates. Classrooms and teachers exist within the larger structure of the school and function within the structure and organization of school-level practices and policies. Maehr and Midgley and their colleagues have shown that school-level focus regarding achievement has implications for students' achievement, engagement, and emotional well-being (Eccles & Roeser, 2003; Maehr & Midgley, 1996; Roeser et al., 1996). For instance, schools which stress achievement through competition, social comparison, and recognition of relative ability create a school-level environment that is ability focused. In contrast, schools in which learning and discovery, effort, and improvement are stressed create a school-level climate that is mastery focused. Findings have shown that an ability-focused school environment was linked to a decline in student achievement, engagement, and self-esteem and an increase in student's psychological distress (Roeser & Eccles, 1998; Roeser, Eccles, & Sameroff, 1998). Eccles and Roeser note that while an ability-focused school environment may serve the needs of higher ability students, the significant number of students who perform at lower levels may be at increased risk of alienation and distress. School-level emphasis on mastery, in comparison, appears to promote the achievement and engagement of a larger segment of students and is associated with lower distress, anxiety, and frustration. Also, students in mastery-oriented schools were more likely to perceive that their teachers are socially and emotionally supportive, which in turn was linked to students' school attachment (Eccles & Roeser, 2003). School-level emotional support is another aspect of school environment that has been linked to school achievement and engagement. Stewart (2008) found that school cohesion was a significant predictor of academic achievement. Similarly, Way et al. (2007) found that decreases in teacher and peer support were linked to declines in adolescent psychological and behavioral adjustment. Also, findings have shown that school climate (including, among other factors, school cohesiveness and friction) was significantly associated with adolescents' school connectedness, which in turn was linked to students' conduct problems (Loukas, Suzuki, & Horton, 2006). Thus, the more students perceived that their school was positive and supportive, the more connected and engaged they were in school, and the less likely they were to engage in problem behavior.

14.3.2. **Tracking**

Tracking involves the practice of grouping students in classes based upon their ability level. For adolescents in secondary school, between-class tracking is common and involves the organizational sequencing of classes based upon expected trajectories of post-secondary placement (e.g., college preparatory, general, and vocational tracks). Students in separate tracks are exposed to different curricula and instruction and different teachers and peers (Eccles, 2004). The impact of tracking on student engagement and achievement is mixed and complex (Eccles, 2004; Fuligni, Eccles, & Barber, 1995; Gamoran & Mare, 1989). According to Eccles, the impact of tracking depends on, among other factors, the outcome assessed, the duration of the investigation, and the group considered. In terms of general conclusions, it appears that there are some advantages that accrue to being in high within-class ability groups and in college preparatory tracks (Fuligni et al., 1995; Gamoran & Mare, 1989). For example, Gamoran and Mare obtained findings that revealed that: tracking attenuated initial differences between students assigned to college and noncollege tracks; lower- compared to higher SES students were more likely to be placed in lower tracks, and tracking widened the achievement gap between high- and low-SES students; average rates of achievement and graduation favored college track over noncollege track students. For students placed in low-ability or noncollege tracks, lower engagement and achievement were more likely and there was a greater likelihood of problem behavior (Eccles, 2004; Oakes, Gamoran, & Page, 1992). Eccles notes that the negative impact of tracking on school engagement and conduct problems is mediated by differences in the educational experiences associated with tracking. Thus, students placed in lower tracks are likely to receive lower quality instruction and support. They are also more likely to be grouped with students who, because of academic and adjustment histories, are more challenging for teachers. These differences in the characteristics of the students make the assignment to lower track classes less desirable for teachers.

Finally, a number of researchers have noted that tracking may disproportionately impact the school experiences of ethnic minority youth (Eccles,

2004; Oakes et al., 1992; Swanson, Cunningham, & Spencer, 2003). Thus, early placement in lower tracks in a child's academic career may place minority youngsters, especially African American and Latino American males, on trajectories that limit their educational experiences and opportunities in secondary school and beyond (see Eccles, 2004; also Swanson et al., 2003). Dornbusch (1994) also reported several troubling findings regarding tracking and its impact on the schooling of ethnic minority adolescents. Dornbusch found there was little movement between tracks in high school, with approximately 85% of students remaining in the same track across the time period. Dornbusch also found that many average students, particularly average ethnic minority students, were incorrectly assigned to lower track courses. Importantly, the sequence of courses in the lower tracks placed students off track in meeting state higher educational system admission requirements.

14.3.3. **Extracurricular activities**

Schools sponsor activities, including clubs and sports, which help form the school's identity among its students and the larger community, potentially impacting adolescents' school engagement and achievement. Indeed, in many schools, maintaining attendance, good conduct, and adequate grades may be requirements for participation in extracurricular activities. Mahoney, Cairns, and Farmer (2003) have argued that participation in extracurricular activities requires a commitment of time and exertion of effort that by its nature is likely to deepen adolescents' attachment to and engagement in school. Also, Eccles (2004) has noted that after-school extracurricular activities may also provide adolescents with structured opportunities. These activities may prevent high-risk behaviors, which are more likely when adolescents have unstructured time to fill.

Research has revealed that there is a positive association between participation in extracurricular activities and educational outcomes and adolescent social adjustment for males and females. For example, results have shown that participation in prosocial activities (e.g., sports and performing arts activities) was positively associated with the amount of education completed—high school and beyond (Barber, Eccles, & Stone, 2001). Similarly, consistent participation in extracurricular activities throughout high school was associated with adolescents' educational aspirations during the 12th grade and their college attendance (Mahoney et al., 2003). Darling (2005) also found a positive link between participation in extracurricular activities and educational outcomes, including grades, school engagement, and academic aspirations. In terms of social and emotional adjustment, participation in prosocial activities was associated with higher self-esteem and lower social isolation (Barber et al., 2001). Also, participation in extracurricular activities was significantly associated with adolescents' interpersonal competence (e.g., avoidance of problem behavior, popularity).

Recent research has shown that the positive effects of participation in activities are more apparent the longer adolescents are involved (Gardner, Roth, & Brookes-Gunn, 2008) and are apparent whether schools or other organizations serve as sponsors. Finally, it is important to note that along with positive outcomes for participation in extracurricular activities, research has shown links to some problem behaviors (misbehavior in school, drug and alcohol use). Eccles (2004) has noted that participation in extracurricular activities places adolescents in greater social contact with groups or clusters of peers. Peer crowds may have shared values with which adolescents identify. The norms and values of some groups may be linked to risky behaviors (drug or alcohol use) that endanger youngsters' adjustment.

14.4. **CONCLUSION**

Research on the social contexts that are linked to adolescents' school achievement has grown substantially in recent years. Social contexts, including the family, classroom, and school, were examined in this chapter. In the family, the authoritative style of parenting (e.g., parenting combining warmth, responsiveness, and demandingness) has been shown to have positive links to adolescents' school achievement and engagement for European and to a less extent African, Asian, and Latino American youngsters. In authoritative homes, parents may enhance adolescents' academic competence and engagement through their responsive, engaging communicative style and their efforts to emphasize the value and importance of developing academic skills. For ethnic minority families the weaker link between authoritative parenting and school performance may exist because parents engage in alternative styles of parenting which are shaped by cultural values and social forces (e.g., economic disadvantage and racial discrimination) prevalent in the social environments they occupy.

Research on parenting practices, the behaviors through which parents convey their values or parenting style, has shown that parental emotional support, control, and monitoring are positively linked to school engagement. Also, the creation and maintenance of order and structure in the home and parental involvement in schooling have also been linked to adolescents' school achievement and engagement. Finally, parents are more likely to engage in more adequate parenting (support, control, organization) when they live in higher quality neighborhoods (e.g., low crime and poverty, high community involvement) and when the family has access to supportive social networks.

Research on the association of factors in the classroom with students' engagement has revealed that teachers' effectiveness is significantly associated with students' competence and engagement. Also, teachers' expectations for student achievement have a significant link to performance and engagement and are more prone to be erroneous and undermine the achievement of ethnic minority, female, and low-socioeconomic-status students. Research on the social climate of classrooms has revealed patterns of findings that mirror the findings on family environment. Emotionally supportive classrooms, in which teachers control and monitor behavior effectively and maintain order and routine, tend to have students who are more competent and engaged in school. Also, classrooms that are mastery-oriented and that stress learning and personal growth, compared to those which are performance-oriented and stress external standards and comparative evaluation, tend to have the most positive outcomes for student achievement and engagement. Findings on the impact of ethnic group relations in schools further reveal that the more that African American students perceived the existence of a racially discriminatory job ceiling and the more they had experienced racial discrimination, the lower their school engagement. However, the more that adolescents reported anticipating discrimination in the future, the higher their school engagement.

Research linking school-level variables to student engagement has shown that schools stressing competition and comparison (ability-focus) compared to those stressing learning discovery and effort (mastery-focus) may enhance the engagement of high-ability students and undermine the engagement of those who perform at acceptable but lower levels. Also, school-level focus that stresses the importance of students' emotional well-being being and support has been associated with school achievement and engagement.

Tracking as a school-wide process involves the practice of grouping students in classrooms according to their ability level. Research suggests that tracking tends to attenuate differences between students and benefits those in college compared to noncollege preparatory tracks. Differences in achievement and engagement appear to be at least partially explained by differences in the quality of teaching students experience, favoring those in college tracks. Also, tracking appears to disproportionately impact the school performance and engagement of ethnic minority adolescents.

Finally, the provision of extracurricular activities in schools (sports, clubs, school-sponsored activities) may deepen adolescents' attachment and engagement in school. Indeed, findings have revealed that adolescents' engagement in school and the completion of schooling beyond high school have been associated with participation in extracurricular activities. It is also important to note that there are potential negative outcomes that are residual effects of extracurricular activities. Because activities bring adolescents in greater contact with groups or clusters of peers, the potential for exposure to individuals engaging in risky behavior also increases.

REFERENCES

Amato, P. R., & Fowler, F. (2002). Parenting practices, child adjustment, and family diversity. *Journal of Marriage and Family, 64,* 703–716.

Ames, C. (1992). Goals, structures, and student motivation. *Journal of Educational Psychology, 84,* 261–271.

Ardelt, M., & Eccles, J. (2001). Effects of mothers' parental efficacy beliefs and promotive parenting strategies on inner-city youth. *Journal of Family Issues, 22,* 944–972.

Aston, P. T. (1985). Motivation and teacher's sense of efficacy. In C. Ames & R. Ames (Eds.), *Research on motivation in education* (Vol. 2). Orlando, FL: Academic Press.

Baldwin, A., Baldwin, C., & Cole, R. E. (1990). Stress-resistant families and stress-resistant children. In J. J. Rolf, A. S. Masten, D. Ciccetti, & S. Weintraub (Eds.), *Risk and protective factors in the development of psychopathology* (pp. 257–280). Cambridge, UK: Cambridge University Press.

Barber, B. L., Eccles, J. S., & Stone, M. R. (2001). Whatever happened to the Jock, the Brain and the Princess? Young adult pathways linked to adolescent activity involvement and social identity. *Journal of Adolescent Research, 16,* 429–455.

Barber, B. L., Stolz, H. E., Olsen, J. A. (2005). Parental support psychological control and behavioral control: Assessing relevance across time, culture, and method. In *Monographs of the Society of Research in Child Development* (Series 282, Vol. 20), Willis F. Overton (Ed): Boston, MA: Blackwell Publishing.

Baumrind, D. (1991). The influence of parenting style on adolescent competence and substance use. *Journal of Early Adolescence, 11,* 56–95.

Bean, R. K., Bush, K. R., McHenry, P. C., & Wilson, S. M. (2003). The impact of parental support, behavioral control, and psychological control on the academic achievement and self-esteem of African American and European American adolescents. *Journal of Adolescent Research, 18,* 523–541.

Bean, R. A., Barber, B. K., & Crane, R. D. (2006). Parental support, behavioral control, and psychological control among African American youth. *Journal of Family Issues, 27,* 133–1355.

Bohn, C. M., Roehrig, A. D., & Pressley, M. (2004). The first days of school in the classrooms oftwo more effective and four less effective primary-grades teachers. *Elementary School Journal, 104,* 269–287.

Boyce, W. T., Jensen, E. W., James, S. A., & Peacock, J. L. (1983). The family routines inventory: Theoretical origins. *Social Science and Medicine, 17,* 193–200.

Bradford, K., Barber, B. K., Olsen, J. A., Maughan, S. L., Erickson, L. D., Ward, D., et al. (2003). A multi-national study of interparental conflict, parenting, and adolescent functioning: South Africa, Bangladesh, China, India, Bosnia, Germany, Palestine, Colombia, and the United States. *Marriage and Family Review, 35,* 107–136.

Bradley, R. H., Corwyn, R. R., Burchinal, M. R., Pipes McAdoo, H., & Garcia Coll, C. (2001). The home environments of children in the United States Part II: Relations with behavioral development through age thirteen. *Child Development, 72*, 1868–1886.

Brody, G. H., Chen, Y., Murray, V. M., Simons, R. L., Ge, X., Gibbons, F. X., et al. (2006). Perceived discrimination and the adjustment of African American youths: A five-year longitudinal analysis with contextual moderation effects. *Child Development, 77*, 1170–1189.

Brody, G. H., & Flor, D. L. (1997). Maternal psychological functioning, family processes, and child adjustment in rural, single-parent African American families. *Developmental Psychology, 33*, 1000–1010.

Bronfenbrenner, U. (1979). *The ecology of human development.* Cambridge, MA: Harvard University Press.

Bronfenbrenner, U. (1986). Ecology of the family as a context for human development: Research perspectives. *Developmental Psychology, 22*, 723–742.

Brophy, J. (1986). Teacher influences on academic achievement. *American Psychologist, 41*, 1069–1077.

Ceballo, R., & McLoyd, V. C. (2002). Social support and parenting in poor, dangerous neighborhoods. *Child Development, 73*, 1310–1321.

Chao, R. (2001). Extending research on the consequences of parenting style for Chinese Americans and European Americans. *Child Development, 72*, 1832–1843.

Chao, R. K. (1994). Beyond parental control and authoritarian parenting style: Understanding Chinese parenting through the cultural notion of training. *Child Development, 65*, 1111–1119.

Chao, R. K. (2000). The parenting of immigrant Chinese and European American mothers: Relations between parenting styles, socialization goals, and parental practices. *Journal of Applied Developmental Psychology, 21*, 233–249.

Chavous, T. M., Rivas-Drake, D., Smalls, C., Griffin, T., & Cogburn, T. (2008). Gender matters, too: The influences of school discrimination and racial identity on academic engagement among African American adolescent boys and girls. *Developmental Psychology, 44*, 637–654.

Clark, R. M. (1983). *Family life and school achievement: Why poor children succeed or fail.* Chicago, IL: University of Chicago Press.

Crosnoe, R., & Huston, A. (2007). Socioeconomic status, schooling, and the developmental trajectories of adolescents. *Developmental Psychology, 43*, 1097–1110.

Darling-Hammond, L. (1997). *Doing what matters most: Investing in quality teaching.* New York, NY: National Commission on Teaching and America's Future.

Darling, N. (2005). Participation in *extracurricular activities* and adolescent adjustment: Cross-sectional and longitudinal findings. *Journal of Youth and Adolescence, 34*, 493–505.

Darling, N., & Steinberg, L. (1993). Parenting style as context: An integrative model. *Psychological Bulletin, 113*, 487–496.

Davalos, D. B., Chavez, E. L., & Guardiola, R. J. (2005). Effects of perceived parental school support and family communication on delinquent behaviors in Latinos and white non-Latinos. *Cultural Diversity and Ethnic Minority Psychology, 11*, 57–68.

Dornbusch, S. M. (1994). *Off the track.* Presidential address at the biennial meeting of the Society for Research on Adolescence, San Diego, CA.

Dornbusch, S. M., Ritter, P. L., Liederman, P. H., Roberts, D. F., & Fraleigh, M. J. (1987). The relation of parenting style to adolescent school performance. *Child Development, 58,* 1244–1257.

Durkin, K. (1995). *Developmental social psychology: From infancy to old age.* Malden, MA: Blackwell.

Eccles, E. S., & Roeser, R. W. (2003). Schools as developmental contexts. In G. Adams & M. Bersonsky (Eds.), *Black handbook on adolescence* (pp. 129–148). Malden, MA: Blackwell Publishing.

Eccles, J. S. (2004). Schools, academic motivation, and stage-environment fit. In R. M Lerner & L. Steinberg (Eds.), *Handbook of adolescent psychology* (pp. 125–154). Hoboken, NJ: Wiley.

Eccles, J. S., Early, D., Frasier, K., Belansky, E., & McCarthy, K. (1997). The relation of connection, regulation, and support for autonomy to adolescents' functioning. *Journal of Adolescent Research, 12,* 263–286.

Eccles, J. S., & Midgley, C. (1989). Stage-environment fit: Developmentally appropriate classrooms for young adolescents. In C. Ames & R. Ames (Eds.), *Research on motivation in education: Goals and cognitions* (Vol. 3, pp. 139–186). New York, NY: Academic Press.

Eccles, J. S., Midgley, C., Wigfield, A., Flanagan, C., Buchanan, C. M., Reuman, D., et al. (1993). Development during adolescence: The impact of stage/environment fit on young adolescents' experiences in schools and in families. *American Psychologist, 48,* 90–101.

Eccles, J. S., & Wigfield, A. (1985). Teacher expectations and student motivation. In J. B. Dusek (Ed.), *Teacher expectancies* (pp. 185–226). Hillsdale, NJ: Erlbaum.

Eccles, J. S., Wigfield, A., & Schiefele, U. (1998). Motivation to succeed. In W. Damon (Series Ed.) & N. Eisenberg (Volume Ed.), *Handbook of child psychology: Vol. 3. Social, emotional, and personality development* (5th ed., pp. 1017–1095). New York, NY: Wiley.

Elliot, A. J., & Church, M. A. (1997). A hierarchical model of approach and avoidance achievement motivation. *Journal of Personality and Social Psychology, 72,* 218–232.

Elliot, A. J., Kirkov, Valary, Kim, Y, & Sheldon, K. M. (2001). A cross-cultural analysis of avoidance (relative to approach) personal goals. *Psychological Science, 12(6),* 505–510.

Emmer, E. T., Evertson, C. M., & Anderson, L. M. (1980). Effective classroom management at the beginning of the school year. *The Elementary School Journal, 80,* 219–231.

Epstein, J. L., & Becker, H. (1982). Teachers' reported practices of parent involvement; Problems and possibilities. *Elementary School Journal, 83(2),* 102–114.

Evertson, C. M., & Emmer, E. T. (1982). Effective management at the beginning of the school year in Junior High classes. *Journal of Educational Psychology, 74,* 485–498.

Fan, X. (2001). Parental involvement and students' academic achievement: A growth modeling analysis. *Journal of Experimental Education, 70,* 27–61.

Fordham, S., & Ogbu, J. U. (1986). Black students' school success: Coping with the "burden of acting White". *The Urban Review, 18,* 176–206.

Fuligni, A. J., Eccles, J. E., & Barber, B. L. (1995). The long term effects of seventh-grade ability grouping in mathematics. *Journal of Early Adolescence, 15,* 58–89.

Gamoran, A., & Mare, R. D. (1989). Secondary school tracking and educational inequality: Compensation, reinforcement, or neutrality? *American Journal of Sociology, 94*, 1146–1183.

Gardner, M., Roth, J., & Brooks-Gunn, J. (2008). Adolescents' participation in organized activities and developmental success two and eight years after high school: Do sponsorship, duration, and intensity matter? *Developmental Psychology, 44*, 814–830.

Glasgow, K., Dornbusch, S., Ritter, P., Troyer, L., & Steinberg, L. (1997). Parenting styles, dysfunctional attributions, and adolescent outcomes in diverse groups. *Child Development, 67*, 507–529.

Goodenow, C. (1993). Classroom belonging among early adolescent students: Relationships to motivation and achievement. *Journal of Early Adolescence, 13*, 21–43.

Gorman-Smith, D., Tolan, R. H., & Henry, D. B. (2000). A developmental-ecological model of the relation of family functioning to patterns of delinquency. *Journal of Quantitative Criminology, 16*, 169–198.

Gray, M. R., & Steinberg, L. S. (1999). Unpacking authoritative parenting: Reassessing a multidimensional construct. *Journal of Marriage and the Family, 61*, 574–587.

Greene, M., Way, N., & Pahl, K. (2006). Trajectories of perceived adult and peer discrimination among Black, Latino, and Asian American adolescents: Patterns and psychological correlates. *Developmental Psychology, 42*, 218–238.

Grolnick, W. S., & Slowiaczek, M. L. M. (1994). Parents' involvement in children's schooling: A multidimensional conceptualization and motivational model. *Child Development, 65*, 237–252.

Guidubaldi, J., Cleminshaw, H. K., Perry, J. D., Nastasi, B. K., & Lightel, J. (1986). The role of selected family environment factors in children's post-divorce adjustment. *Family Relations, 35*, 141–151.

Gunnoe, M. L., Hetherington, E. M., & Reiss, D. (1999). Parental religiosity, parenting style, and adolescent social responsibility. *The Journal of Early Adolescence, 119*, 199–225.

Jackson, C., Henriksen, L., & Foshee, V. (1998). The authoritative parenting scale: Predicting health risk behaviors among children and adolescents. *Health Education and Behavior, 25*, 319–337.

Jeynes, W. (2007). The relationship between parental involvement and urban secondary school student academic achievement: A meta-analysis. *Urban Education, 42*, 82–110.

Journal of Applied Developmental Psychology, 21, 233–248.

Juang, L. P., & Silbereisen, R. K. (2002). Academic capability beliefs, parenting, and school outcomes. *Journal of Adolescence, 25*, 3–18.

Jussim, L., Eccles, J., & Madon, S. (1996). Social perception, social stereotypes, and teacher expectations: Accuracy and the quest for the powerful self-fulfilling prophecy. *Advances in Experimental Social Psychology, 28*, 281–388.

Kerpelman, J., Eryigit, S., & Stephens, C. (2008). African American adolescents' future education orientation: Associations with self-efficacy, ethnic identity, and perceived parental support. *Journal Youth and Adolescence, 37*, 997–1008.

Kotchick, B. A., Dorsey, S., & Heller, L. (2005). Predictors of parenting among African American single mothers: Personal and contextual factors. *Journal of Marriage and Family, 67*, 448–460.

Kurdek, L. A., & Fine, M. A. (1994). Family acceptance and family control as predictors of adjustment problems in young adolescents: Linear, curvilinear, or interactive effects? *Child Development, 65,* 1137–1146.

Lamborn, S. D., Mounts, N. S., Steinberg, L., & Dornbusch, S. M. (1991). Patterns of competence and adjustment among adolescents from authoritative, authoritarian, indulgent, and neglectful families. *Child Development, 62,* 1049–1065.

Lamborn, S., Dornbusch, S., & Steinberg, L. (1996). Ethnicity and community context as moderators of relations between family decision making and adolescent adjustment. *Child Development, 67,* 283–305.

Larson, R. W., Dworkin, J., & Gillman, S. (2001). Facilitating adolescents' constructive use of time in one-parent families. *Journal of Applied Developmental Science, 5,* 143–157.

Lee, V. E., & Smith, J. (2001). *Restructuring high schools for equity and excellence: What works?* New York, NY: Teachers College Press.

Leung, K., Lau, S., & Lam, W. L. (1998). Parenting styles and academic achievement: A cross-cultural study. *Merrill-Palmer Quarterly, 44,* 157–172.

Loukas, A., & Prelow, H. M. (2004). Externalizing and internalizing problems in low-income Latino early adolescents: Risk, resource, and protective factors. *The Journal of Early Adolescence, 24,* 250–273.

Loukas, A., Suzuki, R., & Horton, K. D. (2006). Examining school connectedness as a mediator of school climate effects. *Journal of Research on Adolescence, 16,* 491–502.

Maccoby, E. E., & Martin, J. (1983). Socialization in the context of the family: Parent-child interaction. In E. M. Hetherington (Ed.), *Handbook of child psychology: Vol. 4. Socialization, personality, and social development* (pp. 1–101). New York, NY: Wiley.

Maehr, M. L., & Midgley, C. (1996). *Transforming school cultures.* Boulder, CO: Westview Press.

Mahoney, J. L., Cairns, B. D., & Farmer, T. W. (2003). Promoting interpersonal competence and educational success through *extracurricular activity* participation. *Journal of Educational Psychology, 95,* 409–418.

Mandara, J. (2006). How family functioning influences African American males' academic achievement: A review and clarification of the empirical literature. *Teachers College Record, 10,* 205–222.

Mandara, J., & Murray, C. B. (2002). Development of an empirical typology of African American family functioning. *Journal of Family Psychology, 16,* 318–337.

Manongdo, J. M., & Ramirez Garcia, J. I. (2007). Mothers' parenting dimensions and adolescent externalizing and internalizing behaviors in a low-income, urban Mexican American sample. *Journal of Clinical Child and Adolescent Psychology, 36,* 593–604.

Mason, C. A., Cauce, A. M., Gonzales, N., & Hiraga, Y. (1996). Neither too sweet nor too sour: Antisocial peers, maternal control, and problem behavior in African American adolescents. *Child Development, 67,* 2115–2130.

McCaslin, M., & Good, T. L. (1992). Compliant cognition: The misalliance of management and instructional goals in current school reform. *Educational Researcher, 21,* 4–17.

McLoyd, V. C., Toyokawa, T., & Kaplan, R. (2008). Work demands, work-family conflict, and child adjustment in African American families: The mediating role of family routines. *Journal of Family Issues, 29,* 1247–1267.

Midgley, C., Feldlaufer, H., & Eccles, J. (1989). Change in teacher efficacy and student self- and task-related beliefs in mathematics during the transition to junior high school. *Journal of Educational Psychology, 81*, 247–258.

Midgley, C., Kaplan, A., & Middleton, M. (2001). Performance-approach goals: Good for what, good for whom, under what circumstances, and at what cost? *Journal of Educational Psychology, 93*, 77–86.

Midgley, C., & Urdan, T. (1995). Predictors of middle school students' use of self-handicapping strategies. *Journal of Early Adolescence, 15*, 389–411.

Oakes, J., Gamoran, A., & Page, R. N. (1992). Curriculum differentiation: Opportunities, outcomes, and meanings. In P. W. Jackson (Ed.), *Handbook of research on curriculum* (pp. 570–608). New York, NY: Macmillan.

Ogbu, J. U. (1985). A cultural ecology of competence among inner-city Blacks. In M. B. Spencer, G. K. Brookins, & W. R. Allen (Eds.), *Beginnings: The social and affective development of Black children* (pp. 45–66). Hillsdale, NJ: Lawrence Erlbaum Associates.

Patrick, H., Turner, J. C., Meyer, D. K., & Midgley, C. (2003). How teachers establish psychological environments during the first days of school: Associations with avoidance in mathematics. *Teachers College Record, 105*, 1521–1558.

Pollock, L. L., & Lamborn, S. S. (2006). Beyond parenting practices: Extended kinship support and the academic achievement of African-American and European-American teens. *Journal of Adolescence, 29*, 813–828.

Rivas-Drake, D., Hughes, D., & Way, N. (2008). A closer look at peer discrimination, ethnic identity, and psychological well-being among urban Chinese American sixth graders. *Journal of Youth and Adolescence, 37*, 12–21.

Roeser, R. W., & Eccles, J. S. (1998). Adolescents' perceptions of middle school: Relation to longitudinal changes in academic and psychological adjustment. *Journal of Research on Adolescence, 88*, 123–158.

Roeser, R. W., Eccles, J. S., & Sameroff, A. J. (1998). Academic and emotional functioning in early adolescence: Longitudinal relations, patterns, and prediction by experience in middle school. *Development and Psychopathology, 10*, 321–352.

Roeser, R. W., Midgley, C., & Urdan, T. C. (1996). Perception of the school psychological environment and early adolescents' psychological and behavioural functioning in school: The mediating role of goals and belonging. *Journal of Educational Psychology, 88*, 408–422.

Rosenthal, R. (1969). Interpersonal expectation effects of the experimenter's hypothesis. In R. Rosenthal & R. L. Rosnow (Eds.), *Artifacts of behavioral research* (pp. 192–279). New York, NY: Academic Press.

Ryan, A. M., & Patrick, H. (2001). The classroom social environment and changes in adolescents' motivation and engagement during middle school. *American Educational Research Journal, 38*, 437–460.

Spera, C. (2005). A review of the relationship among parenting practices, parenting styles, and adolescents school achievement. *Educational Psychology Review, 17*, 125–146.

Steele, C. M. (1997). A threat in the air: How stereotypes share the intellectual identities and performance. *American Psychologist, 52*, 613–629.

Steinberg, L., Dornbusch, S. M., & Brown, B. B. (1992). Ethnic differences in adolescent achievement: An ecological perspective. *American Psychologist, 47*, 723–729.

Steinberg, L., Elmen, J., & Mounts, N. (1989). Authoritative parenting, psychosocial maturity, and academic success among adolescents. *Child Development, 60,* 1424–1436.

Steinberg, L., Lamborn, S., Dornbusch, S., & Darling, N. (1992). Impact of parenting practices on adolescent achievement: Authoritative parenting, school involvement, and encouragement to succeed. *Child Development, 63,* 1266–1281.

Steinberg, L., Mounts, N., Lamborn, S., & Dornbusch, S. (1991). Authoritative parenting and adolescent adjustment across various ecological niches. *Journal of Research on Adolescence, 1,* 19–36.

Stewart, E. B. (2008). Individual and school structural effects on African American adolescent high school students' academic achievement. *The High School Journal, 9,* 16–34.

Swanson, D. P., Cunningtham, M., & Spencer, M. B. (2003). Black males: Structural conditions, achievement patterns, normative needs, and "opportunities". *Urban Education, 38,* 608–633.

Taylor, R. D. (1996). Kinship support, family management, and adolescent adjustment and competence in African-American families. *Developmental Psychology, 32,* 687–695.

Taylor, R. D., Casten, R., Flickinger, S., Roberts, D., & Fulmore, C. (1994). Explaining the school performance of African-American adolescents. *Journal of Research on Adolescents, 4,* 21–44.

Taylor, R. D., & Lopez, E. I. (2005). Family management practice, school achievement and problem behavior in African-American adolescents: Mediating processes. *Journal of Applied Developmental Psychology, 26,* 39–49.

Taylor, R. D., Seaton, E., & Domiguez, A. (2008). Kinship support, family relations and psychological adjustment among low-income African American mothers and adolescents. *Journal of Research on Adolescence, 18,* 1–22.

Turner, J. C., Meyer, D. K., Midgley, C., & Patrick, H. (2003). Teacher discourse and sixth-graders' reported affect and achievement in two high-mastery/high-performance mathematics classrooms. *Elementary School Journal, 103,* 357–430.

Urdan, T., Midgley, C., & Anderman, E. M. (1998). The role of classroom goal structure in students' use of self-handicapping strategies. *American Educational Research Journal, 35,* 101–122.

Varela, R. E., Vernberg, E. M., Sanchez-Sosa, J. J., Riveros, A., Mitchell, M., & Mashunkashey, J. (2004). Parenting style of Mexican, Mexican American, and Caucasian-Non-Hispanic families: Social context and cultural influences. *Journal of Family Psychology, 18,* 651–657.

Walker, J. M. T. (2008). Looking at teacher practices through the lens of parenting style. *The Journal of Experimental Education, 76,* 218–240.

Way, N., Reddy, R., & Rhode, J. (2007). Students' perceptions of school climate during the middle school years: Associations with trajectories of psychological and behavioral adjustment. *American Journal of Community Psychology, 40,* 194–231.

Witkow, M. R., & Fuligni, A. J. (2007). Journal Achievement goals and daily school experiences among adolescents with Asian, Latino, and European American backgrounds. *Journal of Educational Psychology, 99,* 584–596.

Wong, C., Eccles, J. S., & Sameroff, A. (2003). The influence of ethnic discrimination and ethnic identification on African American adolescents' school and socioemotional adjustment. *Journal of Personality, 71,* 1197–1232.

Chapter 15

Religious and spiritual development in diverse adolescents

Pamela Ebstyne King, Casey Erin Clardy and Jenel Sánchez Ramos

School of Psychology, Fuller Theological Seminary, Pasadena, CA

I think that it [being spiritual] means, to me, that God is at the center of what I'm all about, that God is the center of what I do and what I think. . . One of the best things is to get close to God. – Christian girl, USA

Spirituality means how well, to me, you can follow a set of morals that everyone pretty much has in common, and how well you can live up to I guess good standards for moral settings. So that would be a kind of spirituality. And how well you can connect with God. – Hindu boy, USA

It doesn't matter where I am, even if it's supposedly similar and I feel that connection everywhere. . .and feeling certain prayers that evoke certain emotions. And it's just like a feeling you get, sort of shivering. . . . But the community has always been such an important part of me, and being able to find that community. And it's been a model for all my social relationships. – Jewish boy, USA

My spirituality motivates me to provide impassioned service, from a religion of compassion not of compulsion. I take all that is a part of who I am and put it into a life of service work. I am interested in finding the internal compassion that is the 'god' of every major religion. All religions have some concept of God and that he will always love you. I try to add to that internal compassion with my daily life. – Humanist boy, USA[1]

---

[1]These quotations come from a study on adolescent spiritual exemplars (King, Ramos, & Clardy, 2008).

These quotations reflect an important part of adolescence, namely spiritual development. They suggest that young people search for meaning, ask questions about ultimate concerns in life, experience something beyond the ordinary of everyday life, embed themselves in religious narratives, and feel connected to something beyond the self. Furthermore, these experiences of spirituality seem to make a difference in their lives, motivating them to care, reach out, and serve others.

Despite evidence pointing to the centrality of spirituality in the lives of young people, the scholarly community has generally overlooked this domain of human development (Roehlkepartain, King, Wagener, & Benson, 2006). However, it is timely that this volume includes a chapter on adolescent religious and spiritual development (RSD), as conceptual development and empirical research in the area are growing (see King & Roeser, 2009; Lerner, Roeser, & Phelps, 2008; Roehlkepartain et al., 2006). However, one of the conundrums, we as the authors face at the time of publication of this volume, is the ambiguity of terms. Historically, spiritual development and religious development have been used synonymously. However, at this point in time, both within the field of developmental psychology and the psychology of religion, scholars are striving to dissect or distinguish these terms from each other. An additional reality we face is that the existing empirical research in the area almost exclusively includes measures of religiosity rather than spirituality. Consequently, within this chapter we will explore the emerging conceptual differences between spiritual and religious development, but when examining existing research we will use the general term adolescent RSD unless otherwise noted.

Regardless of terms used, transcendence is an important part of adolescence. Many youths are engaged with the pursuit of making meaning, finding purpose, seeking God, growing in self-awareness, connecting with others, caring for nature, and other existential and/or transcendental experiences. This chapter addresses RSD as an important process of adolescence. An examination of demographic data paints a convincing picture of the importance of religion in the lives of American young people. After presenting a case for the importance of religion and spirituality in adolescent development, we highlight the dominant theoretical perspectives on RSD during adolescence and present a developmental systems perspective as a helpful framework for understanding adolescent spiritual development in contemporary research. Then we explore the ecology of RSD by examining the different contexts in which it takes shape. Special attention is given to the role of culture and ethnicity, in addition to other sociopolitical and contemporary influences. The chapter then examines how RSD might make a difference in the lives of youth, specifically looking at how RSD is related to thriving, buffers against risk behaviors, and assists in coping with life struggles. Looking at RSD in its entirety we candidly address potential negative aspects of religion and spirituality during adolescence. Finally, we discuss future directions for research.

15.1. SIGNIFICANCE OF ADOLESCENT RELIGIOUS AND SPIRITUAL DEVELOPMENT: DEMOGRAPHIC TRENDS

Two nationally representative landmark studies of American youth have documented that 84-87% of US adolescents are affiliated with a specific religious group (Smith & Denton, 2005; Wallace, Forman, Caldwell, & Willis, 2003). The remaining 13-16% of religiously unaffiliated youth is a significant minority, but the number appears to be rising (Smith & Denton, 2005; Wallace et al., 2003). Of the religiously affiliated youth, the National Survey of Youth and Religion (NSYR) results mirrored US adult religious affiliation patterns (see Smith & Denton, 2005), with most American youth identifying themselves as *Christian* (75%). Of the Christian youth, 52% identified themselves as *Protestant* and 23% as *Catholic*. In addition, 2.5% of the religious youth reported being *Mormon*, 1.5% as *Jewish*, 0.5% as *Muslim*, and another 1-2% identify with other religions (e.g., *Jehovah's Witnesses, Hindus, Buddhists, Eastern Orthodox Christians, Unitarian Universalists*). Furthermore, results showed that approximately 3% of adolescents self-identified with at least two different religions. Sociologists suggest this finding is due to the increase in inter-religious marriages in US society (Eck, 2007). In the NSYR, of the 13-16% nonreligious youth, 10% identified themselves as "just not religious," 3% as "unexplored or uncertain of their religious identity," 1.5% as "atheist," and 1.5% as "agnostic" (Smith & Denton, 2005).

15.1.1. Religious centrality and attendance among US adolescents

Beyond identifying oneself as part of a religious tradition, the most studied variables indexing religiosity include religious salience and religious attendance. Religious salience refers to how important religion is to a young person, and religious attendance refers to their frequency of attendance or the amount of time spent in religious services or activities. Based on national probability samples of 3290 US teenagers, including 267 in-depth interviews between 2001 and 2005, Smith and Denton (2005) reported that approximately half of all US adolescents aged 13-17 years reported a strong, positive subjective orientation to matters of religion, faith, and religious experience in their lives. Similarly, using estimates derived from Monitoring the Future (surveying national probability samples of 15,000–19,000 high school seniors collected annually since 1975) and Search Institute datasets (surveying 20,020 US 6th-12th graders from 1999 to 2000), Benson, Roehlkepartain, and Rude (2003) found 50-60% of US adolescents to be "strongly religious" as indicated by measures of religious salience and attendance (see also Wallace et al., 2003).

Although a significant portion of US youth report being engaged and valuing being religious, this is clearly not the case for all adolescents. Smith and Denton (2005) remind us that "the other half of US teenagers express weak or no subjective attachment to religion and have fewer or no religious experiences" (p. 68). In addition, Benson et al. (2003) also found sizeable proportions of teens that reported high attendance at religious services and low personal importance of religion. For these adolescents, Benson et al. postulated that their attendance in religious programs, activities, and services is most likely motivated by parental pressures and the social benefits that participating in religious activities with same-aged peers can provide. In addition, Smith and Denton found that most American youth describe themselves as religious. However, 8% of their sample responded "very true" when asked if they considered themselves as "spiritual but not religious" and 46% said "somewhat true."

Gender differences

Several studies reveal that gender differences in religiosity are evident among adolescents in terms of both frequency and salience (Smith & Denton, 2005; Wallace et al., 2003). Specifically, in comparison to adolescent males, the NSYR found that adolescent girls aged 13-17 years old reported more frequent (1) religious service attendance, (2) religious youth group involvement, (3) personal prayer time, (4) periods of feeling closer to God, and overall more likely to have (5) made a personal commitment to live life for God (Smith & Denton, 2005).

Age differences

In contrast to consistent patterns across genders, there are ambiguous findings in religiosity across age groups. For example, in a longitudinal study of 370 youths, Benson et al. (2003) found that roughly two-thirds of youths reported continuous levels of religious importance from the middle to high school years, leaving one-third of its sample reporting discontinuous attitudes, changing from both favorable to unfavorable and *vice versa* across this time period. Wallace et al. (2003) also reported less attendance among 12th graders in comparison to both 10th and 8th graders. Smith and Denton (2005) posited that adolescent declines in religiosity as reported in other studies may begin after age 17, when youth often leave home in order to attend college, whereas they found minor age-related differences across various indicators of religiosity within their own cross-sectional, national study of 13-17 year olds.

Geographic trends

Again in the nationally representative studies, the NYSR and Wallace et al.'s (2003) analysis of Monitoring the Future data, youth living in the Northeast were generally found as least religious and those living in the South as most religious, leaving youth in the Midwest and West somewhere in between (Smith & Denton, 2005; Wallace et al., 2003). Specifically in the NSYR dataset, Smith and Denton found that adolescents living in the Midwest and West reported intermediate levels of religiosity, whereas in the Monitoring the Future dataset, Wallace et al. found that adolescents living in the West and Northeast reported lower levels of religiosity than those living in the South and Midwest. Research also shows that US adolescents living in more rural and sparsely populated counties tend to be more religious than those living in more populated, urban environments (Smith & Denton, 2005; Wallace et al., 2003). Overall, the existing literature has suggested that adolescents living in the South, the Midwest, and to some degree the West, as well as less densely populated, more rural areas of the country are more religious than youth of other geographic regions.

15.2. **THEORIES OF SPIRITUAL DEVELOPMENT**

Despite the prevalence of research suggesting that spirituality and religion are significant factors in the lives of diverse young people, reaching conceptual consensus remains a significant challenge in the study of spiritual development during adolescence. Nonetheless, several key theoretical strands can be discerned in current research on spiritual development. Given the aims of this volume, this chapter offers an overview of the conceptual approaches to understanding adolescent RSD and then presents a developmental systems perspective as a helpful framework for understanding religious and spiritual development in contemporary research. Thorough reviews of the history of the study of adolescent RSD can be found in Oser, Scarlett, and Bucher (2006) and King and Roeser (2009).

Although the subfield of psychology of religion has existed for decades, the study of religious and spiritual *development* has not been a focus of study within any field of study within psychology. Consequently, it is not surprising that there are many approaches to understanding the ontogeny of these transcendent domains in the lives of young people. Specifically, RSD has been discussed in terms of (1) a relational system affording security and anxiety reduction (i.e., Freud, Rizzuto, Attachment Theory); (2) a meaning system addressing existential issues (i.e., Bering, Pargament, Mahoney); (3) the development of cognitive schemas indexing conceptions of religious phenomena such as prayer and God (i.e., Barret, Bloom, Johnson); (4) the development of faith as an identity-motivation system organized around particular religious and spiritual goals, values, and ultimate concerns (i.e., Fowler); (5) social-cognitive-affective self-schemas or representations (i.e., Eccles, Roeser, Templeton); (6) states and stages of awareness that transcend ego-consciousness (i.e., Wilbur); and (7) a dynamic developmental systems perspective in which RSD is seen in relation to multiple contexts, people, symbol systems, and opportunities and risks that foster or frustrate such development across the life span (i.e., Benson, King, Lerner). In addition, not all current scholarship about RSD is theoretically framed. Accordingly, we begin this discussion by describing two atheoretical definitions that nevertheless have served as a point of departure for more theoretical approaches.

15.2.1. **Atheoretical approaches and the study of religion and spirituality**

A proliferation of atheoretical, descriptive taxonomies of RSD and the question of how to distinguish religion and spirituality in human development characterize the field of psychology of religion and spirituality today (Paloutzian & Park, 2005). Traditionally, the field of psychology of religion subsumed the terms *religion* and *spirituality* under the construct of religion (Spilka, Hood, Hunsberger, & Gorsuch, 2003). However, recent years have seen a divergence in these constructs, both in the culture as well as in the sciences (Koenig, McCullough, & Larson, 2001; Zinnbauer & Pargament, 2005).

One prominent atheoretical approach to distinguishing between religion and spirituality is to conceptualize religion at the level of an organized sociocultural-historical system, and spirituality at the level of individuals' personal quests for meaning, happiness, and wisdom. For instance, in Chapter 1, "Definitions" of the *Handbook of Religion and Health* (Koenig et al., 2001), religion is defined as:

> ... *an organized system of beliefs, practices, rituals, and symbols that serve to (a) to facilitate individuals' closeness to the sacred or transcendent other (i.e., God, higher power, ultimate truth)*

*and (b) to bring about an understanding of an individual's
relationship and responsibility to others living together in
community (p. 18).*

From this perspective, religiousness or religiosity refers to the extent to which
an individual has a relationship with a particular institutionalized doctrine about
ultimate reality. This relationship occurs through affiliation with an organized
religion, participation in its prescribed rituals, and ascent to its espoused beliefs
(Benson & Roehlkepartain, 2008). Religious development then has to do with
the systematic changes in how one understands and utilizes the doctrines,
practices, and rituals of a religious institution (King & Benson, 2006).

In contrast, spirituality is defined as:

*. . . a personal quest for understanding answers to ultimate questions
about life, about meaning, and about relationship to the sacred or
transcendent, which may (or may not) lead to or arise from the
development of religious rituals and the formation of community (p. 18).*

This aligns with Pargament's (2007) view of personal religiousness or
spirituality as a "quest for the sacred" in which the "sacred" is defined
in terms of individuals' "concepts of God, the divine and transcendent
reality, as well as other aspects of life that take on divine character and
significance by virtue of their association with, or representation of, divinity" (Pargament, 2007, p. 32). It is also consistent with the often-cited
definition put forth by Benson et al. (2003):

*Spiritual development is the process of growing the intrinsic human
capacity for self-transcendence, in which the self is embedded in
something greater than the self, including the sacred. It is the
developmental "engine" that propels the search for connectedness,
meaning, purpose and contribution. It is shaped both within and
outside of religious traditions, beliefs and practices (pp. 205–206).*

15.2.2. **Developmental systems theory**

Developmental systems theory (DST) focuses on transactions between individuals and their various embedded sociocultural contexts of development
(Bronfenbrenner, 1979; Lerner, 2006). Central to DST are the roles of plasticity, context, and developmental regulation (Lerner, 2006). *Plasticity* refers to
the potential for individuals to change systematically in both positive and negative ways throughout their lives. Such plasticity is important in that it legiti-
mates the optimistic search for characteristics of people and contexts that
promote their positive development generally and RSD specifically.

Also foundational to DST is the significance of *context* and transactions between person and context. From a developmental systems perspective, spiritual development occurs through the ongoing transactions between the person and her or his multiple embedded sociocultural contexts of development (Lerner et al., 2008). It is the goodness of fit between person and environment that is of primary concern in determining different developmental trajectories. In particular, optimal development occurs when the mutual influences between person and environment maintain or advance the well-being of the individual and context. This bidirectional relation is referred to as *adaptive developmental regulation*. From a DST perspective, RSD is best characterized by the transactions between individuals and their various embedded contexts over time. If the transactions of the young person and his or her context leads to adaptive developmental regulation, Lerner et al. posit that youth will gain a growing sense of transcendence—a sense of connection to something beyond themselves as well as a growing sense of self or identity. This experience of transcendence is hypothesized to motivate a growing commitment to contributing to the well-being of the world beyond themselves and central to spiritual development.

Based on the notion that the central task of adolescence is identity development (Erikson, 1968), researchers have used a DST perspective to hypothesize that youth whose interactions with their contexts are adaptive—mutually beneficial to the young person and society—are more likely to commit to a sense of identity that promotes reciprocity with their family, community, and society (Lerner, Alberts, Anderson, & Dowling, 2006). This idea was originally Erikson's, in that he hypothesized that youth who successfully resolve the identity crisis gain a sense of fidelity, a sense of loyalty to an ideology that engages the young person in the world beyond themselves (Furrow, King, & White, 2004; King & Furrow, 2004; Youniss, McLellan, & Yates, 1999). Such an understanding of spirituality is more than a feeling of transcendence; it is a growing sense of identity or awareness—that motivational force that propels individuals to care for self and others and contribute to something greater than themselves. As such, spiritual development involves the processes of growing in awareness of self (i.e., identity) and others, transcending the self and connecting with God and others, as well as a way of living that is characterized by a sensitivity to others (i.e., God, religion, community, family) (Benson & Roehlkepartain, 2008). As such, spiritual development nurtures a sense of thriving (see King & Benson, 2006; Lerner et al., 2006) in young people by providing the awareness of responsibility and the passion to initiate and sustain commitment to agency.

15.3. **ECOLOGY OF ADOLESCENT RELIGIOUS AND SPIRITUAL DEVELOPMENT**

From a developmental systems perspective, RSD is embedded within networks of social relationships in different settings across the life span. In this section, we review existing evidence on how relationships with parents, peers, mentors, and experiences in schools and youth organizations shape religious and spiritual development during adolescence.

15.3.1. **Family influences**

Parents play an important role in religious and spiritual development of adolescents. Parental beliefs and practices provide a foundation for young people's development of their own beliefs and practices (Ozorak, 1989) through processes like teaching, discussion, role modeling, and coparticipation in spiritual rituals (Dollahite & Marks, 2005). The quality of parent-child relationships is key to the religious and spiritual socialization process. Important factors identified in this process include frequent interaction, trust, and close relationships (Hoge, Petrillo, & Smith, 1982; King & Furrow, 2004), as well as family cohesiveness (Ozorak, 1989). Research suggests that mothers are more important in the religious socialization of adolescents than fathers (Boyatzis, Dollahite, & Marks, 2006; Erickson, 1992; Hertel & Donahue, 1995), perhaps because women have not only been traditionally more religiously engaged than men, but they have held the responsibility of organizing the religious education of their children inside the home (Slonim, 1991). Both mothers and fathers perceived as accepting by their children had equal influence on these adolescents in the religious domain (Bao, Whitbeck, Hoyt, & Conger, 1999). Other sources of influence in the family, including grandparents, are important to consider in the religious and spiritual development of youth (Boyatzis et al., 2006). For example, African American men report the significant influence of their grandmothers, in addition to their mothers, in their religious upbringing (Mattis, Cowie, Watson, & Jackson, 2008). Many studies have documented the importance of parents in early development, yet longitudinal findings have failed to support the importance of family life in long-term patterns of religiosity in children (O'Connor, Hoge, & Alexander, 2002).

15.3.2. **Peer influences**

Research on the effects of peers on adolescent religiosity is equivocal. Although many studies suggest that parents are more influential than peers on adolescent religiosity, King, Furrow, and Roth (2002) found that participation with friends in informal religious activities explains significant variance in religious commitment above and beyond parental influences. Similarly, Schwartz (2006) found that not only did friends' spiritual example and dialogue account for significant variance in adolescent religious belief and commitment, but that these factors actually mediated the influence of parents on religiousness. Also, adolescents with friends who talk about religion and spirituality have been linked to higher self-reported religious beliefs and commitment than youth who do not talk about their faith (Schwartz, Bukowski, & Aoki, 2006). The NSYR notes that in the United States, young people report having peers that share similar religious beliefs (Smith & Denton, 2005), and religious youth report higher levels of positive social interaction, shared values, and trust with their closest friends when compared with their less religious peers (King & Furrow, 2004). Peer church attendance is an important predictor of youth church attendance (Regnerus, Smith, & Smith, 2004) and early adulthood religiosity (Gunnoe & Moore, 2002). Although this body of research is in its nascent stage, the emerging findings suggest that peers are an important part of teen religiosity or spirituality.

15.3.3. Mentors

An even smaller body of literature examines the roles of adult mentors in adolescent RSD. Nevertheless, research has documented that the relational quality of the mentoring relationship impacts the level of influence on spiritual development. In a study of over 3000 Christian adolescents—participants who described their relationship with their youth pastors as instructive, imitative, and intimate—also reported this specific relationship contributed significantly to their spiritual development (Schwartz, 2006). Similarly, Cannister (1999) found first-year college students who were involved in a formal mentoring relationship with a professor intent on nurturing the young person's spiritual growth reported enhanced spiritual development. King and Furrow (2004) also found that for religious youth, relationships with adults that were characterized by higher levels of social interaction, trust, and shared values had more influence on adolescent moral development. These studies and others indicate the importance of nonparental role models in the religious and spiritual development of adolescent youth.

15.3.4. School influences

Studies examining schooling's effects on the religious and spiritual development of youth are typically divided into two foci—understanding the direct effects of attending a religious school on adolescents' academic development and understanding how the religious composition of the student body may exert indirect effects on adolescents' religious lives. Benson, Yeager, Wood, Guerra, and Manno (1986) found that Catholic high schools serving low-income youth affected the young people's religious development if the school stressed both academics and religion. In a study of an African American Muslim school, Nasir (2004) found that teachers viewed students as spiritual beings waiting to be developed. This social positioning based on a spiritual ideology afforded these young people a unique set of supports and identity position from which to move forward despite adversity. In a study examining the "religious climate" of schools, Regnerus et al. (2004) found that the level of religiosity among classmates predicated individual religiosity; furthermore, aggregate student body religiosity was a more powerful predictor of individual religiosity than attending a religious school. Similarly, Barrett, Pearson, Muller, and Frank (2007) suggested that the private religiosity of popular schoolmates may foster a community in which religious matters are normative and valued.

15.3.5. **Youth organizations**

Organizations other than congregations, such as youth programs, faith-based and non-faith-based youth groups, and camps, can intentionally or unintentionally promote adolescent RSD. For example, some studies have shown that religious youth organizations help integrate adolescents into the greater community (Regnerus, 2000; Smith, 2003). Moreover, Larson, Hansen, and Moneta (2006) found that youth involved in faith-based youth programs were significantly more likely to be engaged in positive relationships and in adult networks than youth not participating in faith-based programs. These authors also discovered that youth participating in faith-based organizations stated that the activities improved their relationships with parents or guardians and helped them form new connections with nonparental adults in their faith communities and as assisted them in identity formation.

15.4. **CULTURAL AND CONTEMPORARY ISSUES IN ADOLESCENT RELIGIOUS AND SPIRITUAL DEVELOPMENT**

There is neither a prescribed trajectory of optimal RSD nor a replicable formula for religious and spiritual thriving in adolescence. Religious and spiritual development does not exist in a vacuum, but instead is influenced by historical, cultural, and sociopolitical differences. Key concerns and influences of adolescent RSD are context-dependent and vary by culture and time. In this section, we discuss current cultural and contemporary issues relevant to studying adolescent RSD.

15.4.1. **Ethnicity and culture**

Religions reflect a variety of geographical, historical, national, and ethnic/racial influences and are thus deeply cultural in nature (Geertz, 1973). Therefore, studying religious and spiritual development apart from culture is to miss something fundamental about its origins and manifestations. For example, some cultures recognize that spiritual development begins before birth. Thus, those cultures often emphasize the spiritual vulnerability of children and may engage in practices intended to protect the spirits of young people (Mattis et al., 2008). Given the diversity of American youth, special attention to the relationship between culture, ethnicity, and spirituality is vital for a thorough understanding of adolescent RSD in the United States. Accordingly, the following sections review existing literature in the presence of adolescent RSD within the context of African American, Asian American, and Latino ethnicities and cultures.

African American adolescents

As the mainstay of African American culture, the church plays an important role in the identity formation process of its adolescents by serving as a refuge and support system. Recent research appears to indicate that African American adolescents maintain higher baseline rates of religious activities and beliefs when compared to their White, Hispanic, or Asian peers (Bachman, Johnston, & O'Malley, 2005; Smith, Faris, Denton, & Regnerus, 2003). In a study of college freshmen conducted by UCLA (Bartlett, 2005), results indicated 95% of African American students believe in God, compared with 84% of Latinos, 78% of Whites, and 65% of Asian Americans. Additionally, religion seems to be salient for many African American adolescents according to data reported by Bachman et al. Their findings suggest that 56% of African American high school seniors believe religion is important, and 45% attend religious services regularly.

Smith et al. (2003) conducted a study on 8th, 10th, and 12th graders and found that 78% of African American adolescents found religion to be "pretty" or "very" important. In addition, 72% reported praying one to seven times a week. Although the majority identify themselves as Baptists, African American adolescents participate in various religions, including Catholicism, Islam, and other forms of Protestantism (Constantine, Lewis, Conner, & Sanchez, 2000). According to Billingsley and Caldwell (1991), the Black church, in the form of megachurches and rural churches, holds considerable moral sway among African Americans, even among those who are not official members or regular attendees, due to its purpose and the empowerment it instills. They assert that the church is one of the strongest social influences within African American communities. However, this does not preclude the fact that some African American adolescents may believe in God or a supreme being and hold no particular church or religious affiliation (Moore-Thomas & Day-Vines, 2008).

Spirituality is especially important to the African American community because the culture maintains a sense of interconnectedness reminiscent of the more traditional African values of communalism and interdependence (Doswell, Kouyate, & Taylor, 2003; Frame & Williams, 1996). Because of racism and persecution throughout history, social support has been central to African American culture. Religion and spirituality played an integral role in this support as a source of hope, freedom, consolation, and a place of gathering during times of slavery (Moore-Thomas & Day-Vines, 2008). More recently, spirituality framed the African American response to social injustices such as racism, discrimination, and inequality. Today, adolescents are still directly and indirectly affected by a cultural memory that prizes connectedness. A specific example of how this connection fosters a sense of group identity is the manner in which African American adolescents often have "play cousins," "aunts," and "uncles" that exist outside the family, but are afforded the same socializing responsibilities as family members (Moore-Thomas & Day-Vines, 2008). In contrast to Western thought, African American adolescents define who they are as individuals through the value of social interconnectedness; essentially, as African American adolescents interact with significant others, they gain a clearer sense of self (Wheeler, Ampadu, & Wangari, 2002). For African American adolescents, school-church connections may provide opportunities for youth to define themselves and to gain a clearer understanding of others through a deepening awareness of personal spirituality (Moore-Thomas & Day-Vines, 2008).

Asian American adolescents

Asian American youth, in general, tend to be less religious than youth from other racial and ethnic groups (Smith & Denton, 2005), though variation in religiosity among Asian Americans is evident in certain parts of the country (e.g., Juang & Syed, 2008). For instance, second-generation Chinese immigrants, and to a lesser extent, other Asian immigrants, tend to come from wealthier families with more secular backgrounds (Portes & Rumbaut, 2006). Even though Asian American youth may be less religious than other racial and ethnic groups, religion and spirituality play a significant role in some of their lives. For example, religious youth groups provide Asian American adolescents with a sense of community and an important sense of religious identity that often supersedes cultural identity. One study revealed that in Korean American Christian congregations, young people may see their Christian identity as separate and superior to their Korean identity (Park, 2004).

Although there is little research on spirituality in Asian American adolescent populations, existing research on spirituality in Asian American adult populations provides insight to the role of religion and spirituality in the lives of Asian American adolescents. Specifically, research suggests that within the Asian American adult population, spirituality is used as a coping mechanism for psychological distress and as a means of social and cultural integration for immigrant populations. Specifically, Asian Americans tend to use spiritual coping sources such as religious leaders and church groups to handle the stresses of daily life (Solberg, Choi, Ritsma, & Jolly, 1994). In addition, research indicates that Korean American adults faced with acculturative distress commonly seek emotional and social support from the Protestant churches in the United States (Bjorck, Cuthbertson, Thurman, & Lee, 2001; Chong, 1998; Hurh, 1998; Park, Murgatroyd, Raynock, & Spillett, 1998).

In addition, people of Asian descent sometimes reject Western approaches in favor of native healing practices that are rooted in traditional spiritual beliefs and traditions (Chung, Bemak, & Okazaki, 1997). In some cases, Christian and animistic beliefs coexist side by side. Oftentimes, the animistic tradition is strongly embedded in specific Asian cultures, reinforcing the existence of spirits. For example, in Filipino culture, parents commonly teach young children the various purposes of spirits; moreover, a typical belief is that children can act as mediums, able to receive messages from deceased persons (Atuel, Williams, & Camar, 1988). In another study, Edman and Johnson (1999) found Filipinos that attributed supernatural roots to specific mental health problems and tended to prefer using spiritual methods to deal with such issues.

Latino adolescents

Similar to Asian American populations, a paucity of research exists on spirituality in Latino adolescent populations. In addition, Latino American spirituality is quite diverse. Although Roman Catholicism is the predominant religion within Latino culture, Latinos and Latinas are involved in indigenous spiritualities, African-based traditions, Protestantism, Santería, Spiritism, and Curanderismo, among many others (Baez & Hernandez, 2001; Zea, Mason, & Murguía, 2004).

Furthermore, we do know that Latino youth report being religious, but attend church less frequently than their African American peers (Smith & Denton, 2005). Religious and spiritual beliefs are transmitted more through culture and family. For example, Latinos and Latinas tend to identify the family and home as places where they learn spiritual practices that affirm their identities and offer spiritual support (Knight, Author, Bentley, & Dixon, 2004). Spiritual lessons are taught and learned from family members, primarily in homes and communities (Villenas & Moreno, 2001). Specifically, spirituality is sustained and developed in family pedagogies by using *cuentos* (stories) and *consejos* (advice) (Norton, 2006).

Research also documents that young Latinos' religious involvement has been found to deter drug use and spirituality seems to protect Latino adolescents from marijuana and hard drug use (Hodge, Cardenas, & Montoya, 2001; Wallace, 1999). This is consistent with research on adult Latino Americans that has found religiosity associated with positive outcomes (Marsiglia, Kulis, Nieri, & Parsai, 2005). Another study showed that religious institutions and beliefs provide Latino adults with support during stressful times (De La Rosa & White, 2001). Although not a large body of literature, existing research suggests that religion and spirituality play important roles in the lives of ethnic young people in America. Not only is taking the role of ethnicity and culture into consideration important, but also there are historical and sociopolitical issues that also play into adolescent RSD.

15.4.2. **Sociopolitical influences**

Sociopolitical issues are influential in the development of adolescent spirituality. Adolescents are uniquely positioned in that they have developed the intellectual capabilities of developing complex belief structures, yet there are many areas of life in which they have yet to solidify their opinions (Arnett, 2002). Therefore, sociopolitical influences are particularly salient to the formation of adolescent beliefs, values, and attitudes, all of which are critical for spiritual development. In this section, we explore such influences by reviewing the literature pertinent to adolescent RSD and its relationship with globalization, immigration, terrorism, and traumatic life events.

Globalization

The spread of people, ideas, languages, and goods is taking place with unparalleled speed and depth in today's global society due to the increased extent of migrations, global travel, multinational corporations, worldwide media, and tourism travel. Scholars have argued that because adolescents tend to show more interest in television, movies, music, and the Internet than adults do, they are at the forefront of the latest globalization trends, which are strongly influenced by popular and media culture (Schegel, 2001). Taken together with the process of adolescent identity and belief formation, the religious and spiritual lives of adolescents are highly susceptible to exchanging or syncretizing premodern, indigenous, and familial value systems with the plethora of spiritual and value options available within postmodern society (see Jensen, 2003).

However, the spread of globalization has contributed to an increase in adolescent RSD in indirect ways. The increasingly multicultural society has forced various ethnic and minority groups to attempt a peaceful coexistence within America, which has led to the inevitable rise in the disenfranchisement of the rights of certain minority groups. Historically, ethnic and minority discrimination has often led to increased levels of involvement in and connection to the church as a place where individual voices and talents can be recognized as contributing to the overall good of the group (Boyd-Franklin, 1989).

Immigration

Roeser, Lerner, Jensen, and Alberts (2008) theorized that religious institutions serve as primary "contexts of reception" for immigrant adolescents in their new homeland, affording them "refuge, resources, and respect" with which to bond within both their ethnic community and mainstream culture through service and other activities (Jensen, 2008; Putnam, 2000; Suárez-Orozco and Suárez-Orozco, 2002). The strong role of religion in the Latino community is not surprising, given the high levels of immigration among this community and the strong historical ties of Latin Americans with the Catholic Church.

Research shows that congregations not only play the important role of incorporation for immigrants and their offspring, but they also create opportunities for maintaining and building ethnic identification and preservation. For example, although the church as an ethnic enclave is stronger among foreign-born and Spanish-speaking Latin Americans, Latino-oriented worship is also prevalent among native-born and English-speaking Latinos (Pew Forum, 2008). In addition, evidence shows that participation in youth groups among immigrants is associated with social service activities that offer young people various forms of social support such as tutoring or medical services (Roeser, Issac, Abo-Zena, Brittian, & Peck, 2008).

Furthermore, Latin American immigrants, who currently constitute more than one-third of all Catholics in America, are transforming the nature of the Catholic Church in the United States, which has been historically heavily influenced by immigrant groups like the Irish and Italians. The brand of Catholicism is now being imported is more charismatic in nature (Pew Forum, 2008). One implication is that many Latino/a youth who identify as Catholic may differ in their beliefs and practices than Catholics who are not relatively new to the United States. In addition, for these young people, their spirituality is often experienced as part of their cultural identity as well as their religious identity.

As immigrants are exposed to new cultures, the phenomenon of dissonant acculturation applies to changes in belief and value structures. Dissonant acculturation refers to the tendency of adolescents to change their beliefs in response to exposure to a new culture more rapidly than their adult counterparts do. For example, Phinney, Ong, and Madden (2000) found that in comparing the value systems of recently immigrated Vietnamese and Armenians, greater value discrepancies occurred between the Vietnamese and Armenian parents and adolescents who had lived in the United States for longer periods of time. Given that current estimates of children and adolescents in the United States suggest that approximately 20% and rising are foreign-born or have foreign-born parents (Portes & Rumbaut, 2006), immigration issues are critical to adolescent development within the United States.

Terrorism

Research indicates that religious and spiritual development can serve as both an explanatory factor and a coping mechanism in response to terrorism. An increasing number of adolescents are committing brutal, violent acts of terrorism and citing their religious and spiritual beliefs as justification of their behavior. Youth struggling with spiritual principles underlying the presence of good and evil in the natural world may be more likely to participate in religious terrorism as supported by their understanding of their personal connection to the divine and their role in seeking justice and revenge (Schmid & Jongman, 1988; Silke, 2003). Interestingly, adolescent understandings of morality, meaning making, justice, and revenge are often closely related to the decision to participate in acts of terrorism, particularly among certain religious groups that have a more vengeance-oriented doctrine (i.e., Cota-McKinley, Woody, & Bell, 2001).

In response to the heightened awareness and perceived threat of terrorism—particularly after September 11—this particular type of trauma has surfaced as a precipitating factor for enlisting various coping mechanisms, some of which are religious in nature. Falsetti, Resick, and Davis (2003) found that young adults who have experienced one traumatic event emerged with either weaker or stronger religious beliefs. Victims who were more likely to question God and rage against a higher power as to *why* these negative events were allowed to occur were more likely left with weaker religious beliefs resulting from trauma (Ganje-Fling & McCarthy, 1996; Wright, Crawford, & Sebastian, 2004). In comparison, young adults who experienced more than one traumatic event were more likely to hold very strong religious beliefs as opposed to weaker ones (Falsetti et al., 2003). Therefore, it seems that the rising concerns of terrorism in the United States may in fact encourage adolescent RSD as a healthy coping mechanism to reduce anxiety and find meaning in the face of traumatic events.

Further research is necessary to understand the differences between those who deepen and those who reject their spiritual beliefs in response to traumatic life events and the impact on adolescence's RSD. However, scholars have theorized that using spirituality to reframe traumatic events is a method of meaning making that serves as a coping mechanism (Falsetti et al., 2003; Maynard, Gorsuch, & Bjorck, 2001). Spirituality can often serve as a resource for youth, allowing them to reframe traumatic events as building toward an eventual positive outcome as orchestrated by a divine, higher power (Snyder, Rand, & Sigmon, 2002).

Similarly, negative or adverse events are often attributed to demonic forces or powers in efforts to maintain one's religious beliefs in an all-good, all-powerful transcendent being. For example, in a 9/11 study of college students' religious appraisals of the terrorist attacks, Mahoney et al. (2002) found that 50-60% of students had demonized the perpetrators in some way, believing that the terrorists were somehow aligned with or confused by the devil and his work. Interestingly, however, the more strongly students identified with these religious appraisals, the more strongly they reported posttraumatic symptoms (Mahoney et al., 2002).

15.5. **CORRELATES OF ADOLESCENT RELIGIOUS AND SPIRITUAL DEVELOPMENT**

A substantial body of evidence suggests that religion serves as a protective factor, buffering young people against health-compromising behavior and promoting their engagement in health-promoting behavior (e.g., Benson et al., 2003; Kerestes & Youniss, 2003; Smith, 2003; Spilka et al., 2003). Studies have generally revealed that measures of religious attendance and religious importance are inversely correlated with indicators of risk behavior such as substance use, sexual activity, and delinquency, as well as positively correlated with positive outcomes such as thriving, meaning and identity, and contribution. In the following section, we examine studies of adolescent RSD across indices of protective, positive, and problematic youth development with a specific focus on health, risk-taking behaviors, and positive youth development.

15.5.1. **Health**

Evidence shows a strong correlation between congregational attendance and health in adolescents (for a review, see Weaver, Pargament, Flannelly, & Oppenheimer, 2006). In an ethnically and racially diverse longitudinal sample, Jessor, Turbin, and Costa (1998) found that both male and female adolescents' frequency of church attendance and their reports on the importance of religious teachings and values were strongly correlated with their engagement in healthy lifestyle behaviors, such as maintaining healthy diet and exercise, adequate sleep and dental hygiene, and the use of seatbelts (see also Wallace & Forman, 1998).

Further, the relationship between religiosity and mental health has also been clearly demonstrated in adolescents (Cotton, Zebracki, Rosenthal, Tsevat, & Drotar, 2006). Adolescent religiosity, assessed in terms of church attendance and reported importance of religion, has been overwhelmingly demonstrated as inversely related to feelings of depression, hopelessness, and loneliness and positively related to life satisfaction (for reviews, see King & Roeser, 2009; Sinha, Cnaan, & Gelles, 2007; Smith & Denton, 2005). Specifically, in a study of 615 ethnically and denominationally diverse adolescents, Kelley and Miller (2007) found that frequency of spiritual experiences in the context of daily life (e.g., seeing the sacred in others) was associated with life satisfaction.

15.5.2. **Risk-taking behaviors**

A solid body of evidence has documented a negative relationship between adolescent RSD and risk-taking behavior. It is not that religious or spiritual youth are not taking risks or engaging in dangerous activities; but rather, research has suggested that they do so to a lesser extent (e.g., Bridges & Moore, 2002; Donahue & Benson, 1995). Studies have shown that indicators of religiosity such as attendance and salience are associated with lower levels of fatalism, suicidal ideation, and fewer suicide attempts in both Caucasian and Native American adolescent populations (see Jamieson & Romer, 2008).

Substance use

Cross-sectional research has demonstrated that more highly religious adolescents are significantly less likely to smoke cigarettes regularly, drink alcohol weekly, or get drunk in comparison to less religious adolescents, who are more likely to smoke marijuana (e.g., Sinha et al., 2007). However, Rostosky, Danner, and Riggle (2007) cautioned against over-generalizing the protective effects of religion to all adolescent populations, given that in their study of gay, lesbian, and transgendered adolescents, religion did not mediate substance use in the same way it did in heterosexual adolescents.

Sexual activity

Although religious youth engage in sexual behaviors, they tend to be less sexually active, have fewer sexual partners, and have a higher age at initial sexual activity than their less religious peers (e.g., Donahue & Benson, 1995; Lammers et al., 2000). Smith and Denton (2005) documented that almost all youth who demonstrate high levels of religious commitment (i.e., church attendance and religious salience) believed in, but did not necessarily practice, sexual abstinence until marriage, in comparison to 56% of religiously unengaged youth's belief that sexual activity is permissible given that both partners are emotionally prepared. In Latin American, African American, European American, and Caucasian American samples, research has shown that adolescents who attended church, valued religion, and held strong religious beliefs had lower levels of sexual experience and held conservative attitudes about sexual activity (Bridges & Moore, 2002; Edwards, Jarrent, Fehring, & Haglund, 2008).

Delinquency

The inverse relationship between religiosity and delinquent behavior, particularly violent problem behavior, among adolescents has also been well established (e.g., Johnson, Jang, Larson, & Li, 2001; Regnerus & Elder, 2003; Sloane & Potvin, 1986). Johnson et al. found that adolescent religiosity was negatively correlated with adolescents' attitudes toward delinquent behaviors, their association with delinquent peers, and their engagement in delinquent behaviors after controlling for their sociodemographic backgrounds.

The striking pattern of adolescent spirituality serving as a protective factor for problem behaviors begs the question of how it impacts positive behaviors. In the next section, we examine the relationship between adolescent RSD and positive developmental outcomes.

15.5.3. Positive youth development

Within the current growing body of positive youth development literature, the term thriving has referred to a pattern of highly adaptive functioning indicative of an individual's ability to adapt to environmental opportunities, demands, and restrictions in a way that satisfies the needs of self, other, and society. Specifically, a thriving young person is one who is developing a positive identity, a meaningful and satisfying life, a sense of well-being, and personal competencies, and is making a contribution to his or her family, community, and/or society (King et al., 2005; Lerner et al., 2006).

Thriving

Dowling et al. (2004) found that adolescent spirituality and religiosity had direct effects on an omnibus measure of thriving, which suggests that both spirituality and religiousness may play roles in the development of thriving. Although most existing research has confirmed the positive role of religion, this study demonstrated that spirituality may have an influence on youth thriving beyond that of religion. In another study, Benson, Scales, and Sesma (2005) found that religious salience and importance were positive predictors of the following eight thriving indicators across sex and racial/ethnic subgroups of youth: school success, exhibiting leadership, valuing diversity, maintaining good health, helping others, resisting danger, delay of gratification, and overcoming adversity.

Meaning and identity

Adolescent RSD can contribute to thriving by influencing psychosocial identity development and the broader search for purpose, meaning, and fidelity characteristic of adolescence (see Roeser et al., 2008). Religion has been shown to have a positive impact on adolescents' development of a sense of personal meaning, commitment, and hope for the future in comparison to nonreligious youth (e.g., Furrow et al., 2004; Smith & Denton, 2005).

Contribution

Several studies have indicated a positive relationship between religion and indicators such as community service and altruism (e.g., Kerestes, Youniss, & Metz, 2004; Youniss et al., 1999). Using Monitoring the Future data, Youniss et al. reported that students who believe that religion is important in their lives were almost three times more likely to participate in community service than those who do not believe that religion is important. Similarly, Smith and Denton (2005) reported that highly committed religious youth performed twice the national average of acts of service to homeless and needy people and significantly more acts than less religious youth. This positive trend in the research on adolescent service and religiosity is likely due to the structured opportunities for service provided by religious institutions, as well as the value of altruism within a religious belief system.

Given the scope of the extant literature on the correlates of adolescent RSD, we must be prudent to consider how religion and spirituality may both help and hinder positive development in young people.

15.6. **NEGATIVE OUTCOMES OF ADOLESCENT RELIGIOUS AND SPIRITUAL DEVELOPMENT**

It is important to consider adolescent RSD in their entirety, lest we identify religion and spirituality as a social panacea. Although there is plenty of evidence to make the case for the beneficial role of religion and spirituality in adolescents, RSD may also lead to problematic social outcomes and developmental forms of psychopathology (see Oser et al., 2006; Silberman, Higgins, & Dweck, 2005; Wagener & Malony, 2006). The notion of DST involves plasticity, contexts, and person-environment fit in different sociocultural and historical environments and is useful for understanding both positive and negative forms of religion and spirituality.

This perspective is an important lens for spirituality. Unfortunately, adolescents are sometimes co-opted into, and become faithful to, things that are actually destructive to those beyond the in-group, as in the case of child soldiers or neo-Nazis in America. Thus, it is important to note that a DST provides a helpful framework for thinking about negative spiritual development as well. Just as a youth may interact with their family, peers, and society in such a way that brings about a moral spiritual sensitivity, transactions between individuals and their contexts may bring about deleterious forms of spirituality. For example, families may interpret and enact religious ideologies to create cultures of abuse (i.e., "Spare the rod; spoil the child") or cultivate generosity and a spirit of gratitude and contribution.

History is full of examples where youth have been socialized with an immoral and destructive spiritual sensitivity. For instance, Tibet changed from a nation of warriors to a nation of Buddhist contemplatives; and in Nazi Germany, religion was used to mobilize the Hitler youth (*Hitler Jugend*). A complex, multilevel, sociocultural-contextual, and historical systems analysis is required to understand how both societies transformed themselves in the direction of spiritual worldviews, one becoming a place in which the ethics of universal compassion and nonviolence thrived, and the other one where pseudospeciation and the Holocaust unfolded (King & Roeser, 2009).

We assume that optimal religion and spirituality affirms both individual development and engenders social contribution. This balance is important, for if one violates the other, healthy development does not occur. For example, if a religious tradition emphasizes the faith community, without valuing the uniqueness of its members, youth may not have the necessary opportunities to explore different aspects of identity. When youth are not given the freedom to explore, and are either forced or pressured into adopting a specific ideology, social group, or expression of spirituality, identity foreclosure is a risk.

Other manifestations of spirituality may not necessarily be deleterious for youth development or for society. Rather, they lack the rich social context that is so effective for optimal development. Forms of spirituality that do not connect youth with a social group or a transcendent experience of other may not promote a self-concept that fully integrates a moral, civic, and spiritual identity.

A developmental systems perspective highlights not only the goodness of fit between an individual and a religious/spiritual tradition, but also between a religious/spiritual tradition and the greater society. If such a spiritual tradition causes detriment to others, such as the case with prejudice and terrorism, then spirituality has gone awry.

15.7. **FUTURE DIRECTIONS FOR RESEARCH**

The role of religion and spirituality in informing and shaping the development of adolescents is only beginning to be explored in a systems view of developmental science, in which biology, psychology, and social ecology play equally important roles. Research now shows that religion and spirituality are important for the course of youth development (Smith & Denton, 2005). However, more nuanced knowledge is required to better elucidate the precise individual and contextual relations that account for youth RSD and its positive outcomes. In this section, we highlight what we see as a few key areas for future research that would strengthen this emerging area of scholarship.

The scientific study of religion and spirituality in human health and development necessitates definitional clarity of the key concepts of religion, religiousness, spirituality, and spiritual. In the wake of stage-structural theories falling out of favor in the developmental sciences, there is a need for renewed theory in the area of what constitutes religious and spiritual development during adolescence. Innovative new approaches that incorporate and expand on these previous works exist (e.g., Wilbur, 2006), but have yet to be examined during adolescence. Exploration of the development and influence of religiously "moored" and "unmoored" spiritualities is required for full understanding of both the substantive and functional uniqueness of spiritual and religious development in young people.

There is also a great need for longitudinal research in this area. Understanding the developmental precursors and sequelae of religious and spiritual development will be critical for untangling patterns of influence and pathways of continuity and change in this aspect of human development. Some of the most comprehensive studies to date remain cross-sectional in design (e.g., Benson et al., 2005; Lerner et al., 2008; Smith & Denton, 2005). A focus on particular subgroups of interest, such as those who are particularly spiritually precocious, those who undergo conversion experiences, or those who leave religion and decide they are atheists, may be one way that such studies advance understanding of not only normative, but also diverse patterns of religious and spiritual development across adolescence (e.g., King et al., 2008).

Given that religion and spirituality are key facets of ethnicity, race, and culture (Mattis et al., 2006; Slonim, 1991), a key direction for future research concerns the intersection among young people's development of ethnic/racial, cultural, and religious and spiritual identities in shaping patterns of positive or problematic youth development. Virtually no research has examined the intersection of such identities with adolescents (e.g., Abo-Zena et al., 2008). New research in this area would enhance our understanding of the roles that religion and spirituality can play in the positive development of ethnically, racially, and culturally diverse youth (e.g., Nicolas & DeSilva, 2008). For instance, despite the centrality of the church in African American history, little research focuses specifically on Black adolescents with respect to religion and development today (Taylor, Chatters, & Levin, 2004).

Although the relationship between religion/spirituality and positive outcomes for youth is well documented at this time, the mechanisms behind this association have not been well explored. Although there is evidence that social support, such as social capital or developmental assets, may mediate the effect of religious participation or religious salience on positive development in young people (see King & Roeser, 2009), further research is needed to clarify how social support might work for different youths in different settings. Other questions about mediating factors exist as well. Do the ideology, worldviews, and moral order available through religion and spirituality help young people navigate through the waters of adolescence? Is there a significant interaction between ideology and social support available through religious or spiritual contexts (King, 2008)? Longitudinal studies exploring these issues are needed to understand causational effects of these potential mediating factors.

15.8. **CONCLUSION**

There is renewed interest in the study of religious and spiritual development. For far too long, the field of developmental science has overlooked these important aspects of being an adolescent. As the field moves toward consensus on the conceptualization of spirituality and religiousness, social scientists will be able to advance the operationalization of these complex constructs. Our hope is that the not-too-distant future will see the rise of creative and rigorous methodologies that will begin to answer some of the questions raised in this chapter.

Varying approaches to data gathering and analysis will allow scholars to examine the presence, development, and impact of spirituality and religion in the lives of diverse young people. Increased understanding will elucidate how spirituality may serve as a potentially potent aspect of the developmental system, through which young people can gain a better understanding of themselves and their connections to the world in ways that foster a sense of responsibility and compassion to the greater good.

REFERENCES

Abo-Zena, M. M., Roeser, R. W., Issac, S. S., Alberts, A. E., Du, D., Phelps, E., et al. (2008, March). *Religious identity development among religious majority and minority youth in the United States.* Poster presented at the Society for Research on Identity Formation, Chicago, IL.

Arnett, J. J. (2002). The psychology of globalization. *American Psychologist, 57,* 774–783.

Atuel, T. M., Williams, P. D., & Camar, M. T. (1988). Determinants of Filipino children's responses to the death of a sibling. *Maternal-Child Nursing Journal, 17,* 115–134.

Bachman, J. G., Johnston, L. D., & O'Malley, P. M. (2005). *Monitoring the future: A continuing study of American youth (8th, 10th, and 12th-grade surveys), 1976–2003 [Computer files].* Conducted by University of Michigan, Survey Research Center, Ann Arbor.

Baez, A., & Hernandez, D. (2001). Complementary spiritual beliefs in the Latino community: The interface with psychotherapy. *American Journal of Orthopsychiatry, 71,* 408–415.

Bao, W. N., Whitbeck, L. B., Hoyt, D. R., & Conger, R. D. (1999). Perceived parental acceptance as a moderator of religious transmission among adolescent boys and girls. *Journal of Marriage and the Family, 61,* 362–374.

Barrett, J. B., Pearson, J., Muller, C., & Frank, K. A. (2007). Adolescent religiosity and school contexts. *Social Science Quarterly, 88*(4), 1024–1037.

Bartlett, T. (2005). Religions views vary by race, survey finds. *Chronicle of Higher Education, 52,* 38.

Benson, P. L., & Roehlkepartain, E. C. (2008). Spiritual development: A mission priority in youth development. In E. C. Roehlkepartain, P. L. Benson, &

K. L. Hong (Eds.), *New directions for youth development: Special issue on spiritual development.* San Francisco, CA: Jossey-Bass.

Benson, P. L., Roehlkepartain, E. C., & Rude, S. P. (2003). Spiritual development in childhood and adolescence: Toward a field of inquiry. *Applied Developmental Science, 7*(3), 204–212.

Benson, P. L., Scales, P. C., & Sesma, A. (2005). Adolescent spirituality. In K. Moore & L. Lippman (Eds.), *What do children need to flourish? Conceptualizing and measuring indicators of positive development.* Boston, MA: Kluwer Academic.

Benson, P. L., Yeager, P. K., Wood, M. J., Guerra, M. J., & Manno, B. V. (1986). *Catholic high schools: Their impact on low-income students.* Washington, DC: National Catholic Education Association.

Billingsley, A., & Caldwell, C. (1991). The church, the family, and the school in the African American community. *Journal of Negro Education, 60,* 427–440.

Bjorck, J. P., Cuthbertson, W., Thurman, J. W., & Lee, Y. S. (2001). Ethnicity, coping, and distress among Korean Americans, Filipino Americans, and Caucasian Americans. *Journal of Social Psychology, 141,* 421–442.

Boyatzis, C. J., Dollahite, D., & Marks, L. (2006). The family as a context for religious and spiritual development in children and youth. In E. C. Roehlkepartain, P. E. King, L. Wagener, & P. L. Benson (Eds.), *Handbook of spiritual development in childhood and adolescence* (pp. 297–309). Thousand Oaks, CA: Sage Publications.

Boyd-Franklin, N. (1989). *Black families in therapy.* New York, NY: Guilford Press.

Bridges, L. J., & Moore, K. A. (2002). *Religion and spirituality in childhood and adolescence.* Washington, DC: Child Trends.

Bronfenbrenner, U. (1979). *The ecology of human development.* Cambridge, MA: Harvard University Press.

Cannister, M. W. (1999). Mentoring and the spiritual well-being of late adolescents. *Adolescence, 34,* 769–799.

Chong, K. H. (1998). What it means to be Christian: The role of religion in the construction of ethnic identity and boundary among second-generation Korean Americans. *Sociology and Religion, 59,* 259–286.

Chung, R., Bemak, F., & Okazaki, S. (1997). Counseling Americans of Southeast Asian descent: The impact of the refugee experience. In C. C. Lee (Ed.), *Multicultural issues in counseling: New approaches to diversity* (2nd ed., pp. 207–231). Alexandria, VA: American Counseling Association.

Constantine, M., Lewis, E., Conner, L., & Sanchez, D. (2000). Addressing spiritual and religious issues in counseling African Americans: Implications for counselor training and practice. *Counseling and Values, 45,* 28–38.

Cota-McKinley, A. L., Woody, W. D., & Bell, P. A. (2001). Vengeance: Effects of gender, age, and religious background. *Aggressive Behavior, 27,* 343–350.

Cotton, S., Zebracki, K., Rosenthal, S. L., Tsevat, J., & Drotar, D. (2006). Religion/spirituality and adolescent health outcomes: A review. *Journal of Adolescent Health, 38,* 472–480.

De La Rosa, M. R., & White, M. S. (2001). A review of the role of social support in the drug use behavior of Hispanics. *Journal of Psychoactive Drugs, 33,* 233–240.

Dollahite, D. C., & Marks, L. D. (2005). How highly religious families strive to fulfill sacred purposes. In V. Bengtson, A. Acock, K. Allen, P. Dillworth-Anderson, & D. Klein (Eds.), *Sourcebook of family theory and research* (pp. 533–541). Thousand Oaks, CA: Sage.

Donahue, M. J., & Benson, P. L. (1995). Religion and the well-being of adolescents. *Journal of Social Issues, 51*, 145–160.

Doswell, W., Kouyate, M., & Taylor, J. (2003). The role of spirituality in preventing early sexual behavior. *American Journal of Health Studies, 18*, 195–202.

Dowling, E. M., Gestsdottir, S., Anderson, P. M., von Eye, A., Almerigi, J., & Lerner, R. M. (2004). Structural relations among spirituality, religiosity, and thriving in adolescence. *Applied Developmental Science, 8*, 7–16.

Eck, D. (2007). Religion. In M. C. Waters & R. Ueda (Eds.), *The new Americans: A guide to immigration since 1965* (pp. 214–227). Cambridge, MA: Harvard University Press.

Edman, J. L., & Johnson, R. C. (1999). Filipino American and Caucasian American beliefs about the causes and treatment of mental problems. *Cultural Diversity and Ethnic Minority Psychology, 5*, 380–386.

Edwards, L. M., Fehring, R. J., Jarrett, K. M., & Haglund, K. A. (2008). The influence of religiosity, gender, and language preference acculturation on sexual activity among Latino/adolescents. *Hispanic Journal of Behavioral Science, 30*, 447–462.

Erikson, E. H. (1968). *Identity: Youth and crisis*. New York, NY: Norton.

Erickson, J. A. (1992). Adolescent religious development and commitment: A structural equation model of the role of family, peer group, and educational influences. *Journal for the Scientific Study of Religion, 31*(2), 131–152.

Falsetti, S. A., Resick, P. A., & Davis, J. L. (2003). Changes in religious beliefs following trauma. *Journal of Traumatic Stress, 16*, 131–152.

Frame, M. W., & Williams, C. B. (1996). Counseling African Americans: Integrating spirituality in therapy. *Counseling and Values, 41*, 16–28.

Furrow, J. L., King, P. E., & White, K. (2004). Religion and positive youth development: Identity, meaning, and prosocial concerns. *Applied Development Science, 8(3)*, 17–26.

Ganje-Fling, M. A., & McCarthy, P. (1996). Impact of childhood sexual abuse on client spiritual development: Counseling implications. *Journal of Counseling and Development, 74*, 253–258.

Geertz, C. (1973). *The interpretations of cultures*. New York, NY: Basic Books.

Gunnoe, M. L., & Moore, K. A. (2002). Predictors of religiosity among youth aged 17–22: A longitudinal study of the National Survey of Children. *Journal for the Scientific Study of Religion, 41*, 613–622.

Hertel, B. R., & Donahue, M. J. (1995). Parental influences on god images among children: Testing Durkheim's metaphoric parallelism. *Journal for the Scientific Study of Religion, 34*, 186–199.

Hodge, D. R., Cardenas, P., & Montoya, H. (2001). Substance use: Spirituality and religious participation as protective factors among rural youths. *Social Work Research, 25*, 153–161.

Hoge, D. R., Petrillo, G. H., & Smith, E. I. (1982). Transmission of religious and social values from parents to teenage children. *Journal of Marriage and the Family, 44*, 569–580.

Hurh, W. M. (1998). *The Korean Americans*. Westport, CT: Greenwood Press.

Jamieson, P. E., & Romer, D. (2008). Unrealistic fatalism in U.S. youth ages 14 to 22: Prevalence and characteristics. *Journal of Adolescent Health, 42*, 154–160.

Jensen, L. A. (2003). Coming of age in a multicultural world: Globalization and adolescent cultural identity formation. *Applied Developmental Science, 7*, 189–196.

Jensen, L. A. (2008). Immigrant civic engagement and religion: The paradoxical roles of religious motives and organizations. In R. M. Lerner, R. W. Roeser, & E. Phelps (Eds.), *Positive youth development and spirituality: From theory to research*. West Conshohocken, PA: Templeton Foundation Press.

Jessor, R., Turbin, M., & Costa, F. (1998). Risk and protection in successful outcomes among disadvantaged adolescents. *Applied Developmental Science, 2*, 194–208.

Johnson, B. R., Jang, S. J., Larson, D. B., & Li, S. D. (2001). Does adolescent religious commitment matter: A reexamination of the effects of religiosity on delinquency. *Journal of Research in Crime and Delinquency, 38*, 22–43.

Juang, L., & Syed, L. M. (2008). Ethnic identity and spirituality. In R. M. Lerner, R. W. Roeser, & E. Phelps (Eds.), *Positive youth development and spirituality: From theory to research*. West Conshohocken, PA: Templeton Foundation Press.

Kelley, B. S., & Miller, L. (2007). Life satisfaction and spirituality in adolescents. *Research in the Social Scientific Study of Religion, 18*, 233–261.

Kerestes, M., & Youniss, J. E. (2003). Rediscovering the importance of religion in adolescent development. In R. M. Lerner, F. Jacobs, & D. Wertlieb (Eds.), *Handbook of applied developmental science. Vol. 1: Applying developmental science for youth and families*. Thousand Oaks, CA: Sage.

Kerestes, M., Youniss, J., & Metz, E. (2004). Longitudinal patterns of religious perspective and civic integration. *Applied Developmental Science, 8*(1), 39–46.

King, P. E. (2008). Spirituality as fertile ground for positive youth development. In R. M. Lerner, R. W. Roeser, & E. Phelps (Eds.), *Positive youth development and spirituality: From theory to research* (pp. 55–73). West Conshohocken, PA: Templeton Foundation Press.

King, P. E., & Benson, P. L. (2006). Spiritual development and adolescent well-being and thriving and well-being. In E. C. Roehlkepartain, P. E. King, L. M. Wagener, & P. L. Benson (Eds.), *The handbook of spiritual development in childhood and adolescence*. Newbury Park, CA: Sage Publications.

King, P. E., Dowling, E. M., Mueller, R. A., White, K., Schultz, W., Osborn, P., et al. (2005). Thriving in adolescence: The voices of youth-serving practitioners, parents, and early and late adolescents. *Journal of Early Adolescence, 25*, 94–112.

King, P. E., & Furrow, J. L. (2004). Religion as a resource for positive youth development: Religion, social capital, and moral outcomes. *Developmental Psychology, 40*(5), 703–713.

King, P. E., Furrow, J. L., & Roth, N. H. (2002). The influence of families and peers on adolescent religiousness. *Journal of Psychology and Christianity, 21*, 109–120.

King, P. E., Ramos, J. S., & Clardy, C. E. (2008). *Exemplars of spiritual thriving in adolescents: Findings from an exploratory study.* Paper presented at the 20th Biennial International Society for the Study of Behavioural Development Conference in Wurzburg, Germany on July 15, 2008.

King, P. E., & Roeser, R. (2009). Religion & spirituality in adolescent development. In R. M. Lerner & L. Steinberg (Eds.), *Handbook of adolescent psychology, 3rd edition, Volume 1: Development, relationships and research methods.* Hoboken, NJ: Wiley.

Knight, M., Author, N., Bentley, C., & Dixon, I. (2004). The power of Black and Latina/o counterstories: Urban families and college-going processes. *Anthropology & Education, 35*, 99–120.

Koenig, H. G., McCullough, M. E., & Larson, D. B. (2001). *Handbook of religion and health.* New York, NY: Oxford University Press.

Lammers, C., Ireland, M., Resnick, M., & Blum, R. (2000). Influences on adolescents' decision to postpone onset of sexual intercourse: A survival analysis of virginity among youths aged 13 to 18 years. *Journal of Adolescent Health, 26*, 42–48.

Larson, R., Hansen, D., & Moneta, G. (2006). Differing profiles of developmental experiences across types of organized youth activities. *Developmental Psychology, 42*, 849–863.

Lerner, R. M., Alberts, A. E., Anderson, P. M., & Dowling, E. M. (2006). On making humans human: Spirituality and the promotion of positive youth development. In E. C. Roehlkepartain, P. E. King, L. Wagener, & P. L. Benson (Eds.), *The handbook of spiritual development in childhood and adolescence* (pp. 60–72). Thousand Oaks, CA: Sage.

Lerner, R. M., Roeser, R. W., & Phelps, E. (Eds.) (2008). *Positive youth development and spirituality: From theory to research.* West Conshohocken, PA: Templeton Foundation Press.

Mahoney, A. M., Pargament, K. I., Ano, G., Lynn, Q., Magyar, G., McCarthy, S., et al. (2002, August). *The devil made them do it? Demonization and the 9/11 attacks.* Paper presented at the American Psychological Association, Washington, DC.

Marsiglia, F. F., Kulis, S., Nieri, T., & Parsai, M. (2005). God forbid! Substance use among religious and nonreligious youth. *American Journal of Orthopsychiatry, 75*, 585–598.

Mattis, J. S., Ahluwalia, M. K., Cowie, S. E., & Kirkland-Harris, A. M. (2006). Ethnicity culture, and spiritual development. In E. C. Roehlkepartain, P. E. King, L. Wagener & P. L. Benson (Eds.), *The handbook of spiritual development in childhood and adolescence* (pp. 283–296). Thousand Oaks, CA: Sage.

Mattis, J. S., Cowie, S. E., Watson, C. R., & Jackson, D. R. (2008, August). *The social ecology of young African American men's spiritual development.* Paper presented at the American Psychological Association, Boston, MA.

Maynard, E. A., Gorsuch, R. L., & Bjorck, J. P. (2001). Religious coping style, concept of God, and personal religious variables in threat, loss, and challenge situations. *Journal for the Scientific Study of Religion, 40*, 65–74.

Moore-Thomas, C., & Day-Vines, N. L. (2008). Culturally competent counseling for religious and spiritual African-American adolescents. *Professional School Counseling, 11*, 159–165.

Nasir, N. (2004). "Halal-ing" the child: Reframing identities of opposition in an urban Muslim school. *Harvard Educational Review, 74*(2), 153–174.

Nicolas, G., & DeSilva, A. M. (2008). Spirituality research with ethnically diverse youth. In R. M. Lerner, R. W. Roeser, & E. Phelps (Eds.), *Positive youth development and spirituality: From theory to research* (pp. 305–321). West Conshohocken, PA: Templeton Foundation Press.

Norton, N. (2006). Talking spirituality with family members: Black and Latina/o children co-researcher methodologies. *The Urban Review, 38*, 313–334.

O'Connor, T. P., Hoge, D. R., & Alexander, E. (2002). The relative influence of youth and adult experiences on personal spirituality and church involvement. *Journal for the Scientific Study of Religion, 41*, 723–732.

Oser, F. K., Scarlett, W. G., & Bucher, A. (2006). Religious and spiritual development throughout the lifespan. In W. Damon, R. M. Lerner (Series Eds.), & R. M. Lerner (Volume Ed.), *Handbook of child psychology, 6th Ed. Vol. 1, Theoretical models of human development* (pp. 942–998). Hoboker, NJ: John Wiley & Sons.

Ozorak, E. (1989). Social and cognitive influences on the development of religious beliefs and commitment in adolescence. *Journal for the Scientific Study of Religion, 28*, 448–463.

Paloutzian, R. F., & Park, C. L. (2005). *Handbook of the psychology of religion and spirituality*. New York, NY: Guilford Press.

Pargament, R. I. (2007). *Understanding and addressing the sacred*. New York, NY: Guilford Press.

Park, H. S., Murgatroyd, W., Raynock, D. C., & Spillett, M. A. (1998). Relationship between intrinsic-extrinsic religious orientation and depressive symptoms in Korean Americans. *Counseling Psychology Quarterly, 11*, 315–324.

Park, K. J. (2004). Yellow on white background: Korean American youth ministry and the challenge of constructing Korean American identity. *Journal of Youth and Theology, 3*, 23–37.

Pew Forum on Religion and Public Life. (2008). *U.S. Religious Landscape Survey*. Washington, DC: Pew Research Center.

Phinney, J., Ong, A., & Madden, T. (2000). Cultural values and intergenerational value discrepancies in immigrant and non-immigrant families. *Child Development, 71*, 528–539.

Portes, A., & Rumbaut, R. G. (2006). *Immigrant America* (3rd ed.). Berkeley and Los Angeles, CA: University of California Press.

Putnam, R. (2000). *Bowling alone: The collapse and revival of American community*. New York, NY: Simon & Schuster.

Regnerus, M. D. (2000). Shaping schooling success: A multi-level study of religious socialization and educational outcomes in urban public schools. *Journal for the Scientific Study of Religion, 39*, 363–370.

Regnerus, M. D., & Elder, G. H. (2003). Religion and vulnerability among low-risk adolescents. *Social Science Research, 32*, 633–658.

Regnerus, M. D., Smith, C. S., & Smith, B. (2004). Social context in the development of adolescent religiosity. *Applied Developmental Science*, *8*, 27–38.

Roehlkepartain, E. C., King, P. E., Wagener, L., & Benson, P. L. (2006). *The handbook of spiritual development in childhood and adolescence*. Thousand Oaks, CA: Sage Publications.

Roeser, R. W., Issac, S. S., Abo-Zena, M., Brittian, A., & Peck, S. J. (2008). Self and identity processes in spirituality and positive youth development. In R. M. Lerner, R. W. Roeser, & E. Phelps (Eds.), *Positive youth development and spirituality: From theory to research*. West Conshohocken, PA: Templeton Foundation Press.

Rostosky, S. S., Danner, F., & Riggle, E. D. B. (2007). Is religiosity a protective factor against substance use in young adulthood? Only if you're straight!. *Journal of Adolescent Health*, *40*, 440–447.

Schegel, A. (2001). The global spread of adolescent culture. In L. J. Crockett & R. K. Silbereisen (Eds.), *Negotiating adolescence in times of social change*. New York, NY: Cambridge University Press.

Schmid, A. P., & Jongman, A. J. (1988). *Political terrorism* (2nd ed.). Oxford, UK: North-Holland.

Schwartz, K. D. (2006). Transformations in parent and friend faith support predicting adolescents' religious faith. *International Journal for the Psychology of Religion*, *16*(4), 311–326.

Schwartz, K. D., Bukowski, W. M., & Aoki, W. T. (2006). Mentors, friends, and gurus: Peer and nonparent influences on spiritual development. In E. C. Roehlkepartain, P. E. King, L. Wagener, & P. L. Benson (Eds.), *The handbook of spiritual development in childhood and adolescence* (pp. 310–323). Thousand Oaks, CA: Sage.

Silberman, I., Higgins, E. T., & Dweck, C. S. (2005). Religion and world change: Violence and terrorism versus peace. *Journal of Social Issues*, *61*, 761–784.

Silke, A. (2003). Becoming a terrorist. In A. Silke (Ed.), *Terrorists, victims, and society* (pp. 29–54). New York, NY: Wiley.

Sinha, J. W., Cnaan, R. A., & Gelles, R. J. (2007). Adolescent risk behaviors and religion: Findings from a national study. *Journal of Adolescence*, *30*, 231–249.

Sloane, D. M., & Potvin, R. H. (1986). Religion and delinquency: Cutting through the maze. *Social Forces*, *65*, 87–105.

Slonim, M. (1991). *Children, culture, and ethnicity*. New York, NY: Garland.

Smith, C. (2003). Theorizing religious effects among American adolescents. *Journal for the Scientific Study of Religion*, *42*, 17–30.

Smith, C., & Denton, M. (2005). *Soul searching: The religious and spiritual lives of American teenagers*. New York, NY: Oxford University Press.

Smith, C., Faris, R., Denton, M. L., & Regnerus, M. (2003). Mapping American adolescent subjective religiosity and attitudes of alienation toward religion: A research report. *Sociology of Religion*, *64*, 111–133.

Snyder, C. R., Rand, K. L., & Sigmon, D. R. (2002). Hope theory: A member of the positive psychology family. In C. R. Snyder & S. J. Lopez (Eds.), *Handbook of positive psychology* (pp. 257–276). New York, NY: Oxford University Press.

Solberg, V. S., Choi, K. H., Ritsma, S., & Jolly, A. (1994). Asian-American college students: It is time to reach out. *Journal of College Student Development, 35,* 296–301.

Spilka, B., Hood, R. W., Hunsberger, B., & Gorsuch, R. (2003). *The psychology of religion: An empirical approach* (3rd ed.). New York, NY: Guilford Press.

Suárez-Orozco, C., & Suárez-Orozco, M. M. (2002). *Children of immigration: The developing series.* Cambridge, MA: Harvard University Press.

Taylor, R. J., Chatters, L. M., & Levin, J. (2004). *Religion in the lives of African Americans: Social, psychological and health perspectives.* Thousand Oaks, CA: Sage.

Villenas, S., & Moreno, M. (2001). To valerse por si misma between race, capitalism, and patriarchy: Latina mother-daughter pedagogies in North Carolina. *Qualitative Studies in Education, 14,* 671–687.

Wagener, L. M., & Malony, H. N. (2006). Spiritual and religious pathology in childhood and adolescence. In E. C. Roehlkepartain, P. E. King, L. M. Wagener, & P. L. Benson (Eds.), *The handbook of spiritual development in childhood and adolescence.* Newbury Park, CA: Sage Publications.

Wallace, J. M., Forman, T. A., Caldwell, C. H., & Willis, D. S. (2003). Religion and American youth: Recent patterns, historical trends and sociodemographic correlates. *Youth and Society, 35,* 98–125.

Wallace, J. M., Jr. (1999). The social ecology of addiction: Race, risk, and resilience. *Pediatrics, 103,* 1122–1123.

Wallace, J. M., Jr., & Forman, T. A. (1998). Religion's role in promoting health and reducing risk among American youth. *Health Education and Behavior, 25,* 721–741.

Weaver, A. J., Pargament, K. I., Flannelly, K. J., & Oppenheimer, J. E. (2006). Trends in the scientific study of religion, spirituality, and health: 1965–2000. *Journal of Religion and Health, 45,* 208–214.

Wheeler, E., Ampadu, L., & Wangari, E. (2002). Lifespan development revisited: African-centered spirituality throughout the life cycle. *Journal of Adult Development, 9,* 71–78.

Wilbur, K. (2006). *Integral spirituality: A startling new role for religion in the modern and postmodern world.* Boston, MA: Shambhala Publications.

Wright, M. O., Crawford, E., & Sebastian, K. (2004, April). *What promotes positive resolution of childhood sexual abuse experiences? The role of coping, benefit finding, and meaning making.* Paper presented at the annual meeting of the Midwestern Psychological Association, Chicago, IL.

Youniss, J. A., McLellan, J., & Yates, M. (1999). Religion, community service, and identity in American youth. *Journal of Adolescence, 22,* 243–253.

Zea, M. C., Mason, M. A., & Murguía, A. (2004). Psychotherapy with members of Latino/Latina religions and spiritual traditions. In P. S. Richards (Ed.), *Handbook of psychotherapy and religious diversity* (pp. 397–419). Washington, DC: American Psychological Association.

Zinnbauer, B. J., & Pargament, K. I. (2005). Religiousness and spirituality. In R. Paloutzian & C. Parks (Eds.), *Handbook of psychology and religion* (pp. 21–42). New York, NY: Guilford Press.

Unit 4

Structuring and Facilitating Supportive Systems

From research to practice: The treatment of adolescent psychopathology

Sheree L. Toth and Erin L. Pickreign

Mt. Hope Family Center, University of Rochester, Rochester, NY

16.1. **OVERVIEW**

Although adolescence is a time of rapid and dramatic psychological, biological, and social role changes, most individuals negotiate this developmental period successfully without developing extreme problems or psychological dysfunction (Cicchetti & Rogosch, 2002; Kendall, 2000). For those who do experience difficulties beyond the normative range, the numerous changes that occur during this time may afford an important window for providing intervention that can foster adaptive functioning (Cicchetti & Toth, 1998).

Although efficacious treatments do exist for adolescent psychological disorders, many of these treatments are modifications of programs originally designed for adults or children (Carey & Oxman, 2007) and do not incorporate developmental theory or account for the unique developmental capacities of adolescents (Toth & Cicchetti, 1999). It has become increasingly accepted that outcomes for adolescents are optimal when interventions are *evidence-based*, signifying that they are derived from the scientific method, and sensitive to the distinctive psychological, biological, and social processes that characterize adolescence (Holmbeck, Greenley, & Franks, 2003; Toth & Cicchetti, 1999).

Shifts toward increasing diversity in the United States demand that clinical and developmental psychology evolve to meet the needs of a more diverse adolescent population (Whaley & Davis, 2007). Therefore, theorists, clinicians, and researchers must routinely integrate culturally relevant considerations into their investigations and treatment of adolescent

Adolescence: Development During a Global Era

psychopathology. Specifically, with respect to the provision of intervention, clinicians must increase their awareness, knowledge, and skills to work effectively with diverse groups (Bernal & Saez-Santiago, 2005; Day-Vines et al., 2007). Cultural awareness and sensitivity may be especially important for engaging adolescents who are members of ethnic/racial minority groups in treatment, as these individuals historically underutilize mental health services (Fisher et al., 2002).

The path toward developmentally and culturally relevant clinical practice begins with the incorporation of these themes in theory and in research design (Toth & Cicchetti, 1999; Whaley & Davis, 2007). This chapter highlights the utility of a developmental psychopathology perspective for informing research and clinical interventions of adolescent mental health disorders from early to late adolescence. The chapter begins with an overview of developmental psychopathology and its implications for intervention approaches with adolescents. The importance of evidence-based treatments for adolescents is then discussed, along with a detailed look at some of the evidence-based psychosocial treatments for adolescents. While a variety of such treatments is currently available, this chapter primarily focuses on cognitive-behavioral, interpersonal, and parent training interventions, as these are the most extensively researched and supported. Next, considerations for the engagement of adolescents in mental health treatment are explored. The involvement of parents or other family members in treatment is then discussed, and ethical considerations regarding treating adolescents are addressed. Finally, future directions in adolescent mental health research and intervention are proposed.

16.2. DEVELOPMENTAL PSYCHOPATHOLOGY PERSPECTIVE

Developmental psychopathology is a framework that integrates multiple areas of scientific inquiry in order to elucidate the ways in which typical and atypical developmental processes contribute to the emergence or avoidance of psychopathology over the course of human development (Cicchetti, 1993; Rutter & Sroufe, 2000; Sroufe & Rutter, 1984; Toth & Cicchetti, 1999). A developmental psychopathology approach to adolescence considers the ways in which the varying developmental capacities of adolescents evolve over time, from early to late adolescence, and contribute to adaptive or maladaptive functioning (Cicchetti & Rogosch, 2002), while recognizing that some adolescents may vacillate between psychopathological and nonpsychopathological modes of functioning. Additionally, the developmental psychopathology perspective highlights how family, community, and cultural contexts transact with an adolescent's psychological, biological, and emotional functioning to influence well-being.

Developmental psychopathology utilizes the organizational perspective as a framework for conceptualizing development. The organizational perspective highlights the importance of integration within and among cognitive, biological, and socioemotional systems for promoting healthy, nonpsychopathological development (Toth & Cicchetti, 1999; Werner, 1948). The perspective also underscores that development does not simply entail resolving a series of tasks that then become unimportant, but rather involves a series of stage-salient tasks that become hierarchically integrated and that influence adaptation and functioning over time (Cicchetti, 1993; Toth & Cicchetti, 1999). Stage-salient tasks that are central in adolescence include academic achievement, the formation of close friendships, the establishment of psychological autonomy, the development of self-identity (Masten & Coatsworth, 1998), and the formation of romantic relationships (Cicchetti & Rogosch, 2002). The successful resolution of an early stage-salient task increases the probability of subsequent successful adjustment, whereas failure to resolve a stage-salient task heightens the probability of maladaptive functioning. It is important to note that developmental psychopathologists do not view organizational development as deterministic. Rather, it is a probabilistic framework recognizing that some adolescents remain on relatively stable, adaptive trajectories, others on maladaptive trajectories, while others fluctuate between healthy and problematic functioning (Cicchetti & Toth, 2006).

Additionally, developmental psychopathology considers the effects of *equifinality* and *multifinality* over the course of development. *Equifinality* refers to the concept that multiple pathways may lead to the same outcome, while *multifinality* refers to the fact that similar risk factors may result in different outcomes (Cicchetti & Rogosch, 1996; Toth & Cicchetti, 1999; Von Bertalanffy, 1968). Because of individual and contextual variations in development, equifinality and multifinality are more the rule than the exception (Cicchetti & Rogosch, 2002). Clinicians working with adolescents must be sensitive to the variability in the etiology and trajectories of maladaptation and psychopathology in order to adequately select appropriate interventions for adolescents with diverse histories, capabilities, and needs.

Knowledge of typical adolescent development is essential for understanding how psychopathology emerges in adolescents, as well as for providing effective interventions (Cicchetti & Rogosch, 2002). Unfortunately, the

Diagnostic and Statistical Manual of Mental Disorders—4th Edition (DSM-IV) offers little guidance for clinicians as to how to incorporate developmental considerations into diagnostic and treatment decisions. Without a broad understanding of what constitutes typical adolescent behavior, as well as how behavior may change from early to late adolescence, clinicians may inadvertently over- or underdiagnose mental disorders in adolescents (Kendall, 2000). For example, it is common for adolescents to experience some mood disruptions, increased risk behaviors, and conflict with parents. However, it is not normative for adolescents to sever ties with parents or to develop clinically significant psychopathology (Arnett, 1999). Similarly, while some obsessive-compulsive tendencies and rituals are within the typical range of behavior for children, these are not normative behavior for adolescents (Holmbeck et al., 2003; Kendall, 2000). Finally, some boundaries between typical and atypical adolescent development are blurry, such as the boundary between normative experimentation with substances and substance abuse (Cicchetti & Rogosch, 2002). Comparing and contrasting typical and atypical functioning over the course of adolescent development may help provide insight into the causal processes that lead to psychopathology (Cicchetti & Rogosch, 2002). Moreover, knowledge of normative behavior possesses implications for helping clinicians make informed decisions regarding treatment selection. For example, treatments that focus on the development of self-control may be more developmentally appropriate for older adolescents than behavioral programs that involve parents in treatment, which may be more useful with younger adolescents (Holmbeck et al., 2003).

It also is imperative for developmental psychopathologists to distinguish between culture and pathology when making diagnostic and treatment decisions (Bernal & Saez-Santiago, 2005). The progression of stage-salient tasks during adolescence may vary from culture to culture. For example, Puerto Rican cultures operate in the context of familism, where it may be more adaptive for Puerto Rican adolescents to remain dependent on parents for longer periods and to be less autonomous than adolescents from other cultures (Rossello & Bernal, 1999). At the same time, developmental psychopathologists must be careful not to make assumptions regarding the extent to which an individual identifies with a particular culture. Efforts must be made to be sensitive to within-group differences as well as to bicultural self-identification (Fisher et al., 2002).

Unless diagnosticians and therapists are cognizant of cultural practices, normative, and, in some instances, culturally adaptive behaviors might be misdiagnosed as psychopathological. For example, after the death of a family member, some ethnic and cultural groups continue to view the departed loved one as present, and may even report seeing and talking to the individual. If this common practice is not understood, it might be considered as consistent with a thought disorder. In the psychotherapeutic arena, focusing on the importance of differentiating from parents might be completely contrary to cultural practices. For example, the age at which children are expected to sleep in their own beds may be later in some Mexican American families than in most European American families (Wood, Chiu, Hwang, Jacobs, & Ifekwunigwe, 2008). Without the knowledge and respect of diverse cultural practices and norms, diagnosticians and clinicians may erroneously identify cosleeping in Mexican American families as a symptom of separation anxiety. Issues such as these must be considered when working with diverse cultural groups.

Finally, developmental psychopathologists are as interested in individuals at high risk for the development of psychopathology who do not manifest a disorder over time as they are in individuals who develop an actual disorder (Cicchetti & Rogosch, 2002). Individuals who maintain adaptive psychological functioning despite chronic or severe adversity are thought to display *resilience*. Adolescents with high intellectual functioning and histories of positive parenting often are found to exhibit resilience in a variety of domains, even in the context of adversity (Luthar & Sexton, 2007; Masten et al., 1999).

16.2.1. Incorporating developmental psychopathology into treatment

Incorporating developmental psychopathology into the treatment of adolescents may not necessarily be straightforward. In order to develop and provide interventions that are based on a developmental psychopathology perspective, clinicians must continually integrate knowledge of developmental psychology, as well as family and cultural systems, into their clinical armamentariums (Koocher, 2003). This task is complicated by the fact that children and adolescents are "developmental moving targets" and are continually evolving (Holmbeck et al., 2003). Moreover, developmental level is not necessarily consistent across ages, so that two teenagers of the same age have the potential to vary considerably from one another with respect to cognitive, psychological, and social functioning (Holmbeck et al., 2003). Finally, cultural factors may influence the relative importance of stage-salient tasks as well as how psychopathology is experienced and manifested (Rossello & Bernal, 1999).

Ideally, psychological interventions for adolescents should take into account developmental norms and stage-salient tasks while maintaining a degree of flexibility so that therapists are able to prioritize the treatment of presenting problems based on the degree to which each symptom is developmentally atypical within an individual's context (Weisz & Hawley, 2002). For example, Holmbeck et al. (2003) recommend that if an adolescent is presenting for treatment with both parental conflict and poor anger management, then therapist should first address the anger management, as this presenting problem is developmentally less normative for an adolescent. At the same time the therapist must consider the context within which the adolescent is developing. However, if the adolescent's culture values a sense of familism, then the therapist may choose to prioritize the parental conflict issues.

16.3. **EVIDENCE-BASED APPROACH TO TREATMENT**

Empirically supported treatments are defined as psychological interventions that have been shown to be efficacious in controlled research trials (Chambless & Hollon, 1998). The gold standard for scientifically assessing the efficacy of treatments is the *randomized controlled trial* (RCT), in which participants are randomly assigned into treatment groups to ensure that known and unknown confounding factors are evenly distributed among treatment conditions. Typically, the treatment groups consist of a group that receives the intervention of interest and a no-treatment comparison or wait-list group. Sometimes, individuals in the comparison group are assigned to a "treatment as usual condition," allowing researchers to compare the efficacy of the intervention of interest to the care an individual would typically receive in a community setting (Whaley & Davis, 2007). Most RCTs are summarized in terms of *effect size* (ES), a standardized index of the direction and magnitude of the treatment impact (Weisz & Gray, 2008). Effect sizes can be averaged across multiple studies, in meta-analyses, to determine an overall ES for a particular intervention.

Randomized clinical trails are known as *efficacy* studies and by design utilize a high degree of scientific control over variables in order to maintain internal validity so that researchers may more confidently infer that observed changes are due to the treatment of interest. Efficacy studies typically utilize manualized treatment modules, enlist well-trained, highly skilled clinicians, limit or exclude comorbidity in the treatment sample, and employ strict measures of treatment fidelity. Although these conditions may be the most ideal for making causal inferences, they may not be representative of community mental health practice (Whaley & Davis, 2007). Therefore, efficacy studies may have limited generalizability.

The reduced generalizability of efficacy studies has led to increased attention on *effectiveness* research, which attempts to maximize external validity by incorporating more typical clinical settings into the research study design. In evidence-based practice there is an attempt to balance internal and external validity (Whaley & Davis, 2007), and this may be a critical step toward establishing best scientific practices. A recent meta-analysis confirmed that evidence-based practice is overwhelmingly superior to usual care (Weisz, Jensen-Doss, & Hawley, 2005).

In an attempt to assist with the dissemination of evidence-based practices, the Substance Abuse and Mental Health Services Administration (SAMHSA), a federal agency, launched a searchable online registry of evidence-based programs and interventions that have been rated by independent reviewers based on the quality of research in support of each intervention and their readiness for dissemination. The National Registry of Evidence-based Programs and Practices (NREPP) can be located at http://nrepp.samhsa.gov. The NREPP website helps clinicians, researchers, policy makers, and consumers of mental health services evaluate the quality of evidence supporting submitted interventions by providing ratings for the reliability and validity of outcome measures used, the extent to which intervention fidelity was systematically measured, how well the investigators controlled for potentially confounding variables, the appropriateness of statistical procedures utilized, and whether or not the study results have been replicated. The website also provides information for clinicians regarding each intervention's readiness for dissemination. Interventions and programs that are deemed the most ready for dissemination according to NREPP guidelines have quality implementation materials, such as treatment manuals, readily available and have adequate training, support, and supervision opportunities for clinicians who wish to utilize these evidence-based interventions. It is important to note that the absence of a particular intervention from the NREPP list, or similar lists, does not necessarily indicate that it is ineffective. Quality interventions for adolescents may simply be in the early stages of scientific evaluation, have yet to be evaluated in a large group, or are in the process of follow-up data collection. Furthermore, at the time of preparation of this text, the waiting list for submissions to NREPP was well over a year. It is also important to note that the declaration of a particular treatment as evidence-based does not necessarily mean that it will yield equal outcomes for all patients. Clinicians must consider the appropriateness of interventions based on their clients' developmental, cultural, and contextual circumstances.

The psychological interventions that have been most extensively researched and supported for the treatment of adolescent mental health disorders include cognitive-behavioral therapy (CBT), interpersonal psychotherapy for adolescents (IPT-A), and parent training interventions (Weisz & Gray, 2008).

16.3.1. **Cognitive-behavioral therapy**

Evidence has demonstrated that CBT is a successful treatment for adolescent anxiety, depression, and conduct problems (Brent et al., 1997; Kendall, Hudson, Gosch, Flannery-Schroeder, & Suveg, 2008; Lewinsohn, Clarke, Hops, & Andrews, 1990; Rossello & Bernal, 1999). Effect sizes for adolescents in CBT are nearly twice the magnitude of effect sizes for children in CBT (Shirk, 2001), perhaps because adolescents are more advanced in their cognitive development and may be better able to understand the utility of the concepts presented in CBT. Moreover, cognitive sophistication may enhance an adolescent's receptivity to psychotherapy, especially a CBT treatment that emphasizes cognition and the capacity to link cognitions with behavior (Cicchetti & Toth, 1998).

CBT for adolescent anxiety

CBT helps adolescents who experience anxiety to identify and alter cognitions that contribute to their anxiety symptoms, to alter maladaptive behaviors (such as avoidance, poor coping skills, and negative parent-child interactions) that sustain anxiety, as well as to develop and evaluate plans to cope with anxiety symptoms (Kendall, & Hedtke, 2006). Some CBT treatments also incorporate relaxation techniques and psychoeducational components that aim at reducing stigma by helping adolescents manage and understand their anxiety. Typically, CBT is administered individually or in a group format. Additionally, Howard, Chu, Krain, Marrs-Garcia, and Kendall (2000) developed a family-based cognitive-behavioral treatment (FCBT) that utilizes many of the components of individual CBT while helping parents modify maladaptive beliefs and expectations regarding their child's anxiety and increasing effective parent-child communication. In a randomized clinical trial, both individual CBT and FCBT were found to be superior to a family education and support program in reducing anxiety symptoms in children and young adolescents 7-14 years of age (Kendall et al., 2008). FCBT was superior to individual CBT only if both parents experienced anxiety disorders. Treatment outcomes were maintained at 1 year posttreatment. In addition to the growing body of evidence that exists for the efficacy of CBT to treat adolescent anxiety disorders in general, CBT has also been reported to be similarly effective when used with African American, Hispanic/Latino, and Caucasian adolescents (Graczyk, Connolly, & Corapci, 2005). For example, Pina, Silverman,

Fuentes, Kurtines, and Weems (2003) reported equivalent treatment effects for Hispanic/Latino and European American youths (aged 6-16 years old) in the treatment of phobic and other anxiety disorders as measured by diagnostic recovery rates, clinically significant improvement and child- and parent-completed questionnaires. CBT for anxiety disorders embodies principles about thought and behavior change that are likely to be fundamentally relevant to individuals across cultures (Munoz & Mendelson, 2005), which may contribute to the efficacy of CBT across ethnic groups, provided that the concepts are presented in a culturally sensitive manner.

CBT for adolescent depression

CBT is one of the most extensively tested and supported treatments for adolescent depression (Weisz & Gray, 2008). Evidence has shown that CBT significantly reduces the severity of depression and increases the rate of recovery (Stark, Sander, Yancy, Bronik, & Hoke, 2000). RCTs have demonstrated that CBT is superior to nonspecific supportive therapy, systemic behavior family therapy, and waitlist conditions for the treatment of adolescent depression (Brent et al., 1997; Lewinsohn et al., 1990; Rossello & Bernal, 1999). An example of an evidence-based CBT intervention for adolescent depression is Adolescents Coping with Depression (CWD-A; Clarke, Debar, & Lewinsohn, 2003). CWD-A is a modification of an adult treatment program and is administered in group format over the course of 16 sessions lasting 2 h each. CWD-A helps adolescents to identify and alter overly negative thoughts that contribute to depression, to improve social skills, and to identify and engage in pleasurable activities that improve their mood. Adolescents who participate in this intervention are also given homework assignments that promote the generalization of skills learned in therapy to other settings, a common component of CBT interventions.

16.3.2. **Interpersonal psychotherapy for adolescents (IPT-A)**

IPT-A is an adaptation of interpersonal psychotherapy (IPT; Weissman, Markowitz, & Klerman, 2000), a manualized, brief treatment for adult depression that is based on the premise that improving current interpersonal contexts can lead to recovery of depression symptoms. IPT-A (Mufson & Dorta, 2003) emerged due to increasing evidence documenting the role that interpersonal events and skills play in the development of adolescent depression (Hammen, 1999). IPT treatment typically focuses on one of four interpersonal domains: grief, role transitions, interpersonal disputes, or interpersonal deficits. IPT-A also offers single-parent family focus as a domain of treatment, although this can be seen as a type of role transition. IPT-A has a large psychoeducational component and is structured in such a way that the adolescent can assume an increasingly more active role in the treatment as the course of therapy progresses (Mufson & Dorta, 2003). Parental involvement in IPT-A is flexible and can range from no involvement to attendance at several sessions (Mufson & Dorta).

Gallagher (2005) reported that IPT-A was superior to nonspecific supportive therapy, relaxation training, family therapy, and wait-list conditions for the treatment of adolescent depression. Additionally, Rossello and Bernal (1999) found that IPT-A performed significantly better than a wait-list control condition at increasing self-esteem and improving social adaptation in depressed Puerto Rican adolescents when the manual was modified to be sensitive and relevant to the Puerto Rican culture. Moreover, David-Ferdon and Kaslow (2008) reported positive treatment effects for IPT-A regardless of modality (individual, group, family) or extent of parental involvement.

16.3.3. **Behavioral parent training**

Family interventions for adolescent conduct disorders have been found to be efficacious in RCTs and typically involve the adolescent much more in the treatment process than do family interventions with younger children (Carey & Oxman, 2007). However, outcomes may differ considerably from early to late adolescence, as the peer group assumes increased significance and relatively less time is spent in the presence of parents (Holmbeck et al., 2003).

Behavioral parent training for conduct disorder

Behavioral parent training programs are among the most extensively supported treatments for conduct disorders. These treatments typically build closeness in the parent-child relationship so that rewards and consequences have more meaning than they may have if the relationship were strained. One such intervention is Family Behavior Therapy (FBT; Azrin et al., 2001). FBT is a treatment that adolescents attend with their parents and typically involves 15 sessions over the course of 6 months. FBT helps parents to create an environment in which their adolescent's prosocial behavior and abstinence from drug and alcohol use is reinforced. FBT also helps adolescents to develop skills for establishing social relationships with peers who do not use drugs and for increasing school attendance or employment.

Multisystemic therapy (MST) for Juvenile Offenders (Henggeler, Melton, & Smith, 1992) works toward ameliorating adolescent behavior problems by identifying and improving dysfunctional family relationships as well as social determinants of an adolescent's conduct problems. MST is conducted within the family's home whenever possible and is typically delivered over the course of 4 months. This treatment demands a high level of therapist involvement and usually requires several therapist-family contacts every week. MST for Juvenile Offenders has evidenced superiority to treatment as usual in reducing adolescent arrests, increasing family cohesion, and reducing adolescent aggression (Henggeler et al., 1992).

16.3.4. **Dissemination of evidence-based treatments**

Despite the research in support of evidence-based treatments for adolescent psychopathology, most such interventions have not been exported into real world clinical settings, nor are they widely taught to graduate students in doctoral training programs (Weisz & Gray, 2008; Whaley & Davis, 2007). There are several possible reasons for the paucity of dissemination of evidence-based treatments.

First, there is some concern that manualized treatments do not provide sufficient flexibility for clinicians to adequately meet the individual needs of their adolescent clients. However, this assumption is not consistent with that held by proponents of evidence-based treatments. For example, Kendall (2000) maintains that treatment manuals are not rigid but are designed to provide structure for therapy (with goals and suggested pace) in order to optimize treatment outcomes while maintaining a balance between flexibility and fidelity.

Another concern of clinicians regarding the utilization of evidence-based treatments pertains to the feasibility of incorporating these treatments into their community-based practices. The vast majority of evidence-based treatments have been developed to treat specific disorders, while the typical clinician serves clients with a variety of psychopathologies and comorbidities. Clinicians fear that it would be expensive and time consuming to learn and utilize multiple treatment manuals in their practices (Weisz & Gray, 2008).

Finally, there is some concern regarding the generalizability of evidence-based treatments to the general clinical population. It is conceivable that adolescents who are recruited for efficacy trials and accept treatment randomization may differ from adolescents referred to clinical care settings in terms of symptom severity (Weisz & Gray, 2008). The National Institutes of Health (NIH) has made a commitment in recent years to move toward more *translational research* that is designed to bridge basic research with clinical care in order to address this growing concern (National Advisory Mental Health Council, 2000).

16.3.5. **Treatments that may cause harm**

While meta-analyses consistently demonstrate that the positive effects of psychotherapy exceed those of no treatment or placebo treatments (Westen, Novotny, & Thompson-Brenner, 2004), treatment evaluation remains an essential step for ensuring that clinicians do not utilize treatments that may cause harm to adolescent clients (Lilienfeld, 2007). Some highly publicized treatments have been shown to increase undesirable outcomes for adolescents and yet they continue to be widely utilized, perhaps due to the mere face validity of such programs. For example, evidence has revealed an increase in arrest rates for at-risk adolescents who have participated in "Scared Straight" programs, which attempt to frighten adolescents away from crime by exposing them to prison life, compared to at-risk adolescents who did not participate in the program (Petrosino, Turpin-Petrosino, & Buehler, 2003). Similarly, Drug Abuse Resistance Education (DARE) programs, which use uniformed police officers to teach children about the risks of drug use and the impact of peer pressure, may actually lead to increases in drug and alcohol use in adolescents (Werch & Owen, 2002). Other programs such as "Boot Camp" interventions for adolescents with conduct disorder have consistently revealed mixed results, with some meta-analyses revealing null results and some evidencing iatrogenic effects (Bottcher & Enzell, 2005). Dissemination is particularly important, not only to prevent the utilization of treatments that are ineffective or that cause harm, but also to promote the utilization of treatments that benefit adolescents (Lilienfeld, 2007).

The utilization of psychopharmacological interventions with adolescents also has been debated. Selective serotonin reuptake inhibitor (SSRI) medications are often used to treat adolescents with major depressive disorder. Although they are approved by the U.S. Food and Drug Administration (FDA) for use with adolescents, SSRI medications have been associated with increased risk of suicidal behavior (suicidal ideation, suicide attempts, and intentional self-harm), but not with suicide completion, in adolescents (Asarnow et al., 2005; Kane, Fagen, & Wolf, 2007), causing controversy over the appropriateness of these medications for adolescent use. A large randomized controlled trial concluded that SSRI medications are efficacious in treating adolescent depression and that the combination of SSRIs and CBT is more efficacious in treating adolescent depression than either treatment alone (March et al., 2004). However, recent FDA warnings regarding the association between SSRI medications and suicidal behavior have led to a decrease in prescriptions of SSRIs to adolescents. Some researchers and clinicians feel that this may be responsible for an increase in suicidal behavior among adolescents in the years following the FDA warnings (Gibbons et al., 2007). However, others point out that in 2004 when suicide completion rates increased, there was no significant drop in SSRI prescribing and that, in fact, in 2005 when SSRI prescriptions decreased, fewer people under the age of 25 committed suicide (Jureidini, 2007). It is important to note that the FDA warnings refer to the association between antidepressant use and suicidal behavior (suicidal ideation, suicidal attempts, and intentional self-harm) only, and not to suicide completion.

The National Institute for Health and Clinical Excellence (NICE) guidelines suggest that a specific psychological therapy such as CBT or IPT should be utilized for the treatment of all cases of moderate-to-severe adolescent depression and that antidepressant medication should not be offered except in combination with one of these therapies (NICE, 2005). The NICE recommendations dovetail with the Asarnow et al. (2005) finding that when a sociodemographically and ethnically diverse group of 13- to 21-year-olds were offered both psychotherapy and medication in primary care settings, psychotherapy was preferred by the adolescent. This finding was significantly different from similar studies with adults. Asarnow et al. noted that since this investigation took place before SSRIs were linked to suicidal ideation that the preference for psychotherapy was not due to controversy, but rather was a function of developmental difference between adolescents and adults.

16.3.6. **Culturally sensitive evidence-based treatment**

Cultural beliefs about the nature of mental illness may influence the way some adolescents manifest and experience symptoms of psychopathology. In particular, cultural beliefs may affect some adolescents' willingness to seek treatment and how they view the course of their treatment once it is in progress (Bernal & Saez-Santiago, 2005). Additionally, risk and protective factors may exert differential impacts on adolescents, depending on cultural norms and values (Cicchetti & Rogosch, 2002).

Diversity in attitudes and experiences of mental health services calls for the increase in more culturally sensitive evidence-based treatments. In 1994, the NIH required that all grant applications for federally funded research include minorities in their samples or provide a strong justification for not doing so. This enactment sought to increase the external validity of research findings for individuals of racial or ethnic minorities. However, as Whaley and Davis (2007) assert, the simple inclusion of minorities in research does not necessarily ensure the development of culturally sensitive interventions. The effectiveness of evidence-based interventions may be improved by considering cultural and ethnicity issues, such as the impact of discrimination on well-being, in the conceptualization and development of interventions from their inception. For example, evidence suggests that, due to cultural attitudes, the inclusion of family members in therapy may be a deterrent for African American individuals to remain in treatment (Hatch, Friedman, & Paradis, 1996). Some evidence suggests that retention rates could be improved by allowing African American clients the choice to designate any person with whom they feel comfortable to participate in therapy rather than restricting treatment involvement to family members only (Hatch et al., 1996). Moreover, researchers must make an effort to include culturally sensitive assessment tools and avoid research designs that utilize data from middle-class, Caucasian samples as the standard of mental health (Fisher et al., 2002; Garcia-Coll, Akerman, & Cicchetti, 2000). The failure to utilize culturally appropriate research paradigms can result in inaccurate portrayals of adolescent functioning (Spencer, Dupree, Cunningham, Harpalani, & Munoz-Miller, 2003), thereby compromising the development of treatment strategies.

16.4. ENGAGING ADOLESCENTS IN TREATMENT

Alarmingly, evidence suggests that less than one-third of youth in the United States with serious mental health concerns receive the professional care that they need (Weist & Evans, 2005). Several common barriers to engaging adolescents in treatment have been identified. These include the mistrust adolescents sometimes experience with respect to mental health professionals, the stigma many adolescents associate with psychotherapy, and the lack of choice adolescents often feel regarding their care (Oetzel & Scherer, 2003).

16.4.1. The therapeutic relationship

As is true of therapy more generally, it is essential for therapists to make an active effort to establish trust, rapport, and a collaborative relationship with adolescent clients. However, the engagement process with adolescents may be particularly challenging. The quality and strength of the therapeutic alliance has been associated with positive outcomes for adolescents in psychotherapeutic treatment, regardless of type of treatment

(Shirk & Karver, 2003). There is little available evidence, however, for determining what specific therapist behaviors contribute to the establishment or maintenance of a therapeutic alliance between a therapist and an adolescent client (Diamond, Siqueland, & Diamond, 2003). It is becoming increasingly recognized that therapeutic techniques for engaging children and adults in therapy are not effective with adolescents due to the distinctive characteristics of this developmental group (Oetzel & Scherer, 2003). Therefore, it is essential for therapists to actively assess the salient developmental features of their adolescent clients such as the unique manifestations of adolescent psychopathology and problem behaviors, their cognitive abilities, the awareness and value they place on consequences, and the quality of their coping strategies that may promote or hinder therapeutic engagement (Oetzel & Scherer, 2003). Moreover, they must recognize how these developmental features vary from early to late adolescence, as well as the heterogeneity between adolescents of the same age.

A therapist's ability to convey empathy is empirically supported as being necessary for establishing a therapeutic alliance with adolescent clients. However, empathy alone is not sufficient for maintaining a working alliance (Greenberg, Watson, Elliot, & Bohart, 2001). Therapists must also be genuine and nonjudgmental regarding their adolescent clients' experiences (Diamond et al., 2003). This may involve a delicate balance, as therapists must establish themselves as their clients' allies while being certain to avoid condoning antisocial or maladaptive behaviors (Greenberg et al., 2001).

An emerging body of research highlights the importance of therapists addressing cultural factors with their clients in establishing a therapeutic alliance. When therapists actively acknowledge and encourage their clients to explore the ways in which issues of diversity impact their presenting circumstances, their clients view their therapists as more credible, are more satisfied with their treatment, have an increase in depth of personal disclosure, and are more willing to continue treatment than clients whose therapists ignore the impact of diversity concerns during the course of treatment (Day-Vines et al., 2007; Thompson, Worthington, & Atkinson, 1994). Wintersteen, Mesinger, and Diamond (2005) evaluated the quality of the therapeutic alliance among 600 adolescent substance abusers and their therapists. They found that gender-matched dyads reported higher alliances and were more likely to complete treatment than were mixed-gender dyads. They also discovered that matching race between adolescent clients and their therapists predicted greater retention, but not patient-rated alliance. Therapists in racially mismatched dyads rated therapeutic alliance significantly lower than did therapists who were of the same race as their adolescent clients. This underscores the importance of clinicians committing themselves to becoming aware of how culture and ethnicity may impact the care that they provide to adolescents (Whaley & Davis, 2007). In situations where race or ethnicity differs between the therapist and the client, it is important to address this openly and to ascertain how these differences may impact upon the therapeutic process. For example, early in therapy it is important to discuss any prior therapeutic experiences that a client may have had. By trying to help the client elaborate on what they found to be effective or something they may have wanted to change, the client may feel comfortable talking about aspects of the prior therapeutic relationship that related to cultural understanding or misunderstanding. This, in turn, can provide a window for the therapist to acknowledge that she is not as familiar with a particular culture and welcomes the opportunity for the client to help her gain a better understanding of the cultural milieu. During the course of therapy, opportunities may also arise for talking about cultural values. When working with parents and their children, for example, emphasizing that the parent is the expert on their child and on their family beliefs and that it is therefore critical that the parent and therapist work as a team may enable a parent to feel more comfortable expressing their cultural values. Additionally, it is important for clinicians to remain mindful of cultural attitudes and norms regarding authority figures. It is common for parents in certain Hispanic/Latino groups to refrain from voicing disagreement with a mental health provider's treatment plan in order to maintain a cordial relationship (Wood et al., 2008). A clinician who is not aware of this cultural expectation may not give the family an opportunity to provide adequate input into the treatment plan, which may lead to noncompliance with treatment recommendations and termination of treatment.

Engaging adolescents in a therapeutic alliance and increasing their involvement in treatment (Chu & Kendall, 2004) have been shown to lead to more adaptive developmental trajectories for adolescents referred for mental health care. Unfortunately, the majority of strategies utilized to engage adolescents in treatment are imported from the adult literature (Shirk & Karver, 2003). The field would benefit from future investigations that include developmentally relevant strategies for assessing the therapeutic alliance between therapists and adolescent clients (Shirk & Karver, 2003).

16.4.2. **Adolescent involvement in treatment planning**

Many adolescents enter therapy in the "precontemplative" stage of change, meaning that they are unaware that a problem exists and have no intention of changing their behavior (Oetzel & Scherer, 2003). Further, because most adolescents do not seek treatment on their own accord but rather are referred by an adult (Koocher, 2003), this may work against their attempts to achieve autonomy (Tan, Passerini, & Stewart, 2007). It is essential for therapists to attend to adolescents' strivings for autonomy by cultivating a mutually collaborative therapeutic environment and actively involving adolescents in their treatment planning (Prinz & Jones, 2003). Kendall (2000) suggests that therapists assume the stance of a coach or consultant while working with adolescents in order to capitalize on adolescents' needs for independent development. In order to accomplish this, therapists should take a supportive stance, help adolescents develop and evaluate their own solutions, give them opportunities to try out their solutions, and provide feedback during the course of treatment (Kendall, 2000). Additionally, it is essential for therapists to involve their adolescent clients in setting treatment goals in order to avoid passive compliance in, or active resistance to, treatment.

Parental involvement

There has been some debate in the literature regarding to what extent, if any, parental involvement in adolescent mental health treatment is appropriate. According to data from the National Longitudinal Study of Adolescent Health, the quality of an adolescent's relationship with his or her parents is a strong predictor of health outcomes (Resnick et al., 1997). These findings suggest that parental involvement may be an essential component to treatment success (Oetzel & Scherer, 2003). However, an adolescent's presenting problem and developmental level may have an impact on the amount of parental involvement needed for optimal treatment results. For example, Kendall (2000) postulates that younger adolescents with conduct disorder may derive more benefit from treatment when parents are present, while older depressed adolescents may benefit more when parents are not included in sessions.

It is also important to note the moderators of parental involvement in adolescent mental health treatment. For example, while some evidence has shown greater parental involvement to be associated with improved outcomes in CBT (Clarke et al., 2003), others have demonstrated that the positive effects of parental involvement in CBT were weakened for adolescents whose mothers were depressed at the time of treatment (Weersing & Brent, 2003). Similarly, it is likely that the involvement of maltreating parents in their adolescent's mental health treatment may be inappropriate or possibly iatrogenic.

The optimal level of parental involvement may also vary by culture. The results of Rossello and Bernal's (1999) RCT suggested that, since parental dependence is extended in Puerto Rican culture, there may be a need for more parental involvement in CBT and IPT-A treatment for depressed Puerto Rican adolescents than for depressed Caucasian adolescents.

Moreover, in many African American families, grandparents, aunts and uncles, and adult siblings are the primary care providers for adolescents, even if they do not possess legal guardianship (Fisher et al., 2002). Therefore, interventions must be sufficiently flexible to be relevant for nontraditional family constellations.

Even if it is determined that it is not in the best interest of the adolescent client to have a parent present during sessions, the therapist-parent alliance remains important. Many adolescents are minors and therefore not legally able to make decisions regarding their clinical care. Young adolescents are also unable to drive. Therefore, many adolescents rely on their parents for attendance at therapy sessions. Diamond, Diamond, and Liddle (2000) suggest that therapists meet alone with parents and empathetically explore personal challenges (psychopathology, marital conflict, poverty) that impact parenting while helping parents feel supported and understood in order to improve treatment retention for the adolescent client. Regardless of the extent of parental involvement in the adolescent's treatment, it is critical that the therapist addresses this issue with the adolescent. Unless both parents and adolescent are clear on the parameters of parental involvement, the course of treatment is likely to be compromised. Of course, "parental involvement" does not assume a two-parent family, nor does it limit involvement to nuclear family members. Rather, the involvement of individuals that are important to the adolescent and seen as caregivers and/or supports can and should be encouraged.

16.4.3. Use of Internet/technology to engage adolescents

There has been tremendous growth in adolescent's access to the Internet in recent years. This has sparked some interest in the clinical community regarding utilization of the Internet as a mode of treatment delivery, particularly for this age group. Some clinicians believe that this novel channel for intervention has the potential to help adolescents overcome many common barriers to seeking treatment. First, it is theorized that many adolescents, particularly those with anxiety-related problems, would find the anonymity of online treatment appealing, as it may reduce the stigma some adolescents associate with seeking care from a mental health professional. Furthermore, it is thought that adolescents who have limited access to clinical care, particularly those residing in rural communities, would be able to receive treatment over the Internet, whereas they may not otherwise receive treatment at all.

Ritterband et al. (2003) noted that most online treatments target specific behavioral concerns, such as smoking cessation, weight loss, posttraumatic stress, tinnitus, and panic disorder. Behavioral treatments are often highly structured interventions that focus on changing specific behaviors to reduce symptom distress and therefore seem to be most adaptable to Internet delivery (Ritterband et al., 2003).

While some investigations have found online treatment to be ineffective (Patten et al., 2007), others have reported online interventions to be promising in both feasibility and effectiveness (Ritterband et al., 2003). However, most empirical investigations of online treatments have only compared the effectiveness of treatment online to no treatment at all. Investigations that have compared the effectiveness of treatment delivered over the Internet to the current gold standard of treatment in a face-to-face context have been few, primarily limited to adult samples, and have found face-to-face treatment delivery to achieve stronger results than similar treatments provided online (Ritterband et al., 2003).

Evidence suggests that the therapist-client relationship is one of the strongest and most consistent factors predicting successful treatment outcome (Okiishi, Lambert, Nielsen, & Ogles, 2003). Critics of online therapy have noted the seemingly impersonal nature of the therapist-client relationship and the barriers to establishing rapport and a cohesive therapeutic alliance in an exclusively online therapy format. Evidence has bolstered this argument, indicating that clients who met face-to-face with their therapists were more satisfied with the therapist-client relationship than were those who only met with therapists over the Internet (Leibert, Archer, Munson, & York, 2006).

It is also important to consider the potential risks associated with mental health treatment via the Internet. Accessibility to information could encourage adolescents to attempt to self-diagnose. Errors in assessment and misdiagnosis could prevent adolescents from receiving the proper treatments. Unsupervised sites have the potential to attract adults who may take advantage of vulnerable adolescents. Moreover, clinicians without the proper credentials could administer therapy. All of these concerns call for strict ethical and professional guidelines regarding online treatment delivery for adolescents. It is also clear that the field must first demonstrate the efficacy of online psychotherapy through rigorous empirical testing.

16.5. **ETHICAL CONSIDERATIONS IN TREATMENT OF ADOLESCENTS**

The provision of intervention to adolescent clients entails a number of ethical and legal challenges for clinicians, particularly with respect to consent and confidentiality. Sometimes clinicians must strike a balance between what they believe to be therapeutically appropriate and the desires of the families with whom they are working. Moreover, there is often a lack of convergence between the goals of adolescent clients and the wishes of their parents. Finally, ethical codes and legal mandates do not always align with one another, leaving clinicians to grapple with difficult decisions.

16.5.1. **Consent**

The ability to provide *informed consent* to treatment is a basic right for all adults seeking services in mental health. Informed consent involves agreeing to take part in a particular treatment after being apprised of the treatments risks and benefits as well as the alternatives available in the absence of coercion and in the presence of the capacity to make treatment decisions (Tan et al., 2007). While most adolescents have the cognitive ability to understand treatment options, developmental theory suggests that many adolescents, particularly those who are younger, lack the developmental autonomy to make treatment decisions independently (American Academy of Pediatrics Committee on Bioethics, 1995). They may not perceive themselves as having the ability to refuse treatment, or they may consent to treatment in order to please their parents or therapist. Moreover, most adolescents are minors and therefore cannot legally consent to treatment. Because the majority of adolescents cannot provide informed consent to treatment, many clinicians choose to obtain *assent*, a minor's agreement to participate in treatment. Obtaining assent provides adolescents with an opportunity to ask questions and express their wishes, without imposing an inappropriate burden on them to independently make treatment decisions (Tan et al., 2007). The process of assent can also serve as the beginning of the establishment of a treatment contract and can be facilitative of a mutually collaborative relationship.

16.5.2. **Confidentiality**

Since most adolescents do not seek treatment on their own accord, clinicians often must negotiate multiple relationships when working with adolescents. For example, clinicians may need to interface with the client, parents, teachers, and social workers. It is imperative that the therapist and adolescent client discuss terms of confidentiality at the onset of treatment and that the therapist explicitly describes his or her role with whomever else might be involved in the treatment (Koocher, 2003). This is of utmost importance because maintaining confidentiality is not only ethical but can also influence the effectiveness of care (Tan et al., 2007). It is also important for clinicians to note the limits of confidentiality by remaining aware of legal and professional regulations (Oetzel & Scherer, 2003) such as mandated reporting of child or elder abuse, policies regarding self-harm, and the therapist's duty to warn others of possible danger.

16.6. **PUBLIC POLICY**

When attempting to increase the availability of evidence-based interventions to adolescents, a number of issues must be considered if such treatments are to be more widely disseminated. First, issues related to funding of services must be addressed. Unfortunately, the demands associated with fee-for-service billing have resulted in greatly increased clinical case loads for many therapists. It is not uncommon for therapists in community settings to have caseloads of 40-100 individuals, all with complex, multiproblem histories (Hromco, Moore, & Nikkel, 2003). The demands that accompany such workloads and the associated expectation for the generation of billable hours severely limit the ability of even the most motivated therapist to devote time to learning new treatment approaches. This is particularly problematic as graduate programs continue to lag behind in training students on evidence-based models of intervention. Therefore, many professionals are totally unprepared to implement empirically supported interventions. If funders are truly invested in ensuring that evidence-based treatments are available, then they must be willing to provide resources for educational initiatives. Such commitment requires that a long- versus short-term vision on cost-effectiveness be cultivated.

Even when organizations are interested in supporting staff members in developing expertise on evidence-based models of treatment, training opportunities may be difficult to obtain. In addition to obstacles associated with freeing time for clinicians to learn new approaches, training may not be readily available or affordable. Although practicing clinicians may attend single-day workshops, such short-term exposure for complex clinical treatments is not likely to yield competent service provision.

As interventions are exported to the broader clinical communities, it is critical that they continue to be evaluated in these new contexts. This is an essential step in moving from efficacy to true effectiveness trials. In fact, it is likely that some evidence-based models will need to be modified in order to be delivered effectively in settings quite different from those in which their efficacy was first demonstrated. Again, a financial investment is necessary. Community mental health clinics typically do not have personnel capable of conducting treatment evaluation studies. Fortunately, researchers do possess the skills needed to evaluate community programs and often can garner financial resources, such as grants, to conduct research and support the work of community providers. Thus, by creating university/community partnerships, researchers can access diverse populations, and intervention and prevention programs can undergo effectiveness trials in the community. In the absence of supportive partnerships to assist community providers in evaluating newly incorporated evidence-based models, it will be nearly impossible to ascertain continued effectiveness.

It is also important that community administrators trying to import evidence-based services recognize that efforts—both in time and money—must be expended to ensure that such treatments are maintaining fidelity to the original evidence-based models. Ongoing supervision and continuing education, as well as utilization of fidelity assessments, are needed if drift from the empirically supported treatments is to be prevented. Administrators and researchers alike should be aware that implementation may fail because of insufficient resources and that this will only hinder the adoption of future evidence-based programs.

Ultimately, the exportation of research-informed treatment methods into real-world contexts requires solid partnerships among scientists, administrators, funding sources, and practicing therapists. The absence of a single link in this chain will doom the broader dissemination and maintenance of evidence-based practices to populations that sorely need them.

16.7. **FUTURE DIRECTIONS**

Although empirically supported interventions for the treatment of adolescent psychopathology are increasingly available, they are not being consistently provided in real-world clinical contexts. Therefore, it is critical that clinical researchers conduct not only efficacy trials, but that they also increasingly devote their energies to fostering the exportation and continued evaluation of these interventions in broader clinical contexts. In order to promote the incorporation of evidence-based interventions into clinics, collaborative partnerships among university researchers, clinicians practicing in community settings, and policy makers are critical. It is only when mutually trusting and respectful relationships exist that true exportation and evaluation of evidence-based interventions are possible.

In addition, administrators and funding agencies must be willing to direct resources into educational endeavors for clinical staff. A true commitment to the cultivation of expertise in the provision of evidence-based interventions requires that clinical caseloads be reduced to free up time for training and for supervision. Currently, many evidence-based interventions necessitate attendance at educational trainings, subsequent supervision, and the purchase of expensive manuals and materials. Unless administrators are dedicated to supporting these initiatives, it is impossible for clinical staff to acquire new skills. Efforts to contain costs by minimizing staff time availability or omitting adequate supervision will undermine the likely effectiveness of the intervention.

Because many evidence-based interventions for adolescents had their origins in approaches developed for adults, it is necessary to determine whether current approaches to treating adolescent psychopathology could be improved by the incorporation of a developmental focus during the actual development of treatment strategies. Research initiatives that compare such treatments with those currently being utilized might yield important new insights on efficacious treatments.

Finally, although researchers and practitioners have become increasingly sensitive to the importance of examining intervention efficacy as it relates to diverse ethnic and economic groups, much more effort needs to be directed toward ensuring that evidence-based models for adolescent psychopathology are designed to meet the needs of varied groups of adolescents. As the scientific base in support of interventions for multiethnic and cultural populations grows, it is likely that the receptivity to implementing such evidence-based models will also increase.

REFERENCES

American Academy of Pediatrics Committee on Bioethics. (1995). Informed consent, parental permission, and pediatric practice. *Pediatrics, 95*, 314–317.

Arnett, J. J. (1999). Adolescent storm and stress, reconsidered. *American Psychologist, 54*, 317–326.

Asarnow, J. R., Jaycox, L. H., Duan, N., LaBorde, A. P., Rea, M. M., Murray, P., et al. (2005). Effectiveness of a quality improvement intervention for adolescent depression in primary care clinics: A randomized controlled trial. *Journal of the American Medical Association, 293*, 311–319.

Azrin, N. H., Donohue, B., Teichner, G. A., Crum, T., Howell, J., & DeCato, L. A. (2001). A controlled evaluation and description of individual-cognitive problem solving and family-behavior therapies in dually diagnosed conduct-disordered and substance-dependent youth. *Journal of Child and Adolescent Substance Abuse, 11*, 1–41.

Bernal, G., & Saez-Santiago, E. (2005). Toward culturally centered and evidence-based treatments for depressed adolescents. In W. M. Pinsof & J. L. Lebow (Eds.), *Family psychology: The art of the science* (pp. 471–489). New York, NY: Oxford University Press.

Bottcher, J., & Ezell, M. E. (2005). Examining the effectiveness of boot camps: A randomized experiment with a long-term follow-up. *Journal of Research in Crime and Delinquency, 42*, 309–322.

Brent, D. A., Holder, D., Kolko, D., Birmaher, B., Baugher, M., Roth, C., et al. (1997). A clinical psychotherapy trial for adolescent depression comparing cognitive, family, and supportive therapy. *Archives of General Psychiatry, 54,* 877–885.

Carey, T. A., & Oxman, L. N. (2007). Adolescents and mental health treatments: Reviewing the evidence to discern common themes for clinicians and areas of future research. *Clinical Psychologist, 11,* 79–87.

Chambless, D. L., & Hollon, S. D. (1998). Defining empirically supported therapies. *Journal of Consulting and Clinical Psychology, 66,* 7–18.

Chu, B., & Kendall, P. (2004). Positive association of child involvement and treatment outcome within a manual-based cognitive behavioral treatment for children with anxiety. *Journal of Consulting and Clinical Psychology, 72,* 821–829.

Cicchetti, D. (1993). Developmental psychopathology: Reactions, reflections, projections. *Developmental Review, 13,* 471–502.

Cicchetti, D., & Rogosch, F. A. (1996). Equifinality and multifinality in developmental psychopathology. *Development and Psychopathology, 8,* 597–600.

Cicchetti, D., & Rogosch, F. A. (2002). A developmental psychopathology perspective on adolescence. *Journal of Consulting and Clinical Psychology, 70,* 6–20.

Cicchetti, D., & Toth, S. L. (1998). The development of depression in children and adolescents. *American Psychologist, 53,* 221–241.

Cicchetti, D., & Toth, S. L. (2006). Developmental psychopathology and preventative intervention. In K. A. Renninger, I. E. Sigel, W. Damon, & R. Lerner (Eds.), *Handbook of child psychology* (pp. 497–547). Hoboken, NJ: Wiley.

Clarke, G. N., DeBar, L. L., & Lewinsohn, P. M. (2003). Cognitive-behavioral group treatment for adolescent depression. In A. E. Kazdin & J. R. Weisz (Eds.), *Evidence-based psychotherapies for children and adolescents* (pp. 120–134). New York, NY: Guilford Press.

David-Ferdon, C., & Kaslow, N. J. (2008). Evidence-based psychosocial treatments for child and adolescent depression. *Journal of Clinical Child and Adolescent Psychology, 37,* 62–104.

Day-Vines, N. L., Wood, S. M., Grothaus, T., Craigen, L., Holman, A., Dotson-Blake, K., et al. (2007). Broaching the subject of race, ethnicity, and culture during the counseling process. *Journal of Counseling and Development, 85,* 401–409.

Diamond, G. M., Diamond, G. S., & Liddle, H. A. (2000). The therapist-parent alliance in family-based therapy for adolescents. *Journal of Clinical Psychology, 56,* 1037–1050.

Diamond, G., Siqueland, L., & Diamond, G. M. (2003). Attachment based family therapy for depressed adolescents: Programmatic treatment development. *Clinical Child and Family Psychology Review, 6,* 107–127.

Fisher, C. B., Hoagwood, K., Boyce, C., Duster, T., Frank, D. A., Grisso, T., et al. (2002). Research ethics for mental health science involving ethnic minority children and youths. *American Psychologist, 57,* 1024–1040.

Gallagher, R. (2005). Evidence-based psychotherapies for depressed adolescents: A review of clinical guidelines. *Primary Psychiatry*, *12*, 33–39.

Garcia-Coll, C., Akerman, A., & Cicchetti, D. (2000). Cultural influences on developmental processes and outcomes: Implications for the study of development and psychopathology. *Development and Psychopathology*, *12*, 333–356.

Gibbons, R. D., Brown, C. H., Hur, K., Marcus, S. M., Bhaumik, D. K., Erkens, J. A., et al. (2007). Early evidence on the effects of regulators' suicidally warnings on SSRI prescriptions and suicide in children and adolescents. *American Journal of Psychiatry*, *164*, 1356–1363.

Graczyk, P. A., Connolly, S. D., & Corapci, F. (2005). Anxiety disorders in children and adolescents: Theory, treatment, and prevention. In T. P. Gullotta & G. R. Adams (Eds.), *Handbook of adolescent behavioral problems: Evidence-based approaches to prevention and treatment* (pp. 131–157). New York, NY: Springer.

Greenberg, L. S., Watson, J. C., Elliot, R., & Bohart, A. C. (2001). Empathy. *Psychotherapy: Theory, Research, Practice, Training*, *38*, 380–384.

Hammen, C. (1999). The emergence of an interpersonal approach to depression. In T. Joiner & J. Coyne (Eds.), *The interactional nature of depression: Advances in interpersonal approaches* (pp. 22–36). Washington, DC: American Psychological Association.

Hatch, M. L., Friedman, S., & Paradis, C. M. (1996). Behavioral treatment of obsessive disorder in African Americans. *Cognitive and Behavioral Practice*, *3*, 303–315.

Henggeler, S. W., Melton, G. B., & Smith, L. A. (1992). Family preservation using multisystemic therapy: An effective alternative to incarcerating serious juvenile offenders. *Journal of Consulting and Clinical Psychology*, *60*, 953–961.

Holmbeck, G. N., Greenley, R. N., & Franks, E. A. (2003). Developmental issues and considerations in research and practice. In A. E. Kazdin & J. R. Weisz (Eds.), *Evidence-based psychotherapies for children and adolescents* (pp. 21–40). New York, NY: Guilford Press.

Howard, B., Chu, B. C., Krain, A. L., Marrs-Garcia, M. A., & Kendall, P. C. (2000). *Cognitive-behavioral family therapy for anxious children: Therapist manual* (2nd ed.). Ardmore, PA: Workbook.

Hromco, J. G., Moore, M. W., & Nikkel, R. E. (2003). How managed care has affected mental health case management activities, caseloads, and tenure. *Community Mental Health Journal*, *39*, 501–509.

Jureidini, J. (2007). The black box warning: Decreased prescriptions and increased youth suicide? *American Journal of Psychiatry*, *164*, 1907.

Kane, E. P., Fagan, H. B., & Wolf, D. G. (2007). Should we use SSRIs to treat adolescents with depression? *The Journal of Family Practice*, *56*, 759–760.

Kendall, P. C. (2000). Guiding theory for therapy with children and adolescents. In P. C. Kendall (Ed.), *Child and adolescent therapy* (pp. 3–27). New York, NY: Guilford Press.

Kendall, P. C., & Hedtke, K. A. (2006). *Cognitive-behavioral therapy for anxious children: Therapist manual* (3rd ed.). Ardmore, PA: Workbook.

Kendall, P. C., Hudson, J. L., Gosch, E., Flannery-Schroeder, E., & Suveg, C. (2008). Cognitive-behavioral therapy for anxiety disordered youth: A randomized clinical trial evaluating child and family modalities. *Journal of Consulting and Clinical Psychology, 76*, 282–297.

Koocher, G. P. (2003). Ethical issues in psychotherapy with adolescents. *Journal of Clinical Psychology, 59*, 1247–1256.

Leibert, T., Archer, J., Munson, J., & York, G. (2006). An exploratory study of client perceptions of internet counseling and the therapeutic alliance. *Journal of Mental Health Counseling, 28*, 69–83.

Lewinsohn, P. M., Clarke, G. N., Hops, H., & Andrews, J. (1990). Cognitive-behavioral treatment for depressed adolescents. *Behavior Therapy, 21*, 385–401.

Lilienfeld, S. O. (2007). Psychological treatments that cause harm. *Perspectives on Psychological Science, 2*, 53–70.

Luthar, S. S., & Sexton, C. C. (2007). Maternal drug abuse versus maternal depression: Vulnerability and resilience among school-age and adolescent offspring. *Development and Psychopathology, 19*, 205–225.

March, J., Silva, S., Petrycki, S., Curry, J., Wells, K., Fairbank, J., et al. (2004). Fluoxetine, cognitive-behavioral therapy, and their combination for adolescents with depression: Treatment for adolescents with depression study (TADS) randomized controlled trial. *Journal of the American Medical Association, 292*, 807–820.

Masten, A. S., & Coatsworth, J. D. (1998). The development of competence in favorable and unfavorable environments: Lessons from research on successful children. *American Psychologist, 53*, 205–220.

Masten, A. S., Hubbard, J. J., Gest, S. D., Tellegen, A., Garmezy, N., & Ramirez, M. (1999). Competence in the context of adversity: Pathways to resilience and maladaptation from childhood to late adolescence. *Development and Psychopathology, 11*, 143–169.

Mufson, L., & Dorta, K. P. (2003). Interpersonal psychotherapy for depressed adolescents. In A. E. Kazdin & J. R. Weisz (Eds.), *Evidence-based psychotherapies for children and adolescents* (pp. 148–164). New York, NY: Guilford Press.

Munoz, R. F., & Mendelson, T. (2005). Toward evidenced-based interventions for diverse populations: The San Francisco General Hospital prevention and treatment manuals. *Journal of Consulting and Clinical Psychology, 73*, 790–799.

National Advisory Metnal Health Council. (2000). *Translating behavioral science into action: Report of the National Advisory Mental Health Counsel's behavioral science workgroup (no. 00-4699)*. Bethesda, MD: National Institutes of Mental Health.

National Institute for Health and Clinical Excellence (NICE). (2005). *Depression in children and young people: Identification and management in primary, community and secondary care. Quick reference guide*. London: Author. Retrieved 20 July 2008, from http://www.nice.org.uk

Oetzel, K. B., & Scherer, D. G. (2003). Therapeutic engagement with adolescents in psychotherapy. *Psychotherapy: Theory, Research, Practice, Training, 40*, 215–225.

Okiishi, J., Lambert, M. J., Nielsen, S. L., & Ogles, B. M. (2003). Waiting for supershrink: An empirical analysis of therapist effects. *Clinical Psychology & Psychotherapy, 10*, 361–373.

Patten, C. A., Croghan, I. T., Meis, T. M., Decker, P. A., Pingree, S., Colligan, et al. (2007). Randomized clinical trial of an Internet-based versus brief office intervention for adolescent smoking cessation. *Patient Education and Counseling, 64*, 249–258.

Petrosino, A., Turpin-Petrosino, C., & Buehler, J. (2003). "Scared Straight" and other juvenile awareness programs for preventing juvenile delinquency. *Annals of the American Academy of Political and Social Science, 589*, 41–62.

Pina, A. A., Silverman, W. K., Fuentes, R. M., Kurtines, W. M., & Weems, C. F. (2003). Exposure-based cognitive-behavioral treatment for phobic and anxiety disorders: Treatment effects and maintenance for Hispanic/Latino relative to European-American Youths. *Journal of the American Academy of Child and Adolescent Psychiatry, 42*, 1179–1187.

Prinz, R. J., & Jones, T. L. (2003). Family-based interventions. In C. A. Essau (Ed.), *Conduct and oppositional defiant disorders: Epidemiology, risk factors, and treatment* (pp. 279–298). Mahwah, NJ: Lawrence Erlbaum Associates Publishers.

Resnick, M. D., Bearman, P. S., Blum, R. W., Bauman, K. E., Harris, K. M., Jones, J., et al. (1997). Protecting adolescents from harm: Findings from the National Longitudinal Study on Adolescent Health. *Journal of the American Medical Association, 278*, 823–832.

Ritterband, L. M., Gonder-Frederick, L. A., Cox, D. J., Clifton, A. D., West, R. W., & Borowitz, S. M. (2003). Internet interventions: In review, in use, and into the future. *Professional Psychology, 34*, 527–534.

Rossello, J., & Bernal, G. (1999). The efficacy of cognitive-behavioral and interpersonal treatments for depression in Puerto Rican adolescents. *Journal of Consulting and Clinical Psychology, 67*, 734–745.

Rutter, M., & Sroufe, L. A. (2000). Developmental psychopathology: Cocnepts and challenges. *Developmenta and Psychopathology, 12*, 265–296.

Shirk, S. R. (2001). Development and cognitive therapy. *Journal of Cognitive Psychotherapy, 15*, 155–163.

Shirk, S. R., & Karver, M. (2003). Prediction of treatment outcome from relationship variables in child and adolescent therapy: A metaanalytic review. *Journal of Consulting and Clinical Psychology, 71*, 452–464.

Spencer, M. B., Dupree, D., Cunningham, M., Harpalani, V., & Munoz-Miller, M. (2003). Vulnerability to violence: A contextually-sensitive, developmental perspective on African American adolescents. *Journal of Social Issues, 59*, 33–49.

Sroufe, L. A., & Rutter, M. (1984). The domain of developmental psychopathology. *Child Development, 55*, 17–29.

Stark, K. D., Sander, J. B., Yancy, M. G., Bronik, M. D., & Hoke, J. A. (2000). Treatment of depression in childhood and adolescence. Cognitive-behavioral procedures for the individual and family. In P. C. Kendall (Ed.), *Child and adolescent therapy: Cognitive-behavioral procedures* (pp. 173–234). New York, NY: Guilford Press.

Tan, J. A., Passerini, G. E., & Stewart, A. (2007). Consent and confidentiality in clinical work with young people. *Clinical Child Psychology and Psychiatry, 12*, 191–210.

Thompson, C. E., Worthington, R., & Atkinson, D. R. (1994). Counselor content orientation, counselor race, and Black women's cultural mistrust and self-disclosures. *Journal of Counseling Psychology, 41*, 155–161.

Toth, S. L., & Cicchetti, D. (1999). Developmental psychopathology and child psychotherapy. In S. Russ & T. Ollendick (Eds.), *Handbook of psychotherapies with children and families* (pp. 15–44). New York: Plenum Press.

Von Bertalanffy, L. (1968). *General systems theory*. New York: Braziller.

Weersing, V. R., & Brent, D. A. (2003). Cognitive-behavioral therapy for adolescent depression: Comparative efficacy, mediation, moderation and effectiveness. In A. E. Kazdin & J. R. Weisz (Eds.), *Evidence-based psychotherapies for children and adolescents* (pp. 135–147). New York, NY: Guilford Press.

Weissman, M. M., Markowitz, J. C., & Klerman, G. L. (2000). *Comprehensive guide to interpersonal psychotherapy*. New York, NY: Basic Books.

Weist, M. D., & Evans, S. W. (2005). Expanded school mental health: Challenges and opportunities in an emerging field. *Journal of Youth and Adolescence, 34,* 3–6.

Weisz, J. R., Doss, A. J., & Hawley, K. M. (2005). Youth psychotherapy outcome research: A review and critique of the evidence base. *Annual Review of Psychology, 56,* 337–363.

Weisz, J. R., & Gray, S. J. (2008). Evidence-based psychotherapy for children and adolescents: Data from the present and a model for the future. *Child and Adolescent Mental Health, 13,* 54–65.

Weisz, J. R., & Hawley, K. M. (2002). Developmental factors in the treatment of adolescents. *Journal of Consulting and Clinical Psychology, 70,* 21–43.

Werch, C. E., & Owen, D. (2002). Iatrogenic effects if alcohol and drug prevention programs. *Journal of Studies on Alcohol, 63,* 581–590.

Werner, H. (1948). *Comparative psychology of mental development*. New York: International Universities Press.

Westen, D., Novotny, C. M., & Thompson-Brenner, H. (2004). The empirical status of empirically supported psychotherapies: Assumptions, findings, and reporting in controlled clinical trials. *Psychological Bulletin, 130,* 631–663.

Whaley, A. L., & Davis, K. E. (2007). Cultural competence and evidence-based practice in mental health services: A complementary perspective. *American Psychologist, 62,* 563–574.

Wintersteen, M. B., Mensinger, J. L., & Diamond, G. S. (2005). Do gender and racial differences between patient and therapist affect therapeutic alliance and treatment retention in adolescents? *Professional Psychology: Research and Practice, 36,* 400–408.

Wood, J. J., Chiu, A. W., Hwang, W., Jacobs, J., & Ifekwunigwe, M. (2008). Adapting cognitive-behavioral therapy for Mexican American students with anxiety disorders: Recommendations for school psychologists. *School Psychology Quarterly, 23,* 515–532.

Chapter 17

Understanding adolescence: A policy perspective

Malik C. Edwards

Charlotte School of Law, Charlotte, NC

Advocates for children are often forced to make two contradictory arguments in the policy arena: "kids are just different" and "kids are like adults." As identified by Poncz (2008), this conflict in "advocacy strategies mirrors the inconsistent legal treatment of youths" (p. 276). As a result there is no national policy in place to guide decision making involving the rights of children, with the result being that "decisions involving children are haphazard at best and inequitable or even damaging to children at worst" (Walker, Brooks, & Wrightsman, 1999, pp. 12-13). I argue that these conflicts are even more pressing when dealing with adolescents because they exist in a space between childhood and adulthood.

As Scott (2000) notes: "American lawmakers have had relatively clear images of childhood and adulthood—images that fit with our conventional notions. Children are innocent beings, who are dependent, vulnerable, and incapable of making competent decisions" (p. 547). Most aspects of the legal regulation of childhood are based on this dichotomy. Children are commonly held unaccountable for their choices; as reflected in their inability to contract.[1] They are also legally assumed unfit to exercise the rights and privileges of adults, and thus are not permitted to vote, drive, or make their own medical decisions. There is a departure from the child-adult dichotomy in legal policy toward youths' criminal conduct.

---

[1] For purposes of contract law, contracts by minors were void at early common law and then voidable by the minor. At common law, age of majority was 21; following the passage of the 26th Amendment in 1971 most states lowered the age to 18 (see Perrillo, 2002, § 27.2).

Adolescence: Development During a Global Era

Privileged children may be given the assumption of infancy and not be held accountable for their behavior, while poor and minority youths are treated as adults. This departs from a belief that all children need care, support, and education in order to develop into healthy productive adults.

For purposes of this text the picture is further complicated by the fact that policy makers have no clear image of adolescence. As identified by Scott (2000), politicians ignore the "transitional developmental stage, classifying adolescents legally either as children or as adults, depending on the issue at hand" (p. 548). So we see adolescents captured in legal rhetoric of infancy, indistinguishable from young children, and subject to paternalistic policies based on assumptions of dependence, vulnerability, and incompetence (Cunningham, 2006; Scott, 2000), whereas in other contexts, adolescents are treated as fully mature adults, who are competent to make decisions, accountable for their choices, and entitled to no special accommodations.[2]

While adolescents may appear physically mature and rational, our knowledge of human development belies these perceptions. Our knowledge, however, cannot overcome our fear of "other people's" children (Woodhouse, 2002). Although serious violent crime has decreased over the past few years, there is still a call on the part of policy makers and the public at large to get tough on delinquents (Woolard, Fondacaro, & Slobogin, 2001). These "get tough" policies deny adolescents what Zimring (1982) refers to as a "learner's permit" period. He posits that there "are a few of the things we cannot learn to do well without practice: making decisions, making love, driving, flying, practicing law, parenting, taking risks, saying no, and—most important— choosing the path of our lives in a free society" (pp. 89-90). He urges that we use the metaphor of the "learner's permit" to remind ourselves that learning to live, like learning to drive, is a risky process. To maximize our gains, we need to give adolescents opportunities to road test their autonomy. To best serve adolescents we need legal policy that "preserves the life chances for those who make serious mistakes, as well as preserving choices for their more fortunate (and more virtuous) contemporaries" (pp. 91-92). Woodhouse identifies the discriminatory aspects of these new policies: "Historically, when a youth was guilty of bad conduct, we were culturally predisposed to allow a second and often a third chance, hoping he or she would eventually get it right. This is no longer true for poor children and children of color" (p. 744).

---

[2]See Taylor-Thompson (2003), "Between 1992 and 1995 forty jurisdictions moved to extend adult court jurisdiction over juvenile offenders by reducing the minimum age for prosecution in criminal court, and twelve states now have no minimum-age requirement for transfers to adult court for prosecution" (pp. 143-144).

The purpose of this chapter is to explore how developmental theory can be used to guide juvenile justice policy. This is done through an examination of the historical development of today's juvenile justice system, the theoretical basis for adolescent development, and finally, an examination of the US Supreme Court's (2005) decision in *Roper v. Simmons*, which examines the interaction of developmental theory and legal policy development.

17.1. **ADOLESCENT JUSTICE?**

The concept of a special system of juvenile justice is largely a twentieth century development, with the first juvenile court being established in Chicago in 1899 (Clark, 2005). Until the very late nineteenth century, US law tended to treat children either as property or as little adults. In the late nineteenth century, jurisdictions in several states experimented with separate procedures in the criminal trials of juveniles, and by the 1920s, separate juvenile justice systems were established in nearly every state (Brink, 2004; Whitehead & Lab, 2006).

Unfortunately, this policy evolution has not always been guided by an understanding of adolescent development. As Taylor-Thompson (2003) has noted, "societal attitudes about adolescent capacities have changed dramatically over time, principally in reaction to perceived political imperatives" (p. 145). The result has been a reactionary system that never fully embraces a contextual human development approach.

17.1.1. **Common law conceptions**

At common law, youths were divided into three age categories; under 7, 7-14, and 14 and older (Cunningham, 2006). Generally, children under the age of 7 could not be found criminally liable. This protection was grounded in both property and capacity concepts. The property conception was eloquently captured by Clark (2005) as "child is chattel, young children (birth until 7) were regarded as the property of their parents, to be treated, like other property, at the discretion of the owner" (p. 622). From a capacity standpoint these youngsters had a nonrebuttable legal presumption of infancy, which held that the accused is not personally culpable because of lacking the mental capacity to understand the likely physical consequences of his or her action or its wrongful nature (Bazelon, 2000; Robinson, 1984; Thomas, 1997).

Children between the ages of 7 and 14 could also avail themselves of the defense of infancy, but for these youths, the defense only provided a rebuttable presumption (Cunningham, 2006). To rebut this presumption, the state had to provide affirmative evidence that a preadolescent child was capable of formulating the requisite *mens rea*[3] with respect to a crime. These were individualized determinations in which the court looked to determine if the youth had "the intelligence to apprehend the consequences of acts; to reason upon duty; to distinguish between right and wrong; if the consciousness of guilt and innocence be clearly manifested, then this capacity is shown" (*State v. Aaron,* 1818 WL 1527, *11 (N.J. 1818)).

Courts presumed children over age 14 possessed the requisite capacities for criminal intent. Once convicted, young offenders, like their adult counterparts, faced the full range of penalties. Although the death penalty for children was rarely carried out, "some children between the ages of 10 and 12 were executed in early America" (Taylor-Thompson, 2003, pp. 145-146).

17.1.2. **Progressive conceptions**

We can see the political imperatives identified by Taylor-Thomas above in the impact of the Progressive movement on children in the US criminal justice system. The nineteenth century was marked by great societal change as a result of industrial revolution. Economic modernization, urbanization, and industrialization forced people to live in closer proximity to one another, and the social challenges that accompanied an urban lifestyle resulted in changes in both family structure and the function of the family in society. These changes in family structure, specifically the supports of extended family, had a significant impact on children. The state quickly recognized the need to deal with children who were considered incorrigible or who posed a problem to their families or communities (Clark, 2005).

In direct response to this recognized need, the states of New York, Massachusetts, and Pennsylvania established Houses of Refuge (see Clark, 2005). These privately funded houses were designed to act as custodians for children, usually in the 7- to 14-year-old group mentioned above, who had committed criminal offenses, who were found to be runaways or vagrants, or whose parents simply were unable to control them. The purpose of these institutions was to save children from a life of crime

---

[3]Mens rea is defined as the mental state required to make the perpetration of a blameworthy act a crime as defined by law. See, LaFave and Scott (1972, § 2), at 7 "Action alone without a bad mind cannot be the basis of criminal liability; crime requires some sort of mens rea (guilty mind)."

and the harsh consequences of incarceration with adults. Reformers were more concerned with protecting young people than with punishing them for their wrongdoing. They believed that a child's poor living environment, rather than his willful behavior, caused juvenile delinquency.

By the late nineteenth century, the way children were treated in the criminal justice system attracted the attention of the Progressives. This was part of a large system of reform proposed by Progressive activists to address "the social, legal, and economic problems associated with industrialization" (Taylor-Thompson, 2003, p. 146). These reforms addressed child labor, children's health and well-being, as well as the methods that the state employed to address delinquent behavior by children (Feld, 1999). The Progressive reformers identified the punitive impulses that defined the US justice system's approach to juvenile crime as an area for reform. They questioned the wisdom and utility of exposing young children to adult trials, convictions, and long prison sentences in the company of hardened criminals.

To address these concerns the Progressives worked to change the prevailing conception of youthful offenders. They developed a view of youths as misguided innocents. To this end they openly endorsed the idea of adolescents as not fully formed individuals. Given their youth, Progressives argued, adolescents were less responsible than adults and more likely to benefit from treatment and intervention.

The progressive ideology was captured by Judge Julian Mack (1909) in one of the earliest articles on the new concept of the juvenile court:

> [T]he child who has begun to go wrong, who is incorrigible, who has broken a law or an ordinance, is to be taken in hand by the state, not as an enemy but as a protector, as the ultimate guardian, because either the unwillingness or inability of the natural parents to guide it toward good citizenship has compelled the intervention of the public authorities (p. 107).

This nascent developmental argument was supplemented by a parental deficit theory, which presupposed that what delinquent children lacked was adequate parental guidance and care. Therefore, the youth's inappropriate conduct could best be addressed by the state through remedial rather than punitive measures.

The Progressives' "common sense and casual observation" were supported by emerging psychological insights that genuine differences existed between a child and an adult (Taylor-Thompson, 2003, p. 146). Clark (2005) presents the generally held belief that "Progressive reform thus reflected some basic changes in the ideological assumptions about the sources of crime and social deviance, and demonstrated a fundamental belief in the benevolence of state action and faith that the government could correct social problems" (p. 665).

For those who accepted this view of benevolence, the juvenile justice system was constructed around ideas about the education and socialization of children, in general, and wayward children, in particular. This is seen in the emergence of cottage reformatories and the Houses of Refuge that dealt with wayward children by combining discipline, education, and vocational training, and later through the development of juvenile courts. Juvenile courts differed from their adult counterparts in several ways, and these differences reflected the assumptions that juveniles were not as mature as adults. Procedurally, juvenile courts were more informal and less adversarial. Substantively, they focused less on punishment and more on rehabilitation and socialization (Brink, 2004).

This historical interpretation is not a universally held view. Sutton (1985) suggests that the juvenile court was not a substantive reform but served primarily to extend conventional means of child control through the legitimizing vocabulary of Progressivism. He uses descriptive analysis of state statutes[4] to show the derivative, ambiguous nature of the juvenile court as a legal phenomenon, and to illustrate that neither functional need nor social movement influences provided a convincing explanation for the rapid institutionalization of the court (p. 107). Instead the juvenile court was ideologically based, taking on "the least controversial aspects of the general progressive reform agenda" (p. 109).

In either case juvenile courts operated under the doctrine of *parens patriae*,[5] and so adopted a more paternalistic attitude toward juvenile offenders. As a result the treatment of juvenile offenders was different from adult offenders; juvenile correctional facilities "stressed educational and vocational training, sentences were often shorter, courts made greater use of probationary and other diversionary alternatives to incarceration, and the criminal records of juvenile offenders were not made a matter of public record in order to prevent stigmatization that might interfere with successful rehabilitation" (Brink, 2004, p. 1559).

---

[4]The development of the juvenile justice system was done on a state-by-state basis.

[5]Parens patriae means the "state as father," and it is the basis for the child welfare systems across the United States. Parens patriae is also the basis of the state's jurisdiction over juvenile delinquency proceeding. See Poncz (2008).

The paternalistic focus of juvenile courts lent itself to procedural inform-alities that did not acknowledge the developmental complexities of adoles-cent development. By adopting an adult-child binary, the ways in which adolescents could participate in their own defense or rehabilitation were overlooked, and juvenile offenders were not afforded the same procedural safeguards before and during trial as their adult counterparts (Brink, 2004). These due process concerns were noted almost from the beginning of the development of a system of juvenile justice. The first such case, *Ex parte Crouse* (1839), predates the first juvenile court by 60 years. Mary Ann Crouse, a minor, was detained in the Philadelphia House of Refuge based on her mother's allegation that she was an incorrigible child. Mary Ann's father challenged the constitutional basis for her commitment, arguing that she should not have been committed without affording her a trial by jury consistent with due process. The Pennsylvania Supreme Court raised the *parens patriae* power of the state, asserting: "The infant has been snatched from a course which must have ended in confirmed depravity; and, not only is the restraint of her person lawful, but it would be an act of extreme cruelty to release her from it" (Ex Parte Crouse 4 Whart. 9, 11, 1839). The court's rationale was that because the goal of detention was reformation and rehabilitation rather than punishment, the Constitution did not prohibit restraints imposed for a child's own welfare.

17.1.3. **Modern juvenile justice**

This precedent held until the 1960s, when the Supreme Court was willing to recognize due process rights in juvenile proceedings. In *Kent v. United States* (1966), the US Supreme Court insisted that in any judicial transfer from juvenile to adult criminal court the accused is entitled to a hearing, the assistance of counsel, and a statement of the reasons for the transfer.

In the seminal case of *In re Gault* (1967), the Court held that juveniles enjoy the Fifth Amendment right against self-incrimination and the Sixth Amend-ment rights to notice of charges, to confront and cross-examine accusers, and to the assistance of counsel. And in *In re Winship* (1970), the Court not only affirmed the requirement that adult criminals be convicted only by the standard of guilt beyond a reasonable doubt but also extended this evidentiary requirement to juvenile proceedings in which incarceration is a possible outcome (Brink, 2004; Whitehead & Lab, 2006).

Contemporary juvenile justice distinguishes juveniles from adults and recognizes distinct forms of juvenile offense (Whitehead & Lab, 2006). The Model Penal Code ("MPC") (1962), for instance, identifies juveniles as those under the age of 18 (§ 4.10 cmt 3). While juveniles under the age of 16 are usually to be tried in juvenile court, the MPC provides for the possibility of judicial waiver of juveniles between the ages of 16 and 18 to adult criminal court. In much the same way preadolescents and early adolescents were treated at common law, 16- and 17-year-old youths are examined on a case-by-case basis, in which the prosecution bears the burden of proof in justifying the waiver (§ 4.10 cmts 1, 3). A substantial majority of states have followed the MPC in identifying juveniles as those under 18 years of age.[6]

Juvenile courts recognize two main kinds of juvenile offense. Juvenile crime is simply criminal activity committed by a juvenile. The rules for adult and juvenile crime are the same; the only difference is the age of the offender. By contrast, status offenses comprise acts whose legality depends upon the status of the actor. Juvenile status offenses involve acts that would be legal if performed by an adult but are illegal for juveniles, such as truancy, running away from home, curfew violations, smoking, drinking, and swearing. The trend of trying juveniles as adults applies only to juvenile criminal conduct, not juvenile status offenses (Cunningham, 2006).

17.1.4. **Developmental perspective**

While the beginning of this chapter is legal and historical, the need for a developmental perspective is infused. As much as Progressives are given credit for developing the concept of adolescence, particularly within policy contexts, they failed to articulate the precise factors that differentiated youths from adults (Taylor-Thompson, 2003). They did not capture the complexity of adolescent reasoning but utilized a strategy that "depend [ed] on selectively invoking images that emphasized—and at times exaggerated—the child-like characteristics of youthful offenders" (Taylor-Thompson, 2003, p. 146). This binary approach, while effective viscerally, has not made for good policy.

Good policy must move beyond emotion and address the substantive ends and have a research base. So, in seeking to reform juvenile justice and support protections for youth, one could start with the concept of capacity. Understanding children's capacities in legal contexts is an urgent priority for psychology and the law (Woolard, Reppucci, & Redding, 1996). The concept of competency as defined by Cunningham (2006) asserts that

---

[6]Ten states (GA, IL, LA, MA, MI, MO, NH, SC, TX, and WI) identify juveniles as those under 17 years of age, and three states (CT, NY, and NC) identify juveniles as those under 16 years of age. See Brink (2004).

"competency is central" to an understanding of an adolescent's rights and responsibilities, because the law looks to determine if the youth is "capable of exercising certain rights or being held accountable for their actions" (p. 278). Woolard et al. provide guidance for using the concept of capacity for research purposes:

> *The distinction between capacity and performance is discussed in light of two research goals: (a) identifying children's capacities relevant to law; and (b) identifying the circumstances under which their performance varies. This discussion leads to three fundamental research issues that are explored. First, in addition to general capacity, the effect of specific legal contexts on performance requires investigation. Second, capacities research must take a developmental approach using appropriate, ecologically valid target and comparison samples. Third, legal standards and their inherent developmental assumptions about children's capacities must be operationalized and investigated from both legal and psychological perspectives (p. 219).*

Steinberg and Cauffman (1996) classify adolescent immaturity in two broad categories:

> *those attributed to cognitive differences between adolescents and adults (i.e., differences in the way they think), and those attributed to psychosocial differences (i.e., differences in their social and emotional maturity). These differences are assumed to reflect differences in competence due to differences in developmental status (independent of experience), differences in experience (independent of developmental status), or some combination of both (p. 250)*

Steinberg and Cauffman (1996) argue that cognition and maturity go hand-in-hand:

> *An individual facing a particular decision may have the cognitive skills to evaluate the costs and benefits of various courses of action, but if the individual is especially impulsive, he or she may not make a wise decision. By the same token, even the most responsible and temperate individual will not make competent decisions if he or she lacks the requisite cognitive skills or access to relevant information (p. 251).*

Even when adolescents engage in an adult-like process of decision making, they may not reach the "right" results. Steinberg and Cauffman have identified a number of factors that may influence decision-making outcomes in a negative way. Adolescent decision making differs from adult decision making because of increased peer influence and different perceptions of risk and time (Scott & Grisso, 1997). Adolescents are also more likely to engage in risky behaviors than adults (Arnett, 1992). This occurs not because they do not recognize the risks of their conduct, but because they believe other factors outweigh the risk (Steinberg & Cauffman, 1996, p. 258).

Cunningham (2006) suggests that additional research is particularly needed in the area of decision making and delinquency. This is supported by the research of Scott (2000), who has found that most children who engage in delinquent acts will outgrow such behavior by adulthood (p. 591). While some youths' delinquent behavior will grow into adult criminality, we know very little about why certain children fall into one category as opposed to the other (Scott & Grisso, 1997). As Cunningham points out, research on the influence of psychosocial factors affecting judgment is "sketchy" (Cunningham, 2006, p. 285)

An area warranting further exploration is whether capacity should be limited to process or whether we should examine an individual's outcomes as well. Much of our appreciation for capacity flows from the medical context, in which informed consent rests on process, not whether the individual reaches the "right result." Beauchamp and Childress' definition, likewise, focuses on the mental process of deliberation. Steinberg and Cauffman's work, therefore, creates a twofold question: (1) Do children reach different results because of their immaturity? and (2) Do we care (i.e., is reaching the right result relevant to one's capacity)?

Human development theory or developmental psychology theory can be divided into linear and nonlinear developmental theory. Linear developmental theory presumes that all humans develop in a similar fashion, demonstrating an upward developmental trajectory tied to chronological age. Nonlinear developmental theory asserts that chronological age alone cannot necessarily be tied to assumptions about development because development is an inherently social process that occurs in a particular real-world context (Wertsch, 1985). A linear approach is usually preferred by policymakers because it is considered less contextual. We can pass a law based on all 16-year-olds as competent. Although a linear approach is preferred, the treatment of some adolescents has allowed for developmental context from common law to model penal code. In addressing this concept of linear versus nonlinear, a brief overview of key theories is presented here.

Nonlinear developmental psychology theory is perhaps best reflected in the work of Vygotsky, Bronfenbrenner, and Bandura.

Linear developmental theory

Linear developmental psychology theory, as demonstrated by the work of Jean Piaget, creates an age-contingent, lock-step trajectory for human development (James & Prout, 1997). Piaget may be the most influential researcher in the area of juvenile justice. This can be attributed to the congruency of his linear approach with the common law conception of capacity. Piaget divided development into four periods with distinct stages therein, and named these periods of development the sensorimotor period, the preoperational period, the concrete operational period, and the formal operational period (Cunningham, 2006; Miller, 1989). In the "sensorimotor stage," infants learn about the world around them through touch, taste, and other interactions. From ages 2 to 7, children undergo the "preoperational stage," in which they learn to communicate. They do not, however, have the ability to understand the consequences of their actions. In the "concrete operational stage," children ages 11-12 begin to think logically and can order their worlds into hierarchies. The last stage, the "formal operational stage," is considered developed by age 15. Children learn to think hypothetically, reasoning through a series of options by considering likely outcomes. Piaget theorized that by age 15 a child has amassed adult-like cognitive ability (Cunningham, 2006; Miller, 1989). At this point in a linear developmental paradigm, the cognitive processes necessary for adult functioning are complete. Therefore, middle adolescence signals the highest level of development in a linear paradigm, when full development is "achieved" (Piaget, 2001).

Erikson, in contrast, focuses on psychosocial development, and while conceptually considered a linear theorist, acts as a bridge between linear and nonlinear theorists. He frames development through identification of eight stages/dichotomies of human development and identity formation: (1) basic trust versus mistrust; (2) autonomy versus shame; (3) initiative versus guilt; (4) industry versus inferiority; (5) identity versus role confusion; (6) intimacy versus isolation; (7) generativity versus stagnation; and (8) ego integrity versus despair (Erikson, 1950, pp. 247-274).

Erikson's first three stages represent early stages, when the individual is not yet capable of interacting with "cultural tools."[7] Because young children are not generally subject to court jurisdiction, this has not traditionally been a problem, but zero-tolerance policies at schools have seen the introduction of younger children into the juvenile justice system.

---

[7]Cultural tools are a Vygotskyian concept discussed in the next section through which children's participation in cultural activities with the guidance of more skilled partners allows children to "internalize the tools for thinking" (Rogoff, 1990, p. 13).

The eighth stage is similarly a stage in which the individual is primarily conquering internal dynamics, and, therefore, interaction with culture, its tools, and other individuals is not the primary focus of the stage.

The focus from a policy prospective would probably fall most heavily on the intermediate, fourth through sixth, stages; where the individual is learning from and making a place in society. The child becomes a different person in each stage with different cognitive capacities and progressively achieves a greater ability to interact with a wider range of people. For Erikson (1950) the ego can only remain strong through interactions with cultural institutions that enable the development of the child's capacities and potential (pp. 190-204). Although theoretically linear, Erikson's stages are not bound to chronological age.

Nonlinear developmental and identity theory

Critics find Piaget's stage-like theory of development too rigid, suggesting, instead, that cognitive development occurs gradually and incrementally (Hartman, 2000). This is seen in the work of developmental theorists with nonlinear approaches who hold important insights contrary to the views of Piaget and other linear developmental theorists. Unlike the lockstep approach of linear theorists, nonlinear theorists take a dynamic approach. An individual interacts with and within a particular social context to generate development in an emergent manner.

Vygotsky (1986), a contextualist and a contemporary of Piaget, introduced the importance of analyzing development in a cultural context. The smallest unit of analysis for Vygotsky (1978) is the child in a particular social context, an inherently variable construction across environments and individuals (pp. 86-90). Learning and development occur through interactions inside the "zone of proximal development." The zone of proximal development refers to the distance between the child's actual ability level and the child's potential ability with help from adults or more advanced peers. In this process, help in development comes not only from humans in the environment but also from self-help using cultural tools (Vygotsky, 1978, pp. 86-90).

For Vygotsky, humans master themselves from the outside through psychological and technical tools, which allow individuals to achieve more in their specific context. These tools, however, also vary, depending on culture and social contexts. In other words, the focus of assessment using a Vygotskian developmental paradigm is less on the static notion of who the child currently is but more on the dynamic question of who the child can become, depending on context and tools (Vygotsky, 1978). This matters greatly when looking to determine the tools and supports necessary for adolescents in the juvenile justice system.

An elaboration on the evolving, nonlinear nature of social contexts that shape development can be found in the work of Bronfenbrenner (1979). Bronfenbrenner presents an ecological model that illustrates the importance of reviewing multiple levels of social context. He identifies four levels of analysis: (1) macrosystem, (2) mesosystem, (3) exosystem, and (4) microsystem (Bronfenbrenner, 1979, pp. 7-8). Analysis at the macrosystem level requires examination of culture as a whole, along with belief systems and ideologies underlying cultural rules and norms (p. 258). This provides context not only for developing reforms but also to understand the actions of adolescents. The analysis focuses on the mechanisms of social governance and the worldview prevalent in society. Analysis at the mesosystem level focuses attention on interpersonal dynamics and the dynamics between the individual and secondary settings, such as the school. A policy prospective analysis at the exosystem level contemplates interactions that are outside the primary sphere of analysis but that nevertheless affect, or are affected by, what happens in the primary setting. At the microsystem level, analysis is primarily focused on individuals and their psychological development in a particular context. It must be remembered that the influences within and across all four levels impact an individual and, consequently, developmental processes because of their interactions with one another.

Bandura's (1986) Social Learning Theory presents a consonant analysis for policy development. The theory views the interaction between individuals and environments as a three-way exchange in which the person, an entity with unique characteristics, performs a behavior in an environment which responds back to the person and the behavior in a process of reciprocal determinism; it is an idiosyncratic interaction. According to Bandura, models can serve to instruct, motivate, disinhibit, inhibit, socially facilitate, and arouse emotion in a process of vicarious reinforcement (Bandura, 1986). Essentially, development is a process of quantitative change, during which learning episodes gradually accumulate over time. Although Social Learning Theory does not directly address historical or cultural context, it reflects the tradition of Vygotsky and contextualist approaches. It remains important because it recognizes the dialectical processes of development where individuals work within and are shaped by an environment; a triadic reciprocal determinism occurs among behavior, cognitive factors, and the environment (Bandura, 1986, pp. 194-196).

In nonlinear perspectives, development is continuous and universal behaviors are rare. This causes problems for policy development because each child must be addressed as a unique individual, but it is necessary if one accepts that children are developmentally malleable, but only within constraints of biology and environment. Nonlinear developmental theories offer useful analytical lenses for (re)theorizing juvenile justice reform and adolescent-focused policies more generally.

17.2. DEVELOPMENT AND ADOLESCENT-FOCUSED POLICIES

Much of the earlier juvenile justice reform process was done through the legislative process. The legislative process has been examined in the work of Sutton (1985) and Taylor-Thompson (2003) and, as they note, the process is often slow and ideologically based. I present in this section an examination of a policy change in the treatment of late adolescents in the limited context of the death penalty.

This raises the question, Why examine the reform when most policy is made through the legislative process? A possible answer is provided by Elmore and McLaughlin (1982), who explain that "recourse to the courts marks an end run around institutions, notably state legislatures, which are politically unresponsive to the equity-based grievances of traditionally unrepresented interest" (p. 15).

While the legitimacy of the courts' role in making policy has been debated, I accept that courts are policy makers and attempt to build on Bosworth's (2001) finding that "courts do not merely reflect larger political and social forces: they help shape those forces" (p. 1).

In examining the Supreme Court's juvenile death penalty jurisprudence, we observe what Cunningham (2006) describes as a shift from "individual determinations to categorical incapacity" (p. 298). The sentence of death for individuals who commit crimes while under the age of 18 was ruled unconstitutional by the US Supreme Court in *Roper v. Simmons* (2005). Prior to *Roper*, juvenile defendants could be executed for crimes committed while age 16 or above.[8] Juveniles who were tried as adults and convicted of capital crimes could at the discretion of individual juries and judges be sentenced to death. Capacity was determined on a child-by-child basis.

---

[8]The Court had set the age at 16 in *Thompson v. Oklahoma* (1988).

While youth (i.e., age constituting a minor) was a mitigating factor, as explained by the Court in *Eddings v. Oklahoma* (1982):

> *[Y]outh must be considered a relevant mitigating factor. But youth is more than a chronological fact. It is a time and condition of life when a person may be most susceptible to influence to psychological damage. Our history is replete with laws and judicial recognition that minors, especially in their earlier years, generally are less mature and responsible than adults. Particularly "during the formative years of childhood and adolescence, minors often lack the experience, perspective, and judgment" expected of adults (pp. 115-116).*

It did not protect mid and late adolescents from the ultimate judicial penalty, death.

Examinations of legal decision making have traditionally relied on the legal model (Epstein, George, & Kobylka, 1992, 2003). The underlying assumption of this model is that judges apply statutes and precedents to the facts of the cases before them without regard to personal preferences or political pressures. Koski (2003) explains it thusly:

> *It is straightforward deductive reasoning from the major premise (the command of the written law) to the minor premise (the facts of the present case) to the conclusion (the ruling based on force of logic. "Through this simple, almost mechanical process, the judge does little more than announce the ruling that already existed-either by virtue of preordained moral principles or by irrefutable logic." (p. 22, citing Stumpf & Paul, 1998).*

This theory is grounded on the principle of *stare decisis*, which requires courts to abide by precedent laid down in previous cases. Pursuant to the legal model, judicial decision making should be constrained by constitutional and statutory law as well as prior case law and precedent.

Based on this understanding, cases with the same facts and legal issues should reach the same result. We can see that this is not always true when we see how, as understandings of adolescent development evolved, in less than 20 years we moved from a system where most adolescents were death penalty-eligible to a system where no one under the age of 18 could be executed in the United States.

In 1988, the Supreme Court established a categorical rule of incapacity in *Thompson v. Oklahoma*. The case concerned Thompson, a 15-year-old accused of murdering his brother-in-law and disposing of his body in a river. Although he was legally a child in Oklahoma,[9] a judge ordered him to stand trial as an adult, finding that he was competent and that he knew and appreciated the wrongfulness of his conduct (1988, p. 819). Thompson was sentenced to death.

Thompson's death sentence was overturned by a plurality of the Court, who found that it was cruel and unusual punishment to execute Thompson, who was 15 years old at the time of the offense. In undertaking their Eighth Amendment[10] analysis, the Court noted that Oklahoma law prevented 15-year-olds from voting, sitting on juries, marrying without parental consent, and purchasing alcohol or cigarettes and concluded that there was near uniformity in the view that 15-year-olds are categorically different from older adolescents.

The plurality also drew upon its own sense of experience and belief about children, stating, "All of this legislation is consistent with the experience of mankind, as well as the long history of our law, that the normal 15-year-old is not prepared to assume the full responsibilities of an adult" (pp. 824-825). The findings were also consistent with other state statutes. At the time of the decision, all states that legislated a minimum age for the death penalty set the age at 16 or higher (p. 829).

The Court's holding built on conceptions of traditional paternalistic notions as well as understandings of capacity. The following passage captures the essence of the Court's *parens patria* concerns:

> *It is in this way that paternalism bears a beneficent face, paternalism in the sense of a caring, nurturing parent making decisions on behalf of a child who is not quite ready to take on the fully rational and considered task of shaping his or her own life.... [The law] reflects this basic assumption that our society makes about children as a class; we assume that they do not yet act as adults do, and thus we act in their interest by restricting certain choices that we feel they are not yet ready to make with full benefit of the costs and benefits attending such decisions. It would be*

---

[9]Oklahoma Stat., Tit. 10, § 1101(1) (Supp. 1987) provides: "'Child' means any person under eighteen (18) years of age, except for any person sixteen (16) or seventeen (17) years of age who is charged with murder, kidnapping for purposes of extortion, robbery with a dangerous weapon, rape in the first degree, use of a firearm or other offensive weapon while committing a felony, arson in the first degree, burglary with explosives, shooting with intent to kill, manslaughter in the first degree, or nonconsensual sodomy."

[10]U.S. Const. amend. VIII ("Excessive bail shall not be required, nor excessive fines imposed, nor cruel and unusual punishments inflicted.").

ironic if these assumptions that we so readily make about children as a class—about their inherent difference from adults in their capacity as agents, as choosers, as shapers of their own lives— were suddenly unavailable in determining whether it is cruel and unusual to treat children the same as adults for purposes of inflicting capital punishment. Thus, informing the judgment of the Court today is the virtue of consistency, for the very assumptions we make about children when we legislate on their behalf tells us that it is likely cruel, and certainly unusual, to impose on a child a punishment that takes as its predicate the existence of a fully rational, choosing agent, who may be deterred by the harshest of sanctions and toward whom society may legitimately take a retributive stance (p. 825, n. 23).

The following passage captures the plurality's concern with capacity:

Thus, the Court has already endorsed the proposition that less culpability should attach to a crime committed by a juvenile than to a comparable crime committed by an adult. The basis for this conclusion is too obvious to require extended explanation. Inexperience, less education, and less intelligence make the teenager less able to evaluate the consequences of his or her conduct while at the same time he or she is much more apt to be motivated by mere emotion or peer pressure than is an adult. The reasons why juveniles are not entrusted with the privileges and responsibilities of an adult also explain why their irresponsible conduct is not as morally reprehensible as that of an adult (p. 835).

As noted by Cunningham (2006), the Court's conception of adolescent development would appear to be at odds at with Piaget's conclusion that by midadolescence a child's cognitive capacity is as developed as a young adult's. While the Court cited the work of Lewis et al., as well as the work of other researchers, it made no reference to the methods and conclusions of those studies, nor did the Court address Piaget's conclusion that midadolescents are nearly identical, from the standpoint of cognition, as adults.

A year later, *Stanford v. Kentucky* (1989) presented the question of whether the categorical exception for 15-year-olds should be extended to a 16-year-olds; the Court declined to rule that 16-year-olds were categorically incapable of receiving the death penalty. Instead, the Court left in place the case-by-case framework from *Eddings* (1982). The Court's reasoning was not based on developmental evidence but instead on a belief that there was no national consensus "as evidenced by the actions of state legislatures and sentencing juries" against the juvenile death penalty (1989, p. 374).

In 2005, only 16 years later, the Supreme Court, in *Roper v. Simmons*, declared the juvenile death penalty unconstitutional altogether. In order to explain its departure from the precedent of *Stanford v. Kentucky*, the Court reasoned that since *Stanford*, a national consensus had developed that the juvenile death penalty was altogether "cruel and unusual punishment" (2005, p. 551). As Cunningham (2006) notes, *Roper* involved "familiar debates about whether the juvenile death penalty was inconsistent with other areas of juvenile law, whether the Court should apply its own judgment of what is cruel and unusual punishment, [and] how much deference is owed to the states" (p. 308). I disagree with his assertion that developmental theory did not affect the Court's decision.

The *Roper* Court noted three major differences between adolescents under 18 and adults: immaturity and recklessness, susceptibility to external influences (i.e., peer pressure), and capacity for continued development (p. 1195). Marrus and Rosenberg (2005) examined the Court's examination of each of these factors. The Court cites Arnett (1992), *Reckless Behavior in Adolescence*, to support their belief that adolescents act impulsively and therefore cannot accurately assess the consequences of their behavior.

The second characteristic the Court focused on in differentiating juveniles from adults was the effect of outside influences on the child's behavior. This has led scholars and reformers to look for other areas where this should impact juvenile justice. In looking to argue against the growing policy of moving adolescents under age 18 to adult, Court Marrus and Rosenberg examined additional studies to support the Court's finding. They analyzed multiple studies to support adolescents' susceptibility to peer pressure as inextricably linked, examining studies from clothing fads to antisocial behavior. They argued that "to be different is to be an outcast and excluded from the 'in cliques.' Street gangs, with their colors and their initiation rites, exemplify the power of peer pressure" (pp. 1164-1165). The result, at least in the death penalty context, is that an adolescent's "understanding of death is intellectual, not emotional" (Marrus & Rosenberg, 2005, p. 1165; citing Goldman 2004, pp. 169-171).

The most examined aspect of the Court's identified differences is the capacity for continued development. Much of the policy work has concentrated on expounding knowledge on brain development. Marrus and Rosenberg argue that the "most telling and objective difference between adults and adolescents is in brain development" (p. 1165). The Court would appear to agree, since they cite the work Baird et al. (1999), a developmental neuroscientist at Dartmouth. In Baird's studies, adults and children aged 12-17 were asked to identify emotions on faces in photographs. As they observed the faces, their brain functions were monitored by an MRI scanner that enabled scientists to determine which parts of the brain were being used.

When adults viewed the faces, the amygdala section of the brain activated, alerting the person that the image was important, then the frontal lobe assessed the situation, checking the person's memory and other parts of the brain so as to "coordinate a response." Adults were able to identify the emotions being displayed accurately. Adolescents, however, often misidentified the emotions. For example, "when shown a face expressing fear... they would identify it as surprise, or even happiness. In this situation, a teen's amygdala, the brain's alarm system, works properly, but the prefrontal cortex, the brain's interpreter, does not. The amygdala zeroed in on the faces as something important, but the frontal lobes couldn't focus enough to get the identification right." (Marrus & Rosenberg, 2005, p. 1166).

The American Academy of Child and Adolescent Psychiatry (AACAP), in an amicus brief filed with the Court in *Roper*, argued that the brain does not physically stop maturing until a person is about 20 years old. Marrus and Rosenberg used this to support an argument that an "adolescent's personality and character are not static. Therefore, punishing adolescents the same as adults is akin to punishing them for a developmental lag" (2005, pp. 1166-1167).

17.3. **CONCLUSION**

While *Roper* provides an interesting case study, I argue that it just touches the surface. Policy makers need research-based evidence to provide proper supports for adolescents during a crucial developmental period. They must overcome the public's fear of adolescents in the criminal justice context and also provide greater understanding of mitigating factors. The brain development described earlier in Chapter 2 (Harrell et al.) can be severely retarded by abuse and neglect. As one might guess, most juvenile offenders who were on death row were impacted by such neglect (Penalty, 2005). Research allows courts and policy makers to understand how psychology and biology work in tandem.

The American Academy of Pediatrics has identified several risk factors that can incite violence in adolescents, including: exposure to domestic violence and substance abuse within the home, sexual or physical assault, and a lack of adult supervision (Violence, 1999). Developmental theory provides the tools to explain why.

REFERENCES

Arnett, J. (1992). Reckless behavior in adolescence: A developmental perspective. *Developmental Review, 12*, 391–409.

Baird, A. A., Gruber, S., Fein, D., Maas, L. C., Steingard, R. J., Renshaw, P. F., et al. (1999). Functional magnetic resonance imaging of facial affect recognition in children and adolescents. *Journal of the American Acadamy of Child and Adolescent Psychiatry, 38*, 1.

Bandura, A. (1986). *Social foundations of thought and action: A social cognitive theory*. Engelwood Cliffs, NJ: Prentice-Hall.

Bazelon, L. A. (2000). Exploding the superpredator myth: Why infancy is the preadolescent's best defense in juvenile court. *New York University Law Review, 75*, 159–198.

Bosworth, M. (2001). *Courts as catalysts: State Supreme Courts and public school finance equity*. Albany, NY: State University of New York Press.

Brink, D. O. (2004). Immaturity, normative competence, and juvenile transfer: How (Not) to punish minors for major crimes. *Texas Law Review, 82*, 1555–1585.

Bronfenbrenner, U. (1979). *The ecology of human development: Experiments by nature and design*. Cambridge, MA: Harvard University Press.

Clark, C. A. (2005). The baby and the bathwater: Adolescent offending and punitive juvenile justice reform. *University of Kansas Law Review, 53*, 659–725.

Cunningham, L. (2006). A question of capacity: Towards a comprhensive and consistent vision of children and their status under law. *University of California Davis Journal of Juvenile Law and Policy, 10*, 275–377.

Eddings v. Oklahoma, 455 U.S. 104 (U.S. Supreme Court 1982).

Elmore, R. F., & Mclaughlin, M. W. (1982). *Reform and retrenchment: The politics of California school finance reform*. Cambridge, MA: Ballinger.

Epstein, L., George, T. E., & Kobylka, J. F. (1992). *Public interest law: An annotated bibliography and research guide*. New York, NY: Garland Pub.

Epstein, L., & Kobylka, F. F. (1992). *The Supreme Court and legal change: Aboration and the death penalty*. Chapel Hill: University of North Carolina.

Erikson, E. (1950). *Childhood and society*. New York, NY: W.W. Norton Co.

Ex Parte Crouse, 4 (Supreme Court of Pennsylvania January 3rd, 1839).

Feld, B. C. (1999). The transformation of the juvenile court—Part II: Race and the "crack down" on youth crime. *Minnesota Law Review, 84*, 327–395.

Goldman, L. (2004). Counseling with children in contemporary society. *Journal of Mental Health Counseling, 26*, 168.

Hartman, R. (2000). Adolescent autonomy: Clarifying an ageless conundrum. *Hastings Law Journal, 51*, 1265–1362.

In re Gault, 387 (U.S. Supreme Court May 15, 1967).

In re Winship, 397 U.S. 358 (United States Supreme Court March 31, 1970).

James, A., & Prout, A. (1997). New paradigm for the sociology of childhood, provenance, promise and problems. In A. James & A. Prout (Eds.), *Constructing and reconstructing childhood: Contemporary issues in the sociological study of childhood*. London: Falmer.

Kent v. United States, 383 U.S. 541 (United States Suprem Court March 21, 1966).

Koski, W. S. (2003). *Fuzzy standards, institutional constraints, and judicial attitudes: The politics of state Supreme Court decision-making in educational finance reform*. Unpublished dissertation. Stanford Univesity, Palo Alto.

LaFave, W. R., & Scott, A. W. (1972). *Handbook on criminal law*. St. Paul, MN: West Publishing.

Mack, J. W. (1909). The juvenile court. *Harvard Law Review*, *23*, 104–122.

Marrus, E., & Rosenberg, I. (2005). After Roper v. Simmons: Keeping kids out of adult criminal court. *San Diego Law Review*, *42*, 1151–1183.

Miller, P. H. (1989). *Theories of developmental psychology*. New York, NY: W.H. Freeman and Company.

Oklahoma Stat., Tit. 10, § 1101(1) (Supp. 1987).

Penalty, N. C. (2005). *Fact sheet: Juvenile death penalty*. Washington, DC: National Coalition to Abolish the Death penalty.

Perrillo, J. M. (2002). *Corbin on contracts*. Albany, NY: Matthew Bender.

Piaget, J. (2001). *Studies in reflecting abstraction*. Hove, UK: Psychology Press.

Poncz, E. (2008). Rethinking child advocacy after Roper v. Simmons: "Kids are Just Different" and "Kids are like Adults" advocacy stratagies. *Cardoza Public Law, Policy and Ethics Journal*, *6*, 273–343.

Robinson, P. H. (1984). *Criminal law defenses* (Vol. 2). Eagan, MN: West Publishing.

Rogoff, B. (1990). *Apprenticeship in thinking: Cognitive development in social context*. Oxford: Oxford University Press.

Roper v. Simmons, 543 U.S. 551 (U.S. Supreme Court March 1, 2005).

Scott, E. S. (2000). The legal construction of adolescence. *Hofstra Law Review*, *29*, 547–598.

Scott, E. S., & Grisso, T. (1997, Fall). The evolution of adolescence: A developmental perspective on juvenile justice reform. *Journal of Criminal Law and Criminology*, *88*, 137–189.

Stanford v. Kentucky, 492 U.S. 361 (United States Supreme Court June 26, 1989).

State v. Aaron, 1818 WL 1527 (Supreme Court of Judicature of New Jersey September 1818).

Steinberg, L., & Cauffman, E. (1996). Maturity of judgment in adolescence: Psychosocial factors in adolescent decision making. *Law and Human Behavior*, *20*(3), 249–272.

Stumpf, H. P., & Paul, K. C. (1998). *American judicial politics* (2nd ed.). Upper Saddle River, NJ: Prentice-Hall.

Sutton, J. R. (1985). The juvenile court and social welfare: Dynamics of progressive reform. *Law and Society Review*, *19*(1), 107–146.

Taylor-Thompson, K. (2003). States of mind/states of development. *Stanford Law and Policy Review, 14*, 143–173.

Thomas, T. A. (1997). Defense of infancy in juvenile defense proceedings. *American Law Reports 4th, 83*, 1135–1145.

Thompson v. Oklahoma, 487 U.S. 815 (U.S. Supreme Court June 29, 1988).

Violence, A. A. (1999, January). *The role of the pediatrician in youth violence prevention in clinical*. Retrieved July 26, 2009, from http://aappolicy. aappublications.org/cgi/reprint/pediatrics;103/1/173.pdf

Vygotsky, L. (1978). Mind in Society: The development of higher mental processes. In V. J.-S. M. Cole (Ed.), *Mind and society: The development of higher mental processes*. Cambridge, MA: MIT Press.

Vygotsky, L. (1986). In A. Kozulin (Ed.), *Thought and language*. Cambridge, MA: MIT Press.

Walker, N. E., Brooks, C. M., & Wrightsman, L. S. (1999). *Children's rights in the United States: In search of a national policy*. Thousand Oaks, CA: Sage Publications.

Wertsch, J. V. (1985). *Vygotsky and the social formation of mind*. Cambridge, MA: Harvard University Press.

Whitehead, J. T., & Lab, S. P. (2006). *Juvenile justice: An introduction* (5th ed.). Cincinnati, OH: Anderson Publishing.

Woodhouse, B. (2002). Youthful indiscretions: Culture class status, and the passage to adulthood. *DePaul Law Review, 51*, 743–768.

Woolard, J. L., Fondacaro, M. R., & Slobogin, C. (2001). Informing juvenile justice policy: Directions for behavioral science research. *Law and Human Behavior, 25*, 13–24.

Woolard, J. L., Reppucci, N. R., & Redding, R. E. (1996). Theoretical and methodological issues in studying children's capacities in legal context. *Law and Human Behavior, 20*(3), 219–228.

Zimring, F. E. (1982). *The changing legal world of adolescence*. New York, NY: The Free Press.

18

Program considerations for youth-focused professionals

Tina J. Kauh

Senior Research Associate,
Public/Private Ventures, Philadelphia, PA

Youth-focused prevention programing can take on many forms and can be implemented in several different contexts, ranging from the classroom setting to after-school programs that take place on school grounds or in community-based organizations in youth's neighborhoods. These programs vary widely in terms of their goals and missions and, accordingly, the scope of services they provide to youth. While some programs aim simply to provide youth with a safe haven during the after-school hours in which they can freely spend their time as they wish in a safe environment, others might provide opportunities for mentoring or a menu of activities from which youth can choose. Still other programs may offer activities through "manualized" curricula that target specific behaviors, assets, or problems, including substance use, delinquency, academic performance, sexual activity, or positive youth development more generally. Such programs involving manualized curricula have been delivered both during the school day and in after-school settings and by a wide range of staff, including both professionals and paraprofessionals. Manualized curricula typically consist of lessons that enhance youth's skills and knowledge and build on their personal assets, with the goals of reducing risks and increasing strengths. The bulk of this chapter focuses on the design and delivery of manualized curricula, particularly as they meet the needs of racial and ethnic minority youth.

18.1. APPROACHES TO PREVENTION

Prevention programing during adolescence follows one of three major approaches: primary, secondary, or tertiary models (Gordon, 1987; Kumpfer

& Baxley, 1997). Each differs in terms of the kind of population it targets. *Primary prevention* programs, also sometimes referred to as "universal programs," are designed for the general population, regardless of background or risk. The goal of universal prevention is to deter the onset of problems by providing all individuals with the information and skills necessary to prevent the problem from beginning. A major assumption of the primary prevention model is that *everyone* shares the same general risk for the problem, and programs are delivered to individuals without any prior screening for risk level. For example, a primary gang prevention program would be delivered to all sixth graders in a school, regardless of their personal characteristics or their prior history in delinquent behavior.

Secondary programs, sometimes also called "targeted" or "selective programs," are intended for individuals considered "at-risk" of experiencing a behavioral or mental health problem as a result of their membership in a particular group. Youth can be determined to be "at-risk" based on numerous factors, including biological (e.g., gender), psychological (e.g., risk perception), social (e.g., peer group), or environmental (e.g., living in a low-income neighborhood) characteristics. For instance, youth who have a history of demonstrating less serious delinquent behavior and who live in a high-crime neighborhood may be selected to participate in a secondary gang prevention program.

Tertiary programs, or "indicated programs," are designed for individuals already demonstrating problems and typically address risk factors associated with the individual and less so with environmental influences. For example, a tertiary gang prevention program would target youth who have been involved in more serious acts of delinquency or violence or who are already affiliated with gangs.

18.2. A FOCUS ON RACIAL AND ETHNIC MINORITY YOUTH

Because many adolescent prevention programs aim to address problem behaviors, it is important to understand which populations are most commonly afflicted with those problems and, presumably, would benefit most from receiving prevention-related services.

18.2.1. Are minority youth in special need of prevention programs?

Problem behaviors among adolescents tend to be more prevalent among lower income youth. For instance, in 2006, high school students living in low-income families were more than four times more likely to drop out before the following school year than their peers from high-income families (9.0% vs. 2.0%) (Laird, Cataldi, Kewal-Ramani, & Chapman, 2008). As Figure 18.1 illustrates, minority youth (those under the age of 18 years), particularly those from African American, Latino, and American Indian backgrounds, were disproportionately more likely to come from disadvantaged backgrounds compared to youth from nonminority families in 2006 (Fass & Cauthen, 2007).

Further, despite the fact that Whites make up the vast majority of adolescents between the ages of 12 and 17 years, based on the 2007 US Census Bureau (Figure 18.2), minority youth are three times as likely to live in poverty as Whites (Figure 18.3) (Fass & Cauthen, 2007).

Not surprisingly, the prevalence of many problem behaviors among lower income youth is mirrored in racial group differences. In 2006, 10.7% of African American youth and 22.1% of Latino youth between the ages of 16 and 24 years had not earned and were not working toward a high school degree, compared to only 5.8% of Whites in the same age group (Laird et al., 2008). Similarly, Whites (92.6%) between the ages of 18 and 24 years who were not enrolled in high school were more likely than their African American (84.8%) or Latino (70.9%) peers to have earned a high school diploma or equivalent (Laird et al., 2008). In fact,

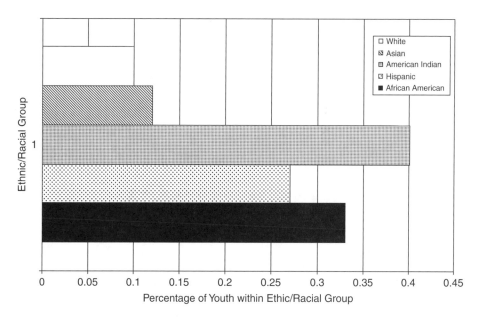

■ **FIGURE 18.1** In 2006, youth from racial and ethnic minority backgrounds under the age of 18 years were disproportionately more likely to come from families living in low-income households. Source: Fass and Cauthen (2007).

■ **FIGURE 18.2** Among adolescents (aged 12-17 years), Whites comprise the single largest racial/ethnic group in the United States at 59%. The next two largest racial/ethnic groups are represented by Latinos and African Americans, who each make up nearly one-fifth of the US adolescent population. Asian, American Indian, and multiracial youth each make up less than 4% of the remaining population. Source: US Census Bureau (2007).

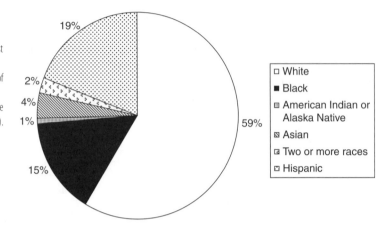

■ **FIGURE 18.3** Although White youth represent the single largest racial/ethnic group living in poverty, minority youth as a whole are twice as likely as Whites to be poor. Source: Fass and Cauthen (2007).

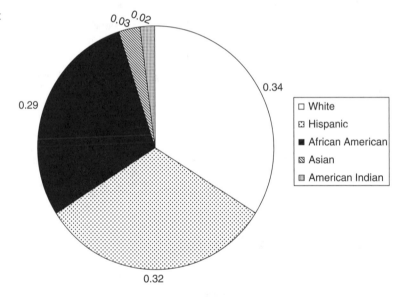

Figure 18.4 illustrates that Latino and Black youth have had consistently higher high school dropout rates than Whites since the early 1990s (U.S. Department of Education, 2008).

This pattern can be seen in other areas of youth's lives as well. For instance, Figure 18.5 shows that in 2007, Black and Hispanic youth overall showed greater risk for poor physical health than Whites, showing lower physical activity, greater sedentary activity, and higher likelihood for

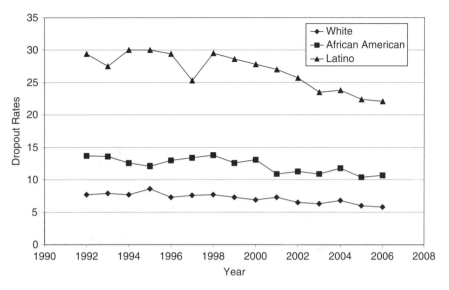

■ **FIGURE 18.4** From 1992 to 2006, African American and Latino individuals were more likely than Whites to have dropped out of high school before receiving a degree or GED. Source: Planty et al. (2008).

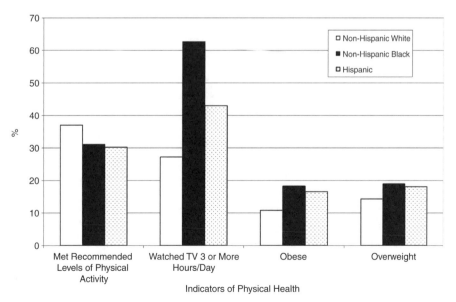

■ **FIGURE 18.5** Black and Hispanic youth demonstrate more unhealthful habits and poorer health than nonminority youth. In 2007, the National Youth Risk Behavior Survey found that compared to their White peers, fewer Black and Hispanic youth reported meeting recommended levels of physical activity, watching 3 or more hours of television per day, being more likely to suffer from obesity and overweight. Source: Centers for Disease Control and Prevention (2008).

■ **FIGURE 18.6** In 2004, non-Hispanic Black and Hispanic teenage girls between the ages of 15 and 19 years were between two and four times as likely as their White peers to have experienced a pregnancy or to have given birth. Source: Ventura et al. (2008).

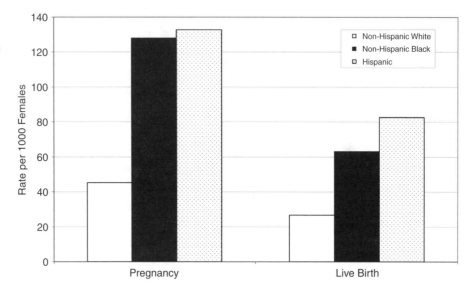

overweight and obesity problems (Centers for Disease Control and Prevention (CDC), 2008). The CDC further found that most of these racial/ethnic group differences exist for both boys and girls separately.[1]

Similarly, non-Hispanic Black and Hispanic females between the ages of 15 and 19 years reported the highest national levels of teenage pregnancy and live births in 2004 (Figure 18.6) (Ventura, Abma, Mosher, & Henshaw, 2008).

Although these figures illustrate that racial and ethnic groups differ in terms of the extent to which they exhibit problem behaviors, less is known about the etiology, or the causes, of these differences, as the bulk of etiological studies have focused on White middle-class youth. The lack of research on Asian American and Native American youth, for instance, is quite significant. Harachi, Catalano, Kim, and Choi (2001) found that, although some local and state-level epidemiological surveys include Asian American respondents, the most extensive national surveys of adolescent drug use (e.g., National Household Survey on Drug Abuse sponsored by the Substance Abuse and Mental Health Services Administration, and Monitoring the Future sponsored by the National Institute on Drug Abuse)

---

[1]The only racial/ethnic group difference that did not persist when examining boys and girls separately was for prevalence of overweight. White, Black, and Hispanic males did not differ in their likelihood of overweight (CDC, 2008).

exclude them as an ethnic category when reporting research findings. Epidemiological research is crucial in properly designing intervention programs that adequately address the needs of unique ethnic populations. Of the limited research that has examined this issue, initial results suggest that many etiological factors are similar across ethnic groups but that the relative importance of these factors varies across groups.

The extent to which prevention programs, regardless of the model they are based on or the location in which they take place, are tailored to be appropriate for ethnic minority youth greatly varies. Despite the disproportionate prevalence of problem behaviors among racial and ethnic minority youth, the majority of prevention programs that target a wide range of problem behaviors are originally developed for and evaluated with nonminority youth (Hammond & Yung, 1993). These programs typically deliver materials and information in a culturally neutral way with the assumption that doing so enables the programs to be relevant to the widest audience, including youth from multiple racial or ethnic groups. In the following section, results from evaluations of culturally generic drug prevention programs that included racial and ethnic minority participants are summarized.

18.2.2. **Effectiveness of culturally generic programs for minority youth**

Recent approaches to alcohol, tobacco, and other drug (ATOD) prevention typically focus on resistance skills training, personal and social skills training, or both. Resistance skills training aims to (1) increase youth's awareness of internal and external influences for substance use and (2) teach skills for resisting those pressures. Programs that focus on instilling personal and social skills in adolescents through cognitive-behavioral techniques assume that substance use achieves instrumental goals for youth, such as helping them deal with anxiety or low self-esteem. These kinds of programs seek to enhance youth's social competencies across multiple personal and social domains, including decision making, anxiety-coping, and communication skills. While studies evaluating these intervention strategies have suggested positive outcomes for preventing or delaying alcohol, marijuana, and, in particular, tobacco use, they have focused disproportionately on White, middle-class suburban youth and include only small samples of ethnic minority adolescents, if any at all (Botvin, Schinke, & Orlandi, 1995; Ellickson & Bell, 1990). When program participants have included minority youth, the substantive program components have not been tailored to that population, with the assumption that the programs' curricula are skills from which all youth can benefit, regardless of their personal backgrounds.

Although limited in number, a few studies with large samples of minority youth somewhat support the generalizability of these programs' effectiveness to various groups of minority adolescents, including African Americans, Latinos, Native Americans, and Alaskan Natives. For instance, Botvin, Batson et al. (1989) exposed seventh-grade students from three New Jersey schools, who were primarily African American urban youth (86%), to the Life Skills Training (LST) curriculum. The results from the evaluation indicated that the intervention was more successful in reducing smoking, increasing knowledge, and changing normative attitudes about smoking than the usual school-based health education program.

Studies have found similar results with generic-skills programing involving Latino youth. For instance, Gilchrist, Schinke, Trimble, and Cvetkovich (1987) extended the generalizability of generic skills training programs to Native American and Alaskan Native adolescents from the Pacific Northwest. Their skills enhancement intervention targeted this ethnic group using 10 program sessions, which consist of concepts similar to those covered by LST (i.e., alcohol and drug knowledge, attitudes, and normative beliefs; communication and social skills). After the program, youth reported greater drug knowledge and interpersonal skillfulness compared to their peers who were not in the program. Moreover, program participants also reported lower rates of alcohol, marijuana, and inhalant use 6 months following the end of the program.

Similarly, in another evaluation of LST, Botvin et al. (1992) replicated previous findings in a sample of predominantly Latino (56%) seventh graders from 47 New York City schools. At the end of the program, fewer LST participants had smoked in the past month or had initiated smoking since the start of the program than had their non-LST peers. Botvin et al. also found no differences in the program's impact on participants by ethnic composition within schools. In other words, programs in schools that had low, medium, or high percentages of Latino students were equally effective, providing additional support for the effectiveness of a culturally generic program.

Although these evaluations suggest that culturally generic programs can be successful among youth of different racial and ethnic backgrounds, there is still reason to believe that minority youth could benefit from tailored programing. For instance, as a result of the scant research examining possible differences in causes for substance use across ethnic groups, an entirely distinct strategy focusing on different protective and risk factors may be necessary for different racial and ethnic groups (Botvin et al., 1992).

In other words, it is possible that the core components of a program that would be most successful with African American youth may be quite different from those of a program that was developed for White, Latino, Asian, or American Indian youth.

18.2.3. **Importance of cultural issues**

Although the incorporation of race and ethnicity into prevention and intervention programs began in the 1980s, prevalence in this type of programing began to increase in the mid-1990s. Prevention and intervention programs began to acknowledge that racial and cultural backgrounds may influence the effectiveness of program content and started tailoring their program practices. The way in which programs address cultural issues, however, can vary a great deal. Regardless of which method is chosen, each is intended to increase cultural relevance and sensitivity for their participants. Doing so may enhance the target population's receptivity of the program and its goals, thereby improving program recruitment, retention, and impact (Harachi, Catalano, & Hawkins, 1997; Kumpfer, Alvarado, Smith, & Bellamy, 2002). Programs can enhance their cultural sensitivity and relevance through changes in either (1) *surface structure* or (2) *deep structure* (Resnicow, Saler, Braithwaite, Ahluwalia, & Butler, 2000). The following section discusses these different methods of addressing cultural issues in prevention and intervention programing.

Surface structure

Surface structure refers to superficial aspects of a program that involve the way in which materials are presented and delivered to the target audience (Resnicow et al., 2000). For instance, programs working with Latino youth might consider translating their materials into Spanish or to deliver the program through staff who share similar demographic characteristics to those of the target population. "Manualized programs" may use images in their curricula of youth who demographically resemble their participants. The apparent success across ethnic groups of culturally generic interventions described earlier in this chapter may reflect the degree to which programs had been culturally sensitive for their participants. When being implemented within minority populations, these intervention programs maintained their core fundamental components, which were initially developed for White middle-class youth. However, they each underwent a modification process to enhance their cultural sensitivity to their respective target groups, which brought about changes to their surface structure. Often, these kinds of modifications are determined by a review of the materials by experts in the field as well as focus groups that include members of the target audience. For instance, before its implementation, Botvin, Batson et al. (1989) and Botvin, Dusenbury et al. (1989) conducted an extensive review of LST by multiple psychologists as well as African American and Latino health educators, cultural experts, and adolescent focus groups. Similarly, in order to enhance the cultural relevance of generic life skills, Gilchrist et al. (1987) utilized indigenous community leaders and Native American or Alaskan Native staff members to conduct and deliver the program sessions.

Deep structure

In contrast to the culturally generic interventions previously described, some school-based programs targeting racial and ethnic minority youth encompass distinct components specific to their target population. These aspects of a program refer to cultural, social, psychological, environmental, and historical factors unique to the target audience that may influence their behaviors (Resnicow et al., 2000; Yashui & Dishion, 2007). Similarly, Tucker (1985) argues that the unique life conditions of a particular ethnic group (e.g., reservation residence, poverty, or discrimination) undoubtedly have implications for the prevalence and patterns of problem behaviors within that group. For this reason, Tucker and others (e.g., Newcomb, 1996; Szapocznik, Scopetta, & King, 1978) emphasize the need for treatment and prevention models that focus on "the special needs of minority populations" (p. 1025) and that "reflect...the everyday realities of [racial and ethnic minority] youth" (Schinke, Moncher, Holden, Botvin, & Orlandi, 1989) rather than merely on generic or superficial concerns (i.e., surface structure). Issues such as acculturation, family cohesion, and sense of hopelessness become important risk or protective factors to varying degrees across different ethnic groups (Kim, Coletti, Williams, & Hepler, 1995).

Racial- and ethnic-specific factors

Youth from different racial and ethnic groups vary widely in their histories, their cultures, their attitudes, and their values, all of which bring with them both risk and protective factors that could influence youth's behavior. Programs can integrate these racial and ethnic-specific factors into their curricula by either minimizing the risks or bolstering youth's sources of strength.

For instance, some researchers have suggested that, as a reaction to their history of oppression in the United States, African Americans may reject institutions that are dominated by the mainstream culture, like the educational system, and that achieving academic success and having positive attitudes about education may be seen as "acting white" (Fordham & Ogbu,

1986). In turn, African American youth may disengage from school and other educational activities, resulting in school failure and/or school dropout. A program that aims to prevent high school dropout among African American youth might consider challenging those attitudes and providing positive African American role models who have succeeded academically.

Along similar lines, Latino, Asian, and American Indian youth may be influenced by values associated with their cultural background. For instance, Latino youth face challenges associated with expectations around *machismo*, *marianismo*, and *familism*. *Machismo* refers to expectations for Latino males with regard to their masculinity—males are expected to be strong, assertive, and dominant, and to act as their family's protector. In contrast, Latino culture encourages *marianismo* in females, a demure, pure, and nurturing demeanor (Castro & Alarcon, 2002; Cuellar, Arnold, & Gonzalez, 1995). In addition, Latino youth are also socialized toward *familism*, in which individuals are encouraged to focus on obligations to the family, both immediate and extended family members, over the personal preferences or goals of the individual. Programs targeting Latino males to prevent gang violence might challenge the *machismo* image and could discourage violence by highlighting how gang membership negatively affects the family.

Similarly, American Indian youth may face challenges associated with their need to show respect for elders, their emphasis on interdependence, and their desire for harmony and balance (Wise & Miller, 1983). American Indian culture emphasizes the family, which often extends past blood relatives into close family friends (Manson et al., 1996). Further, individuals' obligations often are not only to the family but to the tribe to which they belong and their broader community, and individual achievements are less celebrated than putting other's needs above one's own. Harmony and balance are reflected in the culture's belief that problems arise as a result of imbalance among the child, the family, and the community, and family members must work together to regain that balance. Because of this, programs targeting American Indian youth might consider intervening at multiple levels of youth's lives, incorporating participation from youth, their families, and their community members.

Finally, youth from Asian backgrounds must often deal with cultural expectations around *filial piety*, family obligations, and the desire to "save face." *Filial piety* can be linked back to the Confucian ethics that act as the basis for Asian values that guide many behaviors. Individuals are expected to show respect for and obey their elders, particularly their parents. Failing to do so dishonors the family. In addition, Asian families also instill a sense of interdependence in which family members develop a particularly strong sense of obligation to assist, respect, and support their families (Fuligni, Tseng, & Lam, 1999). Youth's sense of filial piety and family obligations could act as mechanisms for deterring problem behaviors. Along similar lines, however, concerns around "saving face," or the desire to prevent public shame, may deter youth from seeking help from others.

Table 18.1 summarizes these, and other issues discussed later, that could influence youth's behavior; professionals should consider these issues when working with youth of different ethnic and racial minority backgrounds.

Table 18.1 Unique Factors that Influence Behavior Among Ethnic/Racial Groups

	Unique ethnic/racial-specific factors
African Americans	• History of oppression, discrimination, and racism • Poverty • Attitudes about masculinity • Religiosity and spirituality • Ethnic glossing • Racial identification
Latino Americans	• Immigrant or refugee status • Discrimination and racism • Poverty • Ethnic glossing • Racial identification • Cultural values • *Familism* • *Machismo* • *Marianismo*

Asian Americans	• Authoritarian parenting
	• Immigrant or refugee status
	• Emphasis on academic achievement
	• Ethnic glossing
	• Racial identification
	• Cultural values
	   – *Filial piety*
	   – *Obedience*
	   – *Saving face*

Native Americans	• History of cultural genocide
	• Poverty
	• Habitation on reservations
	• Storytelling and transmission of legends
	• Ethnic glossing
	• Racial identification
	• Cultural values
	   – *Respect for elders*
	   – *Interdependence*
	   – *Harmony and balance*

In designing culturally tailored intervention programs, program developers should acknowledge these differences and emphasize issues that more strongly influence the behaviors of youth from their target group. (Table 18.2 provides a brief list of youth-focused curricula for African American, Latino, American Indian, and Asian American youth that have integrated cultural issues in their deep structure.)

Further, intervention programs that target ethnic minority youth must ensure that their curricula are *congruent* with those of the ethnic culture. For instance, *Competence Through Transitions* (CTT; Zane, Aoki, Ho, Huang, & Jang, 1998) represents a program targeting Asian American youth and their parents. One component of the program aims to enhance youth's life skills, which can lead to youth's increased sense of empowerment in that

Table 18.2 Examples of Culturally Tailored Programs

Racial/ethnic group	Problem behavior	Program name	Program description
Latino	Substance use	*Keepin' it REAL*[a]	*Keepin' it REAL* is a multicultural, school-based substance use prevention program for students aged 12-14 years old. The program consists of 10 lessons that are taught by trained classroom teachers in 45-min sessions over 10 weeks, with booster sessions delivered in the following school year. The curriculum is designed to help students assess the risks associated with substance abuse, enhance decision making and resistance strategies, improve antidrug normative beliefs and attitudes, and reduce substance use. The narrative and performance-based curriculum draws from communication competence theory and a culturally grounded resiliency model to incorporate traditional ethnic values and practices that protect against substance use.
Latino	Violence	*Movimiento Ascendencia*[b]	*Movimiento Ascendencia* (upward movement) provides at-risk and gang-involved girls between the ages of 8-19 years with positive alternatives to substance use and gang involvement. The program aims to increase cultural awareness, instill mediation or conflict resolution skills, and enhance self-esteem and social supports.

Continued

Table 18.2 Examples of Culturally Tailored Programs—cont'd

Racial/ethnic group	Problem behavior	Program name	Program description
African American	Sex Violence Delinquency	*Aban Aya Youth Project*[c]	The *Aban Aya Youth Project* is designed for African American middle school-aged youth and was developed to address multiple problem behaviors such as violence, substance abuse, delinquency, and sexual activity simultaneously in a 4-year intervention specifically for African American youth. The curriculum consists of 16-21 lessons per year and teaches skills to build self-esteem and empathy, manage stress and anxiety, develop interpersonal relationships, resist peer pressure, develop decision-making, problem-solving, conflict resolution, and goal setting skills, and apply these skills to avoid violence, delinquency, and unsafe sexual behaviors. The curriculum also focuses on developing a sense of self and purpose by addressing career planning, feelings, personal strengths, and cultural pride. Cultural values and history are also addressed.
American Indian	Suicide	*American Indian Life Skills Development*[a]	*American Indian life Skills Development* is a school-based suicide prevention curriculum aimed at reducing suicide risk and improving protective factors among American Indian adolescents 14-19 years old. The curriculum includes anywhere from 28 to 56 lessons covering a range of topics, including building self-esteem, identifying emotions and stress, increasing communication and problem-solving skills, recognizing and eliminating self-destructive behavior, learning about suicide, role-playing around suicide prevention, and setting personal and community goals. Lessons are interactive and incorporate situations and experiences relevant to American Indian adolescent life. Lessons are delivered by teachers working with community resource leaders and representatives of local social services agencies, which ensures that the lessons have a high degree of cultural and linguistic relevance even if the teachers are not Native American or not of the same tribe as the students.

Table 18.2 Examples of Culturally Tailored Programs—cont'd

Racial/ethnic group	Problem behavior	Program name	Program description
American Indian	AIDS and substance abuse	*The Native American Prevention Project Against AIDS and Substance Abuse*[b]	The Native American Prevention Project Against AIDS and Substance Abuse (NAPPASA) program consists of a 24-session school-based curriculum that addresses multiple issues facing Native American communities. Classroom sessions build knowledge, the ability to acquire and practice prevention skills with peers, and foster new positive peer group norms for preventive communications and behaviors in the context of Native American values.
Asian American		*Youth-PASS*[d]	Preventing Asians from Smoking and Secondhand Smoke (Youth-PASS) was designed as a school- and community-based prevention/intervention program aimed at preventing and reducing tobacco use among Asian youth, especially new innmigrants. The curriculum focuses on knowledge about tobacco use as well as the tobacco industry's marketing methods for Asians. The program incorporates several cultural aspects into its curriculum, including reasons why Asian teens smoke; awareness of tobacco industry's marketing of tobacco products to Asian youth; use of posters, pictures, display boards symbolizing Asian images and faces; and reference to famous Asian celebrities and other role models. The program is delivered by Asian peer health educators.

[a]Substance Abuse and Mental Health Services Administration (SAMHSA) National Registry of Evidence-based Programs and Practices: http://nrepp.samhsa.gov/find.asp.
[b]Office of Juvenile Justice and Delinquency Prevention (OJJDP) Model Programs Guide: http://www.dsgonline.com/mpg2.5/search.htm.
[c]The National Campaign to Prevention Teen and Unplanned Pregnancy: http://www.thenationalcampaign.org/EA2007/desc/default.aspx.
[d]Ma, Lan, Edwards, Shive, and Chau (2004).

they feel a greater ability and right to make their own decisions and solve their own problems. Flanagan (1986, as cited in Eccles, Lord, & Buchanan, 1996) found that young adolescents' perceptions of the extent to which they should have a role in family decisions were positively correlated with their perceptions of autonomy and negatively correlated with their perceptions of parent-child conflict and high parent control. In other words, youth who felt more autonomous believed that they should have a role in making family decisions and that their parents were less controlling. These youth also reported lower conflict with their parents. Such findings illuminate a problem that may arise for Asian American youth when they try to transfer their newly refined life skills (greater empowerment) into their family domain. Given the emphasis that Asian culture places on obedience and respect for elders, these youth's family environment may display low acceptance of and tolerance for such autonomy. Although CTT might increase these youth's *sense* of empowerment, the youth may not really *be* empowered due to cultural limitations placed by their parents that emphasize deference to hierarchy and interdependence.

In addition to designing culturally sensitive programs that adhere to the values of ethnic groups, interventions that aim to enhance ethnic identity by strengthening ethnic pride should be cautious about creating feelings of ethnocentrism, in which an ethnic group is seen as superior to the dominant culture; this can lead to racism, prejudice, and discriminatory behaviors (Tajfel, 1982). Rather, Gonzales and Cauce (1995) suggest that "multiethnic environments should strive to foster ethnic pride *while at the same time* facilitating mutual respect and cooperative existence…[by including] instruction that is culturally contextualized and features multiple ethnic perspectives without overemphasizing category boundaries" (p. 155).

Similarly, programs must also balance the goal of creating the best fit between their curricula and their participants with the need to maintain *fidelity* to the programs' core components (Castro, Barrera, & Martinez, 2004). Program fidelity refers to the extent to which a program's curriculum is implemented as it was intended. Although adaptations to a program to address special needs or interests of a racial or ethnic minority group may lead to greater receptivity among its participants and to cultural relevance, they may also lead to such significant changes that the program is no longer effective (Botvin, 2004). In fact, research has found that programs implemented with greater fidelity lead to stronger impacts (Elliott & Mihalic, 2004). Both fidelity and cultural tailoring are therefore essential elements to prevention programing for racial and ethnic minority youth.

18.2.4. Other concerns for professionals working with racial and ethnic minority youth

In addition to addressing cultural values and attitudes relevant to racial and ethnic minority youth, professionals working with this population must also consider other cultural and contextual issues that could influence youth's behavior. Such factors include ethnic self-identification, ethnic glossing, immigrant generational status, and community characteristics like poverty (see Table 18.1).

Chapter 9 presented the notion of adolescence as a critical period during which youth must negotiate the process of forming an identity across multiple life domains. For ethnic minority youth, forming a racial or ethnic identity may represent an important aspect of determining "who I am" and have important implications for well-being. Many research studies have used self-identification (i.e., response to the question, "What is your ethnicity?") as a means of assessing ethnic identity (Stephan & Stephan, 2000). In addition, individuals from certain nations (e.g., Japan) have older generations of immigrant residents in the United States compared to others (e.g., Koreans). Prior research has found generational differences in levels of "Americanization" so that younger generations of immigrants are likely to be more acculturated to American values, norms, and customs than older generational members of their ethnic group (e.g., Kim, Huhr, & Kim, 1993). Assessing ethnic identity based solely on ethnic ancestry may thus incorrectly assume that all youth from the same racial or ethnic group equally identify with that culture when, in reality, these youth likely vary a great deal in terms of their individual ethnic identity. Davis, Nakayama, and Martin (2000) argue that for many ethnic minority youth, "class, gender, and sexual orientation differentiates the experience (and identity) of people within ethnic categories" (p. 529).

In addition to heterogeneity resulting in cultural differences within broad ethnic categories, individuals within racial and ethnic subgroups (e.g., Korean Americans) also vary in their ethnic identity, or the extent to which an individual identifies with his or her ethnic group, depending on the extent to which they acknowledge, express, and act on common cultural values (Tanaka, Ebreo, Linn, & Morera, 1998). Ethnic self-identification represents only one part of ethnic identity and is a relatively "crude approximation" (Cauce, Coronado, & Watson, 1998, p. 312) of it, providing little information regarding the extent to which individuals adhere to cultural norms or practices that influence well-being. Cauce et al. argue that "knowing with which specific group an individual identifies best hints at the cultural practices and social norms to which he or she adheres...[but] it is not appropriate to base research or social policy on hints" (p. 312). Rather, Tanaka et al. argue that ethnic identity should be assessed as a general characteristic, which is comprised three distinct domains: (1) affect, (2) cognition, and (3) behavior (Sue, Mak, & Sue, 1998). The *affective* domain includes individuals' sense of belonging and commitment to the ethnic group (Ibrahim et al., 1997; Phinney, 1990), pride in and attitudes toward group members (Phinney, 1990; Ying & Lee, 1999), and issues of self-identification (Phinney, 1990). The *cognitive* domain consists of interest in and knowledge about one's ethnic group, including its history, language, traditions, norms, and values (Phinney, 1990). Lastly, individuals' degree of competent ethnic involvement in cultural practices and activities are reflected in the *behavioral* domain.

Further, the majority of research within and across racial and ethnic minority populations has had the tendency to pool individuals from certain racial and ethnic groups into a single group, ignoring the heterogeneity that potentially exists within those groups. For instance, much of the research noted earlier in this chapter refers to broad categories of racial and ethnic groups like "Latinos" or "Asians." However, according to the annual American Community Survey, the Asian category includes over 16 different Asian countries, ranging from eastern, southern, and southeastern regions of the continent. This tendency, to which Trimble (1995) refers as "ethnic glossing," reduces researchers' ability to interpret data within the context of a cultural framework. Although members of the same broad ethnicity may share some similar basic cultural characteristics (East Asians, for instance, may share values of filial piety), they often possess unique languages, histories, religions, and traditions. For instance, individuals from different nationalities frequently differ in reasons for immigration. Southeast Asian refugees, for example, have migrated to the United States as a result of political conditions in their native country, often having experienced a great deal of trauma prior to their migration, and have entered the United States with few resources. In contrast, many individuals from East Asian nations (e.g., Koreans, Japanese) have chosen to immigrate to the United States to further their education and often enter the United States with greater personal and economic resources. Similarly, African Americans vary a great deal in terms of how and when they arrived in the United States. While some may have been born in the country after a lineage dating back to ancestral slavery, others may have recently immigrated to the United States.

Further, immigrant generational status identifies the generation in an individual's family that first immigrated into the dominant culture. For instance, "third-generation immigrant" indicates that an individual is the third generation of his or her family to reside in the United States (i.e., grandparents were the first to immigrate). Several studies (e.g., Brindis, Wolfe, McCarter, Ball, & Starbuck-Morales, 1995; National Research Council, 1998) have used an individual's immigrant status as the sole indicator of ethnic identity, which provides only an *indication* of how integrated an individual may be within the dominant culture. For instance, individuals who are raised by parents who have recently immigrated versus those who have been raised in the United States markedly differ in their socialization experiences, and acculturation generally increases with immigrant generation. Similarly, different facets of ethnic identity, like cultural values, cultural knowledge, and behavior, erode over time at different rates (Phinney & Rosenthal, 1992). In addition, immigrant status also acts as only a crude measure of ethnic identity and fails to provide information regarding how or why it would influence either adolescent well-being or the effectiveness of an intervention program. Given these concerns, those who design intervention programs targeting broad categories of ethnic groups should ensure either that their curricula encompass basic ethnic components that apply to all ethnic subgroups within their target population or that they include unique program components that target and serve a *specific* subgroup to receive the program.

Finally, as noted earlier in this chapter, racial and ethnic minority youth are disproportionately more likely to live in poverty than Whites. Similarly, children of immigrants are also disproportionately more likely to live in low-income households than children of parents who were born in the United States. In fact, 57% of children of immigrant parents live in low-income families, while only 35% of children of native-born parents live in poverty (National Center for Children in Poverty, 2007). Because of this, professionals and programs working with minority youth must be cognizant of the cultural and racial issues that affect these youth, as well as any contextual challenges and barriers that these youth may face on a daily basis. For instance, disadvantaged youth often (Sampson, 2004; Sampson, Raudenbush, & Earls, 1997):

1. lack adequate community resources like high quality and safe schools and safe places for youth to spend their free time outside of the school hours;
2. have higher exposure to crime, violence, delinquency, and drug use;
3. lack adequate health- and dental care;
4. suffer from higher unemployment rates and limited job opportunities; and
5. lack positive role models to whom they can refer.

Professionals working with disadvantaged racial and ethnic minority youth can tailor their programs to address some of these issues by taking the following steps (Kauh, 2009):

- *Make programs easily affordable.* Low-income youth will likely be unable to afford enrollment or other program fees; therefore, programs should be free or be willing to waive the fee for those who cannot afford to pay.

- *Support youth's financial needs.* Economically disadvantaged high school-aged youth must often forego their interest in after-school programing because they need to financially contribute to their family. By paying participants' stipends for their participation, programs allow older youth to supplement their incomes while engaging in enriching after-school activities, many of which directly help to prepare them for life after high school through occupational and job training (e.g., After School Matters in Chicago, IL).
- *Make programing relevant to older minority youth.* Programs need to not only be fun to youth, but must also be personally relevant to them both in content and structure. Because economically disadvantaged youth often reside in areas in which job options are limited, programs that teach skills relevant for gaining employment or learning about career options can be especially valuable.
- *Hire staff with whom youth can personally relate.* Although the extent to which youth can relate to program staff may have a lot to do with similarities in racial and ethnic backgrounds, shared experiences like having grown up in similar disadvantaged communities matter.
- *Provide nurturing environments.* Because youth living in poor communities often lack positive role models and supportive adults, programs can reach youth better by making them feel valued and cared for through highly dedicated staff who demonstrate their commitment to youth both within and outside of the program.

18.2.5. Do culturally tailored programs really work better?

Much of this chapter has focused on the various ways in which programs can be tailored to address the unique needs and interests of racial and ethnic minority youth. However, a logical question may be to what extent does tailoring really lead to better impacts? Unfortunately, few studies have empirically compared the relative effectiveness of a culturally tailored program with that of a culturally generic program. This section summarizes the evidence that exists.

Forgey, Schinke, and Cole (1997) compared the Culturally Tailored Intervention (CTI) with that of LST (Botvin, 1997) for ATOD prevention among minority youth (Botvin, Schinke, Epstein, & Diaz, 1994; Botvin, Schinke, Epstein, Diaz, & Botvin, 1996). CTI is a school-based program that targets African American and Hispanic seventh graders and, through professional storytellers, rap videos, and peer leaders, presents culturally relevant stories with which youth can relate in order to prevent substance use. Multicultural stories describe myths from ancient African, Spanish, and Greek cultures, which convey the usage of skills and competencies taught by the curriculum in a culturally relevant context. Students also listen to historical and modern-day biographies of African American and Latino heroes and heroines who overcome obstacles similar to their own (e.g., discrimination, poverty) using the skills demonstrated in the program, thereby further enhancing the personal relevance of the curriculum. Whereas the mythic component functions to increase students' race consciousness and cultural pride, the biographical component addresses the sense of hopelessness from which so many inner-city minority youth suffer as a result of social limitations imposed by poverty and discrimination (Forgey et al., 1997). Botvin et al. (1994) chose to compare CTI and LST due to their similarities in content and structure. CTI closely resembles LST in the sense that it attempts to instill in youth the personal and social skills that allow them to better cope with social influences of substance use through the development of cognitive-behavioral skills. The two programs differ, however, in several other ways based on the "preferences, socio-demographic features, and interpersonal characteristics of high-risk youths" (Botvin et al., 1994, p. 119), to which CTI tailors itself. For instance, LST focuses on a general population, regardless of risk, in contrast to the high-risk population targeted by CTI. In addition, LST includes an informational knowledge component regarding alcohol, tobacco, and marijuana, whereas CTI does not. Further, whereas LST utilizes a more traditional teacher-centered approach, CTI incorporates several different media into its curriculum, including professional storytelling, music, video, and peer-led demonstrations. The results from the evaluation suggested that both interventions were equally effective immediately following the program but that 2 years later, youth who participated in the culturally tailored program, CTI, drank less, reported lower intentions for future alcohol use, and demonstrated less risk-taking behavior than those in LST. Such impacts are interesting, particularly given that CTI excluded any direct training in drug-related issues.

In another evaluation of a substance use prevention program (*Keepin' it REAL*; Hecht et al., 2003), three versions of the same program were delivered: Mexican American, combined African American and European American, and Multicultural. The core components of the program included resistance and life skills training using narrative and performance-based strategies. The different versions of the program all incorporated traditional ethnic values and practices that promote protection against drug use, including communication style, respect for elders, and *familism*. The results from the evaluation suggested that, although the culturally tailored curriculum did lead to impacts on youth substance use, it was not more effective for youth whose racial and ethnic backgrounds matched those of the curriculum to which they were exposed. In other words, Latino youth who participated in the Mexican American curriculum experienced program impacts that were no different from those of White or African American youth who received the same curriculum.

Lastly, Kumpfer et al. (2002) also compared a culturally generic version of the Strengthening Families Program (SFP) with four versions of SFP that were each culturally tailored for African American, Asian/Pacific Islander, Latino, and American Indian, respectively, through both surface and deep structural modifications. SFP is an intervention program that teaches children and their parents, both individually and as a family, skills that improve communication and disciplinary skills. Changes to the program's surface structure included using culturally relevant graphics in program materials, holding program sessions in locations frequented by the ethnic group members and translating materials into ethnic language. Deep structure modifications focused on emphasizing specific cultural values like respect for family traditions. Overall, results from the evaluations of each culturally tailored version of SFP suggested that they were not more effective at improving family skills than the culturally generic program; however, those programs experienced better recruitment and retention of some of their racial and ethnic minority participants.

Because the current evidence is so limited, it is impossible to say whether or not culturally tailored programs are more effective than culturally generic programs at this time. However, we can say definitively that programs cannot have an impact on youth if they are not exposed to them. If culturally tailored programs lead to greater involvement of racial and ethnic minority participants, then integrating cultural issues into program designs may be a critical and necessary step to take in yielding benefits for racial and ethnic minority youth.

18.3. CONCLUSION

Youth-focused prevention programs can take on many forms and can take place in a wide range of locations, ranging from school grounds to community-based organizations. While some programs may be less structured, for example, by offering youth opportunities to simply hang out with friends in a safe place or matching youth with positive, older role models with whom they can interact (i.e., mentors), others have set manualized curricula that are delivered to youth through program staff. Racial and ethnic minority youth may be important populations to target for prevention-related programs, as evidence suggests that they may be at disproportionately higher risk of engaging in problem or risk behaviors. This chapter has provided an overview of how race and ethnicity have been incorporated into the design and delivery of youth-focused programs. While some programs have integrated race and ethnicity into their curricula and overall design via modifications to their surface structure, other programs have been specifically designed for use within a particular racial or ethnic population through the integration of components that acknowledge the unique values and experiences of those racial and ethnic groups. Professionals working with youth should remember to consider how racial and ethnic-specific characteristics like cultural values, attitudes, history, and current environment might influence the relevance and, consequently, the effectiveness of their programs for their participants. Currently, there is not enough evidence to suggest that culturally tailored programs are more effective than culturally generic programs. However, tailoring program content and delivery to best match the backgrounds of the participants may increase the receptivity of participants to the program, thereby improving recruitment and retention among racial and ethnic minority youth. Finally, although this chapter has focused on how youth-focused programs can address the special needs of racial and ethnic minority youth in particular, it is important to remember that culture, or the combination of a group's traditions, experiences, rituals, values, and beliefs, extends past racial and ethnic boundaries. Culturally cognizant programing should therefore extend beyond simply race and ethnicity and account for a variety of youth's life circumstances, such as poverty, religion, and geographic region.

REFERENCES

Botvin, G. J. (1997). *Life skills training: Promoting health and personal development (years 1-3)*. Princeton: Princeton Health Press.

Botvin, G. J. (2004). Advancing prevention science and practice: Challenges, critical issues, and future directions. *Prevention Science, 5*(1), 69–72.

Botvin, G. J., Batson, H. W., Witts-Vitale, S., Bess, V., Baker, E., & Dusenbury, L. (1989). A psychosocial approach to smoking prevention for urban Black youth. *Public Health Reports, 104*(6), 573–582.

Botvin, G. J., Dusenbury, L., Baker, E., James-Ortiz, S., Botvin, E. M., & Kerner, J. (1992). Smoking prevention among urban minority youth: Assessing effects on outcomes and mediating variables. *Health Psychology, 11*(5), 290–299.

Botvin, G. J., Dusenbury, L., Baker, E., James-Ortiz, S., & Kerner, J. (1989). A skills training approach to smoking prevention among Hispanic youth. *Journal of Behavioral Medicine, 12*(3), 279–296.

Botvin, G. J., Schinke, S. P., Epstein, J. A., & Diaz, T. (1994). Effectiveness of culturally focused and generic skills training approaches to alcohol and drug abuse prevention among minority youths. *Psychology of Addictive Behaviors, 8*(2), 116–127.

Botvin, G. J., Schinke, S. P., Epstein, J. A., Diaz, T., & Botvin, E. M. (1996). Effectiveness of culturally focused and generic skills training approaches to alcohol and drug abuse prevention among minority adolescents: Two-year follow-up results. *Psychology of Addictive Behaviors, 9*(3), 183–194.

Botvin, G. J., Schinke, S. P., & Orlandi, M. A. (1995). School-based health promotion: Substance abuse and sexual behavior. *Applied and Preventive Psychology, 4*, 167–184.

Brindis, C., Wolfe, A. L., Mccarter, V., Ball, S., & Starbuck-Morales, S. (1995). The associations between immigrant status and risk-behavior patterns in Latino adolescents. *Journal of Adolescent Health, 17*, 99–105.

Castro, F. G., & Alarcon, E. H. (2002). Integrating cultural variables into drug abuse prevention and treatment with racial/ethnic minorities. *Journal of Drug Issues, 32*(3), 783–810.

Castro, F. G., Barrera, M., Jr., & Martinez, C. R. (2004). The cultural adaptation of prevention interventions: Resolving tensions between fidelity and fitx. *Prevention Science, 5*, 41–45.

Cauce, A., Coronado, N., & Watson, J. (1998). Conceptual, methodological, and statistical issues in culturally competent research. In M. Hernandez & M. R. Isaacs (Eds.), Promoting cultural competence in children's mental health services. *Systems of care for Children's mental health.* (pp. 305–329). Baltimore, MD, US: Paul H Brookes Publishing.

Centers for Disease Control and Prevention. (2008, June 6). Youth risk behavior surveillance—United States, 2007. Surveillance Summaries. *MMWR, 57*(No. SS-4), 25–30.

Cuellar, I., Arnold, B., & Gonzalez, G. (1995). Cognitive referents of acculturation: Assessment of cultural constructs in Mexican-Americans. *Journal of Community Psychology, 23*, 339–356.

Davis, O. I., Nakayama, T. K., & Martin, J. N. (2000). Current and future directions in ethnicity and methodology. *International Journal of Intercultural Relations, 24*, 525–539.

Eccles, J. S., Lord, S., & Buchanan, C. M. (1996). School transitions in early adolescence: What are we doing to our young people? In J. A. Graber & J. Brooks-Gunn (Eds.), *Transitions through adolescence: Interpersonal domains and context* (pp. 251–284). Mahway, NJ: Lawrence Erlbaum Associates.

Ellickson, P. L., & Bell, R. M. (1990). Drug prevention in junior high: A multi-site longitudinal test. *Science, 247*, 1299–1305.

Elliott, D., & Mihalic, S. (2004). Issues in disseminating and replicating effective prevention programs. *Prevention Science, 5*(1), 47–52.

Fass, S., & Cauthen, N. K. (2007, November). *Who are America's poor children? The official story.* New York, NY: National Center for Children in Poverty.

Fordham, S., & Ogbu, J. U. (1986). Black students' school success: Coping with the "burden of 'acting white'." *The Urban Review, 18*(3), 176–206.

Forgey, M. A., Schinke, S., & Cole, K. (1997). School-based interventions to prevent substance use among inner-city minority adolescents. In D. K. Wilson, J. R. Rodriguez, & W. C. Taylor (Eds.), *Health promoting and health compromising behaviors among minority adolescents* (pp. 251–267). Washington, DC: APA.

Fuligni, A. J., Tseng, V., & Lam, M. (1999). Attitudes toward family obligations among American adolescents with Latin American and European background. *Child Development, 70*, 1030–1044.

Gilchrist, L. D., Schinke, S. P., Trimble, J. E., & Cvetkovich, G. T. (1987). Skills enhancement to prevent substance abuse among American Indian adolescents. *The International Journal of the Addictions, 22*(9), 869–879.

Gonzales, N. A., & Cauce, A. M. (1995). Ethnic identity and multicultural competence: Dilemmas and challenges for minority youth. In W. D. Hawley & A. W. Jackson (Eds.), *Toward a common destiny: Improving race and ethnic relations in America* (pp. 131–162). San Francisco, CA: Jossey-Bass/Pfeiffer.

Gordon, R. (1987). An operational classification of disease prevention. In J. A. Steinberg & M. M. Silverman (Eds.), *Preventing mental disorders*. Rockville, MD: U.S. Department of Health and Human Services.

Hammond, W. R., & Yung, B. (1993). Psychology's role in public health response to assaultive violence among young African American men. *American Psychologist, 48*, 142–154.

Harachi, T. W., Catalano, R. F., & Hawkins, J. D. (1997). Effective recruitment for parenting programs within ethnic minority communities. *Child and Adolescent Social Work Journal, 14*(1), 23–39.

Harachi, T. W., Catalano, R. F., Kim, S., & Choi, Y. (2001). Etiology and prevention of substance use among Asian American youth. *Prevention Science, 2*(1), 57–65.

Hecht, M. L., Marsiglia, F. F., Elek, E., Wagstaff, D. A., Kulis, S., Dustman, P., et al. (2003). Culturally grounded substance use prevention: An evaluation of the *keepin' it R.E.A.L.* curriculum. *Prevention Science, 4*(4), 233–248.

Ibrahim, F., Ohnishi, H., & Sandhu, D. S. (1997). Asian American identity development: A culture specific model for South Asian Americans. *Journal of Multicultural Counseling and Development, 25*(1), 34–50.

Kauh, T. (2009, February). *How after-school programs successfully recruit and retain older boys of color: A first look at promising strategies*. Internal report to the Collaborative for Building After School Systems. Philadelphia: Public/Private Ventures.

Kim, K. C., Huhr, W. M., & Kim, S. (1993). Generation differences in Korean immigrants' life conditions in the United States. *Sociological Perspectives, 36*(3), 257–270.

Kim, S., Coletti, S. D., Williams, C., & Hepler, N. A. (1995). Substance abuse prevention involving Asian/Pacific Islander American communities. In G. J. Botvin, S. Schinke, & M. A. Orlandi (Eds.), *Drug abuse prevention with multiethnic youth* (pp. 295–326). Thousand Oaks, CA: Sage Publications.

Kumpfer, K. L., Alvarado, R., Smith, P., & Bellamy, N. (2002). Cultural sensitivity and adaptation in family-based prevention interventions. *Prevention Science, 3*(3), 241–246.

Kumpfer, K. L., & Baxley, G. B. (1997). *Drug abuse prevention: What works?* Rockville, MD: National Institute on Drug Abuse.

Laird, J., Cataldi, E. F., Kewal-Ramani, A., & Chapman, C. (2008). *Dropout and completion rates in the United States: 2006 (NCES 2008-053).* Washington, DC: National Center for Education Statistics, Institute of Education Sciences, U.S. Department of Education. Retrieved September 12, 2008 from http://nces.ed.gov/pubsearch/pubsinfo.asp?pubid=2008053.

Ma, G. X., Lan, Y., Edwards, R. L., Shive, S. E., & Chau, T. (2004). Evaluation of a culturally tailored smoking prevention program for Asian American youth (Smoking Prevention For Asian-American Youth). *Journal of Alcohol and Drug Education, 48*(3), 17–38.

Manson, S., Beals, J., O'Nell, T., Piasecki, J., Bechtold, D., Keane, E., et al. (1996). Wounded spirits, ailing hearts: PTSD and related disorders among American Indians. In A. Marsella, M. J. Friedman, E. T. Gerrity, & R. W. Scurfield (Eds.), *Ethnocultural aspects of posttraumatic stress disorder: Issues, research, and clinical applications* (pp. 255–283). Washington, DC: American Psychological Association.

National Center for Children in Poverty. (2007, September). *Basic facts about low-income children: Birth to age 18.* New York: Columbia University. Retrieved September 20, 2008 from http://www.nccp.org/publications/pdf/text_762.pdf

National Research Council. (1998). *From generation to generation: The health and well-being of children in immigrant families.* Washington, DC: National Academy Press.

Newcomb, M. D. (1996). Drug use etiology among ethnic minority adolescents: Risk and protective factors. In G. J. Botvin, S. Schinke, & M. A. Orlandi (Eds.), *Drug abuse prevention with multiethnic youth* (pp. 105–129). Thousand Oaks, CA: Sage Publications.

Phinney, J. S. (1990). Ethnic identity in college students from four ethnic groups. *Journal of Adolescence, 13,* 171–183.

Phinney, J. S., & Rosenthal, D. A. (1992). Ethnic identity in adolescence: Process, context, and outcome. In G. R. Adams & T. P. Gullotta (Eds.), *Adolescent identity formation. Advances in adolescent development* (Vol. 4, pp. 145–172). Newbury Park, CA: Sage Publications.

Planty, M., Hussar, W., Snyder, T., Provasnik, S., Kena, G., Dinkes, R., et al. (2008). *The condition of education 2008 (NCES 2008-031). National Center for Education Statistics, Institute of Education Sciences.* Washington, DC: U.S. Department of Education.

Resnicow, K., Soler, R., Braithwaite, R. L., Ahluwalia, J. S., & Butler, J. (2000). Cultural sensitivity in substance use prevention. *Journal of Community Psychology, 28*(3), 271–290.

Sampson, R. J. (2004). Neighbourhood and community: Collective efficacy and community safety. *New Economy, 11*(2), 106–113.

Sampson, R. J., Raudenbush, S. W., & Earls, F. (1997). Neighborhoods and violent crime: A multilevel study of collective efficacy. *Science, 277,* 918–924.

Schinke, S. P., Moncher, M. S., Holden, G. W., Botvin, G. J., & Orlandi, M. A. (1989). American Indian youth and substance abuse: Tobacco use problems, risk factors and preventive interventions. *Health Education Research, 4*(1), 137–144.

Stephan, C. W., & Stephan, W. G. (2000). The measurement of racial and ethnic identity. *International Journal of Intercultural Relations*, *24*, 541–552.

Sue, D., Mak, W. S., & Sue, D. W. (1998). Ethnic identity. In L. C. Lee & N. W. S. Zane (Eds.), *Handbook of Asian American psychology* (pp. 289–323). Thousand Oaks, CA: Sage Publications.

Szapocznik, J., Scopetta, M. A., & King, O. E. (1978). Theory and practice in matching treatment to the special characteristics and problems of Cuban immigrants. *Journal of Community Psychology*, *6*(2), 112–122.

Tajfel, H. (1982). Social psychology of intergroup relations. *Annual Review of Psychology*, *33*, 1–29.

Tanaka, J. S., Ebreo, A., Linn, N., & Morera, O. F. (1998). Research methods: The construct validity of self-identity and its psychological implications. In L. C. Lee & N. W. S. Zane (Eds.), *Handbook of Asian American psychology* (pp. 21–79). Thousand Oaks, CA: Sage Publications.

Trimble, J. (1995). Toward an understanding of ethnicity, ethnic identity and their relationship with drug use research. In G. Botvin, S. Schinke, & M. Orlandi (Eds.), *Drug abuse prevention with multi-ethnic youth* (pp. 2–27). Newbury Park, CA: Sage.

Tucker, M. B. (1985). U.S. ethnic minorities and drug abuse: An assessment of the science and practice. *The International Journal of the Addictions*, *20*(6 & 7), 1021–1047.

US Census Bureau (2007). *The American Community Survey 1-Year Estimates*. Retrieved October 25, 2009: http://factfinder.census.gov/servlet/ DTSubjectShowTablesServlet?_ts=274526468676.

Ventura, S. J., Abma, J. C., Mosher, W. D., & Henshaw, S. K. (2008). Estimated pregnancy rates by outcome for the United States, 1990–2004. *National Vital Statistics Reports*, *56*(15), 1–26.

Wise, F., & Miller, N. B. (1983). The mental health of the American Indian child. In G. J. Powell (Ed.), *The psychosocial development of minority group children* (pp. 344–361). New York, NY: Bnumer/Mazel.

Yashui, M., & Dishion, T. J. (2007). The ethnic context of child and adolescent problem behavior: Implications for child and family interventions. *Clinical Child and Family Psychology*, *10*(2), 137–179.

Ying, Y. W., & Lee, P. A. (1999). The development of ethnic identity in Asian-American adolescents: Status and outcome. *American Journal of Orthopsychiatry*, *69*(2), 194–208.

Zane, N., Aoki, B., Ho, T., Huang, L., & Jang, M. (1998). Dosage-related changes in a culturally-responsive prevention program for Asian American youth. *Drugs and Society*, *12*(1–2), 105–125.

Afterword
Adolescent Development
and Geocultural Interpretations

William F. Tate IV
Washington University in St. Louis

> *Geocultural construction work and critique were early ingredients of the discipline [anthropology] in Europe as well as in North America, in continental* Kulturkreislehre, *as well as in the careful mapping of trait distributions to establish the culture areas of Native Americans. Yet in those days, a century or so ago, these were mostly activities of the ivory tower, where scholars would argue over matters of conceptualization and categorization with their peers. In more recent times, it seems to me that geocultural imagination has become more volatile, occurring in both academic and public areas and also crossing boundaries between them and more readily, and more ambiguously. (Hannerz, 2009, p. 269).*

The epigraph is part of an argument put forth by Hannerz that called for the careful examination of discourse and scholarship related to how geocultural scenarios are established empirically as well as promoted in public discussions. The purpose of this Afterword is to comment on the notion of "development in a global era" in light of the book's content and major themes. The global era concept is part of a larger geocultural project. Typically in the social sciences and humanities, culture has focused on more bounded processes and entities: normative processes and related contexts such as cultures of communities, performances, or textual writings. The notion of geocultural is simply stated a macro view toward cultural organization and cultural processes. More specifically, the concept of geocultural is akin to fairly large-scale mapmaking, where the distribution of objects or occurrences cultural, by some means cultural, over regions and their human populations is central to the inquiry. It strikes me that in a volume focused on human development titled, *Adolescence: Development in a Global Era*, that Hennerz's recommendation is most relevant. Hennerz (2009) argued that it is very important to understand the academic roots as well as institutional origins of arguments associated with the global era. His warning is especially challenging in that scholars and traditional news providers along with nontraditional (e-news) producers now contribute to the circulation of information association with geocultural issues.

What themes related to adolescent development in the global era will maintain traction in academic research and with news providers? There is no way to see the future. Instead my intent here is to briefly highlight two subfields that have great potential to influence discussions and understandings of adolescent development. Specifically, I will briefly describe the growing role of genetic-environment research as well as scholarship focused on social origins. These fields are interrelated; however, they are often treated as distinct and disconnected. I will argue they are at times linked geoculturally, and this connection must be acknowledged as important and salient in feature research. In addition, I will examine two areas that are influencing how adolescences are treated in support structures designed to facilitate their development—standards setting and research to practice. These topics appear to be separate concerns. When viewed as geocultural frames they look as if to be more interrelated than at first glance.

The overall approach in this discussion is to focus on adolescent development from a macro view point. A particular focus of my remarks will be on mapmaking, where the distribution of objects cultural across regions is central to the argument. All of my arguments are organized to highlight the four major themes of this book—normative processes, contextual processes, developmental challenges, and supportive systems.

GENE-ENVIRONMENT STUDIES

Harrell, as part of the book's unit on developmental transitions, described biological factors that influence adolescent development. This chapter and related discussions are part of a larger nature-nurture debate. I submit that going forward the field of developmental science will continue to have a strong interest in gene-environment ($G \times E$) research strategies where the goal is to understand the relative influence of factors associated with each domain, as well as how interactions influence individual variation. One very specific reason this area may continue to grow is that funding is available. The NIH Roadmap for Medical Research calls for integrating two or more often disparate scientific disciplines to create a new hybrid discipline.[1] The rationale for this integration is that health and human development problems are growing in complexity so that the traditional cottage industry approach to doing science is not sufficient. Instead, there is a need to create new interdisciplines that directly address the most pressing and challenging research areas. Plomin and Asbury (2005) described how this integration might unfold in behavioral science:

> Behavioral science will be central to the new era of genetic research called the postgenomic era in which the focus will shift from finding genes to understanding how these genes work. Such postgenomic research is usually considered in relationship to the bottom-up strategy of molecular biology in which a gene's product is identified by its DNA sequence and the function of the gene product is traced through cells and then cells systems and eventually the brain. Behavioral science lies at the other end of the continuum in the sense that behavioral research represents an integrationist top-down level of analysis that begins with the behavior of the whole organism rather than a reductionist bottom-up level of analysis that begins with a single molecule in a single cell. For example, behavioral researchers can ask how the effects of specific genes

---

[1] For additional discussion, see http://nihroadmap.nih.gov/.

unfold in development and how they interact and correlate with experience. This top-down behavioral level of analysis has been called behavioral genomics to distinguish it from the often-used phase functional genomics because the latter phrase has become synonymous with bottom-up molecular biology. We suggest that behavioral genomic research is likely to pay off more quickly in prediction, diagnosis, and intervention. . .Bottom-up and top-down levels of analysis of gene-behavior pathways will eventually meet in the brain. The grandest implication is that DNA will serve as an integrating force across all of the life sciences, including the behavioral sciences. (pp. 95–96)

The search for an integrating force across the life sciences is a powerful incentive to continue investing in gene-environment studies—including research on adolescents. This incentive as well as research funding will in part drive the examination of development through the gene-environment lens. Another reason the approaches related to gene-environment studies may continue grow to involve geocultural mapping. How might this emerging, new interdiscipline related to adolescent development inform the geocultural mapping discussion? A forthcoming publication exemplifies the potential contribution. Dick et al. (2009) used data from the population-based Finnish twin study, FinnTwin 12, to examine the significance of socioregional moderating variables on alcohol use measured at age 14, and behavior problems, measured at age 12. Building on prior reports that community-level factors, including urban/rural residency, migration rates, and prevalence of young adults, moderate the importance of genetic effects on alcohol use in 16-18-year olds, this study looked to extend these results by testing for moderating effects of these socioregional factors on alcohol use and behavior problems with a younger sample of adolescent Finnish twins. The point here is that researchers are now extending gene-environment study methodology in an effort to better inform the large-scale mapmaking of adolescent behavior, where the distribution of occurrences cultural or by some means cultural, over regions and their human population is central to the design. Gene-environment research has the potential to inform the geocultural project. Moreover, I submit that research associated with this approach to developmental science will continue to inform the field.

SOCIAL INHERITANCE RESEARCH

There is little doubt that hard work, motivation, and skills are important factors that support productivity in almost every human endeavor. One grand narrative engrained in American folkway is that effort, motivation, and skills as opposed to social inheritance strongly influence life course development. This argument is part of discourses associated with the global era; where in theory the knowledge economy prioritizes merit and ability over demographic characteristics (e.g., SES or race). The argument has been examined in the research literature on social inheritance. Esping-Anderson (2006) stated that in a rare example of disciplinary convergence, sociologists and economists study intergenerational inheritance (or mobility) with the same methods while producing similar results. One difference is that the economist typically focuses on earnings and income, while the sociologist mainly attends to educational, occupational, and social class attainment. Like developmental scientists, sociologists are deeply interested in the mechanisms that connect origins and life-course experiences. This intellectual space is of interest to social scientists from several traditions. All four of the major themes of this book—normative processes, contextual processes, development challenges, and supportive systems—are linked to social origins research. While sociologists are concerned with the intergenerational mobility correlates in the social origins research tradition, their research has broad reaching implications for the study of adolescent development. Esping-Andersen (2006) stated:

> *Most sociologists will interpret inter-generational mobility correlations in terms of two main kinds of social interactions: firstly, the social milieu of the family during childhood and youth (such as family stability, poverty, or 'cultural capital') and, secondly, the characteristics of the social community (neighbourhood class or race segregation, or social networks). (p. 400)*

He described these two main kinds of social interactions as distinct. However, it has been argued that this distinction is blurring. What would this mean for adolescent development research? Douglas Massey's research provides some insight into this question. Massey (2009) argued that the emergence of geographically concentrated affluence and poverty across the world as the primary spatial arrangement of the twenty-first century will have profound implications for the social context in which human development is hosted. He posited that the informal means used in previous societies to conserve public order will break down and disappear as part of rapid urbanization. In its place a new cultural formation linked to the ecological structures of concentrated affluence and poverty will evolve. Several possibilities related to this formation are linked to the purpose and contents of this book focused on adolescent development in a global era. Massey (2009) theorized that as the density of poverty increases in cities across the world, so will the density of joblessness, crime, family dissolution, drug abuse, alcoholism, disease, and violence. He put forth an argument that an alternative status system is nearly certain to form.

> *Under circumstances where it is difficult to succeed according to conventional standards, the usual criteria for success typically are inverted to create an oppositional identity. Children formulate oppositional identities to preserve self-esteem when expectations are low and when failure by conventional standards is likely. Thus, in areas of concentrated poverty, students from poor families will legitimize their educational failures by attaching positive value and meaning to outcomes that affluent children label deviant and unworthy. In adapting to the environment created by concentrated poverty, success in school will be devalued, hard work will be regarded as selling out, and any display of learning will be viewed as uncool ... Once such a subculture becomes established, it acquires a life of its own that contributes independently to the perpetuation of educational failure, the reproduction of poverty, and the cultural transmission of low socioeconomic status from person to person, family to family, and group to group. (p. 28).*

Massey's discussion of global demographics is based on the logic of population trend studies. However, his theoretical propositions concerning identity formation and related implications as a result of concentrated poverty and affluence are at best an unsettled empirical project. Massey's argument links geospatial agglomeration, group concentration, moral density, and subculture development. These geocultural relationships associated with social inheritance should be a research and development priority for social scientists and other human service professionals. Moreover, socioregional factors will inform both social origins research and gene-environment studies.

STANDARDS SETTING AND THE GLOBAL ERA

What is a standard? I have argued elsewhere that the term "standard" has multiple meanings in the context of policy, research, and human service settings (Tate, 2003). Since building supportive systems for adolescents is a major theme of this book, I believe some discussion of standards and the global era are warranted. Here are just a few interpretations of the term standard as the word might be used in discussions of adolescent development:

- Standards as idealized practice.
- Standards as part of a theory of action.
- Standards as essential knowledge in a field.
- Standards as descriptors of adolescents' skills and understandings.
- Standards as guides to align system components.
- Standards as curriculum goals for educators.
- Standards as guides in accountability systems.
- Standards as a framework to discuss resources and inputs linked to opportunity.

What do standards have to do with adolescent development in the global era? Bartley (2007) argued that since the 1944 publication of *The Great Transformation*, social scientists have debated the merits of efforts to embed modern capitalism in social standards. He contended that much of the research examines state regulation of the conditions of production. In addition, his position is that new transformations are occurring where standard setting and regulation are increasingly carried out through private means. He argued that transnational private regulation has emerged where nonstate actors codify, monitor, and in some cases certify firms' compliance with labor, environmental, human rights, or other standards of accountability. Over the past 20 years, international debates over sweatshops, child labor, and other issues have spurred the formation of dozens of nongovernmental certification associations. As part of the private sector, this movement has sought to shape corporate social responsibility through (1) voluntary standards, (2) scrutinizing production locations with accredited auditors, (3) certification of participating organizations, and (4) sharing information with consumers and other bodies. However, this transnational movement in the corporate sector is now a part of the mission of schools, informal learning organizations, foundations, and other human service providers focused on adolescents.

For example, it is commonplace for both academics and public news outlets to refer to global shifts and intense global competition as the rationale for curriculum standards or accountability mechanisms. A fairly typical argument is offered as an example. Carnevale and Desrochers (2003) posited that the United States' massive production system is losing its competitive edge. America's golden age of economic production and family income is being mirrored by other countries across the globe, and as a result competition has intensified. This economic battle requires new and different production investment as well as new forms of corporate responsibility and worker skills. Hence, rigorous standards focused on learning and social development are in order. Accountability systems that provide parents and various concerned publics with student outcome information are now mandated by federal law. A central aim of this standards-based effort is to accelerate the production of adolescents prepared to enter and complete tertiary education (Grubb & Lazerson, 2006). The following announcement in the *Hispanic Outlook in Higher Education* (Bill & Melinda Gates foundation invests $22 million, 2009) captures the current trend:

> *The Bill & Melinda Gates Foundation recently announced more than $22 million in investments in research and data systems. The grants are intended to help schools, districts, and states gather and effectively use data to have maximum impact on teaching and learning and create evidence-based links between students, educators, and policymaker. The grants are part of the foundation's efforts to ensure that all students can graduate from high school college-ready and earn a postsecondary credential with real value in the workplace. (p. 28)*

The drive for postsecondary credentials is linked directly to competitive endeavors by regions seeking human capital advantages. Standards as well as related empirical programs of study will continue to inform discussions of adolescent development in the years to come. Moreover, accountability mechanisms where standards serve as guiding frameworks are part of a push to ensure evidence-based practice in the global era.

RESEARCH TO PRACTICE IN THE GLOBAL ERA

I have argued that standards are part of the evidence-based movement. Another way to describe the evidence-based project is research to practice. It would be extremely difficult to argue that research should not inform the practice of professionals who support adolescents. However, despite the press to use science and research to guide practice in human affairs in the global era, unique challenges remain. The technological capabilities in this era are rapidly becoming more sophisticated and accessible. Massive data repositories of information about education, health, and human development exist. New technologies designed to connect these extant data sources, as well as support new information, is a fundamental characteristic of globalization and the knowledge society. In addition, developmental science including many important studies outlined in this book is growing in quantity and methodological rigor. Yet, the research to practice connection includes few successes.

Szanton (2001) outlined an important set of cultural differences between academic and governmental agencies that going forward must be dealt with if research to practice is to emerge as a serious source of social problem solving. While these cultural divides are not transferable to all settings, they are at least a starting point for bridging the research to practice divide. First, the ultimate objective of traditional academic research is respect from academic peers. For governmental officials the central aim is to gain approval from the electorate. As such, academics tend to approach problems as part of long-term projects while government colleagues charged with managing the problem are operating on the basis of much shorter time horizons. Researchers are concerned chiefly with the internal logic of the problem. In contrast, government culture is focused on the external logic of the setting. Academics largely work alone, while the government culture includes a broad range of actors. The scholar wants to produce original insight largely framed in qualified language. The government culture calls for a reliable solution in absolute, yet simple terms. Scholars are very comfortable producing conclusions with multiple possibilities and uncertainties highlighted. The governmental model seeks one best solution with objectives and uncertainties less transparent. Academics are rarely motivated by feasibility, whereas this is a central concern for government officials. Moreover, academics' efforts to insist on technical solutions to political problems create an additional challenge to the evidence-based movement. Scholars tend to want to provide advice through three formal mechanisms: (1) centers or institutes, (2) federally funded projects, and (3) personal consultation with government officials. Yet, informal contacts between researcher and government officials based on less visible, ad hoc relations are more likely to be acted on and sustained. Of course, there are examples of formal relationships that have generated research while informing practice. My point is that the mechanisms to support and advance research-based solutions in organizations (including families) where adolescent development is central are not well established (Kowalski, 2009). This remains a challenge in the global era.

FINAL REMARKS

The chapters in this book provide important insights into scholarship that will help frame future studies and interventions during what Massey (2009) describes as the "Age of Extremes" (p. 29). Geocultural construction work in the developmental sciences will include the four major themes of this book—normative processes, contextual processes, development challenges, and supportive systems. Moreover, I have argued that gene-environment studies and social origins research will inform these four major themes. In addition, I believe standards and research to practice will continue to grow in importance, yet present challenges. Despite growing technological capabilities and scientific knowledge, it is quite ironic that a foundational challenge to evidence-based practice will be one of cultural disconnects between academics and government as well as human service providers. I submit that one of the most pressing problems associated with adolescent development in the global era will be generating research on how to bridge this divide. This book provides a sound evidentiary base to support closing the divide.

REFERENCES

Bartley, T. (2007). Institutional emergence in an era of globalization: The rise of transnational private regulation of labor and environmental conditions. *American Journal of Sociology, 113*, 297–351.

Bill & Melinda Gates foundation invests $22 million in research and data systems to improve student achievement. (2009, April 20). *Hispanic Outlook in Higher Education, 19*, 28–30.

Carnevale, A. P., & Desrochers, D. M. (2003). *Standards for what? The economic roots of K-16 reform.* Princeton, NJ: Educational Testing Service.

Dick, D. M., Bernard, M., Aliev, F., Viken, R., Pulkkinen, L., Kaprio, J., et al. (2009). The role of socioregional factors moderating genetic influences on early adolescent behavior problems and alcohol use. *Alcoholism: Clinical and Experimental Research, 33*, 1739–1748.

Esping-Anderson, G. (2006). *Social inheritance and equal opportunity policies.* In H. Lauder, P. P. Brown, J. Dillabough, & A. H. Halsey (Eds.), *Education, globalization and social change* (pp. 398–419). Oxford: Oxford University Press.

Grubb, W. N., & Lazerson, M. (2006). The globalization of rhetoric and practice: The education gospel and vocationalism. In H. Lauder, P. P. Brown, J. Dillabough, & A. H. Halsey (Eds.), *Education, globalization and social change* (pp. 295–307). Oxford: Oxford University Press.

Hannerz, U. (2009). Geocultural scenarios. In P. Hedström & B. Wittrock (Eds.), *Frontiers of sociology: Annals of the international institute of sociology (volume II)* (pp. 267–288). Leinden, The Netherlands: Brill.

Kowalski, T. (2009). Need to address evidence-based practice in educational administration. *Educational Administration Quarterly, 45*, 351–374.

Massey, D. S. (2009). The age of extremes: Concentrated affluence and poverty in the twenty-first century. In H. P. Hynes & R. Lopez (Eds.), *Urban health: Readings in the social, built, physical environments of U.S. cities* (pp. 5–36). Sudbury, MA: Jones and Bartlett Publishers.

Plomin, R., & Asbury, K. (2005). Nature and nurture: Genetic and environmental influences on behavior. *The Annals of the American Academy of Political and Social Science, 600*, 86–98.

Polanyi, K. (1944). *The great transformation.* Boston, MA: Beacon.

Szanton, P. (2001). *Not well advised: The city as client—An illuminating analysis of urban governments and their consultants.* San Jose, CA: Authors Choice Press.

Tate, W. F. (2003). What is a standard? In F. K. Lester & J. Ferrini-Mundy (Eds.), *Proceedings of the NCTM research catalyst conference* (pp. 15–23). Reston, VA: National Council of Teachers of Mathematics.

Index